Neither East Nor West

NEITHER EAST NOR WEST

One

Woman's

Journey

through the

Islamic Republic

of Iran

CHRISTIANE BIRD

POCKET BOOKS

NEW YORK   LONDON   TORONTO   SYDNEY   SINGAPORE

"Elephant in the Dark" and "Enough Words?" from *The Essential Rumi* originally published by Threshold Books.

Excerpt of *The Legend of Seyavash* by Ferdowsi, translated by Dick Davis. Translation copyright © Dick Davis, 1992 was reprinted with the permission of Penguin UK.

Excerpt from *Fifty Poems of Hafiz* edited by A. J. Arberry reprinted with the permission of Cambridge University Press.

POCKET BOOKS, a division of Simon & Schuster, Inc.
1230 Avenue of the Americas, New York, NY 10020

Library of Congress Cataloging-in-Publication Data

Bird, Christiane
    Neither East nor West : one woman's journey through the Islamic Republic of Iran /
Christiane Bird.
      p. cm.
    Includes bibliographical references.
    ISBN 0-671-02755-7
    1. Iran—Description and travel. 2. Iran—Social life and customs—20th century. 3. Bird,
Christiane—Journeys—Iran. I. Title.

    DS259.2 .B57 2001
    955.05'4—dc21   00-068227

First Pocket Books hardcover printing March 2001

10 9 8 7 6 5 4 3 2 1

Jacket design by Lisa Litwack

Printed in the U.S.A.

To my parents

ACKNOWLEDGMENTS AND
AUTHOR'S NOTE

*T*his book could not have been written without the help of the many, many Iranians I met who welcomed me with such overwhelming hospitality into their country. Everywhere I went, I found women and men eager to assist me in any way they could, from giving me directions and buying me bus tickets to serving as my translator and inviting me into their homes, for all of which I am deeply appreciative.

I would especially like to thank my hosts in Tehran, Bahman and Chris Faratian and Lona and Pari Jalili, whose kindness, good nature, and wit made my first month in Iran so unforgettable. A special thanks, too, to Manouchehr Kasheff, of Columbia University, who first introduced me to the Persian language, read this book in manuscript, advised me on the transliteration of Persian words into English, and, perhaps most importantly, greatly encouraged me to travel to Iran. I am also especially indebted to Farnaz Fassihi, who started as my Persian-language tutor, quickly became my friend, and advised me on all aspects of this book, from traveling in the Islamic Republic to cultural and political issues.

In addition, I would like to thank Mohammad and Haideh Legenhausen, who went far out of their way to help me in Qom; Mohammad "Babak" Azimi in Tehran; the Tabataba'i family in Mashhad; the Jalili family in Tabriz; my hosts in Sanandaj; and Sohi Nikkhah of the Gulitour travel agency in Tehran, who set me up with first-rate tour guides in many cities. Thanks also to British journalist John Simpson and Canadian journalist Fred Reed, whose books on everyday life in the Islamic Republic first inspired me to travel there, and to historian Sandra Mackey, whose book, *The Iranians,* I found to be an especially rich source for background information on Iran.

I am indebted to Mahnaz Afkhami of the Foundation for Iranian

Studies and to Azar Nafisi of the Johns Hopkins School of Advanced International Studies for providing me with contact names in Iran. A note of gratitude, too, to my friends Melinda Brown and Kathryn Paulsen, who encouraged me to take the trip; Jerry Brown, who held down the home front while I was away; Ali Ne'matollahi, who helped me with my Persian; and Barbara Feinberg, Kim Larsen, Page Sampson, and Walker Simon, who all advised me on various sections of this manuscript. Also, I am deeply grateful to my insightful editor and longtime friend, Nancy Miller; to her able assistant, Anika Streitfeld; and to my always responsive and supportive agent, Neeti Madan of Sterling Lord Literistic.

Finally, and most importantly, I would like to thank my parents, and most especially my father, whose adventurous, generous, and open-minded spirit first took my family to Iran so many years ago. This book is dedicated to them.

Because of the current political atmosphere in Iran, I have had to change some names, locations, and identifying details in this book. On occasion, I have also condensed several of my visits into one for the sake of brevity.

Because there is no standard transliteration from Persian to English, I have in general chosen to spell words as simply as possible and according to how they are pronounced in Iran, choosing *Mohammad*, for example, over *Muhammad*, as that is the Persian pronunciation. I have, however, made exceptions with some Anglicized words, such as *Imam*, whose spellings are already familiar to English-speaking readers, and have spelled people's names according to their personal preferences.

Contents

Life is not days past, but days remembered.

—Stranger on bus to Esfahan

Travel is the most private of pleasures.

—Vita Sackville-West, *Passenger to Teheran*

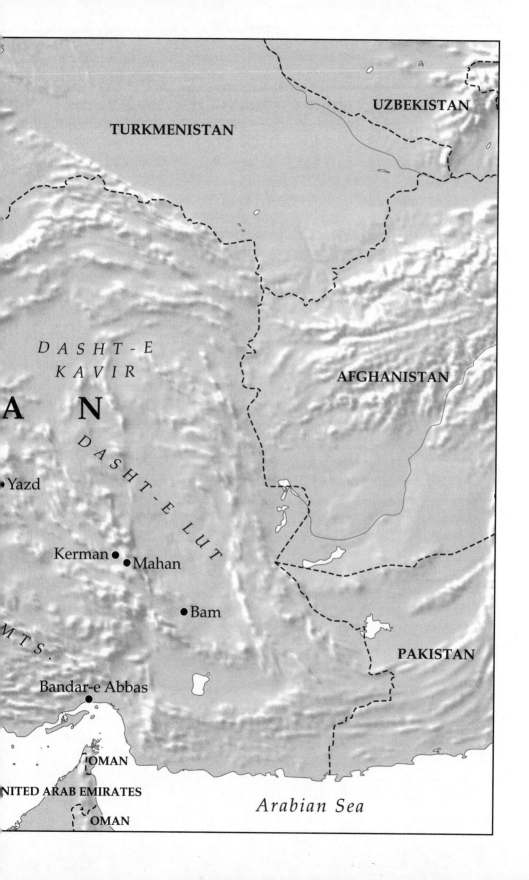

PREFACE

I am on a bus traveling through the desert between Kerman and Yazd when we pull over to a checkpoint. Checkpoints are common along Iranian highways and I've grown accustomed to stopping every hundred miles or so to watch the driver climb out, papers in hand. Sometimes a guard in dark green uniform enters the bus and walks up and down the aisle, eyes flicking from side to side, pistol butt glinting in the shadowed interior light.

This is one of those times. The bus falls silent as a young guard enters, and we all determinedly stare straight ahead, as if by our pretending to ignore the guard, he will ignore us. We listen to his footfalls sound down the Persian carpet runner that lines the aisle, turn, and come back again. He reaches the front of the bus and makes a half-turn, toward the door. But then, just as we begin a collective deep breath, he surprises us by completing his turn and starting down the aisle again, this time to tap various passengers on the shoulder. They gather their belongings together and lurch out of the bus and up the steps of a cement block building.

I sit frozen, hoping that the guard will not notice me and the blond hair sticking out of my *rusari*, or head scarf. I've seen guards pull passengers off buses before, and although it never seems to be anything serious—the passengers always return within five or ten minutes—I'd just as soon remain in my seat.

The guard climbs out of the bus and I relax, wondering what, if anything, he is looking for. I've been told that these searches are usually about drugs and smuggling, but to me, they seem to be more about the display of power.

The guard is back, and intuitively, I know why. He beckons to me.

Me? I gesture, still not completely convinced that he wants me. After two months in Iran, I've learned that—contrary to common Western assumption—the authorities seldom bother foreigners here.

You, he nods.

Copying my fellow passengers, I gather my belongings together and stand up. Everyone is staring at me—as usual, I am the only foreigner on the bus.

I climb out, nearly tripping over my long black raincoat—it or something similar being required wearing for all women in public in Iran. My heart is knocking against my chest. The guard and one of his colleagues are waiting for me on the steps of the guardhouse. At their feet is my lone duffel bag, which they've hauled out of the belly of the bus. It looks like a fat green watermelon.

"Passport," the young guard barks in Persian.

I hand him my crisp, dark blue document, *United States of America* emblazoned boldly across the front. Vaguely, I remember someone back home warning me to get a neutral-covered passport before entering the Islamic Republic. Too late now.

"Visa?"

I show him the appropriate page in my passport.

"Where are you coming from?" His Persian has a strange drawl that I haven't heard before.

"Kerman," I say.

"Where are you going to?"

"Yazd."

"Tourist?"

I nod, thinking there's no need to complicate matters by telling him that I'm here in Iran to write a *safarnameh*, the Persian word for travelogue or, literally, "travel letter." But then immediately I wonder if I've done the right thing. My visa says *Press*.

Slowly, the young guard flips through the pages of my passport, examining the immigration stamps and the rules and regulations listed in the back. He studies my picture long and hard, and then passes my passport to his unsmiling colleague, who asks me the same questions I've just been asked.

"Where are you coming from?"

"Kerman."

"Where are you going to?

"Yazd."

"Tourist?"

I nod again. I can't change my answer now.

The second guard hands my passport back to the first, who reluctantly hands it back to me. I notice a smattering of acne across his forehead and wonder if he's old enough to shave.

"Is this your suitcase?" he says, looking at my bag.

"Yes," I say, and move to open it.

He shakes his head.

All of the other passengers are now back on the bus, and I wonder how much longer the guards will keep me. What will happen, I worry, if the bus leaves without me? We're out in the middle of the desert; there are no other buildings in sight. Hardened dust-white plains broken only by scrub grass stretch in all directions. The sky is a pale steely dome sucking the color and moisture out of the landscape.

Clearing his throat, the first guard stares at me intently. His eyes are an unusual smoke blue, framed by long lashes. They're the same eyes I've noticed before on more than a few Iranians. He nudges his colleague and they whisper together. Sweat is slipping down their foreheads, and down mine.

Then the first guard straightens his shoulders, takes a deep breath, and blushes. "Thank you," he says carefully in stilted, self-conscious English. "Nice to meet you."

"Hello." The second guard is now blushing as furiously as the first. "How are you?" He lapses back into Persian, only some of which I understand. "We will never forget this day. You are the first American we have met. Welcome to the Islamic Republic of Iran. Go with Allah."

SEDUCTION

*The motive of a journey deserves a little attention. It is not the fully
conscious mind which chooses West Africa in preference to Switzerland. . . .
A quality of darkness is needed, of the inexplicable.*
—Graham Greene, *Journey Without Maps*

I went to Iran to flirt with my childhood. I went to Iran to court the
unknown. I went to Iran to see the effects of the Islamic Revolution for
myself.

My family and I had lived in Tabriz, a city in northwestern Iran, for
three years in the 1960s, when I was a young child. Some of my earliest
memories are of Iran—of the mud-brick compound in which we lived, of
the horse-drawn droshkies clip-clopping down the streets, of a shrunken
beggar man with a monstrous swollen hand larger than my head, of a vendor on the corner who sold my brother and me bubble-gum coins wrapped
in bright foil. Silver, pink, green, and gold—the shiny orbs seemed to roll
through the hot desert landscape of my earliest memories, drawing me
back to a time and place far removed from the New York of my present.

I wanted to go back to that place, if not that time. I wanted to reach
through the thick plate glass that separates now from then and remember

I

what life had been like. I could see us all so clearly, moving silently about in a stark, white landscape just beyond the glass: my gentle father, the doctor, who had volunteered his services to the then-undeveloped country through the auspices of the Presbyterian Church; my stylish mother, the lady, who had fled her home in eastern Germany to escape the Russians during World War II; my younger brother, hair the shiny, silvery color of moonlight; and I, an already pensive child yearning to learn how to read.

The world had seemed so orderly then, with well-defined rules and structured roles for everyone. The United States was at the apex of its power, spreading the "light" of democracy and technology into the remotest corners of the developing world; there was no question then about whether America should be in Iran. The sanctity of the nuclear family was as yet unchallenged; my parents' divorce and my own unmarried and childless, though cohabiting, state still lay many years in the future. Economic security and happiness seemed the birthright of every American child; what did I know then about the vagaries of love, work, adulthood, and the freelance writer's life?

But even as I remember order and light, I also remember darkness. The half-comforting, half-frightening darkness of childhood, when most things are still shrouded and the world is filled with secrets. Secrets that sometimes flitted past me when I was out playing in our garden, shaded with almond and pomegranate trees, or listening to a bedtime story, or watching my parents and sensing that there was more transpiring between them than just the exchange of big words. At the beginning of consciousness, I saw the world then—though I certainly couldn't have articulated it—as being filled with dark, mysterious mounds awaiting my excavation.

When my parents told their family and friends that they were going to Iran, most people didn't know where it was. My parents had to pull out a map, only to meet with amazed, concerned—or horrified—stares. Some people told them that they were foolish for going; others said that they were selfish for "risking the lives" of two innocent children.

Pre– or post–Islamic Revolution, Iran has always been a cipher to the West.

∂°℃

Which, as far as my grown-up self was concerned, only added to its appeal. As an adult, I felt pulled by Iran in myriad ways, intrigued and beguiled first by its dual identity, its two distinct traditions, one Persian, the other Islamic. The Persian part dates back to the fifth century B.C., when Cyrus the Great created an empire based on tolerance and justice, where slavery did not exist and men and women were paid equal wages. The Islamic part dates back to the seventh century A.D., when the Arabs arrived in Iran, bringing with them the powerful new religion of the Prophet Mohammad. Most Persians converted to Islam and its egalitarian ideals voluntarily, fed up with a by-then corrupt ruling elite. These two strands of Iranian history are constantly conflicting with each other, and more than a few historians have attributed the 1978–1979 Islamic Revolution to the struggle between the two. During the Pahlavi dynasty (1925–1979), the shahs emphasized the glories of the country's ancient past to the denigration of Islam. The Islamic Revolution turned that approach to history upside down.

I was fascinated, too, by the country's elaborate mix of peoples, geographies, and cultures. Only about half of Iranians are ethnic Persians; the others are Ajerbaijani, Kurd, Lur, Baluchi, Bakhtiari, Mazandarani, Gilaki, Turkoman, Qashqa'i, Shahsevan, Afshar, and Arab. The official language is Persian, or Farsi, but many of these peoples still speak their own language or dialect, and some still live a nomadic life. Over three times larger than France, Iran is mostly mountain, plateau, and two great deserts—one salt, one sand—but to its north lies a fertile crescent that in places resembles Switzerland, and to its south stretches an arid coast lined with palm trees.

As a land bridge between the East and the West, Iran has been invaded countless times, by everyone from the Greeks and the Turks to the Mongols and the Arabs, and yet has never succumbed completely to its conquerors. Instead, the country has coped with invasions by assimilating and adapting those aspects of the conquering cultures that it admired, such as Greek science and Chinese art, and leaving behind the rest. Says a Persian maxim: "Iranians are like wheat fields. When the storm comes, they bend; when the storm passes, they stand up again." Wrote the Greek historian Herodotus: "There is no nation which so readily adopts foreign customs as the Persians. As soon as they hear of any luxury they instantly make it their own."

Perhaps because of this, Iran harbors an extraordinarily complex relationship both with the West and with other Middle Eastern countries, and I was drawn to its contradictions. Despite the Islamic Revolution's highly publicized rejection of the West, Iran is a considerably westernized nation, with an education system, love of technology, middle-class culture, and female work force that greatly resemble our own. Women in Iran have far more rights than do women in many other Muslim countries: Iranian women work as doctors, lawyers, teachers, and politicians; drive cars and vote in elections; keep their own last names after marriage, and comprise nearly one half of the university population. Despite the presence of many Arabic elements in Persian society, many Iranians view their Arab neighbors—who tend to be less educated and less modernized than they—with condescension, if not contempt. Many Iranians draw a firm line of distinction between Persians and Arabs and are offended when Westerners don't recognize the difference between the two. Complicating the matter is the fact that most Arabs are Sunni Muslim, whereas Iran is 90 percent Shi'ite.

I was curious to learn more about Islamic society. What was it like, I wondered, to hear that mournful yet hypnotic call to prayer wafting out over the landscape? (Could I remember the sound? I half imagined I could.) What was it like to see thousands of believers bowing, kneeling, and unfolding in unfaltering rhythm as they prayed? (I couldn't remember that at all.) What was it like to pass clerics in full cloaked regalia on the streets? (One of my favorite books as a child had been *Once the Mullah*, a collection of Persian-Turkish folk tales about the comical yet strangely wise Mullah Nasr al-Din.) What was it like to wear the *hejab*—the Islamic covering for women? (I *could* remember passing those black, enigmatic shapes on the street, and how they'd once filled me with both curiosity and dread.)

Partly because of my family's history and partly because of my own reading, I didn't trust the many negative news reports that had come out of the Muslim world in general and Iran in particular throughout the 1980s and most of the 1990s. As others, most notably the scholar Edward Said, have written before me, Muslims are the last group in our politically correct culture that it is still all right to defile. Most of the world's approximately one billion Muslims are ordinary, peace-loving citizens, and yet Islam is a dirty word in much of the West, synonymous with fanaticism and violence. Though this is just now beginning to change, or so it seems to me, we're still too often told that Muslims will do anything in the name of their religion—bomb, maim, assassinate, take hostages—and are a threat not just to the West but to all civilized society.

And the Iranians, or so common wisdom goes, are among the worst of the bunch. Once one of America's staunchest allies, they have betrayed us as only former friends can.

I thought about the momentous events of recent Iranian history: the

1978–1979 Islamic Revolution that ousted the American-supported Mohammad Reza Shah Pahlavi, notorious for his ruthless secret police and love of ostentatious display; the subsequent homecoming of the ferocious but pious Ayatollah Ruhollah Khomeini, hailed by many as the man who would bring a just and egalitarian order to Iran; the institution of the twentieth century's first theocracy, followed by a horrendous crackdown on personal freedoms and human rights; the 444-day siege of the U.S. Embassy in Tehran, and the embarrassing Iran-Contra affair; an eight-year-long war with Iraq that took the lives of hundreds of thousands of Iranians; the death edict against writer Salman Rushdie; government-sponsored terrorism in the name of Shi'ite Islam.

In the United States, we had heard about these events primarily through the eyes of Western reporters and diplomats, some of whom, according to Said and others, had been hostile to Islam and/or relatively ignorant of Middle Eastern history. Through their reports, and our own prejudices, we had demonized Iran so completely that it no longer seemed to be populated by human beings—all decent Iranians either had been killed or had fled to the West—but rather by evil tyrants and their hypnotized followers. And yet, I thought every time I heard another negative news report, every story has at least two sides, and multiple truths.

I wanted more. More complexity, more informed analysis, more attempts to understand, more details about everyday life. The Iranians my parents had known had been thoughtful, perceptive people, not the one-dimensional fanatics bent on destroying Western infidels that I kept hearing about.

"The Department of State warns all U.S. citizens against travel to Iran . . ." read the government's travel advisory throughout most of the 1990s. "U.S. citizens traveling to Iran have been detained without charge, arrested, and harassed by Iranian authorities." I didn't altogether trust these dire admonitions, but until the election of the Islamic Republic's first moderate president, Mohammad Khatami, in May 1997, my chances of traveling to Iran were extremely remote. Except for some Iranian Americans with family in Iran, reporters on specific short-term assignments, travelers passing through the country in transit, and the very occasional serious scholar, Americans wishing to visit Iran were denied visas.

Then, shortly after Khatami was elected, in a landslide vote that took both Iran and the world by surprise, I read an article in *The New York Times* about American tourists visiting Iran on group visas. Next came a January 1998 interview on CNN in which the new president called for more cultural exchange between Iran and the United States. "Nothing should prevent dialogue and understanding between two nations, especially between their scholars and thinkers," he said in the eloquent language for which he was fast becoming known. I pricked up my ears.

The following semester, I sat in on a Persian-language class at Columbia University. I was often up at the university anyway, finishing work on a master's degree, and as I was in my last semester, I decided that I might as well start to explore this back-burner idea of mine to return to Iran. I'd had it for so long that it no longer seemed like an imminent possibility, but I now realized that it could be a realistic long-term one. I thought I'd simply sit in on the class, absorb a phrase or two, and perhaps one day get myself to Iran.

But I hadn't counted on the seduction of the language, as introduced to me by the irrepressible Dr. Manouchehr Kasheff, an erudite man originally from Shiraz who'd left Iran well before the revolution. During my first week of Persian class, I started to learn the alphabet and delighted in forming the snail-like semicircle with the dot on top that is the *kheh*, the trough with the dot underneath that is the *beh*, the assertive slash sometimes wearing a hat that is the *alef*. Much to my surprise, elementary Persian wasn't particularly difficult; as an Indo-European language, it is much closer to English, German, and French than it is to Arabic, Turkish, or Hebrew—its use of the Arabic alphabet notwithstanding. During my second week of Persian class, I was startled to realize that I could already say a few basic phrases and read a few basic words; never in my wildest imaginings had I envisioned myself being able to decipher this lovely, enigmatic script. During my third week of Persian class, I started visiting the library after class to check out books about Iranian history, art, and culture. After one month of Persian class, I knew that I had to travel to Iran, and the sooner, the better. My tiny grasp of the language had opened up a window for me, and my crazy idea no longer seemed quite so crazy. It could be done.

☙♋☙

Finding out about—and obtaining—a visa to visit Iran wasn't easy. Endless telephone calls to the Iranian Interests Section in the Pakistani Embassy in Washington, D.C., resulted only in busy signals and, one miraculous morning when I finally got through, a recorded message in Persian that I couldn't understand. I therefore decided to take the train down to Washington to apply in person.

Ali, whom I'd met through a friend in Persian class, advised me. To visit the Interests Section, he said, you must wear the *hejab* and arrive there by at least 6 A.M. The office takes only seventy or eighty people a day, and if you're not there early enough, you're out of luck.

The process sounded absurd to me, but I realized that if I hoped to go to Iran, I'd better get used to such practices. I'd dealt with bureaucracies in developing countries before—most notably as a 21-year-old teaching English in Bogotá, Colombia, but more recently as a writer working on travel assignments for the *New York Daily News* and other publications. This, presumably, was the sort of thing that Iranians had to put up with all the time.

I arrived at the Interests Section just before dawn one May morning to find that Ali had been right. There was already a thick line bunched up outside a door marked in Persian letters next to a contemporary furniture store. I'd expected the Interests Section to be housed in a corner of an imposing embassy building or at least a grim office complex, but here it was, squeezed into a strip mall on the D.C.–Georgetown border. A middle-aged jogger in neon green was huffing by, followed by a man out exercising his Airedale.

I took my place at the end of the line, feeling self-conscious. Although I was wearing the same long black raincoat and head scarf that most of the other women were wearing, I was the only full-blooded Westerner in sight. Everyone else appeared to be at least half Iranian, and everyone was speaking Persian. I couldn't understand a word they were saying. How in the world was I going to manage when—if—I got to Iran?

Shahnaz, a tiny, twinkling woman wearing a bright blue scarf just ahead of me in line, befriended me, and after several hours of waiting, we passed through a metal detector to meet a flirtatious man handing out numbers and visa applications. When I told him that, no, I didn't have the apparently required letter of invitation to visit Iran from a friend living there, he didn't want to give me an application, but Shahnaz talked him into it. It's always better to get upstairs, she whispered conspiratorially as we took our papers and entered a narrow stairwell—you can explain to people up there what you want.

We entered a hot and windowless room already crowded with applicants. Framed photographs of bearded ayatollahs and pennants with Qor'anic verses hung from the walls, along with an electronic numbers board. Applicant 8 was now being served; I was number 59 and Shahnaz was number 60; I felt as if we were at the butcher's shop. We sat down next to a trim, bespectacled man—Applicant 63—armed with a thick sheaf of papers that he kept double-checking. He'd already applied for a visa—and been turned down—many times, he said, and had to make sure that he said the exact same thing on every single application; otherwise, "they" might get suspicious.

Shahnaz showed me her Iranian passport. The maroon-tinted pages, inscribed with fanciful borders, looked unremarkable at first, but then she held one up to the light. The ghostly visage of Ayatollah Khomeini glared out at me. People around us chuckled at my surprise, and someone offered me hot tea in a paper cup. Tea is the national drink of Iran and is served in even the unlikeliest of circumstances.

Shahnaz, Applicant 63, and I spent the next two hours discussing everything from the nature of greed to the pros and cons of marriage and the probability of the hereafter. From time to time, one of our neighbors looked up from his or her sheaf of papers—which by then I realized every applicant had—to add a comment or two. Our conversation reminded me of something that a famed nineteenth-century scholar of Persian studies, Edward Browne, wrote in his book *A Year Amongst the Persians*: that Iranians love nothing more than to take an abstract topic and noodle on it for a while. I looked up the exact quote when I got home: "The most striking feature of the Persians as a nation is their passion for metaphysical speculation," Browne wrote. "This passion, so far from being confined to the learned classes, permeates all ranks, and manifests itself in the shopkeeper and the muleteer, as well as in the scholar and the man of letters." Browne is one of the few Western scholars of Persian studies still respected by the Islamic Republic—and even has a street named after him in Tehran.

The minutes ticked by, the numbers on the electronic board flashed higher, and the room went from hot to hotter. I was feeling ridiculously tense, and my basically sleepless night spent on the overnight New York–D.C. train was starting to take its toll. Sweating, I pushed up the sleeves of my heavy black raincoat. Several men stared at my bare arms. I pulled my sleeves back down again.

The board flashed number 50, and our conversation sputtered and died.

"The heart is beating faster," Applicant 63 said. "Things have changed."

This is absurd, I thought to myself, we're only applying for a visa. I reached for an Iranian newspaper that I couldn't read.

Finally, number 59 shot across the board—"Christian! Christian!"

Shahnaz called, in the unlikely event that I'd missed it—and I hurried to the counter to hand my application to a harried, bearded man who'd been fielding questions ever since we'd entered the room. He didn't want to listen to anything I said and flatly turned down my request to plead my case personally to one of the officers in the back office.

Another half hour went by, and Shahnaz, Applicant 63, and I kept completely silent. All of our applications were now under consideration and the air around us had clotted with tension.

"Khanom Bird"—Mrs. Bird—a voice boomed out, and once again I hurried to the counter to the cheerleading of Shahnaz. Without looking up, the bearded man handed me back my application and a photocopied form letter. Rejected, it said.

"What—" I began.

"Try the Iranian Mission to the United Nations," he said, still not looking up. "Or get a letter of invitation."

"Oh, you don't have a letter of invitation?" Shahnaz said when I told her what happened. "You must have a letter of invitation."

"Yes, you must have a letter of invitation," Applicant 63 said.

I didn't know what to say. Earlier, I'd told them both that I had no such letter, and they'd both said that they didn't think it would matter much one way or the other.

ॐॐ

One of the first decisions that I had to make when applying for a visa to visit Iran was what kind of a visa to apply for. As far as I could tell, I had three options—a tourist visa, a student visa, or a press visa—but I had no one to advise me definitely as to which option was best. Given the difficulties of dealing with the Iranian Interests Section, and the nonexistence of United States–Iran diplomatic relations, I didn't even have an official office I could call. Every Iranian American I spoke with had a different opinion regarding the best way to approach the matter, and I worried about the possibility of making the wrong choice and blowing my chances altogether. Complicating things was the fact that I wanted to stay in Iran for a minimum of three months.

I considered the tourist visa first. It seemed the best option, because although I wanted to write a travelogue, I didn't particularly want to label myself a journalist. I wanted to simply meander through the country incognito, gathering impressions without worrying about officialdom. But then I learned that tourist visas were usually issued for only two or three weeks and that to obtain one, I had to either travel in a tour group or travel with a constant guide—not acceptable, as far as I was concerned—or have a letter of invitation from someone in Iran. Even worse, my summer Persian tutor Farnaz told me, was the fact that the Islamic government didn't approve of women traveling alone with no apparent purpose. They would probably turn down my application on that basis alone.

Then, as now, I had no way of knowing whether Farnaz's statement was absolutely correct. Like many things people told me in Iran, it seemed to be both rumor and fact. Other women I met in Iran confirmed Farnaz's statement, but while there, I did hear rumor of two female tourists traveling on their own without guides—a French lady in the citadel city of Bam and a Dutch woman bicycling in the south. I didn't meet either of them, however, and so can't confirm that they actually entered the country alone. For all I know, they could have been tour group travelers gone AWOL.

Farnaz, who'd recently moved to New York from Tehran, also told me that women were not allowed to stay in hotels alone in Iran. I'd read that in one or two books as well, and once I got to the country, many women in Tehran—my first stop, where I stayed with friends—told me the same thing. One even described the travails of a middle-aged lawyer friend who'd had to get a letter from the police in order to stay at a hotel while attending a professional conference. But other people I met in Tehran assured me that all this was pure nonsense—the ignorant opinion of women who hadn't traveled much. Only by incessantly asking around did I eventually arrive at some sort of semisatisfying answer. Both statements, it seemed, were correct. Foreign and middle-aged or older Iranian women usually had no problems staying at hotels alone. But younger Iranian women did. As one hotel owner later confirmed for me, Iranian women in their twenties and thirties most certainly did have to have permission from the police before being allowed to check into his establishment alone.

One of the most unsettling things about traveling—and living—in Iran today is that it's hard to establish the truth about much of anything. Rumors run rampant and conspiracy theories abound. Many Iranians won't answer a stranger's questions directly, and simply calling up a government agency or organization—the hotel association of Iran, say (which doesn't exist, at least in the Western sense)—for more information isn't exactly an option, either. People will want to know who you are and why you're calling.

Making matters worse is the fact that the ground in Iran is constantly shifting. What's true today will not be true tomorrow. And what's true in one town, city, or establishment may not be true in another. For the most part, Iran lacks strong centralized administrative offices and so laws are often elastic and subject to interpretation. Travelers and citizens are frequently at the mercy of petty officials who may or may not grant their requests, depending on how the mood strikes them.

I next considered the student visa. Its main advantage was length, along with relative ease of access. All I had to do was apply to the Persian-language program being offered to foreign students by the Universities of Tehran and Esfahan. Only recently opened up to Americans, the program would allow me to stay in Iran for four blissful months. The only problem was that it would make traveling difficult. I imagined myself skipping out of class for weeks at a time and being put on a blacklist, suspected of being a spy.

In the end, the press visa made the most sense, though it had its drawbacks as well. As a journalist, people would definitely be watching me. I was also initially worried that my amorphous project, involving much unsupervised travel, would not be approved of. But the other options didn't work, and a press visa, I realized at last, would give me more security. No one could arrest me for taking notes, I would have a recognized reason for being in Iran, staying alone in hotels would be easier, and I would have an office to call, should I want to arrange an official interview or obtain hard facts.

As I'd found out in Washington, press visas could be applied for only through the Iranian Mission to the United Nations in New York. Several phone calls and letters there resulted in my connecting with the most helpful Amir Zamani. In charge of media relations, Mr. Zamani approved of my project and sent my request and credentials on to Tehran. Three short weeks later, I had a visa. The only hitch was that it was for only one month. I could, however, apply for an extension once I got there. And what were my chances of getting one? I asked Mr. Zamani when he called with the good news. "It's been known to happen," he said.

I went to meet with Mr. Zamani in the Iranian Mission's offices, housed in a glass-sheathed skyscraper in Midtown. A young bearded man came down to meet me in the lobby and escort me wordlessly upstairs, past an armed guard. We entered a nondescript office furnished with three fat black leather sofas and a wrinkled Persian carpet. On the wall hung side-by-side photographs of Ayatollah Khomeini, President Khatami, and Supreme Leader Ali Khamene'i—the triumvirate whose visages I would later see constantly grouped together all over Iran. Khomeini's face was grim, Khatami's kindly and avuncular, Khamene'i's inscrutable. Appointed Iran's spiritual leader after the death of Ayatollah Khomeini in 1989, the hard-liner Khamene'i—not President Khatami—is by far the most powerful man in the Islamic Republic. He controls the country's security and intelligence forces, the army, the judiciary, and radio and television. But ever since Khatami's election, an intense power struggle has been going on between those who support the president's reformist policies and those who seek to maintain the closed, conservative rule of Khamene'i and his associates.

Mr. Zamani, dressed in a casual green polo shirt and tan slacks, entered the room. He answered all my questions frankly and gave me recommendations about places to go and people to meet in Iran. Then he suggested that whenever I travel outside of Tehran, I travel with a friend; did I have any friends in Iran? Hesitantly, I nodded yes. I had by then collected a list of contacts from my Persian tutors Farnaz and Ali, Professor Kasheff, the Foundation for Iranian Studies—a Washington, D.C.–based educational and research institution—and friends of friends. Once I'd started asking around, it seemed as if everyone I knew had an Iranian friend. One year before, I hadn't known a single Iranian American; since then, I'd met at least a dozen, many with family still in Iran, whom they insisted I look up. Best of all, my father—who was almost as excited about my trip as I was, as if he himself were going—had located a former colleague, who'd promised to meet me at the airport.

But I couldn't consider any of these contacts friends, and I had no intention of traveling with any of them.

"Why can't I travel alone?" I said.

Mr. Zamani paused. "You can, but . . . it would be better to be with a friend."

"Why?"

"In case you have any problems."

"What kind of problems?"

"With the language, with transportation, with the hotels."

That didn't sound too bad. I could handle all that.

"But I am allowed to travel alone?" I persisted.

"Yes." Mr. Zamani looked unhappy. "But it would not be so good. Travel with a friend."

I kept pressing for particulars, but Mr. Zamani didn't give me any, and I left his office wondering exactly what he'd meant by his suggestion. Would I have problems buying bus tickets or eating in restaurants or staying in hotels alone—even with my press credentials? Would the police stop me for walking the streets by myself? Would people assume that I was a prostitute? (Why would I go to Iran to be a prostitute?) Or a spy?

The few journalistic accounts I'd found about traveling in contemporary Iran hadn't mentioned anything about these sorts of problems; in fact, they'd made Iran seem like quite a friendly country. On the other hand, most of those journalistic accounts had been written by men.

Whatever the truth was, I would soon be finding it out for myself. The hour of departure was almost at hand. As I traveled down to Washington again, to physically pick up the visa that Mr. Zamani had brokered, I wondered at the stop-and-start process by which my initially half-baked idea to revisit Iran had metamorphosed into reality. It was no longer a warm daydream but rather a cold fact of my very immediate future. Just how did I get myself into this? I wondered.

သာ

My plane landed at Tehran's Mehrabad International Airport at 2:30 A.M. one hot, velvet black morning in late August 1998. The flight out of London on a worn Iran Air Boeing 747 had been unremarkable, except for a few details. "In the name of God," had begun the standard airline safety announcement—in both Persian and English—and it had been followed a moment later by the phrase "women must dress Islamic." All the women on the plane, myself and the female cabin crew included, were wearing the *hejab*—the covering that all women must wear in public—and the cabin crew's black raincoats with brass buttons matched their male colleagues' preppy blazers. Half dozing off at one point, I noticed a bevy of hooded creatures flowing down the aisle and was struck by how ancient the image seemed.

My seatmate, Nasrin, was an attractive, middle-aged Iranian woman, now living in England, who returned to Iran every year to visit relatives. In contrast to the rest of us women, who were dressed in dark colors, she was wearing a shimmering blue satin coat embroidered with yellow flowers, with plastic shoes that matched. She spent most of the flight flirting with the steward and was excited to hear that I was planning to return to Tabriz.

"Oh, there's something about childhood that's so magical!" she said. "When I was little and still living in Iran, we used to go to the country on the weekends and pick fruit off the trees. The air was so clear and bright, there were no people, we owned the village—it was paradise. I went back there five or six years ago and—bloody hell!—either it had changed or I had changed."

Coming into the Mehrabad terminal, I felt surprisingly calm. The last-minute fears that I'd had before leaving New York, and even the jittery nervousness that had kept me on edge throughout the flight, had evaporated. I was here now and had to deal with whatever came my way. If things proved to be horrifically bad, I'd simply turn around and go back home.

Scanning the large, fluorescent-green hall of passport control, I could spot only two armed guards and two small photographs of President Khatami and Supreme Leader Khamene'i. I felt distinctly disappointed. The face of Ayatollah Khomeini, whom I'd expected to welcome me, was nowhere in sight. People were queuing up neatly and quietly beneath a sign that read PASSPORT in English. We could almost be in any airport in the world.

A short, white-haired man wearing a bright pink shirt seemed to be waving at me from an upper balcony beyond passport control. Who is he? I wondered, still dazed from the flight, and then noticed that he was carrying a large sign that read MS. BIRD, DR. FARATIAN WAITING. Staring, I suddenly realized that this must be Bahman, my father's old friend and medical student, and waved back.

After a surprisingly short wait, I passed easily through passport control, collected my luggage from a crowded carousel, and walked by a wall hung with a big photograph of Ayatollah Khomeini. This is more like it, I thought. Through glass windows facing the street I could see Bahman waiting amid the same jumble of taxis that crowd up against every airport in the world and kiosks lit by a candy-colored neon more playful than anything I'd seen in the West. I crossed under a quotation from the Qor'an and asked a friendly Iranian American walking beside me to translate.

"I hate Arabic," he said, and then I passed out into the night.

BOUNDARIES

There is a red line in Iran that you should not cross. But no one knows where it is.

—Popular saying in Iran

ONE

The first time I stepped out onto the streets of Tehran, I felt like a child again. Lona, Bahman's secretary, had to hold my hand, as people and traffic rushed and roared around us. Jet lag made me unsteady on my feet, and my long, heavy black raincoat seemed to be pulling me down toward a parched pavement that was simultaneously rising up to suck at my hem. The hot August sunlight burned across my shoulders.

The crush of women in black around us was overwhelming. Left and right, shrouded figures were striding purposefully by, carrying purses and briefcases and shopping bags. Because this was fashionable north Tehran, most were dressed as I was, in a *manteau*—the French word for coat that is commonly used in Iran—and a *rusari*, or head scarf. The *manteaus* all looked alike to me, but the *rusaris* came in a wide variety of muted colors and designs, as well as the occasional bright blue or green. Only a few women were wearing the *chador*, the traditional black bell-shaped garment that covers both the head and the body and is held at the chin by a hand or teeth. But whether encircled by a *rusari* or a *chador*, the women's faces shone out like jewels.

I was both one of them and a being apart. In a few days, I would get

15

used to my *manteau* and *rusari* and barely notice them anymore; in a month, in fact, I would feel uncomfortable when in the presence of some men without my covering. In a few days, I would visit other parts of Tehran and know that this crush of people and traffic was nothing. But for the moment, I felt lost and, despite my disguise, horribly conspicuous.

Lona, her seven-year-old daughter Sepideh, and I were heading straight for the *manteau* shop. Though my American raincoat had met with considerable approval from Lona's discerning eye, we'd both agreed that it was far too warm for August. We walked down a smart street, lined with plate-glass shop windows displaying everything from Gucci shoes to Nike baseball caps. We passed by one sidewalk vendor selling hot tea out of a big silver pot, another grilling ears of corn over an electric heater, and a third selling shelled walnuts out of a jar filled with salt water. The shelled walnuts looked naked, like tiny brains.

The *manteau* shop was close and crowded, with the racks of raincoats separated by color. Green, blue, brown, gray, cream, and lots and lots of black. Some had fancy buttons, tassels, and ties, and most had shoulder pads. An embroidered gold panel turned one garment into a semi—evening gown and a nubby hood gave another a schoolgirl look. While I looked around helplessly, not knowing where to begin, Lona tried to convince me to buy one of the black-and-brown animal prints, or at least a light-colored raincoat. To wear light colors in Iran is a mildly liberal political statement, and as a foreigner, I could get away with a lot. But I refused. For all of the colors available in the shop, I'd already noticed that most of the women in the street were wearing black. I didn't want to stand out any more than I already did. And besides, I came from New York.

Finally, I chose the thinnest black *manteau* I could find, and we returned to the street, where I looked around me with a heightened awareness. I could now see differences in the women's attire that I hadn't noticed before. True, most of the *manteau*s were black, but they were of different lengths, styles, shapes, and fabrics. Some clung, some hung, some billowed, some flattered. Some seemed matronly, some youthful, some elegant, and some—that lovely flowing garment with the V-shaped front panel—sexy.

There were other differences in the women's attire as well. Everyone was wearing her *rusari* differently, with various amounts of hair sticking out the front or back. Iranian women have perfected something called the *kakol*, or forelock, which is a pile of teased hair—sometimes several inches high—

that sits atop the forehead. The *kakol* deliberately flouts the whole purpose of the *rusari,* as does the long braid or swish of loose hair hanging out the back that some younger women brandish.

The women's lower extremities also sent out various messages. Some were wearing jeans, some elegant trousers, some heavy socks, and some stockings that were daringly sheer—another liberal political statement. Iran's Islamic dress code decrees that women keep their lower legs and feet well covered, so thin stockings, along with open-toed sandals worn without socks, are forbidden.

Equally diverse were the women's shoes. They ranged from practical flats to stylish designer heels, from sneakers to hiking boots. Variations in these last two were especially popular among the college-age women, and I instinctively knew that each one was sending out a very different signal, which I was too old and foreign to read.

I adjusted the shoulder pads of my new *manteau.* Now that I was wearing a lightweight Iranian garment instead of a heavy Western one, I felt a bit better. I'd also noticed one or two women with light brown, almost blond, hair and realized that Lona was nearly as tall as I was. Perhaps, as a tall, blond American woman, I didn't stand out as much as I'd thought.

A moment later, Lona nudged me and tilted her head toward a parked car against which two men in dark green uniforms without insignia of any kind were leaning. "Pasdaran," she whispered, and I tried not to stare while simultaneously realizing that the men had already noticed me notice them and had registered my Western face. So much for my fleeting hopes of not standing out.

I'd read a lot about the Pasdaran, or Revolutionary Guards, an organization formed after the revolution when the clerics did not trust the regular Iranian army, which had previously supported the Shah. Initially a small unit designed only to protect the new leaders, the Pasdaran had quickly developed into both a powerful internal security force that patrolled the streets for breaches in Islamic conduct and a full-fledged armed troops that fought in the Iran–Iraq War. The Pasdaran's civilian counterpart had been the *komitehs* ("committees"), volunteer organizations formed around mosques and student and workers' groups as a rival authority to the regular police. In the early 1980s, the *komitehs* had roamed the streets, vigilante style, arbitrarily arresting thousands of people for everything from suspected prostitution to antigovernment activities and invading private homes on a whim in search of such incriminating "un-Islamic" evidence as liquor, Western music, and chessboards. The latter were outlawed in the early years of the revolution because of their associations with gambling and royalty.

In the mid-1990s, the Pasdaran and *komiteh*s were merged into a single "disciplinary force," but many people still refer to the uniformed guards as the "Pasdaran" or "*komiteh*" and can tell the difference between them. Some also call them the "morals police." Their street surveillance is far more lax than it once was, but there is still no telling when they might suddenly arrest someone. On another walk just a few days later, Lona, Sepideh, and I would pass by two guards herding three young women with tattoos and heavy makeup into a van. Both tattoos and heavy makeup are officially forbidden in the Islamic Republic, even though cosmetic stores thrive and many women wear far more makeup than do most women in the United States.

From the Pasdaran, Lona, Sepideh, and I passed on to a small, covered bazaar selling inexpensive clothes, shoes, jewelry, and spices. Plastic shopping bags emblazoned with English words hung next to the stalls: *Marlboro, Winston, National.* We passed by a sleepy boy sitting beside a parakeet perched on a box filled with paper packets the size of tea bags. Each packet contained a verse from Hafez, the beloved Iranian poet of the fourteenth century, and for a nominal fee, the boy instructed the parakeet to choose one for me. The Iranians consult Hafez as the Chinese consult the *I Ching*, and each verse serves as an obfuscated fortune that's open to various interpretations. Ambiguity is highly valued in Iran—a fact that delighted the writer part of me.

Later, Bahman loosely translated my fortune for me:

Let us sprinkle flowers around and put wine in the cup.
Let us split the sphere open and start a new design.
If grief arises and sends an army to attack people in love,
We will join with the cup bearer and together we will uproot them.

I didn't know exactly what that verse meant, but overall, I thought, it seemed to bode quite well for the journey ahead of me.

Next to the bazaar stood the Saleh Shrine, its blue mosaic dome sweetly curved and crisscrossed with white. The dome was topped with the cupped logo of the Islamic Republic of Iran, which is a sword bracketed with four crescent moons that stands for the unity and oneness of God. "Unto Allah belong the East and the West, and whithersoever ye turn, there is Allah's countenance. Lo! Allah is All-Embracing, All-Knowing" reads the Qor'an (2:115).

Despite the many modern shops just down the street, the courtyard in front of the Saleh Shrine was teeming, mostly with older women in black *chadors*—bending, pushing, swaying, tittering. The women looked much smaller to me now than they had in childhood, of course, but en masse and with their backs to me, they still elicited the same emotions—curiosity and dread. Later, as I learned more about Iran, I would know better, but those emotions never completely disappeared.

Some of the women were sitting cross-legged on the ground and praying out loud to themselves, some were performing ablutions in a central fountain, and some were taking off their shoes to enter the shrine itself. Men in trim blue uniforms were moving through the crowd, carrying tall, electric-purple feather dusters. I stared at the flamboyant plumes in disbelief—this was the brightest color I'd yet seen in Iran, and I couldn't imagine what they were for. At first I thought the obvious—at about four feet long, the dusters could clean many out-of-the-way spots. But then I noticed that the men were using them to tap certain worshippers disapprovingly on the head, for improper attire or pushy behavior.

Because Lona and I were not wearing *chadors*, we could not enter the shrine. We could, however, enter the courtyard, and after a guard instructed me to pull down my *rusari*, we moved into the hooded crowd. The shrine sparkled in front of us, its *eivan*, or vaulted interior hall, open to the courtyard and shiny with green mosaic glass and crystal chandeliers. A wrinkled woman tried to sell me a booklet of verses from the Qor'an, but I was too busy turning this way and that, trying to take everything in at once. This was my first brush with Islam in action and I had dozens of excited questions for Lona, who spoke English about as well as I spoke Persian—which is to say, barely. We were gesticulating wildly to each other, trying to make ourselves understood, when the dreaded duster descended. Apparently, we'd overstepped the bounds of appropriate Islamic behavior.

Moving out of the courtyard, I noticed several photocopied sheets of paper plastered onto a wall. They all depicted grim bearded men and looked like "wanted" posters. Lona told me, however, that they were death announcements.

৵৽৻

Bahman lived in a brand new five-story apartment building in Zahfaranieh, a wealthy neighborhood in north Tehran. Less than a decade earlier, the area had been a mountain village, and when I awoke on my first mornings in Iran, I could hear the cawing of roosters from other villages located still farther north in the Alborz foothills. More than three decades earlier, when my parents were living in Iran, north Tehran as it is now known did not exist. One of its largest neighborhoods, the now-vibrant Shemiran, was then nothing more than a sparsely populated summer retreat.

Perhaps the most astonishing change that has come to Iran since the Islamic Revolution—even more than politics and religion—is its exponential population growth. Since 1979, the country's population has nearly doubled, from roughly 36 million to almost 65 million, and nearly two thirds of Iran's people are under the age of 25. The explosion is largely the result of government policy, which in the early years following the Revolution encouraged citizens to have as many children as they could. People were needed to help spread the word of Shi'ite Islam and to replace those lost during the Iran–Iraq War. Only in the mid-1980s did the Islamic government realize the full and potentially disastrous consequences of its hasty decree—including widespread unemployment, housing shortages, an inadequate infrastructure, and, more recently, a disaffected youth that may ultimately prove to be the government's undoing. Born after the Revolution, many of these young Iranians have no memories of Khomeini—or the Shah—and are worried more about finding jobs than about politics. The voting age in Iran is 16 and the moderate, reform-minded President Khatami was elected largely by the young, and by women. Today, the Islamic government is aggressively pushing birth control, for which it regularly wins citations from international organizations.

I had originally planned to stay with Bahman and his wife for four or five days, or perhaps a week, tops. That, to my Western sense of hospitality and time, was already a great deal to ask of perfect strangers. My father hadn't spoken to or corresponded with Bahman for thirty years, after all. But Bahman had other ideas. I was hardly a stranger!—I was the daughter of Frank Bird, who had taught him early lessons in medicine. And one week was nothing—in fact, it was less than nothing. I was welcome to stay with him and his wife as long as I liked and to use their apartment as a base in which to store my things when I traveled outside of Tehran. They'd already cleared out a room for me.

Unaccustomed as I was then to the overwhelming hospitality of Persian culture, I felt a little uncomfortable. As I would learn later in my travels, however, Iranians love having houseguests and are often the most generous—as well as sometimes the most tyrannical—of hosts.

Because Bahman's wife, who is English, was in England when I arrived, Bahman asked his secretary Lona and her sister Pari to help him introduce me to life in Iran. Both were handsome, solidly built women in their twenties whose family had known Bahman's family for years. Both were also divorced, and Lona had her daughter Sepideh.

Lona and Pari were eager to assist me in any way they could. From a working-class family in Tabriz, they had lots of questions about America: What kind of food do we eat? Do women always wear short skirts? Is everyone tall and blond? Extremely hard workers, they didn't like to see me perform mundane personal chores, like cleaning my room or doing my own laundry, and they cooked elaborate dishes from their home province of Azerbaijan every night, even after spending long afternoons at the office: *tahchin-e morgh,* a baked chicken-and-rice dish with a crispy crust on top; *kuku-ye sabzi,* a richly textured omelet, thick with herbs; and *kufteh tabrizi,* Tabriz-style meatballs, made with prunes and apricots.

Lona, the older sister, had a flawless oval brown face with large almond eyes and lustrous black hair. Practical and self-confident, she seemed capable of handling virtually any situation; woe to the shopkeeper, I thought on more than one occasion, who tried to pull one over on her. She had a firm opinion on most subjects, sometimes raising her voice to shrill decibels, and an elegant taste that ran to small earrings and slim pieces of jewelry. Pari, in contrast, had a chalk-white complexion, sparkling black eyes, and striking dark eyebrows. She rarely spoke and occasionally seemed nervous. Her taste ran more to the dramatic. The sisters, however, shared a bubbling sense of humor and laughed easily, while Sepideh—a serious child at the top of her class—and I often looked on in mute incomprehension.

Bahman reigned over us women like a benevolent Turkic Persian prince. A short, handsome, and extremely kind man with a heavy mane of white hair, he was also originally from Tabriz, where most people are of a Turkic extraction and speak the Azeri Turkish language. Now a well-known gynecologist, he had been forced to flee Iran during the Islamic Revolution. His English wife, many Christian friends, and good income had made him an obvious probable target of the zealous revolutionaries, and he'd departed the country soon after finding the words *Dr. Faratian must die* written over his office door. He'd returned to Iran only in 1993, at the behest of the Iranian government, who'd extended its invitation to many other expatriated professionals as well. Bahman was one of the few who'd taken the government up on its offer. He'd had a more than comfortable life in England, he told me, but Iran was his country and he wanted to help his people.

Bahman's return to Iran gave him special status both in the community and among government officials, but he was nonetheless in an awkward position. While in England, he'd been part of the infertility team that had developed the world's first in vitro fertilizations. His return to Iran had been especially welcomed because he could bring with him the latest infertility techniques and introduce them to his colleagues. But men are no longer allowed to train as gynecologists in Iran—Islamic law forbids it—and so Bahman was one of a dying breed. All those who attended his lectures were women, and some of those women resented his gender. Some of his techniques, such as artificial insemination, were also highly problematic at first. In a traditional Islamic society, a woman can become legally pregnant only by her husband. Artificial insemination is therefore not allowed, and during his first years back, Bahman had had to obtain a special decree from Supreme Leader Khamene'i himself whenever he'd wanted to perform the procedure.

Bahman talked about my father as a young man in a way that made me catch my breath. He remembered how my father had paced before he was to perform an operation, reviewing human anatomy in his head, and how he'd studied his patients' hands for clues as to their illnesses. He remembered several field trips the two of them had taken together and could still imitate my father's cramped signature perfectly, down to the dashing *F* and illegible *-ird*. My father has always talked about Bahman with a great deal of fondness, but I knew that he didn't remember him in such detail. To my father, then already an accredited doctor from a powerful country, Bahman had been just a student 10 years his junior. To Bahman, the son of a bus driver from a provincial city, my father had been a learned man, representing the then seemingly omnipotent, technically advanced West. Now, though, it was Bahman who was the famous physician.

Despite the wealth of Bahman's neighborhood, it—like much of Tehran—had a cluttered, ragged, unfinished feel. Many of its new apartment buildings sported ersatz resortlike façades, only vaguely protected by flimsy walls that seemed to mock the old Persian ideal of hiding one's home behind thick clay bulwarks. Construction was going on in many of the streets, few of which had sidewalks, and cranes sat like dozing vultures atop at least a half-dozen buildings. Many of these cranes never moved an inch during my stay; running out of money while building is not unusual in inflation-rife Iran.

Along the short, dusty road that descended from Bahman's apartment to the main street ran a *jube,* or concrete water channel. During the spring, when the snow melts in the Alborz Mountains, or after a rain, the *jube* fills with water that then travels downstream to the city center. My parents had told me stories about the *jube*s and how in their time they'd been used both for washing clothes and as sewers, and so I was surprised to see them in the wealthy north. But water is a precious commodity in Iran—the average rainfall is only 12 inches a year—and *jube*s, I later found out, still line many of Tehran's main streets, where they sometimes join with surfacing underground streams. Some of these rushing waterways are three or four feet wide, and I often saw boys playing in them.

A *jube* had run outside our home in Tabriz, I remembered then in a flash, but our parents had never let us get near it, let alone play in it. Not surprisingly, they'd been worried about disease. But we had had two white-and-tan "*jube* dogs"—as the strays were called—as pets, much to the horror of our Iranian servants. Generally speaking, traditional Iranians do not keep dogs as pets. They regard them as unclean.

By the side of the road one block south of Bahman's apartment was a blue box cupped with painted yellow hands, with a plywood dove on top. It sat on a post about three feet tall and had a slit for money. ALMS MAKE YOU RICHER and TO GIVE ALMS IS TO PROTECT YOURSELF AGAINST SEVENTY KINDS OF EVIL EYES read words stenciled on the sides. To give money to the poor is one of the five basic tenets of Islam, and thousands upon thousands of donation boxes fleck the Iranian landscape. Most of the boxes are a standard, machine-made blue and yellow, with a plywood dove, rose, or tulip on top, but I also noticed several homemade-looking versions. Iranians take their obligation of giving very seriously, and people often stop to push faded bills into the money slots. The proceeds go to the Helping Committee of Imam Khomeini, a charity organization that was set up following the Revolution to provide services for the poor. Charitable foundations in Iran have a widespread reputation for mind-boggling corruption—said to run into many millions of dollars—but they are at least somewhat effective: I saw relatively few beggars in the Islamic Republic.

Two blocks south of Bahman's apartment stood a cluster of small gaping shops selling dry goods, vegetables, and meat. The shops had rolling iron grills for doors and sold a mix of Iranian and European wares—Lux, Mazola, Bic, Crest, Nescafé. Next door stood a bakery, dark, ancient, and hot, with a red fire roaring in a clay oven in the back and flour-dusted men tossing balls of dough up front. They were making *sangak*, one of four kinds of Persian flat bread, which is stretched out into the shape of an elongated pizza and baked until it is brown and bumpy on top. Most Iranians buy their bread fresh every day, and wherever I traveled in the country, I passed boys on bicycles, pedaling home with limp slabs of bread big as tabloid newspapers draped across their handlebars.

Actual newspapers and magazines were sold from a kiosk in front of the neighborhood shops. Among the dozens offered were the three English-language newspapers published in Tehran—*Iran News, Tehran Times,* and *Iran Daily*—and the international editions of *Time* and *Newsweek,* sold in sealed cellophane wrappers. The magazines' text was never censored, but all photos that were deemed offensive—those depicting women with cleavage or women with exposed hair, arms, or legs—were blacked out with a marker.

The three English-language newspapers were slim affairs, published primarily for Iran's diplomatic and Western-educated communities. *Tehran Times* was put out by *Kayhan*, a well-established, hard-line newspaper; *Iran Daily* was supported by the moderates; and *Iran News* straddled the philosophical difference between the two. Or so I was told, because in reality I could see only minor differences among the publications, all of which usually supported government policy.

For more controversial news coverage, I would have had to go to the Persian-language newspapers, which, unfortunately, I couldn't read. I was in Iran during a remarkable flowering of the press. In the year and a half following Khatami's election, the number of newspapers published in the country had more than quadrupled, until they numbered over 120. Most popular among them during my visit were *Hamshahri,* supported by Tehran's former mayor, the then recently ousted Gholam-Hosein Karbaschi, and *Tus,* supported by President Khatami. In Iran, newspapers are financed not through advertising and circulation but rather by political parties or organizations.

Every morning along major streets and highways, I saw vendors waving copies of *Hamshahri* and *Tus,* which citizens rushed to buy. Though there had been some muted freedom of the press in the Islamic Republic since the early 1990s, newspapers at the time of my visit were publishing stories that openly criticized the government and/or exposed some of Iran's many social problems. *Hamshahri* took a cautious approach, but *Tus* was frighteningly bold. They're going too far, people whispered among themselves, and they were right. *Tus* was closed down numerous times just before, during, and after my stay—only to be started up again and again under different names. Repression in Iran is far from absolute, and the "new" papers were usually allowed to keep the "old" paper's address, printing presses, and staff. Finally, however, in November 1999, the newspaper's editor, Mashallah Shamsolva'ezin, was put on trial and sentenced to 30 months in prison.*

⊱❧⊰

North Tehran backs up into the embrace of the Alborz Mountains, the most defining physical characteristic of the city. Bone dry and nearly devoid of vegetation in many parts, the Alborz are a living, breathing, shape-shifting presence that seems to stretch, yawn, buckle, and bend as it looms over the metropolis like a giant elephant in repose. One unexpected jerk in the middle of its usually protective sleep and it could kick the entire city right out of its foothills.

Sometimes the Alborz—as high as the American Rockies—are all ridges, valleys, rocks, and sand, with sunlight illuminating a hidden cliff here, an unexpected rockslide there. Sometimes the Alborz are a flat, impenetrable, dun-colored wall, separating Tehran—and by extension, it seems, all of Iran—from the rest of the world. Sometimes the Alborz are sensual, red-hued, and comforting. Sometimes the Alborz are craggy, black, and forbidding.

Sensitive to every nuance of light and atmosphere, the Alborz subtly change color with the day. Though often a dull gray or maroon at first glance, closer looks reveal shifting green streaks, pink splotches, and purple peaks. A cloud passes over, casting down a blue patch.

On especially sunny days in north Tehran, the light of the Alborz reminded me of the light of my early childhood. This was the same stark

---

*In 2000, the situation of the press in Iran changed dramatically. One of the first acts of a new reformist parliament, elected that February, was to propose legislation guaranteeing a free press. But Supreme Leader Khamene'i intervened, blocking the legislation, and by August, 23 reformist publications had been shut down.

backdrop across which my memories were moving. The air was buoyant, the slopes bleak.

On other days, though, as I wandered through the heart of the downtown, I would forget all about the mountains—often rendered close to invisible by horrendous pollution. Along with Mexico City and Bangkok, Tehran is one of the most polluted cities in the world. But then a ray of sunlight would glance off a snowy peak or the sense of a powerful presence would make me look up. And then, there they were again, the Alborz, which have haunted Iran's consciousness since its very beginnings.

The ancient Persians believed that the Alborz grew from the surface of the earth, taking 800 years to reach their full height, as their roots reached deep into the ground and their peaks attached themselves to the sky. The stars, sun, and moon were thought to revolve around these peaks, and they became the mythological home of Mithra, the god of the cosmic order who later became known as the sun god in both Iran and India. Mithra and the creation of the Alborz are described in the *Avesta*, the holy book of the Zoroastrian religion. An ancient faith, founded in what is now Iran between 1000 and 700 B.C., Zoroastrianism was the first known belief system to posit the concepts of life as a perennial struggle between good and evil, individual responsibility for moral behavior, the resurrection of the body, the Last Judgment, and life everlasting. Islam, Judaism, and Christianity all trace many articles of their faiths back to Zoroastrianism.

To the east of Tehran, and visible only from certain angles of the city, is the Alborz's highest peak, Mount Damavand (18,602 feet). A magnificent cone-shaped volcano that is perpetually covered with snow, Mount Damavand is to Iran what Mount Fuji is to Japan and Kilimanjaro is to Tanzania.

Mount Damavand is home to many legendary Persian figures, including the magical bird Simorgh, whose nest is said to be close to the sun, and the evil ruler Zahhak, who is living out eternity bound in chains at the bottom of a well deep inside the mountain. Though a hero as a youth, Zahhak was seduced by the devil, who exploited his ignorance of evil and talked him into murdering his father. In return, promised the devil, Zahhak would become not only ruler of his father's lands but also ruler of all the world. As soon as the pact was made, two black snakes suddenly sprouted out of Zahhak's shoulders. He cut off their heads, but they instantly grew back again and demanded to be fed the brains of two strong men every day. Thereafter began a reign of terror that lasted for 1,000 years, until the arrival of Fereydun, a youth as tall and slim as a cypress tree, with a face as fair as the silver moon. Born in a village on Mount Damavand, Fereydun struck Zahhak with a bull-headed mace and was about to cut off his head when an angel appeared and told him to lock Zahhak inside the mountain instead, as a warning to all future men. Fereydun did so, and there Zahhak lives to this day.

A sort of modern-day equivalent of Zahhak is the notorious Evin prison, situated in the soft brown foothills of the Alborz on the north-western edge of the city. Once part of a suburb, Evin now belongs to Tehran proper and is only a short distance away from the sleek, luxurious Azadi Grand Hotel, many of whose rooms overlook the prison. *Azadi* means "freedom," but when I commented on the obvious irony of its name to my new Iranian friends, they just shrugged. In Iran, people are used to living beside the absurd.

While in Tehran, I passed by Evin prison nearly every day on my way downtown from Bahman's. From the outside, it looked tame and innocuous. Serrated brown walls zigzagged their way up one hillside to disappear into a valley behind, and to reappear again on the far hillside. Inside the walls, the prison appeared to be largely empty space—I caught only occasional glimpses of buildings resembling dormitories and sheds. But at night, everything changed. Bright, hot prison spotlights flicked on, reminding me in one suffocating instant of Evin's horrific history.

During the reign of the Shah, the prison was the stronghold of SAVAK, the ruthless secret police trained by the American CIA and the Israeli Mossad, and after the revolution, thousands of political prisoners were tortured and others put to death there. Today's version of SAVAK, SAVAMA, has nothing approaching the zealous reputation of its predecessor, thought by various human rights organizations to have held between 25,000 and 100,000 Iranians political prisoner in the mid-1970s. However, whereas SAVAK concentrated primarily on political dissidents, SAVAMA keeps tabs on the most mundane details of ordinary citizens' lives. And there are still far too many stories of men and women disappearing into Evin's bowels for inexplicable reasons and unspecified periods of time. For the year that I was in Iran, Amnesty International's annual report on the country read:

> Hundreds of political prisoners, including prisoners of conscience, were held. Some were detained without charge or trial; others continued to serve long prison sentences imposed after unfair trials.

Reports of torture and ill-treatment continued to be received and judicial punishments of flogging and stoning continued to be imposed. . . . Scores of people were reportedly executed, including at least one prisoner of conscience; however, the true number may have been considerably higher.

৵৽

"Da-da-da-da-da-da, da-da-da-da-da-da——" I was on hold with the Foreign Correspondents and Media Department of the Ministry of Culture and Islamic Guidance. It took me a moment to place the jingly tune I was listening to, but when I did, I started—and would have laughed, had I not been so nervous. Scott Joplin's "The Entertainer," here in the Islamic Republic of Iran, which throughout most of the 1980s had banned all popular Western and Persian music from its airwaves. I knew that things had eased up considerably since then, but I still hadn't expected to hear American ragtime music coming from the offices of a government organization. Somehow, it seemed even more surprising to me than the illegal Michael Jackson and Pink Floyd tapes I'd already heard blaring out of taxi cabs.

A Mr. Ali Reza Shiravi came on the line. Yes, he and his colleagues were expecting me. Please be in his office the next morning at 10:00.

I hung up, almost trembling. Someone had already called Bahman earlier that morning to confirm that I was staying with him, as I'd claimed on my entrance papers. And now I was about to meet with the government officials who would be keeping tabs on me during my stay in Iran. I had no idea whether they'd help or hinder my travels, but I expected the worst.

Established shortly after the revolution, the Ministry of Culture and Islamic Guidance is ubiquitous in Iran. Referred to simply as Ershad, or Guidance, by most Iranians, it monitors virtually every aspect of life in Iran, with the intent—as its name implies—of upholding Islamic standards. Among many other things, Ershad censors the media; decides what films, plays, art exhibits, and concerts can be produced; establishes the educational curricula of schools and universities; organizes the tourism industry, including pilgrimages to Mecca; and monitors financial and judicial institutions.

I arrived at one of Ershad's many branches shortly before 10:00 the next morning. My heart was racing and my throat was dry—Just why was it again that I'd wanted to come to Iran? I half asked myself. A grim bearded man at the entrance waved me toward an elevator, and I rode up to the sixth floor, nearly tripping over my *manteau* as I exited its narrow confines. Once I was inside the Foreign Correspondents Department, however, a woman in a *chador* welcomed me with an application form and a smile that put me somewhat more at ease.

As I sat down to fill out the form, sweat trickling down my back, she joined me, along with another woman dressed in a magnificent blue-checked robe with yellow highlights and cuffs, cinched in by a wide sash. Around her face was pinned a pure white hood that gave her a beatific look, and to the top of her head was attached the black *chador*, which streamed behind her like a dramatic cape. Both women wanted to know more about me and my project, and to my surprise, the one in the blue-checked robe wanted me to take back a letter to relatives living in New York.

Later in my travels, I would get used to this sort of request. Despite the image that most Westerners have of Iran as a closed-off society, many Iranians have relatives living in the West, and there is much contact between Iran and its diaspora.

Mr. Shiravi beckoned me into his office. His telephone voice had led me to expect a forbidding, humorless presence, but instead I met a friendly, bemused-looking man in his thirties, wearing a pinstriped shirt and light blue polyester pants pulled up high on his waist. We talked about Iranian poetry for a few moments and then started discussing my itinerary. Mr. Shiravi explained that I would need letters of permission from his office to interview certain people in Tehran and to visit all cities and regions outside Tehran. Tourists, who usually traveled in groups, did not need such letters, and technically speaking, I could travel without them as well. However, as a single reporter asking questions, I might be stopped by local authorities and the letters would provide me with protection. I would also have to be accompanied by a translator-guide. What was the name of my translator-guide?

I had none and nervously told him so. We returned to discussing my itinerary for a moment, but almost immediately, Mr. Shiravi raised the translator-guide question again. He seemed eager to put a name down in my file. I, however, did not want to have a constant companion by my side. I hoped to wander about on my own and hire a translator only when I needed one. But that seemed to be a foreign concept to Mr. Shiravi, used to having journalists in town on a short-term basis to cover specific stories.

I thought about Mr. Zamani back in New York and his insistence that I travel with a friend. Perhaps Mr. Shiravi's concern about my nonexistent translator-guide stemmed from the same kind of worries that Mr. Zamani had—whatever they were. Cautiously I asked Mr. Shiravi if I would be allowed to stay in hotels by myself. Yes, he said, smiling, and then said that whereas I might be able to get away without a translator-guide in Tehran—since I was staying with friends—I would definitely need one when I was traveling. I would also have to provide him with information on where I would be staying when outside Tehran. He was sorry, but his Boss insisted on it.

Oh, no, I thought to myself. I had hoped to travel more spontaneously than that.

I would have to deal with that problem later, however. First, I had to find out about my bigger worry—extending my visa from one month to three. My ideal plan was to spend three to four weeks in Tehran, and then another two months or so traveling around the country. I wanted to make one loop north to the Valley of the Assassins, the Caspian coast, Tabriz, and Sanandaj, and another loop south to Qom, Esfahan, Shiraz, Kerman, and Yazd. I also hoped to visit Mashhad and Gonbad-e Kavus.

"Oh, don't worry about your visa," Mr. Shiravi said heartily as I broached the subject, but his face fell again when I told him how much longer I wished to stay. "I don't know about two months," he mumbled. "You'll have to talk to the Boss about that."

After Mr. Shiravi and I were done, he asked the women in the front office to type up the four initial permission letters I'd requested: one that would allow me to visit Jamaran, where Ayatollah Khomeini had once lived; another for Friday prayers at the University of Tehran; a third granting me leave to interview people on the street; and a fourth giving me permission to interview mourners at the Behesht-e Zahra cemetery. As it turned out, I never had to use either of these last two letters—or most of the other permission letters that I obtained later.

The women typed up the letters while I waited. And waited and waited. The Boss had to sign them, and no one knew where he was. Sitting on Mr. Shiravi's couch, I fretted about my visa—how could I plan my travels if I didn't know how long I'd be in Iran?—while Mr. Shiravi shuffled through papers. It was a scene that would be repeated many times during my stay in the Islamic Republic. The Boss was often out of the office and Mr. Shiravi was often deluged with work. I got used to watching him frown and massage his brow as he plowed through endless details of reporters' itineraries. Every move of every stay had to be carefully documented, with dates, addresses, and names, ID numbers, and telephone numbers of translator-guides.

Finally, the Boss arrived and I was hurried down the hall into a long, L-shaped room. None of the informal friendliness of the outer offices existed here. The Boss, bearded and distant, was all unsmiling business, and once again, I started to sweat. Made of a thin fabric or not, my polyester *manteau* was *hot.*

No, the Boss said in answer to my question, he doubted that I could get my visa extended for two months, because although he personally didn't care how long I stayed in Iran, the Ministry of Immigration would wonder at what an American was doing wandering around the country for three months. Yes, he snorted when I tried to argue the merits of my case, maybe Americans didn't get much news of Iran, but his office had an average of 30 American journalists coming through every month (a number I found hard to believe). Had Mr. Shiravi explained to me that I could not apply for a visa extension until a few days before the old one expired, and that I was not allowed to work with any other journalists while in the country? I should also take several basic precautions: Never show my passport or money to anyone on the street, and never get into a car, even if commanded to do so by someone in uniform. Instead, hail a taxi and follow behind.

Over the next few months, I would visit or telephone the Foreign Correspondents and Media Department many times, and in the beginning, every contact I had with them quickened my pulse. Several times, Mr. Shiravi called me unexpectedly to check up on some point, setting my heart to racing, and often I wondered to what extent my movements were being tracked. Bahman had told me that he'd sometimes suspected his phone of being tapped, and I imagined Ershad noting what kinds of appointments I set up. I worried when, during an early phone call, I inadvertently mentioned the name of a hated opposition leader, and the drinking I'd witnessed in private homes. I also knew that the Foreign Correspondents Department was checking up on my itinerary—staff members had called the family that I was planning to visit in Qom and checked to see whether Lona and Pari were really traveling with me to Mashhad.

But as time went on, I began to realize that to a large extent, the Foreign

Correspondents Department was just going through the motions. Yes, staff members had checked up on Lona and Pari, but they hadn't asked whether they were translator-guides, as I'd implied but not actually said. And yes, they'd called the various tour guides outside Tehran whose names I'd given them to ask if they'd heard of me. But I intended to hire these guides for only a half-day each and spend the rest of my time unsupervised; no one inquired about that. And after my first two trips out of Tehran, the Foreign Correspondents Department stopped asking me where I'd be staying. Was that because its staff was no longer worried that I might be a spy or because they forgot? And why did they want to monitor me anyway? Because they thought I might be up to no good or because they were worried that something might happen to me? The longer I stayed in Iran, the more convinced I became that the latter was the case. Mr. Shiravi and his colleagues seemed genuinely concerned about my welfare and went out of their way to help me as much as they could.

All of which is not to say that someone was not tracking my movements. If not the Foreign Correspondents Department, then perhaps some other branch of Ershad, or the police, or immigration, or intelligence. With the exception of one minor incident in Yazd, which I describe in more detail below, I never noticed anyone following me, but in Iran, as I was told over and over again, you just never know. Someone could always be watching, waiting for you to step over an invisible line.

TWO

*T*ehran is not a city with a simple downtown. Just as the Alborz Mountains sometimes seem like a living, uncontrollable, shape-shifting beast, so does the city, with cluttered avenues, cement overpasses, roaring highways, and teeming traffic circles that seem to writhe in, through, and around the city like body parts that just can't keep still. A building is going up here, another is being repaired there, a badly broken sidewalk disrupts passage along one major avenue, and an abandoned subway project disrupts passage along another. Pedestrians jam the walkways; traffic swells the streets.

And overlooking it all are the faces. Faces of ayatollahs. Faces of martyrs. Faces gazing down at the Qor'an. Faces looking up toward the heavens. Faces surrounded by flowers. Faces surrounded by doves. Faces wearing red headbands, connected to bodies carrying machine guns. Faces atop trucks and tanks.

The art of the mural is highly developed in Iran. Dozens of blank walls in every city, town, and village are covered with carefully executed pictures, many painted in pastels. Some depict the obvious—Khomeini, Khamene'i, Khatami. But many more depict martyrs or scenes from the Iran–Iraq War. Some of these martyrs are famous figures that all Iranians instantly recognize; others are generic young boys with flushed faces and soulful eyes. Small towns and villages proudly display the images of their local heroes, and when there isn't a convenient blank wall available, billboards go up instead. Billboards are especially plentiful around traffic circles, where the martyrs sometimes compete with advertisements for soaps, toothpaste, or tires.

Downtown Tehran is one traffic circle connected to another traffic circle connected to another. There is no one single center, and walking from one circle to another is often impossible—a fact I refused at first to believe. Accustomed as I am to getting to most places in Manhattan on foot, I initially regarded reports about Tehran's immense distances as exaggerated. With a population of about 12 million, I thought, Tehran is the size of New York City, and if I can walk New York, then I can walk Tehran. But what I didn't realize is that Tehran does not have a Manhattan—instead, it is haphazardly spread out over what is the equivalent of the five boroughs, or more.

That said, Tehran does have one predominant thoroughfare, Vali-ye Asr Avenue, which intersects with another major thoroughfare at the centrally located Vali-ye Asr Square. Once known as Pahlavi Avenue, Vali-ye Asr— "the Expected One"—is one of the longest city streets in the world, stretching approximately 12 miles from the cool foothills of the Alborz in the north well into the hot, dusty plateau of the south. Until the Islamic Revolution, the street was rigidly stratified, with the poor keeping to the south, the middle class living near the center, and the wealthy residing in the far north. Since the Islamic Revolution, that segregation has eased somewhat. The poor now come to Vali-ye Asr Square to window-shop, and they picnic in the parks of north Tehran—something that rarely happened in the days of the Shah.

Since the Islamic Revolution, too, many of the street names have been changed. Eisenhower Avenue is now Azadi (Freedom) Avenue, Los Angeles Street is Hejab Street, and Shah Reza Avenue is Enqelab (Revolution)

Avenue. Not all of the new street names have stuck, however. Jordan Avenue is now officially Africa Avenue, but I never heard anyone refer to it as such. Known today for its fashionable shops and cafés, Jordan Avenue was named after Dr. Samuel Jordan, a famous Presbyterian missionary and educator. Living in Tehran in the early 1900s, Dr. Jordan administered the American School for Girls and what later became Alborz College, one of the country's first accredited liberal arts colleges. Dr. Jordan's schools were among the first modern schools established in Iran, and many royal and upper-middle-class families sent their children to be educated there.

My family had stayed in the Presbyterian mission compound in Tehran during our first six weeks in Iran, but I could remember nothing from that period. When I asked my father about it, he just grunted. He'd been sick most of that time. My mother, however, remembered the compound quite well. We'd stayed in a guest house with several other missionaries, she said, while nearby stood the Community School, attended mostly by Muslim children. She also remembered visiting a nearby café, wearing a small golden hat, at the sight of which the Iranians inside started laughing uncontrollably. At that time in Iran, hats had been largely the province of men.

Like many other major cities, Tehran has specific streets devoted to specific businesses. Dozens of electronics stores carrying the very latest in electronics goods, mostly from Japan, pack one section of Jomhuri-ye Eslami Avenue, while farther down are the fishmongers. Ferdowsi Street is known for its leather shops and travel agencies, whereas Hafez Street has many furniture shops. Sidewalk money changers crouch on their haunches at the corner of Ferdowsi and Jomhuri-ye Eslami, calling out "Change, change, dollars, dollars" to passersby. The black market exchange rate is almost twice as high as the official one, and only the very timid change their currency in banks. Until a few years ago, the money changers sat with their *toman* notes piled high before them. (Iran's official currency is the *rial*; 10 *rials* make 1 *toman*; 600 *tomans* were worth about $1 at the time of my visit.) Crime rates are very low in Iran, and no one worried much about being robbed. Since then, however, the government has cracked down on the black marketers and they are more circumspect.

Wandering about on the streets of Tehran, I often felt disoriented, not because I was lost—I had good maps—but because to my Western eyes, most of the buildings looked alike. Boxlike, they crowd close to the sidewalks and, whether old or new, large or small, with plate-glass windows or without, have dull, monotonous façades. Certain blocks are also completely hidden from view by high wooden walls, behind which lies property confiscated from suspected royalists by the Islamic government.

At the same time, I found the streets of Tehran to be greatly liberating. I was far away from the relentless commercialism of New York. Here were no Barnes & Nobles, J. Crews, or Gaps—or their Iranian counterparts—and relatively few luxury shops with out-of-reach price tags to make me feel small. Nor were there any trendy restaurants or bars that I just had to visit or closing exhibitions or shows that I wouldn't have time to see. The restless dissatisfaction that seems to dog everyone in New York—Why aren't I more successful? Why don't I make more money? Why don't I have more fun?—had no place here. People in Iran worry about a lot of things, but achieving great worldly success and having a high social profile usually aren't among them.

Because Tehran has no subway and because buses run only along a few major avenues, most people either own cars or travel by shared or private taxis, whose prices are low enough (20 to 40 cents for a shared taxi, $1 to $2 for a private one) for all but the very poor to afford. The shared taxis travel set routes between major traffic circles, and so to reach your destination, you must know which series of connecting dots will get you there. You must also be bold enough to stand out in the middle of the circles, cars and pedestrians swirling by, and shout out your destination, until the appropriate cab stops. Then you must rush up, fighting off the other supplicants, and squeeze your way into an already crowded back or front seat, hopefully beside a person of the same sex. If that person is not of the same sex, sometimes—but far from always—a shuffling of seats ensues.

As a newcomer, it took me a long time to work up the courage to take the shared taxis, but when I did, the effort was worth it. Many people were eager to help me. Some insisted on walking me to the correct spot on the traffic circle. Some refused to flag down their own cab until I had found mine. And some copassengers even insisted on paying my fare. Don't bother about it! You are a guest in our country! they said, waving away my objections. The latter was a phrase that I was to hear over and over again while in Iran, until by the end of my visit, I was horrified to find myself taking it for granted. I have had the good fortune to visit many countries all over the world, but never have I been treated with anything approaching the hospitality that greeted me—and sometimes overwhelmed and suffocated me—in the Islamic Republic.

Though when it came to hospitality, I also had to be careful. Iranians don't always say what they mean, thanks in part to an elaborate politeness ritual known as *ta'arof*. An Arabic word that means ceremonial courtesy, *ta'arof* involves making extravagant compliments and offering invitations you don't necessarily intend, saying that you don't want something when you really do, and traditionally, though this is changing, turning down an offer three times before accepting it—both to be polite and to make sure that it is genuine. When my fellow passengers volunteered to pay my fare, I knew there was a good chance they meant it, but when my taxi driver said, no, please—I am honored to drive you, it is my privilege, you owe nothing, I knew that he meant no such thing.

Once the taxi is safely negotiated and you are within striking distance of your destination, there is crossing the street to contend with—one of the most terrifying experiences in Iran. Four, five, even six lanes of traffic shoosh by thick and fast, and it is up to you to find an opening somewhere, because traffic lights are few and far between. For the uninitiated, it is wildly intimidating, and I seldom crossed the street entirely by myself. I usually waited for someone else to arrive, to follow in his or her wake. My fellow pedestrians laughed at me, friends took my hand, and more than a few drivers slowed down to an amused extra-slow crawl when they saw me hesitantly appear. And the one time that I almost did get hit, by a motorbike at twilight in Qom, the driver got off his bike, while still in the middle of the street, to apologize profusely.

After a while, though, I began to notice that there is a curious symbiosis between pedestrians and cars in Tehran. Most people didn't wait as I did to cross the street but simply merged into the traffic whenever they needed to. Human forms mingled with metallic ones as if they were one and the same, nudging and bumping up against each other in friendly camaraderie. Usually, but far from always, the traffic in downtown Tehran was moving slowly enough to be relatively safe—one might lose a foot, say, but probably not one's life.

Traffic in Iran has another defining characteristic: The vehicles are old. Very old. Many of the cars on the street go back at least 15 years, and some predate the Revolution. Among them are a fair number of 1970s Mercedes and Chevrolets, navigating the streets like big, aging boats. The most common vehicle, however, is the Peykan, a light, boxy car manufactured just outside Tehran. Several frustrated middle-management types told me that before the Revolution, a man with a good job could buy a

Peykan with the equivalent of four months' salary. Now, that same man with that same job must dole out the equivalent of four years' salary. And so, no one buys much of anything anymore—instead, they repair. The only people who can afford to do otherwise, the managers said, are the *bazaaris*, Iran's traditional merchant class, and the *akhund*s. They laughed nervously. The *akhund*s are the clerics.

೪♡ℰ

One hot afternoon early in my stay in Iran, I set out to explore one small part of downtown. I started in Laleh Park, not far from Vali-ye Asr Square. Tehran may not be the most attractive of cities, but it does have its share of parks, many of which were either established or spruced up during the reign of the city's former mayor, Mr. Karbaschi. A supporter of President Khatami, Karbaschi was put on trial and removed from office shortly before my arrival on what many people believed were trumped-up charges of corruption. As the argument I so often heard went: Yes, perhaps Karbaschi was corrupt, but since all Iranian politicians are corrupt, why did the hard-liners single him out for punishment? Because he is aligned with Khatami, whom they cannot allow to gain too much power.

Paradoxically, however, certain aspects of the Karbarschi trial had seemed to indicate that Iran was moving toward a more open society. Though most trials in the Islamic Republic are held in closed session, this one was televised—and watched by virtually everyone in Iran. And testimony revealed that some of the charges against Karbaschi had been coerced out of his colleagues through torture. Human rights organizations have long accused the Islamic government of torture, but this was the first time that ordinary citizens heard the charge levied in a public forum.*

Once named for the Shah's wife, Farah, Laleh Park is now named for the tulip, a symbol of martyrdom in Iran. At the park's northern end stands the Laleh International Hotel, formerly the Inter-Continental, where international journalists have traditionally stayed to cover everything from political elections to soccer matches. I'd read quite a few of their accounts, many of which had mentioned a prominent DEATH TO AMERICA sign displayed in the lobby, and so on that afternoon, after a moment of hesitation, I pushed through the hotel's big glass doors to see the slogan for myself.

---

*Sentenced to two years in prison, Karbaschi was pardoned by Supreme Leader Khamene'i in January 2000, after serving seven months.

Inside stretched a typical luxury hotel lobby, only a little worn, with a long reception desk. I walked from one end of the lobby to the other, noticing a few plump Middle Eastern guests lingering over afternoon tea, but could see no DEATH TO AMERICA sign. Two hotel employees with grizzled cheeks gave me a half-flirtatious, half-interrogatory stare. Taking a deep breath, I asked them about the sign.

"Gone! Gone!" they said, laughing as if I were asking about ancient history. "You are American?"

"Yes," I said. "Since when?"

"Months ago!"

From the Laleh Hotel, I wandered south and west, past a group of unemployed men loitering on park benches, the Carpet Museum—filled with some of the finest rugs in the world—and the Museum of Contemporary Art. Feeling many eyes on me, I pulled my *rusari* down farther over my face. Already, I had grown more accustomed to my covering, and, in some ways, welcomed its presence. It shielded me somewhat from the curiosity of passersby, some of whom whispered *"khareji, khareji"*—foreigner, foreigner—to each other as I came near. Thinking of the catcalls that had sometimes accompanied me down the streets of Latin countries, or even in New York, I felt surprisingly protected here—albeit still very conspicuous.

For a woman traveling alone, the Islamic Republic of Iran is one of the safest countries in the world. According to Islamic law, unrelated men and women are not allowed to touch each other, and although I did hear many stories about unwanted pinches and gropes in public places, rape or other serious physical attacks are extremely rare. Even those women I met who despised every other aspect of life in the Islamic Republic generally agreed that they felt safe walking the streets any time of day or night—which had not always been the case during the days of the Shah.

Again I adjusted my *rusari*, which had again slipped back on my head. To my surprise, I was finding the scarf far more difficult to adjust to than the *manteau*. The raincoat was hot, to be sure, but otherwise relatively unobtrusive—it just felt like a long dress. But my *rusari* kept slipping or coming undone. It made hearing more difficult and the ties got in the way when I was eating in public places.

At the southern end of Laleh Park stood a tidy outdoor market where cheery kiosks sold everything from hand-woven baskets and buttered popcorn to live birds and portraits of famous ayatollahs. I stopped a young man to ask for directions and then immediately wondered if I'd done the right thing. I'd read that in addition to not being allowed to touch, unrelated men and women are not allowed to converse with each other in public in Iran. Had I already overstepped the boundaries of the Islamic society?

Of course not. I was still far too new to Iran to understand how things worked. The young man answered my halting Persian in passable English and then asked me a few questions about where I was from and what I was doing in Tehran. Short exchanges between men and women are allowed in public, and usually, longer ones go unnoticed as well. Those who have to worry most about harassment from the "morals police" are teenagers and those in their early twenties. Older men and women conversing together are often assumed to be related and so are left alone (though they may be stopped and asked to prove their relationship), and foreigners of any age or sex are rarely harassed, no matter who they're with or talking to.

Similarly, the rules for sexual segregation in Iran's public spaces are far from clear-cut. Some offices and universities have separate sections for men and women, but many others do not, and the sexes often work together side by side all day. Men and women must use separate entrances at airports but can sit next to each other in flight. City buses are segregated— women must sit in back—but inter-city buses are not. And crowded taxis often mean that unrelated men and women sit brazenly next to each other, shoulder to shoulder, thigh to thigh.

Across the street from Laleh Park begins the University of Tehran. At one time a bastion of Western technical knowledge, the University of Tehran is still known for its math and engineering departments and is considered to be the top university in Iran. Tuition is free, and applicants are accepted according to their scores on a national test administered to all potential college students.

After the Islamic Revolution, the University of Tehran, like all universities in Iran, was shut down for two and a half years while its curricula and textbooks were purged of undue Western influences. On reopening in late 1982, the university had fired close to half its teachers and instituted new required courses in religion and Arabic. Dedication to Islam became an important criterion for admission, and a certain percentage of places each year became reserved for children of martyrs from the Iran–Iraq War—practices that many feel have lowered the university's standards considerably.

As I neared the entrance to the university, I noticed a young man in blue jeans and two women in black *manteaus* ten steps ahead of me, constantly turning around to glance curiously in my direction. Equally curious about the threesome—was it permissible for them to be alone together?—I caught up with them at a streetlight and began a conversation in my beginner's Persian. They were all students at the university, and the two women were sisters from Abadan—a city in the south, heavily bombed during the Iran–Iraq War and known for its large Arab population. Don't you notice how beautiful they are, the young man said of the sisters—they're pure Arab. And indeed the women were beautiful, with enormous eyes, translucent skin, and regal carriage. The older one was an actress as well as a student, and the girlfriend of the young man. He put his arm around her, and I nearly lurched to a stop.

"Aren't you afraid to do that?" I said.

"Do what?" He gave me a mocking grin.

"Put your arm around her. The *komiteh*—"

"Oh, the *komiteh*! We don't care about the *komiteh*. When we see the guards coming, we just run away."

The actress looked down her nose at me—she seemed jealous of the attention that her boyfriend was paying to me—while her younger sister took my arm. Both women, I noticed, were wearing far more makeup than was I.

"Of course we worry about the *komiteh*," the younger sister said. "Afshin is just a little wild. And we're probably safe here, at this time. The streets are very crowded. Everyone is going home after work."

"Tell me what you like to drink," Afshin said abruptly. "Whiskey, vodka, bourbon?"

"Well, I like vodka," I said, a little taken aback. "But what about you? Do you drink?" I already knew that although alcohol is forbidden for Muslims in the Islamic Republic, it's widely available on the black market and very popular among the middle class.

"Of course," Afshin said. "And I agree with you. Vodka is the best."

His girlfriend gave me a dark look.

"Are you Muslim?" the younger sister said. "We thought you were Muslim."

We stopped at an indoor shopping strip to wait for Ahmad, a jittery young man who was apparently the younger sister's boyfriend. Ahmad's hooded eyes were badly bloodshot and I wondered if it was from opium—the most popular drug in Iran, usually obtained from Afghanistan. Then we all proceeded down Enqelab Avenue to Vali-ye Asr. The students wanted to invite me for a drink, which in Iran means soda or fruit juice.

We entered a hot, crowded café with a dozen blenders furiously whirring up front. Liquids of pale green, dark orange, creamy yellow, and reds of various hues frothed out into plastic cups. We ordered two melons and three carrots and took seats in the back, single men and women crowded together. The younger sister passed around napkins while Afshin and Ahmad leaned forward to barrage me with questions, only some of which I understood: Are you traveling alone? Why are you traveling alone? How old are you? Where is your husband? Where are your children? How did you get a visa? Why did you get a visa? Why are you here? I felt a little defensive as I tried to answer them, the strangeness of my situation suddenly crashing up against me. Meanwhile, the actress sat with her nose in the air and the younger sister tried to act as interpreter. For some reason, I could understand her Persian much better than I could that of the young men.

"You must be very careful in Iran," she said when the young men had temporarily lost interest in me. "Don't take taxis by yourself."

"Why not?" I said, surprised. I'd already taken quite a few taxis by myself, and all my drivers had been exceedingly friendly, telling me how happy they were to see Americans returning to Iran and welcoming me to their country. One man had been almost in tears as he spoke—I reminded him of his youth, he said, when there'd been many Americans in Iran—and had invited me to come meet his family anytime. Another returned to find me, several minutes after dropping me off, because he'd been afraid that he'd inadvertently taken me to the wrong address.

"There are a lot of bad men in Iran," she said. "And the taxis here are not licensed—did you know that? Anyone who has a car and wants to make some extra money can just go out—"

"But the orange taxis are okay," Afshin said, interrupting, "and so are the white ones with the orange stripe."

"Yes, they're all right," the younger sister agreed. "But you should still be very careful and not go by yourself. I never go by myself."

Afshin nuzzled the actress's neck while I stared at him. His actions had been brazen enough on the street, but here we were in a crowded café.

"You are surprised," the younger sister said, watching me watch him.

"Very," I said.

"Afshin takes many chances," she said. "And he is not so religious."

"Are you religious?" I asked.

"Of course."

"Do you pray five times a day?"

"Of course."

"Do you go to Friday prayers at the university?"

"Of course."

Ahmad took her hand and rubbed her wrist with his thumb. "She likes the mullahs," he said, "but I like her anyway. She is very beautiful."

The younger sister smiled at him affectionately and I wondered what it was that had brought them together, he apparently high on drugs, she apparently high on religion.

⁂

Lona, Sepideh, and I passed out of the bright August sunlight and under a decrepit archway, into the shadows of the Grand Bazaar. Before us stretched a gently inclining paved path lined with shops selling gold. Every shop was immaculate, but they all looked exactly alike—small, with big picture windows up front. Each window was draped with gold pendants and chains and bordered by skinny strips of red neon. Women in *chadors* loitered silently here and there, studying the wares. Gold is especially highly valued in Iran, where it is an important part of every dowry and often purchased for investment.

At the bottom of the incline, the hush of the gold shops ended and the bustle of the rest of the bazaar began—seven convoluted miles of dark covered corridors broken periodically by diagonal shafts of light. Dust danced in the shafts while iron carts rattled, motorcycles roared, and old men bent double with heavy rugs plodded doggedly straight ahead. A barefoot boy tried to sell us tea in plastic cups from an orange basket and a beggar woman flapped a kerchief in my face. Lona shooed her away. *"Kasif,"* she said—dirty. The bazaar is on the edge of south Tehran, and many who frequent it are poor.

Though just a few hundred years old, and therefore one of the youngest bazaars in Iran, Tehran's Grand Bazaar is also the largest. For many years, it was the main focal point of the city—the primary center not only of regional, national, and international trade but also of many social relationships, religion, and politics. Only in recent decades has this begun to change, with some of the more prosperous merchants leaving the bazaar for the fashionable avenues of central and north Tehran. Western-style supermarkets and department stores are also threatening the future of the bazaar.

The Iranian bazaar as it is known today dates back to about the fifth century, when public marketplaces began moving from just outside to just inside city walls. The first bazaars were simple collections of uncovered stalls, but as the centuries progressed, they grew into entire communities within communities, complete with shops, teahouses, restaurants, bathhouses, mosques, religious schools, and caravansaries, or hotel-stables in which traveling merchants stayed with their camels and horses.

The bazaars also soon developed into financial centers, with their own banking, loan, and investment systems. As early as the 900s, members of the elite joined with the merchants to invest in various businesses or loan out money at monthly, weekly, or even daily rates. Today, most financial services that can be obtained at a major U.S. bank can also be obtained in the Grand Bazaar, which also functions as a stock exchange and commodities market. No guarantee or collateral is ever required; a person's reputation is all that matters. The retail business is the least important aspect of trade in the bazaar.

Islam holds merchants in great esteem, and there has always been a close relationship between the *bazaaris* and the clerics. The Prophet Mohammad's first wife, Khadijeh, was a prosperous merchant, and Friday was chosen as the religion's congregational prayer day because it was already the most important trading day in Mecca. From Islam's earliest years, the clerics needed the financial support of the *bazaaris* to fund mosques and theological schools, while the *bazaaris* needed the support of the clerics to maintain their standing in the community. Marriage between the two classes became common, and today, clerics and *bazaaris* often belong to the same family.

Between their great wealth and close links to the clergy, the *bazaaris* wield enormous political power in Iran. Whenever there is a major political crisis, the bazaar shuts down, as it did repeatedly in the months before the Islamic Revolution. With each closing, the Shah lost more and more political control, allowing the militant clergy, who had a strong base in the bazaar, to step into his place. For a few years after the revolution, the links between the *bazaaris* and the government were especially strong. More recently, however, this has changed, owing to the nationalization of foreign trade, antiprofiteering campaigns against the *bazaaris*, and a weak economy. As one *bazaari* explained to me: "Yes, the *bazaaris* support the Islamic government, but we support money more, and it's more difficult to do business now."

Plunging further into the bazaar, Lona, Sepideh, and I wandered from corridor to corridor, each of which was devoted to different wares. Along one alley we saw hundreds of bolts of black fabric for *chadors*, followed by puffy, Western-style wedding dresses—popular all over Iran—hanging from ceilings like satin balloons. A bit further on were kitchen supply shops and spice stores overflowing with open trays. Next came a string of tiny samovar shops, followed by stores selling vacuum cleaners, shoes, buttons, stationery, party decorations, fishing tackle, and plastic *tasbih*, or prayer beads, in bright greens, yellows, blues, and reds. One series of shops was devoted to elaborate mirrors and gold candlesticks—two essential props in any Iranian wedding ceremony—and another to blue jeans. Most of the products said MADE IN IRAN, but despite the Prophet's merchant wife, I didn't see a single woman working anywhere.

At the northern edge of the bazaar stands the Imam Khomeini Mosque, formerly known as the Shah's Mosque. A series of dark winding corridors led us there, and as we neared the sanctuary, the crowds began to change. Women in *manteaus* and *rusaris*—already a minority in the bazaar—all but disappeared, to be replaced by women in *chadors*. Mullahs, or clerics, were more numerous and more men wore the traditional Iranian skull-tight wool cap. Old men sat perched on stools, fingering through trays of prayer beads, while skinny vendors sat crouched on haunches selling prayer stones and prayer mats. Suddenly, I felt out of place.

I remembered a story that my father had often told me about the Tabriz bazaar, which is far older than Tehran's and was once visited by Marco Polo. A colleague who'd had a passion for Persian food had heard of an excellent restaurant hidden deep in the bazaar's bowels, and one day, the two young men set out to find it. Numerous wrong turns later, they finally arrived at their destination, where they were graciously received, and enjoyed a long and delicious lunch. After they were done, however, the owner took them aside. Please don't come again, he said—this restaurant is for Muslims.

A young vendor with a luxuriant mustache stopped us. No religious merchant he—he was selling "Anti-Fat Girdles." The English-language words blared out over and over again from the pile of boxes by his side as he demonstrated to Lona how the stiff, heavy belt worked. It was one of the most uncomfortable-looking devices I had ever seen, but Lona, who was always worrying about her weight, examined it with great interest until I finally pulled her away.

We stepped out into the wide, scruffy courtyard of the mosque. Bathed in the stifling August heat, it was empty except for a few clusters of men and several mullahs sitting in the shadows of its edges. Some were reading the Qor'an, some were counting prayer beads, some were dozing, and some were talking. One man gave us a hostile look. Each side of the courtyard had an *eivan*, or vaulted hall that opened out onto the courtyard, but otherwise, there was nothing to see. The sanctuary was not a tourist attraction.

We headed on to our last stop, the luggage stores. Lona was looking for a backpack for Sepideh, who would soon be starting a new school year. Many of the backpacks featured American cartoon characters and English-language words: *Mickey Mouse, Go Go Rabbit, Champion Bulls, Adidas, God Is Love, Taitanic, Lenordo De.caperio,* and my favorite—*Good for All Chickens, Birds and Children to Go for School.*

As Lona critically examined the backpacks—none of which seemed to be quite right—I heard a sudden commotion coming from the walkway outside. Looking up, I saw a horde of *chador*-clad women seemingly swelling up before my eyes. Where before had been a peaceful stream of people filing by now roiled an angry ball of humanity. A small man, supported by two friends, suddenly broke out of the swirling mass of women and took refuge in a nearby shop.

"What's going on?" I asked Lona, who was giggling.

"That lady says that man pinched her daughter," she said. "She slapped him and wants an apology, but he says he didn't do it and she should apologize."

The tension held for another moment, but then people started to shake their heads, laughing, and the crowd dispersed. Lona finally settled on an appropriate backpack while I thought about Assadollah Lajevardi, once a chief prosecutor for the revolutionary tribunals and more recently governor of Evin prison. Known for his brutality, Lajevardi had been murdered in his shop in the bazaar just a few days before. The murderer had gotten swiftly away after the attack, and several people had told me that that was a definitive sign of the Islamic regime's weakening control. If the *bazaari*s had wanted to stop the assassin, they said, they could easily have done so. I now understood what they meant.

ॐ

The next morning, Lona and I went to visit Sa'dabad, a complex of 18 palaces surrounded by gardens not far from Bahman's apartment. Some of the palaces had been built during the nineteenth century by the Qajar kings, while others had served as summer residences for the Shahs Pahlavi. During the Islamic Revolution, the *komitehs* had stormed the complex, reportedly making off with much of the loot, and set up a headquarters there. Now, Sa'dabad was a museum. As the English-language brochure to the complex read: "The Islamic Revolution, having toppled the aged monarchic system and doing away with so many doors and gates, turned the dreary halls into lively galleries . . ."

Two signs, one in Persian and one in English, stood outside the entrance:

> For Foreigners:
> Price of ticket one Museum—each Person 15,000 *rials*. Price of ticket all museums, each Person 75,000 *rials*.
> Rate of License to take Some memorial Photo—10,000 *rials*.
> This License is valid only For one day.
> To use Pictures only For Personal Purposes
> Please do not take picture of Forbidden Places.
> We wish you success.

Lona wrangled with the ticket seller. Fifteen thousand *rials* was about $2.50, so for me to visit all the museums would cost $12.50—an exorbitant sum for Iran. The price for locals was only about 30 cents per museum. This dual-pricing system is common at visitor attractions and hotels throughout the country, and although I usually felt that slightly higher rates for foreigners were fair, there were times, such as now, when prices seemed out of hand.

Lona argued with the ticket man for a good ten minutes but was not successful at either obtaining a lower rate or at getting me an English-speaking guide—something she thought I should have for my huge outlay of cash. The ticket man assured us, however, that there were lots of English-language signs posted throughout the buildings.

We passed to our first museum, the Museum of Fine Arts, housed in the former Black Palace, once used as the Imperial Court Ministry. Four or five grizzled men sat talking, drinking tea, and reading newspapers at the front desk. Unemployment runs high in Iran.

In the museum's front gallery hung a spotlighted portrait of a melancholy Ayatollah Khomeini, but in the rooms beyond was a fine collection of Qajar paintings, rich in heavy colors and bold forms. Men and women with wide languorous eyes and sensual pouting lips gazed out at us seductively as we passed by. Many of the men had bushy black beards that reached to their waists, and many of the women had thick black eyebrows that met in the middle—a sign of beauty during the Qajar period. Qajar women usually let their eyebrows meet when they were single and plucked them apart once they married.

The Qajars ruled Iran from 1795, when the cruel Aqa Mohammad Khan was crowned shah, to 1925, when Reza Shah Pahlavi rose to power. Aqa Mohammad Khan was the son of a tribal chieftain, captured and castrated as a child by one rival tribe and kept under house arrest by another for 16 years. But after escaping and fighting his way to the throne, he wreaked his revenge: Reportedly, one of his first acts as king was to order 20,000 pairs of his enemies' eyes brought to him on a silver platter. He next moved the country's capital from Shiraz to Tehran, then just a backwater trading center best known for its good hunting.

Although the Qajars did succeed in bringing some economic and cultural stability to Iran, their dynasty was also one of manipulative rulers and rampant corruption. Iran at that time was largely made up of nomadic tribes, and the Qajar kings had no centralized army, government bureaucracy, or even reliable transportation system with which to control their peoples. They therefore had to rely on more indirect methods of rule, such as offering bribes, encouraging infighting, and occasionally forcing recalcitrant but powerful subjects to remain in Tehran for long periods as "guests."

In the early 1820s, an English traveler and diplomat named James Morier traveled throughout Iran and wrote what later became a classic work of the Qajar period, *The Adventures of Hajji Baba of Ispahan.* Professing to be the biography of a young man who leaves the family barbering business to seek his fortune, *Hajji Baba* consists of one tale of greed, hypocrisy, and corruption after another. Almost every page is filled with disparaging satiric comments, made by an equally disparaged narrator, about the people he meets: "The people of Iran are like the earth; they require *rishweh* (a bribe) before they will bring forth fruit" is but one typical comment.

As I passed by the Qajar portraits, I wondered how much of a legacy each historical period leaves to succeeding ones. Corruption is rife in Iran today. I'd been in the country for less than a week, but already I'd heard numerous stories about how the only way to get things done in the Islamic Republic was to slip a little something under the table. One businessman told me about bribing customs officials simply to get basic office equipment into the country. One lawyer told me that she frequently had to grease palms simply to get her briefs read. Another woman told me about how she'd kept the *komiteh* away from her daughter's wedding by paying a hefty bribe in advance. And everyone told me about corrupt mullahs driving Peugeots, owning factories, and socking it away in Swiss bank accounts at rates far exceeding anything seen under the Shahs Pahlavi—hardly an era known for its honesty.

From the Museum of Fine Arts, Lona and I headed to one of the Pahlavi palaces, the Green Palace, built by Reza Shah Pahlavi in 1925. The finest building in the complex, the Green Palace was cozy in size but dazzling, with mirrored glass mosaics covering entire ceilings and walls. The mosaics reflected off one another and off delicate blue furnishings imported from France. Not the kind of residence one would expect from a king who ate with his soldiers out of one pot.

Of all the many unlikely characters who have ruled Iran, Reza Shah—the father of the Shah ousted by the Revolution—was one of the unlikeliest. Of humble origins, he joined the Cossack Brigade, a military force trained by the Russians to protect the Qajars, when he was 15 or 16. A towering, semi-illiterate man with a savage temper, he was nonetheless a natural-born leader and rose quickly to the rank of brigadier general. In 1921, he seized military control of Iran with the approval of the British, who were impatient with Qajar waffling in the face of the Bolshevik threat to their north. In 1925, he was crowned king and chose Pahlavi as his dynastic name. Pahlavi was the language that the ancient Persians spoke before the arrival of Islam.

Though hardly a modern man himself, Reza Shah became obsessed with modernizing his people. He instituted an extraordinary number of changes—some greatly needed, others coming only at a high cost. He established a strong central government; impressive standing army, navy, and police forces; and finance and banking systems; and he changed the name of the country from Persia to Iran—Iran for the Aryan people of central Asia from which many Iranians and Europeans are descended. He weakened the power of the clerics and ordered that the nomadic tribes be forcibly settled. He forbade the photographing of that backward animal, the camel—foreigners might get the wrong impression—and ordered a firing squad to kill a donkey that had inadvertently strayed into one of his fields. He built roads, railroads, hospitals, and schools—for girls as well as boys—and stripped wealthy landowners and clerics of their property, only to expropriate it as his own. By the end of his reign, he was the largest landowner in Iran.

Most radical of all, in the eyes of many, Reza Shah forced his people to adopt a European-style dress. After hundreds of years of wearing the *hejab*, women were commanded to remove it. Most educated women welcomed the decree, but millions of frightened, illiterate women did not, and some refused to leave the house for years. Others fought with the police who tried to tear off their *chadors* in public, and women's prisons were established for the first time in Iran's history. Reza Shah's successor, his son Mohammad Reza Shah, finally repealed the ban on the veil five years later, in 1941, but "the unveiling" was never forgotten and even to this day blazes shamefully in the collective memory of many traditional Iranians.

Down the hill from the Green Palace was the White Palace, a much larger but significantly less impressive edifice that Mohammad Reza Shah used as one of his summer residences. The 54-room building had retained some of its former grandeur—in its elaborate dining rooms, magnificent wall murals, and the Shah's satin-draped bed, built in "The Same Style as Josefin's Bed. The Wife of Napolean Bonapart." But overall, the palace had an aging, cavernous feel. Out front stood a pair of empty shoulder-high bronze boots painted white. A statue of the Shah was to have stood in those boots, but the Revolution started before the statue was finished.

I wondered if Mohammad Reza Shah had chosen the White Palace instead of the Green Palace in which to live in order to escape the overpowering memory of his father. Unlike Reza Shah, Mohammad Reza Shah had been a slight and slender man, shy and hesitant in nature, who'd only gradually grown into the role of a vain, bullying, and ultimately cruel ruler. He'd spent his youth desperately trying to live up to his father's expectations and his early manhood gingerly struggling to maintain control of his state. Only in midlife had he acquired the authoritarianism of his father, and then he applied it full force, greatly augmenting the army, establishing SAVAK, repressing Islam while extolling the virtues of ancient Persia, and, like his father before him, instituting too much reform too fast. Even while introducing such welcomed relief as illiteracy campaigns and rural health programs, he also rammed through an ill-conceived land reform program, spent millions of oil dollars—much needed elsewhere—on a sophisticated military arsenal, and cracked down sharply on freedom of speech and human rights. He demanded absolute allegiance, trusting no one around him, and dismissed the many clerics who did not support him as "lice-ridden mullahs."

To Mohammad Reza Shah's credit, however, he never subjected his people to a bloodbath. When it became clear to him that the vast majority of Iranians supported the 1978–1979 Revolution, he did not unleash the armed forces on them, as some of his supporters advised, but instead left the country.

My family had lived in Iran during the reign of the Shah, but my parents and their colleagues, like most other Americans then in Iran, had never heard a single word of protest uttered against him. Neither had most professional and upper-class Iranians.

Before leaving Sa'dabad, Lona insisted on stopping into the front office. I had my suspicions as to why, and sure enough, as soon as the appropriate manager appeared, she launched into a long tirade about the price of my ticket and what had turned out to be a near complete lack of English-language signage in the complex. As I listened to her rant at the unhappy-looking official, I thought about the Western stereotype of Muslim women as meek, cowering, and repressed, and grinned.

The manager turned to me with an apologetic shrug.

"She is right," he said in heavily accented English. "We must do better. Many, many tourists are coming here now and they want English signs."

"How many tourists?" I said, surprised at what sounded like hordes of visitors.

"We had two French groups here this morning, and an Italian one yesterday. You are Italian?"

I shook my head.

"Russian?"

I shook my head.

"American?"

I nodded, and his apologetic look dissolved into a wide grin.

"Welcome, welcome!" he said. "We love the American people. We have always loved the American people. We have some American students now at Tehran University—they come to speak Persian; they don't want to speak English. That makes me so happy—that is why we love Americans. It is only the American government we don't like. Our governments, they are just"—he picked up two glasses on his desk and placed them far apart—"like this." He placed stacks of books around the glasses. "They build many walls to separate themselves. But the people"—he knocked the books aside and clasped his hands tightly together—"they come together, they love each other. There is only one master of the people and that is God."

CONVERSATIONS IN NORTH TEHRAN

"Before the Revolution, we drank in public and prayed in private. Now we pray in public and drink in private."

—Popular joke in Iran

ONE

*E*very Iranian lives in two worlds—the public and the private. The public is for wearing dark colors, obeying the laws of the Islamic society, and generally presenting a serious and pious face to the world. The private is for wearing bright colors, laughing and socializing with family and friends, and quiet contemplation and prayer. Among some Iranians, most notably the middle and upper classes of north Tehran and other large cities, the private is also for enjoying forbidden music and literature, watching banned videos and TV shows, wearing miniskirts and halter tops, drinking alcohol and doing drugs, and criticizing the Islamic government.

The classic Persian home was protected from the outside world by high clay walls, which kept dangers out and secrets in. Centuries of tribal warfare and invading conquerors had taught the early Iranians to trust no one but their immediate family. The walls' blank enigmatic façade was usually broken only by the front gate, which at one time, and in some houses, had two kinds of knockers. One was round and made a dull clunking sound. The other was rectangular and made an even duller clunking sound. The

51

round one was rung by women and the rectangular one by men, indicating to the listener which sex should answer the door. The hall leading from the gate to the main compound was also often curved, so that visitors would not catch glimpses of the opposite sex by mistake.

Once inside the clay walls, a magical compound opened up. Among the rich, these compounds were often lovely places, filled with lustrous pools, flowering gardens, verdant fruit trees, and nightingales; it is from the ancient Persian word for enclosed garden, *pairidaeza*, that the English word *paradise* comes. But even among the poor, the compounds had enchantment. At their centers, and usually shaded by a tree, shimmered a single shallow pool used for washing. Inside the pool, goldfish darted, their brilliant orange-gold bodies mirroring the sun.

The compounds were divided into two basic parts: the *biruni*, or outer quarter, which among the wealthy was often further subdivided into a reception area for receiving guests and a living area for the male family members, and the *andaruni*, or inner quarter, where the women lived. Strangers were seldom allowed beyond the reception area, and sometimes only the ruling patriarch could frequent all parts of the compound. Women were often kept out of the *biruni*, and only close male relatives could visit the *andaruni*, and then only that section of the *andaruni* where their wives, sisters, or mother lived. If a man had more than one wife, each wife had her own section of the *andaruni* from which the others could be excluded.

Thus, the classic Persian home created boxes within boxes within boxes. The smaller the box got, the more mysterious it became, and the more mysterious it became, or so it seemed to me, the more it both attracted and repelled. Attracted with its unsuspected beauty, sensual pleasures, warmth, intimacy, and exclusive sense of privacy. Repelled with its petty jealousies, unspoken cruelties, and dreary repression. Not so different, perhaps, from the deepest recesses of the human heart.

Some Iranians today continue to live in traditional clay-walled compounds, complete with gardens or pools, but many others, especially in the cities, live in modern apartments. In either case, the rigid dichotomy between the inner and outer life continues, making it difficult for an outsider to understand what's going on.

Certainly I was having difficulty. Impressions were bombarding me from so many directions—religion, politics, economics, history, gender relations—that there were times when I felt as if I were on a kind of a high, immersed in an exaggerated reality. In one short week, the Islamic Republic had been transformed in my mind from the gray, threatening, monolithic presence that it had seemed to be in the United States and into an intricate, multicolored puzzle that I was just beginning to piece together—my own private box within a box.

My head was spinning. I didn't know how to read much of what I saw or interpret what I was hearing. One of my main goals in traveling to Iran was to meet all sorts of people—to gain some sort of understanding—but I knew that I was still far too green to talk to more traditional or conservative Iranians. I would therefore start with people most like me—the denizens of north Tehran, many of whom are more or less bicultural, having either lived in the West for years or studied its history and culture to the point where it is largely their own.

⋘❀⋙

Shirin, a friend of a friend back in the United States, had invited me to dinner. Her daughter, Leila, a university student, would also be there, along with a half dozen of Leila's friends.

Shirin and Leila lived on a quiet lane in north Tehran. Unlike Bahman's neighborhood, where most of the buildings were high-rises with spotlights out front, most of the homes here were low-slung, secluded, and dark, hidden behind thick bushes and spindly trees. My taxi driver and I had a hard time making out the house numbers as we passed but finally stopped before a silent edifice. No one appeared to be home.

I rang the doorbell and waited for a long moment before the door swung slowly open. A bareheaded woman whom I took to be Shirin remained half hidden in the shadows inside, perhaps because my taxi driver was still outside, but then he drove off and I was whisked over the threshold and into a warm, luxuriant room. All around me were gorgeous young women, dressed in revealing T-shirts or tube tops, and slinky black pants, black miniskirts, or tight blue jeans. Some had long, elaborately curled hair and most were wearing a light layer of makeup. All in all, they looked much like fashionable young women in the United States. All spoke a near-perfect English because, I later learned, they'd been taking private language classes for many years.

Laughing and joking, they escorted me through the cheery living room and out onto a small patio surrounded by potted plants and high walls. Overhead, the stars were clearly visible, along with a concave clipping of the moon. We seated ourselves around two round tables while Shirin served a sweet purple liqueur that she'd made herself.

"I'm glad you're staying with friends near here," she said, "because at first, when I heard you were coming, I told my friend, no, I would not go downtown to a hotel to meet you. Someone could have stopped me on the way out and asked me what we were talking about—what I was visiting with a foreigner for. Or they could have asked to see what I had in my bag. It's much better that you have come here."

Like the young women around her, Shirin was fashionably dressed, in black pants and a flattering sweater, and wore her hair long and curled. But although she barely seemed old enough to have a daughter in her twenties, there were tired, discouraged lines around her mouth and an anxious, saddened droop to her eyes. Her shoulders seemed hunched.

"I wanted to invite your friend the doctor, too," she said, "but I didn't know what kind of man he is. Perhaps he is very religious and would not have liked to see alcohol—"

"It would have been all right," I said.

"You see, we have so many problems here. We have to worry about everything. Everywhere we go, everyone we meet . . ." Her words trailed off.

I tried to think of a question that would elicit more details without intruding too much. Still very new to Iran, I was eager to hear more about the difficulties of living in the Islamic Republic, but I also felt embarrassed about asking. My thirst for stories made me feel like a voyeur, excited by the unhappiness of others.

"My mom was arrested at the supermarket once," Leila said. "Tell her, Mummy."

Shirin leaned forward, and suddenly I realized that she was as eager to tell her story as I was to hear it. To talk to me, a Westerner, would relieve the pressure inside her for at least a moment. She spoke with the quiet insistence of one yearning to be heard.

"It happened a few years ago," she said, "when they used to have buses patrolling every day—now they just do it once in a while. I was shopping and I heard someone calling, 'Khanom, Khanom.' I didn't turn around—I didn't want to talk with him, he was just a child—but he said if I didn't go with him, I would get arrested. He took me outside and put me on a bus where they had a checklist with all the things women shouldn't be wearing—lipstick, eyeliner, hair, nail polish. They put those x's against my name. Then they counted how many seats were left on the bus. Ten? They stopped ten more women—the first ones they saw—and took us to an office, but since it was my first time, they just gave me a reprimand. I didn't have to go to court. Leila had to go to court."

I turned to Leila, who shook her head, laughing. The other young women were listening attentively, while watching my reactions, and I got the feeling that they'd told these stories many times before, both to outsiders and to themselves, and that they loved to shock neophytes.

"It was so ridiculous," Leila said. "I was just talking with a girlfriend and two boys from our school on the street when the *komiteh* happened to be driving by. They arrested us, but I wasn't afraid—my mom always said, 'Don't be afraid.' We were laughing, we were interested in what was happening to us. They made us sign a statement saying we wouldn't do it again, but the worst thing was, they said come to court the next day at 6 A.M. We came and waited all day but nothing happened, and then they said come back again tomorrow."

"They'll always let you go if you pay them a little money," added Parvin, a law student with an infectious laugh. "One time, some friends of mine and I were arrested at a party and held in jail for two days and two nights. They threatened us with lashes, but when we said we would pay, they said okay. We paid three thousand *tomans* [about $5] each, but then they said that the kids giving the party couldn't buy their lashes off. So their parents had to go down into the basement with them and pay again."

"Lashes?" I said feebly, suddenly feeling much younger than the university students around me, all of whom seemed to be handling their difficult world with such equanimity.

Parvin grinned at my surprise. "They can't hit too hard," she said, "because they have to hold the Qor'an under their arm."

I absorbed that.

"Were you afraid?" I said.

Parvin shrugged. "Not really. We knew our parents would come. They came with huge baskets of food that we shared with the other women in the cells. They'd been arrested for wearing too much makeup or sunglasses. It wasn't a real prison, anyway—it was just some rooms. And we're used to it. Outsiders are amazed, but to us, this is normal."

That's part of why these young women were so self-possessed, I realized. They'd all been born around the time of the Revolution and had never known any other life.

"But we'd still rather live here than anyplace else," said a slim young woman with enormous eyes. "Most Iranians would."

"Because this is your country?" I said.

"Yes, and because we get together like this every night—not just on weekends. We're always seeing family and friends—and Iranians are so funny. Even with all the problems we have, we're laughing all the time. Whenever I visit my brother in the U.S., I miss Iran so much."

"There's much less stress here," said Mina, who'd recently moved to Los Angeles and was just back visiting. "Studying here is much easier than in the U.S. Here, it's hard to pass the entrance exam, but once you're in, no problem. There's no stress at school and no stress at work."

"But I thought the economy was so bad now," I said. "Everyone's working two or three jobs."

"Yes, they're all working two or three jobs," Mina said, "but they don't get anything done. Last summer when I came back to visit, I wanted to change my return ticket and I had to go back to the airline office six times before they did it—no exaggeration."

"Well, some people do work very hard," Shirin said, disagreeing. "And there is a lot of stress—it's just a different kind. But I could never afford this kind of house in the U.S."

"People think too much about money in the U.S.," Mina interjected. "They're very materialistic and artificial, but I think it's because they're always worried they'll lose their jobs and be out on the streets. They don't have family to take care of them like we do in Iran. Things are more real here. You don't realize it until you go away."

We moved into the house for dinner. The living and dining rooms merged together into one large L-shaped enclosure and were furnished in silvery, brocade-covered couches and chairs, interspersed with coffee tables. Many middle-class Iranians have flamboyant taste, and later in my stay I would visit houses that were way over the top: dining sets that looked like they'd belonged to Louis XIV—sometimes two in the same room—satin-covered sofas, carved mahogany sideboards, rococo-encrusted mirrors, English landscape paintings, candelabras, chandeliers.

Shirin covered the table with dishes: *tahchin-e morgh*, the baked rice-and-chicken dish that Lona had already introduced me to; *khoresh-e bademjan*, an eggplant, lamb, and potato stew; chicken kebab; curried meatballs; stuffed grape leaves; a Western-style salad; a plate filled with raw greens—mint, basil, cilantro, watercress; yogurt; Persian pickles; and two kinds of flat bread. In Iran, it is customary to serve guests much more than they can possibly eat, and sometimes, entire dishes go all but untouched.

The students told me more about their studies at the university. Leila was studying art and had lots of small, mixed-sex classes taught by both men and women. Another friend was studying engineering and had both large and small classes, some mixed-sex, some not. Parvin was studying law and had many large, all-women classes taught mostly by male clerics.

"They're usually looking out the window," she said, laughing, "because they're very religious and not allowed to look at us. So we're always sleeping, talking, painting our nails—"

On Iran's university campuses, men and women are not allowed to speak to each other for more than five minutes at a time, and then only for the purposes of discussing schoolwork. This rule was often overlooked at the private art school that Leila attended but was strictly enforced at the University of Tehran, where the feared Islamic Society was always keeping watch. Composed largely of volunteer members, the Islamic Society usually issued three warnings to a student before he or she was tossed out. The Islamic Society also inspected the students' dress at the campus entrance, where all IDs were checked. Women wearing light-colored *manteaus* were not allowed to enter, and women wearing too much makeup were made to wash their faces.

Shirin pressed more food on me.

"If you can't really speak to men at the university," I said, too fascinated by what the young women were saying to pay much attention to the food, "how do you meet them?" I already more or less knew the answer—I'd read much about Iran before leaving New York—but it felt completely different to be hearing about these experiences in person.

"Through family and friends," Leila said.

"And parties," Mina said. "There are lots of parties in Tehran. When I come back to visit, I go to a party almost every night. We have everything here—music, dancing, drinking—and we dress like this"—she pointed to her skimpy tube top—"or worse." She laughed.

"What about sex?" I asked hesitantly. These women seemed to be just like women I knew back in the United States, but sex is such a loaded topic in Iran. "Are women still expected to be virgins when they marry?"

"Not in Tehran necessarily," Leila said. "But in the villages, sure. They're very religious."

Parvin started giggling. "Everyone who goes to university in Iran has to take religion classes," she said, "and spend a semester studying the last will and testament of Ayatollah Khomeini."

"But we're *not* religious," said the slim woman with the enormous eyes. "We never pray."

"You can get out of prayers if you have your period," said Leila, "and sometimes they ask us, 'Do you have your period three hundred sixty-five days a year?'"

"When I was in high school," said Parvin, "one teacher asked me, 'Why don't you pray?' and I told her, 'My parents don't pray, my grandparents don't pray—why should I pray? Do you want me to be hypocritical?' She just laughed and said she was glad I told her the truth. She didn't bother me anymore after that."

"Parvin is very brave," Shirin said to me quietly as the younger women laughed. "She could have been in a lot of trouble. These people are not joking."

Shirin's aside reminded me of a conversation I'd had the day before with a businessman in his mid-forties. The young are not afraid, he'd said, because they don't remember the very bad times, and so they like to push as much as they can. The younger you are, the more you push. It's exciting for a while, but it gets very tiring, and by the time you reach my age, you're exhausted.

"I'm always fighting," Parvin said. "When I was in grammar school, it was the time of 'Death to America, death to America.' I had a friend who was American and the teacher wanted her to step on the American flag. I said to her, 'What are you doing? She's only six years old. How would you like it if you were told to step on the Iranian flag?' "

After dinner, while the students fell to gossiping in Persian amongst themselves, I studied the books that lined one wall. Many were in English and only too familiar: *I'm Okay, You're Okay, The Celestine Prophecy, Creative Visualization, Hands of Light.* One shelf held several volumes by Deepak Chopra; another featured close to an entire collection of Carlos Castañeda. Shirin, it turned out, was an expert in massage, yoga, and New Age healing, and taught classes in her house. Technically speaking, her classes were illegal; home-based businesses are forbidden in Iran and can result in stiff fines. But Shirin had decided that the risk was worth it—New Age therapy is very popular in Iran and she knew she'd find many clients. She'd obtained some of her books through book fairs in Tehran and others through her friend in the United States.

"How many classes do you teach?" I asked her.

"Oh," she said, with a sigh, "I teach all the time. From eight in the morning until eight or nine o'clock at night. I'm only free tonight because it's the weekend."

"That's a long day," I said lamely. No wonder Shirin looked so exhausted.

She shrugged. "I like it. And at least this way, I don't have to go out. I don't like to go out. Everything is so dirty and the colors are so dark. The streets are ugly and everyone smells bad. It's depressing. I try to stay in my house as much as I can."

I stared at the bookcase, not knowing what to say. Shirin's entire body seemed clenched. I tried to imagine what it would be like to live her life—and couldn't. My imagination didn't stretch that far. To me, Iran seemed fascinating—everything was so different and everyone was so kind; Shirin herself would invite me to dinner several more times. But I didn't have to live here, I thought guiltily. Iran was just an experience for me. For Shirin, it was life.

In the other room, the younger women were laughing and taking pictures of each other as they began gathering up their belongings and getting ready to go. Most were wearing black *manteaus*, and as they put on their coverings, they seemed to change from individuals into representatives of themselves—generic Everywomen, leaving the predictable safeties of a private world for the unpredictable perils of a public one, all while taking the protection of invisibility, of privacy, with them in the form of the *hejab*.

"Are you at all optimistic?" I said to Shirin. "Do you think change will come to Iran?"

"Yes, I believe things will change," she said stonily. "But it will have to happen slowly. Maybe in four to eight years. And that's too depressing for me to think about. I've spent my whole adult life under this Islamic regime."

☙ ❧

Sara and her husband Reza live in a roomy but dark and sparsely furnished apartment in north Tehran. An upright piano stands in one corner and landscape paintings hang from the walls. All the blinds were drawn when I arrived at 2 P.M.

Sara, dressed in a flowing blouse and tan pants, met me warmly at the door and ushered me into the living room, where she had a large spread of fruit and sweets waiting. Her husband was still at work and her teenage son was out with friends.

"I couldn't say this to you on the phone," she said before I even had a chance to sit down. "But be very careful what you write about Iran. Don't say anything negative. Look at what happened to Salman Rushdie."

I felt a twinge of anxiety. The case of Salman Rushdie and the *fatwa*, or official religious ruling, of death that Ayatollah Khomeini had placed on his head had crossed my mind more than once. But then I remembered all the other highly critical books and articles that had come out about Iran— nothing had happened to those authors. Rushdie had been singled out not because he criticized Iran but because he was perceived to have demonized Islam. I said as much to Sara.

"Oh," she said, her voice faltering for a moment. "I didn't know. The only writer we hear about here is Salman Rushdie."

She pressed fruit and tea on me, and although I knew that it wasn't true, I imagined that I saw her hands shaking. She wasn't a particularly slight woman, but something about her seemed disturbingly frail. Her face, framed by large glasses with gold edges, was very pale.

"Has anyone been following you?" she said. Her excellent English, spoken with a slight French accent, was a pleasure to listen to.

"I don't think so," I said.

"Maybe you didn't see them," she said. "But that doesn't mean they're not there. That's why I keep the blinds drawn all day." She laughed nervously.

"You think someone's watching the house?" I said.

"I don't know, but they could be."

To me, that sounded unlikely, but then again, I was a stranger in this country.

"I thought things were getting better," I said. "Since the election of Khatami—"

"Not in my opinion. I know that's what people in the United States think, but all these changes they keep talking about? They're just superficial. Nothing basic has changed at all. We still have no rights. And just last week, I heard that they might make all women wear the *chador* again—no more *manteaus* and *rusaris*."

Educated for many years in France and England, Sara had returned to Iran shortly after the Revolution at the request of her parents, who'd wanted her home in a time of trouble. They and the rest of her family had since managed to leave the country, but she, for reasons that were never made altogether clear to me, had become trapped.

Sara taught French and English at two different universities. She often worked from 8:00 in the morning until 8:00 at night, sometimes teaching for eight hours straight, and brought home the equivalent of about $150 a month—not enough to afford her own car or any new furnishings. Almost everything in the apartment dated back to before the Revolution. Her husband, also trained as a professor, had left his university post years before to work in a private scientific lab, where the money, though not good, was slightly better.

"It's very discouraging to teach here," Sara said, "because the students don't want to learn anything. They're not interested. They only come to my English classes so they can get a good job, not because they want to read literature. We only do one novel or play a semester and still they complain—'It's a foreign language; it's too hard.'"

Her lament sounded distinctly familiar. I'd heard similar complaints from academic friends in New York.

"Sometimes my students come to me and cry when they don't pass classes. They're usually the ones from way out in the backcountry, and I usually feel bad for them and give them a passing grade. Or sometimes my students are the children of martrys, and I've learned to pass them the first time around no matter what. If I don't, the department will come to me and say I have to pass them—it doesn't matter if they failed their exams.

"One of the books that I teach is *Animal Farm,* and I say very clearly at the beginning that this is a criticism of Stalin. I'm very careful not to draw any comparisons to Iran. They can do that for themselves. But one time a girl started whispering, and then said openly, 'This is just like Iran after the Revolution.' I told her after class to be more careful, but she said she didn't care.

"There are spies everywhere. Students from the Islamic Society can come to your class with a tape recorder, and you don't always know who they are. I don't think it's ever happened to me, but I used to teach Greek mythology and one day I was told I couldn't teach it anymore—it had too much sex. Most of the time, though, the Islamic Society leaves me alone because they can't understand that much English. Or French."

The phone rang and hesitantly, Sara picked it up. She put it back down again immediately and for a moment, I worried that the call had been due to me—and those possibly following me. Sara's nervousness was making me nervous.

"A hang-up," she said. "It happens a lot in Iran. It's mostly young kids with nothing to do."

Relieved, I realized that the call had probably been for Sara's son. I'd already learned that the telephone is even more important among teenagers in Iran than it is in the United States. A boy or girl sees someone on the street that he or she admires. They can't speak to each other directly for more than a few minutes and so surreptitiously exchange phone numbers.

"Tell me about the United States," Sara said. "Do you think I could get a job teaching at a university there? Iraj tells me that it is very hard." Iraj was Sara's brother. He was a New York–based photographer whom I'd met through a friend in Persian class, and it was thanks to him that I was visiting here.

"It is hard," I said, not sure whether to encourage her. "But at least there are more options."

Somewhere in the middle of our conversation, I'd realized why Sara seemed so frail. Even more than Shirin, she was badly depressed. I'd been blind not to realize it from the very beginning.

Reza, Sara's husband, came bustling through the door, blue plastic prayer beads in hand. A tall, energetic man, he seemed the antithesis of Sara, and I wondered if his energy made her feel better or worse.

He flicked on the overhead lights and sat down on the other end of the couch while Sara poured out fresh tea, served in typical Iranian fashion, in glasses without lemon or milk. Though not a tea drinker at home, I'd already grown addicted to the smooth, soothing beverage, which I sipped Persian style, through a sugar cube held in the front of my mouth.

I asked Reza, whose English was almost as good as Sara's, if he agreed with her regarding change in Iran.

"Sara is very negative," he said, glancing at his wife, who gave him a wry look. "She doesn't go out much. But things *have* changed. Things *are* improving. Every two or three months Khatami comes on television and talks about our problems—we're not being kept in the dark as much as we were before."

Sara opened her mouth as if to say something, but Reza kept on talking.

"It's true that Iran has a lot of economic problems," he said, "And whenever there are economic problems, people blame the government. But I don't think it's the government's fault. We've just been at war for eight years, and inflation is very bad. Officially, they say it is thirty percent, but I think it's more like fifty percent. Before the Revolution, there were only seventy *rials* to the dollar, and now there are more than six hundred.

"The trouble is that Iran has always depended on oil money and since oil prices are down, we're in big trouble. But we've been making great effort in the last years to develop other things. We've got a lot more factories now, and power plants. We make spare parts for automobiles, we export shoes to France—just five years ago, we imported them from Italy. We make watches and wall sockets—we used to import those from Germany. Our quality still isn't too good, but I believe that will change. Thirty years ago, people used to say things made in Japan were cheap, too."

I nodded, enjoying Reza's positive energy. In the bazaar, I'd seen many of the products that he was talking about and I had read a little about Iran's economy. Iran depends on oil for about eighty percent of its export earnings, and as prices have fallen through the last two decades—from $36 a barrel in 1981 to $11 a barrel in 1998—the country's economy has suffered badly.* One of Khomeini's promises immediately following the Revolution was to reduce Iran's dependency on oil, but the Iran–Iraq War intervened and those plans were put on hold. The nationalization of all major industries, a precipitous drop in foreign investment, and widespread corruption—especially among the country's enormous tax-exempt foundations—have also added considerably to Iran's economic woes.

Sara offered me a small cucumber—a quintessential fruit in Iran—and when I refused, passed me a box of dates. We'd already had melon, tangerines, apples, cookies, sunflower seeds, and nuts. Eating is a constant pastime in Iran.

"Did you support the Revolution when it first began?" I asked Reza. I felt a little strange to be talking only to him. Sara had fallen silent, and I wondered which of them had the more accurate outlook on Iran.

"My father was a high-ranking policeman under the Shah," Reza said, "and the Revolution hurt him and my family very much. Before the Revolution, my father earned about two thousand dollars a month. After the Revolution, he earned about one hundred fifty dollars a month. He hated Khomeini at first, but later he liked him—he was a real man, he said, not like the Shah, who left the country without helping his friends.

"I hated Khomeini, too, and I still hate him because of the changes he brought to Iran. But I also believe he was a great man, a charismatic man, and he did many good things. He helped change some of the superstitions of Iran and I believe that if he were still alive, he could do much more."

---

*When OPEC (Organization of Petroleum Exporting Countries) tightened production quotas in 2000, oil prices rose again to $30 a barrel and more, easing Iran's economic restraints at least temporarily.

I was about to ask Sara whether she agreed with Reza about Khomeini—I strongly suspected she did not—when the doorbell rang. A young man wearing a leather jacket and jeans and carrying a large satchel was at the door. Quickly, he slipped inside, barely saying hello, and headed straight to the kitchen table, where he began unpacking his bag.

Grinning at my surprise, Sara told me that he was a black market entrepreneur who rented illegal videos to about 200 clients all over Tehran. He kept a file on each of his customers, in which he noted their likes, dislikes, and what they'd already seen, and never carried more than 25 videos at a time. In the event that he got caught, 25 tapes were the most he could claim as his personal collection; more than that and he could be charged an enormous, perhaps crippling, fine.

I looked over the videos that he had pulled out: *Spice World, The Fugitive, Jackie Brown, Basic Instinct, The Assassins,* a new version of *Romeo and Juliet* starring Leonardo DiCaprio and Claire Danes, and *Intimate Relations,* which Sara told me was an excellent film that had recently been released in England. She also showed me a thick notebook listing all the movies that she and Reza had rented over the past few years. Alphabetized, with several pages for each letter, it listed hundreds of films both well known and obscure. Most were American and European, and some were so new that they'd still been playing in first-run movie theaters when I'd left New York.

"As you can see, I'm working for American culture," the video man joked. "That's why my life is so stressful."

He did seem jumpy and in a hurry to get out of the house. I had many questions that I wanted to ask him—Had he ever been arrested? Where did he get his videos? Who were his clients?—but he was already halfway to the door and I got the distinct impression he didn't want to talk to me.

"I always have to worry about getting caught," he said, slipping out. "Sometimes, if I hear an area is dangerous, I come very late or I don't come at all."

The door clicked behind him.

In the silence that followed, Sara, Reza, and I started discussing movies and books. We'd all read and seen many of the same things and shared many of the same opinions, making me feel as if I were back in New York, talking with other writers, film buffs, and academic friends. Sara and Reza knew as much about American movies as I did, and considerably more about European and, of course, Iranian film.

"Don't you ever go to the movie theater here?" I asked, struck by the fact that most of what they'd seen had been on the small screen.

"Sometimes," Reza said. "But the best of the Iranian films aren't shown that often—most of what's in the theaters are action movies. And some films, like *Taste of Cherries* by Abbas Kiarostami are banned."

I'd seen *Taste of Cherries*—which concerns suicide, an off-limits subject in Iran—in New York, along with many other Iranian movies. Iranian cinema is currently at the forefront of the international filmmaking scene, consistently winning top prizes at Cannes and other major film festivals. New York has hosted several extensive Iranian film series in the last few years, with the critics lauding the films' freshness, simplicity, moral seriousness, and intellectual ambition. There's something about censorship, I'd thought more than once as the Persian credits rolled, that, like a strict poetic form, can bring out the best in an artist's vision.

"Now that you know about movies in Iran," Reza said, winking broadly at me, "let us show you TV."

"All right," I said, then laughed, glad that he, like many Iranians I met, seemed to find my curiosity about their culture so amusing. "Do you have a satellite dish?"

Satellite dishes are illegal in the Islamic Republic. However, about half the people I met, ranging from the upper middle class to the working poor, had illegal dishes hidden on their roofs—and told me that everyone did. The other half said that they would never dare to have an illegal dish—and that hardly anyone else did either.

When satellite dishes were first introduced in Iran, they were legal. Manufactured near Tehran, they were intended for both national consumption and export. Only on realizing the full potential of the dishes, which can beam down anything from the BBC to CNN, did the clerics outlaw them, in 1994.

"Of course not," said Reza. "They're too dangerous. You have to pay a lot if you're caught."

"But our neighbor has one," said Sara, and got up to make a phone call.

A few moments later, we were traipsing down the hall into a nearby apartment. A slight man wearing heavy glasses welcomed us.

"Look," he said, turning on the TV while we sat down on a wide couch, "We can get everything here."

He flipped by *The Flintstones*, courtesy of TNT; Billy Ocean, courtesy of MTV; American baseball scores, courtesy of CNN; and seemingly endless

Turkish and Indian soap operas, filled with half-naked women. He sub-scribed to an Indian–Turkish satellite package, which is very popular all over Iran.

Settling back with yet another cup of tea, we watched an Indian talk show hostess swoon about the new Bombay Brasserie, a "trendy eatery serving Black Lacy Cutlets," and heard the Indian pop song *Kitaben Bahutsi Venus*, sung by a sex goddess in a miniskirt and halter top. One Turkish advertisement flashed a curvaceous beauty bending over to look in the refrigerator, her frilly underwear showing. Another showed two voluptuous babes driving a new sports car.

Switching to Iranian TV, we saw a stern mullah standing at a podium, pontificating—everyone started to laugh; two stern mullahs sitting at a table, pontificating; a low-key nature show; an even lower-key travel show; and the news, which concentrated on Iran and the Islamic world. At night, Iranian TV does also broadcast Iranian movies, foreign movies, and family shows, but always, everything must be done according to strict Islamic law. Foreign movies are edited so as not to include scenes deemed offensive by Ershad; actors in Iranian programs must wear the *hejab* and cannot embrace or touch, because although the characters may be related on the show, the actors are not related in real life. Programs are interrupted for *azan*, the call to prayer, but not for advertisements, which can appear only between shows.

To me, the illegal Indian and Turkish shows were pure junk and the lack of advertisements on Iranian TV, refreshing. But I could only begin to imagine the pull that the forbidden shows must have on young Iranians used to living in a shrouded world. To them, the sight of bare arms and calves—let alone all the exposed bosoms and thighs and the evidence of so much material wealth—must seem extraordinary. I sighed; both worlds seemed depressing to me.

Sara and Reza drove me home. Night had fallen. Along the way, we passed through a deserted crossroads where skinny teenage boys wearing loose shirts and carrying automatic rifles were lingering. They were mem-bers of the Basij, or voluntary armed forces, first formed during the Iran–Iraq War and made up largely of boys between the ages of 15 and 18. Since the war's end, the Basij has served largely as another arm of the "morals police," and many citizens fear them more than they do the Revolutionary Guards or *komiteh*, as they are more fanatic and less likely to accept bribes. The boys waved their guns at us to slow down as we neared the crossroads, but after taking a good look inside, let us pass. They were looking for young lovers or evidence of alcohol abuse, and we were far too old and sober to interest them.

Later that night, lying awake in bed, I thought more about Sara and Reza and their differing outlooks on Iran. I would encounter similar contradictory opinions again and again in the next few months, with some Iranians praising life in the Islamic Republic to me and others denouncing it, and every time, I felt a restless, gnawing hunger to know which opinion was the "truth." Only when I remembered a poem by one of the greatest of all Sufi poets, the thirteenth-century Persian Jalal al-Din Mohammad Rumi, did I feel some relief. Entitled "Elephant in the Dark," it tells of five people who have never seen an elephant before, touching it in a dark room. The one who touches its trunk declares it to be a "water-pipe kind of creature." The one who encounters an ear describes it as "a very strong, always moving back and forth, fan-animal." A third person, touching the curved back, declares it "a leathery throne." Rumi ends the poem:

Each of us touches one place
and understands the whole in that way.

The palm and the fingers feeling in the dark are
how the senses explore the reality of the elephant.

If each of us held a candle there,
and if we went in together,
we could see it.

৯৯৫৫

Two nights later, five of us, two Christians and three Muslims, went to dine at the Tiare Restaurant, said to be one of the best restaurants in Tehran. Situated on the top floor of the Laleh International Hotel, the Tiare offered an upscale Western setting, bird's-eye views of the downtown, and a cuisine that was advertised as Polynesian, though it tasted a lot more like Chinese-Persian to me.

We ordered Cokes, a move that collapsed the Muslim women among us into piles of giggles, and I stole a look at our mustachioed waiter, wondering whether he suspected anything. One of the Muslims had smuggled in a bottle of vodka in her handbag.

Our Cokes arrived and everyone stiffened, eyes darting furtively in all directions. Luckily, however, the restaurant wasn't very crowded, and so as soon as the waiters' backs were turned—

Out nudged the head of the vodka bottle. Quick, pass the glasses and pour. And pour and pour. Before I realized what was happening, our Muslim friend had filled everyone's glasses almost to the brim. That was seven or eight ounces of vodka per glass, diluted with only an inch or two of Coke. I glanced astonished at the other Christian—and the only other regular drinker at our table—and he grinned mischievously back. We were in for it now. We had to drink up to the last drop because if we left anything in our glasses, it would alert the waiters, who could, if they so chose, call the "morals police."

Drinking in Iran is an elaborate game, filled with code words and intricate rules. Wherever I went, in middle-class homes throughout the country, the subject of alcohol often came up, usually broached obliquely at first and then with more and more confidence as I gave the correct answers. The whole slow verbal dance reminded me of being in high school again or of being offered drugs in certain circles in New York. We were all rebellious teenagers, gleefully slipping the fetters of authoritarian rule. Rewards went to the bold—a fleeting and illusory feeling, of course. As an act of rebellion, drinking doesn't count for much.

Some of the people I met drank relatively openly, in the company of friends, others more clandestinely and only in the company of family, and still others in ways that defied logic. One woman happily imbibed while at her friends' homes but refused to have alcohol in her house, claiming that she never drank of her own volition but only to please her hosts. Another drank only with Christians, who are legally allowed to drink in Iran. The ban on alcohol is a religious one that applies only to Muslims; "They question thee about strong drink and games of chance. Say: In both is great sin," states the Qor'an (2:219).

Long before the arrival of Islam, however, the Persians were a wine-loving people, and the practice has thrived through the centuries despite religious admonitions. The Shiraz grape, now grown mostly in Australia, originated in Shiraz, Iran, and Persian poetry is filled with one reference to wine after another. Wrote the poet Hafez in one typical verse:

The rose has flushed red, the bud has burst,
And drunk with joy is the nightingale—

Hail, Sufis! lovers of wine, all hail!
For wine is proclaimed to a world athirst.

Most drinkers in Iran today consume a homemade brew, made of raisins or grapes. All housewives of a certain class know how to ferment the forbidden beverage, and usually it is viscous and sweet, with a fruity flavor, although I also tasted more vinegary concoctions, with a nutty edge. The tarter brews are meant to be vodkas, and are usually served with a cola or orange soda. The sweeter ones are liqueurs and served straight up or on the rocks.

Other Iranians obtain their liquor through the black market. Bottles of whiskey, vodka, and gin are smuggled in through the Turkish border by truck, to arrive in middle-class homes covered with dust. Most of the time, hard liquor is all that is available; wine and beer aren't cost effective.

Before and after drinking, precautions must be taken. At one party I attended, our host had to leave abruptly to pick up a guest who was bringing homemade vodka. She had no car and was afraid to take a taxi, in case she was searched. Several other times my fellow guests went far out of their way to drive me home. No one liked the idea of my talking to taxi drivers with alcohol on my breath. And when the parties were over, the bottles had to be disposed of carefully. Simply throwing them into the garbage isn't an option—

At the Tiare, we all downed our seven or eight ounces of vodka, cleaned out our glasses with a swill of Coke, and tottered out the door. Luckily, the other Christian, who was driving, could hold his liquor well and we arrived home without incident.

৵৽৻৻

I had an appointment with Mehranguiz Kar, a well-known lawyer, feminist, and writer. Kar had worked as a reformist before the Revolution, but according to the Islamic government, her views hadn't been extreme enough and after 1979, she'd been harshly accused of being against Islam and a follower of the Shah. For years, no Iranian publication would touch her articles and she'd been publicly maligned in print hundreds of times. The attacks had never stopped her from writing for foreign publications, however—usually about women's issues—and although the government had threatened to take away her law license many times, she was still in practice.

We met in her office, a utilitarian space in a quiet neighborhood. A serious and thoughtful woman, Kar was dressed in a dark brown *manteau* and *rusari* that reminded me of something Professor Kasheff had told us back in Persian class. Around the turn of the century, he'd said, women reformers pushing to establish the country's first schools for girls had dressed entirely in brown as an act of protest—and had been vilified. Back then, black and navy blue had been the only outdoor colors for women allowed.

Among the topics that Kar and I talked about was the split between the public and private in Iran.

"Because the religious government closes every door to the people and doesn't give freedom for natural relations, everything is hidden in Iran," she said. "But we have every bad problem here that you have in the West. Maybe you don't see it because of the *hejab*, but it is true. Our problems are getting close to your problems, especially among the young people. I am sure that using drugs is increasing, divorce is increasing, sexual relations between young men and women is increasing. But we don't know the truth because there is no center for getting estimates in Iran. We must research these things and we must talk. But we don't. Why? Because the religious government says we are clean of problems you have in industrial countries."

৶৽৻

One Thursday early in my stay, Bahman suggested that we all go to Shemshak. Situated in the Alborz Mountains just north of Tehran, Shemshak is a world-class ski resort in winter and popular weekend retreat in summer. Many wealthy Tehranis own condos or second homes in the area, and one of Bahman's *bazaari* friends had offered us the day use of his property.

Thursdays in Iran are the equivalent of Saturdays in the United States, as Friday is the Muslim day of public worship. Many Iranians do work on Thursday mornings, however, and most children attend a half day of school before setting out on family outings.

Though I never imagined that I'd have the slightest trouble, I was finding the Iranian calendar surprisingly difficult to adjust to. Trying to set up various appointments for interviews, invitations, and visits to tourist attractions, as well as a travel itinerary, I often got my *shambe*s (Saturdays) and *doshambe*s (Mondays) mixed up or would forget that places would be closed on Thursdays and Fridays. And the months were nearly as bad, as they don't correspond with the West's. The first six months of the Persian calendar have 31 days each; the second five, 30 days each; and the last, 29 days, or 30 in a leap year. I had arrived in Iran on August 26, which in the year 1998 corresponded with the fourth day of Shahrivar. Like the Islamic calendar, however, the Persian calendar begins in A.D. 622, with the flight of the Prophet Mohammad from Mecca to Medina, and so it was not 1998 in Iran but rather 1377. (The Persian calendar begins on the first day of spring, so the difference is usually 621 rather than 622 years.)

Bahman had already shown me around parts of Tehran and introduced me to several of his friends. Always going far out of his way to help others—paying for Sepideh's school supplies, buying socks he didn't need from a down-and-out vendor—he was eager to assist me in any way he could. He had an extremely busy medical practice, however, usually not coming home until after 9 P.M., and so this was the first full day that we were able to get away together.

Piling into Bahman's car, we waved at Naser, our building's caretaker, as he opened the front gates. A young Afghan with a wide grin, Naser had come to Tehran about three years before, to escape the political turmoil in his homeland. As a Shi'ite then living among Sunnis, he'd feared for his life and indeed had a scar across his neck that looked as if someone had once tried to slit his throat. I didn't think the people in our building treated him very well, but he told me that he was happy enough living in Iran. Naser's real dream, though, was to move to America. Almost every day, he wore a T-shirt that said *Beverly Hills*, and he thanked me profusely when I gave him a New York Yankees baseball cap.

Bahman snapped a Louis Armstrong cassette into the tape player, and we inched our way through the streets of north Tehran, stopping for gas at a crowded petrol station, in back of several brand-new sport-utility vehicles. Our tab was about $1.50 for 12 gallons of gas; fuel in oil-rich Iran is subsidized by the government and is extraordinarily cheap, even for Iranians, which helps account for the low cost of transportation throughout the country. A seven- or eight-hour bus ride between major cities usually costs about $2, and most domestic airplane tickets sell for about $20. The government also subsidizes the prices of bread, power, and water—a practice that adds yet another burden to the country's economy.

We eased our way onto one of the many highways that encircle Tehran. Cars packed with people were screeching by in four lanes instead of the designated three, and no one was using signal lights. Between the jostling cars chugged a multitude of motorbikes, most carrying families. Women's *chadors* flapped in the wind as they gripped their husbands' waists, often with a child or two sandwiched in between. Overhead hung green-and-white highway signs identical to those found in the United States, with words in both Persian and English. Though I wasn't the least bit homesick—there was far too much to see—I still found the signs oddly comforting.

"Look! Look!" Bahman said every time another car roared by us or cut us off. "Look how stupid they are! Stupid, stupid!" He was a cautious driver and we were traveling much more slowly than most.

"Stupid, stupid!" Lona cried. She had just recently learned to drive—thanks to Bahman's magnanimity—and enjoyed swearing at the horrendous traffic as much as he did. Driving with either of them was always high drama. We were always just about to be killed.

"Look, look!" Bahman said again as a tiny car covered with rust patches swerved just ahead of us.

"Watch out!" Lona cried.

I half cringed, half giggled, while also feeling disloyal—and concerned. Bahman looked tired and needed a day of rest much more than he needed a day in the country with me.

"See, they don't stay in lanes," Bahman said to me. "They need to be educated."

They was a word I heard often in north Tehran. The middle and upper classes use it frequently to describe their poorer, more conservative, and less educated compatriots—that is, the majority of the Iranian people.

In Iran, the rift between the haves and have-nots is particularly complex—not just a matter of money, education, and family but also a matter of exposure to the West. Ever since the time of Reza Shah, and his emphasis on modernization, the country has been split in two: on the one side, the Westernized middle and upper classes, who in the days of the Shahs were often educated in Europe and still usually speak several languages; on the other, the traditionalist masses steeped in the Qor'an. The Revolution largely came about because there was no communication between the first group—which comprised less than 10 percent of the population but controlled virtually everything—and the second. The Revolution promised to ease the differences between the two, and in some major ways has succeeded. Nearly 80 percent of Iranians are now literate, as compared to 58 percent in 1979, the average life expectancy has risen from 60 to 72 years, and most of Iran's 50,000-odd villages have electricity and roads. Some people believe that these same changes would also have occurred under the Shah, but most do not regret that he is gone. Almost everyone I spoke to agreed that the Revolution, or something similar, was necessary. It is the *Islamic* Revolution, not the Revolution per se, that is controversial.

However, the haves and the have-nots still speak about each other with enormous disdain, and the country remains badly divided between a tiny minority of the very rich, which now includes some clerics, a larger middle class, and the vast majority of the working poor and poor. Because of the country's many economic difficulties, the average income of Iranians in current dollars has fallen nearly a third since 1979, according to the World Bank, and the economy is on everybody's mind. Far more people complained to me about inflation and economics than they did about politics.

Which is not to say that Iran is a desperately poor country. Most Iranians have a standard of living that is much higher than that found in neighboring Pakistan or Afghanistan, as well as in many African countries. I did see destitution in Iran—especially in south Tehran and some of the villages—but it wasn't of the overwhelming magnitude that I'd witnessed in India, Haiti, or East Saint Louis, or even while teaching for a year in Bogotá, Colombia, where packs of orphaned children roamed the downtown streets and some poor soul once stole the glasses off my face.

Bahman got lost several times on the way to Shemshak, circling in detours that took us past homely neighborhood mosques with faded domes, ugly apartment buildings with carpets hanging out front, and a plump boy wearing a T-shirt that said *Think Pink* in English. Then we entered Lashgarak, a military installation area. The flushed faces of innocent martyrs stared down at us from billboards as we drove by lookout towers, military schools, and acre upon acre of barracks protected by barbed wire.

Finally, we reached the turnoff for Shemshak. We rounded a sharp corner, where without warning, a hidden pocket of the Alborz Mountains cracked open before us. Unlike the peaks that towered above the city, these Alborz were a rolling, moving sea of sandy hills flowing smoothly downward, into a hole in the middle of the earth. We were on the top of the pastel-streaked hills, looking down into their depths, and about to descend on a winding road lined with bumper-to-bumper traffic. Vendors parked along the roadside were selling everything from long yellow melons to fresh chewy pistachios, still wrapped in thick red skins. Only when pistachios age do they become hard and acquire a shell.

We started our descent, cut off just before joining the line of traffic by six young men in a shiny white BMW. The slopes spread out before us like fans of light and each was a different color, ranging from maroon, brown, and cream to pink, tan, and green-white. We passed by a parked pickup truck draped with women in *chadors* eating ears of grilled corn and boys selling shelled walnuts out of water jars. Pictures of Khomeini sat beside many of the vendors—just in case we'd forgotten where we were.

Reaching the bottom of the road, we entered a narrow valley filled with poplar and cypress trees. Through the valley flowed a silvery river in which men were trout fishing, boys were swimming, and women and girls were wading, their *manteaus* and *chadors* hiked up to their ankles or, in some daring cases, their calves. Shores and rocks were covered with pretty bits of cloth, spread out for picnicking.

We passed beneath the faded sign of an ugly jagged gun—the logo of the Revolutionary Guards—and by a series of large homes, hidden from the road by high walls. The homes had once belonged to supporters of the Shah but now belonged to their counterparts in the Islamic regime. Here and there were festive restaurants, strung with round, colored lights bobbing on wires.

From somewhere came the sound of *azan*, the call to prayer, and I caught my breath. I'd already heard the call several times in downtown Tehran, but there it had been half drowned out by honking horns and grinding engines. Here, the hypnotic lament made my insides ache—though with what, I couldn't say. I felt glad to have escaped the crazy, frenetic energy of Tehran and to be out in this still, bright landscape that despite the river and trees still seemed desolate and dry.

I thought about Mullah Nasr al-Din from my children's book of folktales, *Once the Mullah*. He had lived in landscape similar to this, though not as dramatic, and had climbed up his minaret five times a day to call the prayers, his voice sometimes cracking a bit on the high notes. "There is no god but Allah and Mohammad is his prophet," he would begin. No one does that in Iran anymore. The calls to prayer are taped and electrified, and every broadcast, perfect.

We stopped into the "Hony Restaurant"—*Hony* for *Honey*—and ordered lunch. On the menu were a large variety of kebabs—lamb, minced lamb, regular chicken, young chicken, fish—a lamb stew, yogurt, salad, pickles, rice, and bread. With minor variations in choice and major variations in quality, this same menu was served by almost every restaurant I entered in Iran. Persian cuisine is enormously diverse, with each region known for certain specialties, but for some reason I was never able to figure out, most restaurants serve nothing but kebabs—or fast foods, including pizza and hamburgers.

The Hony was filled with clean, sturdy tables adorned with plastic flowers, and a well-dressed middle-class crowd. From the walls hung an embroidered picture of Mecca, the Khomeini–Khamene'i–Khatami triumvirate, several cheesy-looking Oriental fans, and a sign admonishing women to dress Islamic. From the ceiling hung plastic beach balls advertising Fanta and Coke, both of which are very popular in Iran, along with several domestic sodas, including my favorite, Zam Zam.

As we ordered our drinks, I thought about the Coca-Cola bottling plant operating under license in the holy city of Mashhad. According to what I'd read, many Iranians had wanted to close the place down, symbolizing as it did American cultural influence. But, as the story went, both Ayatollah Khamene'i and former President Rafsanjani had had friends with financial interests in the plant and had not allowed it to be closed.

I asked Bahman about the plant, but he knew nothing about it. Sitting next to us, however, was a 40-ish, English-speaking Iranian who apparently did.

"Yes, you're correct about that," he said to me, interrupting our conversation. "And did you know that the way they helped solve the problem was to bring in a Muslim from America to run the place? His name was Mohammad Ali Kelly and he was backed by the CIA."

"Mohammad Ali *Kelly?*" I said, trying to hide my disbelief. "The CIA?"

"Yes, of course. The CIA backs everything in Iran, including the Islamic government. Didn't you know that?"

I felt too surprised to say anything. But as I would learn again and again in the next few months, Iranians love conspiracy theories—and the more outlandish, the better. Often, as I listened to their tales, many of which involved the U.S. government, I was reminded of our own stories—Who really killed JFK? Who really killed Martin Luther King Jr.?—and thought about how comforting such conspiracy theories are. If there are only a few sources of evil in the world, then evil can eventually be contained and therefore conquered. All evidence to the contrary, we ordinary folks are— or soon will be—in control. Goodness will prevail.

Our food arrived. Mixed into the yogurt was a pleasant flowery taste, and Bahman told me that it was rose water—a common condiment in

Iran. He also told me, with a roll of his eyes, that according to popular Islamic belief, the first rose was created when a drop of the Prophet's sweat fell onto the earth and a flower sprang in its place. Lona and Pari also rolled their eyes upon hearing this story, whereas I, as a foreigner, had the luxury of simply finding it charming. It wasn't an ignorance that I had to escape from.

As we were leaving the restaurant, a bus filled with young men in loose shirts and women in *chadors* pulled into a nearby parking lot. They made their way down to the river. They appeared to be of university age, and many had a pale, hungry look about them that contrasted sharply with the plump, contented air of the patrons of the Hony Restaurant.

"That's one good thing about the Revolution," Bahman said, watching them. "In the old days, only rich people came to Shemshak. Now, everyone comes."

We drove on, through a narrow gorge, with sheer rock walls rising on either side. Then the gorge opened out into a second valley that reminded me of the Alps, except that the mountains here were dark brown instead of deep green. Flecking the steep slopes were A-frame houses built in an alpine style, and they disappointed me. I knew this kind of architecture from ski resorts in the United States, and it seemed as bourgeois and mundane here as it did back there. I wanted something wilder and strange, something that matched the remote, withdrawn, dramatic landscape rising around us.

Occasionally, we passed a young couple holding hands or picnicking together, and each time, I wondered whether they were illicit lovers. The outdoors has become the refuge of unmarried couples all over Iran, and on the weekends, the Alborz Mountains are filled with young hikers interested more in being alone together than in nature.

Bypassing the A-frames, we pulled up to a dark, uninviting condominium building and parked. Out front was a circular enclosure fitted with a covering of wooden planks. At one time, the enclosure had been a swimming pool, but now, public bathing was considered to be un-Islamic. Young boys were kicking a ball around on the covered pool instead.

Inside, we were apparently expected. The doormen welcomed Bahman by name and handed him a key to his friend's condominium. We rode a creaking elevator up to a top floor and walked down an unlit hallway lined with a worn carpet and peeling paint. The apartment was also in need of fresh carpets and paint, but after turning on the lights, we located a tape player and an assortment of tapes. German language instruction and the Eagles. "I've got a peaceful, easy feeling . . ." wafted out through tinny speakers as Lona and Pari hummed along. I made cups of instant coffee.

Bahman and I settled down on the small balcony, while Lona, Pari, and Sepideh went outside to play badminton—much to my relief. As much as I enjoyed their company, I wanted to be alone with Bahman for a while, so that we could talk freely in English without worrying about being interrupted or being rude. When all five of us were together, there were often two- and three-way conversations going on—in English, Persian, and Azeri Turkish.

Bahman told me more about himself. His bus driver father, though not educated, had been an extremely wise and capable man who'd greatly aided the Americans just after World War II, when Russia tried to seize control of northern Iran. Bahman himself, the first of his family to attend college, had studied with Americans in Tabriz and Shiraz before going to England to complete his medical training. There, he'd met his future wife Chris, and they'd returned to Iran to live for six very happy years before the Revolution broke out. They had two sons—one a teacher in England, the other a medical student in Scotland—and were still in the throes of adjusting to the new Iran.

Bahman didn't regret coming back to Iran, but there was much about his old life in England that he missed: the quiet, the order, certain foods, certain BBC shows, and, especially, his old stone house, with its lovely garden that he'd worked in every weekend. He worried about resettling his wife in Iran and about leaving his sons behind.

"Sometimes I wish I'd never seen the West," he said. "Sometimes I wish I was like the rest of my family here—they own small shops, they drive lorries, they've never been outside Iran—so they can't compare. They're much happier than I am. They don't work so hard. I work too hard. All my life I've worked too hard, and now I am old."

"You're not old," I said, but I was worried about him. He often looked exhausted.

"I think too much," Bahman said.

"I know what you mean," I said wryly. In some ways, Bahman and I were much alike—ambitious, analytical, soft-hearted, sentimental. Throughout my stay in Tehran, we had many far-ranging discussions that lasted long into the night.

In other ways, Bahman reminded me of my mother. As a German reset-

tled in America, she's never quite adjusted to her adopted land, and
Bahman, too, seemed torn between two cultures. Being bicultural, I often
thought while listening to him, is not the easy, oh-so-interesting blending
of two worlds in one person—or one country—that it's sometimes made
out to be. While adding depth and range, it also adds much conflict and
unhappiness.

Relaxing back with his cup of coffee, Bahman told me more about
being a gynecologist in Iran, a profession that often caused his two selves
to clash. Perhaps 80 percent of all births in Tehran were via cesarean section, he said. The practice had begun during the Iran–Iraq War, when
every physician's time was precious, and had continued—in his admittedly
cynical opinion—because the surgery allowed doctors to charge more.

Once, when Bahman was about to perform a cesarean section, the
woman's husband rushed in and demanded that the operation stop.
Though educated at the University of California, Berkeley, he had consulted the poet Hafez and had determined that the timing of the birth was
inauspicious.

Most of Bahman's patients were *bazaaris* because they were among the few
who could afford infertility treatments, the mainstay of his practice, and
they often showered him with expensive gifts that he did not want. The
worst offense had occurred a year before when someone deposited a large
sum of money directly into his bank account without informing him first.

"You see, your life is not your own here," Bahman said, shaking his
head. "People with connections can find out anything about you they
want."

On the more positive side, Bahman told me, medicine in Iran has
advanced a thousand-fold since the days when my father was practicing
there. Back then, there'd been only a few simple hospitals and one incubator in all of Tabriz. Now Tabriz had at least a half dozen excellent hospitals, including one that specialized in heart surgery. In fact, the treatment
of heart disease in general, along with blood transfusions, was something
that Iranian doctors excelled at. They'd perfected their techniques during
the Iran–Iraq War.

As our conversation trailed off, we turned our attention to the outside
world. From our perch, we could see the brown, pastel-streaked mountains
rising and falling in the distance and sport-utility vehicles and BMWs
coming and going in the foreground. One luxury car pulled up to our
building and deposited a woman in an elegant *manteau* carrying a large

DKNY shopping bag. In another, I could see teenage boys and girls passing a joint back and forth.

The scene made me uncomfortable. It had a decadent, languorous feel that made my skin itch. Corruption seemed to weigh heavy in the air.

"There's nothing for people to do here," Bahman said, as if reading my thoughts and apologizing.

True, I thought, but this was precisely the sort of situation that the Revolution was supposed to fix. University professors like Sara and Reza could barely afford to buy meat and yet here were their wealthier compatriots lolling about with all the latest luxuries.

As I got up to turn over the Eagles tape, a young woman named Vida knocked on the door. Nineteen years old, she was related to the people who owned the condominium and wanted to say hello. She spoke excellent English, as she'd gone to high school in London, returning to Iran just one year before.

Taking off her *manteau*, she joined us on the balcony. She was wearing a tight miniskirt with ribbed stockings and heels, and had long, tawny hair that curled sensuously down her back.

"The young people here," Vida said, without my asking her anything, "they don't care about religion and they don't care about the *komiteh*. They just do what they want, and they just want to have fun. And they will not give up. They go out in couples in cars, and when they get stopped, they just pay. If you have money in this country, you can do anything.

"One time I saw a man in a car get stopped. He was very drunk and he had a woman with him. But he only had to pay two thousand *tomans* ($3.50) and they let him go. And another time, in the north, some kids were being bothered by a *komiteh* and they attacked him. They put a shish kebab stick in his stomach and he went into a coma. They were many against one, but they were so proud of what they'd done, they couldn't stop talking about it."

She paused, waiting for me to react.

"That sounds awful," I said. "But terrible things happen in every country." Vida's needling tone was irking me.

Vida continued. "The kids here do a lot of things. And the girls are even worse than the boys. All they want is to get married, have nice cars, and have lots of gold jewelry. They don't care about education—not like my friends in England. They go to parties and do everything"—her eyes flicked to Bahman—"not dancing—other things—and some of them are only thirteen, fourteen years old. Their parents don't care. They'd rather have them at home, safe, and not outside, where they can get caught by the *komiteh*."

I nodded noncommittally, but I knew that her words had validity. The strictures on public dating in Iran encourage young people to stay at home—and there engage in sexual intercourse at a much younger age than they otherwise might.

I was to meet Vida several more times before I left Iran, and with each visit, I became more aware of how deeply unhappy she was. She'd fallen in with a peer group that she couldn't relate to and to a large extent, despised. Iran held many other kinds of individuals besides the friends she had, I already knew, but she was having a hard time finding them. Like many people, she couldn't seem to escape from the social set to which she'd been assigned. Her immediate world was all she could see.

Throughout my travels in Iran, I was constantly struck by how much all of our opinions are formed by our social strata and personal experiences—a truism, of course, but one that's surprisingly easy to forget. As an outsider, I could often see why an individual believed what he or she believed, and how those beliefs—no matter how one-sided—were consistently reinforced by that individual's microenvironment until they became absolute truths.

We took Vida back to Tehran with us, and on the way, we detoured into the city to make a stop on fashionable Jordan Avenue, a hot spot on Thursday nights, with hordes of young people cruising up and down in same-sex packs. Many of the young men that night were sporting tight jeans, new sneakers, and Leonardo DiCaprio haircuts—the movie *Titanic*, though outlawed in Iran, was all the rage. Many of the young women were wearing brightly colored *rusari*s, heavy makeup, and sexy heels. The groups whispered and giggled among themselves as they passed each other, but I saw few direct male–female exchanges.

Vida pointed out an inviting-looking coffee shop that she and her friends had once frequented. They'd stopped going there, she said, because the manager had become a spy for the *komiteh*, watching out for illicit encounters and reporting cars that passed by his shop once too often. Because apparently people cruised Jordan Avenue by wheel as well as on foot, and it took several passes before they were able to flash phone numbers at each other through car windows.

A few minutes later, Bahman nudged me.

"See that man," he said as a middle-aged man on a cell phone drove by. "He's talking to a woman and they'll find somewhere to meet."

"He's not so young," I said, while thinking that for all we knew, the man could be talking to his wife.

"No, and don't let anyone fool you with all their religious talk. I've heard that there's plenty of extramarital sex in Iran. One man even told me that once when he stopped for a red light, a woman jumped into his front seat and opened her *chador*. She was completely naked underneath."

Bahman's story reminded me of others I'd heard in north Tehran, where people seemed to delight in telling me outrageous sexual tales while often implying that they were the Islamic government's fault. One woman told me about a corner in Tehran frequented by transvestites dressed in *chadors*. Another told me about middle-class prostitutes who took their sex from behind so that they were, technically speaking, still virgins. Still another told me about comfortably married women who prostituted themselves for fun—sex being the only enjoyable outlet some women had, she said. It was fascinating to listen to these stories—none of whose activities I witnessed personally—but although they did reflect a large gap between professed Islamic beliefs and practices, I really couldn't see how they were the government's fault. All large cities are part netherworld, hiding within them the most forbidden of private acts.

TWO

One day, I went to visit Goli Emami, a well-known bookseller and translator who'd been in the book business for close to 30 years. Her shop, Zamineh Books, was situated on a narrow back street in north Tehran. Fat and thin hardcovers and paperbacks rose from crowded tables, and shelves overflowed with titles, their cramped spines aswirl with Persian script.

Goli sat behind the cashier's desk. A brisk, handsome woman in her fifties, she wore a light-colored *manteau* and colorful silk *rusari*, out of which stuck a provocative shock of bright white hair.

"Hello, and welcome," she said in excellent English as I came through the door, and she cleared a stack of books off a chair so that I could sit down. "What are you doing here? What else have you written? How much do you know about Iran?"

Like many other north Tehranis I met, including Bahman, Goli wanted to know about my credentials. I found it disconcerting at first, but also realized that it made sense. I was here to write about their country, and they wanted reassurance that I knew what I was doing. But I don't *really* know what I'm doing, I wanted to say sometimes, to break through the polite conversation and acknowledge the not-so-subtle testing going on— I'm just feeling my way along, like we all are.

To write a travel book is a strange endeavor. You know next to nothing when you begin and then, suddenly, a relatively short period of time later, you're an expert. Compared to serious scholars and the culture's citizens, you're still woefully ignorant, and yet, paradoxically, you do often know things that they do not. You see things that they're too familiar with to notice.

I asked Goli about book publishing in Iran, and she told me that there were about 300 serious publishers, about one third of which were women owned. But, she cautioned me, those statistics were very misleading. Most Iranian publishers were single-person operations with shoestring budgets who published only a handful of titles with print runs of 2,000 to 3,000. The publishers, who often had other means of support, did everything themselves, from editing to production, and had no associate editors, pub-licity directors, sales staff, or distributors. Larger publishing companies with offices and staffs did number about 50, but most of those were gov-ernment owned.

Foreign books, Goli went on, comprised about half of the Iranian book market. As in the United States, diet, cooking, relationship, and health books were often the best-sellers, but the Iranians were also especially fond of two foreign novelists: Colombia's Gabriel García Márquez and Czechoslovakia's Milan Kundera. García Márquez's books were often translated into Persian before they were translated into English, and they sold by the thousands, despite horrific mutilation by the censors. The Persian edition of *Love in the Time of Cholera*, a book that chronicles a half-century of unrequited passion between a woman and two men, contains not one single love scene.

Censorship in Iran, Goli said, had followed a strange trajectory. Under the Shah, nothing even tangentially critical of the monarchy had eluded the censors, and all political books had been banned. Therefore, for a short period immediately before and following the Revolution, political books on everything from communism to democracy had poured into the mar-ketplace, most published between blank white covers, as there'd been no time to bother with design. Nonetheless, most of those books had not been big sellers. People had been tired and dazed; they hadn't known what they'd wanted to read.

Then, the Ministry of Culture and Islamic Guidance had been established. The ministry allowed the publication of many political books to
continue but cracked down on books that criticized Islam or the government or described intimate scenes deemed to be un-Islamic.

"At its peak," Goli said, "you couldn't even describe a woman's hair or
her bare arms. Love was eliminated. What is literature if it is not about
love and what is love if it is not about life? Literature started to suffer
enormously."

Censorship, I mused as Goli spoke, is also a way to try to control that
most private of private worlds—the imagination. What happens to an
individual's interior life when his or her personal life is already so strictly
curtailed? Does it become weaker or stronger? Or skew off into some different direction altogether?

In more recent years, Goli concluded as two young men entered the
shop, censorship has eased up somewhat, with more physical description
allowed and some previously banned books available. It was still very difficult to tell, however, whether the change would be permanent.

I was to visit Goli once again, several weeks later, after traveling to the
holy city of Mashhad, a popular pilgrimage site. We met in her home this
time—an artsy oasis filled with plants and books, and as we settled in, I
launched into an enthusiastic description of my visit to the Imam Reza
Shrine. One of the things that had most surprised me, I said, was that
some of the most fervent believers there hadn't been traditional villagers, as
I'd expected, but well-educated teachers and professionals—

Goli looked at me sharply, and I realized that I'd put my foot in my
mouth.

"Don't underestimate Imam Reza," she said. "I have a very special corner in my heart for Imam Reza."

I started. Of course, Goli was Muslim—I'd assumed that from the
beginning—and so why, I wondered now, had I also assumed that she
wasn't religious? What is it about the human mind that likes to categorize
so, neatly slipping people into slots, which in Iran usually translates into:
educated, middle-class, and Westernized = nonreligious; uneducated,
poor, or working-class = religious.

In truth, I don't really know how religious Goli is; we didn't discuss it.
But I did meet other well-educated, middle-class, Westernized Iranians who
were very religious, and each time, though I should have started to learn, it
pulled me up short—especially as the subject usually arose late in our con-

versation or on my second or third visit. Because despite the Islamic government and its constant heavy-handed messages, real religious belief is a
very private thing. Much more private than illicit videos or alcohol, it is not
a subject that most people bring up immediately on meeting a stranger.

ক্ষ্সপ্ৰ

Another afternoon, I went to visit Goli's counterpart in the art business,
Lili Golestan, who operated a gallery in Darrus, an especially exclusive
neighborhood of north Tehran. Flowering bushes peeked out from behind
thick walls and the meandering streets had a genteel, country-gentleman air
about them.

Originally trained as a translator and educated in France during the
time of the Shah, Lili had opened up her gallery in the late 1980s. Her
father had been an art collector, and she'd grown up knowing many famous
artists of the day. In her gallery, which measured perhaps 25 by 15 feet, she
showed everything from sculpture to photography but especially enjoyed
showcasing young painters. She estimated that there were currently about
600 painters and sculptors working in Tehran and about 20 art galleries,
of which 5 could be considered major.

"After the Revolution, the arts became very important in Iran," she said
as I took a seat by her desk in the gallery. Around us was a show of painted
wooden chests, one of the gallery's rare arts-and-crafts exhibits. The chests
were lovely, but I felt disappointed; I had been hoping to see some of the
work of the modern Iranian painters Lili was talking about, and knew that
I might not get another chance. Although Iran boasts many fine museums,
all exhibit either classic Persian and Islamic art or government-sanctioned
artists whose work tends to be wooden and predictable.

"People didn't have that much to do," Lili went on. "Jobs were scarce
and politics were dangerous. Art was a way to forget about the bad things
of the Revolution and later, the war. Especially the war . . ."

The refuge of the private, I thought again. How would any of us survive
without it?

"For the last ten years," Lili said, "the universities have been filled with
art students, and in every neighborhood there are art classes for adults and
kids. Our last mayor, Karbaschi, founded an arts center in each of Tehran's
twenty districts, where young people can go and enjoy themselves without
paying a lot of money.

"Many of our artists are very good. They have a good sense of color and composition, and they especially like the abstract art because the *komiteh* can't understand it. Most of our artists are also very young, in their twenties or thirties so they have plenty of time to develop themselves, and in ten years, if everything goes the way it is going now, with more cultural openness, we will have some very good painters.

"But the bad thing is, their knowledge is not very high. They want to learn, but the government does not give them much. We don't have many art books or films here, and books with nudes are censored.

"Before Khatami came to office, we had to get permission for every show we exhibited here. We had to send in photos. But after Khatami, I wrote a letter to Mohajerani, the minister of culture, proposing to cancel that. He agreed, and now we are free to show what we want. But we must be very careful. Tomorrow, I am opening a black-and-white show and I am a little worried. The photos show hands and feet, and there's not close covering of the head. I hope this will not clash with them.

"I've clashed with the *komiteh* many, many times in the past. Before Khatami, it happened maybe ten times in ten years. Not because of the art—because of the crowd in the street. Two or three hundred people came and there wasn't enough room, they went outside. The *komiteh* came and said, 'Why is this young lady laughing so much?' or 'Pull down your covering!' Then they took me away and everyone went home.

"I'm allowed to show any subject I want except the body. But I'm not afraid to show the body. Some others are afraid and don't show, but I think it's important to do these things. You must do these things. People respect you more if you do."

સૂર્જ

My ride arrived precisely at 8:30 P.M., as promised, and we slid through the streets of north Tehran, past a "morals police" block, and on to a low-slung house hidden behind a high wall. We rang the doorbell and waited in the dark for several long moments until Ali opened the door. He had a mane of black hair that flared out around his face and he was wearing a denim shirt and jeans.

We passed through an unlit courtyard and up an unlit outside staircase into a hot living room. Seven or eight people were crowded around a small table, drinking tea. Most were shaggy-looking men; one, a beautiful woman. All had a hipster edge, as befitted a group of people gathered together to hear live jazz in Tehran.

Technically speaking, jazz is illegal in Iran. Or at least the public performance of it is. Usually. A few years ago, for reasons no one understood, a jazz concert by the same musicians who would be performing here tonight had been allowed to take place at the Bahman Cultural Center, a major venue. No one had any idea, however, as to how that had happened or when or if the next jazz concert might occur.

And so, jazz fans gathered together in this small apartment one, sometimes two nights a week. The apartment belonged to a musician who lived downstairs, and he'd outfitted one of the back rooms to look like an intimate club. Against one wall was a piano, against another a set of drums, and against a third, a sofa and cocktail table. Overhead hung a round red lampshade that threw off streaks of light, disco style.

Friends kept filing in, gradually filling up the apartment, while the musicians and I talked. As far as they knew, they were the only jazz band in the entire city of Tehran. Also as far as they knew, Tehran contained just three oboe players, three trombone players, and six or seven trumpet players. None of the oboe or trombone players played jazz, however, and only one of the trumpet players did. The jazz musicians felt extraordinarily lucky to have a bass player in their group, because he was one of the few bass players in Iran, but were devastated by the fact that he would soon be moving to Canada. They doubted whether they could find a replacement.

Much of the reason for the dearth of players in Iran is the dearth of instruments—and the necessary accoutrements, such as reeds and strings. Most musical instruments were outlawed immediately after the Revolution, and although things have eased up considerably since then, still the only Western musical instruments that can be found with any regularity are the piano and the guitar.

Reza Asgarzadeh, the group's 30-year-old drummer, told me that he'd taught himself to play jazz by listening to LPs and CDs and studying fake books. All were readily available on the black market, he said, while some older jazz recordings were legal and available through music stores.

In addition to the drums, Reza played the piano, flute, accordion, *ney-anban* (Iranian bagpipes), and *duduk* (an Armenian double reed that is a sort of primitive oboe). He also sang in the Tehran Symphony Chorus and played in a baroque group that occasionally performed in the city's foreign embassies and cultural centers. Still, he felt he wasn't being challenged enough musically.

"It's very difficult to play music here," he said. "There's not a lot of stimulation, and most musicians don't know how to practice, to work, to go further and analyze what they're doing."

Proudly, the musicians showed me their one and only CD, "Digitally recorded live in the living room of a jazz devotee, Tehran, June 1998." On it were such standards as "Blue in Green," "Little Niles," and "Days of Wine and Roses." Featured were Reza on drums, Mehrab Moghadassian on bass, and Ali Farvardin on piano. Also involved was composer and pianist Christophe Rezai, half Iranian and half French, who had lived in France for many years before moving back to Iran several years before.

"The trick to recording that CD," Christophe said as the three other musicians wandered away to get set up, "was to find a nice-sounding piano. They're hard to find in Iran, but finally we located a baby grand in a friend's apartment."

Christophe also told me about a jazz score that he'd composed for an Iranian movie called *Fateh*, or *The Conqueror*. The job had come about after the concert at the Bahman Cultural Center, when he'd been approached by a director who was making an action film about a gang of Iranian counterfeiters and their comeuppance at the hands of the Revolutionary Guards. One of the fictional gang members had lived in the United States for many years, another in France, and the paper they'd used for their bills had come from Israel—all standard, state-sanctioned stuff that had probably made it easier for the filmmakers to get permission to use a jazz score.

For *Fateh*, Christophe had composed moody pieces based on jazz from the 1960s and 1970s, using a trumpet, bass, piano, drums, flute, vocals, and *daf*—a large Persian tambourine. The studio in which they'd recorded had been very old, with drums that hadn't been used since before the revolution.

As Christophe moved away to check on the musicians, I thought of Maryam, a perceptive young theater director whom I'd met earlier that day. Many of her observations were still ringing in my ears, and they applied as much to jazz as they did to theater—

"You can't talk about art in Iran today," she'd told me, "because it's constantly changing. Everything depends on who's behind the culture desk. So if someone tells you that you can do something, you have to do it right away. They might say yes today, but no tomorrow, and you'll never know the reason why.

"Everything is very controlled. When you want to put on a play, you have to take three copies of your script to Ershad, and after about two or three months, they will say yes or no. If they say yes, they will research the costs and tell you where it can be staged.

"Most of the censorship is religious. We can't have lots of love stories, or certain themes. And before, there was a rule from Ershad—only Iranian plays could be staged. Now we can do some foreign plays, but we still don't have any modern Western playwrights like Miller or Mamet because there aren't any translations. Dance and musicals are not allowed. So when you follow all the don'ts, there aren't many dos.

"But even with all their rules, I still know lots of people working in the arts in Iran. It's a thriving industry. You can see everything in private houses. Some houses have their own discos. Some houses have their own concert rooms where you can hear Philip Glass, Laurie Anderson. They invite maybe fifty people and then they perform. Whatever you want, you can find it in private houses in Iran."

Ali beckoned to me. The music was about to begin. I made my way into the now-crowded lounge where someone made room for me on the couch and other fans gathered around the door. The musicians nodded at each other, counted in time, and were off. "Night in Tunisia," "Footprints," "So What," "Days of Wine and Roses." A little stiff in the beginning, a little uncertain at times, but otherwise, a real pleasure to listen to, especially when Christophe, a highly accomplished piano player, sat in.

As they played, I was reminded of researching my first book, *The Jazz and Blues Lover's Guide to the U.S.* That journey had taken me into all sorts of clubs in many parts of the country—rich, poor, black, white. I'd covered all the famous spots, of course—the Village Vanguard in New York, the Jazz Showcase in Chicago—but my secret favorites had been the down-and-out holes-in-the-wall. Often located in poor, neglected, African American neighborhoods, the clubs and their people had inspired me with their dedication to the music—and to art for art's sake. Most of the musicians there had known that they'd never get famous, they'd never make any money, they'd never be as good as they'd once hoped to become. Their dream was a private dream only—but it hadn't mattered. They'd played, and their fans had listened and danced, with a passion that was often missing elsewhere. What's inside is often more real than what's outside.

Before leaving Ali's, I asked the musicians whether I could publish their names in anything I wrote, and to my surprise, they said yes. Apparently, though we could have been arrested for our gathering that night, the Islamic government wants the world to know about Iran's hidden cultural life. It's good for Iran's image.

HOUSE CALLS

There is a moment, too, when one is newly arrived in the East, when one is conscious of the world shrinking at one end and growing at the other till all the perspective of life is changed . . .

—Letter from Gertrude Bell to her mother,
Florence Bell, January 29, 1909*

ONE

North Tehran is home not only to many Westernized and professional-class Iranians but also to Jamaran, the neighborhood where Ayatollah Khomeini spent the last nine years of his life. And so, one morning, curious to catch my first glimpse of this other side of Iran, I set out to visit the former leader's abode, armed with my letter of permission from Ershad. Like all my letters of permission, this was a flimsy, photocopied half-sheet of paper with a green Islamic Republic seal at the bottom. I later saw similar flimsy, half-sheet letters in the glass cases at the Museum of the Martyrs, commemorating acts of bravery and martyrdom during the Iran–Iraq War. Then and now, in matters mundane, heroic, and tragic, there was and is no money in Iran for niceties such as stationery.

Once a village separate from Tehran, Jamaran is a rabbit warren of low-slung buildings and winding streets, surrounded by clutches of large, costly

---

*A British citizen, Gertrude Margaret Bell (1868–1926) was a private scholar and archeologist who traveled extensively in the Middle East.

homes that once belonged to supporters of the Shah. After the Revolution, many of these homes were confiscated by the so-called Mercedes-Benz mullahs—wealthy and ambitious men who wanted to live close to Khomeini.

Khomeini moved to Jamaran in 1980, after suffering a heart attack, and thereafter rarely left the area. A hospital was set up next door to his home, and many of his ministers moved into houses across the courtyard from his.

I arrived at Jamaran just before 10 A.M., the time of my scheduled appointment. Lounging by the guardhouse was a young, bored Revolutionary Guard with a Kalashnikov rifle. He signaled to another bored armed guard about 30 yards ahead who signaled to another bored armed guard about 30 yards ahead of him to let me pass along a narrow winding street flanked by mud walls. I came to an office of sorts and two more guards let me into a courtyard dominated by towering trees. No one seemed to know what to do with me. Despite my letter of permission and a scheduled appointment with an English-speaking guide, the guards seemed surprised to see me there. A flurry of telephone calls about "the American" ensued, and finally I was allowed to pass through a curtained entranceway. Unsmiling, *chador*-clad women wearing white gloves patted me down and confiscated my camera. Already the day was hot and sweat trickled down my back as I self-consciously readjusted the shoulder pads of my *manteau*.

Walking as nonchalantly as I could up a short walkway, I came to a jumble of small buildings crowded around a concrete courtyard. Much construction was going on and it took me a moment to locate the narrow, two-storied house in which Ayatollah Khomeini had once lived. I would never have picked it out; like many buildings in Iran, it had a rough and unfinished look. An iron ramp led to a platform that fronted a glassed-in living room the size of a jail cell, and I peered inside to see a low couch, a machine-made carpet, plastic flowers, a Qor'an, and a large pile of neglected-looking oil paintings stacked one against another. The top one depicted the Ayatollah in his prime—as did another painting that sat outside on the platform. Two teenage boys were moving this painting around while taking pictures of it and each other.

I tried to imagine what life had been like when the Ayatollah had lived here. From all accounts, even those of his detractors, he had been an extremely ascetic, pious, and frugal man. He'd eaten simple foods—bread, cheese, yogurt, fruit, *abgusht* (a poor person's stew)—worn simple clothes, and owned only two turbans. He reportedly liked to do his own chores, kept scrupulous financial records, did not accept luxurious gifts of any sort, and scolded others for such things as leaving the lights on or throwing out drinking water. He spent no money on long-distance personal phone calls—not even when his son Mostafa died—and would not tolerate gossip. He followed the same rigid schedule every day and took daily walks of exactly twenty minutes each in his garden. At the end of each walk, he checked his watch to make sure that twenty minutes had elapsed and, if not, went back to take another turn.

Ruhollah Khomeini, whose first name means "soul of God," had lived in this house with his wife Khadijeh, who still resided in the closed-off rooms out back. They'd married in 1929; he by then an up-and-coming cleric in the holy city of Qom, she the daughter of a well-connected cleric in Tehran. Together they'd had seven children, five of whom—two sons and three daughters—had survived to adulthood, and Khomeini had reportedly been a warm and attentive father. As adults, both of his sons had worked for him, and when the elder son, Mostafa, died during the early stages of the Revolution, there were rumors that he'd been murdered by the Shah. Khomeini's three daughters had married into clerical and *bazaari* families.

Khomeini had spent most of his life teaching in Qom. Not until 1963, when he was already in his sixties, did he first enter politics, by harshly criticizing a series of the Shah's reforms known as the White Revolution. His verbal attacks helped to turn the June 1963 religious celebrations into violent protests against the regime. Nearly 100 people were killed, and Khomeini, already under arrest, remained in prison for months. A year later, the Shah extended diplomatic immunity to the many American military advisers then living in Iran, and Khomeini responded with a passionate, now-famous speech that accused the Shah of betraying both Iran and Islam. "They have reduced the Iranian people to a level lower than that of an American dog," he thundered. "If someone runs over a dog belonging to an American, he will be prosecuted. Even if the Shah himself were to run over a dog belonging to an American, he would be prosecuted. But if an American cook runs over the Shah, the head of the state, no one will have the right to interfere with him." The Shah immediately had Khomeini rearrested and deported to Turkey. From there, he moved on to Najaf, Iraq, and then Neauphle-le-Château, France, a village outside Paris, where he remained in exile until 1979.

Ayatollah Khomeini's speech resonated powerfully with the Iranian people because the West and Russia had controlled much of Iran for more than a century. Beginning in the mid-1800s, Iran had served as a pawn between imperial Britain, eager to add yet another notch to its string of colonies, and Russia. Both major powers had lusted over the weaker country, but because neither wanted to risk a war with the other, they finally negotiated the Anglo-Russia Agreement of 1907, which basically divided the assets of Iran between them. Iran was still nominally an independent country, but Russia took over the resources of the north, and Britain, the south. When enormous oil reserves were discovered in the south one year later, the British-owned Anglo-Iranian Oil Company seized control.

Thirty-odd years later, during World War II, the British and Russians simultaneously attacked Iran. Reza Shah had shown strong pro-German sympathies and was forced to abdicate in favor of his son. For the remainder of the war, British and Russian troops occupied Iran.

After the war, the United States took over much of Britain's prewar role and forced Russia to withdraw. U.S. advisory teams had been in Iran since 1942, and the two countries signed an important technical aid agreement in 1950. Five major American oil companies arrived in Iran in 1954, and thereafter, the U.S. government provided the Pahlavi government with hundreds of millions of dollars of economic aid. Many Iranians were deeply unhappy with the heavy military emphasis of that aid, however—much of it targeted against possible Soviet aggression—and with the bloated American bureaucracy that had suddenly arrived in their country.

As I was studying the Ayatollah's living room, a Mr. Mohammad Azimi arrived, sweating and apologizing profusely for being late. Evidently, he was my English-speaking guide. A wiry young man with a ready smile and heavy shock of brown hair that kept falling in his face, he had a beard and was wearing a collarless shirt outside his pants—classic signs of a staunch supporter of the Islamic government. After introducing himself, he immediately launched into a long speech praising Khomeini—who was more a mystic than a teacher or politician, he said—and about the many mistaken ideas that the United States had about Iran. He also agreed that Iran had many mistaken ideas about the United States and felt that the fault on both sides lay largely with the media.

"But," he said, a little self-consciously, "variety is the spice of life. Did I say that correct? Is the first time I use that phrase."

I didn't know quite what to make of him. He seemed very open and friendly, but I was on my guard.

We walked down to the entranceway to retrieve my confiscated camera, and I noticed how the atmosphere around me had relaxed. The formerly stone-faced women guards were now giving me smiles; Mr. Azimi's presence officially sanctioned mine and I had turned from an unknown quantity into a potential friend.

"To come here, you must have a flame in your heart," Mr. Azimi said, and I wondered what exactly he meant by that—and if he were right. Did I have a flame in my heart? Was I perhaps here for reasons that I myself didn't recognize? Was I even in danger of converting to Islam? To me that seemed unlikely, but I had heard enough tales of rational people inexplicably converting to new religions overnight to feel a split second of doubt.

We entered the *hoseinieh*, an informal religious hall, next door to Khomeini's home, where the Ayatollah had addressed his followers. Anyone who wanted to could attend those speeches, Mr. Azimi said to me, but I found that hard to believe. The room wouldn't hold more than a few hundred people.

Now crowded with schoolchildren sitting cross-legged on the floor— the boys in front, the girls (though not yet grown, already in modified *hejab*) in back—the hall was plain and square, with cement walls painted blue, exposed lightbulbs, and naked pipes. A black-and-pastel mural of Mecca covered one entire wall; banners inscribed with calligraphy hung from the others. "Khomeini is a reality which is history alive," "If your leader dies, no problem—you still have God," Mr. Azimi loosely translated for me. The balcony from which the Ayatollah had once spoken ran around the top of the room and was still equipped with his simple desk and a microphone. During the years immediately following Khomeini's death, I knew, the balcony had been enclosed with glass to prevent mourners from climbing up and kissing his chair. Since then, however, the glass had been removed, and I could easily imagine the wizened Ayatollah moving slowly along the rampart to the hushed excitement of the waiting crowd below. Every eye would have been on him; every believer would have caught his or her breath. The plainness of the room would only have added to the power of the man.

"The Imam never let them paint this room while he was alive," Mr. Azimi whispered in my ear. "He believed in simplicity."

I nodded, but I was now more interested in watching the video monitor hanging above our heads. Reading the sign beneath the screen, I was astonished to realize that it was screening an eerie tape of Khomeini's last days. A ghostly figure in striped pajamas and a black cap sat on a big white bed, his hollowed eyes and gaunt face staring out, haunted, as if already beyond the grave. On his large hands, which seemed to float across the screen, he wore immaculate white gloves. A woman in a *chador* was serving him tea.

"The Imam was not like other men," Mr. Azimi whispered in my ear again. "He had no fear. Even during the war, when they monitored his heart every day, it never changed—not even when they bombed Tehran."

Someone nudged my arm and I turned to see a small, beaming woman.

"*Khosh amadi*," she said, clasping my hands tightly in hers—welcome. "Thank you for coming here, to the house of the Imam. You are very good."

This last was a phrase that I was to hear often in Iran, and although it sounds strange in English, it doesn't seem to have the sappy connotation in Persian. Iranians use it often and without the least hint of self-consciousness, and mean it to be a compliment. As such, it is part of *ta'arof*, the politeness ritual I'd encountered in the taxis, which at one time involved using many extraordinarily complimentary and submissive phrases, such as "I will put my eyes under your feet," usually said to a social superior. One of the original purposes of *ta'arof* was to cement the social order; another, to protect the individual from the messy affairs of others. Politeness kept—and keeps—people apart.

From the *hoseinieh*, Mr. Azimi and I proceeded to his office in the nearby Institute for Compilation and Publication of the Works of Imam Khomeini, International Affairs Department. The institute was housed in a small, elegant mansion with an aqua reflecting pool out front and a regal marble staircase inside. The mansion had once belonged to one of the Shah's ministers, and it reminded me—a typical American citizen, in that I'd never experienced real political turmoil—of all the books and movies about revolutions that I had read and seen. The institute's wobbly metal tables and file cabinets contrasted appropriately, I thought, with the building's tall, graceful windows and elaborate chandeliers. In the basement, where stacks upon stacks of cheaply printed books were stored, was a stunning circular staircase and neglected marble fountain.

The purpose of the institute, Mr. Azimi told me as we exchanged our shoes for slippers—common practice in most private homes and some public offices in Iran—was to disseminate the teachings of the Imam throughout the world. The institute had already translated Khomeini's books into 12 languages—including English, German, French, Urdu, Bangladeshi, Bosnian, Chinese, and Japanese—and it collected books about him, pro and con, that had been published elsewhere. In fact, I could do the institute an enormous favor by sending them a list of all the Khomeini-related books that had been published in the United States. The institute would then like to order some of those books through me, for which they would pay, of course.

I grunted noncommittally.

Climbing the marble staircase, we headed down a corridor, past a neat cardboard container hanging on a wall, and I stopped, fascinated. Inside the box were odd-size snippets of paper, on each of which was written the word *Allah*. Among strict Muslims, it is considered inappropriate to simply toss the name of God into the wastepaper basket or onto the floor, and so the word is carefully cut out of any piece of paper on which it appears, to be disposed of more respectfully.

Mr. Azimi shared a large office with a half-dozen other eager young men, and they all looked up with great interest when I came in. Because I'm American? I wondered as someone offered me his chair and someone else served me a cup of tea. Or because I'm a blond woman? My hair was sticking messily out of my *rusari*. Probably both. There didn't seem to be too many women at the institute.

The young men all had at least one master's degree and wanted to talk to me about many things. One had majored in art, another in politics, a third in Persian literature, and Mr. Azimi himself had studied English literature. In addition to his job at the institute, he also worked part time as a writer and translator. He wrote regularly for one of Iran's family magazines, and occasionally for a political one, but his real love was the short story. His favorite writer was O. Henry (!?!, I thought) and he would like very, very much to talk at length to me, a fellow writer, about English literature. Could I possibly join him and his colleagues for lunch later in the week? And would I please call him by his nickname, Babak? It meant "little father."

Eagerly, I agreed. I was as curious about Babak and his colleagues as they were about me. Now that I'd spoken to a number of north Tehranis, I wanted to meet another kind of Iranian. I wanted to be pulled down deeper into the mysteries of Iran.

৵৽

When I arrived at the institute a few days later for lunch, I found Babak anxiously pacing in the lobby. There had been a slight change of plans. His boss wanted to meet me.

Not knowing what to expect, I followed my new friend down the hall and into a large rectangular office where Mr. Mehdi Noroozi was waiting. He had a kind, intelligent face and graying beard and wore a neatly ironed, long-sleeved white shirt outside gray pants, as well as an agate ring—another classic sign of a staunch supporter of the Islamic government. On first impression, I took him to be in his mid-thirties, but later found out that he was 47. I liked him and his quiet demeanor immediately.

"Welcome, welcome," he said in English as the three of us sat down at a long conference table and a small, bent man served us tea. "My dear sister Christiane—you don't mind if I call you sister, do you?—I am so happy to meet you. You know, we respect the Christians and Jesus and Maryam too much. Many women here are named Maryam. A *sura* [book] in the Qor'an is named Maryam. We like Maryam too much."

Too much, I had already learned, was a phrase that Iranians speaking English misuse often. They mean to say "very much." And *sister* was a term from the Revolution, after which all women were referred to as sisters and men as brothers. Nowadays, many disillusioned with the Islamic government use the words ironically.

"I hear you are writing a book about Imam Khomeini," Mr. Noroozi said.

"Well, no, not exactly," I said.

Mr. Noroozi looked slightly disappointed.

"I'm writing a *safarnameh* about my travels through Iran," I said. Much to my delight, I had already discovered that most Iranians, well educated or not, understand exactly what a *safarnameh* is. In the United States, in contrast, many people I'd spoken to before leaving had looked puzzled when I told them I was writing a travelogue about Iran. "You mean a guidebook?" they'd say. "Or a political book? Or a book about women? No? Just an account of your travels? Who will be the audience for a book like that?" In our fast-paced society, the leisurely travelogue, too amorphous for a sound bite, has become a largely marginalized genre read mostly by literary types. In Iran, however, it is still in style.

Mr. Noroozi had his own battery of questions: How much of your book will be about Imam Khomeini? What will be the title? How long will it be? How can the institute best approach the American market? What books should we read to better understand American culture? Would you be available to edit our books and correct our English?

The more questions Mr. Noroozi asked, the more nervous I became. Proselytizers are the same all over the world, and despite the friendly atmosphere in the room, I suddenly felt as if I were being drawn into something I wanted no part of. I imagined dozens of big brown packages from the Institute for Compilation and Publication of the Works of Imam Khomeini arriving at my fifth-floor New York walk-up and shuddered.

But then, as suddenly as he'd started, Mr. Noroozi stopped. The official part of the interview seemed to be over, and he was now sitting back to quietly tell me how much he wished to see more liberalization come to Iran.

"I fought for the Revolution seven years before it happened," he said. "And I can remember a time when I had to hide forbidden books in my socks and lock my door when I wanted to read them. I don't want to see that kind of time in Iran ever again."

I studied his grave face, wondering what exactly he was trying to tell me.

"Are you disappointed that the Revolution hasn't brought more freedom to Iran?" I said cautiously.

"Yes," he said. "Very."

I felt shocked. Mr. Noroozi was the institute's deputy in chief of international affairs, and I'd expected him to toe the party line—especially because I was taking notes.

"We have freedom of speech in our constitution," Mr. Noroozi said. "We should listen to our constitution."

A sudden rain started in the garden outside, and for a moment, I almost forgot where I was. Heavy sheets of rain were slashing against the tall, multipaned windows and the treetops were swaying violently. We could almost be in the tropics, I thought as Babak got up to close the windows, which immediately flew open again. The latch was apparently loose.

"*Kharab*," Babak said with a grin—broken. "Everything in Iran is always *kharab*."

At my prodding, Mr. Noroozi told me more about himself. After finishing high school, he'd joined the air force as a technician and had been sent to train in England, which was where he'd learned his English. Once back in Iran, he'd been stationed on Kish Island, a resort in the Persian Gulf, where he'd had ample opportunity to observe the Shah's decadent lifestyle. The former monarch and his family had vacationed there often,

throwing many profligate parties—while thousands of their countrymen
went hungry. Outraged, Mr. Noroozi had joined an underground resistance group and started reading books by revolutionaries such as Ali
Shari'ati, a brilliant, Paris-trained academic who used classic Marxist argu-
ments to redefine Islam. Shari'ati's theories had influenced many intellectual Iranians to take up the revolutionary cause.

"Ali's father gave me the books," Mr. Noroozi said, nodding at one of
the boys standing in the hallway outside the door. "He was a very good
man. He died in the war. We lost many good men in the war." He stared
silently at the table for a long moment.

"Tell me more about why you think the Revolution was necessary," I
said finally.

"My dear sister Christiane." Mr. Noroozi smiled. "Please forgive me for
saying this, but in the system we were working, we had American supervi-
sors, we were deprived, we were poor, and they could do whatever they
wanted. Their behavior was very bad—especially here in Tehran. Our people were suffering."

I thought more about what I had read. Not all of Tehran's population
explosion is due to increased birthrates. Starting in the 1940s, but swelling
to a tidal wave beginning in the 1960s, peasants had been relocating to the
capital city in search of work. Arriving in south Tehran with deeply traditional Islamic values, they were the army from which Khomeini drew his
greatest support. The tens of thousands of peasants who flowed into the
capital in the 1970s saw Western decadence all around them. Bars served
liquor, women wore miniskirts, and prostitutes preened themselves on
street corners. The price of oil had quadrupled in 1973, but none of the
profits had filtered down to the poor; instead the Shah had gone on a
gigantic military spending spree, purchasing arms at levels never before
seen in international history. The outrageously rich had become even
richer—and so had the Americans, who had high stakes in Iran's oil industry. When my family and I were in Iran, we were a relative rarity, but after
1970, the number of Americans in Iran more than quintupled, with many
earning much more than their Iranian counterparts. Some of those
Americans had also had little respect for the culture in which they found
themselves, wearing shorts or miniskirts while sightseeing in the mosques
and referring to the Iranians as "ragheads" and "sand niggers."

Mr. Noroozi went on with his personal history. After four years on
Kish Island, he'd been relocated to Mashhad, the holy city in northeastern

Iran. There he joined another underground group, which counted Ali Khamene'i among its members. Now the supreme leader of Iran, Ali Khamene'i was then just an ordinary—though prominent—religious scholar. The group met twice a week, to spread its ideas and collect weapons.

I felt a chill at the mention of the stockpiling of weapons.

"What kind of work did you personally do in Mashhad?" I asked, wondering exactly what role this seemingly gentle man had played in the Revolution. Had I misread him?

"One of my jobs was to collect secret information and give it to Mr. Khamene'i, who would pass it on to the Imam," Mr. Noroozi said. "Since the Imam's eyes were very weak, someone would read my information into a tape recorder and he would listen to it."

"What was the Imam like? Did you ever meet him?"

"One time after the Revolution, we went to meet the Imam. 'Dear Imam,' we said, 'you should change the commander of the air force—he is not good.' But he advised us to be patient, he said he would do it after the war. He was very polite, he smiled, he looked at us as his children. As a great leader, he never spoke with us harshly or severely."

"Please forgive me for saying this," I said, and we nodded at each other in mutual amusement. "But in the United States, many people regard Khomeini as evil because of all the assassinations that took place after the Revolution. If he was such a good man, how do you account for those?"

"When a revolution takes place," Mr. Noroozi said, "most things are out of control. The Imam had some ignorant friends and some enemies. I thought he was not satisfied with many things that were done in the Revolution. I know many things that I cannot say. From this point of view and my information about Khomeini, I do not think he was a violent man."

I would later hear this same argument from dozens of other Iranians, rich and poor, educated and uneducated, city dwellers and peasants. With the exception of many intellectuals and Westernized Iranians, most people I spoke to thought Khomeini was a great and just man, incapable of evil. Whatever atrocities had occurred during and after the Revolution had occurred despite, not because, of him, and whatever problems Iran now faces had little to do with the former Ayatollah and everything to with those who have come after him. After a while, the conviction of the many people I spoke with made me question my own assumptions. What, after all, did I really know about Khomeini?

"What about what's happening today?" I said to Mr. Noroozi. "Do you think the Revolution has taken a wrong turn?"

Mr. Noroozi smiled. "I am a Revolution man, and I like my Revolution. But everything happens badly in this country, and sometimes I am worried. Many in our government are young and have little experience. Still, I think we have more freedom now than we had in the time of the Shah. Maybe from an economic point of view, things haven't improved, but economics is not the only thing that satisfies. Man needs many things—morally, intellectually, spiritually."

I knew I liked Mr. Noroozi.

"What things would you most like to see changed in Iran?" I asked. I was beginning to understand that although Mr. Noroozi was well aware of the Islamic regime's many problems, he still believed in it—an outlook, I later learned, shared by many Iranians.

"In the Shah's time, we suffered from injustice," he said. "This building used to be *one* of the houses of the economy minister. In that time, we had too many poor people. And we still have too many poor people. I want to see justice, we should all live at the same level. I have a color TV, my neighbor has a radio—we should both have a black-and-white TV. And we should have open space for declaring our liberty. I would like to see complete freedom of speech. That's what our Qor'an says, it says listen to what your friends say. Our Imam Ali never killed his enemies. Let our people speak freely. What you have in your country, that's what is in our books— we are not real Muslims.

"Many things in Islam are in your country. I have seen the West—meetings are on time, trains are on time. That's what Islam insists on but rarely sees. Boys and girls together—they were together in the Prophet's time, they gathered in mosques, they freely stated ideas. Today, many behaviors in Iran are not in Islam but are rooted in old customs. Islam does not advise to wear black. Women should wear colors—white, pink—and just cover their hair and body."

"Do you still see Mr. Khamene'i?" I said. "Do you tell him these things?"

"No," Mr. Noroozi said. "I don't see him much anymore. It's not good, two such old friends. But we had some differences of opinion—and I liked cultural works too much. That's why I came here."

A young man knocked on the door; it was time for prayer and lunch. Immediately, Mr. Noroozi stood up, but he invited me to come back anytime—to ask more questions, if I liked—and Babak escorted me out of the office, toward the back of the building.

"Mr. Noroozi is a good Muslim," he said. "I respect him very much."

I respected him, too, and wondered what else he would have talked about if we'd had more time together. Like many people I met in Iran, Mr. Noroozi seemed still and deep, layered with more experiences than I could even imagine.

"Could he get in trouble for anything he said to me?" I asked, even though I recognized that Mr. Noroozi had known exactly what he was saying to me.

Babak thought for a moment. "I myself did not expect him to—how do you say?—put the cards on the table. I myself know how what he said was dangerous. But don't worry, no problem—he is a powerful man."

We entered a small office where a young woman named Tuba was working. She was the only woman currently employed by the institute, and despite earlier talk of my having lunch with Babak and his friends, it now appeared that I would be eating here, alone with Tuba. It wasn't that my eating with the men was forbidden, Babak assured me when I looked disappointed; instead, the thinking had been that I'd be more comfortable eating with another woman. Tuba herself had occasionally had lunch with her male colleagues, but she hadn't cared for it much and preferred dining alone in her office. Perhaps, if I liked, I could come back another time to have lunch with the men.

Tuba didn't speak any English and so I muddled by in Persian as best I could. She came from a town near the Turkish border but had moved to Tehran about eight years before to study political science at the University of Tehran. She'd spent her student years sharing a dorm room with five other girls—which she'd enjoyed very much—and now lived by herself in an apartment. No, she said in answer to my questioning, getting an apartment by herself hadn't been difficult, and no, she had no trouble with uncooperative workmen. Her neighbors looked out for her and she was usually very busy, working all day and studying at night for a master's degree.

Tuba's answers surprised me. Several middle-class women I'd spoken with had told me that it was extremely difficult for a single woman to get an apartment in Iran. Even when it did occasionally happen, they said, workmen refused to make repairs and neighbors shunned the poor woman. I wondered if Tuba had some special connections—her job at the institute, perhaps—or whether the middle-class women had been speaking from personal experience or only hearsay. And again I thought about the way in which each individual's opinions are formed.

I also wondered if perhaps Tuba were lying. Over and over again, while traveling in Iran, people told me that their fellow countrymen would never tell me the truth about much of anything. Iranians are secretive, they said, and as a foreigner, I could never get the real story. The Westernized Iranians told me not to trust the traditionalists—who went to Friday prayers just for show, they said—and the poor told me not to trust the rich—who were badly out of touch, they said. The overall effect of all this was to make me second-guess absolutely everything until at times I felt like a dog chasing its own tail. Just how often does anyone anywhere ever tell the whole truth? I grumpily thought then—even on those few occasions when he or she actually knows what it is? Everyone always has some sort of agenda.

Though we were alone in the room, Tuba kept on her covering—a *manteau* and *maghna'eh*, or fitted hood, that some women wear in place of the *rusari*—while we ate our chicken kebab, and so did I. The two black *chadors* hanging by the door were also Tuba's. One was for use only in the building—she put it on over her *manteau* whenever she went out into the halls—and the other was for use on the street. She didn't like to use her street *chador* inside the institute, she said, because it was too dirty.

I asked Tuba how she felt about always wearing the *hejab*, and she told me an analogy that she said she'd figured out while in economics class. Her professor had described two gardens, one filled with ripe fruit because it was protected from robbers by a high wall and the other filled with poor fruit because its low wall made it vulnerable. A woman wearing the *hejab* was like the garden with the high wall, Tuba said.

I asked Tuba if she enjoyed working at the institute and she replied that although she hadn't wanted to work at first—she'd hoped to return to her hometown—economic necessity had dictated that she work, and now she was very happy here. The Imam had changed her life; words couldn't express how very, very deeply she felt about him and his teachings. She also didn't particularly mind being the only woman at the institute. Her male colleagues treated her very well.

As Tuba spoke, I pictured the Ayatollah's homely living room, which to me had looked so unkempt and lacking in even the bare beauty that often accompanies simple things. It seemed strange to realize that for Tuba, in contrast, everything about it and the institute resonated with meaning.

Where I saw only drabness, she saw an elaborate landscape—oh, to work where the Imam had once lived and to help spread his word.

After we'd finished eating, I went into the adjoining bathroom to wash off the right sleeve of my *manteau*, which had gotten in the way during the meal—a frequent problem for me. As I came out again, Tuba started laughing. I'd forgotten to exchange the plastic bathroom slippers that most Iranian bathrooms are equipped with for the slippers that I was wearing while in the institute's other rooms. The faux paux didn't seem particularly funny to me, but Tuba couldn't seem to stop laughing—until I started to feel irked. I'm trying so hard to understand you, I thought. Why aren't you trying to understand me?

Tuba gave me a photocopied questionnaire to fill out. The questions were in English, and surreptitiously, I copied them down into my notebook while she returned to work: What dimensions of the personality of Imam Khomeini are the people in your country familiar with? Which incident related to Imam Khomeini created more waves? What is the level of your people's intellectual and cultural learning? When translating the works of Imam Khomeini for non-Muslims unfamiliar with Islam, what points should be taken into consideration? Would you be willing to work with the institute in the future?

To this last question, I answered "perhaps." To answer no seemed too hostile. But to my enormous relief, no one followed up on my answer. Instead, I left the institute loaded down with reading matter: *Pithy Aphorisms, Wise Sayings and Counsels, Reunion with the Beloved*, and *The Jardiniere of Love* all by Ayatollah Ruhollah Khomeini; *Father! O Standard Bearer of Islam!* by Khomeini's son Ahmad; *Islamic Revolution of Iran* by Dr. Jalalad-Dine Madani; *Self-Recognition for Self-Improvement* by Mohammad Taqi Misbah Yazdi.

I took a look at *The Jardiniere of Love* in the taxi on the way home. Especially in his youth, but also later in his life, Ayatollah Khomeini had written *ghazals*, or short lyric poems, in the tradition of the great poet Hafez. The *ghazal* is used mainly to express love—of the divine kind only, the strictly religious say. Still, it felt strange to read Khomeini's ruminations:

Oh That heart is no heart at all
Which loves thy fair face not
Oh that wise is no wise at all
Who craves not thy beauty spot

Oh for the heart—raptured lover
Rapture's all that's in thy wine
For me save this rapture alone
What else has this life's confine . . .

Who was Ayatollah Khomeini? I thought as I read. And who, for that matter, were Babak, Mr. Noroozi, and Tuba? I had expected Iran to be complex, complicated, and multileveled, but it was exceeding even my wildest imaginings. No one was quite what he or she seemed; everyone was more.

⁂

Two days later, Babak was on the phone. He wanted to come by. He'd located several more books by Ayatollah Khomeini that he thought I should read, and would I be home that evening at about 8 P.M.? I consulted with Lona. We were in her apartment in west Tehran, waiting for Sepideh to return from her weekly visit to her father's. Ask him to come here instead, Lona said, and I relayed the message. Babak agreed immediately, and only later did I realize that the change had cost him at least an extra hour in commuting time.

As soon as I hung up the phone, however, I realized that something else was wrong. Lona and Pari were whispering anxiously together, and Lona was biting her lower lip.

"Are you sure you don't mind if Babak comes by?" I said. The prospect did seem a little strange, even to me. I was at least 10 years older than Babak, but he was unattached and so were we three.

"Of course not," Lona said.

"I could still call him back," I said. I was using Bahman's cell phone, which he'd graciously lent to me for the day; cell phones are very popular among Iran's professionals.

"No, no." Lona shot Pari a worried glance.

"What's wrong?" I said, although I already suspected the answer.

"Nothing," Lona said, and began gathering up our dirty teacups. Then she stopped. "But if he works at Jamaran, he must be *hezbollahi.*"

Technically speaking a word that means "member of the party of God," *hezbollahi* is loosely used in Iran today to refer to any staunch supporter of the Islamic government.

"He probably is," I said slowly. Between his beard, loose shirt, and flat leather slippers, he certainly wore the correct uniform. "But he's been very friendly to me, and he won't stay long."

"He might be a spy," Pari said.

"I guess," I said. Bahman had already warned me that that was a possibility. They're checking up on you, he'd said when I told him about my second visit to Jamaran, and although I knew that that could be true, I still found it hard to believe. Babak's eagerness was a bit wearing at times, but I liked him, and his interest in befriending me seemed genuine. And even if he were a spy, what difference would it make? I wasn't in Iran on false pretenses; there was nothing for anyone to "uncover."

Again I volunteered to call Babak back, and again Lona and Pari refused. They were more concerned with satisfying my every wish than they were worried about the pending visit. We settled down to watch TV. A panel of mullahs was discussing the upcoming election for the Assembly of Experts, and they were followed by the nightly news, delivered by bearded men wearing collarless shirts without ties. No one wears ties in Iran; they are considered to be a symbol of Western oppression.

The picture on the television kept flickering in and out, and finally, Lona turned it off.

"*Kharab*," she said—broken. "Everything in Iran is always *kharab*."

My attention wandered to the furnishings in the apartment. On the floor was a machine-made carpet from Tabriz, and around its edges stood low, shiny, maroon-purple couches. From one wall hung a needlepoint picture of a sad-eyed Romeo and Juliet that Lona had made herself, and from another hung a flashy, pastel-streaked carpet depicting Venice at sunset. Kitsch goes over very well in Iran, perhaps because many Iranians—and, I have to admit, I myself—are sentimental people. Not the most admirable of traits, perhaps, especially in our cool, crisp modern era, but there are worse.

Finally, the downstairs doorbell rang—Babak had arrived. Frantically, Lona and Pari jumped up and ran into the back room, to appear a moment later formally clad in their *manteaus* and *rusaris*. Pari had also wiped the makeup off her face.

Babak, looking tired and disheveled, entered the room, and there was a loud flurry of overenthusiastic greetings and *ta'arof* on all sides. Then he sat down on the couch next to mine and pulled out a copy of Khomeini's last will and testament—the cassette version, in English. He was sweating profusely.

"I think you will like this very much," he said. "And when you listen to it in New York, you will remember Iran."

I opened the elaborately packaged box, entitled "The politico-divine will of the founder of the Islamic Republic of Iran, Imam Khomeini, peace be upon him." Inside were cassette tapes with attractive photographs of the Ayatollah on their covers. Cassettes have a special resonance in Iran. During the years of Khomeini's exile, recordings of his messages were smuggled into the country via cassette, to be circulated from mosque to mosque, city dweller to peasant.

At my encouragement, to help fill the silence in the room, Babak started talking about the publications that he wrote for. Most were women's magazines, he said, because although he hoped to write for political newspapers such as Khatami's *Tus* one day, he hadn't had any luck yet. (*Tus*? I thought, surprised—isn't that awfully liberal for someone who works at Jamaran?) Nervously, he showed me one of his articles, published in the current issue of *Khanevadeh,* or *Family.* It was entitled something to the effect of "Ten Tips for Taking Care of Tots," and his fiancée, Rosita, had helped him write it.

"Oh," I said, glad to hear that he was engaged.

The moments crept by at an excruciating pace. Lona kept giving me *looks,* which I couldn't read, while silent Pari was sitting stiff as a statue against the wall. Poor Babak couldn't seem to stop sweating, and yet he refused to touch the tall glass of soda that Lona had served him. Only later, when Babak and I got to know each other better, did he tell me that he'd been afraid it contained alcohol; Lona and Pari's close connection to a Westernized doctor apparently made them suspect.

Glancing from one of my new friends to the other, I suddenly realized that although I was the reason for their coming together, I was the odd person out here. They were all deeply enmeshed in an emotional drama that I could bear witness to but not truly understand. All three were young and from working-class backgrounds, but that's where their similarities—or at least their perceived similarities—ended. Lona and Pari weren't particularly religious, Babak apparently was, and so the women were as terrified of him as he was of them. The silent dialogue going on among them was drowning out all attempts to be heard.

৵৽৻

One visit usually leads to another in Iran, and Babak called me the next day to ask when I was coming to his house for dinner. He'd already told his mother all about me and she was very eager to meet me. So was the rest of his family—most of them had never met an American before. He, Babak, could borrow a car from a friend and come pick me up whenever I liked.

I agreed, and a few evenings later, Babak, his friend Ahmad, and I were sitting in an ugly traffic snarl on our way to New Tehran on the eastern edge of the city. Because I was a foreigner and it was rush hour, the chances of our being stopped by the "morals police" were minimal.

As we crept along in Ahmad's battered vehicle, he slipped a cassette into a tape player. The sultry voice of Tracy Chapman singing "Revolution" rang out.

"Where'd you get this?" I said, laughing.

"It's not hard," Ahmad said. "American music is everywhere in Iran, and I love Tracy Chapman. Do you love Tracy Chapman? What is your favorite song? I like this one."

If the founding Islamic fathers only knew, I thought.

"Who else do you like?" I asked, and Ahmad told me that among his other favorite American artists were Eric Clapton, Kenny Rogers, and the Bee Gees. He also liked some of Michael Jackson, but only one song from Metallica, and he didn't like rap at all—unlike most young people in Tehran, he said, who liked all of Michael Jackson, most of Metallica, and a lot of rap. Ahmad was also a fan of the old love songs of Elvis Presley and Olivia Newton-John.

From music, we moved on to literature. Babak and Ahmad had both read all of Shakespeare and many of the English classics. "To be or no to be," "A man can be killed but never defeated," Babak quoted—he liked to quote a lot. He was now reading Somerset Maugham because a friend, who was writing his master's thesis on loneliness in Maugham, had gotten him interested. And what he, Babak, wanted to do more than anything else was to move to a small village and write poetry. But that was not possible. He was engaged and had to worry about making a living. Making a living was very difficult in Iran. Despite holding a full-time job and freelancing as a translator and writer, he still was not earning enough money to marry.

I thought about the conversation I'd had with Bahman just before leaving the house. Be very, very careful what you say tonight, he'd said, don't take any chances, and don't come home after midnight—we'll be very worried. But if Babak and Ahmad were spies, they were hiding it very well.

Conversation turned to recent political events. Ataollah Mohajerani, the liberal minister of culture so highly thought of by many I'd met in north

Tehran, had been brutally attacked by a gang of hard-liners several days before and was still in the hospital recovering.

"Do they know who did it?" I said.

Ahmad snorted.

"Will they do anything to them?" I said, feeling extremely naïve.

"Only if the people make them," Ahmad said.

Babak sighed. "Mohajerani is a very good man. He wants to bring more cultural freedom to Iran."

"And you think that's a good idea?"

"Of course." The two men nodded emphatically.

"How much freedom would you like to see?" I asked. "Do you think everything should be allowed in?"

"What do you mean, everything?" Babak asked cautiously.

"All art, all music, all literature, all political books—movies, TV shows, the Internet, pornography—"

"I don't know about pornography," Ahmad said.

"But definitely all books should be allowed," Babak said. "People should read the negative things the West says about Iran and Islam, because then we can debate them and show they are wrong."

"But we don't want a democracy," Ahmad said. "We want the Islamic government."

"We can't have a democracy," Babak said. "Because we have a different tradition."

"We don't need the West anymore," Ahmad said. "We have our own government now. The Revolution gave Iran back its self-respect."

That self-respect, I would conclude months later, after talking to many more Iranians, may well be the single most important legacy of the Revolution.

"What about the *hejab*?" I asked.

The two friends fell silent.

"You think it's good?" I said. "You think it should continue?"

"Not the *chador*," Babak said, waffling. "The *manteau* and *rusari* are enough."

"But the *manteau* and *rusari* are good," I pressed.

Still the young men didn't answer, and a light went off in my head. They don't want to tell me something they think I don't want to hear, I realized.

"Maybe in one hundred years, it can change," Babak said. "But not now."

Finally, after an hour and a half of battling traffic, we arrived in New Tehran, a neighborhood filled with nondescript three- and four-story apartment buildings, one of which had been commandeered by Babak and his family. He and his father, mother, grandmother, and unmarried siblings lived on one floor; a married brother and his family lived on another. A second married brother and his family lived nearby, and they were all coming over to their parents' apartment for dinner. But it wasn't on my account. The entire extended family, which numbered about 20, ate dinner together most nights.

At the front door, we said good-bye to Ahmad and exchanged our shoes for slippers. Neatly waiting by the steps, they were lined up in two rows, from big to small, with the smaller children's ones made of pretty colored plastics and the larger adult ones of plain brown plastic with crisscrossed straps.

Once inside, we climbed to Babak's brother's apartment, where we socialized for several hours, while snacking on fruit, tea, and sweet cream-filled cakes. Iranians often eat very late, at 9, 10, or even 11 P.M., and do most of their socializing before the meal. Sweets are more often served before the meal than after, though sometimes they are served on both ends.

Children with smoke-blue eyes—a legacy from the Aryan tribes of central Asia from which they are descended—ran in and out of the room while the grown-ups talked. Babak's father, a compact man with a scarred face, spoke to me the most, with Babak translating. His father wanted to know how long I planned to stay in Iran, what I thought of his country, how I compared it with the United States, and just what exactly was going on between President Bill Clinton and Monica Lewinsky. (Monicagate was then in full fling; Clinton had finally admitted to having had a sexual relationship with Lewinsky about 10 days before I'd left for Iran.) I asked him what he thought about President Khatami and his plans for liberalizing Iran. Yes, liberalization would be good, he said, because it would bring more economic opportunity for his sons. But Iran also had to be careful; it didn't want the West to gain control of its internal affairs again.

In contrast to his father, Babak's older brother was a tall, thin, sad-eyed man with a full bushy beard who hardly spoke. A superb cartoonist and animator, he sat quietly playing with his son while Babak showed me his work. His videos had a magical, childlike quality filled with rounded shapes and dreamlike sequences, whereas his magazine illustrations had a sharp, satirical edge. One striking cartoon showed a young Iranian man sit-

ting on a pile of books, a fistful of master's diplomas in one hand, a beggar's bowl in another. While I studied it, Babak told me that his brother
had won first place in an international Disney competition several years
before, but that the Islamic government had not allowed him to leave the
country to accept his award.

Each time a new person entered the room, we all stood up. This is common practice in Iranian homes, and the early parts of large social gatherings can often be quite athletic affairs, with much popping up and down.
Until about 25 years ago, each new arrival usually also greeted everyone in
the room individually, starting with the oldest person present, and then
going politely around with "How are you? How've you been? So good to
see you again."

Similarly, most Iranians are too polite to be the first person through a
door. Every time you reach a doorway with anyone else—friends or
strangers; men, women, or both—everyone stops. *Befarma'id, befarma'id,
befarma'id*—After you, after you, after you—everyone says over and over
again, and long moments go by until finally someone has the wherewithal
to go first.

As a foreigner, I tried to play this game, too, but it didn't work. Because
I was always the honored guest, I always had to go first, unless Bahman was
present, in which case, it was a toss-up—although he, too, usually insisted
I go in front.

Babak's sisters-in-law, his fiancée, Rosita, and his mother floated in and
out of the room, all dressed in knee-length skirts or simple pants and
pretty blouses. The younger women wore the *rusari*, but Babak's mother
did not. In more traditional Muslim households, women do not bare their
heads in front of unrelated men, even if they are connected to them by
marriage. Babak's mother could go uncovered because all of the men in the
room were either her husband or sons. I could go uncovered as well
because I was Christian and an honored guest, but I did wish I hadn't worn
a sleeveless blouse. Sleeveless blouses had been fine in all the north Tehrani
homes I'd visited—everyone else wore them, too; it was hot—but here,
things were more traditional. I should have realized. Surrounded by both
men and women wearing long sleeves, my bare arms made me feel near
naked. I'd never realized I had so much flesh, stretching all the way from
my shoulders to my fingertips.

The Qor'an encourages men as well as women to dress modestly.
Muslim men are instructed to cover their arms and their midsections with

loose-fitting clothing that will conceal the bulge of male genitals. Many Iranian men completely ignore this Qor'anic admonition, however, and unlike "badly covered" women on the streets, go completely unchastised.

One of Babak's sisters-in-law kept giving me challenging glances, and finally, she asked me to tell her about America. While I hesitated, wondering where to begin, she asked me if I felt safe living there. "Well, yes," I said, startled by her question, and she gave me an aggressive, disbelieving stare.

"But we see your movies," she said. "We know your country is very violent."

"Yes, it's true that some of our movies are very violent," I said. "but that's not reality."

She shook her head, barely listening as I tried to explain more, and a moment later, she left the room.

"She doesn't understand," Babak said apologetically, "because here in Iran we like quiet movies."

I thought about the many martial arts films that I'd seen advertised in downtown Tehran but said nothing.

Rosita was more sympathetic. A shy, pretty woman with an angelic face that lit up when she smiled, she told me how she and Babak had met. It had happened 14 years before, when they were just children and she'd sat behind him on a bus. She'd noticed him notice her and had waved at him as the bus pulled away. Sometime later she gave him a piece of candy and sometime after that, a flower. They'd lived in the same neighborhood, but it'd taken them well over a year to speak to each other. Whether that was due to shyness or the Islamic government, I couldn't tell. When I asked, they just giggled.

We moved downstairs to Babak's parents' apartment, where dinner was being served. The upstairs living room had been furnished with simple couches, but downstairs, in the older generation's apartment, there was no Western furniture at all. Persian carpets covered the floors, and elongated carpet-covered bolsters were propped up against the walls. On the floor and filling most of the room was a plastic white tablecloth, or *sofreh*, laden with rice dishes, stews, kebabs, salad, yogurt, and bread. Lying flat by each place setting, like a party favor, was an orange soda bottle.

Eating on the floor is a traditional Persian custom, and one that is still widely practiced. About half of the families I visited, especially outside Tehran, ate on the floor, and I immediately fell in love with the casual, playful quality of a typical Persian meal. Eating on the floor made me feel like a kid—especially when we got our soda bottles—sharing in an intimate tea party with my best friends. The grown-ups weren't invited; it was a private affair, open only to those able to cast off their adult stiffness and need for chairs.

Despite the Iranians' reputation for sternness, it often seemed to me that they are a deeply playful people. Not only is there eating on the floor, there is also sleeping on the floor (and in earlier days, on rooftops), a love of bright colors (turquoise, pink) and curious fruits (watermelons, pomegranates), an insatiable national appetite for stories and jokes, an adoration of children, the use of the wondrous Arabic script (with its upside-down heart ♡ for the numeral 5), and picnics. The word *picnic*, which is the same in Farsi and English, comes from a custom that originated in ancient Persia, and even today, Iranians love nothing better than packing up the family, a hamper, and a carpet to dine outdoors. Some of the country's most popular restaurants resemble outdoor picnicking parks, with people eating on carpeted platforms surrounded by globes of light beneath the stars. Some of the world's favorite games—chess, polo, and backgammon—also originated in ancient Persia, which is part of the reason they were outlawed during the early years of the Islamic Republic.

"There is no fun in Islam," Ayatollah Khomeini once gloomily declared, but there certainly is fun in Persia.

We settled down to eat, and halfway through the meal, I noticed both of Babak's parents staring at me—his mother because she thought that I wasn't eating enough and his father because he was suddenly suspicious of me. Or so I thought. Out of nowhere, he started asking me a long string of questions about exactly what I was doing in Iran and how I'd managed to obtain a visa. With Babak serving as translator, I answered him as best I could while feeling my cheeks flush bright red. The rest of the room had fallen silent. Several long moments passed. I tried to think of something neutral to say. Then, suddenly, my elementary grasp of Persian, which had eluded me throughout most of the evening, was back—a gift from the gods. "Which of your children was the most mischievous?" I asked Babak's mother.

It was the right approach. The tension, which had appeared so precipitously—or had I imagined it?—disappeared again, and Babak's brothers started telling untranslatable jokes. By the end of the meal, everyone was laughing and joking, and I—without quite knowing how it had happened—had become a family friend. While I gathered up my belongings to go, people scattered into the back rooms to wrap up presents for me. Babak's parents gave me an engraved copper tray and Babak and Rosita gave me two tapes of their favorite music, a bag of candy, and a Persian grammar book in which they wrote, "Please do not forget us. We love you, dear friend."

"Khoda hafez, khoda hafez"—Good-bye, good-bye—a dozen people, all shorter than I, chorused as they gathered in the doorway to see me off. And a half-dozen more trooped down to the car to wave farewell.

But here there was a short delay. The car, which Ahmad had left for us, had a flat.

"Kharab," Babak's mother said, laughing and hugging my arm. "Everything in Iran is always *kharab.*"

Babak replaced the tire, and off we drove, Rosita and I in the backseat, he alone in the front. To have one of us up front with him at this time of night would have alerted the "morals police."

We crept down the wide boulevards of Tehran, now almost bereft of traffic. As it turned out, our slow speed on the way over hadn't been due just to congestion—the car wasn't capable of going much more than 40 miles per hour.

Tehran by night seemed even more mysterious than Tehran by day. The streets weren't as well lit as streets in the United States and the few corner shops that were still open seemed like caves, illuminated by a single suspended lightbulb. Men hunkered down in them, some squatting on their haunches, and gossiped while conducting the last business deals of the day. Beyond them, buildings hidden behind high walls flashed by, followed by darkened billboards of Khomeini, Khamene'i, Khatami.

We passed by the entrance to a park, lit by the same candy-colored neon that I'd noticed at the airport. Despite the late hour, the park was filled with families, children up far past what to my Western mind was a suitable bedtime. I thought of Luna Park, an amusement park not too far from Bahman's. It, too, was always crowded with people at play, screaming and laughing with the swoop and swirl of the rides. In Iran, where there is not much to do at night, amusement parks are a major attraction. I would later find them in every city I visited, including the holy city of Qom, which has a reputation for fierceness.

Down yet more deserted streets, around a traffic circle, up a short hill, and then three big flashy kiosks lit by bright green and pink bulbs—the colors of the bubble gum coins of my early childhood. Set out in the middle of the sidewalk, the kiosks looked like enormous toys, slyly deposited by an Islamic Santa Claus.

"Hey, wait!" I said to Babak. I knew this street; these kiosks hadn't been here before. "What are those?"

"*Hejleh*," he said, slowing down. "How do you say?—bridal chambers."

I took a closer look. Each of the "bridal chambers" was as tall as I was, twice as wide, and lit by three tiers of light. The panels between the lights seemed to be made of a heavy white cardboard; around the top tier hung glossy black-and-white head shots of a young man, pictured in the same pose over and over again.

"They're for young men who have died," Babak said. "Rich families put them out on the anniversary of their son's death. Each district in the city has a corner for them."

"They're just for men," I said, "not for women?"

"Just for *young* men," Babak corrected me.

"Why are they called 'bridal chambers'?" I asked. The *hejleh*s seemed so magical and filled with light; how could they be about death?

"Because people believe that after death you go to heaven, where there is happiness, and there is happiness also in the bridal chamber."

Although it was after midnight by the time I got home, Bahman and his wife Chris, who'd returned from England by then, were waiting up for me. I could see them sitting on their fifth-floor balcony as we drove up, and as they waved, I felt a rush of affection. We'd known each other for only a short time, but already they felt like family. How quickly the unfamiliar becomes the familiar.

ॐ৯৵

After four visits together, Babak and I had crossed an invisible but universal line. We had a relationship now; we were friends, and even Bahman, Lona, and Pari agreed that Babak was probably not a spy.

Babak had volunteered to help me in any way he could, and one day I told him that I did have one specific request. I wanted to visit a *zurkhaneh*, or "house of strength," where the traditional wrestling of Iran takes place. Women are not usually allowed to attend a *zurkhaneh* session, but I'd heard that because I was a foreigner and a writer, special arrangements could probably be made. Did Babak have any suggestions?

He did. By happy coincidence, his uncle was an avid wrestler. Babak would speak to him and—*ensha'allah*—he and his teammates would issue an invitation.

Ensha'allah, meaning "if Allah wills it," is constantly invoked in Iran when talking about hopes, desires, and future events. In fact, to express a hope or desire without saying *"ensha'allah"* is considered bad luck. I knew the term, but not from Iran—from my later childhood years in Connecticut. My family had imported *ensha'allah* to the United States and we'd used it often—and with the same kind of half-mocking, half-believing laugh that I now heard Iranians using.

In the case of the *zurkhaneh*, I was in luck. Allah did apparently will my visit, for sometime later, I found myself sitting next to Babak in a large, modern room that smelled of sweat. Male sweat. From the walls hung photographs of sports teams, and on the shelves, trophies gleamed. In the middle of the room, beneath a skylight, was a large octagonal pit about three feet deep, lined with heavy wooden clubs shaped like giant soda bottles with lips. Above a door stretched a banner that read, IT IS HE WHO EXTENDS A HELPING HAND TO ANOTHER WHO IS THE TRUE MAN.

Babak and I seemed to be early. All the chairs around us were empty, and the only other people in the room were Babak's uncle and his two friends.

I fidgeted. Because as much as I'd wanted to come, I now felt impatient, irritable, and uncomfortable. Although it was already close to 7:30 P.M. and we'd been waiting well over an hour, nothing was happening. Where was the rest of the audience, I wondered—and the team? And how would I feel when they finally arrived? The sight of the two naked torsos I'd already glimpsed had made me feel distinctly itchy, and suddenly I wasn't at all sure I liked the idea of being the only woman in a roomful of men—most of them half undressed. Apparently, the effects of living in a Muslim society were rubbing off on me.

"You're not drinking your tea," Babak's uncle said. "Would you like coffee instead?"

"No, no," I said. "I'm sorry, I forgot about it." I'd already had at least a half-dozen cups of tea that day.

"Let me get you a fresh cup," he said, and disappeared into the back room.

"He is very polite," Babak said. "There is no coffee. He only offered it because you are a foreigner."

Thank Allah I didn't make that gaffe, I thought to myself. Though I never would have. I'd already discovered that the coffee in Iran is usually either too weak or bitter.

We waited another half hour and then finally, at my renewed prodding,

Babak said something to his uncle, and the team members began to trickle in. Evidently, they'd been socializing in the courtyard and the teahouse next door. Evidently, too, Babak and I were to be the only audience—this session had been arranged especially for me. A lump rose in my throat at that realization and I felt ashamed of my earlier impatience, especially when I saw that the team numbered about 20—and included both a musician and a narrator. The narrator would explain things to Babak, who would explain things to me.

The *zurkhaneh* dates back to pre-Islamic times and each wrestling session is more a series of grueling mental and physical exercises than it is competitive sport in the Western sense. The exercises were initially developed to increase the Persian warriors' ability to fight off invaders and therefore, after the Arab conquest of Iran, the *zurkhaneh* was forced to go underground. With time, however, the sport ceased to be a symbol of Persian resistance and came to represent a bastion of Shi'ite religious values. The athletes were expected to meet certain moral as well as physical requirements—they were expected to be pious, generous, and humble as well as courageous and strong. The sport was especially popular during the Safavid dynasty (1501–1722), when Shi'ism first became the state religion, but it is still widely practiced today. Tehran has about 20 famous *zurkhaneh*s and many smaller ones.

The men filed in, some wearing the traditional knee-length pants made of a carpetlike material with a teardrop design, others; long shorts. To my relief, all had on T-shirts, except for the musician-teacher, or *morshed*, a big, hairy-chested man who sat on a raised platform surrounded by tiny lights beneath a picture of Imam Ali. Ali is central to Shi'ism, and his portrait, usually depicting a soulful-eyed man wearing a flowing green headdress, can be found all over Iran.

The *morshed* began beating his *tonbak*, a large, flat drum, and reciting words that Babak called "poems of humbling," while the men started a slow jog around the pit. They ranged in age from 15 to 80 and came from all walks of life. Among them were a doctor, businessman, and laborer, and they were led by the 80-year-old, a white-haired man with an enormous paunch. Except for the two teenagers, who kept flashing me grins, no one seemed to even glance in our direction, but I was certain that they were watching me. In Iran, I had already noticed, people are aware of everything, even when they don't appear to be.

I still felt a little strange to be the only woman, and a *hejab*-covered woman at that, among so many half-dressed men, but then I took out my notebook and camera, and my professional self took over. I wasn't a woman; I was a journalist. The same thing seemed to be happening to the men. I sensed their awareness of me fade as they turned to the task at hand, transforming themselves from men into warriors. There are many good reasons for role-playing in this life, I thought—including the distancing of self from emotion.

After jogging for about ten minutes, the men laid small wooden planks on the floor, covered them with pieces of cloth, and began doing endless push-ups on them. Some of the old and the young couldn't keep up, but eventually they all stood and began whirling their arms around with chore-ographed precision. Then one especially fit man asked the 80-year-old, "Do I have your permission?" The old man nodded, and the younger man picked up one of the enormous wooden clubs, which weighed perhaps 40 pounds, and began twisting it up and around his head, over and over again. The other men joined in, each choosing the size club that suited his abili-ties, while the *morshed* beat rhythmically on the drum. When all were exhausted, they laid down their clubs and gathered in a circle, with one man in the middle. Stretching out his arms to his sides, he clenched his fists and began whirling furiously while trying to stay in place. When he was done, another took his turn, and then another and another. Some were very good at staying in the center, whereas others flailed wildly about. In the old days, the narrator said, the warriors would whirl like this whenever they lost their swords, to keep their enemies at bay.

Because the session was staged just for me, it was a truncated edition, lasting only about an hour. When it was over, the *morshed* gave a long, for-mal speech welcoming me to Iran, followed by a series of prayers. In one, he asked Allah to protect the health of the people. In another, he prayed for the reappearance of the Twelfth Imam and Jesus Christ. Though the latter was undoubtedly for my benefit, Islam does regard Christ, like Moses and other major biblical figures, as a prophet. Christ is seen as the last great prophet before Mohammad, and as a model of love and humility, though not of divine status. The Qor'an also acknowledges the Virgin Birth, in words very similar to those found in the Bible:

(And remember) when the angels said: O Mary! Lo! Allah giveth thee glad tidings of a word from Him, whose name is the Messiah, Jesus, son of Mary, illustrious in the world and the Hereafter. . . .

>She said: My Lord! How can I have a child when no mortal hath touched me? He said: So (it will be). Allah createth what He will. If He decreeth a thing, He saith unto it only: Be! and it is. (3:45–47).

The men filed out, acknowledging my thanks with gracious nods, and were gone. Suddenly, the *zurkhaneh* was empty again.

Babak and I went off for ice cream, with two of his cousins, young men in their early twenties, who'd been waiting for us in the parking lot. Driving their father's new car, dressed in good-quality clothes, they appeared to have considerably more money than did Babak. Class in Iran is quite fluid, with rich and poor, educated and uneducated often belonging to the same extended family. But many Iranians are also highly class-conscious—and some, prejudiced. One young, vivacious, professional woman even told me that the poor shouldn't be allowed to attend universities—they don't know what to do with an education once they get it, she said.

At the ice cream parlor, two more friends joined us and we took a table in the back. The café was clean, modern, and lined with mirrors, in which we could see our reflections and those of a group of young women at a nearby table. The young men and women kept exchanging glances through those mirrors, sly elliptical looks that slid and collided, sparked and streaked off again—just as they do between the sexes everywhere.

I tried to pay for our desserts, but Babak and his friends wouldn't hear of it. You are a guest in our country, they chorused, and then one young man took Babak and me next door to his china shop. What would you like? he asked me as I admired the delicate dishes—take anything, please, it is my pleasure. I refused three times and then accepted a maroon-and-gold teapot that now sits in my kitchen cupboard in New York. In return, I have since sent Babak, my consummate host, copies of the last three winners of the Pulitzer Prize for literature. It was his one major request of me; he hopes to translate them into Persian at night, after his day job at Jamaran is done.

TWO

*S*ometime later, Bahman, his wife Chris, and I set out to visit the home of Dr. Mohammad Mossadeq, whose name has almost as much resonance in Iran as does Khomeini's. A beloved prime minister, Mossadeq had led—

and lost—a bitter struggle to nationalize Iran's oil industry in the early 1950s. If he had succeeded, Iran would have been a far different country from what it is today.

Acts of imperialism notwithstanding, the deep core of Iran's hostility toward the United States dates back not to the era of Khomeini but to that of Mossadeq, who was ousted from office with the help of the CIA. At that time, the Cold War had just begun, and the United States suspected the new prime minister of being a Communist, with strong ties to the Soviet Union. In fact, Mossadeq was a nationalist, not a Communist, who sought to keep Iran's oil profits in Iran.

Born in 1882, Mossadeq had been educated in France and Switzerland, where he received a Ph.D. in law. He served as a member of Iran's Parliament, and in 1949, helped found the National Front. A loose coalition of political groups strongly opposed to all foreign intervention in Iran, the National Front posed a major challenge to the Shah, who excelled at courting foreign influence. But in the early 1950s, public opinion was running against the Shah. Parliament passed a bill to nationalize the oil industry and the 69-year-old Mossadeq was elected prime minister. Power shifted away from the Shah to the prime minister and the British-owned Anglo-Iranian Oil Company was ousted from Iran.

Britain was outraged. The Anglo-Iranian Oil Company saw to it that Iran was unable to sell its oil on the international market, and the British government seriously considered taking military action. The United States supported the Iranian position at first, but as the crisis dragged on, American advisors began to shift their position and talk with British intelligence about covert political intervention. Things finally came to a head in 1953 when the Shah, facing a constitutional threat from his prime minister, fled the county, and Kermit Roosevelt, grandson of Theodore and chief of the CIA's Near East and Africa division, engineered Mossadeq's downfall. In his book, *Countercoup: The Struggle for Control of Iran*, Roosevelt describes how he used bribery and other questionable techniques to turn public opinion against Mossadeq. He paid high-ranking police and army officers to attack mosques, supposedly in the name of Mossadeq, and offered poor people on the streets 10-*rial* notes to take part in demonstrations supporting the Shah. Many accepted, half out of ignorance and half out of disillusionment with Mossadeq's ineffectual rule; he had not thus far proven himself to be a particularly able leader. By the time Roosevelt was finished, more than 300 people had been killed, the Shah had returned to Iran, and Mossadeq was under house arrest in his family home in Ahmadabad, about 60 miles west of Tehran. There he remained, except for three years spent in prison, until his death in 1967.

During Mossadeq's lifetime, the West had made endless fun of the prime minister, an eccentric man often in poor health. They'd belittled his proclivity for pink pajamas, for holding cabinet meetings while propped up in bed, for crying at the least provocation, and for fainting after delivering an emotional speech. But the Iranians had loved those very same things about him—none of which had hindered his political abilities, after all—along with his shrewd mind, far-ranging intellect, and wry wit. Today, he is remembered by many as the man who could have led Iran to greatness.

Turning off the highway leading toward Ahmadabad, Bahman, Chris, and I rode down a narrow country lane flanked by fields to a small village. Bahman parked the car, and we walked up to a heavy iron gate that to my eyes was unmarked. We rang the doorbell and the gate swung open. Before us stretched a long dirt driveway lined with the tall, black-limbed trees. On either side were empty gardens, bristling with stalks of dead grass and squabbling magpies, and at the end stood a solid two-story brick house with a turquoise door. Built during the Qajar period, the house reminded me of the abandoned abode of an English country squire—and of Jamaran. The Ayatollah's house was built of much poorer materials, of course, and attracted far more visitors, but both homes had the same neglected air and unkempt surroundings—so different from the well-oiled tourist mechanisms of such hallowed American homes as Monticello or Mount Vernon.

A caretaker came out to meet us. He and his family lived in the compound, attending to the house and the needs of the 30 or so visitors who stopped by every month. Up until 1991, the house had been closed to all visitors, including the Mossadeq family. Now, though, there were low-key plans to turn it into a museum.

The Islamic government has always had an uneasy relationship with Mossadeq. No streets or public squares are named after him, he takes up only a few pages in the history books, and his role as leader of the oil nationalization campaign is downplayed as much as possible. In many ways, Mossadeq laid the groundwork for the 1978–1979 Revolution, but he is ignored by today's rulers—largely because he was a secularist. His administration contained no clerics, and he wanted to do away with Islamic law.

With the caretaker as our guide, we entered Mossadeq's cold, dark house and passed through a series of rooms lined with pictures of the former prime minister. His long, intelligent, melancholy face peered down at us from cabinet meetings, family gatherings, political podiums, and sickbeds. In the center of the last room was his simple symbolic tomb, draped with a purple cloth of traditional Iranian paisley design. On top of it stood two crystal lamps and two open Qor'ans.

Bahman and the other Iranian visitors in the room were almost in tears, and I myself could picture Mossadeq shuffling through these rooms in his final years. Exiled from everything he'd loved, he'd lived here all alone with his servants for 14 years, allowed only occasional visits from his wife and children. In this silent, echoing house, he'd metamorphosed from a still-vital 71-year-old into a frail old man.

Mossadeq and Khomeini—two beloved Iranian leaders who'd lived far longer than the usual span of human years. So different in many ways, but so alike in others. One hailed as a savior by the Islamic government, the other more or less ignored, but both still very much alive in the Iranian imagination and both utter enigmas to the West.

Hanging from the wall behind the tomb were two poster-size photographs. One depicted a gaunt, dejected Mossadeq huddled by a drain-pipe outside the house. It had been taken in the late afternoon, shortly before his death at age 85, and his bony hand, gnarled as a chicken's foot, clutched his cane as if it were a lifeline. The other photograph was one that only those visitors well versed in American history—at the moment, just myself, I suspected—could appreciate. It depicted a much younger and happier Mossadeq, smiling as he posed beside the Liberty Bell in Philadelphia, Pennsylvania, the City of Brotherly Love.

ONE WHO YEARNS FOR
DEATH NEVER DIES

Death is a mirror which reflects the vain gesticulations of the living. . . . Tell me how you die and I will tell you who you are.
—Octavio Paz, *The Labyrinth of Solitude*

Lona and I hurried down Enqelab (Revolution) Avenue, on our way to Friday prayers at the University of Tehran—a weekly event that attracts those most committed to the Islamic regime. The street was blocked off, as it usually was on Friday mornings, and dozens of vendors sat crouched along the sidewalks, selling pictures of Khomeini, Khamene'i, Khatami, and Imam Ali; books by Khomeini and other religious leaders; booklets of verses from the Qor'an; and prayer stones and prayer rugs. The vendors reminded me of my walk down a neighboring street just a few days before, when I'd spotted a man selling quite different wares: tattered old paperbacks in English. Among them had been *Gambling Tips from Nick the Greek* and *Food Guide to Tehran*, both published in the 1970s.

Men with beards and loose shirts worn outside their pants were filing by us, many with blue, green, or amber-colored prayer beads clicking in hand. They entered the main gate of the university, with its colorful banner stretched overhead, whereas we turned onto a bleak side street and entered the dark crowded tent that fronted the women's entrance. Inside, a small sea of shrouded figures pushed and pulled against us as we fought to hand our bags over to be searched and present our bodies to be patted down. Arms, children, and flapping *chadors* seemed to be everywhere and it was hard to breathe—the air was close and hot—but finally we collected our bags again and burst back outside, into the sunlight. A woman gave us pieces of halvah, the Middle Eastern sweet made of sesame seeds and flour, without even giving me a second glance, and as I nibbled at it, I flashed back to New York, where halvah is sold in every corner deli. Before, I'd always associated the sweet with Jewish culture, but now Lona told me that halvah is traditionally eaten on days of mourning in Iran. It was being handed out today because following the prayers, there was to be a ceremony honoring 700 martyred soldiers from the Iran–Iraq War. The war had ended in 1988, but their remains had been found just a few days before this day's prayers.

The Iran–Iraq War haunts Iran. The tolls it exacted were tremendous. Estimates on the number of Iranians killed vary from 220,000 to 750,000, and nearly every family lost a son, father, uncle, or brother. The war also precipitated the economic woes that plague the country today and caused even fervent believers to question why Ayatollah Khomeini allowed the tragedy to drag on for eight long years.

Lona had never been to Friday prayers at the University of Tehran before, and although at first she'd wrinkled her nose at the idea of my going, in the end, she'd decided to come along. She was just as curious as I was. Nervously, we both looked around at the hundreds of women filing by us, wondering where we should go, and then showed my letter of permission from Ershad to a monitor standing nearby. Glancing at it without expression, she led us to a roped-off section, where we were searched again, this time by a scowling, pudgy woman half our height who had to stand on a chair to get the job done. Her fingers felt rough as sandpaper as they scraped momentarily against my skin, and she meticulously looked at every item in my bag, including the *tomans* in my wallet, until I felt violated. She had probably been a poor peasant before the Revolution, I thought, watching her blunt, unpleasant face, but now she has power and has to prove it.

Then, to my relief, another woman hurried up, an enormous smile on her face.

"Thank you for coming," she said in excellent English while shaking my hand and shooing away the pudgy woman. "We love having foreign journalists here. Would you like a rug to sit on? Or a glass of water? It is very hot. Where is your camera?"

I winced. Several of Bahman's friends had vehemently warned me not to take my camera along. You don't know what these people are like, they'd said, they're crazy, they're fanatics, they might attack you or destroy your camera. I hadn't altogether believed them, but I hadn't wanted to risk losing my camera, either.

The woman led us to a long paved drive flanked on one side by a high canvas wall hung with banners and on the other by tall trees, a strip of grass, and small brook. Filling the drive and the steps of several faculty buildings nearby were vaguely diagonal rows of women in black and white *chadors*, sitting or kneeling on ground cloths and prayer rugs facing Mecca. Some were eating, some were sleeping, and some were reading the Qor'an, but most were talking quietly with one another. Children ran about while the gentle voices of their mothers mingled with the babblings of the brook.

I looked around in surprise. I had expected something that felt more like an outdoor amphitheater, or at least a gathering of people that had some sort of center. This was just a long line of women parked one row behind another. Then the English-speaking woman beckoned to me, and I climbed up onto a stump to look over the canvas wall. There was the amphitheater, on the men's side. It had an open-sided corrugated roof, a bona fide seating area, and a podium from which the clerics would soon be speaking. This isn't fair, I thought, looking from the comfortable-looking men's side to the uncomfortable-looking women's—no matter how much the Islamic government talks about equal rights for women, situations like this are sending out a different message.

There was one man on "our" side, however, sitting on a platform high above our heads. He was operating a television camera trained on the podium; Friday prayers at the University of Tehran are broadcast live.

Started up immediately after the Revolution, the university prayer meetings, which always begin with a long political speech, are emblematic of the new republic. Throughout the 1980s, the meetings attracted hundreds of thousands of believers who spilled out of the campus and into the side streets in even the worst of weather. Long denied access to the workings of government, the people came to hear their new leaders discuss everything from politics and economics to sexual morality and ethical questions.

They also came to pray and to show their solidarity to the outside world. Today, as disillusionment with the Islamic regime has set in, the crowds at the University of Tehran have dwindled considerably but still number in the low tens of thousands.

Lona and I sat down on a ground cloth provided by our friendly greeter while the women across from us stared at me and giggled. In halting Persian, I asked Lona about what I saw around us and she explained. The many banners on the canvas wall honored Fatemeh, the daughter of the Prophet Mohammad, because this week marked the anniversary of her death. The many white *chadors* that I saw, most sprinkled with pale floral designs, were special prayer *chadors*. Women wore them exclusively for prayer, and they were therefore much cleaner than the ordinary black *chadors* worn on the street. The Friday prayer leader who had just begun speaking was Ayatollah Mohammad Yazdi—a conservative, I knew, and the chief of the judiciary. He was delivering the political speech, and another cleric would follow with midday prayers.

From the loudspeakers above us, the Ayatollah's words descended, to envelop like a comforting glove. His voice was deep, rhythmic, and rich, with the many long vowel sounds of Persian, and his words flowed luxuriantly along, never hesitating, never tripping, as they rose to crescendos and then glided down again. The Shi'ite clerics are trained in the art of rhetoric and, like good gospel preachers in the United States, know exactly how and when to make a point or move a crowd. I tried to understand what Ayatollah Yazdi was saying, but all I gleaned was that he was condemning the U.S. bombing of Osama bin Laden's suspected terrorist lair in neighboring Afghanistan—an opinion that I happened to share. The bombing had occurred only about a week before I left for Iran.

No one else seemed to be listening to the Ayatollah's speech too closely, either, and after about a half hour, I got up to speak with a trio of young women in white *chadors* who were staring at me. They're probably less educated and more tradition-bound than the Iranians I've met so far, I thought as I approached them, though I did notice that one woman was wearing blue jeans.

The women nudged each other excitedly as I sat down among them.

"Where did you learn our language?" they said, and giggled when I tried to communicate, while I fervently wished that I knew more.

One of the women was a housewife, another a secretary, and a third a nurse. They had all gone to high school together and came to Friday

prayer meetings every week without fail. The meetings were very important, they said, both for politics and religion. Then they asked me what I
thought about Iran.

"*Kheili jalebeh*," I said—very interesting. My vocabulary was limited.

I asked them what they thought about America.

"*Kheili khub*," they said—very good.

Seven or eight other women crowded around us. One gave me a com-
memorative *rial* bill, inscribed with the golden outline of a mosque, and
another gave me an apple. Everyone wanted my autograph. As I wrote out
my name over and over again, feeling both touched and foolish, the women
suddenly raised their fists in the air. "*Marg bar Amrika, marg bar Israel*," they
half-heartedly droned in a chant led by the Ayatollah—Death to America,
death to Israel. I froze. The women looked at me apologetically.

"We don't mean you! Or the American people!" they said. "We mean
the American government."

An older woman clasped my arm. "President Khatami says we should
stop this 'Death to America, death to Israel,' " she said. "And he is right. It
isn't good. It doesn't help anything."

I shook my head at the absurdity of it all.

The prayers were about to begin, and so I returned to my seat next to
Lona, who was looking very unhappy. The "Death to America" chant had
upset her more than it had me. Why hadn't it upset me more? I wondered.
Because I hadn't believed it, was the answer. And because I didn't feel it
applied to me, was the even more accurate answer. Yet that is exactly when
bad things happen to people, I thought now, shuddering. It's precisely
when a person is just gliding along, trusting in the goodness of the world,
that something dark and dangerous climbs out of the breach—

"There is no God but Allah and Mohammad is His Prophet."

The women all stood and pulled their *chadors* down farther over their
faces, until they resembled a field full of mummies. Lona and I were the
only women in sight wearing *manteaus* and *rusaris*, not *chadors*, and I was the
only woman not beginning to pray. *Allahu akbar, Allahu akbar*—God is great,
God is great. The women cupped their hands to their ears, symbolic of
hearing the message of God, and then stood with their heads bowed and
their hands by their sides, silently reciting verses from the Qor'an. Next, all
bent forward from the waist, in a long bow with their hands on their knees,
then stood again, and knelt with their foreheads to their prayer stones on
the ground. "Glory to God, glory to God, glory to God," a low rumble

rose up from the men's side, washing over the hundreds of motionless, whispering black and white turtle backs at my feet; men are supposed to say their prayers out loud, whereas women must whisper. I caught my breath at the moment's power—and beauty. *Islam* means "submission," as in submission to God, and for the first time, I caught a glimmering of what that meant. All these thousands of worshippers, united by their belief in a higher good.

A moment later, the women sat back on their heels, stood up, and repeated the cycle all over again. Midway through, in what would have been an act of irreverence in Christian prayer, the monitors began briskly, noisily, taking the banners praising Fatemeh down off the wall.

The prayers ended abruptly, and the canvas wall came down even more abruptly, returning the University of Tehran to its usual workaday appearance—a jumble of gray buildings. A loud chanting came from the men's side, and Lona tugged urgently at my arm. It's time to go, she said, pointing the way to a deserted back entrance, it's going to get very crowded and uncomfortable here. But I didn't want to go—from the milling about me, I sensed something was about to happen—and I talked poor Lona into staying with me as I joined the hundreds of other women already bunched up behind an iron gate that still blocked us from the main drive. On Enqelab Avenue beyond the drive, we could see two waiting floats, draped in red, green, and white—the colors of the Iranian flag. The floats contained the recently found remains of the soldiers from the Iran–Iraq War.

A wailing arose from the women around me as the men slowly began filing out of their section and down the drive, the clerics going first, followed by men in ordinary dress. Then I heard an eerie, escalating, muffled thumping inching its way up into my consciousness, and realized, with both fascination and horror, that the women were beating themselves with their fists on their chests and heads. The sound seemed to reverberate through the entire crowd and through my entire body. Some of the women were sobbing hysterically, sheets of tears glazing their faces, and some were waving photocopied photos of sons and husbands lost in the war. The men kept filing by, the women kept wailing and thumping, wailing and thumping, and a melancholy dirge pounded out of the loudspeakers above our heads. Everyone had changed back into her black street *chador*, and suddenly I, also in black, felt part of an ancient anonymous mass of womanhood, locked into the numbing sorrows of all mothers and wives since the beginning of time. I couldn't really compare myself to the women around me, of course, but we were linked anyhow, through our gender, our gender's history, and the sad, sorry human condition.

Finally, after all the men had passed, the gate opened and we surged out, hundreds upon hundreds of identical black forms streaming down the drive. I couldn't tell us apart, I kept losing Lona, I kept worrying that I might trip or fall, but I did notice one middle-aged woman waving photos of *three* young men—all her sons?—and an old lady with a face so cobwebbed with wrinkles that I could barely make out her features. We reached the teeming avenue, where the floats were just beginning to roll, and saw soldiers on board handing out red, white, and dyed green flowers. Women and men alike screamed to get those flowers; behind the floats milled clerics in flowing capes and rolled turbans, lining up for the procession. Far removed from our sweaty, disheveled crowd, they looked crisp and neat.

After watching for a moment or two, Lona and I hailed a taxi and headed toward home. As we left Enqelab Avenue behind for north Tehran, our driver told us that his last fare had been a *hezbollahi* who'd told him that the floats didn't contain just the bones of the lost soldiers but rather their entire bodies—miraculously preserved by Allah. The driver himself didn't think that the floats contained anything at all. The whole event was completely phony, he said, and staged to try to rekindle the people's dying allegiance to the Islamic government.

ॐॐ

Lona, Pari, Sepideh, and I were in a taxi en route to the Imam Khomeini Holy Shrine and adjoining Behesht-e Zahra, the vast cemetery 12 miles south of Tehran in which soldiers from the Iran–Iraq War and other Iranians are buried. Throughout the 1980s, the burial grounds had been packed with many thousands of mourners daily, along with clerics who praised those martyred for the cause of Shi'ite Islam. As at Friday prayers at the University of Tehran, those crowds had since dwindled considerably, but the shrine and cemetery are still considered sacred to many traditional Iranians, and I wanted to see them for myself.

It had taken us over an hour to negotiate the congested traffic of south Tehran, but at last we were on a multilane highway approaching our destination. Small billboards depicting well-known martyrs began to flash by, one right after another, and Lona called out some of their names while Pari passed out pistachios. A Chevy with a giant red wreath completely covering its front hood zoomed by.

Four golden minarets, a golden dome, a turquoise dome, and three unfinished gray domes appeared, all looking tiny and overexposed under the immense pale sky. They belonged to the Imam Khomeini Holy Shrine and visitors' complex, scheduled to one day include a hotel, bazaar, museum, and supermarket. Already finished were the shrine itself, several restaurants and shops, an emergency health clinic, a post office, a bank, a lost-and-found, and a teahouse, where free tea was served to pilgrims.

After our taxi, rented for the morning, had been parked at the edge of an enormous lot, we walked beneath a graceless arch onto a wide and empty plaza. Everything looked unkempt, with exposed wires hanging here and there and cracks running through the plaza's concrete slabs. To one side stretched a long line of faucets for ablutions, backed by a brilliant blue wall neatly inscribed with bold, black Arabic script. To the other stood prayer boxes with plywood doves on top and a kiosk selling postcards, books, and souvenirs, including rose water, which some believers use to sprinkle themselves and their fellow worshippers.

Along another wall crouched dozens of pilgrims too poor to afford hotels. Having flocked to the shrine from all over the country, they sat or slept with their meager bedding and foodstuffs spread out all around them. Bare-bottomed toddlers ran in and out between pretty floral sheets, hung up to provide at least some privacy, while one scrawny man in brown sat back on his haunches, munching on a giant onion. Watching them, I wondered how they kept their spirits up, out here all day in this hot sun and still air. I hoped their religion was enough.

We entered the shrine, leaving our shoes in one of the hundreds of wooden cubicles up front, and passed quickly through the requisite body search. Before us yawned an echoing space, darkly bathed in a greenish light reflected up off green marble floors. At Khomeini's request, the shrine is a simple place, all but devoid of ornamentation, and feels much like an oversize high school gym. Overhead hung exposed pipes and a few crooked minichandeliers; in niches by utilitarian pillars lay multiple copies of the Qor'an. A few women sat praying and gossiping by the walls while their children slid across the floor on stocking feet. Unlike churches and temples, shrines and mosques are informal places where people come to socialize, snack, study, and sleep, as well as to pray. Neighborhood mosques in particular serve as community gathering places.

We joined the trickle of visitors who were passing from the entrance to Khomeini's tomb, situated about a third of the way in, and back out again.

The size of a large toolshed, the tomb looked like a greenish cage crosshatched with steel bars. Inside lay Khomeini's symbolic casket—the actual body is buried in the ground—facing toward Mecca and covered with a green cloth. Green is the holy color of Islam. Beside him lay the symbolic casket of his son Mostafa, and around them both, swept neatly into the tomb's corners, rose ugly piles of crumpled *toman* bills. They had been pushed into the tomb by pious pilgrims, who had also tied small pieces of cloth—each one a supplication—to the crosshatches.

"Kiss the tomb, kiss the tomb," I heard several women urging their children before demonstrating by example. For once, no one was paying any attention to me, though Lona did tell the one woman who asked that I was Italian, just in case. Despite the fact that most Iranians I met seemed to welcome Americans, there was always a vague worry that if I told the wrong person in the wrong place where I came from, trouble would erupt.

While Lona, Pari, and Sepideh headed back to the entrance, I sat down on the cool marble floor. So this was where the great man was buried. The place felt anticlimactic—mostly because there were so few people. Though most Iranians I met spoke passionately about their high regard for Khomeini, their memory of him is wearing thin. Twenty years is a long time in which to keep revolutionary ideals alive.

From Khomeini's shrine, we proceeded on into the equally deserted Behesht-e Zahra, where everywhere we turned, our *manteaus* drooping in the heat, stretched acres of shiny graves, jammed too tightly together as they pushed inexorably out into the desert. Amid their steady march ran wide, empty boulevards, lined with pine trees and oleander. At the crossroads waited teenage boys selling fancy wreaths, some as big as the boys were and shaped like teardrops or hearts. The perfume of the flowers mingled with the dust of the desert beneath the relentless sky.

Most of the martyrs' graves were marked with awkward aluminum-and-glass boxes mounted on spindly poles. Inside the boxes hung fading pictures of the dead, some only 15 or 16 years old and many looking exceedingly handsome, with brushed-back hair, shining eyes, and the expectant eagerness of the young. Beside their photos lay a few personal effects—a plastic comb, an inexpensive watch, a dusty copy of the Qor'an. In one box, two fat insects wandered over a lace doily. In another, photographs depicted the deceased's bloody body parts. In a third lay a toy gun.

Many of the boxes were framed like dollhouses on the inside, with miniature lace curtains and plastic flowers; from the outside hung the flag of the Islamic Republic, its fabric tattered and its colors leeched by the sun. On the backs of other boxes were plastered identical black-and-white photos of Ayatollah Khomeini, also leeched by the sun. Many Iranians regard these faded flags and photos, along with the dwindling number of visitors to Behesht-e Zahra, as a good sign. No one cares about the war anymore, they say, the craziness of radical Islam has run its course.

When the war began in September 1980, many assumed that it would be over quickly. Saddam Hussein had invaded the oil-rich province of Khuzestan in western Iran in the hopes of catching the fledgling Islamic government off guard. But Iran responded heroically and effectively, regaining control of the invaded territory by the spring of 1982. The hostilities could have ended then and there, had not the still-shaky Islamic government seen the invasion as an opportunity both to rally public support behind it and to spread the Revolution through force. They turned the war from a simple defense of Iranian territory into a ferocious crusade for Shi'ite Islam. The United States and the Soviet Union both supported Iraq against Iran in the belief that it was the lesser of the two evils, and the war dragged on for another six years, finally ending in August 1988 with a negotiated cease-fire that both sides claimed as victory. Most Iranians refer to the long, drawn-out tragedy as the "imposed war," forced on them by Iraq and the world powers.

To the West, the most astonishing aspect of the Iran–Iraq War was the Iranians' willingness to martyr themselves. Iraq was much better equipped militarily, with a well-disciplined army and sophisticated weapons, but Iran had tens of thousands of believers ready to die in battle against the blasphemous Arab infidels. In addition to the regular Iranian army and the Revolutionary Guards, there was also the Basij, composed mostly of teenage volunteers who enrolled through more than 9,000 mosques across the country, often for short periods such as summer vacations. Recognizable by their red or yellow headbands declaring the greatness of Khomeini or Allah, the Basij-is came primarily from a working-class or peasant background; the name of their organization, Basij-e Mustazafin, means "Mobilization of the Deprived." In the early years of the war, the Basij-is became famous for running ahead of the Revolutionary Guards to detonate land mines. Their elders often tried to stop them, but the boys believed that their deaths guaranteed them a place in paradise, and some died wearing a plastic key around their necks—the key to heaven. Later, that kind of extreme fervor died down, but the Iranian armed forces were still able to rely largely on volunteer recruits until the final year of the war.

Before leaving for Iran, I had stumbled across a booklet called "In Memory of Our Martyrs" in the Columbia University library. Published by Ershad in 1982, it contained the last wills and testaments of 47 young men, most still in their teens, written shortly before they died. "I hoped to marry and set up a new life and achieve prosperity. But I see it is my destiny to be martyred in the trenches of the nation," wrote one. "I fight against ignorance as did our Prophet," wrote another. "Today, only a week after my wedding, I am putting on boots and combat gear," wrote a third. In New York, the booklet had seemed like little more than a curiosity—albeit a sobering one—but here, it was all too real.

Lona, Pari, Sepideh, and I wandered from box to box, studying the sad contents while trying not to step on the flat, inscribed gravestones—in Islam, gravestones are always laid flat, as a symbol of the deceased's humility. The first few graves made us catch our breaths, but as one after another of the young, expectant faces slipped by, we became numb, responding only when we saw unusual tragedy—two or three brothers buried together, a 15-year-old, a 14-year-old.

Beside one box stood a large plaque with an Arabic inscription, but when I asked Lona to translate, she couldn't do it and called Sepideh over. Like all children in Iran, Sepideh had started learning Arabic in the first grade and could already read. Arabic is considered paramount to children's education in Iran because it is believed to be the only language in which the complexities of the Qor'an can be fully understood.

We passed by a crossroads where a dry fountain stood. For years, it had gushed a dark red "imitation blood"—only too realistic as it welled up and overflowed from one level into the next. But the Islamic government had turned off the fountain a few years ago, perhaps humiliated by the West's ridicule of the symbol.

Beyond the fountain stretched an imposing, mustard yellow brick building, with sparkling picture windows. Peering inside, like kids looking into a treasure chest, we saw several rows of elaborate tombs, flanked by rich carpets on which groups of schoolchildren were sitting. Several handsome men, on entering the room, knelt by one of the tombs and, with two fingertips touching the stone, began to pray. They were reciting the *fateheh*, the opening chapters of the Qor'an, which Muslims repeat to themselves when remembering the dead.

The mustard yellow building held the remains of Ayatollah Mohammad Beheshti and scores of other Islamic leaders, killed by a bomb in 1981 during a meeting of the Islamic Republican Party. Today's Supreme Leader Khamene'i had lost the use of his right hand during a smaller explosion the night before, and both bombings had been the work of the Mojahedin-e Khalq, a militant terrorist organization of the Islamic left, now based in Iraq.

At the time of his death, Ayatollah Beheshti had been the second most important Islamic leader in Iran. And the Islamic government liked to claim that he had died in an explosion that had killed 72 people because that same number had been killed in the holy battle of Karbala in A.D. 680—the most important event in Shi'ite history. In actuality, however, 74 people died in the 1981 explosion.

The battle of Karbala marked the beginning of Shi'ite Islam. When the Prophet Mohammad died in A.D. 632, he had appointed no heir. His only living child, Fatemeh, had married the Prophet's cousin and first convert, Ali, and some felt that he was the logical choice for caliph, or Mohammad's successor. But instead the caliphate fell first to Abu Bakr, a close companion of Mohammad, and then to 'Omar and 'Othman, two other close companions. Ali did not assume the mantle of the Prophet until 656.

During the reign of the first three caliphs, many leaders in Mecca had become corrupt, neglectful of their religious duties, and enormously wealthy. Ali, in contrast, lived a simple and modest life, devoting himself to religious teaching and study. Like the Prophet, he preached that all believers are created equal and spoke out against the social injustice that he saw all around him. Not surprisingly, much of his support came from the poor, whereas many of the elite bitterly resented his growing power. There upon, the Muslims fell into two camps: those who believed that the caliph should be chosen by consensus, as the first three caliphs were, and those who believed that he should be a direct descendant of the Prophet, as Ali was. The first group later became known as the Sunnis, who now make up over 90 percent of the Muslim world, and the second became the Shi'ites.

Ali was assassinated in 661, five years into his caliphate, and the Muslim leadership fell to Muawiya, the governor of Syria, and the Umayyad dynasty. The followers of Ali then broke away from the mainstream, led by Ali's second son, Hosein, and eventually confronted the Umayyads in battle. The two forces met in 680 at Karbala, a dry, dusty plain south of what is now Baghdad, Iraq. Hosein and his followers numbered only 72, including women and children, whereas the Umayyad army amassed in the thousands. Undaunted, Hosein declared that death was preferable to living under injustice, and he led himself and his followers to slaughter. News of the tragedy banded the remaining followers of Ali together, turning them from an informal group of dissenters into a distinct and separate sect.

The battle of Karbala placed sacrifice and martyrdom at the heart of the Shi'ite faith. To rebel against unjust authority, fighting until the death if necessary, became an intrinsic part of the religion, so much so that the battle lives on today with extraordinary immediacy. For many Iranians, the fate of Imam Hosein has come to personify the fate of all serious Shi'ites, engaged in a noble struggle to do what they believe is right in the face of corrupt, tyrannical power. The Iran–Iraq War was part of that struggle; the stance of religious Iran against the evil West is also part of that struggle.

Every year, Shi'ites commemorate the battle of Karbala during Moharram, a month of mourning, whose climax is Ashura, the day of Hosein's death. Throughout that month, throughout Iran, towns and villages of all sizes stage ta'zieh, or colorful outdoor plays, which recreate the events that led to Hosein's death. Comparable to the passion plays of the West, the ta'zieh are largely enacted by amateurs who don elaborate costumes and speak in verse (the heroes) or prose (the villains) as they reenact weddings, skirmishes, visitations from the angel Gabriel, and death. The whole audience takes part in ta'zieh, laughing and weeping, as if at actual weddings and funerals, and there is no real stage, as the barrier between the actors and the audience is constantly shifting. Finally, on the day of Ashura itself, millions of male mourners march through the streets, beating themselves with fists and chains to lament Hosein's death.

While we were living in Iran in the 1960s, my parents were warned about ta'zieh and Ashura and advised to stay well away. Those fanatic Muslims will tear you to bits, their upper-middle-class Iranian friends told them, and my parents listened. But now I wonder if that advice was well founded. I've since read several accounts of ta'zieh by Westerners who attended the plays in the 1980s and 1990s and wrote only of being welcomed.

Passing beyond the mustard yellow building, Lona, Pari, Sepideh, and I entered another section of the cemetery, where a wiry groundskeeper beckoned urgently to us. We had neared the grave of Shahid (Martyr) Hosein Fahmideh, a famous 13-year-old who had strapped a bomb to himself and rolled under an enemy tank during the first year of the war. Khomeini had praised Fahmideh in one of his speeches. "I am not the leader," Khomeini had said. "Our leader is that thirteen-year-old boy . . ."

The groundskeeper told us to put our hands on the gravestone, which he said smelled of rose water. All the graves of the holiest martyrs in the cemetery apparently smelled of rose water. I pressed my palm to the stone but couldn't smell a thing. Neither could Lona or Pari, and after the groundskeeper left, they rolled their eyes.

"That doesn't make any sense," they said. "Maybe the grave of a holy imam could smell like rose water, but not the grave of an ordinary soldier. They put the rose water on the graves themselves."

Beyond Fahmideh's grave was a museum where wriggling children were watching films made during the Iran–Iraq War. They swung their legs above the floor as the jerky images flashed across the screen—gaunt men huddled in bunkers, exhausted men toiling over trenches, one frail old man getting shot in the chest, a teenager sobbing as he kissed the face of a dead friend. But the giggling schoolchildren paid scant attention. To them, the war was already ancient history.

ॐ

I decided to return to Behesht-e Zahra again, this time on a Thursday, to interview some of the poorer, more conservative Tehranis who visit the cemetery on the weekends. With me, I took along an interpreter, Tannaz, a university student, who suggested that we also attend a funeral—a prospect that intrigued me.

We left early in the morning, to avoid the heat and the crowds, and to avoid attracting too much attention when talking to people. The Boss in the foreign press office had warned me against that.

We headed first to the cemetery's computer center, to see what funerals were planned. Behesht-e Zahra is so large and Tehran so populated that funerals take place constantly throughout the day. In the computer center, we studied a digitized map that showed us where to go and then we passed out back to a bathhouse where bodies are ritually washed before burial. We looked inside the women's section—even in death, the sexes are strictly segregated—but luckily it was empty, except for three chunky attendants wearing light gray uniforms, matching head scarves, and plastic gloves.

Our taxi driver, Ali, a well-spoken man who seemed to know Behesht-e Zahra quite well, drove us straight to the correct plot, where crowds of people dressed in black were milling about. Several funerals and memorial gatherings were in progress. In Islam, mourners commemorate the newly dead with ceremonies on the third, seventh, and fortieth days after their passings. Everyone dresses in black for the funeral and the close family wears black for the succeeding 40 days. Traditionally, a widow remains dressed in mourning for a year, at which point the deceased's family comes to her in a ritualized ceremony, bearing bolts of bright cloth.

Before us stretched a large plot containing rows upon rows of empty, narrow, concrete-lined holes ready for the reception of bodies. Planks of wood led from one section to another and we joined the foot traffic heading to one of the funerals.

No one seemed to question our presence. As we merged into one of the huddled crowds, someone pulled us toward the front, so that we could see better. Teenage boys were passing around dates and halvah while a professional eulogizer, or *madeh,* was extolling the virtues of the deceased. His deep, cadenced voice competed with the deep, cadenced voices of the other *madeh*s nearby, all of whom were projecting their messages with the help of battered-looking loudspeakers perched crookedly atop mounds of earth.

A moment later, "our" body arrived, carried in on a simple stretcher and wrapped in a white burial shroud on which were written verses of the Qor'an; coffins are not used in Islam. Chanting *"La elaha ella Allah"*—There is no God but one God—the men laid him in the earth while the women wailed, their voices thin and eerie in the desolate landscape. Rose water from ordinary glass jars was sprinkled over the body, on whose chest was pinned what looked like an identity card. Then a man knelt beside the grave and began shaking the deceased while reciting verses of the Qor'an—a ritual meant to comfort him. Other men laid cement bricks on top of the body and covered them with mud and earth. The wailing and chanting continued, quieter and yet more insistent than before, and as it did, the women seemed to become one, joining together in their grief— and perhaps lessening their pain—in the same way that the women at the University of Tehran had joined together in prayer. They have an ability to empathize deeply with one another that we Westerners don't, I thought, a bit enviously and sadly.

Tannaz, Ali, and I left. Despite the fact that no one had questioned us, I felt as if we'd trespassed. The deceased had meant nothing to us, but the grief of his family and friends had been real.

Yet my reaction was a Western one; perhaps if I'd been Shi'ite, I might have felt differently. With the battle of Karbala as alive in Shi'ite memory as if it happened yesterday, Iranians are often drawn to suffering and death, and some Shi'ites believe that God confers grace on those who attend funerals and weep for the departed—even if they are strangers.

Grief permeates the Persian side of Iranian culture as well. Many songs and poems lament the futility of all human desire in the face of death. The beloved poet Hafez wrote:

Trust not in fortune, vain deluded charm!
Whom wise men shun, and only fools adore,
Oft, whilst she smiles, Fate sounds the dread alarm
Round flies her wheel; you sink to rise no more.

We Americans, of course, take the opposite approach. Usually, we pretend suffering and death don't exist, and then when that no longer works, half convince ourselves that things can't really be that bad by reading—or writing—self-help books about creative divorce, how to survive the death of a child, how to live with a fatal illness, how to die. Our optimistic attitude can be greatly empowering, giving us the courage and imagination to fight against tremendous odds, but when it falls short—as it ultimately must—it leaves us with little to fall back on.

The Iranians, in contrast, have too much to fall back on. Because when something goes badly wrong, it becomes too easy to passively sink into the comfort of shared grief or belief in inexorable fate or nostalgia for the clear-cut battles of the ancient past.

We drove on to the martyrs' cemetery and parked our taxi beneath a dusty pine tree. Ali settled down for a nap while Tannaz and I roamed the graves, looking for approachable mourners. The artificial nature of our quest struck me with full force.

Our first interviewee was a middle-aged woman whose brother had died in the war at age 27. She seemed pleased to speak to us and said that she was very proud to be the sister of a martyr. The war had been necessary, she said, and she hoped that nothing much would ever change in Iran, because if it did, it would mean that the martyrs had died in vain. The Imam Khomeini had been a very great man—how else could he have succeeded in bringing about the Islamic Revolution?

Next we stopped Mansur Basmechi, age 57, who had lost his father in random gunfire at the beginning of the Revolution. Mansur was very pleased to have Islamic rule in Iran, he said, but he wanted to see his country move more quickly into the modern era. He wanted to see more cultural exchange with the West and more development of technology at home. He thought that President Khatami was the best and most religious leader in Iran and had high hopes for him. He also thought that Imam Khomeini was an extremely great man whose coming had been one of the most important events in world history.

Our next two potential interviewees begged off, one because she only spoke Azeri Turkish, the other because his actions spoke louder than his words. After agreeing to talk to us, he never looked at us once but kept washing his son's grave and whispering to his wife. Then he got up to refill his water bottle.

The threesome at our next stop had come to mourn their brother, a Basij-i who'd died at age 17. They were extremely proud of what he'd done, and the man among them said that he'd wanted to go to war, too, but had had to stay home to help his family. All three were very happy with the increased security and religious laws that the Revolution had brought to their country but unhappy with the economic situation. They doubted whether Khatami could change much—he was just one man. Still, they were glad that they lived in Iran, because Iran had something no other country had.

"What is that?" I asked.

"Islam," they said.

Beyond the threesome was a couple sitting cross-legged by a grave with their eight-year-old daughter. They were eating cucumbers and reading a badly dilapidated copy of the Qor'an. My brother died in the war, the husband said, and although both he and his wife were proud of that fact, they weren't sure that the war had been necessary. They also didn't feel that the Revolution had changed much. They deeply wished that Imam Khomeini were still alive—he had done so much to help them, the poor.

The couple then invited us to join them for cucumbers, but we shook our heads. We have others we want to interview, I said, while also feeling that I didn't have the right to take anything from this couple. They seemed so sad and poor, pale and drawn, with the man's clothes threadbare and the woman's *chador* old and worn. The only decent item of clothing between them was their child's bright red sweater, and I imagined her to be the one spot of hope in their otherwise desolate lives. Despair hung like a shroud around them.

Why is it that some people have to suffer so? I thought angrily as we walked away. Why is it that it is always the poor who die in wars? Power and money—the things that make the world go 'round. No idealist, humanitarian, or religious leader has ever managed to change that.

Tannaz and I walked on, past a water spigot, to a cluster of graves shaded by hoary trees. A moon-faced young woman, tightly wrapped in a *chador*, was standing motionless by one of the graves. She had lost two brothers, ages 15 and 16, in the war.

"They died for Islam," she said, pointing to the fading photos of two moon-faced young men who looked exactly like her, "and everything we have now in Iran, we have from their blood. I believe they are in paradise— I've seen it in my dreams. They are happy. They are the ones who are alive, we are the ones who are dead. We didn't want the war—Iraq wanted the war—but the war was very, very important for Iran. The blood of the martyrs has made Islam come back to every life and every house in Iran."

The ferocity of her words sent a chill down my spine. She seemed to be denying herself the relief of personal sorrow. Even while offering her comfort, the intensity of her religious belief did not allow her to mourn for her brothers, who'd been transformed in her mind from human beings into martyrs.

Tannaz and I returned to the taxi, where Ali was waiting. Eagerly, he asked about our conversations.

We told him, and he shrugged.

"Ninety-five percent of the people who come here are poor," he said, "and although they won't say it to you, they have nothing. They gave their sons to the war and now the government is doing nothing for them. If they had known what would happen after the war, they would never have gone."

I hoped he was wrong. If the mourners believed that their loved ones had died in vain, then they truly had nothing.

"What about you?" I said. "Did you go to war?"

"No. First I was in the university and then when I was finished, I had to work for five years to pay them back."

"Did you want to go?" I said. I wasn't particularly surprised to learn that Ali had a university degree. Several other taxi drivers I'd met had also had university degrees; jobs for the educated are particularly scarce in Iran and many college graduates are unemployed—sometimes deliberately so. Traditionally, Iranians have considered it degrading for anyone who is educated to work with his or her hands, and some insist on working in offices or not at all.

"That's a hard question," Ali said. "Maybe I wanted to at the time, but now I'm glad I didn't."

On the way back, Ali made an unscheduled stop in what appeared to be his neighborhood, on the outskirts of south Tehran. We drove down one narrow lane after another, swerving to avoid a man on a donkey, and pulled up beside a small shop. Ali climbed out while Tannaz and I waited in the hot car, both lost in our own thoughts. *Azan*, the call to prayer, began, drifting lazily out over the mud walls around us.

A moment later, Ali returned, carrying two soda bottles and two shiny packets of cookies.

"I wanted you to see," he said to me as he handed us our complimentary snacks, "that Iran has other things besides Islam to offer. We have hospitality. We have very great hospitality—maybe more than any other country in the world."

I raised my soda bottle to him.

৯৽৽৻

In downtown Tehran, not far from Vali-ye Asr Square, stands the Museum of the Martyrs. Blown-up photographs of the deceased look out of windows onto the main street, while inside sprawl two big floors devoted to those who died during the Revolution and the Iran–Iraq War. The most famous martyrs are downstairs, and the saddest ones, upstairs. One upstairs exhibit case, filled with dog tags and bloody uniforms, honors the Madani family, who lost four sons in the war. Another honors the Afrosiahis, who lost five.

Downstairs, the section on the Revolution begins with the House of Water, a small shrine holding bowls of water that reflect lit candles around them. Water is of utmost importance in the Shi'ite religion. A means of purification, used in ablutions before prayer, it is believed to have preceded creation. During Moharram, when Shi'ites commemorate the battle of Karbala, they distribute cups of water in remembrance of Hosein and his followers, who suffered from an excruciating thirst before being killed. Wealthy Shi'ites build public drinking fountains as pious acts, and these *saqqa-khanehs*—some nothing more than metal barrels with spigots—can be found everywhere.

Beyond the House of Water are exhibits honoring those who died during anti-Shah demonstrations in the 1960s and those who died at the hands of SAVAK in the 1970s. A quote from martyr Mohammad Reza

Sa'idi, a leading cleric killed by SAVAK in 1970, hangs on the wall: "If you kill me, you will see the holy face of Khomeini in every drop of my blood." Sa'idi supposedly said those words moments before he died.

Other quotes hang here and there: "One who yearns for death never dies," martyr Shaikh Hosein Ma'an. "Martyrdom and being ready for martyrdom are necessities of the Revolution," Imam Khomeini. "A martyr is a symbol of having goals, making an effort, and perseverance," Imam Khomeini again, in a Dale Carnegie–esque moment.

ॐ

One block directly east of the Museum of the Martyrs stands the former U.S. Den of Espionage—a.k.a. the former U.S. Embassy. Now being used as a military training site, the enclave is surrounded by tall, dun-colored walls that start soon after the museum and then continue and continue, past flimsy lookout towers manned by armed guards and the U.S. State Department seal, defaced by bullet holes. Graffiti on the wall reads DEATH TO AMERICA; across the silent street, and stretching nearly the entire block, is a long line of moribund handicraft shops, patiently waiting—or so it seems—for the return of prosperous American tourists.

On the morning of November 4, 1979, eight months after the return of Ayatollah Khomeini to Iran, a group of *chador*-clad women began encircling the embassy. Belonging to a group called Muslim Students Following the Imam's Line, they chanted "Death to America" over and over again, to distract the handful of U.S. Marines guarding the compound. Meanwhile, another group of students slipped through a basement window and into the main building where they blindfolded and bound the wrists of every American inside. Staff members in the two neighboring buildings began frantically shredding documents until they, too, were seized. Fifty-two Americans were held as hostages for a tense, frightening 444 days.

I could remember the grim news reports of that period, with their grainy pictures of young, wild-eyed Iranians and uncertain, pale-faced Americans. I could also remember how surprised and angry my father had been. Surprised because he, like most Americans, had had absolutely no sense of what was going on in Iran. Angry because the daily news reports had simply repeated the same sensationalist facts of the case over and over again, without attempting to search for explanations.

One afternoon shortly after my arrival in Iran, I walked down the length of the embassy wall, acutely aware of the guards in the lookout towers above my head, of my blond hair sticking out of my *rusari,* and—especially—of my bare knee occasionally flashing out of my *manteau.* Each time I saw it, I felt a split second of pure horror. I was wearing knee socks beneath a long skirt, but the skirt did not button all the way down the front and I'd forgotten to pin it.

Finally, after what seemed like half an hour, though it was only about ten minutes, I came to the corner of Mofatteh Avenue, formerly Roosevelt Avenue, and stopped before a small, neglected shop that looked permanently closed. Pressing my nose against the glass, I realized that this was the modern version of the old "Center for the Publication for U.S. Espionage Dens Documents" that I'd read about. The center had once published dozens of volumes of reprinted reports and memoranda confiscated from the American Embassy, and sold them to the general public as proof of the "superdevil's" tyranny.

In truth, most of the reprinted documents had dealt only with mundane affairs, but during the height of revolutionary fervor, they were used to discredit hundreds of Iranian moderates who'd had contact with the U.S. Embassy. Many innocent people had been arrested and tortured, and some had been killed. The documents had also revealed the sorry state of U.S. diplomatic policy and intelligence in Iran. Few of the diplomats could speak Persian, and most were woefully unaware of what ordinary Iranians were thinking. As little as two months before Khomeini returned to rule Iran, U.S. Ambassador William H. Sullivan had reported that "we doubt Khomeini personally commands all the power that is often attributed to him."

Ayatollah Khomeini had not ordered the takeover of the embassy, but he had used it to full advantage to help reunify his then-fragmenting public support. America was the Great Satan, he thundered, and anyone who opposed the takeover or his proposed constitution for the new Islamic Republic was collaborating with the enemy. One month later, in December 1979, 16 million voters approved the new constitution by a reported 99 percent, turning Iran into the world's first modern theocracy, or state governed by officials who are believed to be divinely guided. Four months later, the Americans sent eight helicopters to a desert airstrip 275 miles from Tehran. The helicopters were to be the vanguard of a hostage rescue mission, but instead, a surprise sandstorm disabled three of the aircraft and sent eight servicemen crashing to their deaths. Khomeini declared the sandstorm an act of Allah designed to protect the new republic and didn't release the hostages until the following year. By then, the Iran–Iraq War had started and the hostages weren't needed anymore.

ॐॐ

The third and last time I visited Behesht-e Zahra, I went at the invitation of Lona's friend Maryam. She had had a 17-year-old son who'd died in the war, and every year, she organized an anniversary gathering at his gravesite.

Lona, Pari, and I arrived early, along with three or four other members of the mourning party. The deceased's niece, who hadn't been born at the time of her uncle's death, washed off his grave with water from a nearby faucet, and then we all sat down around the wet stone, the hot sun burning through our dark *manteaus* and *rusaris*.

The cemetery was considerably more crowded than it had been on my earlier visits. It was Friday afternoon—a favorite time for families to picnic at Behesht-e Zahra—and people were bustling to and fro, cleaning off graves, arranging flowers, spreading out rugs, and handing around fruit, cakes, dates, and other snacks. The scene reminded me of visiting my grandmother in Germany once when I was ten. Like many other Germans, she'd spent most Sunday afternoons at the cemetery, cheerfully looking after my grandfather's grave; as a child, accustomed to regarding cemeteries as scary, haunted places, that had astonished me. Yet in early U.S. history, I now knew, Americans had also found cemeteries to be pleasurable places. Before the establishment of parks, landscaped graveyards such as Woodlawn Cemetery in the Bronx had been so crowded on weekends that they had required traffic cops. I wondered at what point the American attitude had changed, and whether it had more to do with a fear of death or an infatuation with youth. Or, as seemed most likely, with a whirlwind, self-centered lifestyle that left people with little time or inclination to pay tribute to their dead. I myself have never visited my American grandparents' gravesites.

A slight man wearing a jacket with brass buttons appeared and began scolding us.

"Many sisters made great sacrifices for the Revolution," he said to Lona and the others, "and here you come only in *manteaus*, without your *chadors*. And you"—he turned to me—"cover your head better."

We giggled together as he left, but I did pull down my *rusari*, and so, I noticed, did the others.

One of the things that is most infuriating to many women in Iran today is that anyone—man or woman—has the right to stop them at any time and demand that they cover themselves better. This man appeared to be employed by the cemetery, but he could just have been an ordinary citizen. And from what I'd heard, the self-appointed female enforcers were even worse than the men.

The rest of the party suddenly arrived—by the dozens. Swooping down on us, they began rolling out heavy carpets, setting up a fat-bellied samovar, and opening up multiple cartons, bags, and baskets overflowing with food. Most of the women were wearing *chadors*, and many went out of their way to welcome me. Maryam, whom I'd met several times before, gave me a warm hug. A charming, middle-aged woman with apple cheeks and chocolate-brown eyes, she had an unusual smile that made me feel as if she knew all my darkest secrets but liked me tremendously anyway.

"Maryam is a very, very good friend," Lona said, watching her. "When I got divorced and had no place to stay in Tehran, she took me and Sepideh in. We lived with her and her family for four months."

I nodded. It didn't surprise me. Maryam seemed like exactly the sort of woman who would do anything for others. Her kindness also helped to explain why, despite a twenty-year age difference, she and Lona were such good friends.

"What will happen here?" I said. "Will there be a ceremony?"

"No, I don't think so," Lona said. "I think this is just a party."

We were speaking our usual mix of pidgin Persian and pidgin English, and although we were both frequently frustrated by our inability to understand each other, we could usually at least get the basics.

"Is this typical?" I said. "Do all Iranians do this on the anniversary of a death?"

"All Iranians remember the dead," Lona said, "but most don't give such a big party. It is only because Maryam is very generous and her son was very young when he died. She couldn't give him a wedding, and so she is giving him this instead."

A woman handed me a plump plum, and I took a bite.

"She's had a very hard life," Lona said. "Her husband took a second wife."

I stopped chewing.

"She lives in Arak," Lona said. "About three hours away. That's where he is now."

"But this is his son—"

Lona shrugged. "He spends most of his time with his new wife. They married about ten years ago and have three children. All of Maryam's children are grown."

Or dead, I added silently. I felt stunned. I'd known that under Islamic law, men are allowed four wives. "Marry of the women, who seem good to you, two or three or four; and if ye fear that ye cannot do justice (to so many) then one (only)," reads the Qor'an (4:3). Many people had assured me, however, that the practice rarely occurred in Iran anymore, except among the poor and uneducated. Maryam was hardly either one of those. And of all people to have to suffer such an indignity . . .

"Do many men in Iran have second wives?" I asked.

"Some," Lona said matter-of-factly.*

Later, I realized that it was Lona's straightforward tone that had surprised me as much as anything. To me, the idea of multiple wives was outrageous. To Lona, it was simply a fact of life that had to be dealt with.

The women were handing out more food, and round after round went by. Cakes, apples, oranges, grapes, cucumbers, more cakes, dates, nuts, tea. Our group had commandeered an area of at least 10 graves, and down at the far end, a big bearded man with a loud guffaw and jiggling belly had set up a cauldron that was at least three feet high. He was heating up the *ash*—a thick, sour soup-stew made of noodles, beans, spinach, and chives. He ladled it out into plastic quart-size containers big enough to feed four, of which we each got one, and then began serving the mourners at other gravesites nearby. We passed them our extra fruit and cakes as well. The sharing of both food and grief is a Behesht-e Zahra tradition.

While we were eating and talking, I noticed a mountain of a double-chinned woman with bad skin staring at me. But every time I looked up, she looked guiltily away, and once or twice, I heard her mutter something about "the American." Finally, I caught her gaze and gave her a determined smile. She gave me a wobbly smile back. A few moments later, however, she started in on a rambling, incoherent tirade about the hateful United States. I couldn't understand exactly what she was saying and so, gritting my teeth, I responded with a generic statement: America had some good points and some bad points, I said, just like Iran. Quizzically, she stopped talking, cocked her head, and stared at me even harder than before. She seemed

---

*In truth, having multiple wives is rare in Iran. One statistic I found later in the *Encyclopedia Iranica*, published in the United States, put it at about 24 men per 1,000 in 1986.

confused and I imagined that she was trying to reconcile me—an apparently harmless person—with the image of the big, bad American that she had in her head.

"Oh, don't listen to her!" The other women were suddenly all speaking at once. "She doesn't know what she's talking about! We love you. You are very good—it's only the American government we don't like! Please, have another plum! Have some more cake! Have some more tea!"

One pale older woman with glasses leaning against a pine tree seemed especially embarrassed by her neighbor's outburst, and after the excitement died down, I asked Lona about her. She had a wan, remote look to her that saddened me.

"She lost a son in the war, too," Lona said. "He and Maryam's son and two other friends died on the same day. They are all buried here. She was very depressed about it for a long time."

She's still depressed about it, I thought as I took another look at the woman, who now seemed lost in her own thoughts. Then I turned my attention to the rest of the group. Except for the cook at the cauldron and the small coterie of males around him, most in our gathering were women.

A shiver started at the top of my spine.

"How many women here lost sons in the war?" I asked Lona, suddenly suspecting that there was far more going on here than I had realized.

She looked around, counting.

"Four," she said. "No, five."

We looked at each other for one long, unhappy moment—one of us an American, the other only 18 years old when the war ended, and both removed from this tragedy. Of the 20 or so women around us, perhaps half looked old enough to have had sons of fighting age during the Iran–Iraq War. Five out of 10, I thought, and that doesn't even count dead brothers, fathers, uncles, nephews, grandfathers, and friends.

THE COMPANY
OF WOMEN

In the deep places of the heart, two forces, fire and water, struggle together.
—Ferdowsi

My father and Jerry, the man I live with, had been calling. Back home, there were rumors of war between Iran and Afghanistan. The *Washington Post* had reported that 70,000 Iranian troops had amassed on the Iran-Afghanistan border and that battle was imminent.

"You're not going anywhere near there, are you?" Jerry asked.

I hesitated for a moment.

"Are you?"

It felt strange to be hearing his familiar voice, with its heavy New York accent. Even though our telephone connection was excellent—he could be just down the street—he and my New York life seemed very far away, shadows from a half-forgotten past, and I didn't like the crack that was opening up inside me as we spoke. In just a couple of weeks, much distance had developed between us—partly, I thought, because I couldn't really explain to him what was happening to me here. Telephone calls are too short and awkward even under the best of circumstances, even when not worrying about the possibility of someone else listening in.

"No," I lied. It was no use explaining that I was planning to be in the holy city of Mashhad, located about 100 miles from the Afghanistan border and Taliban headquarters, the next day. I knew what news about Middle Eastern hostilities sounded like in the United States. Telling the truth would only cause him and my family needless worry.

"Is Afghanistan in the news there?" Jerry asked.

"Oh, yes," I said. All the news outlets had been delivering daily reports on the Afghanistan situation. The Taliban, the militant Islamic movement that controls Afghanistan, had captured 11 Iranian diplomats and one journalist, and there were rumors that they had been killed. Iranian officialdom was threatening serious retaliation if that was the case, but most ordinary citizens didn't seem to be overly concerned, and I was taking my cues from them. Let's just wait and see what happens seemed to be the general attitude; Iranians have been through too much in recent decades to excite easily. Besides, with only 40,000 men under arms, the Taliban—whom most Iranians regard as a backward, ignorant group—was not a serious military threat to the Islamic Republic.

"And you're not worried?" Jerry said.

"Not really," I said, while thinking that in truth, if I'd been planning to travel to Mashhad entirely by myself, I might have postponed my trip. But Bahman, Lona, Pari, and Sepideh were coming with me—or rather, we four women were going with Bahman. He had a medical conference to attend and had invited us to come along. We would be staying with a wealthy *bazaari* family who were related to neighbors down the street.

I had mixed feelings about our communal trip. Although I was very eager to travel to Mashhad—Iran's most popular pilgrimage site—and greatly enjoyed my hosts' company, I was getting restless. I wanted to start traveling on my own. But I seemed to be the only one excited by that prospect. Bahman, Lona, and Pari—not to mention everyone else I'd met—looked unhappy every time I mentioned the subject.

"Is everything else all right?" Jerry said, interrupting my thoughts.

"Definitely," I said, feeling a little guilty that he was worrying about me. "In fact, things are more than all right. This is an amazing country."

"But don't you have to wear that outfit?"—his word for the *hejab*. "Isn't it hot?"

"Yes," I said. "But . . . it's hard to explain. That doesn't really matter as much as I'd thought." I barely even noticed my *hejab* anymore. "In fact, a lot of women here are really strong. They work or they're in school, and they talk back all the time—"

"But you said before that the guards can stop women whenever they want—"

"I know, I know," I said, trying to crystallize my complex thoughts. "And there is a lot of repression here. People are tense—but that's still not really what this place is about. There's so much else going on."

It was as if, I thought later, pondering most Americans' view of Iran, all that an outsider knew about the United States was its horrendous racial history, its violence, its drug abuse, its divorce rates, and the obscene wealth of some citizens compared to the dire poverty of others. All those things would be true, but the outsider would still be missing—and by a wide, wide margin—what the United States is about. Politics and related issues are only one part of any culture.

"Huh," Jerry grunted. I couldn't tell what he was thinking. "Just don't go anywhere near Afghanistan."

We hung up.

৵৽৻৻৻

On the evening of our scheduled departure from Tehran, Lona, Pari, and I were sitting on Bahman's balcony, trying not to look at the clock. All of our bags were packed and a taxi was standing by, but we still had no airline tickets. They were due to arrive by motorbike any minute now, for a flight that was leaving in less than two hours.

In the Islamic Republic, where there are too few flights for too many people, flights are often sold out months in advance. Getting a ticket on shorter notice, especially to a popular destination like Mashhad, is often a matter of knowing someone. And because in Iran, everyone always knows someone, successful transactions become a question of just how important the someone that you know is. In Bahman's case, it was a highly ranked immigrations official who'd promised—absolutely, no problem—to provide the tickets but still hadn't delivered.

Finally, about 20 minutes later, the motorbike arrived, driven by a young man with peroxided hair—the first I'd seen in Iran. Grabbing our tickets, we leaped into the waiting taxi and sped toward the airport. Though it was now completely dark, men were busy sweeping the streets with brooms made of twigs and the garbage trucks were out. By the roadside sat vendors selling fruits, hurricane lamps, and spiffy orange lawn chairs.

At the airport, a crowd had already gathered by the Mashhad gate. Among them were many women in *chadors*, a few clerics, several people in wheelchairs, and a boy on a stretcher. All were going to Mashhad to pray, and some were hoping for miracles.

The holy city of Mashhad, situated on a high, cool plateau in northeast Iran, is visited by about 12 million believers each year. They come to honor Imam Reza, the Eighth Imam of the Shi'ite religion, who was buried here in A.D. 817, just one year after being nominated to become the next caliph for all Muslims, both Sunni and Shi'ite. According to tradition, Imam Reza died after eating a bunch of poisoned grapes, given to him on the orders of the Abbasid leader Ma'mun, an Arab. Reza was then buried in a tower in the small village of Sanabad, which soon began to attract Shi'ite pilgrims, who regarded the deceased as the victim of Arab injustice. The village grew into a town and the town into a city, which became known as Mashhad, or "Place of Martyrdom." By the 1500s, the city was known all over the Shi'ite world.

The Shi'ites believe that the Prophet Mohammad was succeeded by 12 spiritual and earthly leaders, or Imams. The first Imam was Ali, who was also the fourth caliph and is buried in Najaf, Iraq; the third was Hosein, who is buried in Karbala, Iraq; and the eighth was Imam Reza. Najaf and Karbala are also major Shi'ite pilgrimage sites, along with Qom, Iran, where Fatemeh, the sister of Imam Reza, is buried. In addition, like the Sunni Muslims, the Shi'ites revere the holy cities of Mecca, Medina, and Jerusalem, and strive to make a pilgrimage to Mecca during their lifetimes.

All of the Shi'ite Imams lived during medieval times except for the Twelfth, who is believed to be still alive and "in occultation." At the end of time, this Twelfth Imam, also known as the Mahdi, or savior, will reappear to establish a reign of justice and save the faithful on Judgment Day. When Ayatollah Khomeini returned to Iran, many referred to him as the "Imam," but for the most part, this was an honorific title only; many Friday prayer leaders are also called "Imam."

In addition to being a major pilgrimage site, Mashhad is also Iran's second largest city and industrial center. Everything from car parts to Coca-Cola, canned fruits to blood serum is produced here, and surrounding the city—population 2.1 million—are hundreds of small saffron farms, for which the region is famous.

When we arrived in the holy city, we found two of our hosts, Azar and Shahla Tabataba'i, waiting, and they greeted us with warm cries and kisses on both cheeks, as is the Iranian custom. Shahla, a bubbling woman with a singsong voice, had given birth six weeks earlier and proudly introduced us to her baby, pointing out its miraculous fingers and toes. While the others were busy admiring it, her older sister Azar took my arm. She had a quiet and serious air about her that reminded me of myself.

"I am very happy to meet you," she said to me in English. "I want to talk to you about many things."

From the airport, we drove down a wide boulevard lined with bright streetlights. Mashhad is one of the wealthiest and best-lit cities in Iran because of the many donations made to the Holy Shrine of Imam Reza; Shahla's family, for one, had donated her weight in gold when her baby was born.

In the medians along the boulevard slept hundreds of pilgrims, dreaming—of what? I wondered—under blankets and carpets, their belongings tied up in neat bundles nearby. Watching them flash by, I imagined each small band preparing to make this pilgrimage—gradually saving up its money, gathering up its family, taking dilapidated transportation to get here.

At the end of the boulevard shimmered the domes of the Astan-e Qods-e Razavi, or Holy Precinct of Imam Reza. The large dome was onion-shaped and the color of the Caribbean. The small one was squarer and made of pure gold. Both were flanked by skinny ghostly minarets, outlined in hazy white against the night sky.

Despite their wealth, the Tabataba'is lived in a simple house not far from the shrine. Four smallish rooms surrounded one center room, with a kitchen, bathroom, and sitting room at one end. The bathroom contained the traditional squat toilet found all over Iran and the Middle East, and except for in the sitting room, there was no furniture anywhere. Instead, the rooms were filled with carpets, laid out side by side, some big, some small, most gorgeous, a few not, and *poshti*, or carpet-covered bolster cushions.

As Persia's most famous handicraft, carpets blanketed the floors of most homes I visited. In the poorer homes, the carpets were often machine-made, of synthetic fibers and artificial dyes—a modern and much decried development—but in the wealthier homes, the carpets were wool and knotted into intricate designs. Each region of Iran has its own distinct rug-

weaving patterns, which are often floral, to reflect the classical Persian garden—oases in a largely arid land. Valued as much as an investment as for
their beauty, Persian carpets have traditionally been used as a kind of savings account, to be sold off in times of need and stockpiled in times of
plenty.

In the Tabataba'i sitting room stood a clutch of green velvet chairs, a
coffee table, a TV, and a large picture of the oldest son, killed in the
Iran–Iraq War. Other, smaller pictures of the same son hung in most of
the other rooms as well, casting a quiet but constant pall.

When we arrived, a little after midnight, fully dressed children were
sleeping here and there, spread-eagled on the carpet. Sleeping in traditional
Iran is an informal affair—a leftover habit, perhaps, from the days when
most people lived in villages and had no pressing schedules to attend to.
Children and adults often fall asleep whenever they want, wherever they
want, which in traditional Iran, often means the floor.

Azar and Shahla introduced us to their mother, Haji Khanom, a gentle,
slow-moving woman with a faraway look in her eyes. *Haji Khanom* is a term
of honor used when addressing women who have been to Mecca; *Haji* is
the term used for men. Often, the title *Haji* is also used in a more general
sense, for all respected older men and women, but in Haji Khanom's case,
she had visited the most holy of holy cities many years before. Today,
because of Iran's politicized view of Islam and the resultant violence that
erupted in Mecca in 1987, Saudi Arabia allows only a small quota of
Iranians into the holy city each year. Their names are chosen by lottery, at
the Hajj (pilgrimage to Mecca) division of Ershad.

Bahman pulled out a photograph that I had brought with me from the
United States. The only good picture that my family has of Bahman, it
depicts him as a dark-haired medical student, posing in an Esfahan garden
beside my mother, my American grandmother—who had come to visit—
my brother, and me, by then age six. My mother and I are wearing identical
polka-dot mother-and-daughter dresses, and I am wearing pigtails, bobby
socks, and Mary Janes. We are too far away from the camera to make out
much of our expressions, but we are all squinting into the sun, and I can
sense our discomfort. At the same time, we look so perfect—a storybook
WASP family with foreign friend.

Bahman always passed around this photograph when introducing me to
new people. I want them to trust you, he had said to me, and this picture
proves that you are who you say you are—otherwise, they will think you're

a spy. Whether that assessment was always correct, I wasn't sure, but I enjoyed seeing the picture over and over again and hearing Bahman's repeated reminiscences about my father and mother. They made me feel warm and protected, as if I belonged.

Azar began pulling out large puffy mattresses from a pile in a store-room. Like the rest of the family, we would be sleeping on the floor. Having five extra houseguests in traditional Iran is no problem at all.

ॐ

The next morning, we packed the mattresses away and replaced them with the white *sofreh,* or plastic tablecloth, on which we would be eating our breakfast. This is a remarkably efficient use of space, I thought as I helped to bring out the flat breads (*sangak,* which I'd already had in Tehran, and *nunghagh,* a special sweet bread from Mashhad), Iranian cheese (similar to feta), honey, butter, jam, and tea.

Azar sat down next to me and explained that a trip to the Imam Reza shrine was not something to be embarked on lightly. We would want to spend many hours there, and on a late summer's day such as today, with the schools still on vacation, the place would be broiling hot and mobbed with pilgrims. Therefore, she suggested that we spend the day visiting Tus and go to the shrine at night.

"Fine by me," I said.

High on my list of places to see, Tus is the burial site of the great poet Ferdowsi, who in A.D. 1010 completed the *Shahnameh,* or *Book of Kings,* the national epic of Persia. Probably the longest poem ever written by a single man, the 50,000-line work, which in the standard edition fills nine volumes, begins with the creation of the world and ends with Arab-Islamic conquest of Iran in the seventh century. Four times longer than the *Iliad,* the *Shahnameh* is matched in scope only by the Indian epics *Mahabharata* and *Ramayana.* Drawing on both a long oral tradition and written sources, Ferdowsi celebrated the lore and history of ancient Persia as he recorded the deeds of its kings and warriors. Much of the poem concerns the Iranians' heroic battles against invaders—including dragons, witches, and the Turks.

One of the most interesting aspects of the *Shahnameh* is the complexity of its characters. Many of its kings both lead and betray, are both wise and foolish. Often the kings' warriors and advisors are shown to be ethically superior to the kings themselves, and one great theme of the book is the complex pull between loyalty and doing what one believes is right. Inner battles are as important as outer ones.

Another interesting aspect of the *Shahnameh* is that it deals only marginally with the early Persian monarchs Cyrus and Darius, and with the southwestern province of Fars where the ruins of Persepolis are located. Westerners who know anything about Persia at all are familiar with Persepolis, but most of the *Shahnameh* takes places in eastern Iran and in what is now Afghanistan and Russia. The first half of the epic is largely concerned with tribal warfare among a collection of peoples who had migrated south from central Asia.

After breakfast, we got dressed and were ready to go. Or rather, the Tehran contingent was ready to go. For the Mashhad contingent, matters were far more complicated. Azar and Haji Khanom had to start stews simmering for dinner. Shahla had to pack and repack the baby's belongings. The older children had to be rounded up, and enough cars had to be found. Because of course the whole extended family was going. In traditional Iran, the whole extended family is always going. Setting off on an outing in small groups of twos and threes is unusual.

"*Tanha?*"—Alone?—said in a voice of pure incredulity might have been the single most frequent comment made to me while I was in the Islamic Republic. Most Iranians, even in Tehran, are deeply communal and the idea of anyone traveling halfway around the world by herself is anathema to them. In Iran, despite rising divorce rates, family is still everything, with kinfolk providing not only love, food, and shelter but also mutual support, solidarity, and a ready-made social circle. *Tanha* in Persian means both "alone" and "lonely."

Sometimes the closeness of the Iranian families I met filled me with envy. They seemed to have so much fun together, always laughing and joking, and provided one another with everything from child care and financial help to a deep sense of identity and self-worth. I had nothing even approximating their communal life back in the United States.

But more often, that same familial closeness made me feel restless and impatient. The large, unwieldy groups made it difficult to get anything done, and it was hard to have a private conversation with anyone. I liked some people I met in families better than others—I wanted to get to know them more than the others—but we always had to interact as a group. That was largely to the good, I supposed, because everyone was always included. But I also wondered about the effect of socializing mostly with one's own family members. What about having close friends from entirely different backgrounds? What about the son of a conservative cleric being best friends with the son of a Westernized doctor, or a Muslim being best friends with a Jew? That sort of thing doesn't happen enough in the United States, either, of course, but from what I could tell, it happens less in Iran—and partly because of the closeness of families.

More difficult for me personally to cope with was the lack of individual privacy—not a valued commodity in Iran. Whether in private homes or on the streets, especially outside Tehran, I seldom had a moment to myself. Wherever I went, someone always adopted me, sometimes for hours, sometimes for days. Before leaving New York, I had worried somewhat about traveling alone in Iran—Would anyone speak to me? Would I be lonely?—but one of the first things I learned about traveling alone in Iran is that one is never traveling alone. Someone is always on hand to be your friend.

Two hours later, we were finally ready to go—all 11 of us, ranging in age from 6 weeks to over 70 years. We divided up into two cars, one of them a 1970s Buick.

I sat beside Azar on the front seat of the smaller car as we drove out of Mashhad. The street scenes around us were much the same as in Tehran but with one important difference. All the women were wearing *chador*s. No, it wasn't the law, Azar said when I asked, but it was the custom. In Mashhad, women dressed in *manteau*s were regarded with suspicion. She herself usually wore a *chador* as well because although she didn't like it, she needed it to keep her favorite teaching job, at a good school near her house. If she wore the *manteau*, someone might report her to the school's director and she would be demoted. The only reason she wasn't wearing her *chador* today was that we were going to Tus, where chances were she wouldn't be recognized.

"People in Mashhad talk too much," she said as we left the city behind. "Always people are talking. They say, Why do you wear the *manteau*? Why do you have long nails? What are you doing with a mobile phone? What are you doing with nice shoes? Where do you get your money? You are rich. I must pretend I am not rich.

"Five years ago, it was very bad. Now it is better. But still we must have more freedom. Because many people are leaving Iran. Who will live here in the future? Only mullahs."

Holding a master's degree in mathematics, Azar taught at three different schools for girls and women. One was a religious school run by the clerics, another was a night school for the wives of martyrs, and the third was a school for gifted students. She estimated that ten years earlier, 80 percent of her students were *hezbollahi*. But now, of a class of 40, usually only 5 or 6 fell into that category.

"Many of my students are very clear and intelligent," she said. "They ask many questions, and I want to help them. Sometimes people ask me, 'Why don't you go abroad?' My brother and sister live abroad—many people I know live abroad. But I feel very sorry. My people are poor. Their life is very hard. I can't go abroad."

Haji Khanom, seated in the backseat, took out a bag of sweets, and Azar's teenage son Turaj passed them around. I'd already noticed how attentive and considerate he was. He was the one who'd organized the cars and gathered the younger children together and who took the baby from Shahla whenever she looked tired.

"How old were you when the Revolution began?" I asked Azar.

"I was eighteen. I was *enqelabi* (a revolutionary). I was guiding other university students in the streets, shouting, 'Allahu akbar, Khomeini akbar.' "

Women, I knew, had played a major role in the Revolution. Coming from all social classes, they'd fought not so much for feminist causes as they had to overthrow the regime. Most politically conscious women had assumed, however, that women's rights would be respected after the Revolution.

"I was in support of Khomeini so much," Azar said. "I was working from six in the morning until late at night, in my *chador*, working for *enqelab*. I was thinking that we would have more freedom, poor people would have more money, more jobs."

I identified strongly with what Azar was saying. During my university years, I had taken part in various political demonstrations and spent my summers working with disadvantaged children. My first job had been teaching English to recent immigrants, and for years, I'd toyed with becoming a social worker. If I were Iranian, I thought, chances were good that I, too, would have been *enqelabi*—in which case I might not have survived. In the tumultuous two or three years following the Revolution, many people, aligned with one wrong leader or another, had been killed.

"I made mistakes," Azar said. "So many people like me made mistakes."

She fell silent and gripped the steering wheel.

Some of those mistakes, I thought ruefully, were the mistakes of all youth. Youth who thought they could change the world into something it had never been before. Youth not yet battered around enough to know about deep disappointment and loss and the intractable, insidious nature of injustice in all its multifarious forms.

Before the Revolution, during the reign of Mohammad Reza Shah, women in Iran had gained major political and social rights. In 1963, women had been given the right to vote, and in 1967, the Family Protection Law had been established. Taking issue with the traditional male interpretations of the Qor'an, the law gave women the right to divorce their husbands under certain circumstances, raised the marriage age from 13 to 15, and later 18, and allowed women to serve as judges. Women were also free to dress as they pleased—in short skirts or the *hejab*—and were encouraged to attend the university, work in a wide variety of fields, and serve in government.

But this expansion of women's rights, adapted mostly by the middle and upper classes, did not help with the society's larger, more general problems of human rights violations, poverty, corruption, and the degradation of Iranian culture. As the Shah's regime grew more and more repressive, many educated women began turning away from him and wearing the *chador* as a symbol of protest, both against the regime and against the cultural onslaught of the West.

Ayatollah Khomeini, who'd vehemently opposed giving women the right to vote in 1963, had changed his position by the 1970s. Then, he spoke out in favor of women's rights and encouraged women to demonstrate for the Revolution. Breaking with tradition, he stated that women did not need their male guardian's permission to leave the house for that purpose, and conservative, less educated women poured out into the streets in droves. Meanwhile, their fathers and husbands, who would never have allowed such independence on the say-so of the Shah, nodded their approval. The Ayatollah had spoken. And continues to speak. One of the most positive results of the Revolution is the far greater role that traditional, working-class women now play in public—working, going to school, and even serving in government.

Immediately after the Revolution, educated women were shocked to find many of their hard-won rights gradually being revoked. The *hejab* was made mandatory, the Family Protection Law was suspended, men could once again divorce their wives at will, coeducation in primary and secondary schools ended, and the marriage age was lowered to puberty. Upon reaching age 9, girls were required to wear the full *hejab*, rise for dawn prayers, and fast during Ramadan; boys, considered less mature, weren't required to pray or fast until age 15.

In the years since then, however, women of all classes have fought for and slowly won back some—though far from all—of their former rights, along with a few unexpected others. A man can no longer unilaterally divorce his wife, and a divorced woman has the right to monetary compensation for the years she worked in her husband's home. Women are once again employed as engineers, veterinarians, physicists, and, as of 1998, judges—fields that were closed to them immediately after the Revolution. Sexual segregation has also created an enormous need for more professional women in a wide variety of fields, including teachers and professors, hairdressers, gym instructors, and nurses and doctors. Women now make up about a third of the Iranian workforce, and two-wage-earner families are common. On a professional level, Iranian women have made great strides; it is on the personal level that equality for women falls far short.

"What do you think about Khomeini now?" I asked Azar.

"I think Khomeini was a very big man, a very good man, a gentle man, a kind man. He didn't like war. I met with him once in Qom with another student leader. He said he wanted freedom for all—Muslim, Christian, Zoroastrian."

A small clay-walled village flashed by, followed by a strange brick building with a rounded top that had been built by the Mongols.

"Many of my friends went to war," Azar said. "Many were killed. We didn't know, we thought we were fighting for freedom. I had three brothers studying in England, and when the war started, they came back—they wanted to fight for Iran. One was killed and another lost a leg. And now, is there freedom in Iran? No. For what was all this? So many people coming and going. What is life? Is life important or not? If not, why are we here? If yes, then life is for helping people. Now I don't think about politics. Now I just do my job, take care of my children, take care of my people."

The difficult private struggles as opposed to the celebrated public ones, I thought, imagining the grinding pressures of Azar's daily life today and comparing it to both the excitement of being a student leader and the easier life she could have had living abroad. I remembered the poet Ferdowsi and his story of Seyavash, whose king and father, Kavus, orders him to send hostages taken in good faith after battle back to the Persian court, where they will be killed. Seyavash, who has promised the hostages their safety, cannot in good conscience obey, but he also knows that if he refuses, he will lose both his homeland and his right to the royal throne. Nonetheless, he makes the harder choice:

> He answered them, "The king's command for me
> Is higher than the sun and moon, but nothing—
> Not motes, not lions or elephants—can rise
> Against God's will; the man who disobeys
> His God has wandering wits, he's lost himself."

⟋⟍⟍⟍

We had reached the outskirts of Tus and were driving through a village of disintegrating clay brick walls. Far in the distance, to the east and the west, stretched bumpy mountain ranges, layered in tan. Between us and them extended a windswept plain that seemed more Asian than Iranian to me. The people looked more Asian, too, with flatter, rounder faces, and smaller, more elongated eyes—descendants of the warring tribes of the *Shahnameh*.

The regional capital long before Mashhad, Tus was once a powerful city. But then the Turks and the Mongols came. The city was sacked in 1389 and abandoned in the fifteenth century. Now all that remains are a handful of homes and an eerie ridge of clay running across the plain that marks the ramparts of the ancient citadel.

Ferdowsi was born circa A.D. 940 when Tus was still flourishing. A member of the landed gentry, he spent 35 years writing his masterpiece. Legend has it, however, that his work was not appreciated by the Turkish ruler, Mahmud, who had conquered Khorasan province, and that the poet died a poor and embittered man.

Iranian tourists were bunched up around the gate leading to Ferdowsi's tomb, a large white marble structure standing at the end of a reflecting pool flanked by red roses. To one side was a small museum and to the other a restaurant. Family groups wandered beneath the trees and posed for pictures beside Ferdowsi's statue.

The Shahs Pahlavi had revered the *Shahnameh*, with its celebration of early Persian history, and so in the years immediately following the Revolution, the ayatollahs had tried to debunk the Ferdowsi mystique. Parts of the tomb were defaced, and all inscribed references to kings were covered over with cement. The *Shahnameh* is far too deeply ingrained in the

Iranian collective memory to be erased by anyone, however; for centuries, everyone from preschool age on up has been able to recite at least a few verses, and some, major segments. The Islamic government soon gave up its unpromising campaign, and as our party descended into the spacious tomb, the defacing cement now long gone, I saw two groups of clerics pausing by the poet's gravesite to have their pictures taken and to pray.

We wandered through the tomb and the grounds, with several people coming up to me to welcome me to Iran. Loudspeakers above our heads hummed with the mournful music that precedes *azan*, and I saw a few tourists slip off into quiet corners to pray. Out in the parking lot, families spread out picnics on the hot, shadeless tarmac.

The call to prayer ended and another, more emphatic voice erupted on the loudspeaker. Azar translated for me: Women must wear the *hejab*, boys and girls must not socialize together, and good Muslims do not drink alcohol or take "brown sugar"—that is, opium. If you know someone who does not obey these Islamic laws, please report them by calling the following number.

But except for Azar and me, no one appeared to be listening to the announcement. After centuries of living under despotic rule, most Iranians have a deep distrust of authority and do not inform on one another.

ॐ

Following an enormous lunch of chicken kebab, we drove on, down the bumpy, two-lane "international highway" that runs through Iran between Russia and Afghanistan. We passed by a few small factories manufacturing fruit juice, cheese, and car parts, and a long line of orchards, hidden behind high walls. Mountains zigzagged through a blue haze in the distance as we pulled farther and farther away from human settlement.

The road curved through a wide bright valley and around a bend framed by poplar trees. Then we arrived at another enclosed orchard whose wall had an Islamic Republic logo on top. Azar blew her horn. The orchard belonged to her family and a caretaker lived inside. The logo was for protection. All businesses in Iran prominently display either the logo or, as is more common, pictures of Khomeini, Khamene'i, and Khatami.

An eager, attentive caretaker let us in and brought out carpets, which we spread out between the cars and a squat cement fountain beneath a grove of trees. To my Western eyes, it was a scruffy, even ugly setting. The trees were straggly, the fountain roughly made, and there was no grass. But no one else seemed to notice. To the Persians, who live surrounded by desert, a garden is a garden and always highly prized. Later in my stay, I would visit some of the country's most famous gardens, and although they were certainly more impressive than Azar's orchard, they seldom offered the monumental beauty of the great gardens of the West. Messy rather than manicured, they usually resembled small wildernesses.

We had come to the orchard to take a nap. Most Persians sleep after the midday meal, with many—but far from all—businesses closed between 1 and 5 P.M., before reopening again until 10 or 11 P.M. This often makes for confusion, at least for the foreigner, as it's hard to know which offices and businesses will be closed when. It also explains how Iranians often manage to stay up well past midnight and still arise before dawn to say morning prayers.

The caretaker brought us baskets filled with small apples and grapes from the orchard, all pockmarked with brown spots but far sweeter than any fruits I'd yet tasted in Tehran. Turaj turned the Buick's radio on low and we all lay down, listening to the faint strands of Turkish music mixing with a fresh breeze tousling the leaves above our heads. We women had taken off our *rusaris* for the first time in hours and reveled in our freedom, running our hands through our matted hair. Your hair is so beautiful, the Iranian women called to me—we want it. Well, I want yours, I called back, admiring their thick lustrous manes, shiny in the midafternoon sun.

Bahman fell off to sleep, and a few minutes later, so did Azar. Haji Khanom had retired to the caretaker's cottage, where she'd be cooler, and Sepideh and Azar's daughter had gone off to play. I could hear them whispering, invisible in the trees behind us. Pari massaged Shahla's back, while Lona, Pari, and Shahla gossiped, the baby sleeping peaceably between them.

I stretched out, trying to find a comfortable spot on the hard, bumpy earth. But I didn't want to fall asleep or even daydream. I just wanted to hold the world still, the pale sky above, the dry earth below, while the voices of Iran washed over me. The past, the present, and the past again, reaching back thousands of years.

An hour or so later, the caretaker was back, this time with large cups of steaming tea. We drank the fragrant brew, and then left the orchard, to drive on through the wide valley, now filled with lengthening shadows, and climb up into foothills. We passed through one mud-walled village after another, stopping now and again for me to take pictures of *chador*-clad women riding donkeys, boys herding flocks of sheep, and old men dressed in traditional Persian tunics with black wool caps. Every time I asked to stop, Azar nodded her approval. I would take the exact same photographs you do, she said—you and I are much alike.

The unpaved road grew bumpier and bumpier as flat, purple mountains rose like cardboard cutouts around us, and the air turned crisp and cool. Then we entered an especially large village and Azar began stopping every 50 feet. She seemed to know everyone. One young woman asked for help finding a job. A middle-aged man asked for help getting his son into high school. Another man asked for medical assistance for his wife. Azar promised them all that she would do what she could.

As she did so, she drew on an air of authority that hadn't been there before. Azar is a powerful woman, I suddenly realized, remembering the many phone calls she'd been making on her mobile phone all day.

Before the Revolution, it turned out, Azar's father had owned the village we were now passing through. Such proprietorship had once been common among wealthy Iranians, and in true feudal fashion, Azar's father, like his father before him, had provided his villagers with everything they needed, from electricity to a health clinic, in return for their labor. Now that he was dead, Azar—not her brothers, not her husband—had taken over his responsibilities. She no longer had the same financial resources that her father had had—the Revolution had seen to that—but she still had influence and power. Especially since she was *enqelabi,* or a revolutionary. A white card in her file in a government office identified her as such.

We passed by small dark shops lit by round fluorescent lightbulbs hanging on strings, wooden ladders leading from one flat mud roof to another, and people squatting in a tea shop, smoking the *ghalyan,* or hubble-bubble. Smoking the three-foot-tall water pipe, with its bulbous belly and skinny stem, is indulged in by both sexes in Iran, and many people while away long afternoons on its mild tobacco high.

At the edge of the village snaked a dirt road that led to the Tabataba'i family villa, perched on a cliff surrounded by zigzagging purple peaks. Beneath the cliff lolled a lush valley ripe with walnut, almond, pear, apple, and plum trees.

After Azar had parked the car, we walked out onto a porch overlooking the valley. The villa itself was boarded up, doors and windows covered with raw ugly wood. Once, the Tabataba'is had spent nearly every weekend here, relaxing and entertaining friends, and it was easy to imagine the bright lights, infectious laughter, and huge platters of food that must have filled the place then. Now, the family only drove out a few times a year.

Haji Khanom left the group and wandered away into a small clump of trees—a lone figure wrapped in dark blue. Sadly, I wondered what exactly she was remembering. She and her family had lost a great deal after the Revolution. The Islamic government had confiscated almost all of their property, and her husband, who'd been a high-ranking government official under the Shah, had spent his last days running a small factory. One son had died during the Iran–Iraq War, and a second son and a daughter had emigrated. And still, she had to count herself lucky. Only Azar's work as an *enqelabi* had saved her and her family from losing much more.

༺❀༻

The next evening, at 9 P.M., all 11 of us stood at the edge of Beit al-Moghaddas Square, a small fountain dancing immediately before us, the domes of the Holy Precinct of Imam Reza resplendent in the darkness far ahead. It had taken us nearly three hours to get dressed, gather the children and Haji Khanom together, pile into the cars, and find two parking spots—parking in downtown Mashhad is as difficult as in Midtown Manhattan. But we had finally made it and stood primped and preened, dressed in our best beneath our *hejab*—no matter that no one would see.

I watched mesmerized by the traffic around us. The streets were teeming with Shi'ites from all over the world. Pakistanis in sandals and loose-fitting tunics and pants. Afghans in brown suits and turbans with loose strands hanging like pigtails down their backs. Syrians in flowing white caftans. Bevies of women in the ubiquitous *chador*. Mullahs of all shapes and sizes—one old and frail in a black turban and worn cape, another short and pudgy with thick glasses and a bushy beard, and a third tall, lean, and breathtakingly handsome as he picked his way across the street in fine yellow slippers, his gauzy black cape billowing out behind him like a puff of smoke.

And then there was the vehicular traffic, honking and screeching around the traffic circle beneath neon signs advertising tourist hotels. Cars, buses, and trucks in varying stages of disrepair swept by, along with mullahs on motorcycles, mullahs on bicycles, and mullahs crowded five or six together in listing Peykans. By the sides of the circle bustled men, dressed in blue, sweeping up litter; in the middle lounged two Revolutionary Guards, their

Kalashnikovs propped up on their thighs as they leaned back against their car. Two other guards were searching a scrawny man in the cab of a truck nearby. Apparently, he'd been accused of pickpocketing. Tears streamed down his poverty-ravaged face as the guards tore off his shirt.

Crossing the street, we entered the tourist bazaar, where men and women were jostling rudely together as they examined the wares—garish wall hangings quoting the Qor'an, prayer rugs embroidered with the outline of the Imam Reza shrine, heart-shaped prayer stones made of Mashhad earth. In one shop, you could get your picture taken beside a cardboard Khomeini, and in another, you could purchase Halloween masks imported from the West. Azar insisted on buying me a small turquoise ring, while Pari bought two new pillowcases—in the hopes that she might marry again, Bahman whispered. I bought myself a pendant inscribed with a verse from the Qor'an; it would bring me luck, Azar told me. One time she'd been wearing a similar pendant on a flight to Singapore. The plane had caught fire and the pilot had said there was nothing he could do. Everyone else started screaming, but Azar remained calm and began writing out the pendant's verse over and over again. Watching her, her Spanish seatmate had said that if her prayers were answered, he would fly her to Spain for a free vacation, and Azar was still hoping to take him up on it.

I didn't know what to make of the story. It had the ring of superstitious fable, but this was Azar I was speaking to. She was no fool.

Leaving the bazaar, we started down the long walk to the Holy Precinct of Imam Reza. Construction surrounded us—evidently the city was building a new parking lot—and so after several blocks, we were forced to turn onto a stony path that led us down dark twisting alleys lined with mudbrick buildings. Dozens of other pilgrims were marching along with us, footsteps sounding loud in the near dead of night, as en masse we passed by a hole-in-the-wall store selling fresh ribbon candy and a blazing hot bakery where men were slapping *sangak* onto nails on a wall to cool.

At the main gate to the shrine, we women checked our handbags and put on *chadors* over our *manteaus* and *rusaris*. This was the first time that I had donned the long, slippery, semicircular garment, and it weighed down surprisingly heavily on my head. Lona and Pari had to help me position it correctly, and then, while the others expertly grasped their *chadors* with one hand at the chin, Lona fastened mine with a pin. As on my first day in Iran, I felt like a child again.

We proceeded through the tented "Sisters Entrance," where Lona was ordered to wipe the makeup off her face and an angry fuss was made over seven-year-old Sepideh, who one guard said was too old to enter the shrine covered only in a *rusari*. I kept my face assiduously down throughout the search. According to everything that I'd read, non-Muslims weren't allowed to enter the shrine's innermost sanctum, and I was afraid that someone might stop me here, at the main gate. It was close to 11 P.M.—no time to be a tourist.

But no one noticed me and we passed through without further incident, to join a sparse crowd moving slowly along a wide circular walkway in the direction of the holy shrine. The entire holy precinct is a large walled island, complete with multiple courtyards, mosques, prayer halls, and other buildings, but the holy shrine, where Imam Reza is buried, is the main attraction. Overhead, a near full moon was glowing, its white light obliterating the golden light of the domes and minarets. Down at foot level, however, it was dark.

We passed by a bank of telephones—all free, Azar said, provided for excited pilgrims to call home—and a group of young girls skipping arm in arm. Boys were racing or playing tag while the grown-ups were bending their heads closely together, laughing under their breaths. Everyone was on holiday.

Turning a corner, we saw a new blaze of lights marking the promenade that led to the Imam's tomb. Several young clerics were sitting beneath the lights, reading the Qor'an, while drumbeats sounded from somewhere. In earlier times, *naqqara*, or kettledrums, were beaten whenever the kings had announcements to make; now, the drums are a regular feature at the shrine, beaten at dawn, sunset, and—as presumably was happening now—whenever a sick pilgrim is healed.

At the end of the promenade towered thick wooden doors, which all the pilgrims touched, and many kissed, as they passed. I, too, ran my hand along the shiny wood as I neared the threshold—to do otherwise would have been to call attention to myself. We were getting closer and closer to the inner sanctum and I was becoming less and less certain about whether I should be here. My Lonely Planet guidebook read, "Do *not* attempt to enter the Holy Shrine unless you are a Muslim, and can prove it (probably in Farsi) if asked," and I didn't want to be disrespectful of Islam. But when I mentioned my concerns to Azar, for the second or third time that evening, she just shrugged, also for the second or third time, and I decided that if my presence didn't bother her, Shahla, and Haji Khanom—

all devout Muslims—then my transgression couldn't be all that serious.

I passed beyond the wooden doors, surrounded by dark heads and hoods, most shorter than I, and then stopped, astonished. Before me stretched a large, roiling courtyard that the half-empty promenade had not prepared me for. Every inch of the expanse was teeming with slight bearded men, rounder *chador*-clad women, and children of all ages sitting, standing, praying, talking, eating, and sleeping on carpets, cushions, and blankets. Voices, laughter, whispers, and cries swirled from one end of the courtyard to the other, beneath a parapet that stood out starkly against the stars. A soft hazy light illuminated some of the walls' arcades, hinting at intricate mosaics too dark to make out, whereas others were completely engulfed in black.

Each side of the courtyard had its own *eivan*, or arched open hall, while in the middle stood gilded fountains in which people were performing ablutions—washing their hands, face, and feet, in preparation for prayer. All the arched halls were distinctive, but dominating everything was the blazing southern *eivan*, on fire with the reflected light of thousands of gold-coated silver bricks.

To one side of the *eivan* huddled the disabled or seriously ill. Some were weeping, but most seemed beyond grief—still, frightened, and yet tenaciously hopeful. In the narrow spaces between their thin forms crowded wheelchairs, crutches, and artificial limbs. One small teenager with stumps for legs sat swaying silently from side to side, his white face tight as a fist.

"Here you are alone," Azar said to me. "You have no country. You have no family. Just Imam Reza and Allah."

Leaving Bahman, Haji Khanom, and the baby behind to wait for us by the fountain, we passed through another set of wooden doors. The crowds around us thickened to the density of tapioca as we all bobbed and bumped our way along, before finally slipping into the women's entrance, where we relinquished our shoes. I gave mine to Lona to hand in. I didn't want anyone to see my face.

I thought of Robert Byron, a writer and architecture buff distantly related to Lord Byron. Robert Byron had traveled through Iran in 1933 and visited the holy shrine disguised as a working-class Persian. But his visit had been extremely brief. Almost as soon as he'd entered, he'd left again, afraid that the other pilgrims had grown suspicious of him. I had no idea how many non-Muslims had visited the holy shrine since then, but I knew that it couldn't be too many. Except for the occasional scholar, VIP, or illicit visitor such as myself, the inner sanctum had been off-limits to non-Muslims even before the Revolution. I felt extremely privileged to be here. My heart was racing.

Inside, the octagonal anteroom leading to the tomb was a riot of shrouded murmuring flesh. Hundreds of women in black and white *chadors* were sitting, bowing, or crouching turtle-backed on the floor, reading the Qor'an or saying prayers. There was no passageway between them and so to cross the room, we had to step over one back after another, hoping each time that the woman wouldn't suddenly reach that part of the prayer that caused her to stand up. I lost my balance several times and felt several strange women grab at my *chador* when they, too, almost went down. Broken prayer stones were scattered here and there, and strong whiffs of stockinged feet rose in the air. Walls and ceilings swirled with arabesques tumbling through turquoise tiles.

And then I saw the sunken shrine room itself, its walls dazzling with blues of every persuasion beneath an arched ceiling of mirrored mosaics. A big grilled tomb with a gilded roof sat in the middle under a bright green chandelier. But it wasn't the room that captured my attention. Before me seethed a sea of tightly packed women screaming, wailing, and waving arms pale as tentacles in the air. Writhing from side to side like an enormous tortured beast, they seemed to be sucked up against each other, the tomb, and the walls. Some women had climbed onto other women's backs. Some women's faces were sheets of tears. One woman dove out into the crowd, to be momentarily caught by her neighbors before landing on her feet. Others tied their *chadors* around their waists before plunging in. The smell of rose water overpowered the smell of stockinged feet.

"Do you want to go closer?" Azar shouted above the roar.

"Are you crazy?" I shouted back. I felt as if I was suffocating as it was, with women crashing against me like waves and almost tearing off my *chador*. For the first time in the presence of Islam, I felt frightened, but not so much because of what could happen to me—Azar and the others were nearby and I felt safe inside my *chador*. Rather, I felt frightened because here before me raged the raw fanatical power of Islam—the power that could turn an otherwise peace-loving people into a violent, wild-eyed horde.

"Look at the wall," Azar shouted, and I looked at the sheet of Plexiglas that separated the women's side from the men's. On top of it gleamed watches, bracelets, necklaces, and rings.

"Pure silver and gold," Azar shouted, and I realized that the jewelry had been donated to the shrine, along with the millions of *tomans* that had been shoved into the tomb. Sometimes, I'd been told, and now wholeheartedly believed, the tomb was filled to the brim with cash.

Azar, Lona, and I would return to the holy precinct the next day to take a closer look at its exquisite mosaics, visit the cavernous hall where pilgrims are served free meals, and tour the underground cemeteries where wealthy Shi'ites who've paid a small fortune to be near Imam Reza are buried. We would also meander through a peaceful, sun-splashed courtyard, filled with thousands of silent believers neatly lined up in rows. A bearded cleric would be speaking, his quiet, measured voice wafting out, and watching, I would have a hard time equating the humbly bent heads before him with the screaming, hysterical women I saw before me now. Two of the many sides of Islam.

Retreating back to the anteroom, which now seemed almost peaceful, we somehow squeezed out a space for ourselves on the floor—Azar and the others wanted to pray. About ten feet to our left sat an old mullah, the only male in the room, who was speaking with a young woman with a troubled look on her face.

"He is here to answer religious questions," Azar said, noticing me notice him. "And for *sigheh.*"

ஃஒ

Sigheh, or *mut'a,* is the exclusively Shi'ite custom of temporary marriage. Usually sanctioned by a cleric, it can last as little as an hour and as long as 99 years, with the man usually paying a mutually agreed-on bride-price to the woman. Temporary marriage does not obligate the husband to provide financial support for his wife, but if a child is conceived by their union, it is considered to be fully legitimate and theoretically has the same rights of inheritance as do its half siblings born of a permanent marriage. A Shi'ite man is allowed to have several temporary wives at the same time, in addition to four permanent wives, but a Shi'ite woman can have only one husband—permanent or temporary—at a time. *Sigheh* is also used to solve infertility problems, to allow a Shi'ite man to marry a non-Muslim woman, and to allow a woman to appear without the *hejab* (but fully clothed; no sex involved) in front of an otherwise forbidden man, such as a relative sharing the same house.

Though for the most part a marginalized activity, *sigheh* has been a hotly debated subject in Iran since 1990, when then-President Hashemi Rafsanjani made a speech in which he urged war widows and young people who had not yet earned enough money for marriage to engage in *sigheh*. Most middle- and upper-class Iranians took vehement issue with the president's comments, equating temporary marriages with legalized prostitution and the degradation of women. On the opposite side, more conservative elements argued that *sigheh* was a religiously legitimate way of taking care of human needs—and far more just than the alternatives of prostitution and "free love."

Though it might seem ironic to many Westerners, Islam abhors celibacy, which it regards as evil and unnatural, and celebrates sexual enjoyment, which is the publicly acknowledged objective of *sigheh*. In fact, the *hejab* is meant not to negate a woman's sexuality but rather to protect it—and to guard men against its inordinate power. Women are regarded as highly sexual creatures. "Almighty God created sexual desire in ten parts; then he gave nine parts to women and one to men," said Imam Ali, according to popular belief.

In the privacy of her home, the married woman is encouraged to make herself beautiful for her husband, to wear slinky clothes and sexy lingerie. Both married women and men are urged to enjoy sex in all its variations, including extensive foreplay, which according to tradition, the Prophet himself recommended. "When any one of you has sex with his wife," he said, "then he should not go to them like birds; instead he should be slow and delaying." Islam also has few sexual taboos for married couples (though gay and extramarital liaisons are strictly forbidden) and is one of the only religions to include sex as a reward of afterlife—though only for men.

Islam's celebration of sex makes a lot more sense to me than does the Christian monastic tradition, I thought as I watched the old mullah. And to some degree, *sigheh* also makes sense. A temporary marriage contract is preferable to prostitution. But the trouble with *sigheh* is that—like many other things—it sounds better in theory than it operates in practice. Yes, *sigheh* promises to protect potentially illegitimate children, and yes, it provides widowed, divorced, and poorer women—its most frequent female practitioners—with legally sanctioned physical and financial pleasures. But most Iranian women are still expected to be virgins when they permanently marry and men sometimes deny the paternity of their *sigheh* children.

Though no one knows how common *sigheh* is in Iran, most everyone agrees that it is most prevalent in the holy cities of Mashhad and Qom, because of their large transient populations. Like adultery in the West, *sigheh* is not socially acceptable in most parts of Iran, and so those who indulge frequently do so while on vacation—which in Iran often means a pilgrimage. Said to be the most frequent practitioners of *sigheh* are the clerics themselves, who have more opportunities than do most Iranians to visit the holy sites. More than one person warned me to be on my guard against lecherous mullahs, and at one point I was approached, albeit in a roundabout fashion, by a jolly cleric in Qom, who suggested that we travel together to Esfahan, where he knew a nice, private hotel.

Sometimes, a woman interested in *sigheh* wears her *chador* inside out and lingers by certain well-known spots. Two common pickup points in Mashhad are said to be the grill overlooking the Imam's tomb and the Plexiglas wall inside the holy shrine. I had kept my eyes open at both these sites during my visit but had seen nothing out of the ordinary.

Common rumor in Mashhad also has it that there is—or once was—an office on a main street near the shrine equipped with several photo books. Each book supposedly contains pictures of sexually available women, all carefully covered with the *hejab*, and their bride-prices. According to one popular joke, one day a man from the provinces comes in and chooses a picture. Later that evening, he arrives for his assignation at the designated hotel room, only to find his scantily clad wife waiting for him. He had failed to recognize her photographed in her *hejab*.

Not surprisingly, one of the by-products of *sigheh* is said to be sexually transmitted disease—an unacknowledged problem in Iran. One of Bahman's medical colleagues, who'd specialized in sexually transmitted disease while studying abroad, told me that he'd heard of many cases of syphilis, gonorrhea, and AIDS in Mashhad, Qom, and Tehran. But he could give me no hard facts because he had not been allowed to practice his specialty since his return to Iran. His was not a reputable field, the Islamic government had told him, and besides, syphilis, gonorrhea, and AIDS did not exist in Iran—it was an Islamic country.

When my companions had finished praying, we left the holy shrine, picked up the rest of our party, and exited the complex. Stepping outside the main gate, I took off my *chador*, relieved to be free of the heavy fabric, and folded it over my arm. As I adjusted my *rusari*, I noticed two young women eyeing me angrily. They turned to whisper to their companions, and suddenly, four or five women were staring angrily at me, their eyes stone cold. Cover yourself again, Azar whispered, and then she and the others closed protective ranks around me and we hurried away.

࿐࿐࿐

At my request, there'd been talk of going to Neishabur to visit the grave of another famous Persian writer, Omar Khayyam, whose name means "Omar the Tentmaker." Born about A.D. 1047, Khayyam is best known in Iran as a mathematician and astronomer—he developed the first solution to the quadratic equation and reformed the Iranian calendar to correct its accuracy to within 1 day in every 5,000 years. But in the West, Khayyam is best known as a poet. In 1859, writer Edward FitzGerald loosely translated Khayyam's *Rubáiyát* into English, and the book became a phenomenal best-seller, influencing many major poets of the day, including Dante Gabriel Rossetti and Robert Browning. It is to Khayyam that we owe the line "A Jug of Wine, a Loaf of Bread—and Thou." One of his most famous stanzas reads:

Oh, come with old Khayyam, and leave the Wise
To talk; one thing is certain, that Life flies;
One thing is certain, and the Rest is Lies;
The Flower that once has blown for ever dies.

Because aside from the holy precinct, Mashhad has little to offer in the way of tourist attractions, I'd assumed that I'd have plenty of time to visit Khayyam's grave as well as Ferdowsi's. As it turned out, however, there were complications.

First of all, I couldn't go by myself. That was apparently out of the question. I was an honored guest, and the family couldn't possibly have me wandering about by myself. They would have to come with me—all of them.

Then again, the family was tired from our earlier excursions. They didn't really want to organize another expedition. Wouldn't I reconsider? We could just stay home and enjoy one another's company instead.

For two whole days? I thought—but didn't say. As far as I was concerned, we'd already spent quite a bit of time just staying home and enjoying one another's company. And if I couldn't go by myself, why couldn't Lona come with me? She wanted to go, too.

No, that was apparently just as bad. Lona was a guest, too. If I really wanted to go that much, Azar and her son Turaj would take me. We would leave the next morning at 8 A.M. The drive to Neishabur took a little over two hours.

But the next day, Bahman decided that he wanted to come, too, and because he had medical conferences in the morning, we wouldn't be able to leave until about noon. That sounded fine to me. We'd still have plenty of time.

Little did I know. In Iran, even the best-laid plans have a tendency to dissipate under the weight of long, lazy mornings and afternoons spent drinking tea, gossiping with family and friends, and vaguely running errands and doing housework. In Iran, there's always plenty of time until it suddenly runs out.

Azar and I did pick Bahman up at noon, but then we had to eat lunch, and lunch was not ready until 1:30—Haji Khanom was cooking a special stew. And after lunch, we had to take a nap, of course. Everyone was very sorry, but I could see, couldn't I, that there just wasn't enough time to go to Neishabur today? Perhaps tomorrow.

While we were waiting for lunch, Shahla's husband, who'd been on business in Tehran, arrived, pausing outside the living room to give Lona and Pari enough time to cover themselves. Haji Ali is very *hezbollahi*, Azar whispered to me before he entered the room, and he had once been an important officer in the Revolutionary Guards.

A tall man with a paunch and round bearded face, Haji Ali greeted me warmly and asked me a few friendly questions. He laughed and joked a lot. But as our visit wore on, I also sensed that he could be a bully and had a fierce temper hidden beneath his congenial demeanor. The women and children seemed afraid of him; Turaj had turned off the radio, tuned to a forbidden Turkish station, when he'd entered the room.

Prior to our arrival in Mashhad, the Tabataba'is had assured us that they'd have no trouble booking our return flights to Tehran. But now it appeared there was a problem—this was the height of the tourist season, hadn't we realized that? Haji Ali, Shahla, and I spent all that afternoon visiting one travel agency after another in search of tickets, but all we were able to locate was one for Bahman. The rest of us would just have to stay in Mashhad a few extra days.

I fretted. I didn't have a few extra days. I had an appointment at the Ministry of Tourism in two days regarding my visa, which would run out in less than a week.

"What about trains?" I asked Azar when we got back to the house.

"Sold out," she said.

"Buses?" I asked.

"I will try," she said, looking dubious.

⊰०ॐ

After our nap, the men went off somewhere, and as the last of their voices retreated out the door, I felt the atmosphere in the house relax. The place once again belonged to us women, and as we proceeded to while away the afternoon drinking tea, eating fruit, and gossiping, I thought about how much modern womankind has lost. Yes, we women can now become doctors, lawyers, and company presidents; make a lot of money or a name for ourselves; compete in the puffed-up, self-important world of men. But what about gentle, lazy, companionable afternoons like this? What about exchanging ideas and advice, and learning how to cope with life from one another? What about simply enjoying the company of other women? But no modern Western woman, least of all me, has the time for that anymore, and even if we did, we wouldn't do it. It would seem too idle, too boring, and depending on our temperament, we'd soon have to get up to go to a movie or on a shopping expedition or to a bar to look for men.

Azar brushed and braided her daughter's hair while Shahla looked at a fashion magazine, and Pari and Lona told us more about their failed marriages. Pari had been married at age 15 and divorced eight months later. She'd barely known her husband before or even after marriage because he'd spent most nights out with his friends, smoking opium. Lona had married at age 20 and divorced seven years later. Her husband had been a good man, but he hadn't earned enough money to support his family yet refused to get a second job, as most Iranians did, and wouldn't let Lona work, either. Now he paid nothing for child support, and although Lona was gainfully employed, she worried that if she remarried, he'd try to take Sepideh away from her. Under Islamic law, men have automatic custody of children in divorce cases, and though a woman can take her husband to court over the issue, she must be able to prove he is an unfit father. Lona did have a clause in her divorce contract giving her custody of Sepideh, but still she worried.

As Lona spoke, I thought about what one older woman in Tehran had told me. Women have changed a lot since the Revolution, she said— they've become more independent, they can take care of themselves, they've grown up. Yet men haven't changed much at all. They're still just like their grandfathers. They still think they have the right to tell their wives what to do and what to wear and to reprimand them if they talk too loudly. They still think a woman's main job is to keep a man happy.

Both Pari and Lona had been smart, Azar said to me in English while the conversation continued around us in Persian, not to stay in their home-town of Tabriz after their divorces. Though divorce was now common in Iran and younger divorced women often remarried, the gossip about divor-cées anywhere except Tehran was horrendous. She should know. After her divorce from her first husband, the neighbors' malicious gossip had rail-roaded her and her parents into arranging her second marriage far too quickly. She'd known next to nothing about her second husband before marrying him; theirs was not a "love marriage."

"Where is your husband?" I said. "Why haven't I met him?"

Azar shrugged. "He is working, he goes with friends."

I hesitated and then asked, "Other women?"

"No, but we don't talk. We have no love." She sighed and kissed her daughter. The braiding was finished. "Sometimes I think, 'Why me? Why not love for me?' My brother, he married for love, and it is very, very beau-tiful. I wish for love for me."

I wanted to tell her that she still had time. She was only 37. But I knew that chances were she didn't have time—or opportunity. That was just my American optimism speaking.

"I am old now," she said, as if reading my thoughts.

"Not so old," I said. I couldn't let that optimism go.

"Middle," she said. "We are both middle."

She passed me a basket of apples that had come from her orchard.

"What about you?" she said. "Do you and Jerry have a love marriage?"

"I guess so . . ." I said, a little startled. Lona had apparently told Azar about Jerry. "But we're not married."

"You are lucky. I think most people in the West are lucky. I think most people in the West have a love marriage?" She looked at me hopefully, questioningly.

I didn't know where to begin. "Well, more people than here at least," I said at last. "But you know, even in the West, love isn't so easy to find. Many of my friends aren't married or even—"

"But why not?"

"I don't know exactly why not." How could I possibly explain? "But maybe it's because many people in the West are very self-absorbed. We only think about ourselves and what we want, and don't want to bother with anyone else. We want to be young forever, have fun, go out with many people—"

Azar was staring at me, trying to understand, but I knew that what I was saying didn't compute. For the most part, Iran doesn't have a "singles scene"; most people are married by age 25.

"Plus, it's hard to meet people," I said, and then realized how ridiculous that sounded. In Iran, where young single men and women can't even have coffee together in a café, it's hard to meet people. What exactly was it again that we in the West were always complaining about?

"But there are many love marriages?" Azar asked again, more insistently, and when I finally nodded yes, she smiled, a dreamy look coming into her eyes.

She needs to believe in it, I realized ruefully—despite all her strengths and many accomplishments. Someplace there is a land where people are in love.

The doorbell rang, and Bita arrived. A striking, outgoing woman with thick dark eyebrows, she had known Azar since their university days together as *enqelabi*s. But her revolutionary status hadn't helped her much during her first marriage, she said, on hearing the topic of our conversation. Shortly after their wedding, her husband had started locking her into her room. Yes, you are *enqelabi*, he'd said to her, but you come from a bad family—your father is rich. Somehow Bita had found a way to escape and take her husband to divorce court, but the clerics had supported him, not her, and he'd continued locking her in for another six months. Only after taking a second wife had he finally let her go.

By law, every Iranian woman has the right to include a clause in her marriage contract giving her the power to initiate divorce on 12 different grounds, including her husband's failure to provide maintenance, desertion, and life-threatening physical abuse. The Islamic government itself makes available to all marrying couples a model marriage contract that includes this clause. However, many of Iran's family courts routinely rule in favor of men, and women cannot initiate divorce for such flimsy reasons as incompatibility or "routine" physical or mental abuse.

A Muslim woman who marries can keep her own money and property and take it with her on divorce. While married, she can also demand that her husband pay her for her housework, refuse to work outside the home, and refuse to breast-feed her child, in which case her husband has to hire a wet nurse. Some less educated women don't know about these rights, however, and others are too intimidated to insist on them.

Most other Islamic laws are heavily weighted in favor of men. A woman's testimony in court is worth only half that of a man's, and if a woman is murdered or accidentally killed, the "blood money" that must be paid to her family is only half that of what must be paid to a man's. Daughters inherit only one half of what their brothers inherit, and widows, one fourth of their husband's estate if he has no children and one eighth if he has children. Iran's Passport Law, which was also in effect under the Shah, requires that a woman obtain written, notarized permission from her male guardian (usually her father or husband) whenever she wishes to leave the country.

The heft of tradition weighs heavily on some Iranian women as well. Tradition—not Islam—states that an ideal woman should be seen, not heard; should remain uneducated and in the home; and should be self-effacing, passive, and at the beck and call of men.

After Bita finished telling her story, there was a long moment of silence and then Shahla fetched fresh cups of tea. Haji Khanom, who'd been cooking in the kitchen, turned on a lamp.

Azar started laughing. "I know the story of one Iranian man who married an English lady," she said, "and after 11 years, he went to court for a divorce. He said, 'She must pay me much money—she has turned my hair white.' How crazy is this country?"

Lona started laughing. "I have one friend who is not allowed to visit her family. Her husband is angry because her family took too many pictures at their wedding. 'Your family is too Western,' he said. 'We don't do that in Iran.' "

Bita started laughing. "I know one woman who can't even take a bath without her husband's permission."

Looking from one woman to the other, now all doubled over with giggles, I made a feeble attempt to join in, while both wondering at their mirth and realizing that it was one of their only outlets. Powerless to change much of anything, they could at least enjoy the absurdity of their situation.

"You see," Azar said, turning to me with tears in her eyes. "I told you you are lucky."

"I know," I said, feeling guilty.

"No, really. I mean it. You are very, very lucky. You should thank Allah."

I fell silent. My acknowledgment of luck had been automatic, not deeply felt. If I couldn't even imagine what it would be like to be an independent woman like Shirin in Tehran, I certainly couldn't imagine what it would be like to be a married woman in the provinces. I was so used to going my own way, living as I pleased. I didn't even have children to tie me down.

"Eastern people are not like Western people," Azar said.

"No," I said, a bit discouraged, contemplating the gulf between us.

"But I think you are like Eastern people. You have kind heart, hot body, like us. My son Turaj feels it, too."

I didn't know what to say. I felt enormously touched, even though I wasn't quite sure what Azar meant by "hot body"—or what evidence she had of mine. Not that I wanted an explanation. I liked the phrase the way it was.

Bita left, and afternoon turned into evening. Haji Khanom took away the bowls of fruit and replaced them with *nabat*, a crystallized sugar from Mashhad, and crispy cookies from Tabriz. Every city in Iran has its own special sweet, with Tabriz being the acknowledged capital, as many candy factories are located there. Qom is known for *sohan*, a pistachio brittle flavored with saffron, and Yazd for *baklava*. Esfahan is the home of *gaz*, a nougat flavored with rose water and pistachios, and Kerman offers treats made of dates. Saffron-flavored ice cream can be found all over the country, while Mashhad and Esfahan are known for *faludeh*—a strange frozen treat made of starch, sugar, and rose water that looks like a pile of spaghetti and tastes like perfumed ice milk.

Slowly, the conversation turned to religion. Lona and Pari wanted to know more about the Imam Reza shrine, and Azar and Shahla had many, many tales to tell, only parts of which I understood. As I sat back, watching and listening, I thought of the *Arabian Nights*, which is part Persian in origin, and narrated by a woman, Scheherazade, who succeeds in saving her life by spinning tales for a tyrannical king. Storytelling among women in Iran has a long tradition. The Tabataba'i sisters professed their stories to be true, but to me, they had the rhythm and cadence of folk tales.

When Azar did finally translate for me, she told one story of a foreign lady, terminally ill with a mysterious disease, who'd traveled to the holy shrine. Falling asleep in front of the Imam's tomb, she dreamed of meeting a man who said, follow me, before moving out into the courtyard. Waking up, the lady traced the path the man had taken in her dream and was miraculously cured. Next came the story of a woman with cancer in one of her fingers. Her doctor had advised her to chop it off, but she was resisting, and one afternoon in the bank, she met an old man with a long white beard. He gave her two pieces of sugar, of which she ate one, and the cancer vanished.

While Azar was telling this story, Shahla slipped off to pray. Out of the corner of my eye, I saw her don her white prayer *chador* and stand stock-still, cupping her hands to her ears. Despite the noisy presence of all of us in the neighboring room, she seemed completely private, self-enclosed, alone. An invisible veil, much more impenetrable than the cloth itself, had cast itself around her, in a way that seemed extraordinary to me. It would be a good thing, I thought as I watched her, to be able to do that.

As Shahla knelt to the ground, her forehead on a prayer stone, Azar told about the sacred hour she'd once spent working in the holy precinct. To work there is a great honor, she said, not granted to just anyone, and many influential doctors, lawyers, managers, and government officials volunteered to do menial labor for Imam Reza. Once, she'd even seen a former minister of state pushing a broom. Azar's influence had been enough to buy her only one hour's worth of work, but during that hour, she'd had the enormous good fortune to see a blind boy be cured.

"So maybe you understand," she said to me, "why I can never leave this city. I like Imam Reza so much. So very much. I go to him two, three times a week, very late, at night. It is quiet. I can pray. I am lucky."

ॐ✿

Haji Ali had bad news. In Afghanistan, the Taliban had killed the Iranian diplomats and journalist. No one knew exactly what that would mean, but he thought that I should leave Mashhad the next day, as originally planned. He didn't want the responsibility of having an American in his house should anything happen. He'd get me on an army transport if he had to.

But Azar had already located a bus ticket for me. I'd be leaving the next evening at 10 P.M. to arrive in Tehran by 7 A.M., in time for my appointment at the Ministry of Tourism. Bahman would be flying out that same evening, and Lona, Pari, and Sepideh would be leaving by bus the following day. Bahman didn't want them remaining in Mashhad any longer than they had to, either.

Before I left, the Tabataba'is performed a traditional departure ceremony for me. On a tray they placed a mirror, sugar, and the Qor'an, and held the tray over my head as I passed beneath it three times. Then they had me look in the mirror, for light; kiss the Qor'an, for guidance; and eat a piece of sugar, for happiness. As I left the house, they poured out a glass of water after me, to ensure my safe return, and warned me not to reenter. If I did, bad luck would certainly follow.

We drove to the bus station, passing by an army base on the way. I could see no movement there at all, and at first I thought that that was a good sign—the reports of hostility must be exaggerated, I concluded. But then I wondered if perhaps the opposite was true—maybe everyone was at the front.

WE GO TO TRIP—GOOD BYE, WELCOM TRIP, YA MOHAMMAD (OH, MOHAM-MAD) read the signs in English on the backs and sides of the buses, as we fought our way through the crowds to find Azar's "connection"—the man who had somehow located a ticket for me. Azar insisted on paying for it and put me on a spic-and-span vehicle, run by the country's top bus cooperative, with a red Persian carpet runner lining the aisle and red plastic trash buckets swinging beneath every other row of seats. Each seat was also equipped with a plastic-wrapped drinking cup and a snowy seat cover. Above the driver hung a modern TV on which we would later watch the English comedy show *Mr. Bean*—a favorite in Iran—and an Iranian crime drama.

"From now on," Azar said to me. "Don't talk to anyone. It is better."

Oh, no, I thought, not Azar, too.

"Really," she said. "I mean it. It is dangerous for you."

"All right," I said, but only to please her.

We kissed three times on alternating cheeks and hugged for a long moment. Neither one of us wanted to say good-bye. Then I promised that I would write and Azar made me promise that if Jerry and I were to marry, I would send her a wedding invitation. "I will come—really," she said, clasping my hands.

As the bus pulled out of the station, the blaze of Mashhad receded and a midnight blue descended. A man in a crisp striped shirt walked down the aisle, handing out bottles of Coca-Cola and small cakes. I'm alone at last, I thought, and then sighed contentedly and stretched out my legs. No one could even sit down beside me. The bus had a double row of seats on one side, a single row on the other, and I was in one of the single seats. For the next ten blissful hours, I didn't have to smile or talk or listen to anyone. I could just think and sleep and daydream . . .

Though I did have one short conversation with the *chador*-clad woman sitting behind me, after she offered me half a sandwich and inquired where I was from. She and her four daughters, all high school and university students, were returning from their annual visit to Imam Reza. For three days, they'd done nothing but visit the holy shrine from early morning until late at night—as did most pilgrims in Mashhad, she said.

As our conversation died down, I thought about what Azar had said about not talking to anyone on the bus. And about what Bahman had said about Babak's possibly being a spy—and others thinking I was a spy. And about what Mr. Shiravi in the press office, Mr. Zamani back in New York, and numerous friends of friends had said about not traveling alone in Iran. All their admonitions didn't have as much to do with real danger, I was beginning to realize—though that could also be there—as they did with distrust. Like the warring tribes of the *Shahnameh,* and the early Persians who hid their homes behind thick clay walls, most Iranians are suspicious of others. Whereas the first American impulse is often to trust—sometimes stupidly so—the first Iranian impulse is often to distrust—also sometimes stupidly so. "Be suspicious, the better to escape another's trickery," says an old Persian maxim.

Shi'ite Islam further strengthens that maxim, I knew, through a principle known as *taqiyeh,* or concealment in the defense of faith. *Taqiyeh* developed during periods of repression when the minority Shi'ites, living under majority Sunni rule, had to lie about their religion to protect it. While outwardly performing Sunni rituals, they inwardly performed Shi'ite ones. Over time, *taqiyeh* was gradually extended into other arenas, until it basically became, and still sometimes is, a license to lie whenever necessary—or convenient. Hardly the kind of atmosphere that encourages confidence in others.

ೞ෴ಌ

I would arrive back in Tehran in time for my meeting at the Ministry of Tourism, which would lead to another meeting and a certified letter, and to several trips back and forth between the Foreign Ministry and the Foreign Correspondents and Media Department, where the certified letter went perfunctorily ignored. Several officials would tell me that a two-month visa extension was impossible, and I would spend two weeks traveling outside Tehran without either my passport or visa—but with an official letter—while my fate was being decided. During that time, someone would visit Bahman to ask him exactly how well he knew me, and upon my return to Tehran, I would make two more trips to the Foreign Correspondents office before Mr. Shiravi located my passport and handed it to me. "I am very surprised," I would exclaim with delight on seeing my new two-month visa. "Why?" Mr. Shiravi would reply, with his bemused smile.

As for the Afghanistan situation, tensions would remain very high for the next two weeks before gradually dying down and fading away. And the next time I talked to Jerry, I could truthfully tell him that I'd arrived in Tabriz, the city of my early childhood, and had no intention of going anywhere near Afghanistan.

A SECRET SHARED

People who know nothing about these things will tell you that there is no
addition of pleasure in having a landscape to yourself. But this is not true. It
is a pleasure exclusive, unreasoning, and real: it has some of the quality and
some of the intensity of love: it is a secret shared . . .
> —Freya Stark, *The Valleys of the Assassins*

ONE

In May 1930, the British writer and adventurer Freya Stark set out to explore the ancient Isma'ili fortresses of Alamut, an isolated valley in the Alborz Mountains about 80 miles northwest of Tehran. With her were her muleteer-guide, Aziz, and his two assistants. The foursome traveled by foot and by mule, scrambling over a barren and often forbidden terrain to penetrate deep into a "closed place shut off from all the world."

Stark went to Alamut because of its former inhabitants—the Assassins, known more correctly as the Nezari Isma'ilis. A heretical sect of the Isma'ilis, who had themselves split off from the Shi'ites, the Assassins were a legendary cult infamous for dispatching killers to murder leading political and religious figures. Part of Western folklore since the time of the Crusades, the sect's leaders were said to drug their followers with hashish in a beautiful secret garden before sending them out on homicidal missions. The leaders supposedly convinced their followers that this garden was paradise, and the place to which they would return, should they die while carrying out their assignments. The Assassins were said to have

182

killed hundreds of important people throughout the Middle East, and the English word *assassins* was assumed to have been derived from the Arabic word *hashishiyun,* or smokers of hashish.

Scholars today dispute many aspects of the Assassin legends, attributing them to the hostility of the Muslims toward the Isma'ilis and the ignorance of the Europeans. Modern-day research reveals that although the cult at its height did extend from Iran to Syria, its reign of terror was not as widespread as it was reputed to be and was largely a response to a dangerous environment; as a religious minority, the Isma'ilis themselves were often the victims of massacres. The garden in all likelihood did not exist, and the probability of the Persian founders' using hashish is slim. The drug was apparently not introduced into Iran until the thirteenth century, when the Sufis brought it with them from India. A later branch of the Assassins based in Syria, however, did use hashish.

But whatever the individual facts of the Assassins' history may be, the core of their legend remains undisputed, to resonate powerfully in modern-day Iran. The founder of the Assassins was Hasan Sabbah, a theologian and philosopher born in the mid-eleventh century in the holy city of Qom. After spending several years in Egypt, he returned to Iran to wage war against its Seljuq rulers, who had entered the country some 50 years earlier and were both Sunnis and Turks. The Assassins regarded Sunni Islam as evil and corrupt and wished to replace it with a just society based wholly on the Qor'an. Directed by a *da'i,* or representative of the Imam, they committed murder in the name of religion, often assassinating their enemies in public and at Friday prayer meetings.

Searching for a secure base for his terrorist operations, Hasan Sabbah chose Alamut. Access to the valley was difficult because of the surrounding gorges and peaks, and the region was already equipped with mountaintop fortresses built in the 800s by the Dailamites, a fierce mountain dynasty. The main castle was named *alamut,* from the word *aloh,* meaning "eagle," because legend had it that an eagle had brought a Dailamite leader to the site.

The Nezari Isma'ilis took over Alamut in 1090, and two years later, committed their first assassination. Assembling his 60-odd followers around him, Hasan Sabbah asked for a volunteer to kill Nezam al-Molk, the powerful Seljuq vizier. A man called Bu Tahir Arrani stepped forward, and shortly thereafter, fatally stabbed the vizier with a poisoned dagger as he was being carried by litter to his wives' tent. "The killing of this devil,"

Hasan Sabbah reportedly said on hearing the news, "is the beginning of bliss."

⅌

I had first heard about the Assassins as a teenager and had read Freya Stark's book, *The Valleys of the Assassins*. The legends surrounding the cult fascinated me, and I was determined to trace the earlier writer's footsteps. I knew that Alamut was no longer the wild and untamed land that it had once been, but the journey would still allow me to both catch a glimpse of history and see something of rural Iran.

Yet I couldn't just go to Alamut and hire a muleteer. My Persian wasn't good enough, my maps were incomplete, and Ershad would not give me a letter of permission to visit the valley unless I gave them the name and phone number of my guide. I therefore needed to find someone in Tehran who could help me arrange the journey. No one I spoke with at first seemed to have any ideas, and so finally, acutely aware of the passing of time, I contacted the Mountaineering Federation of Iran, cited in my Lonely Planet guidebook as "an absolute mine of information and advice."

The Mountaineering Federation's offices were located downtown, near the sports stadium, in a large office building filled with echoing corridors and dim fluorescent lights. A government organization established by the Shah in the 1960s, the federation acts as a clearinghouse and sponsors climbing expeditions throughout the region. The federation also helped to coordinate Iran's first Mount Everest expedition, which took place in the late spring of 1998, about four months before my arrival. Mountain climbing is a very popular hobby in Iran, and many of those who work for the federation are volunteers—and climbing fanatics.

I met with Mr. Golkar, the federation's director, and his colleague Mr. Bakhtiari, there to serve as translator. Mr. Golkar was a fit, middle-aged man with a pocked face and thick brown beard. He was wearing a checked brown shirt and missing his two front teeth. Mr. Bakhtiari was young, strikingly handsome, and, I thought on first impression, somewhat slick. He was wearing a cream-colored sports jacket that contrasted nicely with his jet-black mustache and hair, and he had the aquiline features of a classic Persian warrior.

Both men went out of their way to shake my hand. Because conservative Muslim men do not shake hands with strange women, as it is forbidden in Islam to touch an unrelated member of the opposite sex, their gesture sent a message. Exactly what message, I was never able to figure out, either then or later in my stay. Several seemingly Westernized men I met surprised me by refusing to shake my hand, while several seemingly conservative ones—including a cleric in Qom—pointedly did. I couldn't find any absolute correlation between handshaking and friendliness, either; some of the most helpful officials I dealt with never offered me their hand.

Hezbollahi? I wondered to myself about Mr. Golkar as the three of us sat down. I'd heard that *hezbollahi* were often in positions of power over underlings much more capable than they, and Mr. Bakhtiari certainly seemed to be better educated than Mr. Golkar. As our conversation progressed, however, I realized that Mr. Golkar did have extensive mountaineering expertise.

I explained to Mr. Golkar what I wanted, and Mr. Bakhtiari translated. They both nodded. They both understood. They had heard of Freya Stark and knew the Alamut valley well. It was one of the most beautiful regions in Iran and an excellent area for hiking. They had taken another group there just last week and would be happy to arrange my trip. It would take about six days, and because I was a writer and a woman traveling alone, Mr. Bakhtiari would personally serve as my guide. He'd been a member of Iran's Everest team and was one of the best guides the federation had. We would also hire a local muleteer and mules to carry our gear.

I felt suspicious. It had all been too easy. I pulled out the tiny, hard-to-read map that I had photocopied from Stark's book and showed them exactly where I wanted to go. They pulled out an immense topographical map of the same region written in Persian. Many of the villages on Stark's map were not on the topographical map. Mr. Golkar looked perplexed but suggested that we inquire about these villages—whose names must have changed, he said—as we went. It wouldn't be too hard. The first part of Stark's route, where most of the villages were located, was now a paved road.

We mapped out a tentative itinerary. Mr. Bakhtiari and I would travel by car the first day, stopping at the villages in the morning and climbing up to the main castle in the afternoon. Then, the next day—

"Hey, wait a minute," I said. "Half a day is not enough time to drive from Tehran to Alamut"—a good three hours away—"and visit four or five villages."

"No problem," Mr. Golkar said. "You can leave at 6 A.M. if you'd like and climb up to the castle the next morning if necessary."

Mr. Bakhtiari nodded. "You are the only client. We will do whatever you want."

Feeling somewhat mollified, I listened to the rest of the proposed itinerary. Days 2, 3, and 4 would be spent hiking over the Alborz, day 5 on the Caspian coast, and day 6 in the historic mountain village of Masuleh—said to be one of the most picturesque spots in Iran. Stark had not visited Masuleh, but it was on my list of places to see, and I was glad to add it to my itinerary.

The rest of my proposed trip I felt less certain about. Although Mr. Bakhtiari kept assuring me that we would follow Stark's route as closely as possible, I wasn't sure that he understood exactly what that meant. His English, though good, was far from perfect, and some of my questions went unanswered. I also couldn't tell if our tentative hiking trail was the same as Stark's; between the changed names, Stark's tiny map, and a topographical one written in Persian, it was hard to be sure. When I mentioned this to Mr. Bakhtiari, he just shrugged.

"We can always change the route once we get there," he said.

What the hell, I decided, and plunked down what for Iran—and a freelance writer—was an exorbitant sum of money. One way or another, on or off Freya Stark's trail, I was going to Alamut.

ॐ

As I left the Mountaineering Federation, Mr. Kashan hurried up to me, an anxious look on his kind, gray face. I'd met him an hour or so earlier while waiting outside Mr. Golkar's office. Fluent in English, Mr. Kashan had introduced himself as a poet and translator who worked in the international affairs department of a government agency down the hall.

"You are a writer," he said, with a courtly half bow. "Come with me, please."

Expecting to be shown anything from incriminating government documents to a hidden torture chamber, I followed Mr. Kashan down a dim hallway, into an office crowded with boxes, bookcases, and dented metal desks. A bearded clerk looked up sleepily as we came in and Mr. Kashan asked him to fetch me a cup of tea. Then he sat me down, opened a bottom drawer, and drew out a large sheaf of dog-eared papers.

"These are some of my poems," he said, flicking nervously through the pages. "I'd like to know what you think. Can you get them published for me?"

Before I could answer, he turned around, reached into another desk behind him, and pulled out several more thick sheafs of paper.

"I've been writing for thirty years," he said. "In English and Persian and French."

I was not particularly surprised. In addition to Babak, I'd already met quite a few poets. The middle-aged foreman of the construction site next door to Bahman's apartment was a poet, and so were several taxi drivers and museum guards I'd encountered, not to mention a number of students who'd befriended me at various tourist attractions. All had told me that they'd been writing poetry for years and years.

In Iran, poetry is considered to be the highest form of literature, heir to an ancient verse tradition that began with the Avesta, the sacred Zoroastrian text. The first verses in literary Persian appeared in the ninth century, and by the twelfth century, several poetic forms had been perfected. Among them were the *qasideh,* a long panegyric that played an important role in the royal courts; the *ghazal,* a much shorter lyric form used mainly to express love; and the *masnavi,* or narrative. In addition to knowing sections of the *Shahnameh* by heart, many people I met in Iran could recite long verses from Hafez and Sa'di—the uncontested masters of the *ghazal,* of which Khomeini was also a practitioner—and from Rumi— the brilliant Sufi master of the *masnavi.* Always, people were disappointed when I couldn't reciprocate in kind. But we thought you were a literature major, they would say, their faces falling, as I tried to explain the low status of memorization in American education today.

"I'm fluent in German, French, and Italian, too," Mr. Kashan went on, "and I'm also a translator. Perhaps if you don't like my poems, you will like my translations."

He pulled out yet another stack of papers and I noticed that the wrinkles of his gray, ill-fitting suit matched the wrinkles of his gray, careworn face. Fabric and skin were matted with the same webs of fine lines, broken here and there by deep black furrows.

"These are some of the most famous poets working in Iran today," he said. "So I'm sure you can get them published."

Suddenly I wondered if perhaps this were some kind of a test, if the poems were anti-Islamic diatribes and Mr. Kashan a government agent, sent to gauge my reactions. Then I wondered if perhaps, just perhaps, the poems and/or the translations were the real thing, literary gems that I could help bring to the attention of the Western world.

A quick glance at the first few pages assured me that neither was the case. The translations were very rough.

Mr. Kashan was watching me expectantly. "What do you think? Can you help me?"

"I don't know," I said, stalling. "It's hard to publish poetry in the United States right now. No one reads it anymore."

"But you will try?" He stared at me, unblinking.

"What about publishing it here?" I said.

"Oh!" he said. "The state of poetry in Iran is very bad. It has no content. It's written in the style of the past, very dogmatic, with much exaggeration. Or it pretends to be psychological or philosophical but is only empty, an abyss. When people can't express themselves . . ." His words trailed off.

"Was it better in the Shah's time?"

"No, it was worse. It's much easier to publish now than before the Revolution. Now the only one thing that's taboo is to insult the religion or the religious state. In the Shah's time, if you handed in a naturalistic poem and it had a certain word in it, it was rejected. Many words were rejected at that time—*partisan, blood, night*—"

A knock came from the door and a tall, bearded young man stuck in his head. He was wearing a dark suit that broadened his shoulders, and tinted glasses that obscured his eyes. In his hand were bright blue *tasbih,* or prayer beads, made of plastic. Controlled by his thumb, they moved smoothly, silently, through his closed fist.

Unsmiling, the bearded man looked at us and said something about me, the American, and something about 4:00. He closed the door again.

Mr. Kashan smirked. "My chief, the assistant director. We have a meeting at four o'clock."

"He knows I'm American?"

"Everyone knows you're American." He shook his head. "Did you notice how young he is? Twenty-six. He knows nothing. And the director is thirty-two. He knows nothing. He makes many mistakes. He can't even speak English—the director of international affairs!—and I know English, French, German, Russian, Italian—I'm a second-class citizen here."

"So he's *hezbollahi*?"

"*Hezbollahi*," he spat out the word. "*Hezbollahi* is a story, nobody is *hezbollahi*. They don't believe. They just see money or sex, they take advantage, and if they do something for you, they want the favor back in two days."

"So how did they get where they are?"

"Maybe their brothers were ayatollahs, or maybe they fought in the war."

"Did you support the Revolution when it first began?"

"Surely I supported the Revolution. Most intellectuals did, and now some people blame them—'the vapor comes from the sea, but it's the cloud that rains . . .' "

I looked at him quizzically, but he didn't notice.

"Alas," he said, "as Brecht says, the people that want to make life beautiful, they themselves are not beautiful."

ক্ষ্বৈ

Mr. Homayoun Bakhtiari, whose last name means "prosperous," was supposed to arrive at 6 A.M., but he arrived at 8, dressed inappropriately, I thought, in olive green dress slacks, a pinstripe shirt with a Ralph Lauren logo, and polished leather shoes. On his soft, white hands, he wore a gold wedding ring with a diamond in the middle. This is a man who climbed Everest? I thought to myself. He was riding shotgun in a battered blue pickup truck piled high with more provisions than three people could possibly use in one week.

Part of the reason for the provisions, and the delay, were Bert and Bart, two tall lanky Dutchmen in their late twenties, now introducing themselves. They'd stopped into the Mountaineering Federation several days after I had to arrange a trip to Alamut and we would all be traveling together for the first three days. They were not interested in Freya Stark, but their trip, Mr. Bakhtiari assured me as I looked at them dubiously, would most definitely not interfere with mine. Couldn't I see that they had their own guide—the tall, grinning Shir Mohammad, or "Lion Mohammed"—and their own car—a dejected-looking Peykan riding too low to the ground? We would still have plenty of time to visit the villages mentioned by Stark, and if by chance I disagreed with the Dutchmen regarding our itinerary, we would simply part company. He, Mr. Bakhtiari, was there to serve me.

Repressing my doubts, I watched as Shir Mohammad and the Peykan's driver jump-started their car and the two smiling Dutchmen climbed in back. Then I got into the pickup truck beside Mr. Bakhtiari and our driver, a slight balding man with a raucous laugh. With the Peykan following laboriously behind, we were finally off, inching our way through the usual snarl of Iranian traffic. But not for long. About 45 minutes outside Tehran, we stopped at a crowded gas station to fill up the truck, half-falling into a ditch as we did so. I groaned as the ground careened up beneath me—we were dangling off the turnoff ramp—but no one else seemed at all perturbed. Slapping each other gaily on the back, Shir Mohammad and the driver pushed us out, and we were off again, only to stop at another gas station about 30 minutes later—this time to fill up the Peykan.

By the time we finally reached the exit road to Alamut, we were a good four hours behind schedule. But I tried to convince myself that I didn't care. The landscape was turning from dry, ugly, and factory-studded to dry, enigmatic, and spare. We passed a man on a donkey riding through a forest of electric towers, and by a clutch of abandoned mud-brick houses, their walls half melted, like sandcastles worn down by the sea. A bus with the English words I LOVE YOU on the back and a dozen men on top chugged past, its horn emitting the playful *whee, Whee, WHEE* sound that is characteristic of all Iranian buses. Then came an orchard filled with cherry and walnut trees, and a sea of tan hills, splashed with pastels. Pale green, pinks, blues, whites.

The well-paved road took a sharp turn to the right and we started to climb, winding our way up and around in lonely isolation. Each turn brought a sharp new vista that made my breath catch in my chest, and the hills took on a golden sheen. Empty of vegetation and habitation, they were rounded parabolas smooth as dunes, shaped by a giant's hands.

Along one empty stretch of road, we passed a homemade donation box with a plywood rose on top. Though I'd already seen dozens of such boxes in Tehran and Mashhad, I was still astonished to find one here, among the mountaintops. Mr. Bakhtiari and our driver, who'd been cackling conspiratorially together, seemed surprised at my surprise, and they told me what I later learned was a popular Tehran joke. One day a pious man, knowing that God will protect him if he makes a donation, drops money into a donation box. A moment later, he is hit by a car. As he lies there, unable to move, another man comes up to make a donation. "Don't do it," the pious man calls out. "It's broken."

Just beyond the prayer box was a freshwater spring, marked by a hand-painted sign. Its crooked white letters quoted a verse from the Qor'an: "He it is Who sendeth down water from the sky, and therewith We bring forth buds of every kind" (6:100).

Beyond the springs, the road rose to the top of a ridge, and the hills of Alamut spread out—a sea of pale red now instead of tan. There were still no trees or shrubs to speak of, just an army of electricity poles marching single file toward the horizon, sometimes sticking obediently to the road, other times veering rebelliously off to wander through the undulating valleys lapping at our feet. I tried to imagine what it had been like to be Freya Stark, hiking instead of driving through this isolated country—then devoid of electricity poles—and felt a piercing jealousy.

We descended into the Alamut valley, to find surprisingly green fields alternating with more dry and dusty land. The Shahrud River runs through the valley and is used to irrigate fields of millet, rice, and wheat. Rustling poplar trees rose like spears beside rounder, shorter trees bearing citrus fruit.

We stopped in Rajaidast, a strikingly ugly village of cement block buildings and raw storefronts. Beside a gas station stood a walled complex sporting the jagged gun logo of the Revolutionary Guards; behind it, three young women in *chadors* were raking rice in an empty lot. Between the Revolutionary Guards and the women was an unpainted room where I spotted the bare feet of a half-dozen men crouched in prayer.

By this time, I had given up on the idea of finding the first few villages that Freya Stark had visited. No one we had spoken to had heard of them, and besides, I thought defensively, Stark had given so few details about them, it was hardly worth tracking them down. Instead, I would focus on the villages that she *had* described in detail and that *were* on the map: Gazor Khan, situated at the base of Alamut rock, on which the castle was built, and Garmrud, where she had lived for several weeks. Garmrud was also the site of a second Assassin castle, Nevisar Shah.

An hour or so later, the road now dirt and ridden with yawning gullies and holes, we finally saw it—Alamut rock, a gloomy, striated hump that from our vantage point resembled a pile of giant cow dung patties. Driving to near its base, we entered the village of Gazor Khan, centered on a dirt plaza. WELCOME TO KOHSARAN MOTEL read a sign in English on an unassuming home to the right; to the left was the largest house in town—a lovely, though abandoned and dilapidated, blue-gray building with a balcony. It was only later that I noticed the building's many bullet holes and wondered what life in this isolated village had been like during the Revolution.

On the southern end of the square squatted a homely brick mosque and a cavernous store piled high with lightbulbs, tissue paper, and soap. Next door rose an iron tower topped with a microphone. "Mr. Aftari, call from Tehran. Mr. Aftari, call from Tehran," the microphone blared out as we pulled up. Like many Iranian villages, Gazor Khan had only one telephone and all calls were announced via this high-rise PA system.

The villagers rushed up, to have their pictures taken and to talk. The women were in traditional village dress—colorful flowered blouses, black skirts, and scarves. A few had *chadors* tied around their waists, but most did not.

I asked the women whether their lives were better before or after the Revolution, and one old woman, her face as brown and wrinkled as the walnut she was eating, answered.

"After," she said, "because now we have electricity, a road, a phone." She paused, pressing a gift of walnuts into my hand. "And what about in America? Is life there better after the Revolution, too?"

"First we will have lunch," Mr. Bakhtiari said, coming out of the Kohsaran Motel, where he'd just made arrangements for us to stay the night, "and then we will climb to the castle." He'd finally changed out of his city clothes and into hiking boots.

"What about Garmrud?" I said, panicking. It was already after 3:00.

"We have no time for Garmrud," Mr. Bakhtiari said. "I'm sorry."

"Tomorrow then," I said.

"No time tomorrow, either. The muleteer is coming at eight o'clock to take us over the pass."

"But you said—" I began, and thereafter began a tense half-hour wrangle over who had said what. Mr. Bakhtiari seemed to have forgotten all about his earlier promise to take me wherever I wanted to go, and there seemed to be great confusion over exactly where Garmrud was anyway. One villager told us it was three hours away, and another estimated that it was only an hour. No one had heard of the Nevisar Shah castle.

I took out Freya Stark's map and showed it to Mr. Bakhtiari.

"But she went down through Seh Hezar Valley," he said, studying it, "and that's why she went to Garmrud. We're going down through Do Hezar."

"What?" I said, close to tears. I had agreed to descend through Do Hezar, but only because I hadn't understood where one valley ended and the next one began.

By the time the dust had settled, Mr. Bakhtiari had agreed to drive with me to Garmrud that afternoon and I had agreed to hike down through Do

Hezar. Apparently, despite earlier assurances, all the arrangements had already been made and to change the itinerary now would cause great difficulty. If only I'd researched this more carefully, I thought as I shouldered my backpack.

Leaving Bart and Bert behind, Mr. Bakhtiari and I left for Garmrud in the Peykan. The driver gave me a dark look as I climbed into the back, and that look grew darker as we drove on. Garmrud turned out to be a good hour and a half away, and with each mile, the gutted, dirt road grew progressively worse. I scrunched down deeper into my seat each time we scraped over yet another bump.

Finally, about one mile before Garmrud, we stopped. The road was now too bad to continue; we would walk the rest of the way. Silently, we proceeded down a rocky red road, passing first a bent old man carrying an open egg carton and then a boy on a donkey. A young shepherd, holding his crook like a gun, saluted at us, and young girls in kerchiefs climbing a tree called out hello. The sun was already setting—shadows growing long and dark—and I could see snow on a distant mountaintop.

We turned the corner to see Garmrud before us, and I pulled out Freya Stark. "We came to Garmrud in the sunset," she wrote. "An immense precipice which closes it in at the back and through which the Alamut River finds a narrow cleft to enter, was shining like a torch in the last sunlight. The flat houses on the slope at its feet were also made rosy in the glow."

Except for electricity lines, nothing much had changed since then. Down the steep banks to our right were the winding Alamut River and a patchwork of bright green fields. Before us was the village, still filled with flat-roofed houses, now the color of gold. Beyond the village was the jutting precipice and mountains shaped like giant thumbs.

A woman tending the fields came up to talk to us, and I was struck by the gulf between her and Mr. Bakhtiari and our driver. They were city people; she was a farmer and had little more in common with them than she had with me. She was wearing a long black skirt, a long-sleeved red blouse, and a kerchief that said *flowers* in English over and over again. Slinging her hoe onto her shoulder, she told us that thanks to the Revolution, Garmrud had had electricity for the past three years and a high school for the past ten. The village had a population of about 150 and was the next-to-last settlement in the valley that could be reached by road. As for Nevisar Shah castle, it was that pile of white rocks on the mountain just behind us.

I turned to look at the former fortress that Stark had climbed to and could almost understand why no one else in Alamut had been able to tell us where it was. From ground level, it looked very small, very destroyed, and very inaccessible. I was just as glad that we didn't have time to climb to it, though I did want to wander through the village. Someone there might have heard of Stark or her guide, Aziz. I didn't dare suggest it, though. Mr. Bakhtiari and the driver were looking pointedly at their watches and muttering together; although we'd only just arrived, we had to leave immediately. Driving back in the dark would be impossible.

☙❧

By the time we returned to Gazor Khan, it was twilight and the dust-blue central square was filled with men and boys exchanging the news of the day—no women or girls in sight. The mosque was open and lit by a harsh white light, with the women's section separated from the men's by ragged black *chadors* pinned onto a clothesline. In front of the lovely blue-gray house stood two sturdy orange buses. Gazor Khan was the end of the valley's bus line, and the vehicles would be parked there overnight.

Taking off our boots, we climbed to the flat roof of the Kohsaran Motel, which was a motel in name only. The Kohsaran had no beds, just a room with a carpeted floor and broken prayer stones in the corners, and a rooftop on which to lay out sleeping bags. The toilet out back was the usual hole in the ground, and the sink was outdoors. But the place was clean and friendly, and a guest book in the "dining room" was filled with comments from the many travelers, mostly Japanese, who had passed this way before us.

That evening, over a dinner of rice and lamb served on the roof, Mr. Bakhtiari told us more about his climb up Everest. But I still had problems picturing him on the rugged expedition. He seemed so smooth and meticulously groomed and lacked Shir Mohammad's lean, muscular physique. I also wondered who exactly had paid for his trip—was he perhaps the spoiled son of wealthy *bazaaris*?

Bert, Bart, and I exchanged stories. They'd already spent three weeks traveling all over Iran and were returning to Holland immediately after our trip. They'd had a terrific time—visiting nomads, camping out in peasants' fields, staying in cheap guest houses, and hitching rides in the backs of pickup trucks. As they spoke, the limitations of my sex in Iran hit home to me for the first time. It would be much harder for me to camp out in peasants' fields and ride in the backs of pickup trucks.

After dinner, when the others had gone to bed, I sat on the edge of the roof and looked out over the village. Lights pinpricked their way up the hulking black mountainside, illuminating a clay wall here or a wooden ladder there, with courtyards and flat rooftops in between. I heard the sounds of water running, dogs barking, leaves whispering, and a distant voice slowly releasing the deep, round notes of a mournful melody. The notes seemed to stretch out before me like beads on a string. Overhead, the sky was crowded with the Milky Way and shooting stars.

A sudden commotion sounded at the edge of the square, and I noticed a group of four or five men, loitering. Someone flashed a light at me, and then the group started toward the motel. Mr. Bakhtiari appeared out of nowhere. "You should move away from the edge of the roof," he said. "They can see you." I looked at him blankly and then remembered that I wasn't wearing my *rusari*. It hadn't occurred to me that anyone would notice me up here in the dark, or that anyone in this isolated village would care.

ॐ∞

The next morning, our muleteer, Lohraseb, appeared, two sad-eyed mules in tow, and we said good-bye to the crowd of villagers who had gathered to see us off. To reach the base of Alamut rock was an easy 20-minute walk, but the steep and scrambling climb up the mountain wedge itself left us sweaty and winded. I stopped to rest many times along the way but noticed that Mr. Bakhtiari and Shir Mohammad stopped only once, midway, in a flat saddle area that had once marked the entrance to the castle. Perhaps Mr. Bakhtiari had climbed Mount Everest after all.

Up top was a narrow ridge about 400 yards long, with near-vertical cliffs falling off on all sides. The castle had once stretched along about a fourth of this ridge, and though its walls were almost completely destroyed, it was possible to make out the layouts of some of the former buildings.

Tracing them with my eyes, I wondered which one had once housed the cult's founder, Hasan Sabbah, who for 34 years had never left the castle and only twice left his house—to go up to the roof. Instead, he spent his time praying, fasting, studying, writing—and ordering the murder of his enemies. Life at Alamut was extremely ascetic; alcohol was not allowed, and Sabbah even put one of his own sons to death for drinking wine.

I also wondered what life at Alamut had been like in the 1250s, when Hulagu, Genghis Khan's grandson, arrived. After first entreating the

Assassins to surrender, Hulagu and his Mongol armies laid siege to the castle for three years, achieving victory only when the Assassins ran out of food. In 1256, Alamut was burned to the ground; among the buildings destroyed was a famous library housing many valuable books, including Hasan Sabbah's autobiography.

The destruction of Alamut, however, did not mark the end of the Nezari Isma'ilis. Though the sect went underground for six centuries, it reemerged into the public arena again in the 1850s, when the forty-sixth Nezari Imam, known by the title of the Aga Khan, rose to national prominence—largely through sheer force of personality. Allying himself with the British against the Qajar Shah, the Aga Khan promised to deliver control of Iran to England without a fight. He then moved to India, where he succeeded in raising huge amounts of money, attracting a loyal following, and becoming well known in British diplomatic and political circles. His grandson, Aga Khan III, later became president of the League of Nations and spokesman for the Muslim movement that led to the creation of Pakistan. One of the Aga Khan's great-grandsons, the former Ali Khan, was a notorious playboy who was married to actress Rita Hayworth, and another, Karim Al Hussaini Shah, is a respected Muslim leader who still reigns as Aga Khan IV and the forty-ninth Nezari Imam today.

Bert nudged my arm. On a distant slope far below us, a line of dark sheep, tiny as jellybeans, was threading its way through a steep ravine. We could just barely make out the sheepdog at its head and the shepherd at its rear, but the sound of bells rang out loud, musical and clear.

Something white flicked across the periphery of our vision, and we turned to see an eagle soaring down through the valley at our feet. Then we spotted another, this one cruising in a slow-motion semicircle around the rock. The Assassins' castle was gone, but the eagles that it was named after remained.

Descending from the castle, we headed up the mountainside behind it, past steep terraced fields to a dry pebbly incline that seemed to rise straight up into the sky. Wiry, middle-aged Lohraseb, dressed in a bright blue sweater and rubber shoes, moved easily ahead, picking out a zigzagging path as he called out encouragement to his mules. Shir Mohammad loped just behind him, lean legs flashing in bicycle shorts, while Bert and Bart, sporting T-shirts, followed at a slower but steady pace.

I, meanwhile, laboriously brought up the rear, struggling to survive in my long black, polyester *manteau*. The hot sun beat down on my covered head and I fought for breath in the thin air, the altitude being about 7,000 feet. Mr. Bakhtiari was just ahead of me, politely keeping to my pace, but I imagined that I could sense his impatience and I cursed under my breath, angry at him for being there, at "them" for making me wear the "covering," and at myself for not putting in a better showing for my sex. Just how much good were my thrice-weekly workouts at my local YMCA doing me anyhow? Sweat trickled down my back and under my armpits. My *rusari* slipped from side to side. I tripped. But I wasn't "allowed" to take off my covering until we passed the last village—a tiny hamlet located a good 90-minute hike straight up from Gazor Khan. No wonder we women hate men so much, I thought, as I finally tore off the garments and stuffed them ignominiously into my knapsack.

By the time we stopped for lunch, we had climbed several more steep inclines. My legs had turned to rubber and my T-shirt was soaking wet. But we had reached the top of the world. Jagged red peaks jutted up all around us, scratching the roof of the big blue sky, and an oval emerald oasis lay before us. The first patch of green we'd stumbled on in hours, it was watered by an all-but-invisible spring. Lohraseb unloaded the mules and let them loose to roll in the grass, while Mr. Bakhtiari and Shir Mohammad unpacked lunch. Iranian cheese, flat bread, rubbery sausage, pickles, tomatoes, and tea. Before eating, Shir Mohammed consulted his compass and slipped away to pray, rolling out his prayer rug behind the privacy of a boulder.

Bert asked an innocent question regarding the mules and Lohraseb replied with a quick "what a stupid comment" jerk back of his head, chin up in the air. Bert, Bart, and I looked at each other and laughed. We'd all encountered that same gesture many times in Iran—I myself had noticed it in everyone from 7-year-old Sepideh to grandmothers. Sometimes the gesture was accompanied by a roll of the eyes or "tsk" of the tongue, but always it seemed to connote unbridled arrogance. And yet was that really the case, Bert, Bart, and I wondered to each other in a politically correct way, while I secretly, guiltily, thought that it was. Despite their kindness, many Iranians I'd met seemed cocksure of their opinions, and some were only tangentially interested in what I had to say—interrupting me when I described life in the United States or compared Iran with the West. Others I barely knew weren't at all shy about asking for favors—would I please send them English-language videos/cassettes/books?—whereas some asked me far too many personal questions: How much money did I make?

How much did my camera cost? Why didn't I have children? Most usually backed off quickly, however, whenever I declined to answer.

A flock of black crows settled on the slope behind us, their wings making a dark, muffled sound. There are 14 species of crow in Iran, and they've generated much folklore: When sick, a crow eats human feces and feels better. A plaster of crushed crows' eggs will blacken hair. Drink the blood of a crow and you'll want no more wine. See a crow in the morning and it will bring bad luck. See two crows any time of day and it will bring good luck.

By the time we finished lunch and had a short nap, it was almost 4:00. The mountains had turned from red to brown and we pulled out sweatshirts before starting across the rocky ridge that led to Sialan Pass, altitude 10,500 feet. Thick tufts of thorny grass brushed against our ankles as we walked and the shadows grew cold and dark. The sun was setting behind a distant peak, and I worried about making camp before nightfall. But then Sialan Pass appeared, a small nick cut as neatly as a door into the mountains, and we passed over to the other side.

A blaze of red lay before us. The long rays of the setting sun had lit a fire across an elongated valley lined with what looked like giant sand dunes. As smooth and as untouchable as the Sahara, the rounded, barren slopes rose and fell, rose and fell, into shadow and out, as they unfolded vertically across the valley. Red turned to maroon turned to black turned to pink. Then the rays shifted, the sand slipped, the dunes intensified in color, and I felt an absurd urge to embrace them somehow, pull them down deep inside me—looking wasn't enough. But there was no time to linger. Night was coming quickly, and the others were already well ahead, doll-size figures hurrying down a shadowed slope toward another vast valley.

This valley was green instead of red but equally deep and almost as mystifying. Its rounded slopes, fat as well-fed rumps, descended gently down, down, into a bottom we couldn't see, with black creased ravines and lichen patches. To the east loomed the giant peaks of Mount Alam, a vertical glacier clinging to its side, and Takht-e Soleiman, or "Throne of Solomon," its summit vaguely shaped like a big black chair. Legend has it that old King Solomon could not persuade his young Queen of Sheba to make love to him and so sent out the birds of the air to find him the coldest place on earth. The next morning, all returned except the hoopoe, who didn't fly in until dusk. Bowing before the king, he told of a mountain so cold that when he'd alighted, his wings had frozen to the ground. Only the sun of midday had thawed them. Immediately, the king built a bed atop the summit that bears his name and traveled there with his queen. And that night, unable to bear the cold, she finally crept into his bed.

Freya Stark had described seeing Takht-e Soleiman—at 15,000 feet, the third highest peak in Iran—"glistening in the solitude of its snows at the head of an unmapped valley." But she'd described little else about the valley and had mysteriously failed to mention the sheer magnificence of the landscape that I saw all around me.

A small man dressed entirely in white, holding a tall staff and leading a white donkey, crossed our paths.

"Salaam alaikum," he said—peace be with you.

"Salaam alaikum," we replied.

We made camp in a small, protected bowl situated at the intersection of three yawning valleys. Darkness and cold were falling fast, and there was barely time to put up the tents and pull on winter parkas, hats, and gloves before the landscape around us disappeared. At 10,000 feet, the air was icy, brittle, and thin. The stars overhead seemed close enough to touch, and the mountains crouched invisibly, disquietingly, around us. Flashlights illuminated hands opening up tin cans and unzipping backpacks. Heavy, booted feet crunched over rock and sand.

Too cold to last outside another moment, we crawled into an Arctic tent and ate a bubbling mushroom, pea, tomato, and hot dog concoction out of one pot. The air around us grew warm and moist with our bodies and breath. Outside, a low humming wind started up, and I felt a surge of affection for these five men whom I'd met only two days before and would probably never see again after a few days hence. Winking, Shir Mohammad carefully rationed out a half cup of orange soda for each of us, and I was reminded of camping expeditions back in the United States. There, the carefully rationed liquid lugged up mountainsides had always been alcohol.

"Bekhor!" Lohraseb suddenly bellowed at me—eat! He was sitting beside me, smelling of mules and the wind, and ferociously tearing off pieces of flat bread, which he kept pushing at me. His whole face rumpled in and out as he chomped, but he stopped eating long enough to tell me how worried he'd been when I'd had trouble on the lower slopes, trudging along in my *manteau* and *rusari*. His eyes filled with concern and he gave the rest of the tent an angry glance. *"Khanom,"* he said—lady—and patted my hand with his thick, worn fingers, before shoving another piece of bread at me.

In halting Persian, I asked him about himself and he told me that he'd been born in Gazor Khan, where he'd learned his trade from his father. He was now 48 and owned four mules, which he used to transport people and products such as rice and honey over the mountains. Each mule could carry up to 80 kilos and he was always careful not to overload them. He also had five children, two of whom—a son and a daughter—were studying engineering at Qazvin University.

A son *and* a daughter, I thought, impressed. Before the Revolution, villagers like Lohraseb had seldom sent children of either sex to the university.

We slept three to a tent, with Shir Mohammad and Mr. Bakhtiari leaving close to one half of our tent to me. As I tossed and turned, unable to sleep despite my exhaustion, I wondered about that space around me and about my companions. Tents are intimate environments, small and close and far away from home. Had Shir Mohammad or Mr. Bakhtiari ever gone camping with nonfamily women before? Had either of them ever shared a tent with a single Western woman before? Just how uncomfortable was my presence making them?

The more I wondered about these matters, the more uncomfortable *I* became. My earlier surge of affection for my companions notwithstanding, I suddenly began to question what *I* was doing here with all these men. Had my proposed trip been the topic of much worry and discussion at the Mountaineering Federation? Had there been much relief when Bert and Bart appeared, to at least add other Westerners to the mix? And why did I want to retrace Freya Stark's journey so much anyway? Except for a few luminous passages, I'd found much of her book to be tedious and in need of an editor. I admired her intrepid spirit far more than I admired her prose style.

From the other side of Shir Mohammad, Mr. Bakhtiari said something about how hard it was to sleep—the thin air was making it difficult to breathe, he said, and that's why we kept waking ourselves up. He seemed eager to talk, and I tried to ask him about what I'd been thinking but felt too shy and couldn't get beyond the basics: Did many women hike in Iran? (Yes, of course, hiking was very popular with women and there were even women hiking teams.) Did Muslim women wear their *manteau*s when hiking? (No, of course not. They took them off past the last village, just like I had.)

Mr. Bakhtiari told me that his wife was a nurse and that they were very happily married, with an eight-year-old daughter. His wife enthusiastically supported his passion for climbing, though she herself was not a hiker and understood what many Iranian women did not: Money was not all that important. She'd understood when he'd turned down a well-paying job to climb Everest and understood that he now wanted to return part time to graduate school.

I was beginning to understand that I had seriously underestimated Mr. Bakhtiari.

಄ೲ

The next morning, after a breakfast of tea, bread, and fresh honey, we loaded up the mules and struck out across a barren ridge, to head down into a valley filled with thistle. Here, a sharp-faced shepherd dressed in army surplus was minding his flock, and he and Lohraseb embraced, kissing on alternating cheeks. While they exchanged news, Shir Mohammad pointed out Sialan Peak, glittering with rock and ice in the distance. We would be passing just below its summit, at an altitude of 11,400 feet.

We pushed on, zigzagging our way up another sheer mountainside and across another short ridge. Then we came to a wide valley capped with a pale sky. The views here were enormous, and the light so clear and bright that it seemed to paint a white outline around everything. Shielding my eyes, I stepped out into that brightness and was nearly blown over by a ferocious wind that then followed me all across a half-mile-long slope littered with bear-size boulders. The others were far ahead of me as usual— tiny green and purple dots—and I felt deliciously, greedily, voluptuously alone. Everywhere I looked there was nothing but stern peaks and craggy rock. Everywhere I looked there was nothing but desolation. Yet I felt enormous exhilaration. The strong wind pushed and pulled against me, isolating me even more within its roar, but I barely noticed. I was in a dream and could see myself toiling down below, an ant of a figure just like all the others, stubbornly forging ahead, refusing to be pushed down.

Another hard climb up another arid slope and I passed beneath the dark and watchful presence of Sialan Peak, into the upper reaches of Do Hezar Valley. The others were waiting for me by a sheet of melting ice, and with a sigh of regret, I realized that we'd left the Alamut valley and its dry desert landscape behind. Before us lay a steep rocky incline, flanked by vegetation that would steadily thicken as we descended, followed by a towering fir forest, and the Caspian Sea. Because the Alborz Mountains block the clouds of moisture that rise from the sea, its southern slopes are nearly devoid of moisture, and its northern ones, blanketed with trees. Wild boar and jackal roam the forests' remotest reaches, along with the occasional leopard and the very occasional Asian tiger—now near extinction. The English word *jungle* comes from the Persian and Hindi word *jangal*, which in Iran was originally applied to this region.

The descent down through Do Hezar proved to be brutal—boulders and loose rock nearly the entire way. We all slipped and slid, falling many times. I felt much worse for the mules, though, than I did for any of us, and hated watching the poor animals stop and start, stop and start, hesitating before each new stretch of rock. Where to put those long, skinny legs with the heavy hooves weighting the ends, and how to cope with those bulky loads shifting precariously on their backs? I shivered every time I heard a mule slip or watched one fall, certain that there would come a moment when a leg would snap.

The descent took many hours. We had planned to camp somewhere along the way, but there proved to be no suitable spot. Everywhere was steep, hard rock; nowhere was a stream. And so finally, at about 5 P.M., Mr. Bakhtiari pointed to a green plateau that was still far away. "That's where we'll camp," he said.

I groaned silently to myself and more vocally to Bert and Bart, who were also not too happy about our distant campsite. Their knees hurt and I felt as if I were losing my toes. We passed by a rock enclosure used by shepherds, and our first example of Islamic graffiti. WHEN IN THE MOUNTAINS, THINK OF ALLAH, it said.

"Faster, faster," Mr. Bakhtiari called as he and Shir Mohammad began running down the slope. We were finally past the loose white rocks, and Lohraseb and the mules were already far ahead. But as far as I was concerned, the grassy incline was still steep and pockmarked with sudden holes. Besides, my toes had turned from painful to numb, and I was exhausted. Except for a brief lunch, we'd been hiking for almost 10 hours.

"Come on," Mr. Bakhtiari called again, and Bert and Bart ran ahead. But if anything, I slowed down. I didn't care if it was getting dark. They could come back and get me by flashlight.

At my own pace, I trekked through the pastures, past clumps of jostling sheep, and entered a grove of fir trees where Mr. Bakhtiari was waiting for me. Companionably, we proceeded on down the darkening path, pitched at an acute angle and thick with fallen needles. I could hear a river roaring below us and remembered that although Freya Stark had written little about this part of her journey, she had compared this particular section to the Pyrenees. The comparison still seemed apt, and I was about to say so to Mr. Bakhtiari when Shir Mohammad came hurrying back.

"Manteau, manteau," he said breathlessly. *"Rusari!"* Apparently, there were soldiers up ahead. Where was my covering?

Anxiously, Mr. Bakhtiari turned to me. Feeling annoyed, I pulled off my knapsack. My *rusari* was inside and I would put it on, but as for my *manteau,* well, my sweatshirt would just have to do. My *manteau* was strapped to one of the mules.

"This is a crazy country," I said in exasperation as I covered my head.

Mr. Bakhtiari's jaw tightened.

T W O

The next day, after a night spent camping by the river, Bert, Bart, and Shir Mohammad left Mr. Bakhtiari and me in the crowded town of Tonkabon, by a clunky but still operating public phone booth made in Japan in 1976. Bert and Bart had a plane to catch, and Shir Mohammad was returning to Tehran. That left Mr. Bakhtiari and me to complete the two remaining days of my "program." As a licensed guide, he had leave to be alone with me, but on a more personal level, the prospect of traveling alone together made us both somewhat nervous. We tried to keep things smooth by constantly referring to our respective significant others.

Our first stop was Ramsar, said to be one of the most beautiful towns on the Caspian coast. Before the Revolution, many wealthy Iranians had owned villas all along the Caspian, and although the government has since confiscated most of these, the sea and its beaches are still a major recreation destination. During the summer, the highways heading to the Caspian are dense with traffic and lined with souvenir stands selling beach toys—green dolphins, pink ducks, buckets and shovels, striped beach balls. The beaches themselves are strictly segregated, however, with women (who usually wear one-piece bathing suits) and children funneled to one side, men to the other.

Ramsar's hotels are among the most expensive in Iran, costing anywhere from $40 to $100 a night, and so Mr. Bakhtiari and I found a guest house renting "suites." I was given a room with four iron cots for the equivalent of $8 a night, and Mr. Bakhtiari, a room with two for the equivalent of $6. I took my first shower in days and found two new uses for my *manteau:* It made for a handy bathrobe when using the communal bathroom and served as a good light blanket when taking a nap.

That evening, Mr. Bakhtiari suggested having a drink—nonalcoholic, of course—at the Ramsar Grand Hotel, built during the time of the Shah on a wooded hill overlooking the sea. Next door to the hotel was the Shah's former palace, and in the lobby, an enormous mural of a stern Ayatollah Khomeini. By far the largest indoor portrait of Khomeini that I saw anywhere in Iran, the mural seemed to serve as a rebuke to the many relatively wealthy tourists sprawled in the lobby's dark orange lounge chairs, vintage 1970s American. Among them was an unhappy-looking British tour group on a 17-day trek through Iran and clusters of plump, lethargic Iranians who looked as if they'd never done a day's work in their life. The British tourists had also just hiked through Alamut—they, too, had read Freya Stark—and I wondered what it is that makes modern travelers so eager to retrace historic journeys. Why aren't our own odysseys enough?

Glancing around the lounge, which was lined with picture windows, Mr. Bakhtiari began to speak about the importance of the *rusari*. "If you're going to wear it," he said, nodding at one Westernized Iranian, "wear it right, not with hair sticking out the front and back."

I looked at him in surprise. This was the most forthright about Islamic matters that he'd been with me the entire trip.

"You believe in the *hejab*, then," I said. Given his Ralph Lauren shirts and good English, I hadn't been sure.

"Of course," he said. "This is a Muslim country."

We sat in silence for a moment.

"But I'm not strict," he added. "My wife takes it off at parties—it's just on the street that I'm talking about."

"And how does she feel about it?"

"The same." He shrugged. "Most people do."

"But what about . . ." I thought of the many women I'd spoken with in Tehran and Mashhad.

"Those are just rich people," he said as if reading my mind.

Our drinks arrived—coffee with ice cream—and he stirred his thoughtfully. Then he stiffened.

"Look," he said, and held out his black-and-gold drink stirrer. The handle read CASPIAN CASINO CLUB.

It took me a moment to understand, and then I realized that the stirrer had to date back to the time of the Shah.

"No, no, it's not that," Mr. Bakhtiari said impatiently. "Look, it says 'Casino Club,' and we don't have gambling here, it's forbidden in Islam. They shouldn't use these sticks. I'm going to complain."

He motioned to the waiter, who was busy with two large groups of Europeans who'd just arrived. I guessed them to be German and French and felt surprised at their presence. I hadn't expected to see so many tour groups in Ramsar.

Giving up on the waiter, Mr. Bakhtiari reached for the bill.

"I don't pray regularly," he said, "and some people say that doesn't make me a good Muslim. But I try to do other things good Muslims do. I don't lie, I don't gamble, and I try to do what's right."

After paying our bill, we left the hotel, and walked down the dark driveway toward the sea.

"Some people say there was freedom under the Shah," Mr. Bakhtiari said. "But it's not true. There were soldiers killing, a curfew . . . now, there are still many problems, but I am comfortable here. I have everything I want—my family, Everest, my university degree. Why should I go? Where should I go? My brother went to Canada, and what for? More money. I don't care about money. I don't want that kind of life. People should live very simply, like Imam Ali. Khomeini lived very simply."

"You supported the Revolution, then," I half said, half asked.

"I believe the Revolution was good. I fought for it enthusiastically. I was only age fifteen, sixteen, but I was going around, putting my nose in. It was a beautiful time—exciting. There was fighting all over Tehran, except in the north where the rich people lived. They opened the arsenal and let the people in. I got a machine gun, I was firing at the tanks. But I couldn't do anything, and afterwards I gave the gun back to the mosque. They asked the people to do that, and my mother didn't want it in the house."

"And then?" I prodded.

He shrugged. "Two years later there was a coup. People got killed. That's when I decided politics wasn't for me." He thrust his hands into his pockets.

People in Iran are tired of politics, I thought then—and many times again later in my travels.

"And then I went to war," Mr. Bakhtiari said.

"You were in the war?" I said, surprised. I hadn't guessed that. But then there were many things about Mr. Bakhtiari that I hadn't guessed.

"I was in the regular army, in Kordestan. We had to worry about Iraq and the Kurds. We didn't know which side the Kurds were on. There was a lot of confusion, hiding and just firing machine guns without looking. I had seen films about Vietnam—and they were right. That's what war is like. I lost many friends—but we had to defend our country."

He fell silent, wrapped in his private thoughts.

We hailed a taxi and took it down to the Caspian Sea, which is not really a sea at all but rather the largest lake in the world, five times bigger than Lake Superior. Night had fallen, and except for an occasional blaze of lights, the shore was a dense velvet black. We pulled into a seaside parking lot surrounded by low-slung buildings. To one side stood a flimsy booth selling sunglasses, to another a sort of recreation center where teenage boys were clumped around games of *fusball*. Behind them were open-air restaurants, an Iranian-style motel (no beds), and the sea itself, lapping surprisingly close to the parking lot. Over the past decade or so, the Caspian has been rising at the alarming rate of 15 to 20 centimeters per year. No one is quite sure why, though one plausible theory has it that the clearing of land for agriculture has led to increased water runoff.

For the most part, Russia and its former provinces dominate commerce and shipping on the Caspian Sea. In one extraordinarily shortsighted moment, Haji Mirza Aqasi, prime minister under Mohammad Shah during the Qajar period, ceded the sole rights to the sea to the Russians, supposedly after discovering that it contained saltwater unfit to drink. "We are not waterfowl that we should stand in need of saltwater," he reportedly said, and followed it up with the equally sage reflection: "It wouldn't do to embitter the sweet palate of a friend for the sake of a handful of saltwater."

The one Iranian industry that does flourish on the Caspian is sturgeon and its precious by-product, caviar, of which Iran produces about 300 tons per year. Now being seriously threatened by pollution, the lucrative business is under the strict control of the Islamic government. But not without controversy. According to traditional Islamic law, the handling and eating of sturgeon is *haram*—forbidden—because it is a fish without scales. Prior to 1979, caviar was readily available but supposedly eaten only by non-Muslims and nonconformists. After the Revolution, the future of the caviar industry remained uncertain until 1983, when Ayatollah Khomeini issued a convenient *fatwa*, or religious ruling, lifting the ban. Basing his decision on the expertise of clergymen and "reliable specialists," who supposedly had access to the latest scientific research, he declared that "caviar fishes . . . have lozenge-shaped scales on parts of their body, especially on the upper lobe of their tail fin."

Mr. Bakhtiari and I dined on the formerly forbidden fish in a romantic garden restaurant not far from the shore. While we ate, globes of colored lights glowing in the trees above us, he told me more about his daughter, whose future he was worried about. He and his wife, educated in coed schools, had known each other for many years before they'd married, he said, and he was concerned that his daughter, educated in a sexually segregated system, would not have that same opportunity. He was also fiercely opposed to the Caspian's segregated beaches—what was the purpose of going on a holiday with his family if they couldn't enjoy it together?

Earlier, Mr. Bakhtiari had told me that he'd spent his honeymoon in Ramsar, and as he spoke, I imagined him and his wife visiting some of the same spots we were now visiting. If Mr. Bakhtiari and I were alone in this kind of setting in America, I thought, the possibility of adultery would be hanging heavy in the air. But here in Iran, adultery without the blessing of temporary marriage was more than just betraying your partner, it was betraying your religion and your country. Here in Iran, even the sanctity of marriage didn't always allow men and women to be alone together.

༄༅

The next morning, Mr. Bakhtiari and I departed Ramsar in the first of the shared taxis that would take us to Masuleh, our final stop. Each shared taxi traveled only to the next village or town, and so we were constantly scrambling in and out of rusting, sagging vehicles. Because we always paid for the entire backseat, the other passengers sat in front, and for one short stretch, I counted five heads bobbing in front of us: a family of three squeezed onto the passenger seat, the driver, and another passenger to his *left*, clutching the driver's side door, which wouldn't close. When I asked one of them to please join us in the back, they wouldn't hear of it, but chorused, "Thank you, thank you," in English.

It was a Friday and the beginning of War Week, which commemorates the Iran–Iraq War. Worn-out tanks and trucks and men in khaki uniforms filled the streets of the towns we passed through, preparing for memorial parades. Green-and-white-and-red Islamic Republic flags alternated with green-and-black banners quoting the Qor'an.

As we neared Masuleh, the land became increasingly fertile. Olive groves gave way to rice fields that gave way to tea plantations. Fat cows grazed beneath spreading maple trees. Then, outside of Fuman, the road began to climb, up into the westernmost spur of the Alborz. We switched from a shared taxi to a crowded minibus, and I was struck by how often the peasant men gave up their seats to the peasant women.

Masuleh clings to a lush, forested mountainside above a rushing river. The gradient is so steep that the town has few streets; instead, the flat roofs of the cream-colored buildings, terraced up the mountainside like a wedding cake, serve as walkways and public gathering places. Rock-hewn staircases lead from one level to the next, and embedded in many of the older homes are carved wooden doors and stained glass windows. Balconies draped with kilims and geraniums look out over the valley below, and the exposed electrical wires—found everywhere in rural Iran—detract only slightly from the overall scene.

Renowned for its beauty throughout Iran, Masuleh is a favorite tourist destination. WELCOME TO MASULE ANCIENT TOWN reads a sign in both Persian and English at its entrance, and aggressive old ladies in traditional dress call out to all passersby. Toothless but shrewd, they are desperate to sell the garishly colored socks and hats that they have painstakingly knitted with gnarled hands during long winter months.

Through the center of Masuleh winds an open-air bazaar lined with booths selling more knitted socks and hats, red leather slippers with upturned toes, kilims, and woven wall hangings. Groups of touring middle-class Iranians armed with cameras stop at these shops, but not at the dark, low-ceilinged teahouses next door, filled with rickety tables and scrawny village men in wool caps. At one end of the bazaar is a milky green marble mosque with two minarets thick as elephant legs. At the other is a roaring orange furnace, stoked by a wiry man wielding a shovel—the *hammam,* or public baths.

I had read much about the *hammam* of Persia. Integral to the country after the advent of Islam, the baths once filled many purposes—religious, hygienic, medicinal, social, and occasionally political, with men or women of intrigue sharing secrets while enveloped in clouds of steam. Some of the baths were simple two-room affairs, with one room for changing, another for bathing, but many others were astonishingly elaborate, with mosaic entranceways, murals from the *Shahnameh,* vaulted ceilings, and two or more bath rooms, each more humid than the last. Most baths reserved some days or hours for men, others for women, whereas others were unisex.

The typical large *hammam* began with a long corridor that led to a hexagonal changing room with stone platforms all around and a small tiled pool in the middle. Bathers left their clothes on the platform, wrapped a towel around themselves, and proceeded to the *hammam* proper—a large chamber with at least one pool, brick and tile walls, a dome roof, and water taps scattered everywhere. Each bather was assigned a corner according to his or her social rank; between them moved attendants whose job it was to shampoo, scrub, massage, or otherwise see to the needs of their clients.

For the Persian women, the public bathhouses were especially important. Mothers, daughters, and grandmothers often spent one entire day a week there, gossiping about suitors and marriage, singing and dancing, telling stories, and coloring their hair with henna. Preparing to go to the *hammam* alone often took most of the day before, as the henna and shampoo mixtures had to be concocted, copper bowls and towels packed, and fruits, drinks, and other foodstuffs prepared. In one popular ritual, celebrated 10 days after a woman gave birth, close friends wrapped a plaster made of egg yolks and chickpea powder around her waist and took her to the baths. There, they rubbed the mixture and a special oil into her body for hours while passing around pastries, fruits, and drinks.

I knew that with the advent of indoor plumbing, the public bathhouse in Iran had gone into serious decline. Most of the bathhouses still operating in the country today cater only to the poor and lack romance. Nonetheless, I wanted to experience one for myself.

Mr. Bakhtiari looked unhappy when I told him of my plan. But I was determined. The baths would give me an opportunity to talk to some of the village women. There's nothing like being naked, I thought, for breaking down barriers between people.

Yet the baths of Masuleh were even simpler than I'd expected. Divided into two rooms, they were dark and built of rough cement walls that had seriously deteriorated in places. The first room, lined with wooden lockers, was presentable enough, but the second contained only a half-dozen shower stalls, all badly chipped. It was lit by a lone lightbulb, hanging crookedly by a black cord, and in the corners hulked piles of rubble.

I half considered retreating, but the women inside were greeting me too warmly. *Biya, biya,* they cried—come in, come in. The bath attendant, a wizened woman missing her front teeth, led me to a locker, talking the whole time, and helped me off with my *manteau, rusari,* and shoes, examining them all closely as she laid them in my locker. She sniffed at the soap I'd brought and made a face—apparently it wasn't sweet enough—and offered me a mitt for scrubbing while I paid the required entrance fee, about 20 cents. Then she called for her teenage daughter, a wet, raven-haired beauty naked except for turquoise bikini underwear, who led me to an empty shower stall and turned on the water. Clouds of steam rose into the air.

The women in the other stalls, circumspect at first, stuck out their heads one by one and stared at me, as the attendant's daughter hovered nearby—my protector. Her long dark tresses, plastered onto her shoulders, and huge black eyes reminded me of the paintings of Qajar princesses I'd seen in Tehran.

"Is the water hot enough?" she asked. "Do you like the scrubbing mitt?"

Yes, I nodded, self-consciously aware of my nakedness, of my blondness, and most of all, of my wealth. I didn't need to be here—I had my own private shower back at the hotel, whereas these women . . .

Slowly, they called out questions while white foam swirled around the central drain and the furnace roared. Where was I from? Where was I going? Why was I alone? Where was my husband? Why didn't I have children? Didn't I like children? Had I seen a doctor?

In return, they answered my questions. Life in Masuleh was very hard. There was no work, and in the winter, the snow rose up to their thighs. Sometimes they didn't leave the house for weeks. Life had become even more difficult after the Revolution—there was no money—but life was better. Women had to wear the *rusari*; before, many had been "very bad." No, they'd never traveled to Esfahan or Shiraz—it was too expensive; only foreigners went there. Most of them lived alone with their children for at least half the year; their husbands, brothers, and fathers were all in the nearby city of Rasht or in Tehran, working or looking for work. Often, and especially during the winter, the only men in Masuleh were the sick and the old.

We retreated back to the locker room. The baths were closing in 20 minutes and a rush was on to dry body and hair vigorously with towels and get dressed—jeans and T-shirts for the younger women, long skirts and blouses for the older ones. The bath attendant, her daughter, and her daughter's friend giggled together as the last of their neighbors left the baths, and then they invited me home for tea.

We climbed up the mountainside, scrambling over rooftops and up rock staircases, to the top of the village, obscured since late afternoon by thick clouds of fog. A string of lights climbed single file up the mountain behind us and dampness clung to our clothes and hair.

Exchanging our shoes for slippers, we entered an old wooden home, where a bevy of women ushered us into an airy room filled with unfinished but gorgeous carved wooden doors, Persian carpets, and stained glass windows. I looked around in surprise—the bath attendant lived here?—but then realized that the house belonged to the family of the daughter's friend. Though originally from Masuleh, they were now well-off Tehranis, for whom this was a second home.

Tea was served, followed by watermelon. I tried to converse but had already exhausted much of my Persian in the baths, and so mostly watched as family members wandered in and out and conversation swirled by just beyond my reach. I thought about the young women who'd brought me here—best friends, they said, since age two—and wondered what would happen to their friendship in years to come. The daughter of the bath attendant had so few options, and her best friend, presumably many more—

Later, I reconnoitered with Mr. Bakhtiari and we returned to the heart of the village. Night was falling, and in the gathering darkness, sounds were growing louder. From below came the rushing of the river and the crowing of a rooster who had misjudged the time of day. From the mosque came the slow, haunting cadence of *azan*.

We stepped into an open storefront hung with carpets of a bold geometric design. A tiny man with a narrow, grizzled face sat cross-legged on a carpet, reading a thick book. He was wearing a black lambskin hat that seemed almost as tall as his torso and the narrowest pair of bifocals I had ever seen. Behind him, and half hidden behind another hanging carpet, were shelves crowded with more books and a telephone; on the floor were a large abacus and tarnished brass scale with matching brass weights.

Mr. Bakhtiari was looking for a kilim to take home to his wife, and while he inquired about prices, I looked around. Between the carpets and kilims were antique Russian samovars and faded black-and-white photographs. Many depicted Ayatollah Khomeini—speaking at a rally, seated with his son. Others depicted Khamene'i or Khatami, and two were snapshots of the shop's proprietor standing by a microphone.

I asked him about these last two. Was he a teacher or political leader?

No, he said gravely, he was a poet.

Mr. Bakhtiari and I looked at each other. We'd been speaking about Persian poetry just an hour before. We sat down, and Mr. Yossef Akhavan told us about himself.

He'd been born in Masuleh and had gone to school in Rasht until the sixth grade. Then he'd married and worked as a shepherd for 25 years because he loved nature and wanted to be close to Allah. During those years, he'd started to read, and what he'd read had been poetry—mostly Hafez and Rumi. In fact, he'd been reading *Interpretations of Rumi* when we'd come in.

"And what about your own poetry?" I asked. "When did you start to write?"

"Not until 1979," he said. The return of Imam Khomeini had inspired him, and since then, he'd written about every major political event that had occurred, including the death of Khomeini and the Iran–Iraq War. He wrote about plenty of other subjects, too. Would we like to hear his poem about Edison, Einstein, and Avicenna, the famed Persian philosopher, doctor, and scientist who'd lived in Hamadan, only about six hours away?

Perching on a stool across from us, Mr. Akhavan drew out a sheet of paper covered with miniature Persian script elaborate as an engraving. Words covered every inch of the page, including the margins, where they were written on a neat slant. Tilting his head, Mr. Akhavan cleared his throat and began to recite. Dark, lustrous words, as deep as the gongs of a bell, resonated around us, filling every crevice of the shop. I could understand little, but it didn't matter. The heft of the poem was enough.

Passersby looked in at us curiously, but they couldn't penetrate our circle, and Mr. Akhavan read on and on, drawing us deeper and deeper into his inner world. He followed his poem about Edison, Einstein, and Avicenna with a poem about Masuleh and a poem about Imam Khomeini. Then he composed a poem about me—his "fellow writer and traveling soul"—thanking President Khatami for my arrival in Iran and asking Allah to bless me in paradise.

ॐ

Two months later, shortly before leaving Iran, I was to meet Mr. Farrokh Mostofi, editor of *Shekar-o-Tabiat,* or *Game and Nature* magazine. Though a grandnephew of Ayatollah Khomeini, Mr. Mostofi had been educated in Berkeley, California, during the 1960s, and tended to dress in jeans and carry a backpack. One of his passions was organizing trips to remote areas of Iran, and he especially enjoyed tracing the journeys of earlier adventurers. Among those writers whose footsteps he'd followed was Freya Stark.

He told me about his trip. Following the route of Stark's second journey, which she'd undertaken in 1931, he'd started in Garmrud, hiked through the village of Pichiban, crossed the Alborz via Salambar Pass, and descended through Seh Hezar valley. He'd met a son of Aziz, Stark's guide, who had a store in Garmrud, and visited Aziz's grave. He'd also found a house where Stark had stayed and a waterfall that she had mentioned. His guide had been the perfect modern-day muleteer: a young man dressed in a *Titanic* T-shirt.

As Mr. Mostofi spoke, my spirits sank. He had followed the Englishwoman's route much more closely than I; in fact, if I were honest with myself, I had failed in my quest rather dismally. But then Mr. Mostofi told me that he had traveled with 30 friends and colleagues. Thirty people had traipsed through Garmrud, and 30 people had camped out on a cold mountaintop beneath the stars. Thirty people had huffed and puffed through Salambar Pass, and 30 people had scrambled noisily down through Seh Hezar.

I thought of our small, congenial band toiling silently through the still, red landscape, lit by that startling white light. And I thought of my conversations with Lohraseb, the women in the bathhouse, Mr. Akhavan, and, especially, Mr. Bakhtiari. There was, I thought, more than one way to recreate a historic journey. Or to create an odyssey of one's own.

Strange Children in a Strange Land

No matter how fast you run,
your shadow more than keeps up . . .

But that shadow has been serving you!
What hurts you, blesses you.
Darkness is your candle.
Your boundaries are your quest.
                    —Jalal al-Din Mohammad Rumi, "Enough Words?"

ONE

My Tabriz story begins at dawn, in a big, lovely, two-story house with a brick fireplace, double-hung windows, and half-furnished rooms with bare walls and floors. My brother and I awaken, simultaneously it seems, and sit up on our iron cots painted white. A triangular yellow candy left over from the night before is stuck to my pillow. Our parents let us have candy right before we go to bed here—a concession to our being strange children in a strange land.

We get up and pad downstairs. Our parents are still asleep. Pans are rattling in the kitchen. Shapur, our cook with the bristling mustache, is already here. Holding our breaths—he will be annoyed if he sees us up this early—we tiptoe through the living room, past the squashed leather hassocks that we like to jump on, and out onto the patio. The bricks beneath our feet are already hot. Our hearts are beating tat-tat-tat. Giggling with fear, we nudge each other—who will do the honors?

I will, of course. I am the oldest. At a half crouch, I approach a shoe-size cardboard box with the holes on top. Something is faintly scratching inside. Right behind me is my brother, gripping my pajama top. I lift the box half an inch, and a shiny black leg sticks out. My brother screams and I clamp the box back down again. But it is already too late. Our prisoner "scorpion" has escaped, scuttling across the white clay patio at the speed of light, surprisingly small.*

❧❧

It is midday, in the "dungeon" beneath the hospital. We children are not permitted to be down here, in this dark basement made up of corridors that twist and turn past one black, silent room after another. There are no overhead lights; the cool musty odor of earth fills the air. Beneath our feet is uneven ground, and we must feel our way along as we penetrate deeper and deeper into the tantalizing forbidden. Sometimes we bump up against some mysterious object and want to scream or shout. But we cannot. If we do, we will alert the handful of men who are working in the occasional lit room.

The light of those rooms, spilling out yellow and lacy with dust into the corridors, is both our salvation and the object of our great dread. Without the light, we would not be able to see a thing and would not have the courage to be down here. But the light also has the capacity to reveal us, to betray us.

And so we approach each lit room with bated breath. The trick is to run past the bright open doorway when the backs of the men inside are turned. They are carpenters busy working with noisy hammers and saws, and so we have a chance. But there are also four of us, my brother and I and our two friends. Four makes the situation more dangerous.

We creep along, to the largest of the lit rooms. My friend and I make it across. Yet my brother and his friend are still on the other side, and they are so small. Urgently, we beckon, but they don't move. They seem frozen, clutched to the wall. My brother's friend is sucking his thumb. We beckon

---

*Probably a spider of some kind. Though scorpions are common in Iran, I doubt my parents would have allowed us to capture one.

again, this time more urgently, and maybe we whisper, because suddenly an enormous man with hunched shoulders looms up in the doorway. A raggedy coat swings around him as he shouts out strange, heavy words. He is the same man who has caught us down here before.

Screaming, we scramble away and somehow find a route back out into the ordinary world—pale and anemic compared to our mysterious kingdom. Running as fast as we can, we reach a clump of trees and collapse, to watch as the man in the raggedy coat follows us out. In the sunlight, he looks dusty and poor, and I feel a pang, even though I know that he is on his way to complain to our father, who will undoubtedly forbid us to enter the "dungeon" ever again. And since this is already the third or fourth time we've been caught, I suspect that this time we'll be forced to obey—or else. Even now, the thought fills me with a sense of loss.

જ્જ્જ

It is evening, and my brother and I are taking a bath in an enormous white tub that I now realize must have come from the West. The tub has clawed feet and smooth curved edges and a snoutlike faucet that reminds me of a pig. We sit surrounded by plastic toys and boats that bob wildly about on waves that we've created. Watch out!, There's a big storm at sea! we cry, rocking excitedly back and forth, when suddenly, splat, a wave sloshes up over the side of the tub, taking our rubber duck with it. We look at each other in dismay. We've already been scolded many times about splashing water onto the floor. And now our duck is out there. We have to rescue him.

Shivering, I stand up—it's much easier for me to get out of the tub than it is for my small brother. Stepping out onto the wet floor, I bend down to pick up the duck. But as I do so, I bump up against the cylindrical water heater that stands in the corner. I hear a soft sizzle and feel a soft heat, gentle as a baby's blanket, passing along my buttocks. Yet there's no pain at all until I sit back down in the tub. And then suddenly, I'm on fire. I stand up, I sit down, I stand up again—and scream and scream. My backside is covered with second-degree burns whose scars will remain with me for the rest of my life.

All these years later, I can't recall the searing pain, but I can remember my enormous surprise, and the flashing sense of betrayal I had that the water made me feel worse, not better. I traipsed crankily around the house for weeks afterward, dragging a pillow behind me. I used that pillow every time I sat down, and although it always seemed soft at first, a split second later, it was as hard as a rock and of no use at all. Still, I never let go of it.

ॐ

These memories come to me as brilliant white flashes surrounded by blackness. No matter how hard I try, I can't remember what came immediately before or after them or exactly where they belong in the continuum of my early life. Crowding in on my few frozen memories were millions of possible others that I've left completely behind, and that makes what I do remember seem arbitrary, paltry, unsure.

ॐ

I remember the compound in which we lived, surrounded by high, mud-brick walls, plastered over with another layer of clay. I can't remember any noise ever coming from beyond those walls, though there must have been some—a rooster, traffic, the call to prayer. I can't remember ever seeing the mountains from inside the compound, either, though they were certainly there—deep red, desert dry, and etched with sinuous ridge. The compound of my memory is hermetically sealed in a hot white light, in childhood.

Later, my father will tell me that our house and the American Hospital where he worked—both owned by the Presbyterian Church—were also made of mud brick, and that the building material is much more sophisticated than it sounds. Baked hard by the sun, the bricks can be used to construct everything from elaborate mosques to arched bridges and, when lined up several feet thick, provide excellent insulation. In Iran's arid climate, mud-brick structures last for centuries.

When one entered the compound, the first building on the left was the hospital—nothing more than a bulky brown block in my memory. Then came a long pathway lined with tall trees inhabited by crows, and a sparse flower garden that wordless groundskeepers in faded blue overalls tended. At the end of the pathway stood our house—flat-roofed and clay white, with shiny windows and a patio on which we often ate breakfast. Beyond our house and a little to the left was the nurses' dormitory, with its own private garden, and in between the two buildings grew dozens of almond trees, which flowered white in the spring and then blanketed the ground with petals of snow. Hugging the walls of our house were pomegranate trees.

Several times a day, the nurses would glide back and forth between their dorm and the hospital—crisp white shapes in white shoes and stiff caps. But otherwise, we children seldom saw them on the grounds. They kept to themselves, except on those occasional afternoons when they invited my mother and us children over for tea. My brother and I always disliked those teas. We hated the way the giggling nurses pinched our cheeks so hard that they stung.

Behind the hospital was an untended area that I thought of as being "wild." Dozens of stray cats stalked through its stiff grasses, and through the hospital "dungeon," sometimes followed by a string of kittens. I longed to have a kitten of my own, and so my father and I embarked on several expeditions to catch me one. I can remember the excitement of setting out, of searching into dark corners with a flashlight, and how it always seemed as if we would never find what we were looking for, until suddenly, we did, and would triumphantly go home bearing a snarling, wild-eyed smidgen of a beast in a precariously tilting box. My father would carry the box in his arms high above my head while I skipped alongside him.

But no matter how young the kitten that we captured was—though we took only those old enough to be weaned—we were never able to tame it. Again and again we tried, but again and again the determined animal wouldn't let anyone near it, lashing out with tiny teeth and claws whenever a human hand entered its box. Warm blankets, saucers of milk, ticking clocks meant to remind it of its mother's heart—nothing worked, nothing soothed the fear. I can remember crouching by the boxes for hours, yearning to pick up the sweet, furry presence before me—to feel its rib cage, its paws, its heart—and it glaring ferociously back at me. After a few weeks, we were always forced to return it to the wild, and only now, as I write this, do I wonder about how it was received or think about the human imperiousness of snatching a kitten from its mother.

We had better luck with our two *"jube* dogs"—named after the gutters that lined the streets. I loved playing with those furry puppies—Spot, one was unimaginatively called, and my favorite, Susie.

Yet the *jube* dogs proved to be problematic, too. Although they made good pets as puppies, they never became house trained and, on reaching adulthood, became tired of games and hugs and began roaming the compound in search of escape. Both of them did eventually do so, slipping out the front gate when the gatekeeper wasn't watching, and I remember constantly scanning the streets whenever we left the compound, looking for one of "our" animals, especially Susie. Sometimes I imagined that I spotted her among a rangy pack, but she always disappeared by the time we drew near.

Often waiting outside the hospital gate was a line of *droshkies*, the Russian word for horse-drawn carriages—the Russian border was only about 80 miles away. More conventional taxis usually waited there as well, but we children always dragged our parents toward the patiently waiting nags, long tails flicking, and their even more patiently waiting drivers, usually small, slight men dressed in layered, dust-covered clothes. The men would smile as we approached, gray grizzled faces cracking open with delight in anticipation of a well-paying fare, and a moment later, leather creaking, the whole carriage tilting, my mother would climb on board. Then, the gleaming metal footstep, as high as my waist, would disappear with a whoosh as someone—my father, the driver—lifted me on board. The worn leather seats burned against my bare legs as I sat down and off we clip-clopped, to the smell of manure, the rattle of wheels, the clucking of the driver's tongue. Sometimes an especially kind man would allow my brother or me to sit beside him on his high driver's seat—a precarious perch with no sides or back—and take the reins. That would set my imagination racing—I was driving a stagecoach through enemy Indian country, I was leading an army across the plain—but as excited as I was to hold the reins, it couldn't compare to the power of the dark, enigmatic presence sitting beside me. His large, rough, and sometimes misshapen hands—so different from my father's. His worn, patched, and baggy clothes—unlike anything we owned. His smell—part wind, part sweat, part poverty, and all unknown.

My parents tell me that people sometimes stared at us as we drove by, startled by the sight of our blond hair—both we children's and our mother's. The *hejab* was not mandatory for women back then, and she, like most Christian women in Iran, dressed as she pleased, though always within conservative parameters, which included never wearing short skirts or pants.

Later, my mother would tell me that many of the Iranian women she met loved to talk about clothes and often plied her with questions about the latest Western fashions, which they wore beneath their *chadors*. She also told me that except for a few familiar streets, she seldom went outside the compound alone.

Early on during our stay in Tabriz, our family set off one afternoon in the hospital Jeep. One of the gardeners was driving—my father had been advised against driving in Iran; if you hit someone, he'd been told, there's no telling what might happen. The Jeep pulled up to my parents' friend's house on the outskirts of town. My parents got out to drop something off, leaving us children behind on an empty street with the driver. But when they returned, less than five minutes later, the Jeep was surrounded by a large crowd of people. "And I mean *hundreds!*" my father always says with wonder when he relates this story, which I myself can't remember at all. The people had come, seemingly out of nowhere, to stare—silently, respectfully—at our blond hair.

We lived next door to the American Consulate. Only a high mud-brick wall separated our compound from theirs and a door stood at the midway point to allow for easy passage between. The American consul at that time was William Eagleton, and he and his wife, Françoise, had five children. The oldest was a girl, Diane, at age 12 or so already half a grown-up, but all the others were boys and the middle two, Robert and Richard, exactly my brother's and my ages, respectively, and our constant companions.

Not surprisingly, all the games that we four children played were traditional boys' games. We were soldiers, we were cowboys, we were explorers, we were adventurers. Though I wasn't a particularly athletic child—as a teenager I would be pathetic—I still imagined myself a tomboy and wanted to be a sailor when I grew up, traveling the high seas in a tall-masted wooden ship.

Inside the consulate gleamed an aquamarine swimming pool—the object of our great longing during the hot, dry summers. We children were not allowed in the pool until after business hours, or during the pool parties that the American Consulate occasionally threw for the international community. Then the poolside lawn would be crowded with half-naked adults, talking and laughing and foolishly, or so we thought, all but ignoring the water. I can remember learning to swim in that pool and how the crowd of adults—who seemed so "other" to me, rather like mysterious, overgrown beasts—clapped when I first swam the dog paddle. I can also remember my mother flirting with a dark, lanky Frenchman. I hadn't liked that.

Years later, when I was just beginning to think of returning to Iran, I came across that swimming pool again. I was sitting in Butler Library at Columbia University, reading the transcripts of the Iranian–American Relations Project, an oral history project that had interviewed prominent

Americans living in Iran just prior to the Revolution. I was half falling asleep as I skimmed along when I came across an interview with Michael Metrinko—and sat up. The principal State Department officer in Tabriz in the late 1970s, as well as one of the American hostages held in 1979–1980, Metrinko had once lived where I had lived, walked where I had walked, and though it sounds ridiculous to admit this, that fact alone astonished me. Tabriz, with its American Hospital and American Consulate, had seemed to be my family's exclusive property all my life, and yet here it was, alive on the page. It actually did exist in the world.

The only U.S. State Department employee then in Tabriz, as the consulate was about to be closed because of inactivity, Metrinko described what I'd always thought of as *our* pool: "this huge swimming pool, with all the changing rooms and shower facilities, sitting in the middle of an almond orchard." He also spoke of what a waste it was to have the pool sitting unused all day and how he therefore decided to open it up to the Iranian schoolchildren.

My cheeks grew hot as I read that and I felt a wave of shame, wonder, and horror. Why had the pool never been opened up to Iranians during our years there? Even worse, why had it never occurred to me that it should be? And still far worse, why did part of me recoil—even as most of me rejoiced—at the thought? Because I regarded my family and our cohorts as Great White Hopes come to save the inferior natives? Or because I regarded us as "special," part of the chosen few allowed into an exclusive club?

During our last six months in Tabriz, I went to first grade at a French school run by nuns. All of my classmates were middle- and upper-class Iranian girls, whereas the boys studied at another school next door—I think. Like so much else about Iran, I remember frustratingly little about the school: Long, polished corridors surrounding a central courtyard framed by arcades. Light and shadow falling in tilting elongated shadows through those arcades. The whisper of a nun's heavy habit sweeping across the floor, and the surprising animation of her face above so much dead cloth—just like a *chador.* Crowded rows of desks with benches, and my young self sitting way in the back. Standing up when called upon to recite. Filling up thin blue notebooks with endless rows of tiny print—too tiny, my American teachers would *tsk-tsk* when I returned to the States.

I knew no French when I entered the school, but my parents tell me that I learned quickly and could soon communicate. Perhaps. Because what I remember is the terror of not being able to understand or be understood. The terror of standing lost and trembling in a corridor unable to explain to the nun before me—the head nun, the scariest nun—where I wanted to go. The terror of being called on in class and standing up because I recognized my name but not knowing what I was being asked to do or say, while all the other girls—all dark hair, dark eyes—stared at me, kept their distance from me.

I did have one friend at school. We played with pebbles in the courtyard. But I don't remember whether we spoke and I don't remember her name. She was the only Iranian playmate that I had. Though we lived in Iran for three years and my parents had some Iranian friends, we—like most other Westerners then in the country—kept mostly to our own kind.

ॐॐ

I open a marvelous old photograph album that my mother keeps on a shelf in her study. The album comes from Iran, or rather, Persia, because its hand-painted magnificence belongs more to a mythic past than to a realistic present. Long and maroon, the album's front cover is framed by a border of red and black flowers, some of which have been worn pink by time. Inside the border are lacy arabesques of gold and red on cream, and inside those, a black shape resembling a Rorschach ink blot, laced with more arabesques, leaves, and flowers of red, blue, green, and much gold. Swirling in the center is a round medallion encircling a mosque flanked by minarets and trees.

The album is filled with lots of family photos—picnics, Christmases, Halloweens, and birthdays, especially birthdays. In the expatriate community in Tabriz, where there was not much in the way of entertainment, any event became an excuse to throw a party, and even a child's birthday ballooned into a major affair, with all children of all ages invited and many adults. I see endless pictures of long picnic tables set up outdoors beneath the almond trees, and crowded with little faces expectantly watching an adult bearing a birthday cake. I also see endless pictures of me dressed in the frilly crinoline party dresses that I hated, and I can still feel the insistent way they scratched against my skin. Often in these pictures, my hair is pulled severely back into a ponytail and tied with polka-dot ribbons, sent to me by my German grandmother. I adored my ribbon collection—white dots on pale blue, dark blue, red, and green, and the unusual blue dots on white.

One or two of the photographs depict the Presbyterian church that we attended—a simple but attractive brick structure with a bell tower puffing out from the front façade like a small belly. A handful of Western people dressed in starched dresses and dark suits is standing around out front, but otherwise, the place looks empty.

I have asked my parents about what it was like to be in Iran under the auspices of the Presbyterian Church. Were they expected to proselytize? No, my father tells me—he was there simply to work as a surgeon; religion had nothing to do with it. No, my mother tells me—she was there to support my father and take part in community life. But, my mother also says, they were both carefully screened before going to Iran and asked extensive questions about the depth of their Christian beliefs.

My parents were not missionaries in the full sense of the word. To be a true missionary then was usually a long-term occupation and one that demanded a deep commitment to the Christian faith. We were just in Iran on a temporary basis, to fill in for a full-time missionary who needed to take a break, and my parents, although Christian, didn't have that kind of religious fervor. They therefore had not received the usual intensive language and cultural training and always felt somewhat apart from the rest of the mission community, which numbered about 6 in Tabriz, including 2 other doctors, and 20 in Tehran. We were also in Iran during the mission's twilight years. The hospital would close down shortly after we left, as large numbers of Iranian doctors were beginning to graduate from medical schools, decreasing the need for foreign medical aid.

Although I don't remember actually attending a service in the Presbyterian church, I do remember playing afterward with my good friend Todd, who figures in a number of our photos, often as a solemn child wearing a round cap. One year younger and two heads shorter than I, Todd was the minister's son, and being with him was much different from being with my friend Richard. With Richard, I was an adventurer. With Todd, I was a storyteller. The two of us told each other tales for hours on end, my mother remembers, often adding embellishments to each other's plots. Thinking back on this now and watching other people's offspring, I am amazed by the way even very young children already know exactly whom they like and dislike, and why. Many of my adult friends are also either adventurers—of the mind and spirit, if not of the physical world—or storytellers, and sometimes both.

Some of our other photographs offer glimpses of our servants—Arabic, our maid, and our cook, Shapur. The idea of servants makes me uncom-

fortable now, but most middle-class people in Iran had servants at that
time—wages for hired help were exceedingly low. I remember Arabic as
being small, dark, quick, and intense, and the photographs confirm this. I
remember Shapur as being large, gruff, old, and gray, with big red hands
and a walrus mustache. But except for the mustache, the photos don't confirm this at all. Shapur is perhaps a little stocky but is of average height and
no more than age 35, with dark hair just starting to go gray.

When I returned to Tabriz as an adult, I learned that Shapur had been
dead for many years. And yet, here he still is in our album, a youngish man.
The camera has captured him in time, as it has all our other friends and
acquaintances, and it is strange to imagine them going on after these photographs to have lives as full as my own, when by rights, it seems, they
belong here, in this frozen world. Sometime ago, when I was in my twenties, my father told me that by pure coincidence he'd run into William
Eagleton, the American consul from Tabriz, and that since Iran, the man
had remarried, had more children, and been posted to other countries all
over the world. But how can that be? I half wondered as I heard the news
with an odd sense of betrayal and disbelief.

I turn another page of the album, to a handsome photograph of my
parents. My mother is wearing a flowered satin dress that I remember—
panes of fabric winking and blinking like glass when she walked—and a
strand of pearls. Her hair is piled up in the same regal style that she wears
now, but her long graceful neck and heart-shaped face are clear and
unlined. My father's rounder face, too, is unlined, and he sports a clipped
black beard that scratched against my face whenever I sat in his lap.

These young parents are gone now. We children are gone now, and
Shapur—and who knows who else?—is dead. Looking at the arrested images
before me, I feel an acute sense of loss. I see happy people living in an idyllic
world, headed toward rocky, not-so-idyllic futures. Yet I know that to a large
extent, this is sentimentalized claptrap. Photographs, like memories, isolate a
few quicksilver moments, separating them from messy lives.

இ௭௸

Along with the exotic Persian photograph album, we also have a second
one—a green utilitarian one, filled mostly with pictures of strangers. In it,
I see images of graduating nurses, sad-eyed burn victims, a plain blue hospital waiting room, and several hospital Christmas parties at which a
Christian Santa Claus is handing out presents to Muslim children on

crutches and in wheelchairs. One hospital employee poses proudly by a giant samovar, another by the only incubator in all of Azerbaijan, and there is our wonderful friend Bahman, a smiling, dark-haired young man, standing with his hands clasped before him.

My father tells me about some of these photographs.

A large percentage of his patients, he says, were peasants, because although some middle- and upper-class Iranians came to the hospital, they also had other private, more expensive hospitals to choose from. The peasants often arrived by donkey, and sometimes with fistfuls of prescriptions from other doctors already in hand. They didn't trust anything they'd previously been told, they said, and all they wanted from my father was another opinion: Which one of these prescriptions was the best? Other peasants, to my father's acute embarrassment, fell to the ground on meeting him, to kiss his feet.

Many of my father's patients were burn victims who had fallen into the *kursi*, or charcoal brazier, that was once found in many homes in Iran. Built into a pit dug in the center of the room, the *kursi* was usually covered over with a low table and large rug. During the cold weather, families often sat around the *kursi* with their feet in the pit and sometimes burned themselves or fell in. Children were the most common victims, although my mother also tells me there were sometimes rumors about unhappy women who deliberately burned themselves to prevent their husband's sexual advances.

The most common operation that my father performed involved removing part of the bowel—often five or six feet—and resecting it. The procedure is necessary when the bowel has twisted back on itself and the affected part must be removed within a few hours or the patient will die. My father saw more cases of this condition in Iran than he ever encountered before or since, and many occurred around the time of Ramadan, when Muslims fast all day and then make up for it by eating heartily, perhaps too heartily, after sundown. The shrewd peasants always demanded to see for themselves whatever it was that my father had removed during their operations—proof that the job had been done.

Sometimes my father visited the villages by Jeep, driving up with another missionary into the mountains surrounding Tabriz. The land was always very dry except for a few magical weeks in spring, when the world turned bright green. He and his colleague were always very well received, with one villager bringing out a rug, another putting up a temporary tent, and a third cooking up an impromptu meal.

My father also treated lepers, who lived quarantined in desolate desert country outside Tabriz. A disease that attacks the nervous system, leading first to lost eyebrows and thickened skin, then to deformed hands and fused joints, leprosy is contagious, but only after prolonged contact. Many peasants, terrified of catching the disease, were amazed when my father touched the lepers and even more amazed when he operated on their misshapen limbs in the hopes of offering them some relief. Most of those operations were only minimally successful, however, and my father was heavily criticized for making the attempt.

A few of my father's patients were mullahs, who liked the fact that he had a beard, a symbol of humbleness in Islam. One mullah even said public prayers for him in a mosque. My father never attended a Friday prayer meeting himself, however, and because he is normally the most intellectually curious and adventurous of people, that strikes us both now as emblematic of the times. Prior to the Islamic Revolution, most Americans in Iran were strangely oblivious to the pervasiveness of Islam—an outlook that was reinforced by the attitude of many Shi'ites, who did not welcome Westerners at their prayer meetings.

Religion was a very loose thing, my father says, remembering—most people didn't go to the mosque. But many Iranians don't go to the mosque today, either. Most Muslims prefer to pray in private, making it easy to underestimate the reach of their religion, which among deep believers permeates everything, from social behavior to judicial law.

When the peasants learned of my father's interest in archeology, they brought him shards of pottery that they'd found while tilling their fields. None was of museum quality or of great value, but some dated back to Neolithic times and now sit on a shelf in his study. My father also owns several tiles from the Blue Mosque—one of the few visitor attractions in Tabriz, built in 1465. Though the tiles would never be allowed out of the country today, they were given to him back then by workmen restoring the mosque. These are old, the workmen had told him—take them if you'd like, we don't need them anymore, we're replacing them with new ones.

Many other photographs in the green album depict graduation ceremonies at the hospital's Nurses' Training School. "Capping," "The Ceremony," "Lamb Roast, Last Picnic with Nurses," read a few of the captions. Like our birthday parties, the graduations take place outdoors, where someone has laid out a large Persian carpet and set wooden chairs, a table, and a microphone on it. About two dozen nurses sit in the chairs, while to another side, fanning themselves, crowd the nurses' families, packed onto long pews.

Now my father tells me something that I've never thought about but should have realized before. Most of the nurses at the school were Armenian; indeed, with the exception of the cleaning staff and various laborers, almost everyone who worked at the American Hospital was Armenian because, generally speaking, Armenians are Christian. That's why no one in any of these photographs is wearing a *chador*.

Armenians have lived in northwestern Iran since the earliest days of the Persian Empire (559–330 B.C.), if not before. However, when the Armenians embraced Christianity at about A.D 200, they suffered first under the rule of the Zoroastrian priests, then the country's religious rulers, and later under the somewhat more tolerant rule of the Islamic conquerors. Since then, Armenians in Iran have struggled through various periods of repression, alternating with periods of peace, but have always managed to hold onto their culture and religion, and generally get along well with their Muslim neighbors. Historically, Armenians have been known as great craftspeople and educators, as well as pioneers in the photography, theater, and film industries.

One big problem at the American Hospital, my father goes on, was that the Armenian Christian nurses sometimes refused to touch the Muslim patients, whom they regarded as "unclean." And the Muslim patients, in turn, sometimes refused to be touched by the Armenian Christians.

Standing beside my father in several of the photographs is a young Iranian doctor, one of the few educated Muslims who worked at the hospital. He and my father were quite good friends until one day, my father made an unforgivable mistake. He criticized the younger doctor in front of others on the staff—standard operating procedure in most American hospitals, where older doctors often correct younger ones, but highly offensive behavior in Iran, where you never criticize anyone in front of their peers. Afterward, though the young doctor remained cordial to my father, their budding friendship was over.

❧❧❧

My mother also has a third album, a small tan personal scrapbook in which she has kept a copy of the first letter that she mass-mailed back to friends in the United States, as well as various newspaper clippings, invitations, and programs of social events. The words evoke a time and place in a way that the photographs do not: "The Director of the British Council Centre, Tabriz, Requests the pleasure of your company at a lecture by Mr. Curtis Harnack on 'HOW TO WRITE A BOOK.' " "The Director of the British Council Centre, Tabriz, Requests the pleasure of your company at a lecture by Mr. P. A. Greenway on 'WALES: ITS LANDSCAPE, HISTORY, AND PEOPLE.' "

Near the front of the album is a thick pamphlet about Howard Baskerville, an American mission teacher killed in Tabriz in 1909 while fighting with Iranian revolutionaries to establish the country's first constitution. In the foreword to the pamphlet, a Senator S. H. Taqizadeh praises Baskerville's courage in fighting for Iranian democracy, especially after being advised against doing so by the then-American consul who "warned him about mixing in the internal affairs of a foreign country and said that he, as an American citizen, could be punished by his government."

Accompanying the pamphlet is a newspaper clipping from *The Tehran Journal* recording a ceremony honoring Baskerville. Among the attendees is the U.S. ambassador to Iran, Edward T. Wailes, who succeeds in completely distancing himself, and by extension the U.S. government, from the position of the earlier American consul. "We Americans like to believe—" Wailes said in a speech praising Baskerville, "and there is a certain amount of history to support the belief—that something in us responds to the call for freedom, justice and the defense of spiritual and moral values."

I am not cynical enough to completely refute the validity of that statement, and yet . . . this ceremony occurred only about a decade after the forced ouster of Mohammad Mossadeq by the CIA, and I wonder how the Iranians in the room felt on hearing Wailes's speech.

Following my mother's collection of invitations and announcements are more pictures, these depicting both Americans and Iranians in formal dress attending events at the Iranian Officers Club, the American Consulate, and private homes. All of the women shimmer in silks and satins, and many of the men stand tall in military dress. Faces beam with pleasure—ah, to be included in such sophisticated company at last. I both admire their style and wonder at the insularity of this Westernized Iranian world.

I ask my father about the Shah. No Iranian ever said a word against him to us, he says. I ask my father about SAVAK. No Iranian ever mentioned it to us, he says, though we did hear about its reputation for torture from the State Department and knew that people were very afraid. I ask my father about the U.S. military presence then in Azerbaijan. We were in a sensitive area, he says, said to be infiltrated with Russian spies, and American lookouts were stationed all along the border—"or so I was told."

Some of the last pictures in the album depict more scenes taken in front of the Presbyterian church. The U.S. ambassador from Tehran is in town, and an entourage of cars, small U.S. flags flapping, crowd into the church's courtyard. Grim, lean Secret Service men in crew cuts and sunglasses are painfully easy to pick out, and one of them seems to be staring belligerently back out at me. Just how are you going to portray the U.S. presence then in Iran? he asks.

TWO

I arrived in Tabriz in the dark, after a 12-hour-long bus ride from Tehran. The landscape had been dry and mountainous most of the way, except for occasional strips of tilled green fields and traffic circles planted with flowers. Yet the mountains had changed character as we went. For hours outside Tehran, that stark, familiar Alborz wall had run steadily alongside us to the north. But beyond Zanjan, the mountains had become smaller and redder, and beyond Meyaneh, rounder and more self-contained, plopped down along an ancient winding riverbed like giant, elongated ice cream balls. We plunged into their depths, diving through elegant tunnels darkly lit and rattling over arched brick bridges centuries old. Blue curtains billowed, children cried, Turkish music blared, and a plastic doll with long brown hair, sunglasses, and bright red lips swayed beneath the rearview mirror. It was hours before I realized that the doll had no body, just long hair.

My seatmate was a kindly older woman, originally from Tabriz, now living in Tehran, who plied me with treats the entire trip—sunflower seeds, cucumbers, cookies, chips, candies, and hot tea. I had a hard time understanding much of what she said, but I quickly caught on that she hated the *hejab*. She had once been *"kheili* chic," she said, *"kheili, KHEILI* chic"—very, very chic—and had loved wearing short skirts with high heels on the street. These poor young women, she said every time another passenger in a *chador* entered the bus.

Nearing Tabriz, we passed out of the red mountains and onto a high coffee-colored plateau. Boys herding flocks of brown sheep flashed by, followed by a small lake. The moon hung like a pale silver pendant in the sky as the last rays of the sun illuminated the mountaintops and then disappeared. Colors faded into gray and black.

Mitra, Lona and Pari's sister, was at the station to meet me. I would be staying with their family, of course. My initial plan to stay in a hotel—I wanted time and space to reflect while in Tabriz—had been hastily brushed aside. In this city, of all places, Lona had said, I had to be well taken care of. To decline the invitation would have been to deeply offend.

Mitra had Pari's sparkling black eyes and pale complexion, and Lona's warm smile. The youngest of the three sisters, she was also the most beautiful, with a slim, willowy form and—I would later find out—thick black hair that reached to her waist. At age 23, she was unmarried and tended to dress in light-colored, knee-length *manteaus* that had a playful, girlish quality.

I'm here, I felt like shouting as I emerged from the bus, I'm actually here! And yet I was nervous at having arrived. The Tabriz of my memory was so spare and clear, unmarred by unnecessary detail. As much as I'd wanted to return, I didn't want to change that.

I also felt oddly surprised, despite reading the Metrinko interview, to see that Tabriz actually existed. It didn't belong to me and my family after all but rather to hundreds of thousands of Tabrizis, some of whom I now saw before me. But what are you all doing here? I rather ridiculously felt like asking—you don't figure into my Iran.

We drove through downtown Tabriz, which, though provincial in feel, looked much like any other modern city anywhere, and much better, to my mind, than either Tehran or Mashhad. The sidewalks seemed wider and the buildings cleaner, the traffic was less congested, and the air was crisp and clear—Tabriz is known all over Iran for its clean mountain air. Thin strips of red neon surrounded spotless, plate-glass windows—there was money here. Nothing even remotely resembled the raw Russian-influenced outpost of our pictures. So much happens in 30-odd years.

Though Mitra, her family, and I would soon become good friends, our first evening together was awkward. No one spoke a word of English and I was tired. A'zam, Mitra's mother, silent and heavyset, sat on the edge of the sofa, chain-smoking Montanas, a cigarette made in Pakistan that comes in what looks like a Marlboro Light box. Majid, her father, wiry and white-haired, sat huddled with Farzad, a family friend, telling private jokes. Yashar, her brother, a dark-eyed 15-year-old both confident and shy, kept staring at me. Dinner dragged on interminably until Farzad suggested that we go for a ride. He, Mitra, and Yashar would take me past the hospital compound where I had once lived.

My heart jumped. I knew that our old hospital and house were gone now, replaced by a nurses' training school, but the old compound walls still remained, as did the former American Consulate.

We piled into the car and drove from the family's boxy, modern apartment complex down a long hill into the city. Traffic was light. All the streets were well paved. I kept expecting something extraordinary to happen—a jolt of memory, perhaps—but the moments passed like any others.

We drove on and on, down one street after another—where? I kept wondering, where?—until suddenly, there it was: nothing more than a wide iron gate in a mud-brick wall. But even that was all wrong. In my memory, the hospital compound had been farther away from the center of things and in a far scruffier locale. There'd been no modern shops or new sidewalks nearby, just a tired old vendor in a windowless shack piled high with bubble gum coins wrapped in bright foil and imprinted with the head of the Shah. Silver, pink, green, and gold.

We stopped the car and I stared, trying to understand.

It's me! I wanted to shout again, I'm back! But except for the ghosts, there was no one to hear. I'd lived in Tabriz before Mitra and Yashar and probably even Farzad, who looked to be about 30, had been born. Most of the people my parents had known were either gone or dead, swept out by the Islamic Revolution and/or time. No one cared that I was here.

Because it was nighttime, the compound was closed, and so we drove on 20 or 30 yards to where the hospital compound ended and the former American Consulate began. Slogans covered the wall: DEATH TO AMERICA read one; WHAT ARE YOU THINKING, AMERICA? IRAN IS FULL OF MOBILIZED PEOPLE read another.

The consulate had been taken over by the *komiteh,* Farzad said, nodding at an armed guard lounging outside, and no ordinary citizen was ever allowed inside. I bit my lip at that and then realized that most ordinary Iranians probably had not been allowed inside the American Consulate, either.

Above the consulate walls peeked a handful of slim, sparse trees, bathed in a sickly light. The trees drew my imagination up over the wall and down their trunks, to the ground where perhaps more *komiteh* men were lounging. Or laughing and smoking Montanas. Or sprawled out on lawn chairs by the swimming pool.

Slowly, we circled the block once, twice. And then we continued our tour, past the army base, past the headquarters of SAVAMA (Iranian intelligence), and past the endless, mute barracks of the Revolutionary Guards, where dust hung in pale yellow umbrellas cast by overhead porch lights and slim figures passed across the windows of seemingly empty rooms. As a nighttime tour of New York City might take in the Empire State Building, Times Square, and the glittering streets of SoHo, so a nighttime tour of Tabriz took in four branches of the military. Farzad rated them in order of danger for me: (1) SAVAMA was the worst, he said, followed by (2) the Revolutionary Guards, (3) the *komiteh*/local police, and (4) the army.

࿔

The next day, Mitra and I returned to the former hospital compound, walking up what had once been "our street" from a main square. The road was now named Shari'ati Street, after the prominent revolutionary intellectual whose books had influenced my friend at Jamaran, Mr. Noroozi. During our years in Iran, the road had been called Shahnaz Street, after the Shah's daughter.

We passed by a modern greeting card shop, an electronics shop, a girls' school hidden behind a high wall, and an Armenian church, also hidden behind a high wall. Lots of Armenians live here, Mitra said, and I thought, of course. It made sense that the Presbyterian hospital would have been situated in a Christian neighborhood.

We entered the old hospital compound easily. The wide iron gate was open now, and no one questioned us or even gave us a second glance. Stopping immediately once inside, I stared to the left and the right. Once, I had been an insider looking out of this compound, but now I was an outsider, looking in. The new nurses' training school was now dead ahead—the old hospital had stood more to the left—and the second entrance gate, the door-size one that Bahman's uncle, Majid, had once guarded, was gone.

I had hoped to meet the 70-year-old Majid, who remembered my family, while in Tabriz. But a sudden funeral had taken him to Tehran two days before I arrived and he wasn't expected back for at least a week.

I'd talked to him by phone instead, with Bahman serving as translator. Yes, Majid had said, he remembered my father very well. Dr. Bird had walked like a champion, as if going up and up, and whenever he came through the gate, he was always the first to say hello, and would say hello again if he passed through again, even if he'd just done so a moment before. That sounded just like my father, I thought. And yes, Majid had said, he remembered my mother, too—she'd walked like a duck. A duck? I'd said, astonished. A duck was the last thing my mother walked like. He probably means she was sexy, Bahman said with a laugh.

My father remembered Majid, too. The gatekeeper had been one of the first to take advantage of the literacy classes that my father had helped start at the hospital, and when the unschooled man had learned to read his first words, he had cried.

We started toward the school, a low-slung edifice built of too much cement and too little glass. Painted on one side was the melancholy mural of a woman's face surrounded by blues—her *hejab*, the sky, the sea. She was mourning the dead from the Iran–Iraq War, and in front of her, as if part of the mural, was a row of geraniums in flowerpots. Our old garden had always been planted with marigolds, I remembered now in a flash, and as a child, I'd never liked the thick flowers, with their woody stems and strange smell.

Circling around the nurses' training school—I had no desire to go inside; it seemed pointless, and someone might stop us—we came to a heavy, concrete complex where the nursing students lived. The complex was situated where our old garden and house had been; somewhere amidst these smooth white walls and this dark inner courtyard, we had once lived. I took a few steps forward, paused, took another step, and then caught my breath, because although I knew that it was probably silly, that I was probably imagining things, I suddenly felt with dead certainty that I'd been here before. I knew this place.

That feeling grew stronger as we passed through the dorm complex, its high impenetrable balconies hung with laundry, and then continued on into a scruffy backyard, to walk along the mud-brick wall that bounded the former American Consulate. I knew this wall, too, no matter if it now had barbed wire on top.

We came to the faint outline of a door, now filled in, and I stopped. How often had I walked through this portal? I wondered. How often had my brother and mother and father? Were we all here now, our younger selves, watching me, wondering at what had become of me? A door, passageway between one reality and the next, seemed an appropriate place for ghosts to linger.

Mitra said something that I couldn't understand and we walked on, coming to what had once been the "wild" patch of my memory, now just more stubbled earth. The "dungeon" of the old hospital was gone, of course, and so were the stray cats. And so, for that matter, I suddenly realized, were the *jube* dogs. I'd seen no street dogs at all since my return to Iran. What had happened to them?

Two nursing students in *chadors*, one white, one black, passed by, and as was so often the case with the enshrouded women I saw, their faces seemed extraordinary to me. Peaceful, angelic, serious, intelligent, and wise beyond their years. They gave me curious glances, and I glanced curiously back, struck by how right it was that they should be here. They had taken over what the Presbyterian Church had started, they had helped to reclaim their nation. It was good that we Americans had once been here, bringing medicine and learning to what had once been a backwater town, but it was right that we Americans were now gone. As if on cue, *azan*, the call to prayer, began.

৵৽৻ঌ

The next day was Sunday and I wanted to go to church. I never went to church back home in New York, but I wanted to go to church here, to meet a few Armenians and talk to them about what it was like to be Christian in post-Revolution Iran. Mitra wanted to go to church, too. She'd never been to a church before. As a Muslim, she was forbidden to do so without special permission. My letter from Ershad, granting me leave to be a journalist in Tabriz, was excuse enough for us both.

We went back to Shari'ati Street and talked to passersby. Where could we find an Armenian service? Someone directed us to Sarkis Cathedral, and we wandered through a tight warren of back streets, flanked everywhere by high walls hiding homes, hiding businesses, hiding lives. We came on a group of young men who flirted momentarily with me and more seriously with Mitra—everyone flirted with Mitra—before passing beyond us and beckoning—come this way, come this way, Sarkis is this way, we're all going to Sarkis. Older men joined our path, followed by a bevy of middle-aged women dressed in elegant, light *manteaus* and bright silk *rusaris*. Everyone was going to Sarkis.

When we entered the church, the pews were already crowded. The service had begun and we took our seats in the back, where we'd be least conspicuous. At the altar stood a handsome priest in a green velvet robe embroidered with gold, and an older man in a purple robe, swinging incense back and forth. Chandeliers hung from the ceiling. Deep-hued paintings covered the walls. And to me, mostly raised Congregational in a sparse, white New England church, the Armenian Orthodox service seemed as exotic as the Shi'ite prayer meetings I'd witnessed in Tehran and Mashhad.

I've never understood the fuss regarding different organized religions. Though nominally a Christian, I view most of the world's religions—and especially Christianity, Judaism, and Islam—as being remarkably alike. Christians, Jews, and Muslims all believe in one god, in doing the right thing, in certain prophets, and in the power of prayer. So how can so much hatred be expended on minor differences when many of the major beliefs are shared? A hopelessly naïve question, I'm sure, but nevertheless—I greatly admire truly spiritual people of all religions but cannot understand their fundamentalist counterparts.

When the service was over, Mitra and I retreated outdoors, into an enormous, stone-paved courtyard where some of the worshippers had already gathered. Here, we met Nora, who spoke excellent English. To my delight, she had once taken Bible study classes at the American Hospital and now taught English medical terms at the new nurses' training school. She did not remember my father but had known some of his colleagues, who'd lived in Iran for much longer than we had. She also remembered Bahman—they'd taken English classes together—and she remembered our house.

"Oh, of course I remember it!" she said. "Those beautiful double-hung windows—and the garden! We had tea dances in that garden, once a month, in the late afternoon. I was so young. I had a special feeling. And every time I go back to teach, I still have a special feeling. Thank you for making me remember my youth."

Nora introduced me to her son, a tall, lanky teenager who wanted to know how he could apply to colleges in the United States. Most of the other worshippers were leaving now, dispersing in different directions across the courtyard.

I asked Nora how the Armenian community, which is the largest Christian community in Iran, had fared since the Revolution.

"The Armenian community is stronger," she said. "Our faith is deeper. The Revolution has made us come together."

"Does the government bother you?" I asked.

"No," Nora said firmly. "This is Armenia. This is our place. We have been here for thousands of years. Iran is only here for a short time. The Islamic Republic is only here for a very, very short time."

"So the government lets you worship as you please?" I pressed.

"The government treats us very well," she said. "They have great respect for us. I couldn't imagine anything better."

Armenians, I knew, are one of the most respected minority groups in the Islamic Republic. Though subject to occasional harassment, they have two representatives in the Majlis, or parliament, and the changes they've had to make since the Revolution due to their minority status have been relatively minimal. Male Armenian hair stylists, who once dominated the beauty business, have had to close up shop (no touching of strange women), and Armenian food businesses must now prominently display signs that say MINORITY RELIGION because they serve pork and other un-Islamic foods. Armenian schools, now administered by Muslims, must also be open on Sundays, as per the Muslim calendar.

Other Christians in Iran, most notably Protestants, have fared far worse under the Islamic regime—largely because many are converts or children of converts from Muslim backgrounds. According to traditional Islamic law, to convert from Islam is a crime punishable by death, and even in the days of the Shah, converts were often shunned by their community. After the Revolution, many converted Christians fled Iran whereas others became targets of hostility and violence. In 1979, the Reverend Arastu Sayyah, pastor of the Anglican church in Shiraz, was murdered in his office, and in 1980, the son of Anglican Bishop Dehqani Tafti was gunned down on the streets of Tehran. In 1993, Christian ministers and priests were forced to sign declarations promising that Muslims would not be allowed to attend their services, and in 1994, two more prominent Christian leaders were killed.

The courtyard was now empty. Nora's son had gone home, and Mitra was looking bored. But Nora and I continued to talk, with Nora telling me about her husband, an Englishman who'd worked in Iran for a few years. Shortly after marrying, the two of them had gone to England to live, but just prior to the Revolution, Nora and her children had returned to Iran—alone.

"I am sorry," Nora said, "but I did not want my children to grow up in England. The English are very selfish, they have no faith. Here faith is very great—Muslims and Christians, living side by side, very deep believers. I am a spiritual person, and here, people are very good, very close, always speaking with God. The English people—they do not speak with God."

I asked Nora if she knew anything about the old Presbyterian church that my family had once attended. My parents hadn't been able to tell me exactly where it was.

"The government shut it down after the Revolution," she said. "They didn't like the Presbyterian church. The people there were speaking Persian, trying to convert. And some Iranians went there for bad purposes—to get a visa. They said they were converts, but how is that possible? To be Christian, you must have Christian parents. To be Muslim, you must have Muslim parents."

My heart sank. Why this insistence on the insurmountable differences between peoples?

"What about marriage between Christians and Muslims?" I asked.

"It happens very little," Nora said. "It is not good . . ."

Why not? I thought dispiritedly.

Leaving the courtyard in silence, we started toward Shari'ati Street, passing by another church on the way. There were six churches in Tabriz in all, Nora had told me earlier. Most were Armenian, and one, Adventist.

"We have always been very good friends with Muslims," Nora suddenly said, perhaps sensing my disapproval. "We go to school with Muslims, we have tea with Muslims, they are our good friends and neighbors. But marriage? No."

At Shari'ati Street, Nora pointed us in the direction of the closed Presbyterian church. It was impossible to visit now, she said, without special permission from Ershad, but we might be able to catch a glimpse of it through the gate.

Nora was right. A glimpse of a neglected façade and darkened bell tower was all that we got. But that was enough for me. Except for the accumulated grime, the church looked exactly the way it did in most of our photographs, right down to the empty courtyard. A plastic bag blew across the steps and was gone.

৵৵৻৻

That evening, I went to speak with an old friend of Bahman's, Manucher, a surgeon whose solid, working-class family had converted from Islam to Christianity before he'd been born. Following the Revolution, Manucher had left the country to live in the West but had returned in 1995, as conditions for converted Christians have improved greatly in recent years.

However, Manucher still keeps his faith under wraps. The authorities know that he was Christian—and don't object, because they welcome his medical expertise—but most of his neighbors do not.

Manucher's family had once attended our Presbyterian church, and he'd taken English and Bible study classes at the American Hospital. He remembered our family.

"Many people now say that the Christians did nothing in Iran, but that is not true," Manucher said, after ushering me into his living room, furnished with brocade couches, and serving me tea and cake. "There were people like your father, people who did much good. And I myself learned much from the missionaries. I learned English, they helped me go to college and medical school. I owe them very, very much."

His face fell. "But they should have left our religion alone. What were they doing here? To convert—what?—maybe one percent of the people? For what?"

I avoided his gaze.

Over the years, my parents have told me many stories about the wonderful people they met through the church while in Iran. The mission people were so much fun, they will say, their eyes crinkling as they remember this or that, and we had as good a time with them as we've ever had with anyone—even though, of course, missionaries don't drink. All that nonsense that you hear about how harsh and humorless missionaries are—it just isn't true. They were some of the best people—some of the kindest, wisest, most intelligent, and most open-minded people—we've ever met.

I don't doubt that this is true, and yet, every time my parents tell one of their stories, I feel uneasy. Times have changed, and I, like Manucher, can't help but wonder about exactly what the Presbyterian Church thought it was doing in Iran. I have enormous respect for the great good that the Christian missionaries brought to the country: The first mission was established in Orumieh, just west of Tabriz, in 1834, and two years later, they opened one of the first modern boys' schools in all of Persia. Another of the mission's boys' schools, established in Tehran in 1873, later developed into Alborz College, one of the country's first accredited liberal arts colleges. In the mid-1870s, at a time when education for girls was all but unheard of, the missionaries also established three girls' schools in Tabriz and Tehran; these schools admitted only Christians at first but eventually became largely Muslim. And as for the mission hospitals—also among the first modern institutions in Iran—they were formally established in six towns and cities in the late 1800s and early 1900s.

The Presbyterians knew and loved the country in a way that most other foreigners in Iran did not. Many missionaries had close Iranian friends, knew Persian history and culture, and spoke Farsi as well as they spoke English. I just wish that these great humanitarians had left religion out of it.

"And they couldn't even convert that one percent!" Manucher went on. "One time, Salman, the brother of your cook Shapur, said, all right, he would convert to Christianity. He wanted to get a better position working for the American Hospital. So the missionaries told him, okay, now to convert to Christianity, you must do this and this. He said, yes, good, no problem, he did what they told him to do. And then, they were all finished and they asked him, "Do you have any final questions?" He said, "No, but can I go now? It's time for me to say evening prayers."

I tried to laugh.

Christians in Iran, I knew, had always been singularly unsuccessful at converting Muslims to Christianity. They'd encountered much hostility on all sides, for in addition to purely religious objections, many Muslims had regarded Christians as second-class citizens and had no desire to convert to that rank. The Armenian and Assyrian Christians had also had little interest in joining the Western churches, as they understandably preferred worshiping in their own languages. Therefore, even in the early 1800s, when most foreign missions began arriving in Iran, they had concentrated primarily on running schools and hospitals—while also, of course, sending out latent messages that they hoped would snare a convert or two. Our church had catered almost exclusively to the expatriate community; Manucher's family had been one of the only Iranian families in attendance.

"When I was very young, fifteen or sixteen," Manucher said, "I was very involved in the church. I went to services every Sunday, I went to classes, I was always talking with the missionaries. . . .

"But they had no business interfering with my life! One time I went out with a Baha'i girl. It was so innocent. We just went for ice cream, but then the Christians said no I couldn't see her anymore. They wanted me to be only with Christian girls.

"Another time one of the missionaries called me aside and said, we have to pray. I said, okay. We started to pray and he said, 'Please Lord, forgive Manucher . . .' I thought, 'What? Forgive me for what? What is he talking about?' More, 'Please, God, he didn't know what he was doing. Please, God, he is young,' and then—'Please forgive Manucher for smoking!' For smoking! And I listened to them!

"They ruined my sister's life. She died at age thirty-two of a broken heart. She had a heart attack. No Muslim would marry her because she was Christian. No Christian would marry her because our family had been Muslim."

Manucher showed me a picture of himself taken with one of the missionaries and a handsome friend whom he'd known since childhood. The two of them had been in Bible study classes together, and the friend had grown up to be a highly successful businessman with many American connections. But during the Revolution, he'd been killed. Everyone had known that his family had converted to Christianity from Islam.

Manucher and his family had been more circumspect. Although some of their friends had known that they were converted Christians, they'd never flaunted it. And as discontent in Iran grew in the 1970s, they'd taken precautions.

"My mother was very smart," Manucher said. "She went to Mecca in 1977, even though she was Christian. She said it was insurance.

"She said, 'I will save you. If the soldiers come to the door, beat me and shout, "Why did you make me go to the Americans? Why did you make me Christian?" '"

My parents, especially my father, would be very unhappy to hear of all this, I thought as I left Manucher. My father's commitment to Iran had been uncomplicated—he'd simply wanted to help people in need, to give something back. But not all missionaries had been as straightforward in their intent as he was, and as too often happens in life, matters outside his and their control had made a mess of things.

৵৽৻ঌ

In the center of Tabriz stands a gloomy, hulking structure known as the Arg-e Tabriz, a sheer brick citadel shaped like an inverted U. Built in the early fourteenth century, it was at one time used as a prison. Criminals were hurled from its rooftop, and legend has it that one woman was saved from death when her *chador* filled with air and lowered her gently to the ground.

It was also at or near the Arg-e Tabriz that Mirza Ali Mohammad, better known as the Bab, founder of a faith which led to the Baha'i religion, was executed in 1850. *Bab* means "gate," and Mirza Ali, a gentle and spiritual man, had proclaimed himself to be the gateway of communication to God, while at the same time renouncing Shi'ism—an act of heresy. He was sentenced to death and suspended by ropes before a firing squad.

Hostility toward the Baha'i religion runs deep in Iran, not only among the clerics but also among many ordinary Muslims, who view its followers as apostates—an attitude hard for outsiders to understand. Now a worldwide religion that bears little resemblance to Shi'ism, Baha'ism has never advocated violence in any form, avoids all political involvement, and preaches a doctrine of tolerance, equality of the sexes, and world peace.

Christians, Jews, and Zoroastrians—whom Shi'ites regard as "People of the Book" because their written scriptures are accepted by Muslims—are far more tolerated in Iran than are the Baha'is. Christians, Jews, and Zoroastrians all have representatives in the Majlis, or parliament, and Article 13 of the Islamic Republic's constitution, though not always enforced, reads that followers of these three faiths "are free to perform their religious rites and ceremonies. . . ." But Baha'ism, as a heretical offshoot of Islam, has never had any such protection, either in the 1800s or today. Twenty thousand followers of the Bab were killed in the nineteenth century; since the Islamic Revolution, more than 200 Baha'is have been executed, over 800 imprisoned, and thousands more persecuted in a variety of ways, including being denied the right to vote and access to higher education.

Interestingly, it was the Bab's rejection of Shi'ism, rather than his claim to be a direct conduit to God, that most infuriated his enemies. In fact, in the movement's earliest days, before the Bab broke with Shi'ism, mullahs were among his earliest converts. They believed him to be the long-awaited Twelfth Imam. But then, like converted Christians, the Bab committed the unforgivable, by turning away from the Prophet Mohammad.

ॐ॰॰

Unlike the youngster Tehran, Tabriz is an ancient city, probably founded around A.D. 250. Named regional capital of Azerbaijan province during the Mongol period (1220–1380), Tabriz was also national capital during the earliest years of the Safavid period (1501–1722), before the courts were transferred to Esfahan, where they'd be less prone to Ottoman attack. Tabriz suffered heavily during the wars between the Safavid and Ottoman Empires and during clashes with the Russians in the nineteenth century.

The Russians also occupied Tabriz several times in the 1900s, including most of both world wars, and in 1946 tried to seize control of Azerbaijan province, only to be foiled by the United States—the event that marked the beginning of the Cold War.

It was during the first years of the Safavid period, when Tabriz was capital, that Shi'ism first became the state religion. Up until then, though there were many Iranian Shi'ites, the majority of Shi'ites were non-Iranian, and most Iranians were Sunnis. Then, the first Safavid ruler, a 14-year-old Shi'ite named Isma'il, came to power. Despite his youth, the charismatic man-boy had convinced his tribal followers that he was the true descendant of the Imam Ali, and after capturing Tabriz for him, they marched south to take over much of the rest of Iran. One of Isma'il's first acts as ruler was to forcibly impose Shi'ism on his subjects, and one of his main reasons for doing so was to distinguish his new kingdom from its foremost political enemy, the Sunni Ottoman Empire. Shi'ism gave Iran the separate identity from the Arabs that it had been searching for ever since the Islamic conquest eight centuries before.

One of the few places in Tabriz where the city feels its age is the bazaar, and one clear, crisp morning, Mitra and I approached the ancient marketplace on a four-lane avenue lined with glass-sheathed buildings. In the distance squatted a dark medieval-looking hump whose enigmatic presence gave me the shivers. Surrounded by smaller structures, it was one of the bazaar's oldest halls—a giant, barrel-vaulted emporium piled high, I discovered as we entered, with carpets. Plump men drinking tea were sitting here and there, negotiating in the shadows, while in an alleyway beside the hall stretched high-ceilinged offices with iron-studded doors.

To one side of the carpet emporium stood about a hundred jewelry stores laden with gold—many more than in Tehran. To another soared the Friday mosque and an attached study center out of which impassive mullahs stared. In between were crowded hundreds of stores selling rose petals, black tea, silk yarns, and the same plastic and domestic wares I'd seen in Tehran. Nonetheless, everything in the Tabriz bazaar felt older and more mysterious.

The people were different as well. Compared to Tehranis, Tabrizis tend to be shorter and of a broader build, with darker and thicker hair. Related to the Turks, they speak an Azeri Turkish language not so different from that which was spoken by Isma'il and his followers. I'd already heard much Azeri Turkish from Bahman, Lona, Mitra, and family, but except for a few isolated words, I couldn't understand much of anything.

Despite their ancestors' role in bringing Shi'ism to Iran, the Azeri Turks remain outsiders in the dominant Persian culture and are the butt of many jokes, most of which make them out to be simple-minded, albeit shrewd, peasants. One joke I heard had a Tabrizi going out to buy a newspaper and bringing back a donkey instead; another had a Tabrizi trying to do push-ups on a swimming pool floor. Wrote Edward Browne in his 1893 classic, *A Year Amongst the Persians,* "The natives of Adharbayjan . . . with their scowling faces and furtive gray eyes, are not popular among the Persians, whose opinion about the inhabitants of their metropolis, Tabriz, is expressed in the following rhyme: . . . *From a Tabrizi thou wilt see naught by rascality; Even this is best, that thou shouldst not see a Tabrizi.*"

Unlike most outsider populations, however, the Azeri Turks wield considerable power. The country's largest minority group, accounting for about one fourth of Iran's population, they also control much of its wealth, as Azerbaijan is a rich province and most *bazaaris*—Iran's traditional merchant class—are descended from Tabrizi families. The Azeri Turks are also well represented in both parliament and the cleric class and are known for their independent thinking. Many of Iran's dissident movements have started or crested in Tabriz, including the Constitutional Revolution of 1906, resistance to the Anglo-Persian Treaty of 1919, and the Islamic Revolution.

"Tehran is afraid of Tabriz," one Tabrizi said to me, "because we are very smart, very brave, very religious, and very powerful. And we like freedom. *Azeri* means 'free.' Tabriz is two thousand years old, Tehran is only two hundred years old, and so they try to keep us down just like the West tries to keep Iran down. That's why the U.S. helped Khomeini come to power, you know. They were afraid that Iran might become too strong."

༄༅

One afternoon, after we'd finished our nap, Mitra and I sat on the living room floor and talked, with the help of my Persian-English dictionary. Mitra's passion was art and she showed me some of her work—well-executed oil paintings and watercolors of landscapes, people, and scenes that she'd copied from magazines. Although traditionally, Islamic societies favor nonrepresentational art, figurative art flourishes in Iran; Persia has a strong artistic tradition that long predates the Arab conquest.

"You should go to art school," I said, impressed, and Mitra beamed with pleasure. She had hoped to go, she said, but hadn't gotten a high enough grade on the national test to enter the public university and didn't have the money to attend a private one.

"What about a job?" I asked, and Mitra shrugged. She had also hoped to find a job, but although she'd searched all over, she hadn't found anything, and since graduating from high school had just lived at home, helping out her mother.

I sighed. It sounded like a boring life for such a lively, talented, beautiful young woman. I could so easily imagine her living in New York City, rushing to classes at the School of Visual Arts or Parsons School of Design, a portfolio swinging by her side.

"What about your friends?" I asked. "Do you see them often?"

"Only sometimes," Mitra said. Most of them weren't working, either—jobs were so hard to find—but her two best friends were married with children.

"Do your parents pressure you to marry?" By Iranian standards, Mitra was getting old.

"No." She shook her head. "They are very good, but—" She got up and closed the door; her mother was sleeping on the sofa outside. "The men here are not good. They complain all the time, and there is no freedom. I don't want to marry."

But without a job or money, I thought without saying anything, what are your options?

"I want to go to America," Mitra said.

"I wish you could," I said, running over in my mind all the obstacles in her way. Hardest of all would be the visa. I'd already heard countless stories from other Iranians about how impossible it was to get a visa to go to the United States.

"Would your parents let you go by yourself?" I asked finally. All the other obstacles that she faced seemed too insurmountable to mention. And as a woman subject to the Passport Law, Mitra couldn't leave the country without her father's permission.

"No," she said. "I will have to marry. I don't want to, but it's the only way. I have to find a good husband who will take me to America."

As Mitra put her paintings away, I thought of the boarded-up American Presbyterian church and of the anti–United States slogans on the American Consulate walls. I thought of all the American pop music I'd heard and of all the Leonardo DiCaprio haircuts I'd seen. I also thought about the fact that, depending on whom I was speaking to, the United

States had either caused Ayatollah Khomeini to come to power or almost prevented him from doing so. The United States hadn't left Iran after all.

ॐ๛

Like Lona and Pari in Tehran, Mitra couldn't do enough for me in Tabriz. She took me everywhere and helped me with everything. Sometimes, in the mornings, her mother A'zam accompanied us on our excursions, whereas in the late afternoons and evenings, after school was over, her brother Yashar often came along, sitting in the front of the city buses with the men while we sat in back with the women. I noticed that Mitra helped extensively around the house whereas Yashar did not, but Yashar was always the perfect gentleman, opening doors for women, running errands for his mother, and walking on the gutter side of the sidewalk whenever we went downtown.

Mitra, A'zam, and I spent one morning in the village of Kandovan, about 30 miles southwest of Tabriz, where the people live in a cluster of "caves" that are actually more like elongated hollow cones, with the downstairs used for animals and the upstairs for humans. Once little known and psychologically remote, Kandovan has more recently become something of a tourist attraction, and it was the only place I visited where people asked for money to have their pictures taken. But life in Kandovan is also extremely hard, especially in the winter, when the heavy snows come. Though most of the caves do have some electricity and cold running water, they are very small and hard to heat and light. The villagers must share a communal bathhouse that is not always open, and they have no access to newspapers or mail.

Another morning, Mitra and I traveled to Maragheh, a former capital of the Mongol dynasty, which in the 1260s established a famous astronomical observatory and university there. Both were destroyed over the centuries by a series of earthquakes, but the town is still studded with four handsome tomb towers, inlaid with tiles, which we had to get special permission from Ershad to enter. A young pilot, whom we met on the bus, couldn't keep his eyes off Mitra and insisted on helping us find our way and paying our taxi fare. Mitra had already told me that she didn't dare talk much to men in Tabriz—the neighbors would gossip—but she seemed to feel more at ease out of town and answered the pilot's questions with shy but animated replies.

One evening, Mitra, Yashar, and I went window shopping in downtown

Tabriz, along with hundreds of other young Iranians; aside from the parks and the occasional movie, there is little else to do in Iran at night. For sale: Crest toothpaste, Fruit of the Loom underwear, Czech crystal, Ray-Ban sunglasses, and framed pictures of Leonardo DiCaprio, hanging next to framed pictures of the Imam Ali. Later, we three had a late kebab dinner with the rest of the family in Shah Goli, a pleasant, hillside park laced with walkways, an artificial lake, simple eateries, and one expensive restaurant— formerly a lovely hotel with an outside bar overlooking the lake. Majid, Mitra's father, had once met his friends there most days after work, to share a drink in the light of the setting sun, carp flashing in the darkening waters beneath their feet. But now the restaurant had no bar and was frequented mostly by wealthy government flacks. Peeking in through a window, I saw a roomful of grim men and two equally grim women. Out in the parking lot lurked gray BMWs, muffled in shadows.

Another evening, we were invited to a dinner party, given in my honor, at the home of the daughter of the schoolteacher who lived downstairs. The daughter had married several steps up in the world and the invitation to visit her plush, gilt-edged home—from our utilitarian, working-class apartment—was apparently a major event, as A'zam, who'd never visited there before, spent all afternoon preparing her outfit, putting on makeup, and styling her hair. You should have seen me when I was young and thin, she said to me as she applied the final touches, I wore short skirts up to here, and little hats, and we went to the disco every weekend. Life under the Shah was good, life under Khomeini was good, but now . . . She shook her head, and I knew she was referring to economics, not politics.

Most of the other women at the party were also dressed in their finest—shiny dresses, high heels, makeup—and there was dancing, inside a wide circle framed by elaborate, rococo chairs. Three friends played traditional Azerbaijani music on a *tar* (a guitarlike instrument with six strings), *kamancheh* (a three-stringed instrument with a round box), and *daf* (a large tambourine), and as the sad, sweet music swelled out, people of all ages stood up to dance, one by one at first, and then together. Hips swayed, arms undulated, fingers swam seductively through the air while the rest of us clapped. One vain young man, preening his well-cut body before us, tried to attract the attention of one young woman after another, but they all subtly turned him down.

As I watched and listened—and for a few moments, danced—it occurred to me that Persian music is much like the visual Persian arts of rug weaving, calligraphy, tilework, and miniature painting. All are filled with much intricate detail and repetition; each builds steadily on itself, ever intimate, intense, and harmoniously balanced. To the neophyte Western listener, much Persian music sounds alike, but in reality, each region has its own distinct musical style, which Iranians recognize instantaneously.

The Persians' love of music can be traced back to at least the 400s, when Shah Bahram Gur imported 12,000 Luri musicians, experts on the lute, from India for his and his subjects' listening pleasure. According to the poet Ferdowsi, the shah gave each Luri a donkey, an ox, and a load of seed corn, and invited them to settle in his kingdom. But the Luris promptly ate the seed corn and the oxen, causing the shah to banish them from his lands, with only their donkeys and instruments to their names. That last part of the story is probably apocryphal, but it is true that the Luris moved west from Iran with the spread of Islam, filtering into Turkey, Spain, North Africa, and Europe, where they became known as Roma, or Gypsies. Today, Gypsy and Persian music, along with Spanish flamenco, still have much in common.

As one song ended and another began—the party would go on until 2 A.M., even though it was a Monday—the hostess and her architect husband sat down beside me, to explain how they felt about things. Yes, we supported the Islamic Revolution, they said—the Shah was very bad, and Khomeini was very great, very good. And yes, we wanted an Islamic society, and we like the modest dress. But no, we did not want an Islamic government, and no, we don't like the full *hejab.* We don't want to be as open as is Turkey—they have lost all their culture—but we do want more freedom.

More freedom, more freedom, more freedom—the mantra that I heard everywhere in Iran, from the liberals to the conservatives, the Westernized to the non-Westernized, the very religious to the not religious at all.

THREE

*I*n all our family's photograph albums are many pictures of the Kurds, a tribal people who lived and continue to live scattered throughout Azerbaijan province, though their better-known stronghold in Iran is Kordestan province. Many of my father's patients were Kurds, and he often visited their villages. One series of photographs shows a traditional hunt that a grateful Kurdish family staged for him—dark handsome men on horseback, lean saluki dogs in S-shaped curves, posed against barren brown hills. Another series show my parents in Kurdish dress. My father is wearing a black turban with knotted strings, my mother an elaborate outfit composed of a heavy skirt, wide belt, red velveteen jacket, and sequined pillbox hat kept in place with a scarf. We took those clothes back with us to the United States, where I used them for dress-up and Halloween.

One story my father tells regards a regal, authoritative, Kurdish woman, the mother of six tall sons. She came into the hospital with those sons one day, racked with abdominal pain. My father opened her up but found her already badly riddled with cancer. And then the race was on to get her home before she died—if she passed away en route, my father would be blamed. I imagine him and the six sons galloping over hills on horseback, the prone, dying woman between them, though of course they traveled by automobile—and arrived before she expired.

Now numbering close to 6 million, or about eight percent of Iran's population, the Iranian Kurds are part of the largest ethnic group in the world—total population about 20 million—that does not have its own state. Spread out over large mountainous areas of eastern Turkey, northeastern Iraq, northwestern Iran, and pockets of Syria and the former USSR, the Kurds are descendants of the central Asian tribes who settled in the area in the first millenium B.C. Historically a nomadic people, traveling between semipermanent summer and winter pastures, the Kurds speak Kurdish and are predominantly Sunni.

Throughout most of Iran's history, the Kurds reigned as a powerful people, both within their own territory and within the courts of various dynasties, where they wielded much influence. But in the 1930s, Reza Shah Pahlavi saw the Kurds—along with Iran's other major nomadic tribes, the Bakhtiari, Qashqa'i, Lur, and Baluchi—as a threat to his authority and an embarrassment in a modernizing world. Using every possible means, he forced settlement on them. The tribes were disarmed, their rulers arrested, and peoples accustomed to herding sheep and cattle pushed onto land that was often unsuitable for cultivation. Especially rebellious groups—most notably the Lur—were decimated and tribal languages banned.

Nonetheless, the government's policies toward the Kurds were only partially successful. Several unruly chieftains managed to retain their power, and in January 1946, with the support of the Russians then occupying Azerbaijan, the Kurds succeeded in establishing the autonomous, short-lived Republic of Kordestan, centered on the town of Mahabad. When the Russians began withdrawing from Iran in April 1946, however, internal conflicts in the republic developed and it fell to the Iranian Army without a fight in December 1946. Three of its three most prominent leaders were promptly hanged.

Initially, many Kurds saw the Islamic Revolution as a chance to regain their autonomy. During the reign of the last Shah, several dissident mullahs hid out in Kurdish territory and the exiled Ayatollah Khomeini expressed some support for the Kurdish cause. But after the Revolution, all such quasipromises were quietly forgotten. Khomeini cracked down on Kordestan as early as August 1979, dispatching an army into the province to bring it under control. In 1983, Kurdish guerrilla fighters lost the last of their territory, and in 1988, a foremost Kurdish leader, 'Abd al-Rahman Ghassemlou, invited to Vienna to negotiate a settlement for Kordestan, was assassinated by a hit squad while at the negotiating table with his Iranian counterparts. Though never the object of wholesale repression, Kordestan has effectively remained under military rule since the early 1980s, with some cultural rights granted but all political activities curtailed.

Visiting Kordestan was high on my list of priorities—I wanted to see this proud and rebellious land that I'd heard so much about. At first, however, the subject had been a sticking point with Ershad. Why do you want to go there? Mr. Shiravi asked me again and again, and my answer—that the family of a good friend lived there (actually the family of an acquaintance of an acquaintance of a good friend) and that my parents had told me many stories—didn't seem to satisfy him. But don't many tourists go there? I asked—I'd heard that the province attracted European backpackers. "Y-e-s-s," Mr. Shiravi reluctantly said, before finally handing me my letter of permission, "but Kordestan is a special place."

The family of my "good friend" reneged on their invitation for me to visit—cold feet? I wondered—and I ended up leaving Tabriz for Kordestan one day later than cited in my letter of permission. I also had no guide (also cited in the letter) and no passport (it was in the Foreign Ministry, awaiting a new visa) and therefore felt somewhat nervous about my credentials, which I might have to produce on the road and would definitely have to produce at a hotel. In Iran, passports and identity cards must be left at front desks upon check-in, often to be perused by the police at night.

But these were relatively minor worries—no one had asked me for my papers yet, after all—and I refused to let them stop me. I'd come this far.

As is customary in Iran, I purchased my bus ticket for Sanandaj, the chief city of Kordestan, one day prior to my departure. As is also customary, I gave the bus company my name for its registry and it assigned me a seat number. And the next morning, when I arrived at the huge, modern Tabriz bus station, teeming with thousands of travelers, I suddenly heard an announcement in English blaring out over the loudspeaker: "Mrs. Bird, please go to platform number five. Mrs. Bird, please go to platform number five. Your bus is arriving." Someone in some back office was worried that I might not find my way. I tried to imagine something comparable happening to a foreigner in a similar-size American or European city—and couldn't.

As usual whenever I traveled by bus in Iran, people started covertly staring at me as soon as I climbed on board. At first, thinking that I hadn't noticed them, they would look long and steady. But then, after I glanced in their direction, the looks would come shorter, sneakier, more surreptitious, and sometimes I heard a whisper or two. This would usually continue until we stopped for lunch—most of my bus rides were all-day affairs—when we would all pile out to use the restrooms, buy kebabs and soft drinks, and, in the case of my traveling companions, say midday prayers—usually in a separate room set aside for the purpose.

And then, one of two things would happen. Either some woman would say hello to me in the restroom or the stares would begin again, in a slightly different manner, with groups of three or four women in *chadors* huddled together, watching me, until I responded with a greeting or question. Either way, as soon as I said even one word of Persian—God bless Professor Kasheff and my Persian tutors Ali and Farnaz—the floodgates would burst open. The women would bombard me with questions, ply me with food and drink, and tell me how happy they were to see me in their country. Often, several men would come over as well, until sometimes by the end of the bus ride, I suspected that everyone on board knew my story. *Man safarnameh raje' beh Iran minevisam*—I am writing a travelogue about Iran. No one seemed to find my project, or the fact that I was a woman alone (as opposed to a person alone) especially unusual, but they were all very surprised that I'd been given a visa. You must be the first American they've allowed back in here, I was told a number of times by provincial travelers unaware of the trickle of Americans now traveling to Iran. In 1998, the year I was there, about 2,000 U.S. tourists visited the Islamic Republic, most on group tours.

In the case of my trip to Sanandaj, the barriers between cultures broke down earlier. Less than a half hour out of Tabriz, a serious, deliberate young woman sitting ahead of me turned around to engage me in a conversation that at first extended just to the people sitting around us and then to the whole back half of the bus. At one point, I turned around to see nearly a dozen men craning eagerly forward in their seats to listen to what we— what I (ha!)—were saying (intercity buses in Iran are not sexually segregated). Most were dressed in comfortable-looking blue-gray jumpsuits with wide woven belts—traditional dress in Kordestan.

Rojeen, the young Kurdish woman who'd first befriended me, was a 19-year-old engineering student studying at a university in Tabriz. She loved her classes, she said, but she and the other Kurdish students had to stick together because there was much prejudice. Many other Iranians disliked them, but not because they were Kurdish—because they were Sunni.

Shortly outside Tabriz we passed Mount Sahand, the tall peak that stands sentinel over the city, and about a half hour later, the crusty shores of Lake Orumieh. Too salty to support anything but the most primitive of creatures, the huge barren expanse blinded with its whiteness. Then came rolling, cultivated valleys filled with grasses, arid hills framed by peaks in the distance, and slopes of chocolate brown and rust red, some stacked with bundles of hay. We passed a shepherd in a jumpsuit praying beneath a tree, a young Kurdish woman driving a tractor, a pickup truck filled with Kurdish men—turban strings flapping—and villages made of mud walls, blue doors, and dark, man-size cones that Rojeen told me were ovens. The closer we got to Sanandaj, the steeper, more rugged, and more beautiful the terrain became.

Somewhere in the midst of our conversation, Rojeen invited me to stay with her and her family while I was in Sanandaj. Are you sure your parents won't mind? I asked her several times, but she considered the matter already settled, and I felt relieved at the thought of avoiding a hotel check-in. No one asked to see my credentials en route either, though armed guards entered the bus several times on routine inspections and we stopped at three or four checkpoints. Simple round military outposts also crowned many of the Kordestan hills. I counted more than 20 in all, though fewer than half appeared to be occupied.

ॐ✿ॐ

By the time we arrived in Sanandaj—a much larger city than I'd anticipated—it was dark, and it was dark when we arrived at Rojeen's home as well. The electricity was out—a frequent occurrence in Sanandaj and, I would later discover, in other poorer Iranian cities as well. But the municipal neglect in rebellious Sanandaj seemed especially bad. The electricity went out three times during my three-day visit there, and many of the sidewalks were badly broken, and the streets, jarred with potholes.

Though Rojeen's family must have been surprised to see me emerge out of the shadows with their daughter, they expressed only a warm, albeit somewhat wary, welcome: Tahmasb, her father, a tall, impressive-looking man with thick white hair; Jaleh, her mother, a soft-spoken woman with expressive eyes; and Rostam, her teenage brother. Like most urbanized Kurds, they dressed in Western clothes.

We travelers deposited our things, and then we all went to visit Rojeen's uncle, carefully picking our way along the dark uneven streets, lit only by the stars. Around us rose blind walls and apartment buildings, all eerily silent; outlined against the night sky were distant mountain peaks.

At Rojeen's uncle's, other extended family members had already gathered, and we numbered over two dozen as we crowded together on the carpeted floor of a typical Persian living room. Candlelight flickered off pale, handsome faces, as tea, fruit, and walnuts were passed around. Everyone had lots of questions for me, as per usual, only some of which I understood, also as per usual, but then, to my relief, I found that Tahmasb spoke some English. He'd learned it while serving in the air force in Tehran and Tabriz for 11 years.

Tahmasb and I exchanged nothing but pleasantries that first evening, but over the weekend, I learned more. Prior to 1979, he'd supported the Revolution, but after it was over, he was shocked to find himself forced out of the air force because he was Kurdish. By then in his early thirties, and the father of two children, he'd had no choice but to return to Kordestan, where he and his wife had struggled for years before saving up enough money to open a small shop.

One of Tahmasb's brothers had been forced to flee to Sweden because of his political activities, the other to Germany. Tahmasb hadn't seen his first brother in close to 20 years, the second one in 15, though his mother—a kind-faced woman usually dressed in gauzy green—had just returned from a visit to Germany. That's why she was always crying, Tahmasb explained. She'd gone with his sister, her only daughter, who'd insisted on staying behind. At age 38, the younger woman had never married because she'd always wanted to live in the West, and now she had no intention of ever coming back to Iran.

In the years immediately following the Revolution, Tahmasb said, life in Sanandaj had been very hard. Now, things were better but still far from good. The Kurds weren't allowed to hold meetings or stage large celebrations and so just gathered together in family groups. The economy in Kordestan was even worse than the economy in the rest of Iran, and many people were unemployed. Women had to wear *chadors* or dark *manteaus* on the streets, even though the *hejab* was not part of the Kurdish tradition, and during Ashura, the Shi'ite month of mourning, not celebrated by the Sunnis, the Kurds had to be extra careful not to call attention to themselves. One of Tahmasb's brothers had once been arrested during Ashura for wearing short sleeves.

"What do you think of Imam Khomeini?" I asked Tahmasb at one point.

"Imam—" He grinned at my use of the honorific title. "I don't like to even hear his name in my ear. I never liked him. Sunnis, Shi'ites—they're both bad, but Shi'ites are more bad. The importance is what a person has in his head and his heart—not just praying."

ॐ

On my first morning in Sanandaj, Rojeen showed me the town. We started in the hillside park above her home, which had a bird's-eye view of the entire city, ringed with brown mountains and equipped with a sprawling army base and downtown prison. Groups of rough-looking young men were roaming by, shouting out epithets as they passed, and Rojeen told me that they came from the villages. They have no culture, she said with a sniff, which was undoubtedly true, but I was more struck by their swaggering air of defiance, the same defiance that I would also notice later downtown, among more urbanized Kurdish men. These people are not cowed, I thought. No wonder they make the Islamic government nervous.

Rojeen and I sat down on a bench for a moment to take in the view.

"No, I never talk to boys," she said in answer to my question. "If you talk to boys here, the neighbors think you are bad. I don't want to be friends with boys anyway—I just want to know one, talk to him about a year, get married, and go to the West. I hate Iran."

"Can you talk to boys at the university?" I asked.

"No," she said. "My school is just for girls. My classes are good, but"— she bit her lip—"everything else is very bad. Some of our teachers are prejudiced. We don't have a gym. I want to get exercise, I want to play basketball, like Michael Jordan." We had spent the morning watching a year-old NBA play-off game, broadcast on regular Iranian television. "I don't want to get fat—I want to be thin like you and all the other American women. Iranian women are very fat."

"Lots of American women are fat, too," I said. "Fatter than here."

"No," she said. "Not like here."

"You'd be surprised."

"No! I see the magazines. I know the American women are very thin and the American children very beautiful."

"But those—"

She interrupted me. "I don't want to get fat! That's why I try not to eat. It's not hard at school. Our cafeteria is very bad." She gave me a mournful look.

"Now you sound just like an American student," I said, trying to sort out her legitimate complaints from her adolescent ones. "We always complain about school food, too."

"It's worse in Iran," Rojeen said, pouting.

Leaving the hillside, we meandered down through a gray, worn town, past a few villagers in traditional Kurdish dress, townspeople in black, professional scribes writing out letters for the illiterate, and armed guards at the major crossroads. I stopped to take a picture of a man making brooms, and a huge crowd gathered to watch me. I stopped to give money to a tiny, muttering beggar sitting all alone in the middle of the sidewalk, her head completely covered by her *chador*, and Rojeen pulled me angrily away. Why did you do that? she said, those people are very bad.

Because it was a Thursday, the bazaar and shops were closing down for the weekend, but we saw the town's few historic sites—the Friday mosque, a small museum, and a mysterious, Qajar-era palace that Rojeen's younger cousin Yalda, whom we'd met at the bazaar, led us to. Built of elaborate brickwork around an overgrown courtyard, the palace had collapsed in some parts but was still inhabited in others. One section of the basement initially seemed to be completely abandoned on the outside, but then opened up on the inside like a fairy tale to reveal an immaculate, well-lit bathhouse with bright blue walls and a circular stone tub. Stumbling in past the rubble, into the sudden light, I half imagined for a second that I'd fallen back into early childhood. Here was a magical "dungeon," like the one I remembered from so long ago.

⧼⧽

The next day, we attended a wedding. I'd told Tahmasb that I was interested in visiting a Kurdish village—I had in mind some isolated mountain spot—but he told me that he had a suggestion and took us all to the outskirts of town, where yet another brother lived. This brother's apartment overlooked what Tahmasb called a village, though it seemed like just another poor extension of the city to me. The houses were cube-shaped and made of concrete, with electricity wires draped in between. The settlement had apparently been established long before Sanandaj had grown so large, however, and was still inhabited by Kurdish peasants who more or less ignored city life.

The wedding was already in progress when we arrived, with perhaps two hundred people in traditional Kurdish dress gathered in a small pasture. To one side were the city's apartment buildings, to the other the village's concrete houses, and to a third and fourth, empty lots strewn with litter. But the people and their costumes, framed by the far-off mountains of their ancestors, transcended their immediate tawdry surroundings. Women in bright reds, pinks, greens, blues, and yellows, embroidered with sequins and silver and gold. Men in black baggy pants, with woven belts and heavy turbans. Boys playing with hoops. Girls dreaming by a bonfire. Musicians on a mournful flute (the *sorna*) and enormous drum (the *dol*), followed by circling men dancing single file, waving handkerchiefs above their heads.

It took the crowd a few moments to notice me and my camera, but when they did, dynamics instantly shifted. The musicians started playing for me, the dancers started dancing for me, and the children jumped up and down in front of my viewfinder, while Tahmasb and his family discreetly disappeared. No, no, go back, go back, I cried to the jumping children, to no avail, but luckily, the bride and groom arrived only a few minutes later, in a shiny white Buick studded with paper flowers. Someone burned *esfand*, or wild rue, someone threw rice, and someone grabbed my hand to lead me after the bridal couple, dressed in Western wedding clothes. What a strange mix of East and West, I thought, as we fought our way up a crowded staircase to enter a dark, close room so packed with shouting, dancing people that I could barely see.

The sharp smell of *esfand* again filled the air; I already knew it well, from private homes and shrines. The smoke of *esfand* is believed to ward off harm, and tradition has it that the herb can cure 72 ailments, including leprosy, epilepsy, and insanity. *Esfand* was once used as an aphrodisiac, and its crushed seeds, as a fertility drug.

The crowd parted for a few seconds, allowing me to take a picture of what was an extremely lugubrious-looking couple, before closing ranks again amidst a din of shouting and singing. I felt tugged on all sides as people pressed against me and then, or so I imagined, subtly pushed me back out the door.

I was welcomed to visit—and to record. But not to stay. I was an outsider.

ॐ

On my last evening in Kordestan, various neighbors and family members came over to visit, while Jaleh and Tahmasb—who often helped around the house—bustled to and fro, serving tea, cake, and candy. I, on the other hand, wasn't allowed to do a thing, though I had managed to fold up my own mattress-bed that morning—a major accomplishment. Jaleh, the consummate hostess, had also tried to buy me my bus ticket back to Tehran. Luckily, though, I'd stopped her just in time. The house was far too spare, furnished only with machine-made carpets and a few sticks of furniture, for her to be buying tickets for strangers.

"I wish I knew more English, or you knew more Persian," she'd said to me after the matter was finally settled. "I have many things I'd like to say to you."

Ruefully, I nodded. Jaleh and I had tried speaking several times but hadn't gotten very far. Though I knew enough Persian to conduct basic conversations, as with Rojeen and Mitra, I couldn't talk about anything in depth and frequently felt stymied by my inability to truly communicate. I had so many questions I wanted to ask, so many answers I wanted to hear, but often, just as a conversation was getting really interesting, my comprehension failed me. The fact that many Iranians spoke some English helped enormously, but at times, as in the case of Tahmasb, their English was only marginally better than my Persian.

As we sat on the floor that evening, drinking tea and eating sweets, a thirtyish, unemployed uncle arrived. He had just obtained a new illegal video featuring Michael Jackson and Madonna, and he snapped it into the VCR, immediately causing our conversation to sputter and die. "Thriller" burst out, followed by "Material Girl" and "Like a Virgin," and with the exception of Tahmasb and Jaleh—both too wise to be easily distracted—

no one in the room could keep his or her eyes off the screen. Watching them, I imagined the thirtyish uncle—who, without a job, couldn't hope to marry—fantasizing about the many half-naked women before him, all apparently so easily available in the United States. I imagined Rostam, Rojeen's teenage brother, fantasizing about all the apparently free beer. I imagined Rojeen fantasizing about all the beautiful clothes and adoring men. And I imagined everyone fantasizing about a world without worries and plenty of money, where people danced in the streets all night and had fun all day.

Just what exactly is it about American popular culture that's so compelling? I wondered, remembering similar scenes I'd witnessed in front of TVs in Tehran. It's taken over the world, we all understand that, but why? And why don't the popular cultures of other nations translate as well?

"How many times have you seen Michael Jackson?" Rojeen asked me when the tape was over.

"Never," I said.

"Never?" Half of those in the room looked at me in astonishment.

"Well, tickets are expensive," I said, suddenly feeling ridiculously apologetic. "And hard to get."

"How expensive?"

"Fifty dollars or more."

"But that's nothing for an American," one of the neighbors said. "I have a cousin who lives in Los Angeles and he makes a hundred thousand dollars a year. Every year!"

"But most Americans don't make that much," I said. "And some Americans are very poor. Life isn't the way it is in those videos."

There was a polite silence.

"We have many problems in the United States, too," I went on. "Most people have to work very hard, and there's poverty and homelessness and . . ." I didn't know the word for "racism" and couldn't remember the word for "prejudice," though I'd learned it since arriving in Kordestan.

Rojeen gave me an annoyed look.

"How can we get a visa to go to the United States?" one of the neighbors interrupted in English. "Can you help us?'

"I'm sorry," I said. "But I really don't know—"

"I have a good education," the neighbor pressed. "I'm a professor. I teach health at Sanandaj University."

I couldn't help but sigh. "You must be very needed here."

"Yes, I am," he said matter-of-factly. "But I don't care. I've been working for ten years and my wife and I still only have one car. It's very old. We want to have more. We want to go to the United States—or Switzerland. We especially like Switzerland."

Just the country that needs another health professor, I thought, though I also knew that I was no one to judge. What did I know about living in a society as restrictive as Iran's?

The neighbor with the rich cousin in Los Angeles disappeared, to return a few minutes later with a photograph album. Inside were yellowing sleeves holding pictures that his cousin had sent him from the United States. Most of the room gathered around to watch as scenes of Los Angeles, Las Vegas, and Disneyland flipped by. Each one seemed glitzier than the one before, and the neighbor ended his show with the coup de grâce—his cousin and his wife, sleek and plump as otters, exiting from a stretch white limousine.

"Look at that car!" someone said.

"How much do you think that cost?" someone else said.

"It's probably rented," I said, feeling like an Eeyore.

"No!" the neighbor said, too excited about the idea of someone he knew owning such a marvelous vehicle to get irritated at me. "He owns it, I'm sure."

"Who is this Michael Jackson?" Tahmasb, the voice of reason, suddenly—finally—interrupted. "Why do people like him so much? Is he a good man? Does he help people?"

The evening wore on, with more talk about visas and the imagined high life in the United States—$50,000 salaries for even lowly office workers, three-day weekends for everyone, two cars in every garage, and plenty of clothes, wide-screen TVs, jewelry, and luxury vacations. It was the same sort of talk that I'd already encountered in Tehran and Tabriz, and I would hear much more of it as I continued my travels. The government's policies are backfiring, I often thought, disheartened, as I listened to the drivel and tried to object—usually to no avail (no matter that I lived in the United States and might know whereof I spoke). By depriving their people of exposure to the West, they are making it seem much more glamorous and forgiving than it really is. People are wasting their lives dreaming about an easy paradise that does not exist—anywhere.

I thought back to what one well-educated Tehrani had told me several weeks before. I tried to live in Canada for several years, he said, but I finally gave up. The competition for work was just so tremendous, and as an immigrant, all I could find were low-paying jobs. Now I miss the freedoms of the West, sure, but life for me is better here.

"You look tired," Tahmasb and Jaleh said when the neighbors and extended family members finally left.

"A little."

"I'm sorry they bothered you with so many questions," Jaleh said.

"It's all right," I said. "I didn't mind. It's just that—"

"Many people here are ignorant," Tahmasb said.

"There are many, many good things about the United States," I said, climbing onto one of my soapboxes, "but materialism and the love of the almighty dollar just isn't one of them. Life isn't about money, life—"

"Now you sound just like an Iranian," Tahmasb said. "We believe in spiritual things."

"I don't know—" I said, thinking about the conversation we'd just heard and about the reputation that Iranians in the United States have for an excess love of luxury.

We all looked at each other, shrugged, and grinned.

∞∞∞

On the bus ride back to Tehran, I took out a black-and-white photograph that Jaleh had given me. It was a picture of a lovely little girl in typical Kurdish dress, staring out—a little frightened, a little surprised—from beneath a heavy headdress hung with jewelry and coins. I had admired the picture while looking through a box filled with family photographs, and Jaleh had handed it to me. No, please take it, she'd said over my objections, this picture was taken so long ago that we're not even sure who she was anymore—some neighbor's child, perhaps. I stared at the little face, a dislodged remnant of the past floating around unclaimed in the present. I wondered who she was then. I wondered who she is now.

TO FIND GOOD ANSWERS TO GREAT QUESTIONS

He who knows is powerful; thanks to his knowledge, the old man's heart is young.

—Ferdowsi

ONE

While back in New York, visiting the offices of the Iranian Mission to the UN, I had been on my way out the door when Mr. Zamani called me back in. He had someone he wanted me to meet. I returned to find a tall, lanky man with red hair, a red beard, and pale, owlish glasses. His name was Mohammad Legenhausen, formerly known as Gary Legenhausen, originally from Queens, New York, now of Qom, Iran. Mr. Legenhausen taught Western philosophy at the Imam Khomeini Education and Research Institute and was, as far as he knew, the only American teaching in the holy city—a place renowned not only in the United States but also in Iran as being a fierce and closed society filled with sour-faced mullahs and religious fanatics. Mr. Legenhausen invited me to look him up when I came to Iran, and recognizing opportunity when it knocked, I promptly did. He was one of the first people I called when I arrived in Iran.

But before I left Tehran for my first visit to Qom, everyone I knew warned me about going. Many Iranians, Tehranis in particular, despise Qom and I heard story after story about how gray and ugly, harsh and intolerant the city was. People won't talk to you there, I was told; they scorn all outsiders. It's a city of hate—all the worst ayatollahs studied there—and death—many pay ridiculous fees to be buried near the Holy Shrine. You'll be lucky if taxis stop to pick you up or if people don't try to knock you down on the streets. The Qomis are extremely ignorant—all that's taught in the elementary schools is the Qor'an—and you'll have to wear a *chador* at all times. According to an old saying, "It is better to be a dog in Kashan than a noble in Qom."

So it was with some trepidation but also great curiosity that I set out for Qom early one morning in a private taxi. Qom is located only about 90 miles south of central Tehran—about a $30 ride by private car—and my Tehrani friends were appalled at my original plan to travel by shared taxi or bus. Qom is not Tabriz or Mashhad, they'd said; you don't know what kind of fanatics you're dealing with here. Once again, and for what I promised myself would be the last time, I acquiesced to their wishes—even when Bahman insisted that Pari come along with me. She had a young married cousin in Qom whom she'd been hoping to visit, and we could stay with her and her husband.

The four-lane highway connecting Tehran and Qom is wide, well paved, and mostly flat. Running first past the Holy Khomeini Shrine and Behesht-e Zahra, it then skirts the edge of the great Dasht-e Kavir, all the way down to Qom. Much of central and southeastern Iran is made up of the Dasht-e Kavir, a salt desert covering about 200,000 square kilometers, and the Dasht-e Lut, a sand desert covering about 160,000 square kilometers. Among the most arid areas in the world, these desert plateaus are all but uninhabitable, with human settlements located only along their edges and around a few oases in the Dasht-e Kavir.

Immediately south of Tehran lies a region that has traditionally been known as the Valley of the Angel of Death—a land that, according to Persian folklore, is inhabited by several species of demons. Of these, the *ghuls* are said to be the most dangerous, for in the days of the great camel caravans that traversed Iran, they supposedly lured travelers away from their companions by imitating the voice of a friend or relative. Crying out piteously for help, the *ghuls* led the unsuspecting to a lonely spot where they tore him, or perhaps her, to pieces and ate him up.

And if a *ghul* didn't get the traveler, perhaps a *palis*, or Foot-Licker, would. The Foot-Licker attacks only those who are sleeping and kills its victim by licking the soles of the feet until it drains away the victim's lifeblood. It is said that on one occasion, two muleteers from Esfahan, finding themselves lost in the desert at night, lay down feet to feet, covering themselves with their cloaks. Soon the Foot-Licker arrived and circled around them again and again, before finally giving up, saying, "I have wandered through a thousand and thirty and three valleys but never yet saw a two-headed man."

Beyond the Valley of the Angel of Death, we came to the Dasht-e Kavir proper, a crusty, bumpy, desert plain stretching out in all directions. With pictures of the Sahara in my head, I felt disappointed—this was not a fine-grained sand desert but rather an ugly, gray wasteland flashing by mile after bleak mile. Nothing but desolation in sight.

Pari and I dozed and woke up, dozed and woke up. The road shimmered with the heat, and the dusty air caught in our breaths, even through the closed windows and air conditioning. Small brown mounds appeared in the foreground and volcanic mountains in the distance. Many of the mounds were inscribed with elaborate graffiti, written with white rocks, which I later learned spelled out the names of army platoons that had once practiced maneuvers in the area. A stark gas station surrounded by a graveyard of dead tires slipped past, followed by a boxy, mustard yellow shrine, built for travelers who wanted to pray en route. And this was a land that one felt the need to pray in. "O mankind! Worship your Lord, Who hath created you and those before you, so that ye may ward off (evil)" (Qor'an, 2:21).

Nearing Qom, we entered a region of blinding white salt deposits, followed by a great white salt lake. Legend has it that the Shah's SAVAK used to drop bodies by helicopter into the lake, though more rational Iranians say that that is unlikely, as bodies will not sink in a lake with such a high salt content. (But what about weights? I wondered to myself when I heard that objection; Iranians aren't the only ones with vivid imaginations.)

Qom appeared, with the usual jumble of shacks, sheds, power lines, and mud-brick walls that mark the outskirts of all Iranian cities. But then I noticed a giant, spinning Ferris wheel to our right and the golden dome and minarets of the Holy Shrine of Fatemeh, or Hazrat-e Ma'sumeh, far ahead. The faces of Khomeini and several martyrs stared down at me. To my consternation, they were beginning to seem almost comfortingly familiar.

We entered Qom proper, following a wide, dry riverbed that runs through the center of the city. Even in earlier years, before the building of a dam upstream, the river flowed only a few months of the year, but now it is dry year round, with the riverbed used in places as a parking lot, marketplace, and playground—while also serving as a sort of symbol. The water in Qom is notoriously bad, owing to its high salt content, and is almost impossible to drink. Salt deposits often form on people's showerheads, and their clothes come out stiff from the laundry. Daily, and in a multitude of ways, Qomis are reminded of the inexorable power of the desert that surrounds them.

A glint of gold, green, and blue flashed, and we passed beneath the dome and minarets of Hazrat-e Ma'sumeh, the shrine where Fatemeh, the sister of Imam Reza of Mashhad, is buried. Traveling through the region in the year 816, Fatemeh became ill and was brought to Qom, then already known as a Shi'ite center. She died 17 days later, and her tomb became an important pilgrimage site. Destroyed by the Mongols in the late fourteenth century, it was rebuilt by Shah 'Abbas I and his successors in the 1600s.

More importantly, though, Qom is Shi'ism's preeminent religious city, home to dozens upon dozens of *madrasehs*, or religious colleges, that train Shi'ism's intellectual elite. The city revolves around scholarship and education, with the streets lined with bookstores and the sidewalks teeming with clerics and clerics-in-training. Everyone from Ayatollah Khomeini to most of today's government leaders studied in Qom, the holy center and unofficial second capital of Iran.

As we passed by Fatemeh's shrine, I caught my first glimpse of the city's many *talabehs*, or students—mostly young men dressed in blue or gray tunics, white turbans, and black cloaks, or *abas*, and carrying stacks of books. Between them passed older clerics, other students and male pilgrims in ordinary dress, and women in *chadors*. All women in Qom must wear a *chador*—a garment that Pari and I, too, hastily put on, over our *manteaus* and *rusaris*. We'd entered a medieval scholastic world, and despite my serious doubts about organized religion in general and Shi'ism in particular, I felt a surge of envy. Oh, to be part of a society that revolved around ideas and books. Oh, to be part of a society that spent its days studying, and its early evenings, when the first dust of twilight descends, congregating in plazas and on sidewalks to discuss what it had read. Many strict Muslims believe that it is harmful to read in the light of the last forty-five minutes before sunset, and so during that time, the students pour outdoors to talk about their lessons before evening prayers.

The *talabeh*s, which means "seekers," come to Qom from all parts of Iran and the greater Shi'ite world, including Iraq, Pakistan, and India. Most arrive when they are 14 or 15 years old, though it's not unheard of for a student to begin later, even in middle age. The length of study varies widely, with the average student staying only a year or two before going back to his village or neighborhood to work as a local mullah (originally a corruption of the Arabic word *maula*, meaning "master," and regarded as a slang word in Persian). In contrast, the more talented students often stay for decades, and ayatollahs study for 40 years or more, while teaching at the same time.

The course of study is rigorous, covering everything from the basic principles of Islam and Aristotelian logic to the intricacies of Islamic law and the definition of a just government. The earliest years are spent study-ing standard texts of grammar, rhetoric, and logic, whereas the middle years are devoted to prescribed books on Arabic, logic, philosophy, theol-ogy, Islamic law, and jurisprudence. Texts by such ancient thinkers as Avicenna, Ptolemy, Aristotle, and the fourteenth-century Arab historian Ibn Khaldun are used, in addition to those devoted to various aspects of Islam. Books by twentieth-century authors play only a minor role in the curriculum.

For the serious *talabeh*, the goal is to graduate to the level of *mujtahid*, or "jurist," a scholar who through his learning has earned the right to inter-pret Islamic law. One *mujtahid*'s interpretation of a religious law can vary greatly from another's, but all are valid as long as they adhere to the Shi'ite tradition. Conflicting opinions are an essential part of Shi'ism, which, con-trary to common Western assumption, believes in the power of reasoning and debate. Students are taught to question the authority of their teachers, and clerics often disagree vociferously with one another. In fact, one debate that has been stewing in Qom ever since the Revolution, but with espe-cially greater urgency in recent years, is whether the clergy should be involved in politics. For every cleric who has become powerful or wealthy through the Islamic regime, there are many others who do not believe in mixing religion with government.

Once a *talabeh* has reached the level of *mujtahid*, he can go still further and rise first to the category of *hojjat al-eslam*, "the proof of Islam," and then to the level of *ayatollah*, "the miraculous sign of God." Only the most admired of clerics ever get that far, and their promotion is based on a vague—and quite democratic—set of criteria, including years of study, how many students their classes attract, the quality of their publications, and, most importantly, the opinion of their peers. From ayatollah, a handful then rise to the level of *marja'-e taqlid*, "source of emulation," or grand ayatollah. To do so, they must exhibit an extraordinary level of piety, wisdom, good character, and charisma; a grand ayatollah must have the ability to lead. There were only seven grand ayatollahs in Iran at the time of my visit, including Grand Ayatollah Shirazi, to whom Ershad had given me a letter of introduction—a fact that both excited and terrified me. What was I going to say to him?

ঙ্কৈৰ্জ্ঞ

Mohammad Legenhausen had invited me to lunch. I was greatly looking forward to it—there was much about Qom and Islam that I wanted to learn—but I was also prepared to be blasted with religious propaganda. Our meeting in New York had been low-key enough, but as the world knows, there is nothing worse than a recent convert, be it a new non-smoker, born-again Christian, or Muslim, and I didn't know what to expect of our visit.

Pari and her cousin, Maryam, insisted on escorting me to Mohammad's. We took the bus, sitting in back with the other women, all of us in *chadors*. I caught a glimpse of our reflections as we passed a shop window, and I marveled at how anonymous we looked—more like a flock of crows than a group of women. The only females not in black were the children, although even girls who looked to be about 9 or 10 were already wearing white *chadors*, with their school backpacks underneath.

As we rode, Pari and Maryam giggled and nudged each other. Close friends, they would spend most of the next few days gossiping, shopping, and trying on each other's clothes and makeup. I knew that they found my interest in Qom to be strange but were nonetheless eager to help me out in any way that they could. Pari, in particular, was constantly checking up on me. *"Khubi,* Christian?" she would ask many times a day—are you good/well/happy?

Disembarking from the bus, we walked down an empty, nondescript street, passing only a small vegetable stand. Unlike all other major cities in Iran, Qom holds few fast-food restaurants, video stores, or fashionable shops—all deemed too frivolous for this most holy of cities, over which even airplanes are not allowed to fly.

Mohammad lived in a typical modern Persian apartment not far from the Imam Khomeini Education and Research Institute, where he worked. When I arrived, he had just gotten home. He introduced me to his wife, Haideh, a gentle woman with jet-black hair and thoughtful eyes, who was preparing lunch. She welcomed me warmly, as did their three-year-old son Ali, who spoke to me in English with a Persian inflection.

Mohammad and I took seats on the carpet, Ali gamboling around us, and talked. Mohammad had been born in Queens in 1953, and studied at the State University of New York, Albany, and at Rice University in Texas, receiving a bachelor of arts degree and master of arts degree in philosophy, respectively. Then he'd gone on to Texas Southern University to teach and finish work on his doctoral thesis, "Matters of Substance in Aristotle and Contemporary American Analytic Philosophy." Founded in 1947 for African Americans studying on the GI Bill, Texas Southern had run into trouble in the 1960s, when many blacks began attending white universities, and started actively courting foreign students. So while teaching at Texas Southern between 1979 and 1989, Mohammad—at first still known as Gary—met everyone from a Nigerian sergeant and an Ethiopian Marxist to many Shi'ites and Sunnis. Soon he, a lapsed Catholic, became interested in his Muslim friends' beliefs and began attending their mosque, finally converting to Islam in 1983.

"Why Shi'ism? What was it about it that attracted you?" I asked, steeling myself to hear an impassioned reply that had something to do with "seeing the light."

But Mohammad was not so easy to categorize. "It was a mostly Sunni mosque," he said, "but I found I had the most rapport with the Iranians. The most interesting conversations I had were with them, and I started doing a lot of reading, especially the *Sermons of Imam Ali* by Nahjul Balagha. It's the most important collection of texts of the Imam Ali and though I had a very bad translation, I still found it fascinating. It's philosophy, mysticism, politics, and justice all mixed up together—I thought that was neat. And what I found especially interesting were issues pertaining to justice. That was important to me—I'd been involved in the Free South Africa movement for years."

At the word *justice* I felt a heightened interest. This great concern for justice, I'd already thought on several earlier occasions, is something that Iranians and Americans have in common. It was a concern for justice that led to both the American and Islamic revolutions, and a concern for justice that fuels many decisions made in both countries today. Most Americans don't see the Iranian struggle that way because they are focused on the atrocities that occurred after the Islamic Revolution and on the harshness of Islamic law. But many Iranians do, because despite those atrocities and strict Islamic law, they still feel that Iran is a more just society today than it was in the days of the Shah.

Mohammad continued with his story. He'd first visited Iran in 1985, to attend a 10-day conference on Shi'ism, and became fascinated with the country as well as with its religion. Back in Texas, he knew that he wanted to return to Iran to live for a while and learn more about Islam, but he didn't know how to go about it. Tension between the United States and Iran was then at its height, and Americans were not welcome in Iran. Not until 1989, when a former student introduced him to Dr. Kamal Kharrazi—then at the Iranian Mission to the UN, now Iran's foreign minister—did he get his chance. Dr. Kharrazi arranged for him to become a fellow at the Iranian Academy of Philosophy in Tehran, where he was given a room, a monthly salary of about $100, and the opportunity to study with the school's director. In return, he taught a course called the Philosophy of Religion.

At first, Mohammad said, everyone he met in Iran regarded him with great suspicion. (I could only imagine.) The conservatives thought that he'd come to spy for the United States, and the liberals thought that he'd come to spy for the conservatives—how else could he have gotten a visa? The academy's gatekeeper locked him into the school compound at night and was very annoyed on the one or two occasions that he climbed over the wall.

There was culture shock to deal with as well.

"I was angry the first two years I was here," Mohammad said. "People would promise to do things and they wouldn't get done. Or people would say they were helping me, but they were taking me in directions I didn't want to go in. There's a saying here about being strangled by a silk thread—"

I knew exactly what he was talking about.

"This is an enormously polite and formal society, and I had to learn how to maneuver through that politeness so that I was both going along with others and getting some room for myself."

Mohammad's next big step came a year or two later, when he was introduced to Ayatollah Mohammad Taqi Misbah, a conservative, pro-government cleric who is actively supported by Supreme Leader Khamene'i. An authoritative firebrand, Ayatollah Misbah frequently speaks out against the country's more liberal thinkers, especially 'Abd al-Karim Soroush, a pro-Khatami scholar who argues passionately for human rights, academic freedom, and the separation of religion and politics. Nonetheless, in one of those ironic twists that occurs so often in Iran, it was Ayatollah Misbah who established the first institute of Western learning in Qom in the mid-1990s (the Imam Khomeini Education and Research Institute), and began the first student seminarian exchange program with the West in 1998 (with Mennonites from Toronto, Canada). His impeccable conservative credentials give him a latitude that more liberal Iranians do not usually have.

Ayatollah Misbah invited Mohammad to teach Western philosophy and religion at his Imam Khomeini Institute. Founded specifically to expose gifted seminary students to Western science and thought, the institute offers courses in 12 fields, including economics, law, history, business management, sociology, political science, and education. Mohammad jumped at the chance; he wanted to get out of Tehran and into an environment where he could both continue studying Islam and improve his Persian—too many people in Tehran spoke English.

At about this same time, Mohammad was introduced to his future wife by a friend. Also a scholar, Haideh holds a master's degree in linguistics, and the two of them hit it off immediately. Her family accepted Mohammad quickly as well, saying that they didn't care where he came from as long as he was Shi'ite. Only some of Haideh's friends were more circumspect—but not about her choice of husband. What's the matter with you, they said, only half joking, you're marrying an American and you're moving to *Qom?* We'll never visit you there.

"We had no idea we'd like it here so much," Mohammad said. "Isn't that right, Haideh?"

Haideh stuck her head out of the kitchen, where she was preparing *fesenjan*, a popular Persian dish made of chicken, walnuts, and pomegranate juice that comes in both a sweet and a sour version. She was preparing the sweet version.

"No, not at all," she said in Persian. "I'm from Gilan in the north and I'd always heard such awful things about Qom. But our neighbors are very kind—and so are the shopkeepers. Just the water is bad." She made a face.

"It helps that we've got good jobs," Mohammad said. "Haideh works on the research staff at the University of Qom and also teaches a course on research methods. And my students are very good. They have a mix of doggedness and openness, and a genuine thirst for learning—not like some I taught in Tehran."

"How about politics?" I asked. "How do people here feel about President Khatami?"

Mohammad nodded, as if waiting for this question. "Even in Qom," he said, "people voted overwhelmingly in favor of Khatami. All the seminary students want less heavy-handed control of cultural affairs. But at the same time, they're worried about Western interests finding a foothold again. Lots of times, the difference in political perspectives here isn't really the difference between liberals and conservatives but between some people being more worried about Western powers coming in and some being less worried."

"What about you? Where do you stand?" I asked a little hesitantly. So far, Mohammad did not appear to be the fanatic I'd feared he might be, but perhaps I just hadn't asked the right questions yet.

"I don't get too involved," he said. "That's not the reason I'm here—"

Ali came careening around the corner on his tricycle, and we had to pull back against the wall to keep from getting hit. He giggled and continued on his way.

I tried again. "But don't you ever question the Islamic government? We hear such negative things in the U.S."

Mohammad paused, watching Ali. "I have friends in the U.S. from all parts of the political spectrum," he said finally, "and some think it's horrible that I'm here, supporting the Islamic government. Sometimes I myself have doubts. But what can I do?" He paused again. "Just try to make things better."

I felt relieved to hear him say that. He seemed to be a thoughtful and intelligent man, and I felt as if I was learning a lot from him. But remembering warnings given to me both in Tehran and the United States, I kept worrying that I was naïvely accepting too much on face value. Surely Mohammad's admission of self-doubt indicated a healthy level of skepticism on his part, I thought, but I knew that some I'd met wouldn't see it that way. He was smart, they'd say, he knew what he was doing. He knew how to manipulate you.

"Most Iranians in the U.S. are considerably more negative than the ones here," Mohammad said, standing up to help Haideh lay the *sofreh* out on the floor. "Here, it's true, many people feel fed up with the system because of economic difficulties. But my villager friends say, 'Yeah, sure, Tehranis, go ahead and complain, but we have electricity now, we go to the university now—that's what the Islamic Revolution did for us.' "

Over lunch, the conversation turned from politics to the *madrasehs*, or seminaries, a subject that fascinated me. I desperately wanted to visit one, and to see the medieval system of "from chest to chest" education (discussion in small groups) in action, but it was proving very difficult to arrange. As a woman, I could visit only a women's seminary, and the main one in Qom had turned down my request—faxed ahead by Ershad. Mohammad and Haideh were now trying to help me through other channels, *ensha'allah*, but hadn't had any luck yet.

"They're suspicious of you," Mohammad said. "As they are of all writers. Many Iranians' worst fear is that someone will embarrass them."

I thought of my father's experience, criticizing a young Iranian doctor in front of his colleagues and thereby all but ending their friendship.

"Isn't there at least some central administrative office I can contact?" I asked. "Someone who could give me an overview of the system?"

"Not really," he said, "because all the seminaries here are autonomous. Each is usually centered around one ayatollah and his top students, who also teach.

"Everything is very loose. The students coming into the seminaries don't even register for classes. It's all free, and they just sit in and decide whether to stay or not, and if not, they move on—sometimes three or four times. Or, they might do the opposite and read a classic text in Arabic with one professor for five years or more. It's a completely separate world here."

"If the seminaries are free," I said, "who pays for the classes?"

"If a director of a seminary accepts you, your classes are paid for out of the school's endowment. You're also given a monthly stipend, but it's minimal, and as soon as you're able to teach, you go back to the town you came from and get money that way, or you get on some sort of preaching circuit. Also, now, a lot of students get positions in the government."

Haideh pressed more *fesenjan* on me. The dish was delicious, with a dark, sweet-sour taste unlike anything I'd had before.

"One interesting problem here," Mohammad said, "is that historically, the seminary students have never gotten grades or degrees—they've gotten permissions. Permission from a teacher to graduate to another level, permission to make legal decisions. You study with a master until he decides you're ready.

"But now, the system is so flooded with students that the seminaries can't operate without grades and exams anymore—especially at the lower levels. Now to go from one step to the next, you have to take an exam. This wasn't so twenty years ago. And now there are also plans to give higher degrees, because a big problem is, without degrees, how do you evaluate someone? How do you compare? Okay, so he's studied for so many years—but what does that mean?

"Many middle-class Tehranis like to say that because of this old system, and the ancient texts the seminaries use, the mullahs are incompetent."

I pricked up my ears, wondering what Mohammad had to say on this subject. I'd heard the complaint many times myself and thought it made sense. How much could a cleric who'd spent 20 years immersed in ancient texts know about governing a modern society? As much as the idea of studying books for years on end appealed to me as a writer and literature major, it didn't seem like effective training for a politician or administrator.

"Do you think the Tehranis' criticism of the clerics is justified?" I asked.

Mohammad shrugged. "Whether or not it's justified, it's a good influence. The mullahs feel this influence coming from society, and it has stimulated them to learn more and gain a more liberal education—by going to our institute or the University of Qom or Tehran. Or even by going abroad to earn a master's or doctorate degree."

Spoken in the true fashion of an ivory-tower professor, I thought, while remembering something a lawyer had told me back in Tehran. It's often very difficult to work with the judges here, she'd said, because they're all clerics and don't know anything about the practical world.

"Although you really can't overemphasize the importance of learning here already," Mohammad went on, "the intellect holds an extremely prominent place in Islam. The first thing that God created was the intellect, and to be a scholar here is a very real honor. In fact, the most important religious narrative begins with a section on the intellect. Here, let me show you."

He got up, returning a few minutes later with a fat volume bound in dark green leather and tooled in gold. When he opened up the book, however, its pages were flimsy and badly printed—an odd but common juxtaposition in Iran, where leather and craftsmanship are cheap but paper is expensive, and printing presses, basic.

The book was the first volume of the eight-volume Usul al Kafi, which Mohammad explained was one of the most reliable of the *hadith*s, or ancient narrations. Collected by early Muslims in the first two centuries after the Prophet's death, the *hadith*s record his every word and deed, from the sublime to the apparently trivial. Because devout Muslims aspire to emulate the Prophet in every way, even his minor acts have significant import, and the *hadith*s are closely studied, with some considered to be much more reliable than others. A whole field of studies in Islam is devoted to sorting through the genealogies of each *hadith* narrator and rating each "true," "good," or "weak."

Mohammad opened to the first chapter and read: " 'When God created the Intellect (*al-'Aql*), He examined it. Thereupon He said to it: "Come forward." It came forward. Then He said: "Go back." It went back. Thereupon He said: "Be My power and majesty, I didn't create any creature dearer to me than thee!" ' "

TWO

With my hopes to visit a women's seminary on what proved to be permanent hold, Haideh had arranged for me to visit the University of Qom, where she taught, and interview its director, Ayatollah Qaadi. We set off early the next morning with Mohammad, who would serve as my interpreter, and Ali, and drove to the outskirts of town, past a bustling marketplace for the buying and selling of sheep, and several igloo-shaped buildings used for the baking of bricks. The University of Qom sat by itself on a small hill, behind an encircling wall.

As we drove, Mohammad provided me with background information. The University of Qom had been started up one year after the Revolution, he said, because there'd been a desperate need for more high school teachers in Iran. Initially a men's college with just 200 students, it had since grown into a co-ed institution with about 1,400 students.

Reaching the university, we drove through the compound gates where a clutch of women in *chador*s stood waiting for the shuttle bus. They were not allowed to walk the long and lonely stretch between the gates and the women's section of the university, Haideh said, because they might run into male students on the way.

"You're kidding," I said.

"But don't write that!" she said, laughing.

Entering a large, modern edifice, the main building of the women's section—I would not be allowed to visit the men's—we were ceremoniously ushered into a formal reception room, furnished with brocade-covered couches and chairs. A six-foot-long spread of fruits, nuts, cakes, and candy sat waiting, and a moment later, amidst a flurry of underlings, black *abas* and *chadors*, Ayatollah Qaadi, the university's director, and Khanom Husayni, the director of the women's section, arrived. Introductions were made and we all nodded politely at each other, but as a strict Muslim, Ayatollah Qaadi did not look directly at me. Instead, he, Mohammad, and I all sat down on the couch like three birds on a wire, with Mohammad in the middle, where he proceeded to turn his head from side to side as he interpreted.

We started with the basics. The University of Qom differed somewhat from most universities in Iran, Ayatollah Qaadi said, in that it offered more courses in religion and many of its professors were clerics. Undergraduate degrees were available in eight areas of study, including literature, mathematics, law, and theology. Master's degrees were available in criminal law, private law, and the Qor'anic sciences, among other areas, and doctorate degrees, in comparative philosophy, Western sciences, and theology. The school had started small but grown quickly, and "thanks be to Allah, we've been successful."

As the Ayatollah spoke, I kept nervously fiddling with my *chador*. Mohammad had told me that one of the Ayatollah's main concerns regarding this meeting was that I should be covered correctly. I was trying my best to comply with his request but I'd sat down too quickly on my *chador* and now it was slipping back off my head—and threatening to pull off my *rusari* as well. This was the first time that I'd had to wear the *chador* all day and I was finding it extremely difficult to adjust to. Standing up and walking weren't so hard, but sitting down and getting in and out of cars were impossible. Later, I would learn that it's necessary to hitch up a *chador* in back before sitting down.

The interview continued, with Ayatollah Qaadi telling me that with the exception of some areas of the law, all courses offered to men were also offered to women. The university's facilities for both sexes were also almost exactly alike. Out-of-town students lived for free in dorms on campus and, as at all public universities in Iran, all students were provided with free tuition, subsidized board, and a monthly government stipend. In return, the students were required, on graduation, to work for two to five years at reduced salaries in government jobs.

The free tuition, room, and board—even when coupled with a required stint in low-paying government jobs—sounded like an excellent plan to me, but sitting there in my slipping *chador*, I wanted to get back to the male–female question. The university's separate-but-equal facilities reminded me of racial struggles back in the United States—a comparison that had already occurred to me several times. Gender relations in Iran are as fraught with tension, both personal and political, and difficult to decode as are race relations in the United States.

"If most classes for men and women are the same," I said, "why can't men and women be taught together?"

"Because there is a difference in cultural background between Iran and the U.S.," Ayatollah Qaadi said. "If we had mixed classes in Iran, women would not feel comfortable asking questions, especially regarding the status of women in religion."

A politic answer, I thought.

"And in fact, I have heard about recent studies in the U.S. and Canada that proved that girls did better in school when separated from boys. What do feminists in the U.S. have to say about those studies now?"

I muddled out some sort of a reply, but I couldn't really answer him. He had a point. He was referring to certain studies that have shown that teachers in co-ed classrooms pay more attention to boys than they do to girls, and that girls perform better in subjects such as math and science when in same-sex classrooms. The radical viewpoint has merged with the ultraconservative one, I thought.

A *chador*-clad underling with a professional camera arrived to take our picture. Oh, no, I thought, making one last-ditch effort to readjust my *chador* before the camera bulb flashed.

Ayatollah Qaadi sat waiting, expecting me to ask more questions about the university, but in reality, I was more curious about him. He was the first cleric I'd met. I'd been sneaking glances at him as he spoke, and it struck me as oddly empowering that I could look at him whenever I wanted to, whereas he couldn't look at me at all. Because he was sitting on the other side of Mohammad, I couldn't see him terribly well, but I knew that he was a serious-looking man with thin cheeks and a short white beard, dressed in a white turban, collarless gray tunic, and black *aba*. Beneath his tunic, I could see light blue pants, dark socks, and slippers, and I wondered about his personal life. Was he married? Did he have grandchildren? Did he eat, sleep, and take showers like ordinary men?

"Did you study in Qom?" I asked. "And if so, what was it like back then?"

"I came to Qom fifty years ago as a young seminarian," Ayatollah Qaadi said, "and at that time, Qom was very small—seventeen thousand, as compared to today's one million. The Shah was doing everything he could to stop the town's development. Up until the time of the Revolution, there was not a single nonreligious institute for higher learning in Qom. Now there are about ten. The number of seminaries has also grown six or seven times and the number of seminarians has increased from six thousand to thirty-five thousand."

"Where did you study?" I asked, hungry to get back to the personal.

"Feiziyeh," he said, as I'd hoped he would. Founded about 600 years ago, Feiziyeh, meaning "Abundance of Goodness," is the oldest and most famous theological college in Qom. Ayatollah Khomeini and most of Iran's other powerful ayatollahs have studied there.

"Did you study with Ayatollah Khomeini?" I asked.

"Yes, of course," Ayatollah Qaadi said, and for the first time, I thought I detected a hint of passion in his voice. "I spent years studying philosophy with the Imam and also attended his very popular ethics class on Friday afternoons. The class wasn't in the usual ethical theory but was rather in morals and was attended by almost all the seminarians then in Qom. Incredibly, the Imam was less than thirty years old! That was unheard of! But he was already a highly respected teacher because of his purity and conviction. His thoughts were not just theoretical—they came from the depths of piety!"

So I'd been right; I had detected passion.

After studying at Feiziyeh for 12 years, Ayatollah Qaadi went on, he had moved back to his hometown, where he began teaching while continuing his studies. But still he traveled regularly to Qom, to listen to the speeches of Khomeini, and when the Imam was exiled to Najaf, Iraq, went there to visit him there four times.

"Khomeini was a very, very great man," he said. "Everyone in Qom knew it from the very beginning, which is why when he returned to Qom after his exile, ninety percent of the people came out to meet him. Qomis have always been the most ardent supporters of the Revolution—and continue to be so."

I still wanted to ask Ayatollah Qaadi more, especially about his personal life, but we'd already been speaking for about 40 minutes and he seemed to be growing restless. So I wrapped things up by asking a more general question or two, sensing as I did so that he was glad to stop talking about himself. Then I broached a more difficult subject.

"Would you like to see better relations between Iran and the U.S.?" I asked.

"Of course Iran wants better relations with the U.S.!" Ayatollah Qaadi said. "But the U.S. refuses to meet even the most basic of conditions! First, we have asked that the U.S. not interfere with our internal affairs, and yet two years ago, the U.S. Congress approved twenty million dollars to get rid of the Islamic government in Iran."

This, I learned later, was only partially correct. In 1995, at the instigation of then-Speaker of the House Newt Gingrich, the U.S. Congress *had* proposed a plan to set aside $18 million of an intelligence-spending bill to destabilize the Iranian government. But, following a wave of embarrassing publicity, the "secret" plan had never been implemented.

"And second," Ayatollah Qaadi said, "the U.S. continues to harbor terrorist organizations working against Iran. Under these circumstances, how can there possibly be better relations between the U.S. and Iran?"

The room fell silent, and the atmosphere grew tense. Ayatollah Qaadi's voice, though low, had been taut with an anger that had erupted out of nowhere. Goose bumps rose along my forearms.

A moment later, Ayatollah Qaadi straightened his *aba* and left without saying good-bye to anyone. That was apparently against protocol. But he did order an elaborate lunch for us, scheduled to arrive in about an hour.

ॐ

In the meantime, Mohammad, Haideh, Ali, and I, along with several guides, set out caravan style to tour the women's section of the university, housed in a clean and very modern facility complete with intimate classrooms, a language lab, computer lab, library, cafeteria, and prayer hall. In the language lab, I spotted English-language videos: *Macbeth*, *Sleeping Beauty*, *The Lion King*, *Meeting Objectives*, and *Effectual Telephoning*. In the library, organized according to the Library of Congress, I saw *The Oxford Book of Essays*, *The Scarlet Letter* by Nathaniel Hawthorne, *The Rover* by Joseph Conrad, *The Man in the Iron Mask* by Dumas, and an assortment of Shakespeare plays. In the computer lab, I counted seven computers, and in the prayer hall, we caught a student sleeping. She got up hastily as we came in, mumbled an apology, and scurried away.

We entered one of the classrooms, and with the flapping of *chador*s, all the students stood up, giggling and smiling at me until I looked at them, when they immediately looked away. The teacher, a male civilian, told us that the current lesson concerned a religious narrative entitled "What Is the Intellect?" from the *Sermons of Imam Ali* by Nahjul Balagha, the same book that had helped persuade Mohammad to convert to Islam. I wondered about the coincidence and about whether religion entered into every course offered by the university. While teaching English in Bogotá, Colombia, I'd attended many classes at the stridently leftist National University, where every lecture from mathematics to art had been imbued with a heavy-handed political message. A stultifying way, I'd thought then, and still do now, of approaching learning.

Outside, we passed a cheery playground where Ali sometimes played while Haideh was working. Like many universities and large offices in Iran, Haideh told me, the university provided free day care, which was especially important for the students, who tended to marry young and have children while still in school. Haideh also said that when Ali was born, she was given four months' maternity leave with pay, though three was standard in Iran, and that health insurance for herself, Mohammad, and Ali cost them about $4 a month.

Why can't we do that? I wondered as she spoke, but I knew exactly why. Much in Iran, including most of its health-care system, is government owned and operated. Private enterprise is limited, and although it is true that health care is affordable, the country lacks many of the sophisticated health services that are standard in the United States. Often, Iranians who can afford to do so go outside the country when they need treatment for serious illnesses.

As we toured the university, I sometimes felt as if I'd stepped back 10 years, into communist Russia or China, where the regime was showing me one of its model facilities. But my tour guides weren't government factotums, and I'd seen enough of Iran by now to know that although perhaps this model university wasn't exactly the norm, it certainly wasn't the exception, either. Increased educational opportunities for ordinary Iranians is one of the Revolution's greatest accomplishments; there are about four million university graduates in Iran today, as compared to about 430,000 in 1979.

౩౨౷౼

My own education continued that afternoon, with a visit to Fatemeh Medical University, an all-women university and hospital. Here, we met with Dr. Tahereh Labbaf, the school director, who, as soon as we arrived, called in six other female doctors, each representing a different specialty. All were dressed in tightly clutched *chadors*, and they presented a formidable presence as they marched into Dr. Labbaf's office and took up a whole bank of chairs across from us. My spirits drooped a little as I saw them. We four were tired from our visit to the University of Qom that morning and Ali was getting cranky. I had hoped to keep our visit to Fatemeh short, but the odds on that had just dropped precipitously.

One of the women snapped on a tape recorder and our session began.

I asked Dr. Labbaf, a brisk and seemingly very competent woman, to give me an overview, and she complied. Iran held 38 centers for training physicians, she said, and although most had a student body that was 40 to 55 percent women, this was the only medical school in Iran whose administration, clinics, hospital, and teaching staff were 100 percent women. In fact, as far as she knew, Fatemeh was the only institute of empirical sciences in the world that was entirely run by women. She had researched the topic, and although she had found medical schools in India, Japan, and elsewhere that accepted only women students, all of those schools had many male administrators and professors.

Fatemeh Medical University had been founded in 1988 by Imam Khomeini and offered degrees in medicine and eight other fields of study, including bachelor of science and technician's degrees. Of the 900 students at the school, 550 were studying to be doctors, 40 were studying to be technicians, and the rest were getting their undergraduate degrees.

Fatemeh Hospital was the largest in the province and treated all major problems, usually for women and children only, though the emergency room took men as well. The hospital had 400 beds, 9 operating rooms, 9 pathology rooms, and separate general surgery, pediatrics, operation, intensive care, critical care, and dialysis units.

One of the major purposes of the school, Dr. Labbaf concluded, was to serve as a showcase. The school wanted to both show the men of Iran what women were capable of and to show the world the independence that Iranian women have.

"How has the school been received?" I asked. "Do you get respect from the rest of the medical community?"

"Whenever you start something new," Dr. Labbaf said, "you get mixed reactions. Our work here has met with much resistance but also with much encouragement—praise be to Allah.

"When we started, there were not only people who opposed us but also people who were worried that we would succeed. Some said that without co-ed competition, we would always stay behind. Some said that since all our instructors were women, and their scholastic levels don't meet those of men's, we would always be behind. However, we have proved them all wrong in the national exams, where we have outperformed most other schools."

The irony of all this, I thought as she spoke, was that whereas if Fatemeh University were in the West, its efforts would be applauded as a strike for feminism, here there was the distinct possibility that it existed primarily as a way to enforce sexual segregation.

"Are there any advantages to having a hospital for women only?" I asked. "What is the purpose, besides serving as a showcase?"

Dr. Labbaf sidestepped the question. "I think the world has done a great injustice to Islam and especially to the women of Iran," she said. "When I went to a medical conference in Germany a few years ago and said that my specialty was surgery as related to childbirth, no one was interested. Instead they asked me, 'Are women in Iran allowed to drive cars?'! Such negative propaganda!"

"I agree with you," I said, sympathizing with her very tangible frustration. "But part of the problem is that the West lumps all Islamic countries together. We hear that women in Saudi Arabia can't drive, so we think all Muslim women can't drive."

Dr. Labbaf glared at me, and I realized that she hadn't heard a word I'd said. She was too angry.

"More than one thousand women work here," she said. "And we all wear the *hejab*. And we all want to wear the *hejab*. This shows that Islam and Islamic dress are no obstacle when it comes to doing good work.

"But when I read articles from the West, I read that women in Iran hate the *hejab*. That women in Iran can't work because of the *hejab*. But this is not true! Please correct this mistaken opinion."

All the other doctors in the room nodded vigorously, and their vehemence reminded me of the many other women I'd met who'd argued just as vehemently against the *hejab*. Even before leaving the United States, I'd known that Iran is deeply divided over this issue, but at that time, I'd attributed it to a basic educated/uneducated, religious/Westernized split.

My conversations with Babak and Tuba at Jamaran, Azar in Mashhad, and Mr. Bakhtiari in Alamut had already alerted me to the fact that things were not quite so simple. But only now, while talking to Dr. Labbaf and her colleagues, did I begin to suspect how very, very complicated it all is. These were highly educated women, and there were many of them.

ॐॐ

The next evening, Mohammad and I visited yet another educational institute, the Computer Research Center of Islamic Sciences, where we met two strikingly handsome clerics with dark beards, dressed in white and black robes so crisp they seemed to crackle. The older one was wearing a white turban, and the younger one, a black turban—a sign that he was descended from the Prophet Mohammad. Ayatollah Khomeini also wore a black turban, and so do Ayatollah Khamene'i and President Khatami.

The two clerics greeted me with considerable graciousness, despite the fact that only a few hours earlier, I'd heard Mohammad arguing with them on the phone. They hadn't liked the suddenness of my visit. Who is she exactly? they'd asked Mohammad, we're getting tired of mild-mannered Western reporters coming here in apparent friendliness and then writing whatever they feel like.

But now that we'd arrived, all earlier reservations were at least temporarily put aside, as the clerics enthusiastically proceeded to explain to me what went on at the Computer Research Center. And as they talked, I grew enthused myself. Here was yet another part of Qom—and Islam—that I'd had no idea existed.

The center's main purpose, the clerics explained, was to disseminate information about Islam to scholars all over the world. Established in 1989, the center had already put 80 percent—or about 1,000 volumes—of the most important Islamic reference texts on computer disc and CD-ROM and was in the process of producing one of the first encyclopedias of Islam written entirely by Muslim, as opposed to Western, scholars. The center also served as an umbrella organization for all companies producing Islamic-related software in Iran, offered computer classes for clerics, organized seminars and exhibitions worldwide, and maintained cybercafés in various countries, including the United Arab Emirates and Germany.

But the most important accomplishment of the center, the clerics went on, was to provide Islamic scholars with indices. None of the major Islamic texts have indices, and in the past, scholars would spend days, and sometimes weeks, searching for a specific passage that they just knew had to be in a certain text somewhere. Now, those same scholars could simply type in a subject, such as *inheritance*, or a concept, such as *existence and identity*, and cut their research time down by as much as 90 percent.

I blinked hard, wondering what this meant for the future of Islamic studies. The idea of doing research without indices—and especially research in those fat, dull-looking Islamic texts I'd seen at Mohammad's—boggled my mind. The amount of time wasted by Islamic scholars before the computer age must have been phenomenal.

Though perhaps they hadn't seen it that way.

"How do most clerics feel about using the computers?" I asked. "Do they accept them?"

"Everyone is very interested," said the white-turbaned cleric. "Sometimes the older ones have a hard time, but the younger ones help them, because everyone understands that whereas before, teachers spent most of their time researching and not so much time thinking, now they can spend more time thinking."

"About sixty percent of clerics in Qom now have computers in their homes," added the black-turbaned cleric, "and others use them in the libraries."

So the clerics can be flexible when they want to be, I thought, and especially when it's to their personal advantage. Everyone else has to suffer under the usual restrictions. From various conversations I'd had, I knew that computers are rapidly catching on in Iran. A growing percentage of the middle class now has e-mail, and Tehran established its first cybercafé around the time that I left Iran. But unrestricted access to the Internet requires an official permit, and users must sign a statement promising not to access "immoral" sites or those "against national security." Permit fees are also too high for most ordinary citizens to afford.

৵৽

While at the University of Qom, I had met Clara, a lovely, blue-eyed Austrian in her early twenties who radiated happiness. Dressed in a fine embossed *chador*, worn over an elegant tunic with a wide sash, Clara had converted to Islam with her family at age four. Two years before our meeting, as a student, she had come to Iran on her own to learn more about Islam, had met her future husband, the son of a prominent cleric, and stayed. Now she was continuing her studies at the university, and when I told her that I was eager to learn more about what it meant to be a religious Muslim woman in Iran, she invited me to come visit with her and her Iranian sister-in-law, Maryam, also a young newlywed.

I arrived at their house at dusk, my taxicab taking me through a neighborhood of unlit winding streets seemingly too narrow to allow for the passage of cars. Dust hung heavy in the air, turning the world into a pointillist painting, as dark figures cloaked in *chadors* and *abas* glided silently past. I could have been in the fourteenth century.

Then a door opened, letting out a wedge of electric light, and I saw Clara's beatific face, wrapped in a white *chador* sprinkled with flowers. A young man, her husband, passed me on the stairs as I entered, and after welcoming me, said that he was going out, to give us women a chance to talk in private.

Clara ushered me into their simple living room, furnished with a small, student-style sofa to one side, books to another. We sat down on a carpet on the floor and Clara offered me a bowl of watermelon. Maryam was still in the other room, seeing to her young son. The two families lived next door to each other.

"What made you decide to come to Iran?" I asked Clara, who was fluent in English as well as Persian. She'd taken off her *chador* and looked like a typical college student, dressed in pants and a blouse. Without her *chador*, she seemed taller than she had before and was of slender build and still lovely. I'd already discovered that it was not always easy to predict what a woman in the *hejab* will look like without it. Sometimes women who seemed as if they'd be extremely pretty weren't especially so, whereas others who appeared to be of only average good looks were striking when their full presence was revealed.

Personal style was often hard to predict as well. One woman whom I'd met several times in public had at first seemed quite elegant to me, always dressed in a neat black *manteau* with gold buttons and a silk *rusari*. But then I met her in private homes on a few occasions, and always, she was dressed in the same oversize Tweety Bird cartoon T-shirt and leggings.

"I wanted to learn more about Islam," Clara said. "It's very difficult to be a Muslim in Austria without knowing much about it."

To me, it seemed strange that she'd been a Muslim in Austria without knowing much about it in the first place, as it also seemed strange that so many believers of all faiths adhere to their religions so doggedly without knowing much about them.

"And you're happy here?" I asked.

"Very," she said. "In the West, they say, 'We are free,' but I've been there, and it's a lie. So many in the West are not satisfied. Love is missing. But here—my husband and I, we have a little paradise."

"Where did you meet?"

She let the question pass. "I don't think a Western woman can understand what it's like to be a Muslim woman in Iran—how appreciated we feel. To my husband, I am a gift that God has given him. A woman for a religious Muslim man is like an angel, just under God. The sky has opened and given her to him. She's the best—and he never compares her with anyone else because he hasn't seen anyone else. That's the purpose of the *hejab*, you know, to make relationships stronger. I feel no fear, no jealousy, this husband is only mine. I feel so loved."

I felt a distinct stab of jealousy. Had I ever felt so loved? Had anyone I'd ever known felt so loved? How much of what Clara felt was due to her youth and how much to her religion?

"But that's not true for many Muslim women," I said.

"No," Clara agreed. "But that's because many men are not good Muslims. And many women here don't accept the Islamic laws, either. They don't understand the meaning. They see only the West, they have no clue. They think the West is free, but they don't understand how difficult it is to be free. They don't know the ways in which the West destroys. They don't know the value of what they have."

I couldn't disagree with any of that.

"Iran is Islamic," Clara went on, "but the percentage of people here who are truly religious is still small. And Iran made many mistakes after the Revolution. Many good religious people were killed. But we are still very young. We need time to change. Iran is the only country in the world that is trying to establish a truly religious state, and we have opposition on all sides. The West tries to destroy us on one side, and tradition tries to destroy us on the other."

Maryam, a slim woman with shoulder-length hair, wearing a long-sleeved blouse and below-the-knee skirt, entered the room and we introduced ourselves. A 24-year-old medical student, she commuted three times a week between her classes in Tehran and her home in Qom. Both her and Clara's husbands were seminary students.

"What you said before about Islam might be true," I said to Clara, as we resettled ourselves. "But it still seems to me that there are many ways in which women here are oppressed. Take child custody cases, for example." I was thinking of Lona.

"You can't pull out one aspect of Islam and criticize it without looking at the whole system," Clara said. "There are reasons for everything in Islam. Our religion says that a man must support his family, and that's why in divorce cases, the child goes to the husband—he must support it. That's also why men inherit twice as much as women—he must support his family.

"A woman does not have to support anyone, and if she works, she has the right to keep her money all for herself. Her husband cannot ask her for it, and if he does, he is only borrowing. Also, a woman has the right to get paid for her housework, or to refuse to do it. And if she refuses, her husband must hire a housekeeper."

"But that only works in an ideal marriage," I said, now thinking of Azar and Shahla in Mashhad. "Most women can't do that—or much of anything without their husband's permission."

"Because they don't know," Clara said. "And because of tradition. For hundreds of years, tradition has said that women must stay in the house, they cannot study or work. But this is not Islam. This is tradition, and one of the things that's most difficult to distinguish here is what's tradition and what's Islam. Many traditional things hurt people very much."

She paused. "For example, Islam says that you must treat guests very well—which is good. But tradition says that you must do everything for your guests—you must give them meat even if you have no money, you must prepare a big meal even if your family goes hungry. And that is not good."

I felt a twinge of discomfort. Were people here treating me so well only because of Islam and/or tradition? Was their kindness toward me only due to a sense of obligation?

Clara stood up and left the room for the nearby kitchen, where she was preparing iced coffee. Though the heat of summer, so oppressive when I'd first arrived in Iran, had subsided in many parts of the country, Qom, the desert city, was still hot.

I turned to Maryam. "What does being a good Muslim woman mean to you?"

"To be a good Muslim woman . . ." She paused. "There's no difference between men and women really. We all want to satisfy God, to get nearer to Allah. But our ways of getting near Allah are different. For women, it is family, taking care of family. If this unit is healthy and okay, then the society will be a good society—

"But this doesn't mean a woman cannot work outside the house," she added quickly, as though anticipating my objection. "I'm outside the house six, seven hours a day. But I always know what is my first duty. We cannot be careless about our children."

"And for husbands?" I asked. "What is their most important duty?"

"For husbands, family is also number one, because whatever you do in the family will have a good and bad effect on the society."

"So there's no real difference between men and women," I pressed.

"Not for families."

"Does your husband help with the housework?"

"Yes, of course. In all good Muslim families, the man doesn't think just of himself. To help is the best way to Allah. The work in the house is not just the woman's. There's no question that the home duties must be divided."

"But from what I've seen, most husbands in Iran don't do this," I said. "Not that they do it in the West." I thought of all the husbands and boyfriends I knew. I could count the ones who helped around the house in a serious way on one hand.

"That's because we are still not an exact Muslim society," Maryam said. "There are many differences between families, and between what husbands and wives want from each other. But at least now, since the Revolution, we are going forward."

Good luck, I thought. When it came to the division of housework, I doubted whether any society anywhere was going forward.

"You spoke before about getting closer to Allah," I said. "How do you do that?"

"It depends on time," Maryam said. "Day by day, step by step, with things that look very simple but will lead to your goal. To pray is the best way to reach God—he is our creator, he knows the secrets of us—but to be a good Muslim doesn't mean just pray, fast. It means taking care of children, doing good work, studying the Qor'an—for men and women. God likes it very much when women study. And anytime any person of any religion does a kind thing, then it's a Muslim act."

"Even if that person is not Muslim," I said, to be sure, while thinking about how in the West, kind deeds are often described as Christian acts.

"Yes, of course."

"It will take time for women to find their real place in society," Clara said, coming back into the room with our iced coffee. "And it will take time to show what women can do in society. Everything is ready, but our capacities are not there yet."

"But it still seems to me," I said, tiring of generalities, "that women here don't have the same rights as men. They can't—"

"That is a typical Western comment," Clara said, suddenly exasperated—needlessly, I thought. "Always in the West, people ask, 'Can a woman do everything a man can do?' If she can, that supposedly means she is free. Freedom means doing what men do. But what is that? That is only a surface freedom. Women in the West are not free at all. In my opinion, they have problems with themselves, they have complexes toward men."

"You might be right," I said. "But when a Muslim woman can't leave the country without her husband's permission—that's not equality."

"Yes, okay," Clara said. "Maybe if you look at Islam from a narrow view, you will think women are not as free here as they are in the West. But if you look at a deeper level, you will see that women here are not trying to imitate men or be something men want them to be. Women here are trying to be themselves, to grow and go further in their own way. That is our aim.

"The measure of an Islamic woman differs from an Islamic man. She has to find her own identity. In the West, men are treated better in society than women, so women think they must have what men have. But here, these measures differ. Men and women can complete each other and make a perfect unit, complementary. And this unit will lead the way to Allah."

Much of what Clara said interested me. I agreed with her about Western women too often defining their successes in terms of men's, while denigrating certain classic feminine traits—gentleness, empathy, inner strength as opposed to surface toughness—because they aren't particularly respected in an attitude-ridden male world. I also didn't think women in the West were especially free, particularly when it came to the tyranny of beauty standards. But there were still many basic questions that Clara was ignoring.

"All right," I said. "But explain to me why a woman's testimony in Islamic court is only worth one half of a man's. How is that fair?"

"Because of emotion," Clara said. "Emotion is higher in women than it is in men, and when a woman comes to a difficult problem, especially if it is about herself, she will cry. Men don't do this, their logic is higher. In Islam, we say this women's emotion is good—it's needed for children and family. But in the West, you say this emotion is bad—women have to be like men."

Hmm, I thought. I liked the part about emotion being good, but I certainly didn't agree that men were universally more logical than women or with the implication that women couldn't separate their emotional and logical sides. It was an argument, however, that sounded only too familiar. Most men I knew had said something similar at one time or another.

"What about the Passport Law?" I asked. "Why can't a woman travel without her husband's permission?"

"It's not easy to explain." Maryam was answering this time. "But in every family, there must be a principal, and that principal must be a man. This does not give him the upper level—my husband and I always advise each other and he will not ignore things I've told him. But there cannot be two principals, and always I will leave the last decision to him. I'm more quiet and peaceful with that. Before my marriage, I did not understand this. But now, I am sure. It's the only way to be a good Muslim."

That argument neither directly answered my question nor made much sense to me. Again, though, it sounded only too familiar. I'd heard plenty of Western men, and some women, making that exact same point.

As I left Clara and Maryam, I thought of the Moroccan feminist scholar Fatema Mernissi. In her book, *The Veil and the Male Elite*, Mernissi argued that the repression of women in Islamic countries had nothing to do with the Prophet and the word of Allah as revealed in the Qor'an, and everything to do with a powerful male hierarchy's interpretations of the Qor'an and the *hadith*s. She pointed out that the Prophet's first wife, Khadijeh, 15 years older than he, was a highly respected businesswoman who asked *him* to marry *her*, urged him not to be afraid of the revelations he heard, and became the world's first convert to Islam. She also pointed out that one of the Prophet's later wives, A'isha, was a leader in battle; that the Qor'an gave Arabian women the right to inherit property in the 600s, a privilege that most European woman did not gain until the 1800s; and that one of the Prophet's great-granddaughters, Sukayna, was a spirited woman who married at least five times and was famed for her interest in poetry and politics.

I suspected that both Clara and Maryam would find much in Mernissi that they agreed with. I also suspected that they'd never read her. Although Mernissi's books are not officially banned in the Islamic Republic, they are not widely available—and then only in Arabic, English, and French. But if

Iran were truly building a new religious world order, I thought, and if Qom were as devoted to learning as it professes to be, Mernissi and others like her would be standard texts in all curricula—thinkers to be embraced, even if perhaps ultimately discarded, because dissent sharpens and invigorates.

The male-female conflict, around since the beginning of time, is not one that is likely to be resolved anytime soon. I disagreed with many of Clara and Maryam's positions, but at the same time, neither could I say that I—or by extension, the West—had all the answers. Some of what the young Muslim women had said had not only interested me but also challenged me to look at both our worlds a little differently. The East and the West have much to learn from each other, I thought. Why, in the name of Allah, isn't there more dialogue going on?

꒰ঌ৵ৎ꒱

One evening, as Pari, Maryam, and I were returning to our neighborhood after grocery shopping, I suddenly saw a small rounded figure in a white turban standing in the shadows by our front gate. Pari and Maryam, who'd been gossiping together, suddenly saw him, too, and fell silent. Our footsteps crunched over gravel.

"Mrs. Bird?" the figure said as we drew closer.

I stared at him. He had a gentle, apologetic manner and was clutching a big shiny briefcase to his chest. I couldn't imagine who he was.

And then I knew.

"Mr. Milani?"

His face broke out into a smile.

I had told Mohammad that I was interested in speaking with one or two *talabeh*s, and he had presented my request to his class, who had all agreed that the best person for the job was their colleague Mr. Milani. He was both a top student who had studied at several seminaries and nearly fluent in English. Over the last few days, I had tried calling him several times but had repeatedly missed him and left multiple messages in broken Persian with his wife.

"How long have you been waiting?" I asked, astonished to see him here.

"Oh, not long," Mr. Milani said, while I continued to gape. Apparently, after receiving my last message, he'd simply come over, in the hopes that I'd return soon. Mohammad had given him the address.

"Thank you so much for coming," I said. "It was very kind of you."

But Mr. Milani just shrugged. He did not seem to consider his action at all unusual.

I introduced him to Pari and Maryam, who nodded distantly. They had pulled their *chadors* more tightly around them and were eyeing Mr. Milani dubiously.

"Is it all right if I invite Mr. Milani in?" I asked Maryam.

But to my great surprise, she didn't answer. In obvious discomfort, she glanced at Pari, who bit her lower lip.

"He's not a stranger," I said, thinking that that was the problem. "He's a friend of Mohammad Legenhausen, whom you met the other day."

Maryam and Pari wouldn't meet my eyes, and I wondered what they were thinking. Did they imagine that Mr. Milani might hurt us in some way? Or did they think that he was here to court me?

"It's all right," Mr. Milani said to me under his breath. "There's a park near here where we can talk."

I said as much to Maryam and Pari, who, after asking me several times if I was sure I'd be all right, turned away with obvious relief and entered the house. The front door clicked shut behind them.

"I'm so sorry," I said to Mr. Milani, feeling embarrassed.

Mr. Milani cleared his throat. "A good Muslim woman does not let a strange man into the house when her husband is away."

"Oh," I said numbly, feeling strangely deflated. I would never have guessed that. Here I was just beginning to think I understood something about Iran, and I'd completely misinterpreted even this simple situation.

We headed toward the park. At age 40 or so, Mr. Milani was much older than I'd expected. But then I remembered that in Qom, the more serious students are often older. Mr. Milani was probably either well on his way to becoming, or already was, a *mujtahid.*

"Are you a teacher as well as a student?" I asked.

"Yes," he said, and added proudly, "and I'm also the father of four children."

Mr. Milani was wearing the soft yellow leather slippers that I'd already noticed on many clerics, and they padded softly alongside my clunky black shoes as we crossed first one street and then another. His briefcase glinted in the light of an occasional street lamp or passing car while I juggled my knapsack beneath my *chador.* Somehow I just couldn't get the pack into a comfortable position. Whether on my back or by my side, it pulled awkwardly against the *chador*'s heavy fabric, making it difficult to keep the garment in place.

Finally, we came to a large concrete bench at the edge of a park—inexplicably closed—and sat down. Traffic was whizzing by uncomfortably close, but it didn't seem to bother Mr. Milani, who immediately launched into a long enthusiastic speech about President Khatami and the importance of more cultural exchange with the West. After listening for about ten minutes, I interrupted him. As interested as I was to learn that he held liberal views, I didn't particularly want to hear all the details. I wanted to know more about his experiences. Why had he decided to become a *talabeh?*

Cocking his head at my interruption, Mr. Milani thought for moment. He didn't seem to be especially interested in talking about himself, but he was polite and eager to please me.

"After I finished high school, I entered the university," he finally said. "I wanted to study physics. But soon, after one year, I changed my mind and went to the *hoseinieh.* I thought, it's better, because by studying the Qor'an and comparative religions, we can answer the major questions. For every human being, there are some major questions. What are we in creation? Who is our creator? What does he want from us? What am I? What's my next future? These are the great questions.

"So for finding good answers to these great questions, I came here. I understood that the questions I have are metaphysical and that the questions that physics answers are only physical."

He paused and looked at me expectantly, waiting for my next question.

"Tell me about your first years here," I said. "What did you study?"

"I went first to Feiziyeh school because it is very old and very famous. Before, when I was in Tehran, I had read the Arabic language for four years. Every student who comes to Qom must know Arabic. And then, in Feiziyeh, I started jurisprudence and rational thought."

I nodded. Mohammad had already explained to me that most of what is taught in Qom is jurisprudence and that there are two major jurisprudence topics. *Fiqh* is Islamic jurisprudence, or the study of rulings from contract law to ritual. *Osul* questions what kind of principles can be used to derive legal ruling from sources. Both sounded disappointingly dry to me.

"What were those years like for you?" I asked, and then, when he looked puzzled, I added, "Was it an exciting time for you?"

"Oh, it was a very exciting time for me! We had lessons about God and the Qor'an. Our spirituality was very high. We used to get up at midnight and pray—supplication with God." He stared at me. "Why is it that when we marry and live individually, little by little we lose that good feeling?"

"I don't know," I said, discomfited. It felt a little strange to be sitting here in the near darkness alone with a cleric, his *aba* occasionally billowing against me in a passing breeze, and I hoped that he wasn't going to start complaining about his wife. "Maybe because everything is so new when we're very young, and when we get older—"

"Yes, yes." He nodded vigorously. "You are right."

A frazzled-looking young man came by and asked Mr. Milani for money. Apparently, he had lost his bag. Mr. Milani gave him a few coins.

I then tried to get Mr. Milani to tell me more about his student years and about his years working as a village mullah, but it was very difficult to pull much else out of him. Like Ayatollah Qaadi and some other men I met in Iran, he seemed reluctant to answer even the simplest of personal queries. Only when we returned to more general topics did he light up and expound without my constant prompting. Like many Iranians, he had lots of opinions and liked to talk about them.

"I think the greatest achievement of the Revolution," he said, "is spiritual more than material. The people in the era with the Shah thought Iran was a Third World country. We cannot be independent, they said. But now we understand that we can. We can stand on our own feet—"

"Now I study Western thought at the Khomeini Institute. It's very important to do so. The Western thought is not very deep. Even Kant and Hegel are not very deep, and we can easily criticize."

Really, I thought, wishing that I knew enough about philosophy to challenge him in a serious way.

"But it is the responsibility of the clerics to know the Western books," he continued, "so we can defend and not let young people go astray. The Western thought can easily make young people go astray—"

I drew in a deep breath. "Many people here have complained to me about the mullahs," I said, trying to be both direct and tactful. "They tell me that they are not very honest or very intelligent, that they don't really think but just memorize the ancient books. What is your opinion?"

Mr. Milani paused, wrinkling his brow. "When the mullahs study," he finally said, "they are very intelligent, very deep. But I don't know why— they don't know about freedom. Islam is free in every aspect of life—economic, women, even sexual freedom. It is unique. But unfortunately, most people don't know this. Even the government doesn't know this. All they know is according to what they take from their parents.

"I know many people in Iran now are angry with the mullahs, and I agree. Some have gone astray from the Islamic path. Some have taken the license from a factory and made a lot of money. Some want too much power. But this does not apply to all mullahs. Or most mullahs.

"I think mullahs should live very simply, like a poor man in a village without electricity. According to our religion, this is a recommendation but not an obligation. I think it should be an obligation. It is an obligation for the Supreme Leader—Khamene'i has no carpets—but for the others, there are no laws."

By *recommendation* and *obligation*, I knew that Mr. Milani was referring to the five different categories of human actions under Muslim law. At one end are acts that are *haram*, or forbidden, such as eating pork or drinking alcohol, and at the other is behavior that is *vajeb*, or obligatory, such as praying five times a day. In between are *makruh*, or discouraged acts, *mostahab*, or encouraged acts, and *mobah*, or neutral acts.

Only after Mr. Milani and I parted company did I realize that I'd forgotten to ask him the most important question of all. Had he found any good answers to great questions? I was looking for those myself.

THREE

*O*n the morning of my visit to Grand Ayatollah Shirazi, I rendezvoused with a young woman named Nasrin. Thin, serious, and extremely pale, she was a student at the University of Qom and had volunteered, through Mohammad and Haideh, to be my interpreter that morning. But as soon as Nasrin and I greeted each other, my heart sank. Despite the fact that she was a senior majoring in English translation, she could barely speak English—a phenomenon that I'd already discovered among quite a few so-called English majors in Iran.

Making our way down a sidewalk crowded with clerics and women in *chadors*, we came to a scruffy side street and an open doorway, half covered with a short curtain. Inside, a clerk was lounging, and we handed him my letter of introduction from Ershad. He looked from it to me with disapproval and clucked something to Nasrin. Nervously, I adjusted my *chador*. Earlier, everyone in Qom had assured me that I did not need an official appointment to visit Ayatollah Shirazi—he's famous for his accessibility, they'd said; you'll have no trouble seeing him if you just stop by. I'd had my doubts about that information but had had no telephone number to call, and now it appeared I'd been misinformed. I most definitely did need an appointment, the clerk said, although perhaps if I took a seat and was patient, the ayatollah could fit me in.

Exasperated with myself for not trying harder to verify what I'd been told, I followed Nasrin into a large waiting room. Here, a second clerk took our shoes, invited us to take seats on the floor, and served us glasses of tea.

I looked around. The waiting room was covered with carpets and informally divided into two parts. At the end of one stood a podium with a phone on top. At the end of the other stood a coffee table with two phones on top. Both tables were staffed by kneeling clerics in white turbans and tan cloaks. And all over the room, sitting cross-legged like giant crickets, were perhaps two dozen more clerics, most dressed in black *abas* and white turbans, and reading books. Two Pakistanis in traditional dress were whispering vigorously together, and a few ordinary citizens sat scattered here and there. Nasrin and I were the only women in the room, but no one had even glanced at us when we came in. Do all these men have appointments? I wondered, with a sinking heart.

Nasrin's husband Rahmin suddenly arrived. I had no idea how he'd found us, but here he was, as thin, serious, and extraordinarily pale as she was, with soft brown eyes, a fuzzy beard, and a threadbare brown suit. Immediately, he and Nasrin began whispering together.

An hour or so passed slowly, with the two of them continually whispering and glancing at their watches. Are you in a hurry? I asked Nasrin several times. No, no, she kept saying, before finally admitting that they had a bus to catch. It left shortly after noon, and it was now nearly 11 o'clock. Why, I wondered, irritated as I heard the news, had Nasrin, with her limited English and time, volunteered to be my interpreter in the first place? But I already knew the answer. She'd been interested in meeting me and had been too polite to turn Mohammad and Haideh down.

Suddenly, Rahmin stood up. The clerk whom we'd first met had entered the room, and Rahmin hurried up to him, to talk excitedly under his breath as he pointed emphatically at me and his watch. My ears burned beneath my *rusari* and *chador*. Here were all these supplicants waiting ahead of me, and yet I had to be first—the impatient American.

But the deed was already done, and a moment later, the clerk, his nostrils twitching, beckoned to us. Putting on our shoes, we crossed an empty street to enter a modern edifice of yellow brick, built around a courtyard.

A pretty blue tile border, the building's only adornment, ran just beneath the roof.

"Where are we?" I asked Nasrin.

"The Imam Hosein *madraseh*," she replied.

So I was in a *madraseh*—seminary—at last. But to my disappointment, there was little to see. Except for a crowded waiting room near the entrance, the sterile building appeared to be completely empty—classes were not in session. Instead, four stories of uniform rooms stared blankly back at me as the clerk hurried us along. We passed a time clock—here? in a seminary? I wondered—and then entered a back room with a cot. Apparently, as women, we were not allowed to wait in the public waiting room.

Gingerly, Nasrin and I took seats on the creaky cot as an old man shuffled in with more cups of tea. Rahmin had disappeared—to fetch their luggage, Nasrin explained, glancing at her watch yet again.

"Why don't you two just go when he gets back," I said. "I'll manage here somehow." Their nervousness was driving me crazy, and I didn't want them to miss their bus.

"No, no," Nasrin said. "You are our guest. We can't just leave you."

Why not? I thought, although I didn't really want them to go. As halting as Nasrin's English was, it was still better than my Persian.

"How did you meet Rahmin?" I asked.

"Through poetry," Nasrin said, and then explained that Rahmin had been the editor of a poetry journal at the University of Qom, when she'd sent in a poem. Impressed, he'd asked to meet her—under supervision, of course—and it had been love at first sight for them both. Nasrin's mother hadn't been too enthusiastic at first, as her daughter had had other prospects, but now that she knew Rahmin better, she loved him so much. And Nasrin loved him so much. And he loved her so much. She couldn't live without him. Without him she would die.

"How old are you?" I asked, startled. Counting Clara, this was the second story about great love that I'd heard in two days. I'd had no idea Iranians were so romantic.

"Twenty," she said. "And Rahmin is twenty-one."

At eight minutes to 12:00, when I'd given up all hope of seeing Ayatollah Shirazi, the clerk came back.

"You can see the ayatollah now," he said. "How much time do you need?"

"Oh, only about five minutes," I said, thinking of Nasrin's bus, of the many other people who were waiting, and of the impossibility of conducting a proper interview under these harried conditions.

The clerk beamed.

"Or perhaps ten," I amended.

His face fell. "Ten minutes is impossible," he said. "The ayatollah breaks for prayers at noon."

Hustling us back down the promenade, he escorted us through the still-crowded waiting room, where I recognized some of the clerics who'd been waiting across the street. They looked at me with what might have been a well-deserved hostility, and then we were whisked into the Grand Ayatollah's office. A huge plastic mural of Mecca shimmered, covering one entire wall. Pale blue rugs covered the floor. By the windows crowded a small metal desk and several simple chairs—the only furniture in the room.

Sitting in one of the chairs was Grand Ayatollah Shirazi, a kindly looking older gentleman with a full beard, heavy brown glasses, white turban, and age spots freckling his hands and face. Despite his high religious standing, he looked directly at us—lowly women that we were—and we began an awkward interview.

Women are extremely important in Islam, Ayatollah Shirazi said, and if anyone ever tells you differently, they are wrong. There is only one limit for women in Islam—if you consider it a limit, because we do not—and that is the *hejab*. Cultural exchange is not bad for Islam and could be good, but Iran must also be careful to keep its own culture. Technology and Islam are not incompatible because history shows that technology arrived first in the East, through Avicenna and others, and was then exported *from* Islamic countries *to* Europe.

As Ayatollah Shirazi uttered these predictable answers to my predictable questions, I felt opportunity slipping away from me, but there was nothing I could do about it. Getting to the heart of anything is difficult even under the best of circumstances, and these were not the best of circumstances. I'd known even before arriving in Ayatollah Shirazi's office that I didn't know enough about the nitty-gritty of Islamic law or Iranian politics to ask as insightful questions as I would have liked, and I had come as much for his presence as I'd come for his words. And he wasn't disappointing me. His was indeed a gentle yet powerful aura, and he seemed to be a true spiritual leader—kind, understanding, charismatic, sorrowful, and wise. Implicitly,

I trusted him, while at the same time recognizing that that kind of gut reaction can be dangerous.

The interview over almost as soon as it had begun, we were escorted back outside and I sat down on a bench near the waiting room to collect myself. A split second later, Ayatollah Shirazi swept briskly by, on his way to noon prayers. Instantly, most of those in the waiting room shot to their feet and hurried after him, calling out religious queries as they went. The Pakistanis were at the head of the pack, followed by a clutch of bobbing turbans and one lone man in civilian dress. Black *aba*s swirled, books banged against thighs, and arms waved in the air.

The pack disappeared out the front gate with what I imagined was a cloud of dust, leaving silence behind. I tucked my notebook away. Nasrin looked at her watch.

Then, suddenly, Rahmin reappeared—without any luggage that I could see.

"Go! Go!" I said as soon as I saw him. "It's only twelve o'clock—you might still catch your bus."

But now it turned out that the bus didn't matter so much after all. There were other buses, Nasrin said, leaving every hour or so, and now that the interview was successfully concluded, she and Rahmin wanted to invite me for a fruit drink. What?!? I thought to myself, not knowing what to say. I'd been needlessly worrying about them and their bus for over an hour.

Nevertheless, I accepted their invitation and we walked down the street, into one of the narrow fruit juice bars that can be found all over Iran, and ordered a pomegranate drink. Out poured the thick, frothy, bloodred beverage. But before more than five minutes had passed, Nasrin and Rahmin started looking at their watches again.

"Hey!" I said, my earlier annoyance returning full force. "What's going on here? I thought you weren't worried about the bus anymore."

"No, no—we're not, don't bother about it," they said, sneaking more glances at their watches.

"Then what's the matter?" I asked, and only after I kept badgering them did they admit that they were now worried about saying their prayers. It was already after midday.

"So go ahead and say your prayers," I said, exasperated. "Don't let me stop you—people say their prayers around me all the time."

Still, the matter wasn't settled yet, because Nasrin and Rahmin couldn't say their prayers at the juice bar—I could understand that—but wanted to go to

Hazrat-e Masumeh, the holy shrine. And they couldn't go to the shrine with me, because I wasn't allowed inside. Though not as important a pilgrimage site as Imam Reza's tomb in Mashhad, Fatemeh's tomb is also off limits to nonbelievers (all other tombs and mosques in Iran are open to visitors).

"Then I'll just wait outside," I said, stating the obvious, at which they looked a little surprised and vastly relieved.

As we made our way to the shrine, Nasrin bombarded me with questions: Don't you want to become Muslim? Why don't you want to become Muslim? What do you think of the Qor'an? What do you think of Allah? Do you like the call to prayer? Some foreigners don't like the call to prayer—they say it is not beautiful. But how can that be? I don't understand. For me, it is the most beautiful sound in the world.

Finally, we reached a side entrance to the shrine, and while Nasrin and Rahmin slipped inside, I waited in the vestibule and watched the foot traffic. As in Mashhad, I spotted Shi'ites from all over the world—Pakistanis, Afghans, Iraqis, and Africans. But the atmosphere here, at this smaller pilgrimage site, in the off season, seemed both less festive and more serious to me than had Mashhad's. Many of the pilgrims filing by me were young men—*talabehs*, perhaps—and I could sense their overwhelming excitement as they bustled in and out, their eager faces shining. I envied them their faith, their certainty, and their sure sense of place in the world, and thought about how, in the West, many of us are too cynical to even recognize the beauty of faith anymore.

The gatekeeper befriended me. Despite my *chador*, he'd spotted me as a Westerner as soon as I'd first approached and had fiercely warned me about trying to enter. But now as we stood there, exchanging pleasantries, he lightened up.

"Why don't you convert to Islam," he said, "and then I'll let you in right away. It's easy, all you have to say is 'There is no god but Allah and Mohammad is His Messenger,' three times."

"I know," I said, contemplating for a moment the simplicity of converting to Islam. "But how can I do that if I don't believe?"

The gatekeeper shrugged. "You believe in one god, don't you?"

"Y-e-s-s," I said slowly. Though a nonpracticing Christian, I don't consider myself an atheist, or even an agnostic.

"Then you should convert to Islam. You'll see. It's much better. You'll be much happier. "

If only life were that simple, I thought.

⸺⸱⸻

I returned to Hazrat-e Masumeh, the holy shrine, a day or two later, this time
in the early evening, walking up the main promenade with Tahereh, another
university student I'd met through Mohammad. En route, we passed a large,
tidy market where vendor stalls sold everything from prayer rugs and prayer
beads to souvenir T-shirts and *sohan*, the flat, sweet pistachio brittle that is a
trademark of Qom. Sold all over the city, *sohan* is usually packaged in round,
flat tins that are then stacked up in piles as high as shop ceilings.

The promenade led to a wide and lovely square, which in the gathering
dusk seemed hushed and dreamlike, with pale yellow lights just beginning
to flick on beneath a pearled sky. Clumps of clerics in white, gray, and
black were gathered together, and as they bent their heads to talk and listen, I realized for the first time that the Iranian turban does not cover the
whole head but is a ring, with a hole in the middle.

Behind the clerics, at one end of the square, rose the arched main gateway to the holy shrine, beyond which I could see three pairs of minarets
flanking three domes—one gold, one pale blue, and one sea green. Doves
swooped from one minaret to another, but I could see no storks—once the
signature bird of Qom, found at the holy shrine and all over the city, but
driven out in recent years by the city's population explosion.

I kept my head down as we walked through the main gate, which I'd
deliberately chosen over the less crowded side entrance, where my gatekeeper friend might again be working. I'd also deliberately chosen to come
under the protective cover of dusk. As in Mashhad, many Muslims in
Qom had assured me that as long as I entered the holy shrine with respect,
I was not really breaking any serious Islamic rule, but I still didn't want to
be recognized.

Once past the gateway, though, my nervousness diminished. No one
was paying the least bit of attention to me, and Tahereh and I wandered,
deliciously anonymous, through a wide and tranquil courtyard, surrounded
by gentle murmurings. The men were vaguely heading toward one side of
the courtyard, the women toward another, but the sexes were quietly conversing with each other as they went, reminding me of being on a hushed
promenade in Colombia or Spain, where the citizens come out at twilight
to socialize.

It is from Qom that the ugliest of the Shi'ite fundamentalist messages
come. It is from Qom that the cruelest terrorists draw their inspiration
and the harshest ayatollahs breathe their fire. Dictums of hatred, dogma,

and intolerance emanate from the city all too often, repressing and some-times destroying lives. Yet to enter Qom's holy shrine is to enter a king-dom of peace.

To one side of the courtyard rose the entrance to Fatemeh's tomb, topped by the gold dome and blue tile minarets. The *eivan,* or open hall, fronting the tomb glittered with tiny mirrors shaped like diamonds and teardrops; the building's façade gleamed with blue tiles embroidered with white arabesques that swirled and spilled over into leaves and flowers. Passing through the women's entrance, we relinquished our shoes, then entered the tomb room—cozier and far less crowded than Imam Reza's. Standing in the back, where I'd be least conspicuous, I watched for a moment as women knelt, prayed, and kissed the tomb, glass chandeliers above them, cool green marble below. And then Tahereh and I retreated to the courtyard. To my mind, it was much more beautiful out here.

The music that precedes the call to prayer had begun, and we took a seat on a marble ledge on the far side of the courtyard, across from Fatemeh's tomb and the main prayer area. To one side of us sat young ani-mated women gossiping with each other while keeping close eyes on their children who were dashing here and there. *"Afarin! Afarin!"*—Excellent! Excellent!—they intermittently cried, clapping, as one child after another performed some extraordinary feat, such as hopping on one foot or twirling in place.

The music continued, more urgently now, and I felt its dark, rich, hyp-notizing lament tugging at my insides like a melancholy blues ballad. The women's prayer area before me, separated from the men's by a sagging sheet on a wire, had become crowded with black and white *chadors,* some women sitting cross-legged, others turtle-backed, many completely still. Amplified words reverberated around the courtyard, echoing everywhere, and the set-ting sun grew more intense for just one moment before the sky gradually dimmed from gray-blue to gray-black.

The prayers began, with some women standing and cupping their hands to their ears, others still gossiping on the ledges around us. The muezzin's voice seemed to be nudging the praying women along, pushing them into each new position, and as he called and they bowed and knelt, stood and bowed again, I noticed that the darker the sky became, the bluer the *eivan* fronting Fatemeh's shrine grew, its mirrored ceiling reflecting the building's tiled façade.

I don't want to go home, I suddenly thought. It's magical here.

ॐ

I visited Qom three times in all, arriving the second time by communal taxi, and the third, by the clacking, overnight Yazd–Tehran train, in which I shared a sardine can of a sleeping compartment with five other women, while a lonesome moonlit desert slipped by outside. Staying up half that night to stare out my smudged upper-berth window, I yearned to hold onto the ghostly landscape with my mind but lost it anyway.

I stayed with Mohammad and Haideh on my second visit, and in a hotel the third, knocking at its shuttered doors one morning at 4:30 A.M., direct from the train station. The man who had shared the taxi from the station with me insisted on paying my fare, while the hotel's sleepy night manager rushed out to help me with my bag.

My Tehrani friends were perturbed by my repeat visits to Qom. Why are you going back there? they asked, it's such an abominable city, and it's not the real Iran.

But I felt that Qom had something important to teach me—if only because, for better or worse, it is the center of Shi'ite Islam. All of the ironies and contradictions that I'd found elsewhere in the country seemed to come to a head here—violence coupled with gentleness, dogmatism with questing, the fourteenth century with the twenty-first, mean grasping politics with genuine spiritual transcendence. There were answers in Qom, I could feel them—elusive shadows as always, traveling just beneath the surface.

IN THE SHADOW
OF KINGS

For in and out, above, about, below,
'Tis nothing but a Magic Shadow-show
Play'd in a Box whose Candle is the Sun,
Round which we Phantom Figures come and go.

—*Rubáiyát* of Omar Khayyam,
rendered into English by Edward FitzGerald

ONE

When I got to Esfahan and Shiraz, everything changed. Suddenly, in these two popular tourist destinations, I found myself among Westerners again, and I wasn't sure I liked it. I had grown accustomed to being the only foreigner around, and to the excessive attention that that brought me. I also didn't like suddenly being cast into the role of tourist, here to see the glories of ancient worlds, created by legendary kings, rather than traveler, here to observe the workings of the Islamic Republic. Most of all, though, after over two months in Iran, the presence of other Westerners disconcerted me. Though I was one of them, their long limbs, pale hair, and use of slang startled me. They seemed foreign to me.

I had checked into Esfahan's friendly Amir Kabir Hotel, a *mosafer-khaneh,* or guest house, listed in the "Places to Stay—Budget" section of my Lonely Planet guidebook. Almost everyone else at the Amir Kabir had found it through the Lonely Planet guidebook also, and most were twenty-something Australian or European "overlanders," making the trek between Nepal and Turkey—still referred to by some in quotes as the "hippie trail." A marginally clean room with two iron cots and a sink, toilets, and showers down the hall cost about $4 a night. Signs in the lobby warned about a nearby restaurant that tried to rip off tourists. The hotel "library" included copies of *A Tale of Two Cities, A Handbook for Motorists, Beginning Japanese, The Picture of Dorian Gray, The Role of the Holy Imams in the Revival of Religion, The Complete Music Catalogue,* and a book about Alfred Hitchcock in Spanish.

As an American and a single woman, however, I still stood out. One of the two plump, jolly brothers who ran the hotel took my passport with glee as he checked me in. "An American!" he said in passable English, "that's *very* unusual." Five years before, he said, the Amir Kabir had catered almost exclusively to Iranians and central Asians, but these days, most of his guests were Western, and now (!) it appeared as if the Americans were coming (!). Good times lay ahead.

A hotel employee led me to my room on the second floor, overlooking a scruffy but pleasant courtyard in which a large group of Australians were laughing and joking together. Two tall Dutchmen with greasy ponytails were lounging outside my door, exchanging travel war stories, while a threesome of Germans sat nearby, smoking cigarettes and drinking tea. Older than most of the other guests and dressed entirely in black, the Germans oozed ultracool and kept giving the Australians—and then me—the kind of attitude-ridden glances that I hadn't seen since New York.

Feeling many pairs of eyes on me—the newcomer—I scurried into my room. I didn't want to talk with anyone. Or at least not yet. I needed time to adjust to this odd new environment, and to clear my head. I'd been traveling by rattling minibus since dawn, through the long stretch of desert that surrounds Esfahan.

I looked around my doll-size room. The stained walls were completely bare, except for one small medallion made of blue paper. On it was a black arrow pointing toward Mecca, and later, I would see similar arrows in all the hotel rooms I stayed in—some on paper, some on plaques, and one simply drawn with a marker on the wall. "And whencesoever thou comest forth (for prayer, O Muhammad) turn thy face toward the Inviolable Place of Worship. Lo! it is the Truth from thy Lord" (Qor'an, 2:149).

By the time I left my room, the courtyard was almost empty, and gratefully I wandered out and down the wide thoroughfare that fronted the Amir Kabir. The northern end of Chahar Bagh Street, built by Shah 'Abbas I in the late 1500s, the boulevard had once been lined with mansions and was still shaded with "sparrow-tongue" trees, so nicknamed because of the chattering noise their leaves made in the wind. I passed through a busy traffic circle and then by a series of tourist-oriented carpet shops, silversmith shops, and restaurants, followed by tourist hotels and kiosks selling soft-serve ice cream flavored with saffron.

As I walked, I realized that Esfahan, population about 1.3 million, was the first Iranian city I'd been in that felt relaxed. The vehicular traffic, though as dense and polluting as ever, seemed to be moving at a slower speed, and people were strolling, rather than striding, down the boulevard. No one seemed to be in a particular hurry; maybe most were tourists, like me. Esfahan is a favorite vacation destination among Iranians as well as foreigners.

Most Iranians, however, have little good to say about the Esfahanis, who have a reputation for avarice and stinginess. As one popular saying goes: "Esfahan is a paradise full of luxuries; there ought, however, to be no Esfahanis in it." A popular admonition warns: "An Esfahani will buy a cucumber, paint it yellow, and sell it as a banana." And a popular joke goes: "An Esfahani goes to interview at the University of Edinburgh, in the hopes of studying economics. The interviewers turn off the lights, saying there's no need to waste electricity while talking. But when they turn the lights back on, they find the Esfahani sitting in the buff—because, he explains, there was no need to wear out his clothes in the dark. 'Congratulations,' the Scotsmen tell him, handing him his diploma. 'We can't teach you anything here you don't already know. Go back to Iran.'"

A motor scooter zoomed by. "Welcome to Iran!" its driver shouted at me in English as he disappeared around a corner in a puff of exhaust.

Crossing through another congested traffic circle, I reached the Zayandeh Rud, a slow, magnificent river that in the late afternoon seemed the density and color of mercury. Immediately before me, and mirrored to perfection in the water, stretched the Si-o-Seh Pol, a bridge built in 1602, its 33 pointed archways marching out in strict precision as they crossed to the other side. In the manicured park that hugged the river, friends and families were gathered together, talking and laughing, while their children flitted between them like bright butterflies. Some had brought portable potbellied samovars with them and were passing around cups of tea.

I joined the lazy foot traffic strolling down the walkway that ran through the park. Before me I could see spic-and-span playgrounds, colorful kiosks selling snacks, and more ancient bridges, all shining golden in the lengthening rays of the sun. Fishermen in rowboats were casting their lines and boys were rolling past on bicycles; a large group of old men sat crouched on their haunches on a small hill, gossiping.

A young woman befriended me and together we walked, exchanging the usual pleasantries. She was on her way to a friend's house and seemed happy to take the long way around, as she led me across the narrow Chubi bridge and showed me the extraordinary, double-tiered Khaju Pol, built in 1660, which was both a bridge and a weir. On its lower level operated a cozy teahouse filled with Persian carpets, hubble-bubbles, and folk art—one of several such establishments tucked into the bridges. Outside, the teahouse sported a faded fresco from the Safavid period; inside, an English-language sign read: A WOMEN DRESSED MODESTLY IS A PEARL IN ITS SHELL.

After the young woman left me, I bought a Fanta from a surly vendor and sat down on a bench—a mistake, I immediately realized, as a man in his late twenties sat down too familiarly beside me. I'd already noticed quite a few Esfahani men staring at me curiously, and much more invasively, than had men elsewhere in Iran. The Esfahanis' curiosity was not the distant, gentle, what's-a-Westerner-doing-here kind that I'd grown used to but rather the more aggressive and avaricious kind that often thrives in popular tourist destinations. As a travel writer, I recognized it well.

"Where are you from?" the young man asked, predictably.

"America," I said, not so predictably.

He stared at me. "American people are very dangerous."

"Some."

"And you're here alone?"

"Yes," I replied, without thinking.

But I got lucky. The man was already standing up.

"This is very strange," he said. "You are from America, and you are here alone. I think you are dangerous. I must go."

"All right," I said, trying not to smile as he rapidly walked away, keeping his head well down. There were many people in the park, and it was, I later learned, a favorite haunt of the plainclothed *komiteh*.

I finished my soda and handed the bottle back to the kiosk vendor, who was looking at me in a much friendlier manner now, as if to say, That was a job well done. He's probably a good Muslim, I thought, who doesn't approve of unrelated men and women socializing together. Westerner though I was, I had perhaps surprised him—or even made his day—by behaving just like a proper Muslim woman should.

৩৮৫৪৮

From the river, I headed back into the heart of the old city, to continue sightseeing. Thought by many to be the most beautiful city in Iran, Esfahan is home to dozens of major Islamic monuments, most of which were built by one man, Shah 'Abbas I, in the late 1500s and early 1600s. According to a famous saying coined around that time, *"Esfahan nesf-e jahan"*—Esfahan is half the world.

Coming to power in 1587, Shah 'Abbas I first pushed out the Ottoman Turks then occupying much of Iran and next proceeded to develop what had hitherto proved elusive: a sense of national identity. Building on the Shi'ism that Isma'il of Tabriz had already instilled in his people, Shah 'Abbas successfully united many of the country's ethnic and tribal groups for the first time, through the celebration of their shared religion. Though the heyday of his Safavid dynasty was short-lived, flourishing only about 100 years, it is considered to be one of Iran's three golden ages (the others being the Achaemenian period, 559–330 B.C., and the Sassanian period, A.D. 224–637).

Transferring the Safavid capital to Esfahan in 1598, Shah 'Abbas immediately set about transforming the already important town into the jewel of the Muslim world. In many ways a just and enlightened ruler, with a deep appreciation of the arts, he encouraged trade with Europe and Asia and ordered the construction of many exquisite buildings, bridges, squares, and gardens. When the French traveler Jean Chardin visited Esfahan in the 1670s, he noted that the city held 162 mosques, 48 colleges, 1,802 caravansaries, and 273 public baths, along with a thriving population that included Muslims, Armenians, Zoroastrians, Indians, Chinese, and Europeans.

But in that marriage of extremes so common among powerful rulers, Shah 'Abbas could also be a ruthless and cruel man, in the habit of executing those who displeased him. As a teenager, he had seen nine of his relatives murdered or blinded by his reigning uncle, and thereafter he developed an extreme fear of ambitious men. He killed one of his sons on suspicion of disloyalty, blinded two others, and incarcerated all the rest in the harem, where they became addicted to sensual pleasures and unfit to rule.

Heading east, I entered the crowning architectural achievement of Shah

'Abbas's reign—Imam Khomeini Square, formerly King's Square—and caught my breath. Before me stretched a vast storybook plaza, twice the size of the Red Square in Moscow and seven times the size of Saint Mark's in Venice. To my immediate left yawned a dark opening, which led to the bazaar, whereas to my right stretched archway after archway, lined up in a delicate double arcade, now rosy with the light of the setting sun. One side was interrupted by a boxy building with spindly pillars out front, the other by a luminous green dome of perfect proportions. Far down at the end of the square rose the imperious Imam Khomeini Mosque, marked by two pairs of slim minarets and a turquoise dome. Horse-drawn droshkies, the same as I'd known as a child in Tabriz, were clip-clopping past, carrying tourists for a ride around the square.

The luminous green dome belonged to the Sheikh Lotfollah Mosque, named after the Shah's favorite theologian, a renowned Shi'ite scholar from Lebanon. The boxy building was the six-story Ali Qapu Palace, on whose wide balcony the Shah and his guests had once sat to watch parades, military maneuvers, fireworks, and—polo games. Polo was invented in Iran, and four thick, smooth, white goalposts, about five feet tall, still stand in the busy square today.

Keeping an eye out for the many motor scooters roaring past— "Welcome to Iran!" the drivers kept calling—I walked toward the Imam Mosque. The arcades on either side of me held dozens of small tourist shops, most selling the hand-printed tablecloths, bedspreads, and other fabrics for which Esfahan is famous. I'd grown up with the Esfahani cloths, one of which was still tacked up on my bedroom wall in New York, and in a strange reversal, seeing the fabrics reminded me of home. I'd never realized, though, how faded my wall cloth had become—the colors here were much more vibrant.

Behind the row of shops ran a dark vaulted corridor and then another row of shops, these selling copper wares. I could see them through occasional breaks in the arcade and hear the coppersmiths banging at their craft. A few Western tour groups were passing in and out, along with clusters of independent Iranian, Japanese, and Western tourists, but most of the shops were completely empty. Esfahan today may attract many more tourists than do most Iranian cities, but it still hosts a fraction of the number who once flocked here.

Climbing the broad stairs that led to the Imam Mosque, I passed through a towering gateway, aswirl with tilework and stalactite moldings, into what is often said to be the most magnificent mosque in Iran. Before me lay a large, quiet courtyard, with a dark pool for ablutions, and the soaring *eivan*, minarets, and dome of an exalted prayer hall, with a marble *mehrab*, or niche indicating the direction of Mecca. On either side nestled smaller *eivans*, arcades, and courtyards, each with its own pools, and every inch of every surface was covered with a dazzling blue tile etched with white or yellow arabesques. At first, all the tiles looked alike, but then I realized that quite the opposite was true. Many of the panels were different from each other, with the blues ranging from light blue, pale green-blue, and turquoise to bright blue, dark blue, and blue-black, and the "yellows" ranging from cream to butter, lime green to forest green.

The Persian mosque, like all mosques, originally evolved from a model based on the layout of the Prophet Mohammad's house in Medina. What sets the Persian mosque apart is its extreme simplicity of design, coupled with its lavish ornamentation, usually in the form of tiles. Because representational art is not part of the Islamic tradition, the tiles are usually geometric or calligraphic in design. The art of calligraphy is highly evolved in Iran and is closely linked with architecture. Several panels of the Imam Mosque consist of hundreds of blue-and-white tiles on which is written the single word *Allah* in a highly stylized form, over and over again.

The mosque was filled with a half dozen tour groups, most European and one Japanese. Europeans, some of whose governments have diplomatic relations with Iran, have an easier time obtaining visas than do Americans and do not, in general, regard the Islamic Republic with quite the same horror. The Japanese, who enjoy good relations with Iran, can usually get three-month visas quite easily and are Iran's predominant non–Middle Eastern visitors.

The tour groups roamed the mosque, all stopping in the center of the prayer hall, where each tour guide clapped his hands, to have the sound echo back seven distinct times. Watching them, I felt superior and territorial. I'm getting to know the real Iran, I all but sniffed; you are just taking in the sights, too protected by your numbers to really see anything. The thought seemed to have validity at first, but the more I ruminated on it, the more I questioned it. Why is it, I wondered, that human beings like to hoard their experiences so, to be the only one to have done this or that? Why did I have this selfish feeling of wanting to keep Iran for myself? And why my emphasis on the "real"? (What makes one experience more "real" than another, anyway?)—an emphasis that I instinctively knew I shared with my fellow travelers at the Amir Kabir. They would feel as superior toward these packaged tourists as I did, I knew, and although it was true that the tour groups' numbers and money buffered them from some of the grit and adventure of unsupervised travel, we were all still tourists in Iran. It was just a matter of degree.

As I left the Imam Mosque, I stopped at a kiosk selling postcards. With the exception of a few tourist sites in Tehran, I'd seen virtually no post-cards for sale anywhere in Iran and was glad to find some at last. Browsing through the offerings, I came across a card depicting a stern-looking Khomeini and bought a half dozen. I've been looking for these! I thought—a lot of people I know back home will get a kick out of receiving the Ayatollah in the mail.

But later that evening, a strange thing happened. Sitting in my hotel room, about to address the cards, I suddenly realized that I couldn't send them. I knew how many people back home would look at them—slyly, ironically, with superiority and condescension toward a people that most Americans perceive as being brainwashed by religion. I myself would have looked at the cards the same way just two, or even one, month before. But whoever Khomeini was or wasn't, the icon that was his face broadcast a too-simplistic, too-harsh, too-alienating image of Iran. He wasn't an unfortunate joke, and neither was the Islamic Republic.

ॐ

The next morning over breakfast, I learned more about my fellow travelers. The large group of Australians was journeying together by chartered bus across Asia, on a budget trip offered several times a year by an Australian tour company. Everyone else was traveling independently—the two young Dutchmen, three young Canadians, two Japanese college students, an older Australian couple, the German trio, and another 18-year-old German with white-blond hair who was bicycling all the way from Germany to India. He'd already been on the road for seven months.

Much of the conversation at breakfast centered on visas. Not knowing what to expect of Iran, many at the table had originally requested only five- or ten-day visas, and were now busy applying for extensions at the Esfahan passport office. This is the best country we've visited so far! they said excitedly, the people are so friendly, we had no idea. So it isn't only me who's having a great time, I thought, a little smugly, as I fielded a barrage of questions about how I'd managed to wrangle a two-month extension.

Other moments at breakfast unsettled me. One Canadian bragged about how he'd outwitted a Revolutionary Guard who'd wanted to see his passport and one Australian joked about how she kept pretending to "lose" her *rusari*. All seemed to agree that the authority figures in Iran were clowns and that the Iranian people unilaterally hated the Islamic government. But it's not that simple, I protested—as tourists, we're treated differently, and we're only meeting certain types of Iranians. But my words seemed to fall on deaf ears, and I soon fell silent, feeling both angry and disturbed. Angry at the easy assumptions that were being made—assumptions that I myself had made not so long ago. Disturbed at the way that I felt like—what? Defending the Islamic government or proving how deadly serious it was? Or both?

I spent the next hour or so puttering around my room and then went down to wait in the tiny lobby. The day before, I'd telephoned a Mr. Hosein Khani, whose name had been given to me by Mohammad Legenhausen in Qom, and he'd promised—*ensha'allah*—that "we" would come by the Amir Kabir at 11:00 to meet me. I had no idea who the "we" referred to—or who exactly Mr. Khani was. My phone Persian was very poor.

At precisely 11 A.M., the front door opened and a woman in a *chador* stuck in her head.

"*Khanom* Bird?" she said—Mrs. Bird?

I nodded, but before I could stand up, she disappeared. A few long moments passed, and then the door opened again, this time letting in a young, bearded cleric in a splendid flowing *aba*, followed by a half dozen women in tightly wrapped *chador*s. The cleric's white turban shone like a moonstone in the darkened lobby and his long, pristine garments seemed to put our well-worn surroundings to shame. Nodding a brief hello, he asked where we could talk, and then we all proceeded down the even darker passageway, the cleric's wide robes nearly touching both walls, and out into the courtyard, which now seemed more scruffy than pleasant to me. All the hotel employees and the few guests still left inside were staring, their jaws dropped, and so was I.

In the garden, more formal introductions were made. *Besmellah al-rahman al-rahim*—In the Name of Allah, the Magnificent, the Merciful—said Mr. Hosein Khani, he wished to welcome me to Esfahan. He'd heard much about me from Mohammad Legenhausen and had brought with him six of his students: Maryam, Zohreh, Zahra, Ladan, Nilufar, and a second Zohreh. All were undergraduates studying medicine at the University of Esfahan and enrolled in his course in Islamic studies.

Shyly, the women smiled at me, nodding and swaying together like a flock of beautiful magpies. Then one of them handed me a magnificent bouquet of flowers as long as my arm.

We sat down around the same rickety table I'd eaten breakfast at, and the women crowded close, while Mr. Khani asked me questions about my background and what I was doing in Iran. I answered him as best I could in Persian, which he reiterated in a clearer fashion for his students. He seemed a little uncomfortable—as was I—and kept glancing nervously around the courtyard, twisting his agate ring. But when I apologized for the simplicity of our surroundings, thinking that perhaps that was it, he just smiled. The students like it, he said.

Then one of the students asked me to write down "my idea of God." Yes, yes, please, please, everyone else said and nodded eagerly; write that down. Oh, no, I thought, half wanting to make a joke—What is my idea of God? Do I even have an idea of God? I tried to hold off the women, but when that didn't work, I wrote down some clichéd pablum that I am too embarrassed to repeat here. Most of the women could read some English, and they stared at my piece of paper—perhaps comprehending, perhaps not—as it was passed around. Then the one who'd asked for it reverentially folded it up and slipped it inside her *chador.* I winced.

Suddenly Mr. Khani stood up. It was 12:00 and time for midday prayers. Where could he pray?

I had no idea, but luckily, one of the hotel employees scurried over to lead him and five of the six students down into a basement prayer room that I suspected was barely used anymore, now that most of the hotel's guests were Westerners.

I was left alone in the courtyard with Maryam. She couldn't pray, she explained to me, because she was having her period, and menstruating women are considered unclean in Islam. "They question thee (O Muhammad) concerning menstruation. Say: It is an illness, so let women alone at such times . . ." (Qor'an, 2:222). The idea irritated me; if women are considered unclean a few days a month, I thought, then doesn't that automatically relegate them to a position lower than that of men? I wished Clara from Qom were here; I wanted to ask her about that.

About 20 minutes later, Mr. Khani and his students reemerged and we left the Amir Kabir, to board two taxis, which Mr. Khani, striding ahead, organized. As he did so, I was reminded of the youth of the women around me; despite their matronly *chador*s, they were still only undergraduates and his charges. The responsibility and, hopefully, success of our meeting together was largely dependent on him, or so *I* imagined *he* imagined, as we headed for lunch, to the home of two recent University of Esfahan graduates.

Arriving at our destination, we exchanged our shoes for slippers, passed behind a curtain, and climbed a narrow staircase to where Mitra and Ahmad Reza were waiting. Graciously, they ushered us into their snug living room, furnished with fat white-and-gold couches. On a coffee table lay a large spread of fruit, pastry, and *gaz*—the nougat candy made of pistachios that is a trademark of Esfahan. How much trouble they've gone to for me, I marveled, once again feeling overwhelmed by the extent of Iranian hospitality. When I'd initially spoken to Mr. Khani on the phone, all I'd expected from our encounter was a short meeting at his office.

We sat down, and I took out my Persian–English dictionary, to help us converse, and my guidebooks—one Australian, the other Iranian—which everyone wanted to look at. I'd already noticed the same reaction in several other situations. People seemed very surprised to see that guidebooks on Iran existed and were curious to know what was included.

Mr. Khani took off his turban, wiping the sweat from his brow—and I froze, feeling shocked. It seemed scandalous to see him sitting there bareheaded, and almost as bad to see his turban curled up beside him, like a sleeping cat. But none of the other women, still cloaked in their *chadors*, seemed to notice, and after a moment, I deliberately pushed my feelings away, wondering where they'd come from. It's as if, I thought later, I've internalized one part of the Muslim message—people must be "covered"—but still don't know exactly how it works and so apply it willy-nilly, in this strange space that I'm now occupying, somewhere between the East and the West.

The women asked me more questions, mostly about religion, and as they did so, I was suddenly reminded of being in north Tehran. Just like the north Tehranis, these women were questioning my credentials—albeit a different set of them: What do you know about Islam? What *suras* (books) do you like best? What is your feeling about the Qor'an? What do you think of Khomeini? What do you think of the *hejab*?

Some of my answers discomforted them. They were amazed to hear that I had read the Qor'an only once, and there was a sharp intake of breath when I said that many Americans thought that Khomeini was *kheili bad-e*—very bad. And when I said that I wanted to write both about

Iranians who supported the Islamic government and those who did not, the women fidgeted.

"But everyone loves the Islamic Republic!" one woman said.

"And life is much better now!" another said.

"And Islam is much stronger!" said a third.

"How about more liberalization?" I asked, once their excitement died down. "Would more freedom be good for Iran?"

"Yes," said one woman, while all the others nodded in agreement. "But it must be within the Islamic framework. We want more free writing and music, but we don't want too much freedom—when there is too much freedom, there is much divorce and drugs, like in the United States."

"Why do people in the United States like President Khatami so much?" Mr. Khani said, interrupting. "He is a good man, but he is new to politics, and he doesn't know much."

I tried to explain, and the conversation continued, ebbing and flowing, with some disagreement and misunderstanding, but mostly goodwill, until I brought up the subject of Salman Rushdie. About one month earlier, President Khatami had announced that Iran no longer intended to carry out the *fatwa*, or religious ruling, of death, that Ayatollah Khomeini had placed on Rushdie's head almost ten years before.

But when I mentioned this, the room fell ominously silent.

"What do you think?" I finally asked Mr. Khani with a sense of foreboding.

"The *fatwa* was necessary," he said. "Rushdie slandered Islam and all Muslim people."

"So you don't think the *fatwa* should have been lifted?"

"No, it has *not* been lifted! It *cannot* be lifted! Only the person who gives the *fatwa* can lift it. Rushdie thinks he is safe, but he is not. He must die!"

"But why?" I said, startled by his outburst. Mr. Khani seemed like such a gentle man, and it was obvious that his students adored him. Where did this hatred come from?

"Why do you care so much what Rushdie wrote?" I asked. "We in America can't understand that. It's just the opinion of one man. What does it matter? He has his opinion and you have yours."

"He slandered us," Mr. Khani said grimly. "And he knew exactly what he was doing. He comes from India. He knows about Islam. He knew that this would happen."

I objected again, but only halfheartedly. My opinion certainly wasn't going to sway Mr. Khani.

This is where I just can't understand any more, I thought heavily. I can understand about the importance of religion and even to some degree about the *hejab*, but this is completely beyond me.

"Do you feel the same way?" I asked the women around me, and they nodded.

"You see," one of them added quietly, in an aside a moment later, "if you are a good Muslim, you must obey the rules. Even if you yourself do not believe Rushdie must die, if you are a good Muslim, you must obey."

"So you can't think for yourself?" I asked.

"Not if you are a good Muslim."

"Do you believe he must die?" I suspected that in her heart she did not.

"I am a good Muslim."

Later, I wondered about her argument. It seemed to me that if Shi'ism allows for different interpretations of the Qor'an and the *hadiths*—as even the most conservative of clerics agree that it does—there could also be various interpretations about the mutability of the *fatwa.*

We moved on to other topics, but my heart wasn't in it. In one short moment, the gulf between my companions and me had grown insurmountably large. What was the use of even trying to communicate? I thought. But the others didn't seem to be much affected by our interchange. A few minutes later, Mr. Khani even made a sort of a joke, in his serious, deliberate way, and gave me his telephone number in Qom, inviting me to visit him and his wife the next time I passed through.

Finally, we sat down to lunch, a lovely and enormous spread of many dishes, including chicken kebabs, a green-bean-and-lamb stew, rice with sour cherries, and yogurt flavored with rose water. The dishes were set out on the *sofreh* on the floor, along with my favorite, the horizontal Fanta bottles, neatly laid at each place setting. The pretty scene cheered me somewhat, and much to the pleasure of everyone, I took pictures and promised to send copies.

Then the women asked me to say a Christian prayer, and when I acquiesced, giggled when I folded my hands. But we open our hands, they said, and spread out their palms, supplications to the heavens.

꒰ꙮ꒱

The next afternoon, I rendezvoused with Mr. R. N. Bakhtiar, a friend of a friend in Tehran. A professional photographer who mostly specialized in industrial shoots, Mr. Bakhtiar had also authored several best-selling books on Esfahan and knew all the city's hidden nooks and crannies. With Ella Fitzgerald playing on his Jeep's tape deck, he took me to the outskirts of town where people living in tents were cooking up huge pots of natural dyes, used to color the Esfahani fabrics, and to an old section of the city built of mud and straw. We also passed by several of the "pigeon towers" that had once encircled Esfahan. In earlier centuries, the now-deserted towers had been used to house pigeons that provided fertilizer for agriculture.

"All this traditional way of life is ending now," Mr. Bakhtiar said as we toured, with the sadness of artists and chroniclers everywhere. "Everything is becoming modernized in Iran—just like in the West."

After leaving Mr. Bakhtiar, I stopped for tea in the Abbasi Hotel, Esfahan's most famous and luxurious hostelry, housed in what was once a caravansary. Out back stretched a marvelous garden filled with meandering walkways, flowering trees, and double-tiered arcades; in a small, fancy teahouse, men in historic costume were serving tea to Iranian and Western tourists. Taking a seat, I fell into conversation with an Iranian American lawyer who had lived in Los Angeles for over 20 years. This was his first trip back to Iran since the Revolution, and he seemed beside himself with excitement, jumping up every other minute to videotape the waiters serving *ash* (a thick soup-stew), his friends smoking the hubble-bubble, and—especially—two beautiful young Iranian women in fashionable *manteau*s and *rusari*s seated across from us.

"I was very scared to come back here," he said to me. "My friends had to make me. But now I love it! It's wonderful! I'm very comfortable here, and I'm taking all these movies to show people back home what Iran is really like." Chuckling, he nodded at the two women. "And I'm especially taking lots of pictures of girls. There are so many pretty girls in Iran! I want to show my son. He could find a very beautiful wife here."

৩৯৫৫

Set in the remains of an old royal park just behind the Imam Khomeini Square reigns Chehel Sotun, a dark and haunting palace with a long reflecting pool, filled with carp. Built in 1647, during the reign of Shah 'Abbas II, the great-grandson of Shah 'Abbas I, the palace holds within it an unforgettable collection of wall frescoes. Most depict scenes of hedonistic banquets—dancing women, inebriated men—and young Persians in love, and so, during the early years of the Islamic Republic, the paintings were kept safely hidden behind scaffolding. The museum authorities feared that the zealous revolutionaries might try to destroy them.

Now, however, the frescoes are not only in plain sight but also being restored, and in the shrouded world that is Iran today, they come as a shock. Wandering about among them, I felt almost guilty looking at their semi-clad, dark-eyed beauties, and glanced around to see how the Iranians were taking it. But no one was expressing any outward surprise—and why, I thought on further reflection, should they? No matter how hard governments try to repress their peoples' past, it is always there, waiting to be rediscovered.

This heft of hidden history, only half submerged, saturates Esfahan.

I found it again at Hasht Behesht, or "Eight Paradises," another Safavid palace. In far poorer condition than is Chehel Sotun, Hasht Behesht was built as a residence for "the princes of the king's harem," and I half imagined I could hear their heavy robes sweeping across the floors as I walked from one empty room to the next. I also spent time in the palace's garden, once known for its nightingales—now long gone—for it was somewhere there that the photograph depicting my family and Bahman had been taken. I recognized the place from the photograph, but I couldn't remember it at all.

And I found it again in Jolfa, the Armenian Christian community located across the river from Esfahan. In the early 1600s, Shah 'Abbas I forcibly moved the entire Armenian community of (Old) Jolfa, located about an hour north of Tabriz, to Esfahan. He wanted them near largely because they were superb craftsmen who could help build his Islamic capital. Tens of thousands died along the way, but those who survived were allowed to practice their religion and to prosper—for at least the rest of the Safavid dynasty. Back then, the town had been known for its flourishing social life and homes of great wealth, but the Jolfa of today feels quiet and subdued.

And I found it again in Abyaneh, an isolated, half-deserted village made of a red clay that hardens with exposure to rain. Largely built in the 1500s and 1600s, Abyaneh is inhabited by a people who speak a unique Persian dialect and dress in an ancient, perhaps old Zoroastrian, style. The men wear loose dark trousers and billowing shirts, and the women, pleated skirts, colorful blouses, and floral kerchiefs that reach below their waists. One of the town's elders took my driver and me on a tour, whispering to me whenever my driver's back was turned about how much he disliked the corrupt Islamic government.

And I found it again in a Sassanian fire temple, built around A.D. 500, perched atop a steep hill on the outskirts of town. It took me a good 15 minutes to scramble up to the small round edifice, large uneven windows cut into its sides, but it offered superb views of the surrounding plateau and the winding Zayandeh River. Later, when I returned to the United States, I found pictures of this same fire temple in our family photograph album, but when I asked my father about it, he looked confused; he couldn't remember it.

But I found it most of all in the Jom'eh Mosque, which before the building boom of Shah 'Abbas I was considered to be the greatest mosque in Esfahan—and to my mind, still is. The mosque has none of the tiles or ornamentation of the Imam Mosque. Its floors are partly packed earth, and its walls and ceilings are a plain, dull brown. But it is vast, complex, and secretive—with elaborate brickwork, pregnant shadows, a cavernous prayer hall too dark to really see, and endless colonnades where shafts of light play with motes of dust. First built by the Seljuq dynasty 1,000 years ago, on the site of a still earlier shrine, the Jom'eh Mosque feels like Iran's subconscious.

৵৹ৎ৾

Some of the students I'd met at lunch with Mr. Khani had invited me to dinner. Two of them lived together with another classmate in an apartment off campus, and as we sat on the floor near the kitchen, socializing, they took turns cooking: Nilufar, whose name means "flower"; Jannat, the Arabic word for "heaven"; and Zahra, which means "brightening." Most first names in Persian have meanings, whereas last names were adopted nationwide only in 1920, on the orders of Reza Shah.

Zahra was my favorite. Small and beautifully proportioned, with high round cheeks and an easy laugh, she reminded me of my best friend from high school. Eagerly, she showed me around the apartment, which in usual Persian fashion was more or less unfurnished, except for carpets, end tables, and dozens of photos and posters on the walls. Some depicted Khomeini, Khatami, and Khamene'i; others, handsome bearded men.

They were *shahids*—martyrs—of course. With shining eyes, Zahra told me their histories, and said that she liked Shahid Avini the best. He'd been a philosopher, artist, and film director as well as a martyr, she said, and she had five of his books in her closet and many, many pictures of him. She gave me a small one as a gift, while I thought of American teenagers and rock/pop/hip-hop stars. Instead of dreaming about Ricky Martin at night, Zahra probably dreamed about Shahid Avini.

Zahra showed me the other books in her closet. One was an art book filled with paintings from the Revolution and the Iran–Iraq war—glossies of a pensive Khomeini, of martyrs dying in battle, of doves flying from tombs to heaven. Others were fat medical textbooks originally published in the United States by major companies such as McGraw-Hill and Macmillan, and offset-printed in Iran. Because Iran does not belong to the international copyright convention, books from other countries are pirated with impunity. Some of Zahra's reference books would have cost at least $100 in the United States, but had cost her only about 15,000 *tomans* ($2.50).

Returning to the kitchen, we rejoined the others, who were now watching the evening news on TV. The election for the Assembly of Experts had just taken place, and the students clapped and hugged each other enthusiastically as one after another of their chosen candidates were declared winners. Meanwhile, I thought about conversations I'd had with many intellectuals a few weeks before in Tehran. They'd been angered because many of the more liberal candidates for the assembly had not been allowed to run, whereas most of the conservatives had. My new student friends might or might not have been aware of that fact, which had been well publicized, but either way, they were probably not politically sophisticated enough to understand its significance.

Although the Islamic government is often viewed as a totalitarian regime by many in the West, that assumption is not correct. For all its flaws, the Islamic Republic is a republic in some major respects. Power does not reside in one man—be he shah or supreme leader—but is spread out over several branches, the most important of which are the supreme leader, the president, and the parliament. Both the president and the parliament representatives are elected by the people—men and women—and although liberal candidates are sometimes blocked from running, several recent elections—including the 1997 election of President Khatami and the 2000 parliamentary elections, largely won by reformists—have delivered surprising results. A certain amount of public debate is also tolerated, and a constitution guaranteeing basic human rights, including the right to vote, is in place.

However, the supreme leader is far more powerful and the constitution, more malleable than their counterparts in stronger republics. Appointed for life, the supreme leader controls the country's security and intelligence forces, the army, the judiciary, radio and television, and is the ultimate interpreter of Islamic law. As such, he can nullify any act of parliament or decision of the court, and though he does not usually choose to do so, the threat is always there. Theoretically, the Assembly of Experts, which is elected every eight years, oversees the supreme leader, but thus far the assembly has been largely controlled by the same hard-line establishment that is behind the supreme leader.

During Ayatollah Khomeini's time, he commanded near absolute powers over the Islamic Republic. However, his successor, Supreme Leader Ali Khamene'i, lacks his predecessor's charisma and religious authority, and as a new generation of Iranians has come of age, calls for reform have intensified a thousandfold. Most Iranians I spoke with, however—young and old, liberal and conservative—want change within the existing system, not an overthrow of the system itself. Another revolution is not on most people's minds.

ॐ

As I wandered around Esfahan, I thought more and more about the *hejab.* The more time I had spent in Iran, the more complex it'd seemed to me, and nowhere was this truer than in Esfahan, which, despite its strong artistic heritage, is highly traditional. If I'd arrived in Esfahan first, I kept thinking, instead of Tehran, I would have had a whole different first impression of the Islamic Republic. Iran, as personified by its *chador*-cloaked women, would have seemed much more impenetrable to me.

Almost all of the women in Esfahan, like almost all of the women in every city I'd visited except Tehran, and later Shiraz, wore the *chador* instead of the *manteau* and *rusari.* And in Esfahan, more than anywhere else, they knew how to wear it. Sweeping across the Imam Khomeini Square or down the streets, they advanced like intimidating sailboats, swooshing everyone else—male or female—out of their wake. The older women were often pugnacious—hard black bodies shoving ahead to get what they wanted. The younger ones were often disdainful—beautiful, alluring women who might deign to swish their *chadors* flirtatiously for just one moment but would then turn their backs. The *chador*, the Esfahani women taught me, was not just a swath of black fabric but rather a formidable garment to be reckoned with.

Before leaving for Iran, I'd imagined that wearing the *manteau* and *rusari* would render me invisible—an idea that greatly appealed to me. I'd fantasized about moving unnoticed through bobbing crowds, an anonymous shadow seeing without being seen, gathering knowledge—and therefore power—without revealing anything. I'd also looked forward to escaping for a few months from the constant Western pressure of wanting/having to look good and yet also, paradoxically, hoping to go unnoticed and not be hassled. None of that, of course, had proved to be the case—far from it—but I sensed that that was the case with many of the *chador*-clad women I saw around me. Their cloaks seemed to give them both invisibility and power.

At the same time, however, in an interesting contradiction, the more the *hejab* covered, the more it seemed to reveal. A woman's face or, even better, just her eyes, surrounded by black, exposed her in a way that her full form did not. I'd noticed from my first days in Tehran how faces shone out like jewels beneath the *hejab,* and how what was covered did not necessarily match what was revealed, but now I realized that it went further than that. Seeing a woman's intelligent eyes or stubborn chin in isolation from the rest of her often gave me a clue to her character that I might otherwise have missed.

Though my *manteau* and *rusari* lacked the power of the *chador,* the combination did share some of its advantages. On a mundane level, I could wear the same clothes underneath for days on end if I so chose—a help while traveling—and didn't have to worry as much about wrinkles or what to wear when. My hair did get dirty more quickly beneath the *rusari,* but then again, unless I took it off, no one noticed. The *hejab* also made me feel more at one with the society around me, and less of a sexual object—two of its main objectives. Women I met who supported the *hejab* praised it for hiding the differences between the haves and have-nots, for protecting them from undue curiosity, and for easing the pressures of the workplace, by making others focus on their minds and talents rather than on their bodies or clothes. I could see all that.

None of which is meant as an apology for enforced *hejab.* Women, like men, should be able to wear what they please. But after several months in Iran, I did see the *hejab*'s advantages—and its appeal.

After living in a strict Muslim society for a while, I also, to my surprise, began to absorb its mores. Getting too close to my hotel window without my *rusari* one night, I felt a strange mix of horror and shame when I noticed a man on the street staring at me; I'd come a long way since that Alamut rooftop, where the villagers' reaction to my bare head had startled me so. Hearing a knock on my hotel door one afternoon, I opened it to a messenger without thinking, and then blushed bright red as I hurriedly shut it again and rushed for my covering. Visiting an Iranian home one day for lunch, I felt some annoyance but mostly acute embarrassment when I thought that an invitation to remove my *manteau* also meant an invitation to remove my *rusari,* and all of the men in the room turned around until I'd covered myself again. The men's disapproval of my bare head made me feel as if I'd been standing before them in my underwear.

Which was both horrifying and oddly exciting. It was degrading to think that there was something so indecent about me that it had to be covered up, but it was also flattering to think that the mere sight of my hair or exposed arms could stir a man with overwhelming desire. Forget about trying to entice someone by wearing a low-cut dress or short skirt—all I had to do was uncover my head.

The history of the veil is as murky and complex as is its meaning and impact. One widespread theory has it that the use of the veil began in Persia during the reign of Cyrus the Great, 10 centuries before the advent of Islam, and was only later adopted by the Arabs. Others believe that the veil began with Islam. Either way, the wearing of the *hejab* in ancient Iran and elsewhere was usually a sign of privilege, as only the elite could afford to veil and seclude their women. Then, as now, too, veiling was mostly an urban phenomenon; peasant women working the fields were in no position to wear the *hejab.*

Though veiled women in pre-twentieth-century Iran were barred from most public arenas, not all were powerless. Wealthy women especially were often in charge of running large households and overseeing the home production of weaving and carpets, whereas others became skilled in areas such as midwifery and healing. Veiled women also played important, if housebound, roles in social movements, including the Tobacco Revolt of 1891 and the Constitution Revolution of 1906.

As for the use of the *hejab* among women in Islam, it is barely mentioned in the Qor'an, and when it is, is used to describe how the followers of Mohammad should deal with his wives. The Prophet has just married a new wife, Zaynab, and is annoyed because one of his believers will not leave them alone. The *hejab*, which means "curtain," is then introduced to protect their privacy: "And when ye ask of them (the wives of the Prophet) anything, ask it of them from behind a curtain. That is purer for your hearts and their hearts" (Qor'an, 33:53).

Elsewhere, the Qor'an does state that women should dress modestly: "And tell the believing women to lower their gaze and be modest, and to display of their adornment only that which is apparent, and to draw their veils over their bosoms, and not to reveal their adornment" (24:31). But nowhere does the Qor'an detail the extent of a woman's veiling or recommend that she cover her entire body. That interpretation only came later, and largely because of a *hadith* in which the Prophet reportedly said that women must cover everything but their face and hands. The extent of the *hejab* could therefore be drastically reinterpreted, should the clerical authorities choose to do so, and many modern Muslim women believe that all their religion requires of them is to dress modestly.

Interestingly, according to the Egyptian scholar Leila Ahmed, Western disdain for the *hejab* only began in the nineteenth century, when some Europeans used what they perceived to be the degraded status of women in Muslim society as an excuse for colonization. To these male imperialists, who had virtually no access to Muslim women and therefore no idea what they were thinking, the veil was "proof" of female subjugation under Islam and, by extension, of the intrinsic backwardness and inferiority of Islam. Though many Muslims themselves were then beginning to question the traditional role of women in their societies, the Western colonialists used the veil as their license to attack and "liberate." As far as they were concerned, the fact that most European women at that time did not have the right to vote or inherit property was beside the point.

৵৽৻৻

Mr. Hosein Khani, his students, and I had a final rendezvous planned, and one evening, he and his wife, a tall, quiet woman with a light sprinkling of freckles across her nose, came to the Amir Kabir to pick me up. In friendly silence, we drove to the outskirts of the city, where a protective mountain peak hulked against the blue-black sky. We were going to the University of Esfahan to visit one of the women's dormitories, which I presumed meant a tour and perhaps an interview with university personnel.

But when we arrived at the dormitory, a dozen or so students were waiting for us on the front steps. Hurrying up in an excited rush, they escorted us into the building and up several flights of stairs. Mr. Khani and his wife got left somewhere behind as I was ushered into a large assembly room where perhaps 20 other students were sitting on a carpeted floor. A conference table with three chairs sat at one end.

I joined the students on the floor and we introduced ourselves. Many were dressed in T-shirts and leggings, and had the easy, relaxed air of women living only among themselves. I could almost be in a dorm in the U.S., I thought. Both the women and the room—modern and utilitarian, with picture windows along one wall—reminded me of universities everywhere.

Then, suddenly, a few minutes into our low-key conversation, most of the women abruptly stood up and whooshed out of the room. I could hear them tittering and giggling as they disappeared down the hall, and I turned to the few remaining students in surprise.

"A man is coming," they said. "They need their *chadors*."

Oh, I nodded. All the women around me already had on their coverings.

That man turned out to be Mr. Khani, and as he authoritatively strode into the room, his black *aba* flowing, the students began filing back in, in much greater numbers than before. Most were now dressed in white *chadors*, which are often used in the home, as well as in prayer.

Ceremoniously, Mr. Khani invited me to take the middle seat at the conference table, while sitting down on my right and arranging his robes around him. A serious-looking student with heavy black glasses sat down on my left. Her name was Zahra and she was an English major, here to translate for me—because it now appeared that I was to give a talk. About a hundred students had assembled on the carpet before us, eager to hear what "the American" had to say.

"*Besmellah al-rahman al-rahim*," Mr. Khani began—In the Name of Allah, the Beneficent, the Merciful. These are the first words of the Qor'an, and the religious pronounce them before nearly every activity of daily life, be it a meeting, a meal, or sexual relations.

Mr. Khani then introduced me and my project, described our luncheon together a few days before, and asked me to tell the students more about myself, the United States, and my impressions of Iran—in Persian, please; "it would be much better."

Startled, I gathered my thoughts together and began, feeling relatively calm. Though in general, my Persian didn't seem to be improving much, I had at least gotten my basic statement down pat—I'd repeated it so many times. I was in Iran to write a *safarnameh*, I said, because people in the United States knew so little about everyday life in the Islamic

Republic. I was more interested in social and cultural issues than I was in politics and was trying to meet people of all backgrounds and points of view—

When I was finished, Mr. Khani invited the students to ask me questions, which Zahra helped interpret: What are the problems of women in America? Why don't blacks in America like Dr. Martin Luther King anymore? Are Muslims in America safe? Why is there so much crime in America? Who is Monica Lewinsky? Why aren't young people interested in politics? Why does America hate Iran? Isn't it true that you have many problems in your country—drugs, divorce, rape—because you don't wear the *hejab*?

Being an American, I was very frank. Even while praising U.S. democracy and its principles, I also spoke about racism, crime, the breakdown of the family, and the widening gap between the very rich and the very poor. I tried to be as fair and honest as I could and paid tribute to certain strengths of Iranian culture that I felt were missing in the United States— the close family ties, the slower pace of life, and, especially, the emphasis on the spiritual rather than the material.

At last, the women were finished, and it was my turn.

"What about here in Iran?" I asked. "What do you think are your country's biggest problems?"

There was a dead silence. The women seemed frozen. Maybe they didn't understand what I said? I thought, and repeated my question.

Finally, one student opened her mouth.

"Sometimes we have a lack of educational resources," she said in a small voice.

"Yes, yes," several other women nodded, as a relieved rustling sounded around the room.

"That's it?" I said, stunned. Here I'd been completely open—too open? I wondered now—and they weren't even beginning to reciprocate in kind. "That's Iran's only problem?"

There was another long silence.

"Nothing else?" I prodded, feeling both foolish and angry. Thanks entirely to me, the United States was coming off far worse in this little interchange than was Iran.

I appealed to Mr. Khani, thinking that perhaps the students were too young or protected to know much about problems in Iran, or to have the courage to speak out.

But Mr. Khani wasn't any help, either. He just elaborated on the lack of educational resources.

"You asked me before about prejudice in the United States," I said, irritated. As much as I myself frequently question various aspects of American life, I couldn't leave it under attack like this. "But you have much prejudice here, too, I know, against Afghans and Jews—"

"No, no," the women protested. "We have no problems with Afghans— Iranians marry Afghans all the time. And the Jews live in peace in Iran. They can worship the way they want and have representation in the parliament—"

Too complex an issue, I thought, and tried again. "But many people have complained to me about life here," I said. "They want more freedom. Don't you think this is a problem?"

The women shook their heads.

"So you don't want more freedom?" I pressed.

But now the women were nodding their heads.

"Yes, we do want more freedom," someone said. "But only within the Islamic framework."

That was the exact same phrase that the students had used at lunch a few days before and I didn't like hearing it again. It seemed like parroting; had Mr. Khani or some other teacher drilled it into them?

"Do you like President Khatami?"

Everyone nodded.

"How about Supreme Leader Khamene'i?"

Everyone nodded again.

"In the United States, many people think Ayatollah Khomeini was evil—" I began.

The women gasped, but I ignored it.

"Why do Iranians like him so much?"

"Because he brought Islam back to Iran," one woman said. "And he brought the people back to themselves. He changed many bad things of the earlier government, and he brought back the *hejab*."

The tensions in the room were rising.

"We like the *hejab*," another woman in the back called out. "Please tell the people of your country we are comfortable with the *hejab*, we feel protected by the *hejab*, we can do anything with the *hejab*."

"Why is the United States so evil?" one woman suddenly said.

"Why did you shoot down our plane?" another woman said, and then, to my astonishment, started sobbing.

"What's the matter?" I turned, bewildered, to Zahra.

"She lost her brother in that plane," she said.

Oh, no, I thought. There was nothing I could possibly say to that. The shooting had been one of those tragic accidents, occurring in 1988, when the USS *Vincennes* had shot down an Iranian Airbus on a scheduled passenger flight across the Persian Gulf.

A moment later, the sobbing woman got up and left the room. We watched her go in silence and then another woman raised her hand.

"Since family is not important in the United States—" she began.

"No, no," I said. Things were going from bad to worse. No one seemed to have understood a word I'd said. "I didn't say family wasn't important— I just said it wasn't *as* important—"

"America is always complaining about Salman Rushdie—" someone else interjected.

"Yes," I said, glad to get back to what I considered to be a cut-and-dry issue, "because we don't understand. We believe in freedom of speech. Everyone has a right to his opinion and—"

"But what about Roger Garaudy?"

"Who?" I asked. The name rang a distant bell, but I couldn't place it.

Mr. Khani sat up. "This is very interesting," he said, addressing his students in a didactic, professorial tone that was all too familiar to me from my own university years. "She is a writer and so must be well informed, but she doesn't know who Roger Garaudy is. This proves that the people in the United States don't get the real news."

Oh, no—score another point for Iran, I thought. I now dimly remembered that Roger Garaudy was a French writer who'd been brought to trial for claiming that the crimes of the Holocaust were a myth, exploited by Zionist groups to create Israel.

"I remember now," I said, hoping I sounded convincing. (Who said writers had to be well informed, anyway?) "But that was France. I don't really know how the law operates in France." Now, though, the Iranians had me wondering. Why exactly had Garaudy been brought to trial?

Later, I looked up the case in New York. According to the *World Press Review*, Garaudy had been prosecuted under the Gayssot Law, which prohibits any "negation" of the "crime against humanity" committed by Germany. The trial had received wide attention throughout the Arab world, where it had been largely viewed—with some justification, I thought—as a witch-hunt.

"You are tired," Mr. Khani said, turning to me with a concerned look as the students began talking among themselves.

"A little," I admitted.

"And it is late. *Besmellah al-rahman al-rahim . . .*" To my relief, our meeting was over, and Mr. Khani was saying a prayer.

A moment later, we all stood up, and dozens of women rushed over to me. I was still feeling tense from our exchange, but no one else seemed to be at all affected by it. Thank you very, *very* much for coming, the women said, grasping my hands. We really, *really* enjoyed meeting you. Will you *please* come back again? Will you *please* be our pen pal? Please, here is our address. Please, write to us. Please, here is a small gift. Someone pressed a prayer stone encased in a green velveteen pouch into my hand.

At least a dozen students came out to the taxi, waving as we drove away, and I felt both moved and saddened to see that. They have such little contact with the outside world, I thought. I was still feeling angered by their refusal to talk openly about Iran—which I later learned was a cultural reticence; Iranians rarely air their dirty laundry in public—but I was also interested to see how little, given their political opinions, they seemed to hold my nationality against me. Iranians really do make a distinction between peoples and governments, I thought, probably because they've never felt that their government represents their interests. Whereas in America, despite widespread cynicism, most people still see the U.S. democratic system as an extension of themselves.

"*Kheili jalebeh, kheili jalebeh,*" Mr. Khani kept saying all the way back to the Amir Kabir—very interesting, very interesting. "Thank you for speaking tonight."

Kheili jalebeh, kheili jalebeh, I kept repeating to myself a half hour later as Mr. and Mrs. Khani and I sneaked up to my bare room at the guest house, carrying take-out hero sandwiches. We had planned to eat out after visiting the dorm, but as it was now after 11 P.M., the restaurants near the hotel were closed, and all we'd found was a take-out shop. I'd initially imagined that we could eat in the hotel garden, but as we neared its entrance, raucous laughter burst out of one dark corner (the Australians, I thought) and I saw Mrs. Khani cringe. I cringed. She didn't want to be stared at. I didn't want to be stared at, or asked any more questions, by either Westerners or Iranians. I was tired of being a tourist in either language, and despite earlier tensions, felt comfortable being alone with the Khanis. And so the three of us crept up the stairs like fugitives, to sit companionably on creaky cots and eat meatball sandwiches, beneath a medallion pointing the way to Mecca.

TWO

Approximately 350 miles south of Esfahan, across more hot dusty plains, lies Shiraz, an easygoing city of wide boulevards and peaceful gardens, surrounded by a fertile valley and the pinkish foothills of the Zagros Mountains. Of all the cities in Iran, Shiraz is said to be the most open-minded and good-natured, the most poetic and learned. Wrote the nineteenth-century Persian scholar Edward Browne of Shiraz: "Its inhabitants are, amongst all the Persians, the most subtle, the most ingenious, the most vivacious."

Shiraz also holds within it the tombs of Hafez and Sa'di, two of Persia's most famous poets, and is the jumping-off point for Persepolis, the ancient capital founded in the fifth century B.C. by Cyrus the Great. Poetry and Persepolis are central to what it means to be Persian—the proud common heritage that all Iranians share, be they Muslim or Jewish, Westernized or traditional—and so Shiraz is, in a sense, the soul of Iran.

I had checked into the Payam Hotel, not far from the city center. Again, I had found the *mosafer-khaneh,* or budget guest house, through my Lonely Planet guidebook, but perhaps because it was buried in the middle of the listings and had received only a modest review, it did not seem to attract many Westerners. The wiry albino manager, wearing glasses so thick that I could barely see his eyes, shouted at me as I asked about a room—thinking perhaps that that would make me understand Persian better—while the lone hotel employee, an older woman with a worn face, gaped. For a few awkward moments, I thought that they weren't going to give me a room, but then suddenly, they did. And then they and the handful of other guests in the lobby—all male—stared at me in silence as I took my key, crossed a tiled inner courtyard with a drain in the middle, and unlocked the door to my simple but adequate room, feigning nonchalance.

They stared at me even harder a half hour or so later, after I'd called Mr. Khorsandi from the hotel's only phone, at the reception desk. His name had been given to me by a friend of Mohammad's in Qom, and if I'd had little idea who Mr. Khani in Esfahan was before meeting him, I had even less idea who Mr. Khorsandi was. It took me at least a day after first contacting him to realize that he was the office manager for the most important cleric of Shiraz, the Friday prayer leader, Mr. Haeri. But the albino manager, who also spoke with Mr. Khorsandi on the phone, realized it right away, and immediately passed the information along to everyone else at the hotel, who began eyeing me with a confused mixture of respect and suspicion.

But my understanding of that, and of the twirling motion above his head, meant to indicate a turban, which one impish guest repeatedly made at me, came later. Leaving the hotel that late afternoon, I meandered down to the wide, leafy Zand Boulevard, which cuts through the city like a life-line, and entered the Arg-e Karim Khani, an enormous fortress with four towers and sloping walls. Built in the mid-1700s by Karim Khan, one of Iran's few truly benevolent rulers, the citadel was once part of the royal courtyard and later used as a prison.

On my way out, a young woman named Fereshteh, wearing a bright green *rusari* and opaque stockings, befriended me. An architect and poet who'd just self-published her first book, she spoke near perfect English, partly because she traveled to Europe every summer. She loved Iran, she said as we headed toward the Shiraz bazaar, but she was tired of all the government regulations—and of President Khatami. She had had great expectations of him at first, but now she was getting impatient.

"He says a lot of nice things," she said. "But he doesn't *do* anything. We still have no freedom, people still have no jobs, and he's still a cleric."

I had heard similar statements from other young people all over Iran. President Khatami's election had roused great expectations—of greater freedoms, a better economy, a better life—and few wanted to acknowledge that systems seldom change overnight.

Still, Fereshteh, also like many other people I met—young and old—had no intention of leaving Iran.

"This is my country," she said, when I asked her if she ever thought of moving to the West. "Where else should I go?"

Leaving Fereshteh to her shopping, I wandered on, through the bazaar and winding back alleys, to the Madraseh-e Khan, a seventeenth-century theological seminary that is open to tourists. The school's romantic court-yard was filled with plane, orange, and towering date trees, some heavy with leaves, and the sounds of swallows; all sides of the building were lined with perhaps a hundred weathered doors, most with plastic slippers out front. Each door led to a student's room, and some were hung with laundry lines.

Under an arch was a carpeted hall where students were studying; on the edge of a reflecting pool sat three ancient mullahs with white turbans and gnarled hands. I asked to take their picture, and to my surprise, they acquiesced.

By the time I returned to the city center, evening had fallen. Wide Zand Boulevard was now illuminated with street lamps that seemed to stretch all the way from the floodlit citadel well into the Zagros foothills, and dozens of fast-food joints were in full operation, slinging hamburgers and pizza, meat pies and kebabs. I stopped to order a meat pie and took a seat in a modern eatery with plastic tables and chairs. Several people gave me curious glances but left me alone. Most restaurants in Iran are not sexually segregated, and the sight of a woman eating alone is not unusual.

I headed back to my hotel, passing through streets that were considerably darker than Zand Boulevard and crowded with open-air bakeries, around which expectant faces were waiting. The flames from the ovens threw leaping shadows across cheeks and foreheads, as the warm, nutty smell of *sangak* enveloped me and young boys called out, "Hello, missus. Where are you from?"

At the Payam, the manager was alone in the lobby, watching a dreamy television show about a *chador*-clad young woman and her bicycle. He had to tear himself away to hand me my key—and the first of many messages from Mr. Khorsandi.

॰॰॰

To tour the sights of Shiraz, as well as to travel to the ancient Sassanian ruins of Firuzabad, located about 100 miles south of Shiraz, I hired a guide and a car with a driver. Everything was located relatively far apart, and I didn't want to waste time negotiating transportation. I was also feeling tired, and somewhat lonely, and the idea of simply relaxing in a car while someone else took care of me appealed to me. I'd spoken with my parents and with Jerry the night before, and hearing their familiar voices had reminded me how far away from home I was.

While traveling alone in other countries, I've often found myself feeling tired, and sometimes very lonely, hungering for people and things I'd earlier yearned to escape from. Much to my surprise, however, these kinds of feelings seldom plagued me in Iran, perhaps because so many people were so extraordinarily kind and hospitable. And when those feelings did finally come, it wasn't until near the end of my trip, as if my subconscious was already preparing me for what would prove to be a long trip home.

Parviz and Mehdi arrived early the next morning, driving up to the Payam in a 1973 Chevy that seemed longer than the entire narrow front of the hotel. The manager rushed out to meet it, thinking perhaps that it contained an emissary from the Friday prayer leader, and we all introduced ourselves. Parviz, the guide, was a trim, compact man with a military bearing. Mehdi, the driver, was tall, handsome, and courtly, though also, I found out later, quite shrewd. Both were longtime business associates whose names I'd gotten through Sohi Nikkhah of Gulitour, a travel agency in Tehran. A New York New School–educated entrepreneur, Sohi had provided me with the names of guides in several cities and had never steered me wrong.

We drove first to the Eram Garden, famed for its tall and slim "flirting cypress" trees; next to the tomb of Sa'adi, a revered thirteenth-century poet, and then to the tomb of Hafez. The latter was a visit I was especially looking forward to, because of all their many, many beloved poets, the Iranians love Hafez the best. They often start memorizing his verses at age four or five and can usually recite a couplet to suit any situation. Many Iranians keep a volume of Hafez next to the Qor'an and consult it for guidance and to tell their fortune, by choosing a verse at random in a ritual known as the *fals* (omens).

The tomb of Hafez felt intimate and congenial. Flanked by dark cypress trees, it was a small open pavilion with a snug cupola shaped like a Sufi's hat. An alabaster tombstone in the center was inscribed with several of the poet's verses. "Though I am old, hold me tight in thy arms, be it for a single night. In the dawn, I will arise, made young by thy caress" read one especially famous couplet.

When we arrived, a dozen or so Iranian tourists were standing reverentially around the tomb, some reciting Hafez quietly to themselves, others touching his tombstone and praying. Volumes of the poet's collected works were also on hand, while behind the tomb stood a library and study center filled with thousands of books on Hafez, collected from all over the world.

Khajeh Shams al-Din Mohammad, or Hafez (One Who Can Recite the Qor'an from Memory), was born in Shiraz about 1324. Educated by top scholars, he soon became deeply interested in both literature and Sufism, the mystical religious movement. Regarded worldwide as the greatest master of Persian lyric poetry, his work appears simple to understand at first, as it is filled with much straightforward imagery about love and women, nightingales and wine. But a closer reading reveals poems of great subtlety that are difficult to translate—or so I'd been told. To truly understand Hafez takes much study, and to me, the poetry of Hafez, like his tomb, was pleasant enough but not deeply affecting—a fact that distanced me enormously from the Iranians around me.

Leaving, we drove south out of the city, which dropped quickly away, to be replaced by fields of wheat and barley, interrupted by villages seemingly glued haphazardly together out of brick and corrugated iron. Then, we began to climb up into dry, white mountain-hills, covered with dusty scrub brush and bony almond trees—two-dimensional shapes outlined against the overhanging sky. Mehdi snapped a cassette into the tape player and the aching lamenting voice of Dariush—one of the most popular of all popular Iranian singers, banned after the Revolution—echoed around the cab of the car. And then, raising the hair along my arms, Parviz and Mehdi mournfully began to sing along: "Your love is like a spear thrust into my heart—no one can cure this attack—I can live without people but not without you." Dariush was outlawed in part because he sings about love, in part because he is perceived to be against the Islamic regime, but many believe that his songs are not so much about his love for a woman as they are about his love for Iran.

Descending from the mountain-hills, I felt a spear thrust into my own heart as we entered a wide, silent plateau, framed on all sides by the red Zagros Mountains. We had slipped though a mountain pass to penetrate a hidden lunar land, etched with the same white light that I'd found hiking in Alamut and remembered from childhood. That light enveloped us like a living, breathing thing, subtly changing slant and color as it turned the plain around us into hundreds of shades of brown, red, and white. There seemed to be no other people or animals or even movement at first, just a frozen, immutable stillness disturbed only by our now-tiny Buick.

I noticed the ruins of a caravansary by the side of the road, and we stopped, to scramble down an incline and wander among ruined foundations and archways. The camel caravans that once crisscrossed Iran by the hundreds used to overnight in caravansaries, a sort of fortified inn, built with stables for camels and horses down below, rooms for humans up above. Caravansaries were once spaced about every 20 miles—a day's march for a camel—and dozens of the ruined structures still dot Iran. The camels themselves have all but disappeared, however, replaced by vehicular traffic.

A clear, light green stream, framed by a single almond tree, ran near the caravansary, and I sat down beside it for a moment, to watch it dance its path across the plain. Immediately, Mehdi approached with a small thermos, cookies, and glasses for tea—a service he would expect me to pay extra for later. He and Parviz then took seats as well, and a moment later, Parviz recited a famous verse from Hafez, in long, dark tones that resonated far deeper than did his usual speaking voice:

Sit down by the side of the stream
And in the rushing of water
Witness the transience of life.

As he spoke, the stream seemed to dance even more beautifully than before, and for a moment at least, I felt at one with Hafez.

We traveled on, red striated cliffs suddenly appearing out of nowhere, to close in on both sides, as we followed a rushing river. About 10 minutes in, Parviz pointed out Sassanian ruins perched on the cliffs above us. "That's the Qal'eh-ye Dokhtar, or Daughter's Castle," he said, which once stood guard over the Sassanian capital of Gur, then located in the valley below.

The Sassanians ruled central Persia from A.D. 224, when Ardashir I came to power, until 637, when the Arabs arrived. The creators of a strong and prosperous empire, the Sassanians developed much small industry and trade, embraced Zoroastrianism as the state religion, established a rigid class order, and, in a precedent that has resonance in Iran today, placed priests at the pinnacle of that social order. The Sassanians were also the first to encourage many of the arts for which Persia is still famous, including architecture, carpet weaving, miniature painting, and poetry.

Emerging from the gorge, we reentered the plain, where the area's foremost Sassanian ruin, the Palace of Ardashir, beckoned in the distance. But before reaching it, we passed through a village filled with women in traditional Qashqa'i tribal dress—bright blouses and skirts of mostly reds and blues—and stopped outside town near what is simply known as "the tower."

Before "the tower" stretched acres of gold—the villagers were drying corn on large tarmac lots in the sun. An old woman dressed entirely in shades of blue, her face a hard brown, sat sifting the bright kernels through her dusty fingers, while an old man in a conical hat—her husband?—tossed rakefuls up into an azure sky, winnowing. Corn is a new crop in Iran, Parviz told me as I watched, introduced only since the Revolution, but has proven to be well suited to the country's climate.

The Sassanian tower itself was a solid brown shaft about 80 feet tall, once believed to mark the spot of a stone fallen from heaven. Around its square sides was some evidence of a spiral ramp, which may have originally led to a fire altar on top, but historians are uncertain as to the tower's purpose. Equally mysterious are the dozens upon dozens of archeological mounds surrounding the tower; they contain the remains of Gur, the walled city built by Ardashir. Writer and archeology buff Robert Byron, traveling through the region in the 1930s, wrote: "I should like to dig here; it must be the richest site in Persia still untouched." And so it remains at the turn of the millennium.

Driving on, we came to the Palace of Ardeshir and entered the clay-white ruins through a dark hall that opened out into two courtyards, divided from each other by domed chambers. Each dome was pierced by a hole, letting in a single shaft of light; a staircase led to rooms overlooking a deep blue pool, around which the Sassanians had once held Zoroastrian ceremonies.

But, as Byron writes, the interest of the palace lies not so much in its beauty as it does in its use of the squinch, or arch built across the angle of two walls. Before the squinch was first developed by the Sassanians, there was no way to build a dome on four square walls whose inside area exceeded that of the dome itself. And without the squinch, many of the world's greatest architectural treasures, including the Taj Mahal in India and Hagia Sophia in Istanbul, not to mention most major cathedrals and capitol buildings, would not exist as we know them.

ॐ

When we returned to my hotel, I found two messages from Mr. Khorsandi waiting for me. Somehow, I wasn't surprised.

Mr. Khorsandi and I had first met on my first evening in Shiraz, after I'd finished sightseeing. A short, round, beaming man, then dressed entirely in brown, he had immediately whisked me home to meet his wife and family, who'd insisted on serving me dinner although it was already almost 11 P.M. And he arrived the next morning at 7 A.M. to take me to the Qor'an Gate, an archway situated on a steep hill that in presmog days had had marvelous views of the city. And he arrived that midday to take me to lunch, and the following morning—though we'd made no prior arrangements—to take me to breakfast. He wanted to know where I'd gone when he'd come by the hotel and I wasn't there, and why I said I wasn't going out one evening and then wasn't in when he called. He couldn't understand why I didn't want to spend all my free time socializing with his family—who also couldn't seem to get enough of me—or why I'd chosen to stay in the down-market Payam when the big and luxurious, though also depressing and expensive, Homa Hotel was just down the street.

Making matters even more difficult was the fact that Mr. Khorsandi and his family were extremely kind. Constantly, they inquired: Was I sure I was comfortable at the Payam? Was I sure I was eating enough? Was I sure I was having a good and productive time? Mr. Khorsandi wanted to chauffeur me everywhere I went, in and out of Shiraz, gratis, of course, even though the reality of the matter was that he had a full-time job. Though in some odd way, I also seemed to be part of his job. Perhaps because I'd been referred to him and his boss, Mr. Haeri, by a friend in Qom, Mr. Khorsandi treated me as if I was his personal responsibility.

"The guest is the donkey of his host," says an old Persian maxim. I'd already run into the truth of that saying elsewhere in Iran, with new friends who didn't want to let go of me, but Mr. Khorsandi drove it home. How to be sociable, appreciative, and kind to him while also getting the time and space I needed for myself? How not to let his desire to control my visit and show me off—for surely in this land of few Americans that was part of it—override my own wishes? How to engage in an elaborate two-step without tripping over myself?

Complicating things still further was the language. Mr. Khorsandi, who knew no English, spoke a slurred, rapid Persian that I could only occasionally comprehend. He addressed me as if I were a native speaker, and whenever I told him that I didn't understand something, he simply chuckled, his plump cheeks jiggling, and repeated it, sometimes even more rapidly and with more asides than before. After a while, I stopped asking him anything and just nodded and smiled and daydreamed while he talked and talked. I didn't really mind; I enjoyed just listening. The sound of the language had captivated me from the very beginning.

Though late one night, returning from dinner, Mr. Khorsandi startled me by saying an English word that I knew only too well. We'd been talking—or rather, *he'd* been talking—about my "husband" and how he must miss me, about his wife, and about movies and TV. I'd followed him for a while, but then he went off somewhere and I went off somewhere, when suddenly—

"Shit," Mr. Khorsandi said in English.

"What?" I said, coming back to reality.

"*Shit.* What does that word mean? I hear it all the time. It's in every American movie, and I don't understand . . ."

ঌৎঌ

On my last day in Shiraz, Mr. Khorsandi and I traveled to Persepolis, located about an hour northeast of the city. I'd put the excursion off until my last day because initially, yet another friend of a friend had promised to take me there then. She had a farm near Persepolis, she said, which she'd like to show me, and we could make a day of it.

But then complications arose. On the day before our planned rendezvous, Mrs. Estakhri Baharloo called to say that something unexpected had come up and although we could still spend the morning at her farm as we'd discussed, I'd have to find someone else to meet me there, take me on to Persepolis, and bring me back to Shiraz.

With time running out, I called Mr. Khorsandi, who dithered at first, refusing to tell me whether he was available, but also getting very upset when I suggested that if he wasn't free, I'd hire my guides from Firuzabad instead. "No, no—don't do that," he said. He was already hurt and annoyed that I'd made that trip without him. "I'll be at your hotel at 8 A.M. tomorrow when Mrs. Baharloo comes to pick you up to talk about this."

The next morning, Mr. Khorsandi drove up promptly on the hour, his one-year-old son sitting like a silent Buddha on the front seat beside him. Like many Iranian men I'd met, Mr. Khorsandi took great pride in his child and often took him with him on errands.

But Mrs. Baharloo was late, only arriving in a dark sport-utility vehicle at about 9:15. A very attractive, deeply tanned woman in her fifties, dressed in practical black jeans and boots beneath her *manteau,* she spoke English to me in a delightful French accent and Persian to Mr. Khorsandi in an imperious yet coaxing tone and immediately beguiled us both. I forgave her for being late and disrupting my plans, and Mr. Khorsandi, who up until then had said that there was absolutely, positively, no way he could meet us before 2 P.M., agreed to be at Persepolis at noon.

How does she do it? I mused about Mrs. Baharloo as she and I rode off, enveloped in her enchanting perfume.

As we drove out of the city, Mrs. Baharloo told me something about herself. For generations, she said, her family had been large landowners living in the countryside, but between the Shah's reform programs and the

Revolution, they had lost much of their land. And after the Revolution, they'd been forced to leave their beloved ancestral home and move to town because of death threats to the landowning class.

As she spoke, I thought about the two sweet, round-cheeked sisters whom I'd met the night before. Both had once been high school English teachers, deeply devoted to their jobs—there's no better profession in the world! they raved to me, their eyes glowing, our jobs were our lives. But both had been ousted from teaching after the Revolution, simply because they belonged to the old guard.

The Revolution broke a lot of lives, I thought.

Nonetheless, Mrs. Baharloo went on, her words surprising me, she'd initially had great hopes for the Islamic Republic and still thought that, despite many problems, it had brought about some positive change.

"This country has developed a great deal intellectually since 1979," she said. "The Revolution taught people how to think. Before, everything was running okay superficially, and so people just went along, like children. But now, they are more mature. They think about themselves and the future of their country."

Leaving Shiraz behind, we passed by a military camp that had once been an equestrian club founded by the Shah, a sugar beet refinery, a refrigerator factory, and the bustling town of Marvdasht, before entering a rich agricultural region planted with corn, wheat, beets, and other vegetables. Black tents for migrant workers, many of them Afghan, were pitched here and there, while framing the plateau were the Estakhr Mountains, from which Mrs. Estakhri Baharloo's family had taken its name.

Many of the fields surrounding us now belonged to her family, and we started making many stops, delivering soda, yogurt, and other much appreciated foodstuffs to workers who seemed to be as charmed by their employer as I was. What I was witnessing, I suddenly realized as I watched, was the remnants of a feudal society. Mrs. Baharloo's workers showed a deference toward her, and she a kindly condescension toward them, that was quite different from the guarded mutual respect some American workers and their employers have for one another. Islamic Revolution or not, Mrs. Baharloo was an aristocrat, albeit a very hardworking one.

Finally, our errands done, we took a road veering off to the left, to arrive at Naghsh-e Rostam. Four tombs hewn out of a reddish cliff about 30 feet above the ground, Naghsh-e Rostam is believed to hold the remains of the Achaemenian kings Darius I, Artaxerxes, Xerxes I, and

Darius II. The Achaemenians founded the great Persian Empire in 559 B.C., with its first king, Cyrus the Great, conquering and ruling over parts of what is now Turkey, Iraq, Greece, Syria, and Israel, and his son also conquering and ruling over Egypt. Another generation later, Darius I expanded the empire still further, to India in the east and the Aegean Sea in the West.

Part of the reason for the Achaemenians' rapid expansion and success was their belief in tolerance and justice; it was Cyrus the Great who freed the Jews from the Babylonians, as mentioned in the Bible, and Plato himself praised Darius I as a good lawgiver and king. Different cultures and religions were allowed to flourish under the Achaemenians as long as they paid tribute to their king, whose duty it was to unite all peoples of the world into one just kingdom. The Achaemenians regarded the king as an institution of God on earth and believed that a king was a king only as long as he ruled righteously. If he did not, he lost the *farr*, or "glory"—the sign of divine favor—and thereby the right to rule.

The concept of the *farr* has survived into the modern era. For many Iranians, a leader has the right to rule only if he is following divine guidance and working to improve the human condition—otherwise, he loses the *farr*. Prime Minister Mossadeq lost the *farr* because of his inexperience and, say the clerics, his failure to wholeheartedly embrace Islam. The Shahs Pahlavi lost the *farr* because of their corruption, ignorance, and greed. The only modern leader who never lost the *farr*, according to many traditional Iranians, was Ayatollah Khomeini.

One of the Achaemenians' most remarkable achievements was the building of a royal road that ran from Mesopotamia through Persia to Asia Minor for a distance of 1,500 miles. Fresh horses were stationed at inns along the way, allowing royal messengers to use a relay system and travel the route in two weeks if necessary. This relay system later became the model for the Pony Express in the United States, and the ancient Persian motto "Stopped by neither snow, rain, heat nor gloom of night" was adapted by the U.S. Postal Service.

Mrs. Baharloo and I rode on, stopping for kebabs in an outdoor restaurant, and then headed for the former center of the Persian Empire, Takht-e Jamshid, better known to Westerners as Persepolis—a place I'd heard about all my life. My father had often spoken of its history and had dozens of pictures of its carved columns, bas-reliefs, winged bulls, and double-headed horses, on which we children had once posed, as if on a carousel. I had always imagined Persepolis to be out in the middle of nowhere, surrounded by desert, but here it was, in the midst of fertile fields, with the smokestacks of Marvdasht not far in the distance. The ancient complex was more compact than I'd imagined, too—only about 300 yards by 500 yards—and I'd forgotten that it was mounted on a platform, as if it were a sculpture or a birthday cake.

We were over an hour late for our scheduled rendezvous with Mr. Khorsandi, but I seemed to be the only one who noticed. Oh, well, Mrs. Baharloo had shrugged when I'd mentioned it over lunch, and Mr. Khorsandi himself, dressed in a bright blue windbreaker, didn't seem to be the least bit put out. Instead, he greeted us with a wide grin that broadened still further when Mrs. Baharloo handed him, as well as me, one of her business cards before leaving. She's a good person to know, he said, winking at me as we both regretfully watched her drive away.

To my horror, Mr. Khorsandi had come equipped with his fancy video camera, which sat propped on his shoulder like a giant egg. He'd already spent hours videotaping me visiting with his family and now it appeared that he was about to videotape me visiting Persepolis: American Woman Discovers Ancient Persia. I tried to convince him to *please* leave the camera in the car, but he wouldn't hear of it. He wanted to videotape the ruins, not me, he said, with a peal of laughter. Right, I thought.

We approached the staircase leading up the sheer-faced platform, on which ruined gateways, towering columns, and groups of tourists—foreign and Iranian—could be glimpsed. The staircase was massive and utilitarian but also beautifully proportioned, so that both horses and humans could walk up and down it with ease.

Begun by Darius I in 512 B.C., Persepolis was never a real city but rather a royal palace complex, built to house the king and his court, and to host royal ceremonies during the spring and autumn (summers were spent at the royal quarters at Ecbatana and winters in Susa). The most important annual event was the New Year celebration of the spring equinox, when envoys from all over the Achaemenian Empire came to Persepolis to pay tribute to the king of kings. "I (am) Darius the great king, the king of kings, the king of lands, the king of this earth, the son of Hystapes" reads one inscription from Persepolis, in words that even now, back in New York, make me shiver—for their power, for their antiquity, for their hubris.

Alexander the Great and his army entered Persepolis less than 200 years later, in 330 B.C., Persepolis was sacked, the royal treasury looted, and the palaces burned to the ground—perhaps deliberately, perhaps accidentally, during an orgy. Some historians see the sacking as the Greeks' revenge for the destruction of the temples of Athens by the Persians in 480 B.C., but others point out that Alexander seldom destroyed the cities he conquered and had nothing to gain by burning Persepolis. In either case, the city was left in ruins and abandoned.

But Persepolis had one more intimate connection with a Persian king— Mohammad Reza Shah, who in 1971 staged a massive celebration here, to commemorate the two thousand five hundredth anniversary of the Persian monarchy. Hoping to tie in his own dynasty with the greatness of the Achaemenian past, he spent at least $50 million on the extravaganza, wining and dining dignitaries and pseudodignitaries from all over the world with French champagne, Iranian caviar, and meals flown in by Maxim's of Paris. It was a disastrous misuse of power and miscalculation of political climate, especially in a drought year when many of his subjects were going hungry. Iranian intellectuals and much of the foreign press ridiculed the over-the-top event. Student demonstrations broke out, to meet with violent repression, and an exiled Ayatollah Khomeini thundered: "Anyone who organizes or participates in these festivals is a traitor to Islam and the Iranian nation."

Reaching the top of the staircase, Mr. Khorsandi and I gazed out across the windswept platform. To one side stood the ruins of the Apadana Palace, where the kings had once received visitors, now roofless and bleached white by the sun. Before us stood the Gate of All Nations, flanked by defaced winged bulls and carved with the graffiti of the dead: "Cap. John Malcolm, Envoy 1800," "Stanley, NY Herald, 1870." And on the plains below, not quite visible from our vantage point, stood the remains of the Shah's tented city, built for his sorry anniversary gala. Empires, kings, and ordinary men—gone, all gone.

We wandered, past more gateways, winged bulls, lions' paws, and double-headed creatures that I now realized weren't horses at all but rather bulls. (On which one of these had younger versions of my brother and myself once sat?) We lingered, at the staircases of the Apadana, famed for their detailed bas-reliefs of the ancient New Year's processions: handsome Syrians, Ethiopians, Libyans, Indians, Babylonians, and emissaries of 18 other peoples, all bearing gifts for the king. And we took pictures, I with my Minolta and Mr. Khorsandi with his video camera, which, despite his earlier assurances, was always pointed in my direction. I had long been looking forward to getting lost in the ancient ruins, to daydreaming in a world that I felt I almost knew, from my father, but every time I glanced up or leaned forward to look at something, the camera's big black eye zoomed in as well, distracting me away from the past and into the present. Stop it! I said to Mr. Khorsandi again and again, and although he always obeyed at first, grinning, a moment later, there he was again, until I finally gave up. I could no longer deny it, I was the donkey to my host, who was examining me with as much curiosity as I was examining him. We were all tourists in the end.

ॐௐ

We had one more stop to make: Pasargadae, the tomb of Cyrus the Great, the founder of the Achaemenian Empire, located on the Dasht-e Morghab, or Plain of the Waterbird. The trip there took us an hour and a half, over badly paved roads, and we raced against the setting sun as it cut shafts of light through the mountains surrounding the plain. The further we drove in the darkening day, the older, wilder, and flatter the land seemed to become, with mysterious mounds of earth appearing out of nowhere, in between forsaken fields and a string of black, bowl-shaped hills.

The turnoff to Pasargadae was badly marked and we almost missed it, but then we caught ourselves just in time, to bump down a dark street that seemed far too wide for the homely village that lined it. At its end, a chain and sign reading CLOSED had already been placed across the entrance to the ancient site, but we climbed over the barricade and walked through an empty field to a simple mausoleum standing completely alone, surrounded by silence.

DESERT CITIES

Allah is the Light of the heavens and the earth. The similitude of His light is as a niche wherein is a lamp. The lamp is in a glass. The glass is as it were a shining star. (This lamp is) kindled from a blessed tree, an olive neither of the East nor of the West, whose oil would almost glow forth (of itself) though no fire touched it. Light upon light, Allah guideth unto His light whom He will. And Allah speaketh to mankind in allegories for Allah is Knower of all things.

—Qor'an (24:35)

ONE

I arrived in the desert city of Kerman at night, following an all-day bus ride from Shiraz that had taken me through more arid plateaus, past shimmering salt lakes even more astonishing than the one I had passed en route to Qom. One was a diaphanous pale blue, rimmed with line after wavy line of salt, emanating out from its shoreline like rings formed by a dropped stone. From the distance, the lake appeared to be a sheet of ice, with swirling mists hovering just above and three jagged peaks reflected in its blinding expanse. As our bus passed by, I spotted a far-off rowboat in the waters. Doing what? I wondered. There could be no fishing or recreation here—the land was so inhospitable.

Another lake was even bigger. Opaque green-white in color and framed by low black hills, it looked as if it was foaming, and I yearned to go down to its shores, to see it up close.

341

Beyond the lakes, the land grew flat and brown, and then flat and red, and then flat and white. We passed through several oasis towns, their main streets lined with trees, and a stretch of cultivated fields. Other buses with signs reading YA MOHAMMED! (Oh, Mohammad!), BEAUTIFUL BUS, and GOD REMEMBER in English *whee-Whee-WHEE*'d by, and in one, I spotted a mullah picking his nose. The woman next to me was reading the Qor'an. The faint face of the moon appeared, and darkness descended.

As the bus pulled into the dimly lit Kerman station, shadows of taxis and people jostling everywhere, I felt as if I'd arrived on the moon. I had no sense of the city but a very palpable sense of the expansive plateau surrounding it. Distant mountains crouched like prehistoric lizards along the horizon, and the night sky, studded with stars, hung low; Kerman is said to have the most beautiful sky in Iran.

ॐॐ

Far removed from Iran's centers of power, Kerman sits on the western edge of Dasht-e Lut, the Great Sand Desert. Founded in the third century A.D. during the Sassanian period, the town was on the ancient Asian trade routes and has close historical ties with India, Afghanistan, and Bandar-e Abbas, Iran's main port on the Gulf of Oman. Marco Polo, traveling through Kerman in the thirteenth century, spoke of its inhabitants' skill "in the manufacture of all the equipment of a mounted warrior" and "embroidering silk of all colours with beasts and birds and many other figures."

After the fall of the Sassanian dynasty, Kerman, like many other Persian towns, was governed successively by the Arabs, Buyids, Seljuqs, Turks, and Mongols, followed by a series of regional despots. Then in 1794, the town suffered horrifically, as the first Qajar king, Aqa Mohammad Qajar, invaded Kerman in pursuit of Loft-Ali Khan, the last ruler of the Zand dynasty. For harboring the popular fugitive, 20,000 Kermanis were reportedly sold into slavery and 20,000 others blinded, their eyes delivered to Aqa Mohammad on silver platters.

ॐॐ

I spent the night in a hotel at the edge of town, and the next morning, walked down a wide, windswept boulevard that led to the city center. The sidewalks were broken, and pedestrians and cars few and far between, except at the traffic circles, where taxi drivers lounged against Peykans in varying stages of disrepair. I passed by a mural of children jumping up and down with glee as they burned the Israeli flag, and grimy storefronts that looked half closed. Kerman is one of Iran's poorer cities.

I was heading to the town's most famous attraction: the Vakil Bazaar, which also houses the Jom'eh Mosque. (Many cities in Iran have a Jom'eh, or Friday, mosque, so named because Friday is the congregational prayer day.) Largely built during the Safavid period, the bazaar begins at a wide, neglected, yet also quite inviting outdoor square framed by two *badgir*—wind towers or, literally, "wind catchers." Found on rooftops all over Iran's desert towns, the *badgir* are playful rectangles made of clay brick, with vertical vents for catching cool breezes. The air is then funneled down into the rooms below, where it provides natural air conditioning.

To one side of the bazaar was the coppersmith's market, where workers were hammering out pots and pans in a cacophony of sound. To another was the Museum of the Baths of Ganjali Khan, a lavish seventeenth-century bathhouse. To a third was the Madraseh of Ibrahim Khan, its courtyard bursting with tiles portraying birds, peacocks, and flowers.

Descending a flight of stairs inside the bazaar, I entered the Vakil Coffeehouse, a plush but empty touristic spot where waiters in historical costume were idling beneath honeycomb ceilings from the Safavid period. Sitting down for a cup of tea, I looked around.

From the mid-1500s to the mid-1900s, coffeehouses flourished all over Iran. Important gathering places, they were not only cafés but also cultural centers where men—no women allowed—met to discuss politics and art, to play chess, and to hear oratory, poetry, music, and religious sermons. Itinerant artists traveled from coffeehouse to coffeehouse, creating folk paintings on large screens, which they used to recite stories from the *Shahnameh*, Iran's national epic. These "coffeehouse paintings," as they became known, are now highly prized by art collectors.

In the beginning, the coffeehouses did serve coffee, but when tea was introduced to Iran in the early nineteenth century, it caught on quickly, and by the late 1800s, few coffeehouses were actually serving coffee. They didn't bother changing their moniker, however, and even today most of Iran's thousands of so-called coffeehouses serve nothing but tea—a fact that few Iranians I met seemed to find at all strange.

The traditional coffeehouse, with its offerings of music, art, and culture, went into a steep decline in the 1960s, largely because of television. The actual physical houses still operated—and operate—but as cafés only. In recent years, however, the government has begun renovating some once-famous spots, like the Vakil Coffeehouse, turning them into tourist attractions—handsome places physically but with none of the life and intellectual vigor that must once have flourished inside their walls.

Leaving the café, I wandered on to the Jom'eh Mosque, strangely situated at the bottom of a steep staircase. At one end towered the mosque's main gate, a fourteenth-century masterpiece covered with elaborate tiles. The dark blue ones with the white geometric designs dated back to the Mongols, the light blue ones to the Safavids, and the ones etched with yellow and pink to the Qajars.

A young man sidled up to me, eyes darting in all directions, and whispered greetings in broken English. He wanted to be my pen pal, he said, but couldn't give me his real address, because that might get him in trouble. He would therefore like to give me his post office box address—which he'd rented specifically for corresponding with foreigners—and hoped to hear from me soon. Nervously, he thrust a piece of paper into my hand and walked rapidly away, while I stared suspiciously after him. Who was he?

As I left the mosque, he approached me again and more or less accompanied me down the long dispiriting blocks back to my hotel. I say "more or less" because every time a guard or a man with a beard drew near—possible *hezbollahi*—my would-be pen pal disappeared. Several times I thought I'd lost him for good, but then, there he'd be again, eager to practice his English. He had to be careful, he said, because he'd already been arrested for talking to foreigners several times by the "information police" dressed in "personal clothes."

I felt startled to hear that, and I wondered if the man's arrests had something to do with the drug trade. Kerman is relatively close to the Pakistan and Afghanistan borders, through which a steady stream of opium, heroin, and hashish flows, some for use in Iran and much for use in the West. As most of Iran's eastern frontier is desert, the drug traffickers find it well suited to their purposes, often driving across at night without headlights, using night-vision goggles. Since 1979, the Iranian authorities say that they have confiscated more than 1,300 tons of contraband drugs. Iran accounts for 85 percent of opium seizures and over 30 percent of heroin and morphine seizures worldwide.

Most Kermanis have nothing to do with drugs or the drug trade, of course, and yet, I thought as I settled into the city, overall the place does have an outlaw feel. For all its apparent austerity, and what I knew to be its religious conservatism—typical of most provincial Iranian cities—a relaxed iconoclast spirit seemed to be bubbling beneath its surface. Later, I was not at all surprised to hear that although Kerman wholeheartedly supported the Revolution, its zeal never approached that of Esfahan, Tehran, Mashhad, or Tabriz. Its isolation protects it from many things.

ॐ

I had a contact name in Kerman: Farhat, an Indian woman originally from Delhi. She had come to Iran as a graduate student around the time of the Revolution, met her future husband, and stayed. Both taught sports at Kerman University and wore fat bouncy sneakers that gave a spring to their steps as they arrived at my hotel to meet me. Farhat had a practical, no-nonsense air about her that reminded me of my own gym teachers from high school, while her husband was a bear of a man with an infectious guffaw.

Driving to the outskirts of the city, we proceeded down a tree-lined boulevard that led to the university, where Farhat had been teaching for 12 years. When she started, she said, she'd been the first "lady sports teacher" the university had ever had, and there'd been only 10 students in the entire athletics program—4 girls and 6 boys. Now, the students numbered over 400, with the ratio still about 4 to 6.

At the gymnasium, Farhat and I parted company from her husband to head to the women's section. Like everything else in Iran, sports are strictly segregated and governed according to a complex set of rules. Iranian women can participate in most sports, but they must be played in an all-women's environment. Many schools and universities have women's basketball and volleyball teams, and large cities have all-women health and swim clubs. Women who are well covered in sweats or baggy shirts and pants can also go jogging and play soccer in the parks, compete in equestrian and target-shooting events, and ski—in parkas and pants—at resorts such as Shemshak, the retreat I'd visited with Bahman. But since most highly competitive sports require more streamlined clothing, opportunities for outstanding athletic achievement, especially on the international level, are limited. Other sports, such as water-skiing, just aren't that much fun when well covered up.

Farhat's students, dressed in a motley collection of T-shirts and shorts, were playing volleyball when we arrived, but as soon as their game was over, they rushed up to me, bursting with questions about the United States. What kind of sports did American women like? Had I ever met

Michael Jordan? Did I belong to a health club where men and women went swimming *together?*

Then, Farhat and I toured the rest of the women's facilities, which were mostly housed in two worn but busy gymnasiums. Next door to the volleyball courts was a second hall where students were playing badminton and basketball. An enormous mural of a patriarchal Khomeini covered one wall, a battleground with dying teenage martyrs covered another.

As we toured, Farhat complained to me about the low standards at the university. "Iranians don't have any drive," she said, in a lament that I'd heard several times before. Some attributed the trait to a perceived lack of opportunity, but most—like Farhat—felt that it had more to do with a cultural heritage that emphasizes taking each day as it comes, as Allah wills it.

Still, Farhat went on, for the most part she was very happy living in Iran. "Iran treats foreigners very well," she said. "As an Indian, I am regarded with great respect. It wouldn't be that same way for a foreigner living in India—or even in the U.S. I have a sister who works in Washington, D.C., so I know. Life is not easy for foreigners in the U.S."

As she spoke, I compared her words with those of a biologist I'd met the night before. Unable to find work in his field since the Revolution, he told me how much he hated the Islamic Republic and longed to move to the United States. He also warned me about his countrymen. Don't depend on their kindness, he'd said, it means nothing—only money talks in Iran.

We passed by two *chador*-clad women.

"Hello, hello," they said to me familiarly.

I looked at them quizzically. Did I know these women?

"You don't remember us?" they asked.

And then I realized that of course—here were two of the students I'd just watched playing volleyball. I hadn't recognized them in their *chadors*—transformed from sweaty athletes into devout Muslims. The human mind does not handle contradiction well.

ॐ

While traveling by bus between Shiraz and Kerman, I had met four pretty teenage women and their mother, all dressed in fashionable *manteaus* and *rusaris*. They were going to Kerman to attend a wedding, which they promptly invited me to attend as well, even though we hadn't exchanged more than a handful of words.

The address that they gave me was situated in a new neighborhood on the outskirts of town, and the manager of my hotel, who called me a cab, was none too happy about my going out there alone at night. "Kerman is not secure," he said, and insisted on making a note of my host's address.

The taxi arrived, and we rode—and rode. As it turned out, the address was not just on the outskirts of town; it was on the far, far outskirts of town, and as the road became bumpier and bumpier, traffic and street lights all but disappeared, to be replaced by an isolated mountain peak, looming up before us like a black iceberg. We had to stop several times to ask directions, and when we finally reached the correct neighborhood, we rode down one dark dirt road after another, ditches on either side, before finally spotting a house ablaze with colored lights.

"*Anja!*" my driver exclaimed—There! He was as happy to have arrived as I was.

Climbing out of the car, I felt discomfited at first, as the bride's grizzled male relatives, waiting in a crowd outside, stared at me without saying a word, having absolutely no idea who I was. But then two of my young friends from the bus, dressed in long, flowing, red-and-black dresses and *rusaris*, came running out and ushered me inside to have a puff on the *ghalyan*, or hubble-bubble. The bride and groom will be here any minute, they said, as I puffed politely, the smoke making me feel dizzy.

On the floor of the main room was spread a large white cloth, covered with objects, and for the first time, I realized that I was not here for the *'arusi*, or secular wedding ceremony, as I'd thought, but rather for the *'aqd*, or marriage contract ceremony. Iranian weddings are divided into these two parts, with the *'aqd* marking the formal legal recognition of a marriage, when a contract is signed. Months or even years can elapse between the *'aqd* and the *'arusi*, and only then do the bride and groom go home together.

I'd read enough about the *'aqd*, which usually takes place before sundown, to know that most of the objects on the white cloth had significance. At the far end stood a sort of canopied throne, covered with roses; at the other was a large brass mirror, "the mirror of luck," which should be the first object taken into the newlyweds' home. Flanking the mirror were two elaborate candlesticks, one said to represent the bride, the other the groom, and before it spread a fine prayer cloth of paisley and gold design. Salt had probably been sprinkled under the cloth—for prosperity—and on top sat a copy of the Qor'an. Also on the white cloth were dishes filled with sweets (for happiness), eggs (for fertility), and greens (to guard against the husband taking a second wife).

A sudden commotion sounded outside, and we all rushed out, along with dozens of other women who had seemingly materialized out of nowhere. The bride and groom were arriving, in a new car covered with pink and white bows. To my consternation, the bride's father slit the neck of a sheep, dragging a bloody line with its body across the driveway—for good luck—and then the wedding car rolled in. The door opened and out stepped the bride and groom, dressed in Western wedding clothes. The women ululated—that high, eerie warbling done with the tongue—and someone held a tray with a Qor'an and burning *esfand*, or wild rue, over the couple's head.

Jostling together, we poured back into the house, where the bride and groom took seats on the canopied throne and the rest of us fought for space on the floor, covered with a thin machine-made rug. The crowd had grown to several hundred, filling up all the rooms of the house and much of the yard. All were women and children; the *'aqd* takes place in the bride's house, and traditionally, the only man in attendance is the groom.

Someone brought out a boom box, big as a suitcase, and as the groom discreetly disappeared, the women stood up to dance two by two while the rest of us clapped. One young matron in a too-tight red dress, her face shellacked with makeup, began slowly rolling her hips, seductively swimming her scarlet nails through the air. Another matron in a violet *rusari* and slinky blue knit followed, and then came a woman who looked like Alice in Wonderland. Her dyed blond hair was piled high, high up, tiered as a wedding cake, and her bright green dress was covered with dozens of pink bows.

I, meanwhile, kept on my *manteau*. Assuming that we'd be in a mixed-sex setting and so remain covered, I'd again worn a sleeveless blouse. As outrageous—and seductive—as some of the women looked to me, none had exposed arms. In fact, most of the women around me were wearing *chador*s. The party was an odd mix between a few Westernized women—the dancers and my new friends—who looked to be solidly middle class, and mostly traditional women, who looked to be quite poor, their faces worn, their hands chapped, their shoes the rubber slippers that could be purchased for a pittance everywhere.

The dancing continued for hours, while various foods were passed around—fruits, cucumbers, sweets, pistachios, and small bundles of rolled-up bread, with cheese and greens inside. But then finally, the formal ceremony began. Everyone stood up, more guests poured in, and an older woman sat down beside the bride to read the marriage contract. Meanwhile, behind the bride stood three other women, two holding a white canopy over her head and a third rubbing two sugar cones together above it—to ensure a sweet future. I also suspected that somewhere in the crowd, one of the bride's relatives was snapping the blades of scissors open and shut beneath her *chador*, in a traditional ritual known as "cutting the mother-in-law's tongue" (to prevent the older woman from offering intrusive advice or gossiping about her daughter-in-law).

The reading over, the bride signed the contract, and the groom, who'd been waiting outside, entered the room. Sitting down beside his bride, he put a ring on her finger and she put one on his. Then he formally presented her with a heavy gold necklace and bracelet, and the room erupted with clapping, ululation, and more traditional music from the boom box.

My new friends and I fought our way outside, to get some much-needed air. This is a very bad *'aqd*, they said with a sniff when we finally reached a small garden strewn with ripe pomegranates—very, very bad. It is much too crowded and there is no place to sit. So many poor, dirty women in *chador*s and the killing of that sheep! They wrinkled their noses and smoothed down their fine red-and-black dresses. Next time, you must come to Shiraz, they said. Then you will see what a real Iranian *'aqd* is like.

৵৽৻৻

The flat, two-lane highway traveling southeast out of Kerman toward Karachi, Pakistan, seems to be heading toward the edge of the world. Arid, dark brown land stretches out forbiddingly on both sides, and in the distance extends a barren mountain ridge. A puff of wind strikes, raising a billowing cloud of dust, and then disappears.

But nothing is quite what it seems in Iran, and 20 miles out of Kerman, the road bumps into the oasis of Mahan. Cradled in a lush green valley flanked by high peaks, Mahan is the burial site of the Sufi mystic and poet Shah Ne'matollah Vali. Founder of the Ne'matollahi order, one of the most influential of Sufi groups, Ne'matollah was born in Aleppo, Syria, and spent much of his life traveling before settling down in Mahan. His shrine, which dominates the peaceful town, tall shade trees rustling everywhere, has been attracting believers from all over the world since his death in 1431.

Mysticism first emerged in the Islamic community in the eighth century, with its adherents known as Sufis, from *suf* (wool), because of the woolen hair shirts that some early believers wore. Reacting against the growing greed of their rulers and Islam's rigid legal traditions, the Sufis emphasized the contemplative, ascetic life and the forging of personal bonds with God. Slowly, Sufism spread throughout the Muslim world, and although tenets varied from place to place, all Sufis believed, and continue to believe, that an individual can attain spiritual union with God through his or her own efforts, and that all people have within them a spark of the divine essence. Nature is seen as witness to God's eternal beauty, and the pious work to reach a state of absolute oneness with their creator while still here on Earth.

At first, Sufis were individuals with transient followers who traveled from place to place without money or food, relying on the kindness of strangers and the Prophet's saying, "My poverty is my pride." Beginning in the twelfth century, however, they began to form sects, with their leaders known as masters or guides, and their members known as dervishes. Some also began to practice extensive forms of fasting, hypnosis, or collective frenzy—for example, the famed whirling dervishes who spin 'round and 'round until they reach a near hypnotic state that they believe can bring them closer to God.

The early Sufis were firmly grounded in Islamic law, but as official Islam became more dogmatic, schisms developed, especially in Shi'ism, because of its emphasis on the holiness of the Twelve Imams. Mullahs began preaching against the Sufis, some going so far as to demand that their masters be assassinated. I had seen evidence of that myself in Kerman, where I had visited the grave of one 32-year-old Sufi guide who had been stoned to death in the nineteenth century for playing music outside the mosque while a prayer meeting was in session. Many Sufis believe that playing music during prayer can bring one closer to God, while traditional mullahs see that belief as blasphemous.

Even today, I had learned from Mohammad Legenhausen in Qom, many Shi'ites regard Sufis with enormous suspicion, associating them with opium smoking, licentiousness, and the disregard of Islamic law. However, at the same time, Shi'ites also have great respect for *erfan*, a highly philosophical form of Sufi mysticism combined with Shi'ite philosophy whose main goal is to break down the barriers between subject and object, to enter a transcendent world in which the seer and seen are one. Many seminary students take private lessons in *erfan*, though only through a sort of semisecretive underworld, as many mullahs are against the tradition—even though Ayatollah Khomeini himself was a practitioner. The Islamic government also pays for the upkeep of several Sufi shrines, including that of Ne'matollah Vali.

Entering the shrine, I found myself in an enormous garden courtyard filled with towering cypresses and umbrella pines. Recessed archways lined the walls, covered with tiles from the Qajar period—brilliant yellows, pinks, and blues—and straight ahead shone a bulbous blue dome framed by minarets. Under the dome echoed a whitewashed hall in which Vali's tomb stood, surrounded by smaller domed halls that led to more tombs and more courtyards, separated from each other by seven ancient wooden doors, originally from India. Exploring the peaceful complex felt like opening up a series of nesting babushka dolls, or different compartments of the mind, with each hall built in a different era, from the early 1400s to the 1840s. Clerics and women in *chadors* were praying here and there, teenage boys were doing their schoolwork, and I spoke briefly with one frail old man who told me that he lived at the shrine, surviving on donations from visitors. He'd once been a man of considerable material wealth, he said, but Allah had told him to leave it all behind.

ॐ⚬ॐ

Southeast of Mahan, the two-lane highway, now almost empty of traffic, continues on through more arid terrain that grows steadily flatter and harsher. The land turns from a dark brown to a dark, dark brown, and gaunt electricity poles, wires drooping like aging flesh, flash by. Flat-topped hills jut up. A black bumpy expanse appears. Seemingly a sea in the distance, it later reveals itself to be a hideous plain, choppy with blocks of broken crust.

Then, out of nowhere, nearly three hours beyond Mahan, Bam appears, flaunting fat date palms. Bam is the date-producing capital of Iran and home to a remarkable, abandoned citadel city that once housed between 9,000 and 12,000 people. It was to Bam that Loft-Ali Khan, the last ruler of the Zand dynasty, fled in 1795 to make his final stand against the cruel Qajar king, Aqa Mohammad Qajar. The governor of Bam betrayed him, however, and Loft-Ali was captured and mutilated by Aqa Mohammad himself before being sent on to Tehran to be executed.

Arriving in Bam near sunset, I checked into Mr. Akbar's Tourist Guesthouse. I had found the hostelry through the guest comment book at the Amir Kabir in Esfahan, and it was by far the loveliest guesthouse I stayed in in Iran. Outside was a wild garden filled with hammocks, date trees, and long tables around which other Westerners were drinking tea. Inside were airy, high-ceilinged rooms with colorful rugs, creaky cots, and plump, mismatched sofas and chairs. A quote or two from the Qor'an hung from the walls, but all the signs were in English because Mr. Akbar, who had traveled the world in his youth, catered only to foreigners. A tall, wiry man with an erect bearing, thick glasses, and curly salt-and-pepper hair, he was a former schoolteacher who'd always dreamed of running the kind of cheap and homey hostelry that he himself had looked for while traveling. The Iranian authorities had told him that his guesthouse would never succeed—what Westerners want are expensive hotels with private baths and amenities, they said—a common assumption throughout Iran. But Mr. Akbar was proving them all wrong, with a nearly full house every night.

Also an excellent cook, Mr. Akbar prepared dinner for his guests, and that evening, about a dozen of us sat outside beneath the date trees and the stars, dining on a tasty vegetarian casserole. Most of my fellow travelers were Europeans in their early twenties, traveling to "find themselves"—a phrase that I distinctly remembered using once myself but that now seemed strange and silly. One of the biggest differences between being in one's twenties and being older, I thought, is realizing how essentially unimportant you are. I fell into conversation with one thirty-five-ish Frenchman, who'd biked all over southern Iran, and with a gregarious New Zealand "panel beater" (body mechanic) and his English girlfriend. The two of them, Shane and Lorraine, also in their thirties, were on a six-month trek across Asia via Land Rover.

The next morning, Shane, Lorraine, and I set off for the Bam citadel in that Land Rover, packed to the brim with camping equipment and other supplies. It's been a crazy experience driving in Iran, Lorraine said as we went. People want to play games or race us on the highway, and when we ask for directions, have us follow them in their cars. Children chase us on bicycles, and everyone loves Shane—I think because of his beard.

At the citadel, a crowd of schoolchildren rushed up to say hello—"Welcome to Iran," they chorused. The parking lot was filled with a half dozen tour buses and I spotted two French tour groups that I'd seen earlier in Kerman.

Before us stood the citadel, built on a rocky outcrop and surrounded by a moat and crenellated wall. Passing through the main gateway, we entered the tan-golden city, clay brick battlements zigzagging everywhere. Around us lay what had once been the homes of the middle class; directly ahead rose the old fortress, where the city's rulers and soldiers had once lived. In between were the former homes of the aristocrats and the ruins of a former school, stables, mosque, and bazaar.

About two thirds of the buildings were wonderful ghostly apparitions, walls worn and pockmarked by time, but another third stood slick and geometric, all cracks and missing sections filled in with new clay and bricks. The Iranian authorities are overrestoring Bam, turning it from a haunting presence into a clean and user-friendly tourist attraction. It seems to be the modern Iranian way; I'd noticed the same disturbing phenomenon in Esfahan, where artists were completely repainting the lyrical fading frescoes at the Chehel Sotun pavilion, using bright new colors. Be careful! I wanted to cry both times—the past is precious—you'll regret it. But there'd been no one there but workers to complain to, and *swish, swish, slap, slap,* the painting and bricklaying inexorably continued.

Shane, Lorraine, and I parted company, to wander individually in and out of the abandoned homes, back and forth from the castle, up into the ramparts to get a better view. Founded during the Sassanian era, Bam gave refuge to many people over the centuries, including a group of Kharijites who'd been hounded out of Iraq, various princes and amirs, the armies of Shah 'Abbas, Sistan and Baluchi tribesmen, and the Zand ruler Loft-Ali Shah. But most had been defeated in the end, sometimes in bloody battles. Bam was abandoned about 1840, whereupon it was converted into a garrison. Reza Shah's soldiers continued to reside there until the 1930s, probably feeling self-deceptively snug.

Reconnoitering, Shane, Lorraine, and I returned to the Land Rover, which even from the distance looked oddly different. Only when we drew close, however, did we realize what it was. Someone had bedecked the vehicle with dozens of yellow wildflowers, draping them over the hood, under the wipers, and around the handles of the doors. Talisman to take with us from the desert.

TWO

*I*f Kerman is a city that is austere on the outside, more easygoing within, Yazd is a city that is romantic on the outside, tradition-bound within. Wedged on a plain between the Dasht-e Kavir and the Dasht-e Lut, Yazd is Iran's quintessential desert city, holding within it both a magical old city filled with tilting wind towers and winding clay walls and a large Zoroastrian community. The Yazdi people speak in a drawling singsong cadence filled with archaic words that other Iranians love to listen to, and are known for both their industry and their piety.

My bus pulled into the Yazd bus station on the outskirts of town in the early afternoon. In one direction stretched sun-baked desert, and in another, cotton fields; Yazd is framed by a few distant mountains, and a complex network of more than 2,500 qanats, or underground canals, funnels the water from those mountains to the fields.

In operation all over the Persian plateau for at least 2,000 years, the qanats are a sophisticated irrigation system dug centuries ago by craftsmen who burrowed through the ground at depths of up to 200 feet. The qanats can carry water 50 miles or more, with little of the evaporation that plagues open-air canals, and as many as 50,000 qanats are still being used today, providing Iran with about one fifth of its irrigation water. I'd seen evidence of the qanats' existence everywhere I'd traveled—mounds of earth piled up like giant inverted bowls at regular intervals across the plains.

For some reason, there were no taxis in sight when I arrived in Yazd, and so I caught a ride into town with a garrulous businessman in a shiny Peugeot who was appalled at my intention to stay in a humble mosafer-khaneh, or guest house. But it was none of his business, and a half hour later, I checked into the Pars Hotel. Situated on the second floor above a noisy street, the Pars was not particularly inviting, thanks to its grouchy manager, unlit bathrooms, and the disheveled man sleeping on its balcony, but my first choice of accommodations had been filled.

I set out to explore the town, and immediately felt a difference between Yazd and the other cities I'd visited. People were closely watching me here, in the same way that people in small towns everywhere watch outsiders. Exactingly familiar with all activities on their streets, they immediately sense when something is different; antennae go up. I hadn't gotten quite that same feeling in Shiraz, Esfahan, Qom, or Tabriz—all considerably larger cities—or even in Kerman, which is about the same size as Yazd, population 320,000, but more spread out. In all of those places, I had been noticed, but not in the same way, with my every move duly noted.

Within easy walking distance of my hotel was the city's Jom'eh Mosque, one of the most extraordinary buildings in Iran. I'd seen pictures of it but still wasn't prepared for its soaring gateway topped with two minarets so tall and slender it seemed they must surely collapse. An elbow-shaped arch supported the gateway to one side; its narrow, tapering portal was covered with dazzling blue tiles.

Inside, the courtyard proved to be nothing special, but the main sanctuary dome, built in the fourteenth century, was covered with more beguiling tilework, this mostly pale turquoise and dark blue. The dome's beauty didn't stop me from noticing the sanctuary's other, less impressive, artifacts, however: a battered space heater, bare lightbulbs, exposed wires, plastic fans, and a Western grandfather clock (what was that doing there?). I'd seen a similar motley array of objects in virtually every mosque and shrine I'd visited, and to my Western eyes, they detracted considerably from the overall aesthetics of the sacred places. As far as I could tell, however, none of the Iranians ever noticed.

Heading out through the back of the mosque, I entered the historic Old City—one of the oldest in the world, according to UNESCO. Suddenly, here was ancient Persia, or at least a sanitized version of ancient Persia. Before me lay a tilting maze of winding alleyways, some open to the sky and lined with smooth clay walls 10 feet high, others covered with low ceilings. The whole area seemed to be deserted at first, but then I heard noises coming from behind the walls and footsteps sounding somewhere.

I walked down one alleyway, and then another, not sure where anything led. My map didn't seem to apply. I passed two or three dizzying *badgir*, or wind towers, and numerous neat house-number plaques. Here and there stood weathered wooden doors with the ancient knockers I'd read about— a round knocker for the women, an elongated one for the men. Most of the streets were impeccably maintained, and overall, the place reminded me of Greenwich Village in New York City—home. I imagined its residents to be mostly families who'd lived there for generations or artsy professionals. As in the West, historic neighborhoods in Iran are rapidly disappearing and a hot commodity among those culturally inclined.

Near the center of the Old City was a small museum, housed in an 800-year-old former theological college. Inside was a mildly interesting collection of historic artifacts, but what arrested me most was a prim and proper sign in English prominently hung at the entrance: IF YOU SEE ANY WRONG DOING FROM EMPLOYEES, PLEASE DO NOT HESITATE TO CALL.

☙❧

In downtown Yazd stands an important focal point, and one of my main reasons for visiting the city—the Ateshkadeh, a Zoroastrian fire temple whose sacred flame has apparently been burning without interruption for over 1,500 years. Ever since the Arab conquest of Iran, which caused many Zoroastrians to flee from more populated areas in search of religious freedom, isolated Yazd has housed a large Zoroastrian community.

Upon arrival at the Ateshkadeh, I at first thought I had the wrong address. The place looked nothing like a temple but was instead a modern, unassuming building set in a garden with a circular pool out front. Wide steps led up to a colonnaded porch, over which—so I *was* in the right place—stretched the classic symbol, or *fravahar*, of Zoroaster. The bearded Prophet, his long hair flowing, stood astride the three-tiered span of feathered wings; the three tiers represent "Good thoughts, good words, good deeds," the motto of Zoroastrianism. He wore a long robe, also made of feathers, and held a hoop in his left hand—a reminder that one should not leave this life empty, without contributing to the greater good.

Inside, the temple was equally unassuming, holding only a full-length portrait of Zoroaster, looking much like a Renaissance Jesus; a few framed plaques quoting verses from the Avesta, the Zoroastrian holy book; and the sacred flame, which glowed in a dark enclosure behind thick glass. A caretaker told me that the fire had to be stoked five or six times a day with a special dry wood, some of it from apricot or almond trees, and that only priests were allowed to do the honors. A nearby sign in English read: ZOROASTRIANS WERE AND HAVE BEEN THEIST AND DO NOT WORSHIP THE FIRE. RATHER THEY REGARD IT AS A SYMBOL OF PURITY. ONLY THE UNIQUE GOD (AHURA MAZDA) DESERVES TO BE WORSHIPED.

The state religion of three great Iranian empires, which dominated the Near and Middle East for over 1,200 years, Zoroastrianism has had a remarkable influence on other faiths. Many of its doctrines were later adopted by Judaism, Christianity, Islam, and some Gnostic sects, and it also influenced the development of northern Buddhism.

Better known to most Westerners by his Greek name Zarathustra, Zoroaster probably lived sometime between 1000 and 700 B.C. An Iranian and a priest, he was born into a pastoral society that revered water, the giver of life, and fire, the source of warmth. The religion at that time was a proto-Indo-Iranian one, which worshipped many gods and believed in a shadowy, subterranean afterlife, ruled over by the first king to reign on earth.

According to tradition, Zoroaster spent many years wandering in search of truth, during which time he witnessed much violence and developed a deep longing for justice and peace. Then, at age 30, a revelation came to him: the world had only one god, Ahura Mazda, an eternal being and the creator of all that was good and light. However, opposing him was an equally powerful being—Ahriman, the destroyer, who was all darkness and evil—and the two supreme forces were engaged in an unrelenting battle for control of the universe. Both had made a deliberate moral choice, and this was the same choice that every man and woman had to make for him— or herself each and every day.

This was an astonishing concept at the time. Earlier, polytheists had been able to blame their bad behavior on the influence of evil or capricious gods, but now, Zoroaster was preaching that all human beings were responsible for their own moral destiny. Salvation depended on the sum of one's words, thoughts, and deeds, and no divinity could intervene in the process. Zoroaster was also the first to teach the doctrines of heaven and hell, the resurrection of the body, the Last Judgment, and life everlasting—all articles of faith later adopted by Jews, Christians, and Muslims.

When the Arabs arrived in Iran in the seventh century A.D., Zoroastrianism was still widely practiced, and part of the reason why Islam spread so quickly is that the two religions have much in common. In addition to a half dozen or so major articles of faith, both religions also advocate praying five times a day and giving alms to the poor, and reject representational images. Some Zoroastrians also converted to Islam quickly to escape their religion's by-then rigid caste system or to avoid paying the heavy poll tax inflicted on non-Muslims.

Today, Zoroastrians live mostly in Yazd, Kerman, and Tehran, Iran— total population about 30,000—and in India, where they are known as Parsees. Although sometimes subject to harassment in Iran, especially immediately following the Revolution, when about 10,000 Zoroastrians left the country, today's Zoroastrians are largely left alone by the Islamic government and have a representative in the Majlis, or parliament.

৵৽ড়৽

On my second evening in Yazd, I met Ali Reza. Coming up to me on the street, he addressed me first in hesitant French but almost immediately switched to Persian. He'd always wanted to learn English, too, he said on learning where I was from, but then he'd met his fiancée and now could think of nothing but her. That remark, and his ready smile, endeared him to me immediately.

Ali Reza was about 20 years old, and one of the most handsome young men I'd met in a country filled with handsome young men. Broad-shouldered and fit, with a jaunty confidence to his walk, gentle eyes, and thick wavy hair, he was self-assured, almost bold, and yet blushed easily. On the day we met, he was dressed in jeans and a cream-colored sports jacket.

He volunteered to show me the Yazd bazaar, famous for its silks and brocades, and as we wandered past stalls overflowing with luscious fabrics, told me that his favorite band was Pink Floyd and that he'd cried while watching the movie *Titanic*. He also showed me the *fravahar*, or Zoroastrian symbol, that he was wearing. It was all the rage among young people in Yazd, he said, but had nothing to do with religion. He himself was one hundred percent Muslim.

Because I'd told Ali Reza that I was interested in buying some Iranian music, we stopped into a music shop, where I purchased several cassettes, much to his consternation. But *I* should be paying for those, he said—you are a guest in our country. And the next day, he made up for it by giving me another cassette and a doll-size pink-and-white teapot, made in the china factory where he worked.

The music shop was near an ice cream parlor where I'd had a friendly talk with the middle-aged manager the evening before, and so I suggested that we drop in to say hello. As we entered, however, the manager gave Ali Reza a brief stare and then refused to look at me. I tried to talk to him, but he pretended to be very busy cleaning an already clean pot. I don't understand it, I said to Ali Reza as we left again.

But less than an hour later, I got my first clue as to the manager's behavior. Ali Reza and I had wandered into a well-lit mall where he stopped to talk to several friends, while I watched and listened. Suddenly, there was a flurry of commotion, the friends all talking at once, and a moment later, Ali Reza was rushing me outside and into a taxicab.

"What's going on?" I asked, astonished, as we hurriedly drove off. Darkness had fallen and the dust-filled streets were teeming with young men on motor scooters, headlights zigzagging in and out with drunken abandon.

"I said I would take you to a museum, remember?" Ali Reza said, glancing anxiously out the rear window.

"Yes, but—what happened back there?"

"Nothing." Ali Reza sat biting his lower lip, and though I questioned him several more times, he still wouldn't answer. We drove most of the rest of the long, dark way in silence.

Arriving at our destination, Ali Reza paid the cab driver and we got out. Seconds later, another cab pulled up. It stopped directly in front of us and a man inside stared at us for a long moment before finally motioning to his driver to continue on.

"He was following us!" I said to Ali Reza, shaken, but he refused to talk about it, and we toured the museum without either one of us mentioning it again—but with one of us at least thinking about nothing but.

And I got my second clue that evening when we returned to my hotel and the manager gave Ali Reza an exceedingly sour look, and my third one the next day when Ali Reza told me that he'd been telephoning me for hours, though I had received no messages. But it wasn't until my final night in Yazd that I finally fully understood what was going on.

I was supposed to have dinner with a family whom I'd met the day before. However, they'd had car trouble on the way over and didn't arrive at my hotel until 9:30—at which point, the hotel owner came out, blocking my way to the front door. A big burly man with grizzled cheeks, heavy jowls, and misshapen jacket whose pockets bulged with bulky objects, he frightened me.

"Enough is enough," he said, or words to that effect. "First, a young man has been calling for you, and now you want to go out late at night. Young women do not talk with young men in Iran, and they do not go out alone late at night."

"I'm not so young," I feebly protested. "I could be Ali Reza's mother." But I didn't push too hard. Who knew who this man was, or what connections he had? Feeling like a child, I obediently waved good-bye to my would-be hosts—I was tired, anyway, and hadn't really wanted to go out—who didn't seem at all surprised at my decision.

Returning to my bare room, a plastic arrow pointing toward Mecca above me, I realized that I'd finally had my first encounter with the sort of moral policing that Iranians, and especially young Iranians, have to put up with all the time. As a Westerner and a tourist, I'd been hitherto exempt, but perhaps because Ali Reza was so young and handsome, or because Yazd was so conservative, it had finally caught up to me here. I still wasn't sure why someone had followed us to the museum, but I suspected that it had more to do with "morals" than with my being a foreigner or possible spy. Ali Reza had told me that, unlike the apparent situation in Kerman, he'd never heard of anyone being harassed for talking to Westerners in Yazd.

I thought back to a conversation that I'd had with a 26-year-old Danish graduate student in Esfahan. She'd been studying at a university there, working on a dissertation about Muslim women, and living in a hotel. She was enjoying her studies very much, she told me over lunch, but not her life. The hotel manager and school officials bothered her incessantly, questioning her about where she went, day or night, and more or less forbidding her to speak with men. When she did speak with men, as she had one evening, joining a soccer team staying at the hotel for dinner, the hotel employees had made her life so unpleasant for days afterward that she hadn't done it again.

As long as you obey the rules in Iran, I thought, life is okay, and often good. But step outside those rules, and be prepared for consequences.

જીજ

Ali Reza had invited me home to meet his family, of which there were many branches. The two evenings I spent in his company, we spent much time shuttling to and fro among various relatives' houses, talking, snacking, listening to music, eating meals, and meeting mostly male cousins, many of whom were about Ali Reza's age and his best friends.

All of which was highly instructive. When we were alone together, Ali Reza was lively and charming. But when we joined the rest of his family, he fell silent, deferring to his uncles and to several older cousins who spoke some English and therefore monopolized the conversation with me. I didn't much like some of his relatives—opinionated men who grilled me incessantly—and so kept suggesting to Ali Reza that we get away from them, to wander the streets again. But Ali Reza never responded.

Sitting down to dinner at the home of one of the uncles one evening, I was shocked to discover that I was the only woman present; apparently, as a foreigner I had special privileges—the other women were eating in the kitchen. Except for my lunch with Tuba at Jamaran, this was the first time that I'd experienced such sexual segregation during meals in Iran, and it disturbed me. I tried to bring the topic up, but the men quickly sloughed it off, by turning it into a joke.

Why here? I wondered when it became obvious that no one would discuss the subject with me. Is it because Yazd is so isolated and conservative, or because this particular family is especially traditional? Or, is this custom still widespread and I've just been lucky not to run into it before?

Though I had had one comparable experience. A student from Shiraz, whom I'd met while speaking at the University of Esfahan, and beseeched me to call her when I got to her city. She'd be home on vacation that week, she said, and would I please, please, *please* come to her house for dinner?

I complied, and the experience turned out to be both unsettling and unforgettable. The student's father was a cleric, and neither he nor his wife appeared throughout my visit. They ate separately in another room—because, I suspected, I was an infidel—while the student's five fervent brothers fired questions at me, challenging me to defend my country and culture. With the sound of the invisible parents' utensils clicking against plates in the background, we seven sat crowded closely together on the floor of what appeared to be a study. The tiny room, the ugly carpet, and the broken bits of dry bread that we ate out of an enormous plastic bag all spoke of grinding poverty. The house was also dirty—one of the few dirty households I visited while in Iran.

Ali Reza's family kept a clean house, but many of the questions they asked me were the same ones that I'd been asked in Shiraz: Are you really free in America? Can you really criticize your constitution? (No one seemed to believe my answers.) But isn't it true that America is very dangerous? Isn't it true that you execute many people? Why can't you keep your hands off the rest of the world?

The biggest topic of conversation at Ali Reza's that evening, however, was the Clinton-Lewinsky scandal. Word about the impending impeachment hearings had just reached Iran, and Ali Reza's family, like many Iranians I'd met, were convinced that the whole debacle was a Jewish conspiracy. Clinton had extended a hand of friendship to the Muslim world and the Jews hadn't liked it. Ergo, they'd sent in Monica to create a mess. Monica was Jewish, wasn't she? That proved it. Why else would Americans—otherwise so prone to bragging about sex—be creating such a fuss over infidelity?

"But that's not why he's being criticized," I said. "It's because he lied under oath."

Ali Reza's uncles and cousins looked at each other.

"You're being very naïve if you believe that," one of the more bombastic uncles said. "It's all politics."

"I agree it's all politics," I said. "But it's partisan politics, between the Democrats and the Republicans, not between the Jews and the Muslims."

We wrangled back and forth, getting nowhere. I'd already had this same conversation with many other Iranians, some much more educated and levelheaded than was Ali Reza's family, but all equally convinced of a Jewish conspiracy in the U.S. Congress.

Many Iranians I spoke with also blamed the Jews for various other things, both major and mundane. One young woman told me that she wanted to apply to dentistry school in the United States. She had the grades and, more importantly, the money. But she didn't have a chance, she said, because she'd heard that the top three directors of the American Dental Association were Jews, who would, of course, never allow an Iranian Muslim to study dentistry in the United States. Even worse, when I protested, her father—a doctor educated in the West—backed her up.

Iran, along with Turkey, is one of the few remaining Middle Eastern nations with a sizable Jewish population, who have been living scattered throughout the country for over 2,500 years. Though many left after the Revolution, decreasing their numbers from about 80,000 to about 30,000 today, they have generally fared better under the Islamic government than many feared. Though discriminated against in various ways—sometimes forced out of places of employment, denied entrance to the university, or worse—they haven't faced wholesale persecution, and their rights are protected under the constitution. This doesn't necessarily guarantee anything in Iran, but close to 30 synagogues do operate in Tehran alone, Jewish schools flourish, and there is a Jewish representative in parliament. Khomeini himself, who initially called Jews "a wretched people," later amended his words, saying that Judaism was an "honorable religion that had arisen among the common folk," as opposed to Zionism, a "political 'ism' that opposed religion and supported the exploiters."

In early 1999, however, shortly after my return to the United States, an incident occurred that could bode ill for Iranian Jews in the future. That February and March, 13 Iranian Jews were arrested on charges of spying for Israel and the United States. Among them were a rabbi, three Hebrew teachers, and a kosher butcher, all initially held for minor infringements of law that then escalated into "proof" of collaboration with the enemy. In July 2000, 10 of the 13 were convicted in a closed trial and sentenced to prison terms of 4 to 13 years. The evidence against the men was kept secret and they were not allowed access to lawyers until just weeks before their trial began. Three months later, following an appeal, the men's terms were reduced by 2 to 6 years.

"How do you feel about the Jewish people?" one of Ali Reza's uncles asked me.

"Well, my husband's Jewish," I said. I'd long before given up explaining my unofficial marital status.

"O-h-h-h." They all chuckled and nodded at each other, as if to say, *that* explains it, and then changed the subject—to Pink Floyd. As it turned out, Ali Reza wasn't the only one who loved Pink Floyd. They all did, even the middle-aged uncles, and made me promise to write out the lyrics for them to "Dark Side of the Moon." Then, someone brought out a *daf*, or large tambourine, and one uncle began to half sing, half recite an Iranian love song, sometimes using his natural baritone, sometimes an eerie, answering falsetto. The other uncles began snapping their fingers to his hypnotic cadence, while Ali Reza and his cousins wrestled on a pile of cushions.

As I watched and listened—the other women still nowhere in sight—I thought more about the many conspiracy theories, involving Jews or not, that I'd been hearing ever since my arrival in Iran. The CIA controlled the Islamic Republic. The CIA controlled Coca-Cola. The mullahs were in cahoots with the British. Khomeini had come to power with the help of the United States. The Shah had been a British agent. Khomeini had been a British agent. The United States imposed the Iran–Iraq War. The West had deliberately caused the deflation of oil prices to ruin Iran. There was a conspiracy between the mullahs and the world powers to destroy what had hitherto been a rapidly developing Persia and/or emasculate true Shi'ism by turning it into an instrument of corruption.

Conspiracy theories, with their absolute views of good and evil, help to explain an incomprehensible world. Exceedingly hard to disprove, they make a sort of easy sense, clicking into place like dominoes—especially in a country like Iran where foreign powers *have* intervened covertly and where it's hard to get much done through standard channels. Everything happens in private, through personal contacts, bribery, back doors.

But in Iran, I thought, something else is also going on. The country's love of conspiracy theories ties in somehow with many of its other passions—with its love of ambiguity, of poetry, of polite circuitous discourse and meanings within meanings, all of which have to be unraveled and recombined over and over again to get to any sort of truth. It's a highly romantic, complex, and literary view of the world, which gives it great appeal, but also an inefficient and potentially dangerous one. It's also the opposite of the typical American approach, with its candor and directness, which when it works well accomplishes much quickly but when it doesn't, burns bridges fast.

෨ඐ

One morning, just after I'd eaten breakfast at a modern teahouse near my hotel, a woman came running up to me. She was middle-aged, pretty, and dressed in an attractive *manteau* and *rusari*.

"Are you Mrs. Taylor?" she said in breathless English.

"No," I said, surprised. I'd stopped to get my shoes shined by a crippled old man on the pavement who'd been calling out to me every time I passed.

"Oh." Her face fell. "I'm sorry. I want so much to find Mrs. Taylor." She stared at me.

"Why?" I said, curious.

"Oh, I see now," she said. "You're American, aren't you?"

I nodded.

"Mrs. Taylor is English, and married to a businessman who works near here."

The shoeshine man gave me a pair of plastic slippers to put on and then took my shoes, which he began polishing vigorously. The small boy beside him, who'd also been calling out to me for days, nodded at me, as if to say, finally you stopped.

"I'm a high school English teacher," the woman went on. "And I want to make language tapes with a native speaker for my class—"

"I'd be happy to help you," I said, while also wondering what exactly I was getting myself into.

"Oh, thank you!" she said. "You are very kind! You will help my students so much! They will thank you so much, and I—"

"When can we do it?" I interrupted, feeling embarrassed. "I'm only here for a few days."

"This afternoon?" she said, and later that same day came by in a 1970s American station wagon to pick me up.

Shahin lived with her husband, Farukh, an urbane older gentleman dressed in an elegant but frayed three-piece suit, and their two teenage children in a large, well-built but gloomy house on the outskirts of town. Much of the Western-style furniture in their living room was covered with plastic, and those pieces that weren't, were well worn. Several rooms appeared to be closed off, and the whole house was in need of fresh paint and multiple repairs. I'd already been in similar houses all over Iran— dispirited semitombs belonging to upper-middle-class Iranians who haven't been able to keep things up after the Revolution. Visiting the homes always saddened me, as did meeting their owners—cultured, learned, and stylish people who once, I was sure, had been filled with vibrant energy and ideas but now seemed weary and tense. The pressures of life post-Revolution weigh down especially hard on the professional middle class, which benefits neither from the Revolution's programs for the poor nor from previous professional connections.

Shahin and I recorded the tapes, with my reading a series of comprehension, pronunciation, and vocabulary drills into a microphone. Then, as her husband Farukh joined us, Shahin served tea and fruits, and I asked them both about life in Yazd.

"Yazd is not a happy city," Shahin said. "We're originally from Mashhad and life is much better there. Here, it is a small town, everyone knows your business. There is no entertainment—only one cinema—and no parks or zoos, like in Mashhad."

"Many Yazdis are very rich," said Farukh. "They own textile factories and farms, but they hide their money and look poor. They're suspicious of strangers and very conservative. Fathers don't let their daughters go out on the streets."

"*Our* daughter doesn't like to go out on the streets," said Shahin, "because everyone stares. She is not a Yazdi, and she doesn't wear the *chador*—just the *manteau*."

Later, I would meet Shahin's daughter, a freshman studying engineering at the University of Yazd, and I would understand why at least some people stared. She was striking.

"It took us over two years to meet people here," said Shahin. "But now it is better, we have good friends. Once Yazdis trust you, they are very kind."

"Why did you move here?" I asked, but Shahin and Farukh evaded the question, and only later did I glean that it had something to do with the fact that they had been quite wealthy pre-Revolution and felt safer living in Yazd. Neither one of them would say a word against the Islamic government. However, Farukh started to at one point, but Shahin quickly cut him off.

I asked about Zoroastrians.

"Zoroastrians are very good people," Farukh said. "Very honest, very frank. If a Zoroastrian says he has no money to lend, he has no money to lend. But if a Muslim says he has no money to lend, maybe he has, maybe not."

"In the government's eye, Zoroastrians and Muslims are equal," said

Shahin. "But in reality, Zoroastrians and Muslims don't get along. Muslims say to Zoroastrians, 'Stay away.' "

"They have a problem with intermarriage," Farukh said. "Because in their religion, they cannot marry Muslims or Christians."

"Only six or seven years ago," Shahin said, "Zoroastrians had to drink out of separate water fountains and sit on separate benches. But that's not true anymore. Things are better now."

ॐॐ

Shahin had promised to take me to her school, to meet her Zoroastrian students, and to the office of a family friend, where a Zoroastrian woman worked. The woman had agreed to talk to me about Zoroastrian life in Yazd.

But when Shahin arrived at my hotel two days later, a squat, square-faced man was with her—one of her superiors, Mr. Ahmad. He'd heard the language tapes that Shahin and I had recorded and now wanted to do other recordings, of better quality, so that they could be distributed all over the province, and perhaps all over Iran.

"We will go to the Ershad office," he said to me, puffing up with self-importance. "They have a soundproof room, and high-quality equipment, and you will read many tapes."

"But we have appointments," I said, my back immediately up. The idea of my voice wafting through high schools all over Iran did amuse me, but it sounded as if he was planning to monopolize my whole day.

"But you will be helping all the people of Iran!" He glared at me. "Don't you want to help the people of Iran?"

"Well, yes," I said, "but—"

"Then first we will go to the high school," he said, interrupting, "where you will speak to the students, and then we will go to Ershad."

"What about your Zoroastrian friend?" I asked Shahin.

"Don't worry," she said. "We will still have time."

"All right," I agreed then, and we set off in a chauffeur-driven school car.

As it turned out, the school that we visited was not Shahin's, because when she'd asked for permission to bring me to one of her classes, it had been denied. Instead, Yazd's superintendent of schools had instructed her to take me to a school for the children of Iran–Iraq War martyrs and to take Mr. Ahmad along.

Our visit to the well-kept facility was uneventful and carefully chore-ographed, with Mr. Ahmad sticking close by my side. After tea with the principal, I spoke to a class, where the students—all girls, of course—had ambitious plans. One wanted to be a film director, another a doctor, a third a chemical engineer.

"You see," Mr. Ahmad said to me, in one of his many explanatory asides, "women can do anything they want in Iran."

"Zoroastrian women, too?" I asked.

"Of course!" he said. "We love the Zoroastrians, we love the Christians, we love the Jews. All religions in Iran are the same, no problem. Only the Bahai's are a problem, and they are not a religion, they are a party." His face darkened.

This is the official line in Iran, used to justify the persecution of the Bahai's, and one that Mr. Ahmad would repeat several times that day.

From the school, we drove to Ershad, to set things up for our recording session that afternoon. The man in charge, apparently a good friend of Mr. Ahmad's, led us through a maze of rooms, unlocking and locking doors behind us as we went, to reach a soundproof room at the center. Many of the walls we passed were lined with videotape cassettes, and later I learned that there was much muttering about taking me, an American, back there. Apparently, the videotapes were recordings of top-secret Ershad meetings—as if I could glean that or anything else from their spines.

After finding the tape recorder and testing my voice, we retreated back outside for a cup of tea. And then another, and another. I kept glancing pointedly at my watch, as I was afraid that Shahin's Zoroastrian friend would soon be leaving her office for lunch. Shahin seemed anxious, too. But Mr. Ahmad was enjoying himself, schmoozing with his friend. Besides, his workday was almost over.

"This afternoon," he said sternly to Shahin, "you will bring her back here and record the tapes. I will be going home for lunch, and it is too far for me to drive all the way back here."

Fed up, I stood up. "We have to go now," I said. "I told you before, we have appointments."

"All right." Mr. Ahmad nodded gravely. "I will be finished in a minute."
Shahin and I retreated back to the car.

"Iranian men are very dictatorial," she muttered under her breath as we went. "How does he know *I* have time to come back here this afternoon?"

We sat in the car and waited. And waited. Mr. Ahmad did not come out for a good half hour, by which point I was fuming. Shahin was also visibly upset, but mostly, I thought, because I was. Despite my prodding, she wouldn't say another word against Mr. Ahmad or consider calling a taxi; he was her superior.

At last, the man came out, all apologies and charm now that he'd gotten his way, and ordered the chauffeur to step on it—we were in a hurry. The car screeching through the back streets of Yazd, we passed over a bridge and down a wide highway to finally pull up to an office on the outskirts of town. It was an architectural firm, run by Shahin's family friend, who was inside patiently waiting for us, along with Farukh, and, somewhat to my surprise, as it was already after 1:00, their Zoroastrian friend, Banu. A tall and slender woman in her early thirties, she had the pale complexion and gray eyes that are typical of Zoroastrians, and was dressed in a cream-colored *manteau* and flowered *rusari*.

"Good-bye," I said with relief to Mr. Ahmad. But then I realized that he was coming inside, too—to translate he said, because Banu spoke no English.

"But Shahin speaks very good English," I protested—better than you, I thought—"and I speak some Persian."

"No, no," he said. "I want to help you. That is my job."

With that, he made a few feeble jokes, as if to cajole me into a better mood, and perched himself on a stool next to my armchair. Everyone else sat down in a semicircle before us.

"Go ahead, ask your questions," he said. "I am ready."

Great, I thought.

Banu looked understandably nervous and so I asked her a few neutral questions about Zoroastrian beliefs and traditions. I'd noticed many Zoroastrian women wearing colorful skirts over wide trousers, with flowing head scarves I said—why didn't Banu dress like that? Too old-fashioned, she said, relaxing a bit, though she still wore the traditional clothes on Zoroastrian holy days, which came not once a week, as in the Muslim and Christian religions, but once a month. On those days, too, many religious people wore a special white dress with no sleeves, pants, and a belt of three strands—

"Isn't that interesting?" Mr. Ahmad said, interrupting his own translation. "The three strings are for good thoughts, good words, good deeds—that's very important in the Zoroastrian religion, correct?" He looked at Banu.

She nodded, and continued as I asked her more. Like Muslims, she said, Zoroastrian girls came of age at 9, and boys at 15. Fire was central to their religion because it represented all that was true and good, and on the last day of the year, just before it got dark, people built small fires on the street and jumped over them, chanting to the sun, "May your red radiance come to me; may my yellow tiredness go to you." Even the very young and the old did that—

"That's part of our No Ruz festival!" Mr. Ahmad said enthusiastically, again interrupting his own translation. "It happens every March—"

"Yes, yes, I know," I said, quickly cutting him off. "I've heard about it."

Held on the vernal equinox, No Ruz, or New Year, is by far the biggest festival in Iran, and though Zoroastrian in origin, is celebrated by all Iranians, no matter what their religion. Families gather together from all parts of the country, and the world, to sit down at a No Ruz table, which holds seven bowls, the number of the holy Zoroastrian immortals. Each bowl is filled with foods or objects beginning with the letter *S*—why *S*, no one knows anymore—and also on the table are two candles representing light and darkness, a mirror to reflect evil, a bowl of goldfish to symbolize life, painted eggs for fertility, and enough food to last for weeks. In addition, Muslim families usually set out a copy of the Qor'an, Christian families a copy of the Bible, and Jewish families a copy of the Torah. A volume of poetry by Hafez is often also on hand.

Shortly after the Revolution, the ayatollahs tried to abolish No Ruz as un-Islamic but were singularly unsuccessful. If anything, the festival is even more popular than before, with the entire country more or less shutting down during the two-week No Ruz period—which includes a nationwide picnic, celebrated on the thirteenth day.

Mr. Ahmad was distracted for a moment, talking to Farukh while helping himself to a cream-filled cake, and so I asked Banu about prejudice— how much of a problem was it? Instantly, her eyes grew distant, and then she said that although it was better now than it had once been, she was worried about her son. A Muslim neighbor had forbidden him to play with her children, and he didn't understand, coming home every day in tears.

Mr. Ahmad, ears like radar, turned back, and Banu quickly added that, of course, there were also plenty of Zoroastrians who were prejudiced against Muslims, too.

"See?" Mr. Ahmad said to me, "I told you. All religions are the same in Iran."

At last, Mr. Ahmad left to go home for lunch—but so did Banu. Her husband and son were waiting for her outside, and regretfully, I watched her go. We would not have a chance to meet again. The rest of us also ate lunch, and then Shahin and I returned to Ershad—as ordered—to record more language tapes.

Inside, an official was waiting for us, a green cloth draped around his neck, symbolizing his descent from the Prophet Mohammad. But apparently, there was to be no retreating into the forbidden soundproof room this time. Instead, we were to sit on the floor of an open prayer hall, people coming and going at the far end, and record. The official also ordered me to read the lessons straight through—no stopping the machine to rest or take a drink of water, he said, as that would detract from the quality of the tapes.

Obviously a man who knows about sound recording, I thought to myself as we began. And later, I was not at all surprised to learn that the tapes didn't turn out well. In fact, they were of much poorer quality than the tapes that Shahin and I had recorded in her home. So much for my voice wafting through high schools all over Iran.

ॐ

On the outskirts of Yazd stand three Zoroastrian "towers of silence," or *dakhmeh*s. Conical in shape, with flat tops enclosed by low stone walls, they are the hills on which the Zoroastrians once exposed their dead. Zoroastrians believe that to bury a body is to defile the Earth—death being an evil brought on by Ahriman, the malevolent being, and the Earth being the creation of Ahura Mazda, or God. Fire is also too sacred an element to come into contact with the dead, and so historically, Zoroastrians laid out their departed on barren hilltops, for vultures and beasts to devour.

Back then, a body would be brought to the base of the *dakhmeh* a few hours after death, and a ritual ceremony performed. Then, the corpse would be carried by priests up to the tower and laid to rest on flat stones, so that there would be no direct contact with the Earth. At the bottom of the hill, a close relative or friend would take up residence in a small cottage for three days, keeping a light in the window in case their loved one had not truly died and needed help. Wealthy Zoroastrians also placed small fires on all the steps leading to the tower, to comfort their departed.

At one time, only priests were allowed into the *dakhmeh*s, but now they are tourist attractions, and on the morning before I left Yazd, my guide Sa'id and I scrambled up to the top of one. To my surprise, the structure was only about 140 years old and had a much wider top—perhaps 30 feet in diameter—than I'd imagined, with a hole in the middle. The bodies had once been placed with their heads toward that hole, Sa'id told me, and if the vultures picked out the right eye of a corpse first, it was considered to be a good omen.

Just below the tower of silence was a small cemetery where today's Zoroastrians bury their dead, in cement-lined coffins that continue to prevent direct contact with the Earth. In 1937, Reza Shah outlawed the *dakhmeh*s, but the towers of silence continued to be used in Yazd until about 1965—if not later. In my mind's eye, I imagined a surreptitious party of mourners illegally sneaking up the *dakhmeh* in the dead of night, or traveling out of town to some remote hilltop, where they could practice their religious beliefs in peace. Much goes unnoticed in the isolated reaches of the Iranian desert.

REENTRY

If you have the means and fail to make the journey, you have not attained completely the happiness and pleasure of worldly riches; indeed, the perfection of pleasure lies in seeing what you have not already seen, eating what you have not hitherto eaten and experiencing what you have not yet experienced. Only by travel can this be achieved.

—Kai Ka'us ibn Iskandar, *A Mirror for Princes*

I had many more places I wanted to see in Iran but only a handful of days left on my visa. The clock had been ticking for the last two or three weeks, and with each passing day, I was becoming more and more aware of a distance growing between myself and my surroundings. I wasn't quite as in touch. I wasn't listening quite so hard. Part of me was already elsewhere.

Back in Tehran, Bahman, Chris, Lona, Pari, and Sepideh were busy going about their lives in a way that surprised me. When I had visited before, it'd been late summer, with all the lassitude that that implies. But now a crisp fall had descended. Bahman's medical practice was more hectic than ever, Chris was sprucing up the house, Sepideh was back in school, Lona was struggling to balance her work and personal lives, and Pari was entertaining a marriage proposal—from the brother of Azar and Shahla Tabataba'i, the family we'd stayed with in Mashhad. He'd noticed her during our visit, and although he barely knew her, he had already proposed. Everyone welcomed me back to Tehran with great enthusiasm and asked many questions about my trip, but had little time to socialize. There was work to do.

Which was fine by me, because I wanted to squeeze in one more trip, to Gonbad-e Kavus, or Tower of Kavus, in northeastern Iran near the Caspian Sea. Architecture buff Robert Byron had traveled to Persia in 1933 specifically to see the Gonbad-e Kavus, which he believed to be one of the world's greatest buildings, and I'd read his book, *The Road to Oxiana*. I'd also seen pictures of the tower—a tall, dark, buttressed column with a wild and primeval look about it that attracted me. Built in 1006, the Gonbad-e Kavus is the tower-tomb of a prince of the Ziyarid dynasty, whose glass coffin was once rumored to have swung, inaccessible to all profane hands, just beneath its 150-foot-high ceiling.

I was also interested because the Gonbad-e Kavus stands on the Turkoman steppe, near the Turkmenistan border, an area that is geographically and culturally quite different from anything else I'd yet seen in Iran. The Turkomans, who are Sunni Muslim, are a tribal central Asian people, once feared for their fierce, marauding ways, and for their bandits who attacked pilgrims en route to Mashhad. Though now mostly settled, the Turkomans still keep largely to themselves and continue to breed what was once central to their culture—the horse. The Turkoman horse is one of the oldest breeds in the world, existing in its present state as early as 3000 B.C. And *ensha'allah*, I thought as I headed to the airport, I'd find not only horses but also horse racing while on the steppe. I knew that the sport existed in Iran and had already tried to find it several times—to no avail—largely because I'd promised Jerry back in New York that I'd do my best to attend a meet. He works in the horse racing industry, and now that I was about to go home, I had to remember such obligations. I was also curious to see the sport for myself, and the illegal gambling that I was sure went on.

The flight between Tehran and Sari, the jumping-off point for Gonbad-e Kavus, took less than an hour, over the Alborz Mountains, which spread out below like crumpled brown velvet. Sari itself was small and inviting, with orange trees planted along major avenues, but I had no time to explore. As luck would have it, the taxi driver who'd picked me up at the airport was a horse player and knew of a meet taking place that afternoon. It was several hours away; we had to leave immediately.

We sped north, through rich agricultural terrain. Bright green cotton and wheat fields stretched out on either side, and I caught glimpses of the Caspian Sea to the left. We stopped for a late lunch at Iran's equivalent of a truck stop—a large cafeteria divided by a curtain. My taxi driver, Nejad, ate on the side for men; I, on the side for women and families. Outside, a 1970s Chevy stood with its engine running throughout our entire meal. The car's owner had trouble turning over the engine, and because gas is so cheap in Iran, he thought nothing of letting it idle for an hour or so.

As we rode on, the terrain grew drier and stonier, the fertile fields began to disappear. The Turkoman racetrack is near Gonbad-e Kavus, and we were now traveling through the same territory that Robert Byron had once explored. He described seeing the tower from 20 miles off—"a small cream needle [standing] up against the blue of the mountains"—but we saw nothing but telephone poles, sagging electrical lines, fields, and highway, followed by shabby storefronts. I'd thought that Gonbad-e Kavus, which is the name of a town as well as the tower, would feel like the end of the world, but it didn't.

The racetrack was on the far eastern outskirts of the town. Built by Australians in the 1970s, its physical facilities looked much like those of any small, local track in the United States: a bit scruffy, run down, dark. But the place teemed. Broken-down vehicles of all shapes and sizes jammed the parking lots and the grandstand spilled over with scrawny men in misshapen jackets and various hats—Russian astrakhans, small woolen caps, and thin-rimmed turbans of checkered white and black, quite different from the turbans the mullahs wore. Later, I learned that these thin-rimmed turbans indicated that their wearer had been to Mecca. A middle balcony was set aside for women, of which there were perhaps 20, but women were also free to wander the grandstand as they pleased.

Nejad and I took up a position on the second floor, where we had a good view of the track. On the grass below us, I could see a dozen or so parked motorcycles and a handful of kneeling men, folding into the fetal position and then up again as they said their prayers. We had arrived at the track in the late afternoon, the time for evening prayers, yet I also couldn't help but wonder if the upcoming race was entering into anyone's conversations with Allah. Mohammad Legenhausen in Qom had told me that in Islam, there is no matter too small or pragmatic to speak with Allah about. One story even tells of a man who prays for money. Allah delivers with a big sack of gold, but it is not enough, and the man prays for more—perfectly acceptable behavior in Islam, Mohammad said.

Nejad and the Turkoman standing beside us, a businessman in the import-export trade with Russia, filled me in on horse racing in Iran. Only one meet per day was allowed in the entire country, they said; that was why I'd had so much trouble finding live racing. Horse racing had been outlawed in the years immediately following the Revolution, but the sport was culturally ingrained and soon came back. The best meets took place here at Gonbad-e Kavus, with serious fans flocking in from all over the country. Some of the horses that raced were Arabian thoroughbreds and some were Turkomans, which were considerably larger than Arabians and best at distance running. The race that was about to go off—the last of the three races that day—was 1,400 meters in length, and the minimum bet 10,000 *tomans*, or about $2.

"Bet?" I said, blinking hard. "I thought gambling was illegal in Islam." From all that I'd heard and read, it is a serious offense.

"Well, that's correct," the Turkoman said, and laughed. "But we have it anyway."

"People aren't arrested?"

"They are if they do it privately. But not if they do it downstairs. Come on, I'll show you."

Astonished, I followed him through a crowd of people, down to the lower level. I had expected to find gambling at the track, but I'd thought that it would take place on the sly, unacknowledged, with people surreptitiously exchanging coded language, pieces of paper, money. I certainly hadn't expected to see anything organized.

Yet suddenly here before me was a dark, cold room filled with a half dozen computers, and women in *chadors* operating those computers. Men were lined up along the counters between them, flashing the thick wads of bills that many people carry in Iran because the currency is badly devalued and the largest-denomination bill is worth only about $2.

"What is going on?" I said, half denying the scene before me. I couldn't understand how this sort of operation could possibly be allowed in the Islamic Republic.

But Nejad and the Turkoman couldn't tell me anything more, and we hurried back upstairs. The last race was about to go off. Standing at the back of a row of seats, I studied the men below us, their various hats bobbing up and down. Many had round or oval faces, elongated eyes, and straight black hair. We were in Central Asia.

"Look," the Turkoman said, and I turned to see two men being arrested by the Revolutionary Guards, whom I'd already noticed posted throughout the grandstand. Apparently, the two men had just been caught exchanging an illegal bet. Betting illegally, said the Turkoman as the two men disappeared, was potentially much more lucrative than what went on in the computer room, where the winnings were very small.

The race was off, with about a dozen horses flying down the track, blue mountains etched against the sky in the distance. A battered truck with officials aboard was following them, and although the jockeys wore some variation of silks, and the horses stayed on course, everything seemed much messier and more relaxed than it would at an American track. Someone won, a few men cheered, and we all poured out of the grandstand, into a dust-filled traffic jam that lasted all the way into downtown Gonbad-e Kavus.

Later, I found out why computerized gambling at the track is allowed: All appearances to the contrary, it isn't exactly gambling. Four or five years ago, the Islamic government, which receives a percentage of the track's entrance fees, came up with an ingenious plan to increase the then-flagging attendance. Would-be bettors could now purchase a small piece of a horse on race days. Therefore, when they won, they were horse *owners* receiving a prize—not *bettors* receiving ill-gotten gains. When the conditions are right, Islam is nothing if not flexible.

ঙৈন্তৈ

I spent the night at a small seaside hotel in Sari, and the next morning, as per arrangements I'd made earlier, my English-speaking guide Farshad arrived to take me to the Gonbad-e Kavus tower. A fortyish man with a jaunty step, he was prone to making jokes that didn't quite translate. With him was his sister-in-law Maryam, along for the ride.

Half Persian and half Turkoman, Farshad suggested that we begin our trip with a visit to his Turkoman relatives, who lived near the tower. Ordinarily, Farshad said, he rarely saw these relatives, but he thought that as a foreigner, I might like to meet them. When he'd been very young, his mother had told him that he'd have to choose between being a Sunni like his Turkoman father or being a Shi'ite like herself, and after much study, he'd chosen Ali—that is, Shi'ism—and cut himself off from his Turkoman roots. It was better, he said, and made his life easier; being a Turkoman and a Sunni was difficult in Iran.

"The Turkomans are a very simple people," Maryam said with a sniff sometime later, en route to the tower, "and they are not clean. I don't know where we're going to eat lunch."

Farshad settled that question as soon as we arrived at his relatives' house. Though he hadn't seen them in years, he more or less ordered them to serve us lunch—and preferably one that included *chekdormeh*, what he called the "domestic food of the Turkomans," because he'd already told me about it. It was similar to Spanish rice, he said, a comparison that proved apt.

We sat down on the floor of the bare house, built of exposed brick walls and cement, sloppily put together. Some of the walls were badly eroded at the bottom and one had a jagged hole near the ceiling. Machine-made carpets covered the floor, and in one corner sat a TV and VCR.

"See," Maryam whispered to me, "I told you. The Turkomans are simple people."

Crowding into the living room to greet us, but disappearing again almost immediately thereafter, were three or four school-age children, their older sister, and their mother, to whom Farshad was related by marriage. Her husband was not home. He worked as a truck driver and only came home every fourth or fifth night.

The oldest daughter, Bedeh, served us tea. Tall, regal, and enigmatic, with a perfect oval face and unblinking eyes, she was dressed in typical Turkoman attire—an ankle-long, form-fitting dress, with a long kerchief, splashed with orange flowers, draped over her shoulders. When outside, the kerchief would be pulled up over her head in place of a *chador*; the Turkoman women do not wear *chador*s.

Bedeh would change clothes twice during our short visit: once into a maroon-and-white checked dress to serve us lunch and then again into a lime-green gown and red-flowered kerchief to go to the Kavus tower. I saw her give my dusty shoes and well-worn *manteau* several disdainful glances and wondered who she was inside. Several other Iranian women, dressed to the hilt, had also given my simple traveling clothes disdainful glances, but they had been city women, caught up in status and class. I hadn't expected to find that sort of attitude here.

I tried to talk to Bedeh, but she seemed suspicious of me and would answer only in monosyllables or not at all. Only gradually did it come out that she was just 17 years old, about to graduate from high school, and planning to be a doctor. She'd already been accepted into a medical program in Tehran.

Meanwhile, after greeting us, Bedeh's mother disappeared into the kitchen. She neither served us nor ate with us, though her daughter did, and sat down for only a brief period after lunch because Farshad insisted on it. She's shy, he explained to me as the careworn woman smiled hesitantly, because she doesn't speak much Persian—only Turkoman. She was also highly traditional. When her father-in-law stopped by a short while later, joining us for a cup of tea, she quickly covered her face and didn't speak to him. Traditional Turkoman women never address either their father-in-law or their mother-in-law, Farshad said to me, laughing merrily—it's a sign of respect.

Oh, wow, I thought, feeling saddened, while imagining all the difficulties and miscommunication that could arise out of that sort of absurd situation. I also wondered how Bedeh and her mother got along. Did Bedeh respect her mother? Or pity her, despise her? How uneasy is the relationship between the old and new Iran?

Some people think they don't need their parents, Farshad said later when I asked him about it. He spoke in a disapproving tone and yet, I thought, here was a man who had himself more or less disowned half of his heritage.

At last we left for Gonbad-e Kavus, taking several wrong turns before finally arriving at a small park. Out front were men with scales, for passersby to weigh themselves for a small fee, and vendors selling sunflower seeds and cheese puffs.

The tower stood on top of an emerald green mound—a tapering circular spear aimed at the heavens. Slender triangular buttresses jutted out from its sides like small fins; around the top and bottom ran rings of neat Kufic script, an angular style of calligraphy found all over Iran. The tower was enigmatic and perfectly formed but also disappointing: It seemed so small and, worse, so tamed, hemmed in by this cultivated park and pedestrians out for a stroll.

I took a closer look at the Kufic script, which proclaims the glory of Qabus ibn Washmgir, a famous historic figure who was both a fierce warrior and an accomplished man of letters. Poet, philosopher, skilled Arabist, and student of astronomy, he was the patron of many artistic and learned men, including Avicenna. Once again, however, as so often in the Persian tradition, Qabus was also extremely cruel. He put his bodyguards to death one by one until almost all were killed, and was exiled from his own lands by his own army for 18 years. Finally returning, he was assassinated in

1012 and his coffin placed in this tower-tomb that he himself had erected (the tower's name, *Kavus*, is a corruption of *Qabus*).

Two generations later, Qabus's grandson Kai Ka'us ibn Iskandar wrote *A Mirror for Princes*, a sort of primer on life, addressed to his son, which would become a classic of Persian literature. Part ethics and part practical advice, the book covers everything from the etiquette of eating and rearing children to how to behave should one become a merchant, astrologer, poet, musician, or king.

One chapter is entitled "On Taking Thought Concerning the Enemy." In it, Iskandar wrote: "Yet always show [the enemy] the semblance of friendship; it is possible for the fiction to become a reality and out of enmity friendship may spring just as enmity out of friendship." Wise words, I thought on reading them, that it would behoove both the U.S. and Islamic governments to listen to. Communication may or may not lead to understanding, but no communication leads nowhere.

We entered the tower and I caught my breath—for no good reason. There was nothing to see inside, just a round brick shaft ascending, to quickly disappear into darkness. But it was here—not outside—that I felt the tower's age, Persia's age, civilization's age, and imagined how it must once have been when the tower stood all alone on this steppe, casting a long shadow, symbol of a far-off power. Cupping his hands to his mouth, Farshad called out, "Qabus," and his echoing voice, banging against the walls, spiraling up, seemed to swirl through the dark centuries, taking me with it.

გიდ

Two days before I left Iran, I met Louise Firouz, a tall, lanky American woman in her sixties who has lived in Iran for more than 40 years. Married to an Iranian who is now deceased, Louise has spent decades researching the origins of the oriental horse. She believes that the Turkoman horse and the Caspian pony, a miniature horse found mostly in Iran, are the oldest horses of Central Asia, and the stock from whose mixture the Arabian thoroughbred descended. Her theory has caused a furor among equine historians accustomed to regarding the thoroughbred as the Middle East's "sole purebred strain," from which all other local breeds descended. Various aspects of her research have been verified, however, by archeologists, the British Institute of Persian Studies, and a scientist studying the DNA samples of horse breeds at the University of Kentucky.

Louise divides her time between her home on the Turkoman steppe, where she has lived for decades, and her horse farm outside Tehran. I had hoped to meet her on the steppe, but schedules conflicted and we rendezvoused at her farm instead. The autumn day was cool and crystal clear, yellow leaves rustling, reminding me of New England—persimmon trees in the front yard notwithstanding. It was Louise and her son, a freelance photographer, who explained Iran's racetrack "gambling" system to me.

Louise also told me other things that surprised me. Jailed at the time of the American hostage crisis in 1979–1980, she went on a hunger strike without telling anyone but was soon let go when her captors saw how thin she was becoming. Since then, the authorities arrest her "whenever they feel like it," but she has no real complaints about it. They treat her well enough, she said, and usually just want to know about some English-language book or movie that has recently come out—What does it really say? Should it be banned? The authorities confiscated all her videos once, including the ones on horses, but the tape they objected to most was—was I ready for this?—*The Sound of Music*. All those short sleeves, all those short dresses—it had seemed pornographic.

After the Revolution, Louise, like all foreigners in Iran, had had to register with the authorities. She'd never thought of leaving the Islamic Republic, however, and had never worried about her personal safety. If you're the kind of person who worries about your personal safety, she said, giving me a questioning glance, you shouldn't be in a place like Iran. Nonetheless, during especially tense periods, she'd made herself scarce on the Turkoman steppe, where she is widely known and respected for her knowledge of horses. In fact, when she'd first arrived on the steppe, the Turkoman culture had been so insular that she'd had to teach those who worked for her Farsi, which they still spoke with an American accent.

The morning wore on as we drank cup after cup of tea beneath the persimmon trees. Occasionally, a stablehand came over to ask a question or Louise popped up to check on lunch—a stew bubbling on a stove inside. But all the while, her stories continued, each one illuminating one small corner of Iranian life.

One time a few years after the Revolution, she said, she'd applied to the authorities for a mobile phone with a long-distance range. She'd traipsed from one office to another, accumulating more and more impressive-looking documents with high-ranking signatures supporting her cause. Everyone kept promising to help her, but the license never arrived and never arrived, and finally she learned that at that time, long-distance mobile phones were illegal. No one had wanted to tell her that; they'd all wished to please her.

Another time, two little girls came up to her while she was grocery shopping. Let us see your tail, they said. What tail? she asked. Come on, they said, please—we know all Americans have tails, we know you're the devil. Just like Americans "know" all Iranians are fanatics, Louise said, laughing.

Before moving to the Turkoman steppe, Louise had spent a winter with her horses in Kordestan—another region known for its fine horsemanship. Here, the horses were kept in semiunderground stables, and the humans slept on the second floor. Snow piled up high against the windowless walls, and wolves hurled themselves against the doors at night. But when Louise suggested killing a wolf or two to scare off the others, her Kurdish friends objected. God put wolves on earth, too, they said.

During the Iran–Iraq War, Louise often went out riding on the red hills surrounding her horse farm. Their elevation gave her excellent views of Tehran—then almost devoid of pollution, because many citizens had fled—and of the missiles streaking over it. One time in particular, she saw Scud missiles flying like lit cigars and landing somewhere in the city, to explode with blackness and light. But around her, the birds kept singing, the sun kept shining. There'd been nothing to do but keep riding.

Louise's two grown daughters now lived in the West, and she herself had last visited the United States 12 years before.

"But I doubt I'll go back," she said. "When I told people where I lived . . ." She paused. "Their reactions were so negative. They were so critical. I was on the defensive my whole visit."

Though I'd been in Iran only a meager three months, I'd witnessed much of what Louise was talking about: the suspicion, the kindness, the absurdity, the generosity, the repression, the tolerance, the occasional danger, and the constant wonder of life in the Islamic Republic.

Her last observation also gave me pause. What would I find when I got home?

⁂

On my last evening in Iran, Lona and Pari invited Bahman, Chris, and me over for dinner. They prepared all my favorite dishes—*tahchin-e morgh*, the baked chicken-and-rice dish; *kuku-ye sabzi*, the rich spinach omelet—and we socialized for several hours on shiny sofas beneath kitsch. We tried not to think about good-byes, we tried to avoid the word *tomorrow,* but it sat heavily between us anyway, dark and inert. I gave Lona and Pari pretty silver boxes that I'd picked up in Esfahan, and Bahman and Chris an antique wooden painting that I'd found in a folk arts store. The gifts were lovely, but I felt embarrassed to give them. They weren't anything approaching enough.

ॐ

On my last day in Iran, I went to visit the Bahman Cultural Center, a large community arts center, housed in a former slaughterhouse, that's often held up as a showcase of the Islamic Republic. I'd heard much about it and wanted to squeeze everything I could out of my last hours in Tehran. But as I toured the spacious, renovated facility—free or inexpensive classes in session everywhere—I could barely pay attention to anything my assigned interpreter-guide was saying. I was flying out at midnight; in fewer than 36 hours, I would be home. I was looking forward to it. I was dreading it.

We went in to interview the center's director, Mr. Shayestenya, a big, forbidding-looking man with a beard, fingering plastic prayer beads. He scowled as I entered the room, and suddenly I wished myself anywhere but here. Why was I putting myself through this? I didn't need another encounter with a grim Islamic official. Another unfriendly bearded man was in the room as well, there to take notes on everything we said, and a tape recorder whirled in the corner.

I introduced myself as a travel writer, primarily interested in learning more about the Iranian people and culture, and we talked awkwardly for a while about the center and arts in Iran. But then I asked a quasi-political question—about Tehran's former mayor, who'd founded the center but now was on the political outs—and Mr. Shayestenya swelled up, glaring suspiciously at me. The man taking notes looked up.

"Why are you asking about politics?" Mr. Shayestenya growled, jowls shaking. "You said you wouldn't ask about politics. You said you were interested in culture."

"I'm just asking about the center's future," I said, startled, and thinking about how closely politics and culture are entwined, even while having little to do with each other. "Who will support it now that Karbaschi has been removed from power?"

Mollified, Mr. Shayestenya embarked on a long-winded answer that I couldn't follow in either Persian or interpreted English. My mind drifted off for several long moments, until suddenly I heard some sense developing out of the director's thicket of words. He was speaking of the many good people that the Islamic Republic has lost since its founding—through politics, terrorism, the Iran–Iraq War, natural causes. Their deaths had been very serious losses, he said, but the country had gone on, because the Islamic people always went on, just like the American people went on. He himself had just returned from a visit to the United States, the Great Satan that supported terrorism against Iran, but to his surprise, had met many good people there whom he did not believe supported that terrorism.

"Iran depends on its people like America depends on its people," Mr. Shayestenya said.

From the Bahman Cultural Center, my taxi driver and I drove north, through the congested streets of south Tehran. It was rush hour and the traffic was even worse than usual. The car crawled along, through streets I'd never seen before, the blue haze of exhaust mixing with the deeper, stiller blue haze of twilight. A boy on a bicycle rolled by, a slab of *sangak* bread draped over his handlebars. Pomegranates spilled out of a fruit store. Two women in *chador*s stopped to converse, and *azan* began. The last call to prayer I was to hear while in Iran, it slipped in through car windows, human hearts, closed doors. The world froze for just a moment, we were united for just a moment—the boy, the women, the cab driver, I—and then the traffic jam broke and we rode on.

᠅

Back in New York, nothing had changed. Had I seen the latest movie? Read the latest book? Heard of the hottest, newest, youngest artist/director/entrepreneur who was setting the world on fire with the most extraordinary, edgiest ideas? And what about that trendy restaurant? Or sleek new clothing store? Could I believe the money people were making—through IPOs, the Internet, some odd product that no one guessed would ever take off? Wasn't it sickening? Wasn't it great? There was so much money to spend, so many new toys to buy. Was this a great country, or what?

It was all so oppressive. I yearned to go back to Iran. Or, at least, to that part of Iran where people write poetry and ask the great questions, where materialism is secondary to spiritualism, where concern for issues larger than the self are often in the air. I could do without the other part: the politics, the repression, the heft of backward tradition.

Not that I think that Iranians are all that different from Americans in most ways. When given half a chance, Iranians are just as rabid consumers as we are—and some were before the Revolution, or still are in the privacy of their own homes. And in the privacy of our own homes, or in the dead of night, we Americans think about the larger issues, too. But this spiritual questing isn't a valued part of our culture; it's pushed out of sight, as something almost shameful, as we forge our way up the more tangible professional, consumer, and self-gratification ladders, denying introspection, denying darkness, denying death. It's one of our greatest strengths as a nation, allowing us to achieve certain kinds of success with surprising ease, but also a great weakness.

Wealth in Iran and many other parts of the world means many things: not only money and material luxury, but also poetry, art, imagination, the intellect, family, friends, nature, a vibrant inner and spiritual life. We in America value those things, too, but they don't make you rich. Only money makes you rich.

When I tried to communicate to my compatriots how I felt about Iran, some recoiled in horror as soon as I mentioned the country's name, whereas others listened in skeptical silence as I tried to explain what I had seen there—the good and the bad. Because many weren't expecting to hear anything good at all, I often sensed that they didn't really believe me or thought that I was being naïve—had gotten sucked in somehow, not seen the real picture, allowed a few favorable experiences to cloud my better judgment. Yet what is it exactly, I sometimes wondered, feeling frustrated and irked, that gives these people their sense of authority, if not superiority?

One of the hardest topics to discuss was the status of women. First, I usually had to explain that yes, Iranian women can drive cars, work, attend college, vote, run for office, own businesses, keep their own money. Having to explain all this seemed fair enough; I hadn't known much before I'd visited Iran, either. But then, inevitably, the conversation turned to the *hejab* and the general oppression of women in Iran and Islam, and here I often floundered as I tried to explain that things aren't exactly what they seem but rather very complex, with some women having a surprising amount of power and many far from being the meek slaves they are perceived to be in the West. I certainly didn't want to unilaterally defend Iran's policy toward women but neither could I completely condemn it.

Some people, especially women, didn't want to hear this. It was as if I was either for women's rights or against them, and by even partially defending Iran, and Islam, had placed myself squarely in the highly unpopular second camp.

Others I spoke with made me feel even worse—as if I were anti–human rights. How could I in any way defend that cruel, totalitarian, fanatically religious state? was the undertone of their comments and questions.

Because that's not what the Islamic Republic is, was my answer. Because our image of Iran has become so politicized, so dehumanized that we can't see the reality for all the propaganda. Iran does have many serious problems, which I don't mean to underplay—beginning with its lack of individual freedoms, persecution of minority religious groups, and some family and Islamic laws so devastating to women. But in general, Iran is not nearly as harsh or brutal a society as it is perceived to be in the United States. Repression there is not what it was in Stalinist Russia or Maoist China, or what it is in Taliban-controlled Afghanistan or in Iraq. A certain amount of dissent and religious freedom is officially allowed, and that which is not, goes on anyway. Especially in recent years, many people in Iran speak out against the government all the time—in taxis, in front of strangers—without fear of repercussion. Others flout the Islamic laws constantly—by listening to forbidden music, reading forbidden books, drinking alcohol—and when they are caught, just shrug, pay a fine or bribe, and do it again.

Sometimes, while in Iran, I felt as if I were in a country of unruly children. Everyone, myself included, was trying to get away with something and hoping that he/she/we wouldn't get caught. The authorities were like parents—distant, often ineffectual, and usually oblivious to what was going on. We were all playing a game—how could guards reprimanding women for wearing lipstick, or armed teenagers stopping cars at intersections, be anything but a game? The problem, however, is that sometimes the game turns deadly serious. And the knowledge of that wears on people, grinds them down, takes spirit and hope out of lives.

లో(ఫ

Being in Iran brought me no real personal epiphanies, just a few sharpened memories and a shimmering of ghosts. The thick glass wall separating yesterday from today is just as impenetrable to me as ever, perhaps even more so, now that I've seen what the past looks like in the present.

But being in Iran brought me something that is at least as valuable—a liberation from self, rather than an encounter with it. Every one of my days there brought with it so much that was new and startling and thought-provoking that I rarely thought about myself or my limited personal world. Something much bigger was playing out on the stage before me and I had to keep all my senses highly tuned at all times to capture as much of it as I could. The tyranny of self, with its constant petty wants and whines, nagging, always nagging, disappeared.

Travel at its best, and especially solo travel at its best, always has this potential. But somehow, most travel never lives up to it. Either mundane details get in the way—arranging hotels and connections, missing hotels and connections—or else one can't get out of one's skin—one is lonely, still half back home, unable to make contact. Traveling in the imagination is often more rewarding than traveling in the real world.

Yet for me, traveling in Iran was precisely like traveling in the imagination, where much is wild and uncharted. Every day, I encountered deep, rich recesses that I'd had no idea existed before. Some of this was due to the overwhelming hospitality and complexity of the Iranian people, some to the depth and variety of their culture, some to the haunting, arid beauty of the terrain—so different from what I was used to. But some of it also had to do with the fact that for Americans, Iran is a forbidden society. Few of my compatriots have been in the Islamic Republic; I was in an illicit land. I had penetrated into the hidden other, the back side of the self, and caught a glimpse of infinite other layers underneath that I would never know or understand.

For me, the veil that had descended over the country after the Islamic Revolution deepened its attraction. Iran was a secret place, an enshrouded place, a very private and enormously rich place to which I, by what often seemed a great stroke of good fortune, happened to have very personal ties. Always I felt it a privilege to be in Iran—the *hejab* seemed a small price to pay. Always I felt it a privilege to be invited into people's homes—whether I agreed with their religious beliefs and politics or not. Sometimes I worried that I was somehow missing the "real" Iran or clomping clumsily about on a culture I didn't understand. But then those moments passed and there I was again, surrounded by an astonishing world.

৩৽ড়

Much happened in Iran after I returned. In late 1998, the opposition leader Dariush Foruhar, his wife, and three dissident writers were killed by a vigilante death squad, whose actions were later condemned by the

Islamic government. In February 1999, reform candidates swept village, town, and city council elections by about 70 percent. In March, 13 Jews were arrested on dubious charges of espionage. In May, popular Culture Minister Ataollah Mohajerani narrowly survived impeachment by conservatives angry at his failure to control pro-reform newspapers. In July, police and vigilante gangs attacked University of Tehran students protesting the closing of a pro-reform newspaper and other issues; it was the largest demonstration since the Revolution, and at least two students were killed, many others injured, hundreds arrested, and four condemned to death. In October, two other students who'd published a satirical essay on the holy Twelfth Imam in a campus newsletter were sentenced to three years in prison. In November, Abdullah Nouri, a close confidant of President Khatami, was found guilty of using his newspaper, *Khordad,* to "insult Islam" and sentenced to a five-year jail term.

Then in February 2000, the reformists swept the parliamentary elections, winning more than two thirds of the 290 seats. For the first time, it appeared as if President Khatami—before, always at loggerheads with a conservative parliament—might be able to implement serious change at last. (Though not without a struggle. Immediately following the election, several acts of vigilante violence occurred, including an assassination attempt on reformist Saeed Hajjarian, and that spring and summer, the hard-liners shut down all major reformist newspapers operating in Iran.)

But until the exhilarating parliamentary election results were finally declared official—over 3 months after the election and 18 months after my return home—much of the news coming out of Iran was dismal, and I listened to it with great dismay. What happened to the tolerance for which Persia was once so famous? I wondered every time I heard another negative news report. What happened to the ease of assimilation that was once the country's hallmark?

The news also dismayed me because once again, here in the United States, the Islamic Republic was being viewed by many in black and white. Once again, it had become a monstrous country. With each negative news story, the possibility of restored diplomatic relations between Iran and the United States—so tangible right after Khatami's election—seemed more and more remote. With each negative news story, even I was having a hard time remembering the people and the country for the politics.

I retreated to my Persian-language class. Though I had no reason now to keep studying the language, I didn't want to give it up. It would be a shame, I told my friends, to throw away the start I've made. But it was more than that. Persian class was the one place I could go where people cared about Iran, understood the complexities of Iran, condemned it and loved it at the same time. Most of my fellow classmates were young Iranian Americans who'd grown up in the United States. Many had never been to Iran, and Professor Kasheff, hailing me a conquering hero, held me out to them as a shining example. See, he said in his exuberant way—sometimes several times in one class—go to Iran, it's not all bad, you'll love it, I mean it.

NOTES

*F*or historical information on Iran, both ancient and modern, I am especially indebted to three excellent sources: *The Iranians* by Sandra Mackey; *The Mantle of the Prophet* by Roy Mottahedeh; and *Roots of Revolution* by Nikki Keddie. I also found *Lifting the Veil* by John Simpson and Tira Shubart, and articles in *The New York Times* especially helpful for information on Iran after the Islamic Revolution. All quotes from the Qor'an are taken from *The Meaning of the Glorious Koran*, translated by Mohammed Marmaduke Pickthall.

In "Boundaries" and "Conversations in North Tehran," statistics on literacy, life expectancy rates, and Iran's economy come from Iran's Ministry of Information, the *CIA World Factbook 1999* (World Wide Web), and *The Iranians*.

In "House Calls," Gertrude Bell's letter to her mother is as quoted in *Kurdistan: In the Shadow of History* by Susan Meiselas (p. 30). The text of Khomeini's 1963 speech is as quoted in *The Eagle and the Lion* by James Bill (pp. 159–160). For information on U.S. involvement in Iran, I relied primarily on *The Iranians, Lifting the Veil*, and, especially, *The Eagle and the Lion* (specific statistics cited are from pp. 114–115, 124, 202, 211). For information on Mossadeq, I relied primarily on *The Iranians, The Eagle and the Lion*, and *Khomeinism* by Ervand Abrahamian.

In "One Who Yearns for Death Never Dies," the quote from Ambassador William Sullivan is as cited in *Lifting the Veil* (p. 179). The figure on multiple marriages from *Encyclopedia Iranica* can be found in volume VII, page 449.

When describing the *Shahnameh* in "The Company of Women," I am indebted to Dick Davis's insightful introduction to *The Legend of Seyavash* by Ferdowsi. *Reconstructed Lives* by Haleh Esfandiari; *Nine Parts of Desire* by Geraldine Brooks; and *Law of Desire: Temporary Marriage in Shi'i Iran* by Shahla

Haeri, all provided me with excellent background on women's history and rights in Iran.

For information on the Assassin legends in "A Secret Shared," I depended primarily on *The Assassins* by Bernard Lewis, and *The Assassin Legends* by Farhad Daftary. *Persian Postcards* by Fred Reed also contains a good detailed account. The quotes attributed to Haji Mirza Aqasi regarding the Caspian Sea come from *A Year Amongst the Persians* by Edward Browne (p. 117). The information on the sturgeon's scales is as cited in the *Encyclopedia Iranica* (vol. V, p. 100).

For the history of Christians in Iran in "Strange Children in a Strange Land," I depended largely on the *Encyclopedia Iranica*; *Christians in Persia* by Robin Waterfield and on *One Hundred Years* by Arthur Judson Browne. For information on the Baha'is, I consulted *A People Apart* by Denis MacEoin; *The Persecution of the Baha'is of Iran, 1844–1984* by Douglas Martin; and *The Baha'i Question* published by the Baha'i International Community. For information on the Kurds, I am especially indebted to *Kurdistan* and *The Kurds: A Nation Denied* by David McDowall.

In "To Find Good Answers to Great Questions," *The Mantle of the Prophet* and *The Iranians* both provided me with excellent background on the seminaries of Qom. When discussing the "secret bill" proposed by Newt Gingrich, I relied on an article in *The New York Times* (January 1, 1996) and *Persian Mirrors* by Elaine Sciolino. The statistics on the number of university graduates in Iran also comes from *Persian Mirrors.*

When discussing the history of the *hejab* in "In the Shadow of Kings," I depended largely on *The Veil and the Male Elite* by Fatima Mernissi; *Roots of Revolution*; *Nine Parts of Desire*; *Women and Gender in Islam* by Leila Ahmed; and *Veils and Words* by Farzaneh Milani. The *World Press Review* article on Roger Garaudy appeared in April 1998 (vol. 45, no. 4). The Ayatollah Khomeini quote regarding the Persepolis celebration is as cited in *The Iranians* (p. 232).

In "Desert Cities," the drug smuggling statistics come from an article in *The New York Times* (August 29, 1999). For the history of the Sufis and *erfan*, I relied largely on *The Mantle of the Prophet* and *Islam: The Straight Path* by John Esposito. For the history of Zoroastrianism, I relied largely on *Zoroastrians, Their Beliefs and Practices* by Mary Boyce, and *The Iranians.* The quote from Ayatollah Khomeini on Jews and Zionism is as cited in *Khomeinism* (p. 51).

BIBLIOGRAPHY

Abrahamian, Ervand. *Khomeinism: Essays on the Islamic Revolution.* Berkeley, CA: University of California Press, 1993.

Abrahamian, Ervand. *Iran Between Two Revolutions.* Princeton, NJ: Princeton University Press, 1982.

Afkhami, Mahnaz, and Erika Friedl, eds. *In the Eye of the Storm: Women in Post-Revolution Iran.* London, England: I.B. Tauris Publishers, 1994.

Ahmed, Leila. *A Border Passage: From Cairo to America—A Woman's Journey.* New York, NY: Farrar, Straus and Giroux, 1999.

Ahmed, Leila. *Women and Gender in Islam: Historical Roots of a Modern Debate.* New Haven, CT: Yale University Press, 1992.

Akbar, Fatollah. *The Eye of the Ant: Persian Proverbs and Poems.* Bethesda, MD: Iran Books, 1995.

Al-i Ahmad, Jalal. *Occidentosis: A Plague from the West.* Berkeley, CA: Mizan Press, 1984.

Attar, Farid ud-Din. *The Conference of the Birds: A Sufi Fable.* Rendered into English from the French translation of Garcin de Tassy by C. S. Nott. Boston, MA: Shambhala Publications, 1993.

The Baha'i Question: Iran's Secret Blueprint for the Destruction of a Religious Community. New York, NY: Baha'i International Community, 1999.

Bahrampour, Tara. *To See and See Again.* New York, NY: Farrar, Straus and Giroux, 1999.

Bakhtiar, Afshin. *Iran and Iranians.* Tehran, Iran: Farhangsara (Yassavoli) Bazaarcheh Ketab, 1996.

Balagha, Nahjul. *Sermons, Letters and Sayings of Imam Ali.* Qom, Iran: Ansariyan Publications, n.d.

Batmanglij, Najmieh. *New Food of Life: Ancient Persian and Modern Iranian Cooking and Ceremonies.* Washington, DC: Mage Publishers, 1998.

391

Bill, James A. *The Eagle and the Lion: The Tragedy of American-Iranian Relations.* New Haven, CT: Yale University Press, 1988.

Bird, Isabella L. *Journeys in Persia and Kurdestan.* London, England: Virago, 1988–89.

Boyce, Mary. *Zoroastrians, Their Religious Beliefs and Practices.* New York, NY: Routledge & Kegan Paul, 1984.

Brooks, Geraldine. *Nine Parts of Desire: The Hidden World of Islamic Women.* New York, NY: Anchor Books, 1995.

Brown, Arthur Judson. *One Hundred Years: A History of the Foreign Missionary Work of the Presbyterian Church in the U.S.A.* New York, NY: Fleming H. Revell, 1936.

Browne, Edward G. *A Year Amongst the Persians.* London, England: Adam and Charles Black, 1893.

Byron, Robert. *The Road to Oxiana.* New York, NY: Oxford University Press, 1966.

Chaqueri, Cosroe, ed. *The Armenians of Iran.* Cambridge, MA: Harvard University Press, 1998.

Chardin, Sir John. *Travels in Persia, 1673–1677.* New York, NY: Dover Publications, 1988.

Curtis, Vesta Sarkhosh. *Persian Myths.* Austin, TX: University of Texas Press, 1993.

Curzon, George N. *Persia and the Persian Question.* New York, NY: Frank Cass & Co. Ltd., 1966.

Daftary, Farhad. *The Assassin Legends: Myths of the Isma'ilis.* New York, NY: Tauris, 1994.

Danziger, Nick. *Danziger's Travels: Beyond Forbidden Frontiers.* London, England: Grafton Books, 1987.

Dodwell, Christina. *A Traveller on Horseback.* London, England: Hodder & Stoughton, 1987.

During, Jean, Zia Mirabdolbaghi, and Dariush Safvat. *The Art of Persian Music.* Washington, DC: Mage Publishers, 1991.

Esfandiari, Haleh. *Reconstructed Lives: Women and Iran's Islamic Revolution.* Washington, DC: Woodrow Wilson Center Press, 1997.

Esposito, John L. *Islam: The Straight Path.* New York, NY: Oxford University Press, 1988.

Faramarzi, Mohammad Taghi. *A Travel Guide to Iran.* Tehran, Iran: Yassaman Publications, 1997.

Farmaian, Sattareh Farman, with Dona Munker. *Daughter of Persia: A Woman's Journey from Her Father's Harem through the Islamic Revolution.* New York, NY: Anchor Books, 1993.

Ferdowsi. *The Epic of the Kings.* Translated by Reuben Levy. Costa Mesa, CA: Mazda Publishers, 1996.

Ferdowsi. *The Legend of Seyavash.* Translated by Dick Davis. New York, NY: Penguin Books USA, 1992.

Fluehr-Lobban, Carolyn. *Islamic Society in Practice.* Gainesville, FL: University Press of Florida, 1994.

Fonseca, Isabel. *Bury Me Standing: The Gypsies and Their Journey.* New York, NY: Vintage Books, 1995.

Greene, Graham. *Journey Without Maps.* New York, NY: Penguin Books USA, 1978.

Greenway, Paul, and David St. Vincent. *Iran.* Oakland, CA: Lonely Planet Publications, 1998.

Haeri, Shahla. *Law of Desire: Temporary Marriage in Shi'i Iran.* Syracuse, NY: Syracuse University Press, 1989.

Hafiz. *Fifty Poems of Hafiz.* Translated by Arthur J. Arberry. London, England: Cambridge University Press, 1953.

Helms, Cynthia. *An Ambassador's Wife in Iran.* New York, NY: Dodd, Mead & Company, 1981.

Hobson, Sarah. *Masquerade: An Adventure in Iran.* Chicago, IL: Academy Chicago Limited, 1979.

In Memory of Our Martyrs. Tehran, Iran: Ministry of Islamic Guidance, 1982.

Iran, A Country Study. Washington, DC: Library of Congress, Federal Research Division, 1989.

Iskandar, Kai Ka'us ibn. *A Mirror for Princes.* Translated by Reuben Levy. New York, NY: E. P. Dutton & Co., 1951.

Johnson, Diane. *Persian Nights.* New York, NY: Plume Books, 1998.

Kaplan, Robert D. *The Ends of the Earth: A Journey at the Dawn of the 21st Century.* New York, NY: Random House, 1996.

Kapuscinski, Ryszard. *Shah of Shahs.* Translated by William R. Brand and Katarzyna Mroczkowska-Brand. New York, NY: Vintage International, 1982.

Keddie, Nikki R. *Roots of Revolution.* New Haven, CT: Yale University Press, 1981.

Khayyam, Omar. *The Rubáiyát of Omar Khayyám.* Rendered into English verse by Edward FitzGerald. New York, NY: Quality Paperback Book Club, 1996.

Khomeini, Ruhollah. *Coupe-Amour; The Jardiniere of Love.* Tehran, Iran: Institute for Compilation and Publication of Imam Khomeini's Works, International Affairs Division, 1994.

Khomeini, Ruhollah. *Pithy Aphorisms, Wise Sayings and Counsels.* Tehran, Iran: Institute for Compilation and Publication of Imam Khomeini's Works, International Affairs Division, 1994.

Levy, Reuben. *An Introduction to Persian Literature.* New York, NY: Columbia University Press, 1969.

Lewis, Bernard. *The Assassins.* London, England: Weidenfeld & Nicolson, 1967.

Loveday, Helen. *Iran.* Hong Kong: The Guidebook Company Ltd., 1994.

MacEoin, Denis. *A People Apart: The Baha'i Community of Iran in the 20th Century.* London, England: Centre of Near and Middle Eastern Studies, University of London, 1989.

Mackey, Sandra. *The Iranians: Persia, Islam and the Soul of a Nation.* New York, NY: Penguin Putnam, 1996.

Martin, Douglas. *The Persecution of the Baha'is of Iran, 1844–1984.* Ottawa, Canada: The Association for Baha'i Studies, 1984.

McDowall, David. *The Kurds: A Nation Denied.* London, England: Minority Rights Publications, 1992.

McGinnies, William G., Bram J. Goldman, and Patricia Paylor. *Deserts of the World.* Tucson, AZ: University of Arizona Press, 1968.

The Meaning of the Glorious Koran. Translated by Mohammed Marmaduke Pickthall. New York, NY: Penguin Books USA, n.d.

Meiselas, Susan, with chapter commentaries by Martin van Bruinessen. *Kurdistan: In the Shadow of History.* New York, NY: Random House, 1997.

Mernissi, Fatima. *The Veil and the Male Elite: A Feminist Interpretation of Women's Rights in Islam.* Translated by Mary Jo Lakeland. New York, NY: Addison-Wesley, 1991.

Milani, Abbas. *Tales of Two Cities: A Persian Memoir.* Washington, DC: Mage Publishers, 1996.

Milani, Farzaneh. *Veils and Words: The Emerging Voices of Iranian Women Writers.* Syracuse, NY: Syracuse University Press, 1992.

Miller, Judith. *God Has Ninety-Nine Names: Reporting from a Militant Middle East.* New York, NY: Simon & Schuster, 1996.

Morier, James. *The Adventures of Hajji Baba of Ispahan*. New York, NY: Random House, 1954.

Mottahedeh, Roy. *The Mantle of the Prophet: Religion and Politics in Iran*. New York, NY: Simon & Schuster, 1985.

Naipaul, V. S. *Among the Believers: An Islamic Journey*. New York, NY: Viking Penguin, 1981.

Naipaul, V. S. *Beyond Belief: Islamic Excursions Among the Converted People*. New York, NY: Random House, 1998.

O'Donnell, Terence. *Garden of the Brave in War: Recollections of Iran*. Chicago, IL: University of Chicago Press, 1980.

Once the Mullah. Retold by Alice Geer Kelsey. New York, NY: Longmans, Green and Co., 1954.

Paz, Octavio. *The Labyrinth of Solitude: Life and Thought in Mexico*. New York, NY: Grove Press, 1961.

Picard, Barbara Leonie. *Tales of Ancient Persia*. New York, NY: Oxford University Press, 1993.

Polo, Marco. *The Travels of Marco Polo*. Translated by Ronald Latham. New York, NY: Penguin Books USA, 1958.

Reed, Fred A. *Persian Postcards*. Vancouver, Canada: Talonbooks, 1994.

Rumi, Jalal al-Din. *The Essential Rumi*. Translated by Coleman Barks, with John Moyne, A. J. Arberry, and Reynold Nicholson. New York, NY: HarperCollins Publishers, 1995.

Rushdie, Salman. *The Satanic Verses*. New York, NY: Viking, 1988.

Sackville-West, Vita. *Passenger to Teheran*. New York, NY: Moyer Bell Limited, 1990.

Said, Edward W. *Covering Islam: How the Media and the Experts Determine How We See the Rest of the World*. New York, NY: Random House, 1997.

Said, Edward W. *Orientalism*. New York, NY: Vintage Books, 1979.

Schimmel, Annemarie. *Islam: An Introduction*. Albany, NY: State University of New York Press, 1992.

Sciolino, Elaine. *Persian Mirrors: The Elusive Face of Iran*. New York, NY: The Free Press, 2000.

Shafii, Rouhi. *Scent of Saffron: Three Generations of an Iranian Family*. London, England: Scarlet Press, 1997.

Shirley, Edward. *Know Thine Enemy: A Spy's Journey into Revolutionary Iran*. New York, NY: Farrar, Straus and Giroux, 1997.

Simpson, John. *Behind Iranian Lines: Travels Through Revolutionary Iran and the Persian Past.* London, England: Robson Books, 1988.

Simpson, John, and Tira Shubart. *Lifting the Veil: Life in Revolutionary Iran.* London, England: Hodder & Stoughton, 1995.

Souresrafil, Omid. *The Islamic Success: The Untold Story of the Islamic Revolution of Iran.* Glebe, Australia: Wild & Woolley, 1996.

Stark, Freya. *The Valleys of the Assassins.* London, England: Wyman & Sons, Ltd., 1947.

Stevens, Roger. *The Land of the Great Sophy.* London, England: Methuen & Co. Ltd., 1971.

Waterfield, Robin E. *Christians in Persia.* London, England: George Allen & Unwin Ltd., 1973.

Wilbur, Donald N. *Iran Past and Present.* Princeton, NJ: Princeton University Press, 1976.

Wright, Robin. *In the Name of God: The Khomeini Decade.* New York, NY: Simon & Schuster, 1989.

Wright, Robin. *The Last Great Revolution: Turmoil and Transformation in Iran.* New York, NY: Alfred A. Knopf, 2000.

Yarshater, Ehsan, ed. *Encyclopedia Iranica.* Boston, MA: Routledge & Kegan Paul, 1985 (vol. I); New York, NY: Routledge & Kegan Paul, 1987 (vol. II), 1989 (vol. III), 1990 (vol. IV); Costa Mesa, CA: Mazda Publishers, 1992 (vol. V), 1993 (vol. VI), 1996 (vol. VII), 1998 (vol. VIII); New York, NY: Bibliotheca Persica Press, 1998–99 (vol. IX).

W9-ANA-853

BY LISA GARDNER

LOVE YOU MORE

LOVE
YOU MORE

A Novel

LISA GARDNER

DOUBLEDAY LARGE PRINT HOME LIBRARY EDITION

BANTAM BOOKS
NEW YORK

Published in the United States by Bantam Books, an imprint of The Random House Publishing Group, a division of Random House, Inc., New York.

BANTAM BOOKS and the rooster colophon are registered trademarks of Random House, Inc.

ISBN 978-1-61129-295-4

Printed in the United States of America

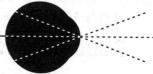

This Large Print Book carries the
Seal of Approval of N.A.V.H.

LOVE YOU MORE

PROLOGUE

Who do you love?

It's a question anyone should be able to answer. A question that defines a life, creates a future, guides most minutes of one's days. Simple, elegant, encompassing.

Who do you love?

He asked the question, and I felt the answer in the weight of my duty belt, the constrictive confines of my armored vest, the tight brim of my trooper's hat, pulled low over my brow. I reached down slowly, my fingers just brushing the top of my Sig Sauer, holstered at my hip.

"Who do you love?" he cried again, louder now, more insistent.

My fingers bypassed my state-issued weapon, finding the black leather keeper that held my duty belt to my waist. The Velcro rasped loudly as I unfastened the first band, then the second, third, fourth. I worked the metal buckle, then my twenty pound duty belt, complete with my sidearm, Taser, and collapsible steel baton released from my waist and dangled in the space between us.

"Don't do this," I whispered, one last shot at reason.

He merely smiled. "Too little, too late."

"Where's Sophie? What did you do?"

"Belt. On the table. Now."

"No."

"GUN. On the table. NOW!"

In response, I widened my stance, squaring off in the middle of the kitchen, duty belt still suspended from my left hand. Four years of my life, patrolling the highways of Massachusetts, swearing to defend and protect. I had training and experience on my side.

I could go for my gun. Commit to the

act, grab the Sig Sauer, and start shoot-ing.

Sig Sauer was holstered at an awk-ward angle that would cost me precious seconds. He was watching, waiting for any sudden movement. Failure would be firmly and terribly punished.

Who do you love?

He was right. That's what it came down to in the end. Who did you love and how much would you risk for them?

"GUN!" he boomed. "Now, dammit!"

I thought of my six-year-old daughter, the scent of her hair, the feel of her skinny arms wrapped tight around my neck, the sound of her voice as I tucked her in bed each night. "Love you, Mommy," she always whispered.

Love you, too, baby. Love you.

His arm moved, first tentative stretch for the suspended duty belt, my hol-stered weapon.

One last chance . . .

I looked my husband in the eye. A sin-gle heartbeat of time.

Who do you love?

I made my decision. I set down my trooper's belt on the kitchen table.

And he grabbed my Sig Sauer and opened fire.

1

Sergeant Detective D. D. Warren prided herself on her excellent investigative skills. Having served over a dozen years with the Boston PD, she believed working a homicide scene wasn't simply a matter of walking the walk or talking the talk, but rather of total sensory immersion. She felt the smooth hole bored into Sheetrock by a hot spiraling twenty-two. She listened for the sound of neighbors gossiping on the other side of thin walls because if she could hear them, then they'd definitely heard the big bad that had just happened here.

D.D. always noted how a body had fallen, whether it was forward or backward or slightly to one side. She tasted the air for the acrid flavor of gunpowder, which could linger for a good twenty to thirty minutes after the final shot. And, on more than one occasion, she had estimated time of death based on the scent of blood—which, like fresh meat, started out relatively mild but took on heavier, earthier tones with each passing hour.

Today, however, she wasn't going to do any of those things. Today, she was spending a lazy Sunday morning dressed in gray sweats and Alex's oversized red flannel shirt. She was camped at his kitchen table, clutching a thick clay coffee mug while counting slowly to twenty.

She'd hit thirteen. Alex had finally made it to the front door. Now he paused to wind a deep blue scarf around his neck.

She counted to fifteen.

He finished with the scarf. Moved on to a black wool hat and lined leather gloves. The temperature outside had just crept above twenty. Eight inches of snow on the ground and six more fore-casted to arrive by end of the week. March didn't mean spring in New En-gland.

Alex taught crime-scene analysis, among other things, at the Police Acad-emy. Today was a full slate of classes. Tomorrow, they both had the day off, which didn't happen much and war-ranted some kind of fun activity yet to be determined. Maybe ice skating in the Boston Commons. Or a trip to the Is-abelle Stewart Gardner Museum. Or a lazy day where they snuggled on the sofa and watched old movies with a big bowl of buttered popcorn.

D.D.'s hands spasmed on the coffee mug. Okay, no popcorn.

D.D. counted to eighteen, nineteen, twent—

Alex finished with his gloves, picked up his battered black leather tote, and crossed to her.

"Don't miss me too much," he said.

He kissed her on the forehead. D.D. closed her eyes, mentally recited the number twenty, then started counting back down to zero.

"I'll write you love letters all day, with little hearts over the 'i's," she said.

"In your high school binder?"

"Something like that."

Alex stepped back. D.D. hit fourteen. Her mug trembled, but Alex didn't seem to notice. She took a deep breath and soldiered on. *Thirteen, twelve, eleven...*

She and Alex had been dating a little over six months. At that point where she had a whole drawer to call her own in his tiny ranch, and he had a sliver of closet space in her North End condo. When he was teaching, it was easier for them to be here. When she was working, it was easier to be in Boston. They didn't have a set schedule. That would imply planning and further solidify a relationship they were both careful to not overly define.

They enjoyed each other's company. Alex respected her crazy schedule as a homicide detective. She respected his culinary skills as a third-generation Italian. From what she could tell, they looked forward to the nights when they could get together, but survived the nights when they didn't. They were two independent-minded adults. She'd just hit forty, Alex had crossed that line a few years back. Hardly blushing teens whose every waking moment was consumed with thoughts of each other. Alex had been married before. D.D. simply knew better.

She lived to work, which other people found unhealthy, but what the hell. It had gotten her this far.

Nine, eight, seven . . .

Alex opened the front door, squaring his shoulders against the bitter morning. A blast of chilled air shot across the small foyer, hitting D.D.'s cheeks. She shivered, clutched the mug more tightly.

"Love you," Alex said, stepping across the threshold.

"Love you, too."

Alex closed the door. D.D. made it down the hall just in time to vomit.

Ten minutes later, she remained sprawled on the bathroom floor. The decorative tiles were from the seventies, dozens and dozens of tiny beige, brown, and harvest gold squares. Looking at them made her want to puke all over again. Counting them, however, was a pretty decent meditative exercise. She inventoried tiles while she waited for her flushed cheeks to cool and her cramped stomach to untangle.

Her cellphone rang. She eyed it on the floor, not terribly interested, given the circumstances. But then she noted the caller and decided to take pity on him.

"What?" she demanded, her usual greeting for former lover and currently married Massachusetts State Police Detective Bobby Dodge.

"I don't have much time. Listen sharp."

"I'm not on deck," she said automatically. "New cases go to Jim Dunwell. Pester him." Then she frowned. Bobby couldn't be calling her about a case. As a city cop, she took her orders from the Boston turret, not state police detectives.

Bobby continued as if she'd never

spoken: "It's a fuckup, but I'm pretty sure it's *our* fuckup, so I need you to listen. Stars and stripes are next door, media across the street. Come in from the back street. Take your time, notice *everything*. I've already lost vantage point, and trust me, D.D., on this one, you and I can't afford to miss a thing."

D.D.'s frown deepened. "What the hell, Bobby? I have no idea what you're talking about, not to mention it's my day off."

"Not anymore. BPD is gonna want a woman to front this one, while the state is gonna demand their own skin in the game, preferably a former trooper. The brass's call, our heads on the block."

She heard a fresh noise now, from the bedroom. Her pager, chiming away. Crap. She was being called in, meaning whatever Bobby was babbling about had merit. She pulled herself to standing, though her legs trembled and she thought she might puke again. She took the first step through sheer force of will and the rest was easier after that. She headed for the bedroom, a detective who'd lost days off before and would again.

"What do I need to know?" she asked, voice crisper now, phone tucked against her shoulder.

"Snow," Bobby muttered. "On the ground, trees, windows . . . hell. We got cops tramping everywhere—"

"Get 'em out! If it's my fucking scene, get 'em all out."

She found her pager on the bedside table—yep, call out from Boston operations—and began shucking her gray sweatpants.

"They're out of the house. Trust me, even the bosses know better than to contaminate a homicide scene. But we didn't know the girl was missing. The uniforms sealed off the house, but left the yard fair play. And now the grounds are trampled, and I can't get vantage point. We need vantage point."

D.D. had sweats off, went to work on Alex's flannel shirt.

"Who's dead?"

"Forty-two-year-old white male."

"Who's missing?"

"Six-year-old white female."

"Got a suspect?"

Long, long pause now.

"Get here," Bobby said curtly. "You and me, D.D. Our case. Our headache. We gotta work this one quick."

He clicked off. D.D. scowled at the phone, then tossed it on the bed to finish pulling on her white dress shirt.

Okay. Homicide with a missing child. State police already on-site, but Boston jurisdiction. Why the hell would the state police—

Then, fine detective that she was, D.D. finally connected the dots.

"Ah shit!"

D.D. wasn't nauseous anymore. She was pissed off.

She grabbed her pager, her creds, and her winter jacket. Then, Bobby's instructions ringing in her head, she prepared to ambush her own crime scene.

2

Who do you love?

    I met Brian at a Fourth of July cookout. Shane's house. The kind of social invite I generally refused, but lately had realized I needed to reconsider. If not for my own sake, then for Sophie's.

    The party wasn't that large. Maybe thirty people or so, other state troopers and families from Shane's neighborhood. The lieutenant colonel had made an appearance, a small coup for Shane. Mostly, however, the cookout attracted other uniformed officers. I saw four guys from the barracks standing by the grill, nursing beers and harassing Shane as he fussed over the latest batch of brats. In front of them were two picnic tables, already dominated by laughing wives who were mixing up batches of margaritas in between tending various children.

Other people lingered in the house, prepping pasta salads, catching the last few minutes of the game. Chitchatting away as they took a bite of this, a drink of that. People, doing what people do on a sunny Saturday afternoon.

I stood beneath the shade of an old oak tree. At Sophie's request, I was wearing an orange-flowered sundress and my single dressy pair of gold sparkling flip-flops. I still stood with my feet slightly apart, elbows tight to my unarmed sides, back to the tree. You can take the girl out of the job, but not the job out of the girl.

I should mingle, but didn't know where to start. Take a seat with the ladies, none of whom I knew, or head to where I would be more comfortable, hanging with the guys? I rarely fit in with the wives and couldn't afford to look like

I was having fun with the husbands—
then the wives would stop laughing and
shoot daggers at me.

So I stood apart, holding a beer I'd
never drink as I waited for the event to
wind down to a point where I could politely depart.

Mostly, I watched my daughter.

A hundred yards away, she giggled
ecstatically as she rolled down a grassy
knoll with half a dozen other kids. Her
hot pink sundress was already lawn-
stained and she had chocolate chip
cookie smeared across her cheek.
When she popped up at the bottom of
the hill, she grabbed the hand of the little girl next to her and they chugged
back up as fast as their three-year-old
legs could carry them.

Sophie always made friends instantly.
Physically, she looked like me. Person-
ality-wise, she was completely her own
child. Outgoing, bold, adventurous. If
she had her way, Sophie would spend
every waking moment surrounded by
people. Maybe charm was a dominant
gene, inherited from her father, because
she certainly didn't get it from me.

She and the other toddler arrived at the top of the hill. Sophie lay down first, her short dark hair contrasting deeply against a patch of yellow dandelions. Then, a flash of chubby arms and flailing legs as she started to roll, her giggles pealing against the vast blue sky.

She stood up dizzily at the bottom and caught me watching her.

"Love you, Mommy!" she cried, and dashed back up the hill.

I watched her run away and wished, not for the first time, that I didn't have to know all the things a woman like me had to know.

"Hello."

A man had peeled off from the crowd, making his approach. Late-thirties, five ten, hundred and eighty, buzz-cut blonde hair, heavily muscled shoulders. Maybe another cop, given the venue, but I didn't recognize him.

He held out his hand. Belatedly, I offered my own.

"Brian," he said. "Brian Darby." He

jerked his head toward the house. "I live down the street. You?"

"Umm. Tessa. Tessa Leoni. I know Shane from the barracks."

I waited for the inevitable comments men made when meeting a female officer. *A cop? I'd better be on good behavior, then.* Or, *Ooooh, where's your gun?*

And those were the nice guys.

Brian, however, just nodded. He was holding a Bud Light in one hand. He tucked his other hand in the pocket of his tan shorts. He wore a blue collared shirt with a gold emblem on the pocket, but I couldn't make it out from this angle.

"Got a confession," he said.

I braced myself.

"Shane told me who you were. Though, to give me some credit, I asked first. Pretty woman, standing alone. Seemed smart to do a little recon."

"What did Shane say?"

"He assured me that you're totally out of my league. Naturally, I took the bait."

"Shane's full of shit," I offered.

"Most of the time. You're not drinking your beer."

I looked down, as if noticing the bottle for the first time.

"Part of my recon," Brian continued easily. "You're holding a beer, but not drinking it. Would you prefer a margarita? I could get you one. Though," he eyed the gaggle of wives, who were well into the third pitcher and laughing accordingly, "I'm a little afraid."

"It's okay." I loosened my stance, shook out my arms. "I don't really drink."

"On call?"

"Not today."

"I'm not a cop, so I won't pretend to know the life, but I've been hanging out with Shane a good five years now, so I like to think I understand the basics. Being a trooper is way more than patrolling highways and writing tickets. Ain't that right, Shane?" Brian boomed his voice, letting the common lament of any state trooper carry over the patio. At the grill, Shane responded by raising his right hand and flipping off his neighbor.

"Shane's a whiner," I said, letting my voice carry, as well.

Shane flipped me off, too. Several of the guys laughed.

"How long have you been working with him?" Brian asked me.

"A year. I'm a rookie."

"Really? What made you want to be a cop?"

I shrugged, uncomfortable again. One of those questions everyone asked and I never knew how to answer. "Seemed like a good idea at the time."

"I'm a merchant marine," Brian offered up. "I work on oil tankers. We ship out a couple of months, then are home a couple of months, then out a couple of months. Screws with the personal life, but I like the work. Never boring."

"A merchant marine? What do you do . . . protect against pirates, things like that?"

"Nah. We run from Puget Sound up to Alaska and back. Not too many Somali pirates patrolling that corridor. Plus, I'm an engineer. My job's to keep the ship running. I like wires and gears and rotors. Guns, on the other hand, scare the crap out of me."

"I don't care for them much myself."

"Funny comment, coming from a police officer."

"Not really."

My gaze had returned automatically to Sophie, checking in. Brian followed my line of sight. "Shane said you had a three-year-old. Holey moley, she looks just like you. No taking the wrong kid home from this party."

"Shane said I had a kid, and you still took the bait?"

He shrugged. "Kids are cool. I don't have any, but that doesn't mean I'm morally opposed. Father in the picture?" he added casually.

"No."

He didn't look smug at that news, more like contemplative. "That's gotta be tough. Being a full-time cop and raising a child."

"We get by."

"Not doubting you. My father died when I was young. Left my mother to raise five kids on her own. We got by, too, and I respect the hell out of her for it."

"What happened to your father?"

"Heart attack. What happened to her

father?" He nodded toward Sophie, who now appeared to be playing tag.

"Better offer."

"Men are stupid," he muttered, sounding so sincere that I finally laughed. He flushed. "Did I mention I have four sisters? These are the things that happen when you have four sisters. Plus, I have to respect my mom twice as much because not only did she survive being a single mother, but she survived being a single mother with four girls. And I never saw her drink anything stronger than herbal tea. How about them apples?"

"She sounds like a rock," I agreed.

"Since you don't drink, maybe you're also an herbal tea kind of gal?"

"Coffee."

"Ah, my personal drug of choice." He looked me in the eye. "So, Tessa, maybe some afternoon, I could buy you a cup. Your neighborhood or my neighborhood, just let me know."

I studied Brian Darby again. Warm brown eyes, easygoing smile, solidly built shoulders.

"Okay," I heard myself say. "I would like that."

Do you believe in love at first sight? I don't. I'm too studied, too cautious for such nonsense. Or maybe, I simply know better.

I met Brian for coffee. I learned that when he was home, his time was his own. It made it easy to hike together in the afternoons, after I'd recovered from the graveyard shift and before I picked up Sophie from daycare at five. Then we caught a Red Sox game on my night off, and before I knew it, he was joining Sophie and me for a picnic.

Sophie did fall in love at first sight. In a matter of seconds, she'd climbed onto Brian's back and demanded giddyup. Brian obediently galloped his way across the park with a squealing three-year-old clutching his hair and yelling "Faster!" at the top of her lungs. When they were done, Brian collapsed on the picnic blanket while Sophie toddled off to pick dandelions. I assumed the flowers were for me, but she turned to Brian instead.

Brian accepted the dandelions tentatively at first, then positively beaming when he realized the entire wilted bouquet was just for him.

It became easy, after that, to spend the weekends at his house with a real yard, versus my cramped one-bedroom apartment. We would cook dinner together, while Sophie ran around with his dog, an aging German shepherd named Duke. Brian bought a plastic kiddy pool for the deck, hung a toddler's swing from the old oak tree.

One weekend when I got jammed up, he came over and stocked my fridge to get Sophie and me through the week. And one afternoon, after I'd worked a motor vehicle accident that left three kids dead, he read to Sophie while I stared at the bedroom wall and fought to get my head on straight.

Later I sat curled up against him on the couch and he told me stories of his four sisters, including the time they'd found him napping on the sofa and covered him in makeup. He'd spent two hours biking around the neighborhood in glittering blue eye shadow and hot pink lipstick before he happened to catch his reflection in a window. I laughed. Then I cried. Then he held me tighter and we both said nothing at all.

Summer slid away. Fall arrived, and just like that, it was time for him to ship out. He'd be gone eight weeks, back in time for Thanksgiving, he assured me. He had a good friend who always looked after Duke. But, if we wanted . . .

He handed me the key to his house. We could stay. Even girl the place up if we wanted to. Maybe some pink paint in the second bedroom, for Sophie. Couple of prints on the wall. Princess rubber duckies in the bathroom. Whatever it took to make us comfortable.

I kissed his cheek, returned the key to the palm of his hand.

Sophie and I were fine. Always had been, always would be. See you in eight weeks.

Sophie, on the other hand, cried and cried and cried.

Couple of months, I tried to tell her.

Hardly any time at all. Just a matter of weeks.

Life was duller with Brian gone. An endless grind of getting up at one p.m., retrieving Sophie from daycare by five, entertaining her until her bedtime at nine, with Mrs. Ennis arriving at ten so I could patrol from eleven to seven. The life of a single working mom. Struggling to stretch a dime into a dollar, cramming endless errands into an already over-scheduled day, fighting to keep my bosses happy while still meeting my young daughter's needs.

I could handle it, I reminded myself. I was tough. I'd gotten through my pregnancy alone, I'd given birth alone. I'd endured twenty-five long, lonely weeks at the live-in Police Academy, missing Sophie with every breath I took but determined not to quit because becoming a state police officer was the best shot I had to provide a future for my daughter. I'd been allowed to return home to Sophie every Friday night, but I also had to leave her crying with Mrs. Ennis every Monday morning. Week after week after week, until I thought I'd scream from the pressure. But I did it. Anything for Sophie. Always for Sophie.

Still, I started checking e-mail more often because if Brian was in port he'd send us a quick note, or attach a silly picture of a moose in the middle of some Alaskan main street. By the sixth week, I realized I was happier the days he e-mailed, tenser the days he didn't. And Sophie was, too. We huddled together over the computer each night, two pretty girls waiting to hear from their man.

Then finally, the call. Brian's ship had docked in Ferndale, Washington. He'd be discharged the day after tomorrow, and would be catching the red-eye back to Boston. Could he take us to dinner?

Sophie selected her favorite dark blue dress. I wore the orange sundress from the Fourth of July cookout, topped with a sweater in deference to the November chill.

Sophie, keeping lookout from the front window, spotted him first. She squealed in delight and raced down the apartment steps so fast I thought she'd fall. Brian barely caught her at the end of the walk. He scooped her up, whirled her around. She laughed and laughed and laughed.

I approached more quietly, taking the time for a last minute tuck of my hair, buttoning my light sweater. I stepped through the front door of the apartment complex. Shut it firmly behind me.

Then I turned and studied him. Took him in from eight feet away. Drank him up.

Brian stopped twirling Sophie. Now he stood at the end of the walk, my child still in his arms, and he studied me, too.

We didn't touch. We didn't say a word. We didn't have to.

Later, after dinner, after he brought us back to his place, after I tucked Sophie into the bed across the hall, I walked into his bedroom. I stood before him, and let him peel the sweater from my arms, the sundress from my body. I placed my hands against his bare chest. I tasted the salt on the column of his throat.

"Eight weeks was too long," he muttered thickly. "I want you here, Tessa. Dammit, I want to know I'm coming home to you always."

I placed his hands upon my breasts, arching into the feel of his fingers.

"Marry me," he whispered. "I mean it, Tessa. I want you to be my wife. I want Sophie to be my daughter. You and her should be living here with me and Duke. We should be a family."

I tasted his skin again. Slid my hands down his body, pressed the full length of my bare skin against his bare skin. Shivered at the contact. Except it wasn't enough. The feel of him, the taste of him. I needed him against me, I needed him above me, I needed him inside me. I needed him everywhere, right now, this instant.

I dragged him down to the bed, wrapping my legs around his waist. Then he was sliding inside my body and I groaned, or maybe he groaned, but it didn't really matter. He was where I needed him to be.

At the last moment, I caught his face between my hands so I could look into his eyes as the first wave crashed over us.

"Marry me," he repeated. "I'll be a good husband, Tessa. I'll take care of you and Sophie."

He moved inside of me and I said: "Yes."

3

Brian Darby died in his kitchen. Three shots, tightly clustered midtorso. D.D.'s first thought was that Trooper Leoni must've taken her firearms training seriously, because the grouping was text-book perfect. As new recruits learned at the Academy—never go for the head and never shoot to wound. Torso is the high percentage shot and if you're discharging your weapon, you'd better be in fear for your life or someone else's, meaning you're shooting to kill.

Leoni had gotten the job done. Now, what the hell had happened to drive a state trooper to shoot her husband? And where was the kid?

Currently, Trooper Leoni was sequestered in the front sunroom, being tended by EMTs for an ugly gash in her forehead and even uglier black eye. Her union rep was already with her, a lawyer on his way.

A dozen other state troopers had closed ranks outside, standing stiff-legged on the sidewalk where they could give their Boston colleagues working the scene, and the overexcited press reporting the scene, thousand-yard stares.

That left most of the Boston brass and most of the state police brass to squabble amongst themselves in the white command van now parked at the elementary school next door. The homicide unit supervisor from the Suffolk County DA was presumably playing referee, no doubt reminding the Massachusetts State Police superintendent that the state really couldn't oversee an investigation involving one of its own officers, while also reminding the commissioner of Boston Police that the state's request for a state police liaison was perfectly reasonable.

In between bouts of marking turf, the head muckety-mucks had managed to issue an Amber Alert for six-year-old Sophie Leoni, brown hair, blue eyes, approximately forty-six inches tall, weighing forty-five pounds, and missing her top two front teeth. Most likely wearing a pink, long-sleeved pajama set dotted with yellow horses. Last seen around ten-thirty the previous evening, when Trooper Leoni had allegedly checked on her daughter before reporting for her eleven p.m. patrol shift.

D.D. had a lot of questions for Trooper Tessa Leoni. Unfortunately, she did not have access: Trooper Leoni was in shock, the union rep had squawked. Trooper Leoni required immediate medical attention. Trooper Leoni was entitled to appropriate legal counsel. She had already provided an initial statement to the first responder. All other questions would have to wait until her attorney deemed appropriate.

Trooper Leoni had a lot of needs, D.D. thought. Shouldn't one of those include working with the Boston cops to find her kid?

For the moment, D.D. had backed off. Scene this busy, there were plenty of other matters that required her immediate attention. She had Boston district detectives swarming the scene, Boston homicide detectives working the evidence, various uniformed officers canvassing the neighborhood, and—given that Trooper Leoni had shot her husband with her service Sig Sauer—the firearms discharge investigation team had been automatically dispatched, flooding the small property with even more miscellaneous police personnel.

Bobby had been right—in official lingo, this case was a clusterfuck.

And it was all hers.

D.D. had arrived thirty minutes ago. She'd parked six blocks away, on bustling Washington Street versus a quieter side street. Allston-Brighton was one of the most densely populated neighborhoods in Boston. Filled to the brim with students from Boston College, Boston University, and Harvard Business School, the area was dominated by academics, young families, and support staff. Expensive place to live, which was ironic given that college students and academics rarely had any money. End result was street after street of tired, three-story apartment buildings, each carved into more units than the last. Families were piled in, with twenty-four-hour convenience stores and Laundromats sprouting up to meet the continuous demand.

This was the urban jungle in D.D.'s mind. No wrought-iron balustrades or decorative brickwork like Back Bay or Beacon Hill. Here, you paid a fortune for the honor of renting a strictly utilitarian box-like apartment in a strictly utilitarian box-like building. Parking was first come first serve, which meant most of the masses spent half their time cruising for spaces. You fought your way to work, you fought your way home, then ended the day eating a microwavable dinner in a standing room only kitchenette, before falling asleep on the world's smallest futon.

Not a bad area, however, for a state trooper. Easy access to Mass Pike, the main artery bisecting the state. East on the Pike hit I-93, west brought you to 128. Basically, in a matter of minutes, Leoni could access three major hunting grounds for the trooper on patrol. Smart.

D.D. also liked the house, an honest to goodness single-family dwelling plunked down in the thick of Allston-Brighton, with a tidy row of three-story apartment buildings on one side and a sprawling brick elementary school to the other. Thankfully, being Sunday, the school was closed, allowing the current mass of law enforcement to take over the parking lot while sparing them from further drama caused by panicky parents overrunning the scene.

Quiet day in the neighborhood. At least it had been.

Trooper Leoni's vintage two-bedroom bungalow was built into a hillside, white-dormered structure stacked over a red-bricked two-car garage. A single flight of concrete steps led from the street-level sidewalk up to the front door and one of the largest yards D.D. had ever seen in downtown Boston.

Good family home. Just enough space to raise a kid inside, perfect lawn for a dog and a swing set outside. Even now, walking the lot in the dead of winter, D.D. could picture the cookouts, the playdates, the lazy evenings hanging on the back deck.

So many things that could go right in a house like this. So what had gone wrong?

She thought the yard might hold the key. Big, sprawling, and completely unprotected in the midst of population overload.

Cut through the school parking lot, walk onto this property. Emerge from behind four different apartment buildings, walk onto this property. You could access the Leoni residence from the back street, as D.D. had done, or by walking up the concrete steps from the front street, as most of the Massachusetts state police seem to have done. From the back, the front, the right and left, the property was easy to enter and easier to exit.

Something every uniformed officer must have figured out, because instead of studying a pristine sweep of white snow, D.D. was currently looking at the largest collection of boot imprints ever amassed in a quarter acre.

She hunched deeper into her winter field coat and exhaled a frustrated puff of frosty breath. Fucking morons.

Bobby Dodge appeared on the back deck, probably still searching for his vantage point. Given the way he was frowning down at the mucked-up snow, his thoughts mirrored her own. He caught sight of her, adjusted his black brimmed hat against the early March chill, and walked down the deck stairs to the yard.

"Your troopers trampled my crime scene," D.D. called across the way. "I won't forget that."

He shrugged, burying his hands in his black wool coat as he approached. A former sniper, Bobby still moved with the economy of motion that came from spending long hours holding perfectly still. Like a lot of snipers, he was a smaller guy with a tough, sinewy build that matched his hard-planed face. No one would ever describe him as handsome, but plenty of women found him compelling.

Once upon a time, D.D. had been one of those women. They'd started out as lovers, but discovered they worked better as friends. Then, two years ago Bobby had met and married Annabelle Granger. D.D. hadn't taken the wedding well; the birth of their daughter had felt like another blow.

But D.D. had Alex now. Life was on the up. Right?

Bobby came to a halt before her. "Troopers protect lives," he informed her. "Detectives protect evidence."

"Your troopers screwed my scene. I don't forgive. I don't forget."

Bobby finally smiled. "Missed you, too, D.D."

"How's Annabelle?"

"Fine, thanks."

"And the baby?"

"Carina's already crawling. Can barely believe it."

D.D. couldn't either. Crap, they were getting old.

"And Alex?" Bobby asked.

"Good, good." She waved her gloved

hand, done with small talk. "So what d'ya think happened?"

Bobby shrugged again, taking his time answering. While some investigators felt a need to work their homicide scenes, Bobby liked to study his. And while many detectives were prone to jabber, Bobby rarely spoke unless he had something useful to say.

D.D. respected him immensely, but was careful never to tell him that.

"At first blush, it would appear to be a domestic situation," he stated finally. "Husband attacked with a beer bottle, Trooper Leoni defended with her service weapon."

"Got a history of domestic disturbance calls?" D.D. asked.

Bobby shook his head; she nodded in agreement. The lack of calls meant nothing. Cops hated to ask for help, especially from other cops. If Brian Darby had been beating his wife, most likely she'd taken it in silence.

"You know her?" D.D. asked.

"No. I left patrol shortly after she started. She's only been on the force four years."

"Word on the street?"

"Solid officer. Young. Stationed out of the Framingham barracks, working the graveyard shift, then racing home to her kid, so not one to mingle."

"Works *only* the graveyard shift?"

He arched a brow, looking amused. "Scheduling's a competitive world for troopers. Rookies get to spend an entire year on graveyard before they can bid for another time slot. Even then, scheduling is awarded based on seniority. Four-year recruit? My guess is she had another year before she could see daylight."

"And I thought being a detective sucked."

"Boston cops are a bunch of crybabies," Bobby informed her.

"Please, at least we know better than to disturb crime-scene snow."

He grimaced. They resumed their study of the trampled yard.

"How long have they been married?" D.D. asked now.

"Three years."

"So she was already on the force and

she already had the kid when she met him."

Bobby didn't answer, as it wasn't a question.

"In theory, he would've known what he was getting into," D.D. continued out loud, trying to get a preliminary feel for the dynamics of the household. "A wife who'd be gone all night. A little girl who'd require evening and morning care."

"When he was around."

"What do you mean?"

"He worked as a merchant marine." Bobby pulled out a notepad, glanced at a line he'd scribbled. "Shipped out for sixty days at a time. Sixty out, sixty home. One of the guys knew the drill from statements Trooper Leoni had made around the barracks."

D.D. arched a brow. "So wife has a crazy schedule. Husband has a crazier schedule. Interesting. Was he a big guy?" D.D. hadn't lingered over the body, given her tender stomach.

"Five ten; two hundred ten, two hundred twenty pounds," Bobby reported.

"Muscle, not flab. Weight lifter, would be my guess."

"A guy who could pack a punch."

"In contrast, Trooper Leoni's about five four, hundred and twenty pounds. Gives the husband a clear advantage."

D.D. nodded. A trooper had training in hand-to-hand combat, of course. But a smaller female against a larger male was still stacked odds. And a husband, to boot. Plenty of female officers learned on-the-job skills they didn't practice on the home front; Trooper Leoni's black eye wasn't the first D.D. had seen on a female colleague.

"Incident happened when Trooper Leoni first came home from work," Bobby said now. "She was still in uniform."

D.D. arched a brow, let that sink in. "She was wearing her vest?"

"Under her blouse, SOP."

"And her belt?"

"Drew her Sig Sauer straight from the holster."

"Shit." D.D. shook her head. "This is a mess."

Not a question, so again Bobby didn't answer.

The uniform, not to mention the presence of a trooper's duty belt, changed everything. For starters, it meant Trooper Leoni had been wearing her vest at the time of the attack. Even a two hundred and twenty pound male would have a hard time making an impact against an officer's body armor. Second, a trooper's duty belt held plenty of tools other than a Sig Sauer that would've been appropriate for defense. For example, a collapsible steel baton, or police-issued Taser or pepper spray or even the metal handcuffs.

Fundamental to every officer's training was the ability to quickly size up the threat and respond with the appropriate level of force. A subject yells at you, you didn't pull your gun. A subject hits you, you still didn't necessarily pull your weapon.

But Trooper Leoni had.

D.D. was starting to understand why the state union rep was so eager to get Tessa Leoni appropriate legal counsel, and so insistent that she *not* talk to the police.

D.D. sighed, rubbed her forehead. "I don't get it. So battered wife syndrome. He hit her one too many times, she finally cracked and did something about it. That explains his body in the kitchen and her visit with the EMTs in the sunroom. But what about the kid? Where's the girl?"

"Maybe this morning's fight started last night. Stepdad started pounding. Girl fled the scene."

They looked at the snow, where any trace of small footsteps had been thoroughly eradicated.

"Calls went out to the local hospitals?" D.D. asked. "Uniforms are checking with the neighbors?"

"It's a full Amber Alert, and no, we're not stupid."

She stared pointedly at the snow. Bobby shut up.

"What about birth father?" D.D. tried. "If Brian Darby is the stepdad, then where's Sophie's birth father and what does he have to say about all this?"

"No birth father," Bobby reported.

"I believe that's biologically impossible."

"No name listed on the birth certificate, no guy mentioned around the barracks, and no male role model visiting every other weekend." Bobby shrugged. "No birth father."

D.D. frowned. "Because Tessa Leoni didn't want him in the picture, or because he didn't want to be in the picture? And oh yeah, in the last couple of nights, did those dynamics suddenly change?"

Bobby shrugged again.

D.D. pursed her lips, starting to see multiple possibilities. A birth father intent on reclaiming parental rights. Or an overstretched household, trying to juggle two intense careers and one small child. Option A meant the biological father might have kidnapped his own child. Option B meant the stepdad—or birth mother—had beat that child to death.

"Think the girl is dead?" Bobby asked now.

"Hell if I know." D.D. didn't like to think about the girl. A wife shooting her husband, fine. A missing kid . . . This case was gonna suck.

"Can't hide a body in the ground," she considered out loud. "Too frozen for digging. So if the girl *is* dead . . . Most likely her remains have been tucked somewhere inside the house. Garage? Attic? Crawl space? Old freezer?"

Bobby shook his head.

D.D. took his word for it. She hadn't ventured into the house beyond the kitchen and sunroom, but given the number of uniforms currently combing through the eleven hundred square foot space, they should've been able to dismantle the structure board by board.

"I don't think this has anything to do with the birth father," Bobby stated. "If the birth father was back in the picture making noise, those would be the first words out of Tessa Leoni's mouth. *Contact my rat bastard ex-boyfriend, who's been threatening to take my daughter from me.* Leoni's said no such thing—"

"Because the union rep has shut her down."

"Because the union rep doesn't want her to make statements that incriminate herself. Totally fair game, however, to make statements that incriminate others."

Couldn't argue with that logic, D.D. thought. "Fine, forget birth father for a second. Sounds like the current household was dysfunctional enough. To judge by Trooper Leoni's face, Brian Darby is a wife beater. Maybe he hit his stepdaughter, too. She died, Trooper Leoni came home to the body, and they both panicked. Stepfather has done a terrible thing, but Trooper Leoni let him, making her party to the crime. They take the body for a drive and dump it. Then get home, get into a fight, and the stress of the whole situation leads Tessa to snap."

"Trooper Leoni helped dump her own daughter's body," Bobby said, "before returning home and shooting her husband?"

D.D. regarded him squarely. "Make no assumptions, Bobby. You of all people know that."

He didn't say anything, but met her stare.

"I want Trooper Leoni's cruiser," D.D stated.

"I believe the brass is ironing that out."

"His car, too."

"Two thousand and seven GMC Denali. Your squad already has it."

D.D. raised a brow. "Nice car. Merchant mariners make that kind of money?"

"He was an engineer. Engineers always make that kind of money. I don't think Trooper Leoni hurt her own child," Bobby said.

"You don't?"

"Spoke to a couple of the troopers who worked with her. They had nothing but good things to say about her. Loving mom, dedicated to her daughter, yada yada yada."

"Yeah? They also know her husband was using her for a punching bag?"

Bobby didn't say anything right away, which was answer enough. He turned back to the scene. "Could be an abduction," he insisted stubbornly.

"Unfenced lot, bordered by a couple hundred strangers . . ." D.D. shrugged.

"Yeah, if just the six-year-old were missing, I'd absolutely run the perverts up the flagpole. But what are the odds of a stranger creeping into the home the same evening/morning the husband and wife have a fatal argument?"

"Make no assumptions," Bobby repeated, but didn't sound any more convinced than she had.

D.D. resumed studying the churned-up yard, which might have once contained footprints relative to their present discussion and now didn't. She sighed, hating it when good evidence went bad.

"We didn't know," Bobby murmured beside her. "Call came in as an officer in distress. That's what the troopers responded to. Not a homicide scene."

"Who made the call?"

"I'm guessing she made the initial phone call—"

"Tessa Leoni."

"Trooper Leoni. Probably to a buddy in the barracks. The buddy summoned the cavalry and the call was picked up by operations. At that point, most of the troopers responded, with the lieutenant colonel bringing up the rear. Now, once Lieutenant Colonel Hamilton got here—"

"Realized it was less of a crisis, more of a cleanup," D.D. muttered.

"Hamilton did the sensible thing and notified Boston turret, given the jurisdiction."

"While also summoning his own detectives."

"Skin in the game, babe. What can I say?"

"I want transcripts."

"Somehow, as official state police liaison, I have a feeling that will be the first of many things I will fetch for you."

"Yes, state police liaison. Let's talk about that. You're the liaison, I'm the head detective. I take that to mean I call the shots, you run the plays."

"Have you ever worked any other way?"

"Now that you mention it, never. So first task, find me the girl."

"Don't I wish."

"Fine. Second task—get me access to Trooper Leoni."

"Don't I wish," Bobby repeated.

"Come on, you're the state police liaison. Surely she'll talk to the state police liaison."

"Union rep is telling her to shut up. Her lawyer, once he arrives, will most likely second that command. Welcome to the blue wall, D.D."

"But I also wear the fucking uniform!"

Bobby looked pointedly at her heavy field jacket, emblazoned *BPD.* "Not in Trooper Leoni's world."

4

I was on my first solo patrol for all of two hours when I received my debut domestic disturbance call. Incident came from dispatch as a verbal domestic—basically the occupants of apartment 25B were arguing so loudly, their neighbors couldn't sleep. Neighbors got mad, neighbors called the cops.

On the surface, nothing too exciting. Trooper shows up, occupants of 25B shut up. And probably drop a bag of burning dog poo on the neighbor's front stoop the next morning.

But at the Academy they had drilled

into us—there is no such thing as a typical call. Be aware. Be prepared. Be
safe.

I sweated through my dark blue BDUs
all the way to apartment 25B.

New troopers work under the supervision of a senior officer for their first
twelve weeks. After that, we patrol
alone. No wingman for companionship,
no partner to watch your back. Instead,
it's all about dispatch. Second you're in
your cruiser, second you exit your vehicle, second you stop for a cup of coffee,
second you pull over to pee, you tell dispatch all about it. Operations is your
lifeline and when something goes
wrong, it's operations that will send the
cavalry—your fellow state troopers—to
the rescue.

In the classroom, this had sounded
like a plan. But at one in the morning,
getting out of my cruiser in a neighborhood I didn't know, approaching a
building I'd never seen, to confront two
people I'd never met, it was easy to
consider other facts, too. For example,
while there are approximately seventeen
hundred state troopers, only six hun-

dred or so are on patrol at the same time. And these six hundred troopers are covering the entire state of Massachusetts. Meaning we're spread out all over the place. Meaning that when things go wrong, it's not a five-minute fix.

We're all one big family, but we're still very much alone.

I approached the building as I had been trained, my elbows glued to my waist to protect my service weapon, my body turned slightly to the side to form a smaller target. I angled away from the windows and kept to one side of the door, where I would be out of direct line of fire.

The most frequent call out received by a uniformed officer is situation unknown. At the Academy, we were advised to treat all calls like that. Danger is everywhere. All people are suspect. All suspects are liars.

This is the way you work. For some officers, this also becomes the way they live.

I mounted three steps to a tiny front stoop, then paused to take a deep breath. Command presence. I was twenty-three years old, average height and unfortunately pretty. Chances were, whoever opened that door was going to be older than me, bigger than me, and rougher than me. Still my job to control the situation. Feet wide. Shoulders back. Chin up. As the other rookies liked to joke, never let 'em see you sweat.

I stood to the side. I knocked. Then I quickly threaded my thumbs into the waistband of my dark blue pants, so my hands couldn't tremble.

No sounds of disturbance. No sounds of footsteps. Lights blazed, however; the occupants of 25B were not asleep.

I knocked again. Harder this time.

No sound of movement, no sign of the residents.

I fidgeted with my duty belt, debated my options. I had a call, a call required a report, a report required contact. So I drew myself up taller and knocked *hard*. *BAM. BAM. BAM.* Pounded my knuckles against the cheap wooden door. I was a state trooper, dammit, and I would not be ignored.

This time, footsteps.

Thirty seconds later, the door silently swung open.

The female occupant of unit 25B did not look at me. She stared at the floor as the blood poured down her face.

As I learned that night, and many nights since, the basic steps for handling domestic violence remain the same.

First, the officer secures the scene, a swift, preliminary inspection to identify and eliminate any potential threats.

Who else is in the home, Officer? May I walk through the house? Trooper, is that your weapon? I'm going to need to take your firearm, Trooper. Are there any other guns on the property? I'm also going to need your duty belt. Unhook it, easy . . . Thank you. I'm going to request that you remove your vest. Do you require assistance? Thank you. I will take that now. I need you to move into the sunroom. Have a seat right here. Stay put. I'll be back.

Scene secured, the officer now inspects the female party for signs of injury. At this stage, the officer makes no assumption. The individual is neither a suspect nor a victim. She is simply an injured party and is handled accordingly.

Female presents with bloody lip, black eye, red marks on throat, and bloody laceration high on right forehead.

Many battered women will argue that they're okay. Don't need no ambulance. Just get the hell out and leave 'em alone. Be all better by morning.

The well-trained officer ignores such statements. There is evidence of a crime, triggering the larger wheels of criminal justice into motion. Maybe the battered woman is the victim, as she claims, and will ultimately refuse to press charges. But maybe she is the instigator—maybe the injuries were sustained while the female beat the crap out of an unknown party, meaning she is the perpetrator of a crime and her injuries and statement need to be documented for the charges that will soon be filed by that unknown party. Again, make no assumptions. The trooper will alert dispatch of the situation, request backup and summon the EMTs.

Other bodies will now start to arrive. Uniforms. Medical personnel. Sirens will sound in the horizon, official vehicles pouring down the narrow funnel of city streets while the neighbors gather outside to catch the show.

The scene will become a very busy place, making it even more important for the first responder to document, document, document. The trooper will now conduct a more detailed visual inspection of the scene, making notes and snapping initial photographs.

Dead male, late-thirties, appears to be five ten, two hundred ten to two hundred twenty pounds. Three GSWs mid-torso. Discovered faceup two feet to the left of the table in the kitchen.

Two wooden kitchen chairs toppled. Remnants of broken green glass under chairs. One shattered green bottle—labeled Heineken—located six inches to the left of the table in the kitchen.

Sig Sauer semiauto discovered on top of forty-two inch round wooden table. Officer removed cartridge and emptied chamber. Bagged and tagged.

Family room cleared.

Upstairs two bedrooms and bath cleared.

More uniforms will assist, questioning neighbors, securing the perimeter. The female party will remain sequestered away from the action, where she will now be tended by the medical personnel.

Female EMT, checking my pulse, gently probing my eye socket and cheekbone for signs of fracture. Asking me to remove my ponytail so she can better tend my forehead. Using tweezers to remove the first piece of green glass which will later be matched to the shattered beer bottle.

"How do you feel, ma'am?"

"Head hurts."

"Do you have any recollection of blacking out or losing consciousness?"

"Head hurts."

"Do you feel nauseous?"

"Yes." Stomach rolling. Trying to hold it together, against the pain, the confusion, the growing disorientation that this can't be happening, shouldn't be happening . . .

The EMT further examining my head,

finding the growing lump at the back of my skull.

"What happened to your head, ma'am?"

"What?"

"The back of your head, ma'am. Are you sure you didn't lose consciousness, take a fall?"

Me, looking at the EMT blankly. "Who do you love?" I whisper.

The EMT does not reply.

Next up, taking an initial statement. A good trooper will note both what the subject says and *how* she says it. People in a genuine state of shock have a tendency to babble, offering fragments of information but unable to string together a coherent whole. Some victims disassociate. They speak in flat, clipped tones about an event that in their own minds already didn't happen to them. Then there are the professional liars—the ones who pretend to babble or disassociate.

Any liar will sooner or later overreach. Add a little too much detail. Sound a bit too composed. Then the well-trained investigator can pounce.

"Can you tell me what happened here, Trooper Leoni?" A Boston district detective takes the first pass. He is older, hair graying at the temples. He sounds kind, going for the collegial approach.

I don't want to answer. I have to answer. Better the district detective than the homicide investigator who will follow. My head throbs, my temples, my cheek. My face is on fire.

Want to throw up. Fighting the sensation.

"My husband . . ." I whisper. My gaze drops automatically to the floor. I catch my mistake, force myself to look up, meet the district detective's eye. *"Sometimes . . . when I worked late. My husband grew angry."* Pause. My voice, growing stronger, more definite. *"He hit me."*

"Where did he hit you, Officer?"

"Face. Eye. Cheek." My fingers finding each spot, reliving the pain. Inside my head, I'm stuck in a moment of time. Him, looming above. Me, cowering on the linoleum, genuinely terrified.

"I fell down," I recite for the district

detective. *"My husband picked up a chair."*

Silence. The district detective waiting for me to say more. Spin a lie, tell the truth.

"I didn't hit him," I whisper. I've taken enough of these statements. I know how this story goes. We all do. "If I didn't fight back," I state mechanically, "he'd wear out, go away. If I did . . . It was always worse in the end."

"Your husband picked up a chair, Trooper Leoni? Where were you when he did this?"

"On the floor."

"Where in the house?"

"The kitchen."

"When your husband picked up the chair, what did you do?"

"Nothing."

"What did he do?"

"Threw it."

"Where?"

"At me."

"Did it hit you?"

"I . . . I don't remember."

"Then what happened, Trooper Leoni?" The district detective leaning

down, peering at me more closely. His face is a study of concern. Is my eye contact wrong? My story too detailed? Not detailed enough?

All I want for Christmas is my two front teeth, my two front teeth, my two front teeth.

The song sounds in my head. I want to giggle. I don't.

Love you, Mommy. Love you.

"I threw the chair back at him," I tell the district detective.

"You threw the chair back at him?"

"He got . . . angrier. So I must have done something, right? Because he became angrier."

"Were you in full uniform at this time, Trooper Leoni?"

I meet his eye. "Yes."

"Wearing your duty belt? And your body armor?"

"Yes."

"Did you reach for anything on your duty belt? Take steps to defend your-self?"

Still looking him in the eye. "No."

The detective regards me curiously. "What happened next, Trooper Leoni?"

"He grabbed the beer bottle. Smashed it against my forehead. I . . . I managed to fend him off. He stumbled, toward the table. I fell. Against the wall. My back against the wall. I needed to find the doorway. I needed to get away."

Silence.

"Trooper Leoni?"

"He had the broken bottle," I murmur. "I needed to get away. But . . . trapped. On the floor. Against the wall. Watching him."

"Trooper Leoni?"

"I feared for my life," I whisper. "I felt my sidearm. He charged . . . I feared for my life."

"Trooper Leoni, what happened?"

"I shot my husband."

"Trooper Leoni—"

I meet his gaze one last time. "Then I went looking for my daughter."

5

By the time D.D. and Bobby finished circling around to the front of the property, the EMTs were retrieving a stretcher from the back of the ambulance. D.D. glanced their way, then identified the Boston uniform standing outside the crime-scene tape with the murder book. She approached him first.

"Hey, Officer Fiske. You've logged every single uniform entering this joint?" She gestured to the notebook in his hand, where he was collecting the names of all personnel to cross the crime-scene tape.

"Forty-two officers," he said, without batting an eyelash.

"Jesus. Is there a single cop left on patrol in the greater Boston area?"

"Doubt it," Officer Fiske said. Kid was young and serious. Was it just D.D. or were they getting younger and more serious with each passing year?

"Well, here's the problem, Officer Fiske. While you're collecting names here, other cops are entering and exiting from the rear of the property, and that's really pissing me off."

Officer Fiske's eyes widened.

"Got a buddy?" D.D. continued. "Radio him to grab a notebook, then take up position behind the house. I want names, ranks, and badge numbers, all on record. And while you two are at it, get the word out: Every state trooper who showed up at this address needs to report to Boston HQ by end of day to have an imprint made of his or her boots. Failure to comply will result in immediate desk duty. You heard it straight from the state liaison officer." She jerked her thumb at Bobby, who stood beside her rolling his eyes.

"D.D.—" he started.

"They trampled my scene. I don't forgive. I don't forget."

Bobby shut up. She liked that about him.

Having both secured her scene and stirred the pot, D.D. next approached the EMTs, who now had the stretcher positioned between them and were preparing to climb the steep stairs to the front door.

"Hang on," D.D. called out.

The EMTs, one male, one female, paused as she approached.

"Sergeant Detective D. D. Warren," D.D. introduced herself. "I'm the one in charge of this circus. You getting ready to transport Trooper Leoni?"

A heavyset woman at the head of the stretcher nodded, already turning back toward the stairs.

"Whoa, whoa, whoa," D.D. said quickly. "I need five minutes. Got a couple of questions for Trooper Leoni before she goes on her merry way."

"Trooper Leoni has sustained a significant head wound," the female answered firmly. "We're taking her to the hospital for a CT scan. You got your job, we got ours."

The EMTs took a step closer to the stairs. D.D. moved to intercept.

"Is Trooper Leoni at risk for bleeding out?" D.D. pressed. She glanced at the woman's name tag, adding belatedly, "Marla."

Marla did not appear impressed. "No."

"Is she in any immediate physical danger?"

"Swelling of the brain," the EMT rattled off, "bleeding of the brain . . ."

"Then we'll keep her awake and make her recite her name and date. Isn't that what you guys do for a concussion? Count to five, forward and backward, name, rank, and serial number, yada yada yada."

Beside her, Bobby sighed. D.D. was definitely toeing a line. She kept her attention focused on Marla, who appeared even more exasperated than Bobby.

"Detective—" Marla started.

"Kid missing," D.D. interrupted. "Six-year-old girl, God knows where and in what kind of danger. I just need five minutes, Marla. Maybe that's a lot to ask from you and your job and from Trooper Leoni and her injuries, but I don't think that's nearly enough to ask for a six-year-old child."

D.D. was good. Always had been. Always would be. Marla, who appeared to be mid-forties and probably had at least one or two kids at home, not to mention how many little nieces and nephews, caved.

"Five minutes," she said, glancing over at her partner. "Then we're taking her out, ready or not."

"Ready or not," D.D. agreed, and sprinted for the stairs.

"Eat your Wheaties this morning?" Bobby muttered as he jogged up behind her.

"You're just jealous."

"Why am I jealous?"

"Because I always get away with this shit."

"Pride goeth before the fall," Bobby murmured.

D.D. pushed opened the front door of

the house. "For six-year-old Sophie's sake, let's hope not."

Trooper Leoni was still sequestered in the sunroom. D.D. and Bobby had to pass through the kitchen to get there. Brian Darby's body had been removed, leaving behind bloodstained hardwoods, a pile of evidence placards, and a thick dusting of fingerprint powder. The usual crime-scene detritus. D.D. covered her mouth and nose with her hand as she skirted through. She was still two ·paces ahead of Bobby and hoped he didn't notice.

Tessa Leoni looked up at Bobby and D.D.'s entrance. She held an ice bag against half of her face, which still didn't cover the blood on her lip or the oozing gash in her forehead. As D.D. walked into the sunroom, the female officer lowered the pack to reveal an eye that had already swollen shut and turned eggplant purple.

D.D. suffered a moment of shock, despite herself. Whether she believed Leoni's initial statement or not, the female trooper had definitely taken a beating. D.D. quickly glanced at the officer's hands, trying to ascertain any signs of defensive wounds. Trooper Leoni caught the motion, and covered her knuckles with the ice pack.

For a moment, the two women studied each other. Trooper Leoni seemed young to D.D., especially wearing her state blues. Long dark hair, blue eyes, heart-shaped face. Pretty girl despite the bruises and maybe more vulnerable because of them. Immediately, D.D. felt herself set on edge. Pretty and vulnerable almost always tried her patience.

D.D. surveyed the other two occupants of the room.

Standing beside Leoni was a super-sized state trooper, his shoulders thrown back in his best tough-guy stance. Conversely, sitting across from her, was a petite gray-suited older gentleman with a yellow legal pad balanced delicately on one knee. Union rep standing, D.D. determined. Union-appointed lawyer sitting. So the gang was all here.

The union rep, a fellow state trooper, spoke first.

"Trooper Leoni isn't answering questions," he stated, jutting out his chin.

D.D. glanced at his badge. "Trooper Lyons—"

"She has provided an initial statement," Trooper Lyons continued stiffly. "All other questions will have to wait until she's been treated by a doctor." He glanced behind D.D. to the doorway. "Where are the EMTs?"

"Getting their gear," D.D. said soothingly. "They'll be right up. Of course Trooper Leoni's injuries are a priority. Nothing but the best for a fellow officer."

D.D. moved to the right, making room for Bobby to stand beside her. A united front of city and state law enforcement. Trooper Lyons didn't look impressed.

The lawyer had risen to standing. Now he held out a hand. "Ken Cargill," he said by way of introduction. "I'll be representing Trooper Leoni."

"Sergeant Detective D. D. Warren," D.D. introduced herself, then Bobby.

"My client is not taking questions at this time," Cargill told them. "Once she has received the proper medical attention and we understand the full extent of her injuries, we'll let you know."

"Understand. Not here to push. EMTs said they needed a few minutes to prepare the stretcher, grab some fluids. Thought we could use that time to cover a few basics. We got a full Amber Alert out for little Sophie, but I gotta be honest." D.D. spread her hands in a helpless gesture. "We have no leads. As I'm sure Trooper Leoni knows, in these kinds of cases, every minute counts."

At the mention of Sophie's name, Trooper Leoni stiffened on the sofa. She wasn't looking at D.D., or at any of the men in the room. She had her gaze locked on a spot on the worn green carpet, hands still tucked beneath the ice pack.

"I searched everywhere," Leoni said abruptly. "The house, the garage, the attic, his vehicle—"

"Tessa," Trooper Lyons interjected. "Don't do this. You don't have to do this."

"When was the last time you saw your daughter?" D.D. asked, seizing the opening while she had it.

"Ten forty-five last night," the officer answered automatically, as if speaking by rote. "I always check on Sophie before reporting for duty."

D.D. frowned. "You left here at ten forty-five for your eleven o'clock shift? You can make it from here to the Framingham barracks in fifteen minutes?"

Trooper Leoni shook her head. "I don't drive to the barracks. We drive our cruisers home, so the moment we take the wheel, we start our patrols. I called the desk officer from my cruiser and declared Code 5. He assigned me my patrol area and I was good to go."

D.D. nodded. Not being a state trooper, D.D. didn't know these things. But she was also playing a game with Trooper Leoni. The game was called establish the suspect's state of mind. That way, when Trooper Leoni inevitably said something useful, and her eager-beaver attorney sought to block that admission by claiming his client was suffering from a concussion and therefore mentally incapacitated, D.D. could point out how lucidly Leoni had answered other, easily verifiable questions. For example, if

Leoni had been able to accurately recollect what time she'd called the desk officer, where she'd gone on patrol, etc., etc., then why assume she was suddenly mistaken about how she'd shot her own husband?

These were the kind of games a skilled detective knew how to play. Couple of hours ago, D.D. might not have used them on a fellow officer. She might have been willing to cut poor battered Trooper Leoni some slack, show her the kind of preferential treatment one female officer was inclined to give another. But that was before the state troopers had trampled her crime scene and placed D.D. squarely on the other side of their blue wall.

D.D. did not forgive. She did not forget.

And she did not want to be working a case right now involving a small child. But that was not something she could talk about, not even to Bobby.

"So you checked your daughter at ten forty-five . . ." D.D. prodded.

"Sophie was asleep. I kissed her on

the cheek. She . . . rolled over, pulled the covers up."

"And your husband?"

"Downstairs. Watching TV."

"What was he watching?"

"I didn't notice. He was drinking a beer. That distracted me. I wished . . . I preferred it when he didn't drink."

"How many beers had he had?"

"Three."

"You counted?"

"I checked the empties lined up next to the sink."

"Your husband have a problem with alcohol?" D.D. asked bluntly.

Leoni finally looked up at D.D., peering at her with one good eye, as the other half of her face remained a swollen, pulpy mess. "Brian was home sixty days at a stretch with nothing to do. I had work. Sophie had school. But he had nothing. Sometimes, he drank. And sometimes . . . Drinking wasn't good for him."

"So your husband, who you wished didn't drink, had had three beers and you still left him alone with your daughter."

"Hey—" Trooper Lyons started to interrupt again.

But Tessa Leoni said, "Yes, ma'am. I left my daughter with her drunken stepdad. And if I had known . . . I would've killed him then, goddammit. I would've shot him last night!"

"Whoa—" Attorney was out of the chair. But D.D. didn't pay any attention to him and neither did Leoni.

"What happened to your daughter?" D.D. wanted to know. "What did your husband do to her?"

Leoni was already shrugging her shoulders. "He wouldn't tell me. I got home, went upstairs. She should've been in bed. Or maybe playing on the floor. But . . . nothing. I searched and I searched and I searched. Sophie was gone."

"He ever hit her?" D.D. asked.

"Sometimes, he got frustrated with me. But I never saw him hit her."

"Lonely? You're gone all night. He's alone with her."

"No! You're wrong. I would've known! She would've told me."

"Then you tell me, Tessa. What happened to your daughter?"

"I don't know! Dammit. She's just a little girl. What kind of man hurts a child? What kind of man would *do* such a thing?"

Trooper Lyons placed his hands on her shoulders, as if trying to soothe. Trooper Leoni, however, shrugged him off. She rose to her feet, obviously agitated. The movement, however, proved too much; almost immediately, she lurched to one side.

Trooper Lyons caught her arm, lowering her carefully back to the love seat while skewering D.D. with an angry stare.

"Steady," he said gruffly to Tessa Leoni, while continuing to glare at D.D. and Bobby.

"You don't understand, you don't understand," the mother/trooper was murmuring. She didn't look pretty or vulnerable anymore. Her face had taken on an unhealthy pallor; she looked like she was going to vomit, her hand patting the empty seat beside her. "Sophie's so brave and adventurous. But she's scared of the dark. Terrified. Once, when she was nearly three, she climbed into the trunk of my cruiser and it closed and she screamed and screamed and screamed. If you could've heard her scream. Then you would know, you'd understand. . . ."

Leoni turned to Trooper Lyons. She grabbed his beefy hands, peering up at him desperately. "She's gotta be safe, right? You would keep her safe, right? You would take care of her? Bring her home. Before dark, Shane. Before dark. Please, please, I'm begging you, *please.*"

Lyons didn't seem to know how to respond or handle the outburst. He remained holding Leoni's shoulders, meaning D.D. was the one who grabbed the waste bucket and got it under the ashen-faced woman just in time. Leoni puked until she dry-heaved, then puked a little more.

"My head," she groaned, already sagging back into the love seat.

"Hey, who's disrupting our patient? Anyone who's not an EMT, out!" Marla and her partner had returned. They muscled into the room, Marla giving D.D. a pointed glance. D.D. and Bobby took the hint, turning toward the adjoining kitchen.

But Leoni, of all people, grabbed D.D.'s wrist. The strength in her pale hand startled D.D., brought her up short.

"My daughter needs you," the officer whispered, as the EMTs took her other hand and started administering the IV.

"Of course," D.D. said stupidly.

"You must find her. Promise me!"

"We'll do our best—"

"Promise me!"

"Okay, okay," D.D. heard herself say. "We'll find her. Of course. Just . . . get to the hospital. Take care of yourself."

Marla and her partner moved Leoni to the backboard. The female officer was still thrashing, trying to push them away, trying to pull D.D. closer. It was hard to say. In a matter of seconds, the EMTs had her strapped down and were out the door, Trooper Lyons following stoically in her wake.

The lawyer stayed behind, holding out a card as they stepped from the sunroom back into the home. "I'm sure you understand none of that was admissible. Among other things, my client never waived her rights, and oh yes, she's suffering from a *concussion.*"

Having gotten his say, the lawyer also departed, leaving D.D. and Bobby standing alone next to the kitchen. D.D. didn't have to cover her nose anymore. She was too distracted from the interview with Officer Leoni to notice the smell.

"Is it just me," D.D. said, "or does it look like someone took a meat mallet to Tessa Leoni's face?"

"And yet there's not a single cut or scrape on her hands," Bobby provided. "No broken nails or bruised knuckles."

"So someone beat the shit out of her, and she never lifted a hand to stop it?" D.D. asked skeptically.

"Until she shot him dead," Bobby corrected mildly.

D.D. rolled her eyes, feeling perplexed and not liking it. Tessa Leoni's facial injuries appeared real enough. Her fear over her daughter's disappearance genuine. But the scene . . . the lack of defensive wounds, a trained officer who went first for her gun when she had an entire duty belt at her disposal, a female who'd just given such an emotional statement while studiously avoiding all eye contact . . .

D.D. was deeply uncomfortable with the scene, or maybe, with a fellow female officer who'd grabbed her arm and basically begged D.D. to find her missing child.

Six-year-old Sophie Leoni, who was terrified of the dark.

Oh God. This case was gonna hurt.

"Sounds like she and the husband got into it," Bobby was saying. "He overwhelmed her, knocked her to the floor, so she went for her gun. Only afterward did she discover her daughter missing. And realize, of course, that she'd just killed the only person who could probably tell her where Sophie is."

D.D. nodded, still considering. "Here's a question: What's a trooper's first instinct—to protect herself or to protect others?"

"Protect others."

"And what's a mother's first priority? Protect herself or protect her child?"

"Her child."

"And yet, Trooper Leoni's daughter is missing, and the first thing she does is notify her union rep and find a good lawyer."

"Maybe she's not a very good trooper," Bobby said.

"Maybe, she's not a very good mother," D.D. replied.

6

I fell in love when I was eight years old. Not the way you think. I had climbed the tree in my front yard, taking a seat on the lower branch and staring down at the tiny patch of burnt-out lawn below me. Probably, my father was at work. He owned his own garage, opening up shop by six most mornings and not returning till after five most nights. Probably, my mother was asleep. She passed the days in the hushed darkness of my parents' bedroom. Sometimes, she'd call to me and I'd bring her little things— a glass of water, a couple of crackers.

But mostly, she waited for my father to come home.

He'd fix dinner for all of us, my mother finally shuffling out of her dark abyss to join us at the little round table. She would smile at him, as he passed the potatoes. She would chew mechanically, as he spoke gruffly of his day.

Then, dinner completed, she would return to the shadows at the end of the hall, her daily allotment of energy all used up. I'd wash dishes. My father would watch TV. Nine p.m., lights out. Another day done for the Leoni family.

I learned early on not to invite over classmates. And I learned the importance of being quiet.

Now it was hot, it was July, and I had another endless day stretching out before me. Other kids were probably living it up at summer camp, or splashing away at some community pool. Or maybe, the really lucky ones, had happy, fun parents who took them to the beach.

I sat in a tree.

A girl appeared. Riding a hot pink scooter, blonde braids flapping beneath a deep purple helmet as she flew down the street. At the last moment, she glanced up and spotted my skinny legs. She screeched to a halt beneath me, peering up.

"My name is Juliana Sophia Howe," she said. "I'm new to this neighborhood. You should come down and play with me."

So I did.

Juliana Sophia Howe was also eight years old. Her parents had just moved to Framingham from Harvard, Mass. Her father was an accountant. Her mother stayed home and did things like tend the house and cut the crusts off peanut butter and jelly sandwiches.

By mutual agreement, we always played at Juliana's house. She had a bigger yard, with real grass. She had a Little Mermaid sprinkler head and a Little Mermaid slip and slide. We could play for hours, then her mother would serve us lemonade with pink curly straws and thick slices of red watermelon.

Juliana had an eleven-year-old brother, Thomas, who was a real "pain in the ass." She also had fifteen cousins and tons of aunts and uncles. On the really hot days, her whole family would gather at her grandma's house by the South Shore and they would go to the beach. Sometimes, she got to ride the carousel, and Juliana considered herself an expert on grabbing the brass ring, though she hadn't actually gotten it yet—but she was close.

I didn't have cousins, or aunts and uncles or a grandmother near the South Shore. Instead, I told Juliana how my parents had made a baby when I was four years old. Except the baby was born blue and the doctors had to bury him in the ground, and my mother had to come home from the hospital and move into her bedroom. Sometimes, she cried in the middle of the day. Sometimes, she cried in the middle of the night.

My father told me I was not to talk about it, but one day, I'd found a shoe box tucked behind my father's bowling ball in the hall closet. In the box had been a little blue cap and a little blue blanket and a pair of little blue booties.

There was also a picture of a perfectly white newborn baby boy with bright red lips. At the bottom of the picture, someone had written *Joseph Andrew Leoni.*

So I guess I had a little brother Joey, but he had died and my father had been working and my mother had been crying ever since.

Juliana thought about this. She decided we should have a proper mass for baby Joey, so she got out her rosary beads. She showed me how to loop the dark green beads around my fingers and say a little prayer. Next, we needed to sing a song, so we sang "Away in the Manger," because it was about a baby and we sort of knew the words. Then it was time for the eulogy.

Juliana did the honors. She'd heard one before, at her grandfather's funeral. She thanked the Lord for taking care of baby Joey. She said it was good he did not suffer. She said she was sure he was having a great time playing poker in heaven, and looking down upon us all.

Then, she took both of my hands in her own, and told me she was very sorry for my loss.

I started to cry, big noisy sobs that horrified me. But Juliana just patted my back. There, there, she said. Then she cried with me, and her mom came up to check on us because we were making such a racket. I thought Juliana would tell her mother everything. Instead, Juliana announced that we needed emergency chocolate chip cookies. So her mother went downstairs and made us a batch.

Juliana Sophia Howe was that kind of friend. You could cry on her shoulder and trust her to keep your secrets. You could play in her yard and count on her to give you her best toys. You could stay in her house and depend on her to share her family.

When I went into labor all alone, I pictured Juliana holding my hand. And when I finally held my daughter for the first time, I named her in honor of my childhood friend.

Juliana, unfortunately, doesn't know any of these things.

She has not spoken to me in over ten years.

For while Juliana Sophia Howe was

the best thing that ever happened to me, turned out, I was the worst thing that ever happened to her.

Sometimes, love is like that.

In the back of the ambulance, the female EMT administered intravenous fluids. She had produced a pan just in time for me to vomit again.

My cheek burned. My sinus cavities had filled with blood. I needed to hold it together. Mostly, I wanted to close my eyes and let the world slip away. The light hurt my eyes. The memories seared my brain.

"Tell me your name," the EMT instructed, forcing me back to attention.

I opened my mouth. No words came out.

She offered me a sip of water, helped clean my cracked lips.

"Tessa Leoni," I finally managed.

"What is today's date, Tessa?"

For a second, I couldn't answer. No numbers appeared in my head and I started to panic. All I could picture was Sophie's empty bed.

"March thirteen," I finally whispered.

"Two plus two?"

Another pause. "Four."

Marla grunted, adjusting the line carrying clear fluids to the back of my hand. "Nice shiner," she remarked.

I didn't answer.

"Almost as pretty as the bruise covering half your ass. Husband like steel-toed boots?"

I didn't answer, just pictured my daughter's smiling face.

The ambulance slowed, maybe ready to turn into the emergency room. I could only hope.

Marla studied me a second longer. "I don't get it," she said abruptly. "You're a cop. You've received special training, you've handled these kinds of calls yourself. Surely you of all people oughtta know . . ." She seemed to catch herself. "Well, guess that's the way these things go, right? Domestic violence happens across all social groups. Even those who should know better."

The ambulance came to a stop. Thirty seconds later, the back doors flew open and I rolled into daylight.

I didn't look at Marla anymore. I kept my eyes on the gray March sky rushing past overhead.

Inside the hospital, there was a lot of activity at once. An emergency room nurse charged forward to meet us, ushering us into an exam room. There was paperwork to be filled out, including the omnipresent HEPA form advising me of my right to privacy. As the nurse assured me, my doctor would not discuss my case with anyone, not even other members of law enforcement, as that would violate doctor-patient confidentiality. What she did not say, but I already knew, was that my medical charts were considered neutral and could be subpoenaed by the DA. Meaning any statements I made to the doctor, which were recorded in those charts . . .

Always a loophole somewhere. Just ask a cop.

Paperwork completed, the nurse turned to the next matter at hand.

Last night, I had spent fifteen minutes donning my uniform. First, basic black panties, then a black sports bra, then a silk undershirt to keep the next layer—

heavy body armor—from chafing my skin. I'd rolled on black dress socks, then my navy blue trousers with their electric blue accent stripes. Next I'd laced up my boots, because I'd already learned the hard way I couldn't reach my feet once I'd donned my vest. So socks, trousers, boots, then back to the top half, adding my bulky vest, which I covered with a state police turtleneck in deference to the weather, then topped with my official light blue blouse. I had to adjust the vest under my turtleneck, then work to get three layers—silk undershirt, turtleneck, and blouse—tucked into my pants. Next I belted my slacks with a broad black belt to hold them in place. Then I got my gear.

Twenty pound black leather duty belt, which I wrapped over my pants belt, and attached with four Velcro keepers. Next taking my Sig Sauer semiauto from the gun safe in the bedroom closet and inserting it into the holster on my right hip. Clipping my cellphone to the front of my duty belt, then attaching my police pager to the clip on my right shoulder. Checking my radio on my left hip, inspecting my two extra ammo clips, the steel baton, pepper spray, one pair of cuffs, and Taser. Then slipping three ink pens into the sewn inserts on my left shirtsleeve.

Finally, the pièce de résistance, my official state trooper hat.

I always paused to study my reflection in the mirror. A state trooper's uniform is not just a look, but a feel. The weight of my duty belt pulling at my hips. The bulk of my body armor, flattening out my chest, broadening my shoulders. The tight band of my hat, pulled down low onto my forehead and casting an impenetrable shadow across my eyes.

Command presence. Never let them see you sweat, baby.

The nurse stripped my uniform from me. She removed my light blue blouse, my turtleneck, body armor, undershirt, bra. She pulled off my boots, unrolled my socks, unclasped my belt, and tugged my trousers down my legs, before doing the same with my underwear.

Each item was removed, then bagged and tagged as evidence in the case the

Boston cops would be building against me.

Finally, the nurse removed my gold stud earrings, my watch, and my wedding band. Can't wear jewelry for the CT scan I was told as she stripped me bare.

The nurse handed me a hospital gown, then bustled away with her evidence bags and my personal possessions. I didn't move. Just lay there, feeling the loss of my uniform, the shame of my own nakedness.

I could hear a TV down the hall broadcasting my daughter's name. Next would come an image of her school photo, snapped just this October. Sophie wore her favorite yellow ruffled top. She was turned slightly sideways, looking back at the camera with her big blue eyes, an excited smile on her face because she loved pictures and she especially wanted this photo, her first since she'd lost her top front tooth, and the tooth fairy had brought her a whole dollar which she couldn't wait to spend.

My eyes burned. There is pain, then there was pain. All the words I could not speak. All the images I couldn't get out of my head.

The nurse returned. She stuck my arms in the Johnny gown, then had me roll to the side so she could tie it in the back.

Two technicians arrived. They whisked me away to the CT scan, my gaze locked on the blur of ceiling tiles whizzing by overhead.

"Pregnant?" one asked.

"What?"

"Are you pregnant?"

"No."

"Claustrophobic?"

"No."

"Then this will be a breeze."

I was wheeled into another sterile room, this one dominated by a large, donut-shaped machine. The technicians didn't let me stand, but hoisted me from the gurney directly onto the table.

I was instructed to lie absolutely still while the donut-shaped X-ray moved around my head, taking cross sections of my skull. A computer would then combine the two-dimensional X-ray images to form a three-dimensional model.

In thirty minutes, the doctor would have a graphic image of my brain and my bones, including any swelling, bruising, or bleeding.

The technicians made it sound very easy.

Lying alone on the table, I wondered how deep the scanner could peer. I wondered if it could see all the things I saw every time I closed my eyes. Blood, appearing on the wall behind my husband, then streaking down to the kitchen floor. My husband's eyes, widening in surprise as he looked down, seemed to actually notice the red stains blooming across his muscled chest.

Brian sliding down, down, down. Me, now standing over him, and watching the light dim in his eyes.

"I love you," I had whispered to my husband, right before the light fled. "I'm sorry. I'm sorry. I love you. . . ."

There is pain, then there was pain.

The machine started to move. I closed my eyes and I allowed myself one last memory of my husband. His final words, as he died on our kitchen floor.

"Sorry," Brian had gasped, three bullets in his torso. "Tessa . . . love you . . . more."

7

With Brian Darby's body removed, and Tessa Leoni whisked off to the hospital, the immediate practicalities of the homicide investigation began to wind down while the search for six-year-old Sophie Leoni ramped up.

With that in mind, D.D. summoned the taskforce officers to the white command van and began cracking the whip.

Witnesses. D.D. wanted a short list from all the uniformed officers of any and all neighbors worth a second interview. She then assigned six homicide detectives to begin those interviews

ASAP. If someone was a credible witness or potential suspect, she wanted them identified and talking in the next three minutes.

Cameras. Boston was riddled with them. City installed them to monitor traffic. Businesses installed them for security. D.D. formed a three-man team whose job was to do nothing but identify all cameras in a two mile radius and skim through all video footage from the past twelve hours, starting with the video cameras closest to the house and working out.

Known associates. Friends, family, neighbors, teachers, babysitters, employers; if someone had ever set foot on the property, D.D. wanted their name on her desk in the next forty-five minutes. In particular, she wanted all teachers, playmates, and caretakers of Sophie Leoni rounded up and cranked through the wringer. Full background checks, a search of their homes if the detective could talk his way through the door. Officers needed to be eliminating friends and identifying foes and they needed to be doing it now, now, now.

Other people out there knew this family. Enemies from the husband's job, felons snagged in Trooper Leoni's patrols, maybe partners in torrid affairs, or longtime personal confidantes. Other people knew Brian Darby and Tessa Leoni. And one of those people might know what had happened to a six-year-old girl who'd last been seen sleeping in her own bed.

Time was not on their side. Get out, hit the streets, beat the clock, D.D. ordered her crew.

Then she shut up and sent them back to work.

The Boston detectives scrambled. The brass nodded. She and Bobby returned to the house.

D.D. trusted her fellow investigators to begin the enormous task of sifting through all the nuances of an entire family's existence. What she wanted most for herself, however, was to live and breathe the victims' final hours. She wanted to absorb the crime scene into her DNA. She wanted to inundate herself with the tiniest little domestic details, from paint choices to decorative

knickknacks. She wanted to set and reset the scene a dozen different ways in
her mind, and she wanted to populate it
with a little girl, a merchant marine father, and a state trooper mother. This
one house, these three lives, these past
ten hours. Everything came down to
that. A home, a family, a collision course
of multiple lives with tragic consequences.

D.D. needed to see it, feel it, live it.
Then she could dissect the family down
to its deepest darkest truth, which in
turn would bring her Sophie Leoni.

D.D.'s stomach flip-flopped queasily.
She tried not to think about it as she and
Bobby once again entered the blood-
stained kitchen.

By mutual consent, they started upstairs, which featured two dormered
bedrooms, separated by a full bath. The
bedroom facing the street appeared to
be the master, dominated by a queen-
sized bed with a simple wooden head-
board and dark blue comforter. Bedding
immediately struck D.D. as more his
than hers. Nothing else in the room
changed her opinion.

The broad dresser, a beat-up oak, screamed of bachelor days. It was topped by an old thirty-six inch TV which was tuned to ESPN. Plain white walls, stark wood floors. Not so much a domestic retreat, as a way station, D.D. thought. A place to sleep, change clothes, then exit.

D.D. tried the closet. Three-fourths of it yielded sharply pressed men's shirts, arranged by color. Then came half a dozen neatly hanging blue jeans. Then a mishmash of cotton slacks and tops, two state police uniforms, one dress uniform, and one orange flower-printed sundress.

"He took up more space in the closet," D.D. reported to Bobby, who was examining the dresser.

"Men have been killed for less," he agreed.

"Seriously. Check this out. Color-coded shirts, *pressed* blue jeans. Brian Darby was beyond anal-retentive and bordering on just plain freaky."

"Brian Darby was also getting seriously huge. Look at this." Bobby held up a framed eight-by-ten portrait with his gloved hands. D.D. finished inspecting the empty gun safe she'd found in the left-hand corner of the closet, then crossed to him.

The framed picture featured Tessa Leoni in the orange sundress with a white sweater, holding a small bouquet of tiger lilies. Brian Darby stood beside her in a brown sports jacket, a single tiger lily pinned to his collar. A little girl, presumably Sophie Leoni, stood in front of both of them, wearing a dark green velvet dress with a ring of lilies in her hair. All three were beaming at the camera, happy family celebrating a happy day.

"Wedding photo," D.D. murmured.

"That would be my guess. Now look at Darby. Check out his shoulders."

D.D. obediently checked out the former groom and now dead husband. Good-looking guy, she decided. Had a military/cop vibe going on with the buzz-cut blonde hair, chiseled chin, squared shoulders. But the impression was balanced by warm brown eyes, crinkling at the corners from the impact of his smile. He looked happy, relaxed.

Not the kind of guy you'd immediately suspect of battering his wife—or, for that matter, ironing his blue jeans.

D.D. handed the picture back to Bobby. "I don't get it. So he was happy on his wedding day. That doesn't mean anything."

"Nah. He was *smaller* on his wedding day. That Brian Darby is a fit one eighty. Bet he worked out, kept active. Dead Brian Darby, on the other hand . . ."

D.D. remembered what Bobby had told her earlier. "Big guy, you said. Two ten, two twenty, probably a weight lifter. So not that he got married and he got fat. You're saying, he got married and he *muscled up*."

Bobby nodded.

D.D. thought about the picture again. "It's not easy to be in a relationship where the woman is the one who carries a gun," she murmured.

Bobby didn't touch that statement, and she was grateful.

"We should find his gym," he said now. "Check out his regimen. Inquire about known supplements."

"'Roid rage?"

"Worth asking about."

They moved out of the master, into the adjoining bath. This room, at least, had a splash of personality. A brightly striped shower curtain was drawn around an old claw-foot tub. A yellow-duckie area rug dotted the tiled floor. Layers of blue and yellow towels warmed up wooden towel racks.

This room also displayed more signs of life—a Barbie toothbrush lying on the edge of the sink, a pile of purple hair elastics in a basket on the back of the toilet, a clear plastic spit cup declaring "Daddy's Little Princess."

D.D. checked the medicine cabinet. She found three prescription bottles, one made out to Brian Darby for Ambien, a sleep aid. One made out to Sophie Leoni, involving some kind of topical eye ointment. A third for Tessa Leoni, hydrocodone, a painkiller.

She showed the bottle to Bobby. He made a note.

"Have to follow up with the doc. See if she had an injury, maybe something from the job."

D.D. nodded. Rest of the medicine cabinet held a plethora of lotions, shaving creams, razors, and colognes. Only thing of note, she thought, was the fairly impressive stash of first-aid supplies. Lotta Band-Aids, she thought, in a lotta different sizes. A battered wife, stockpiling for inevitable repairs, or just life as an active family? She checked under the sink, found the usual mix of soap, toilet paper, feminine hygiene products, and cleaning supplies.

They moved on.

The next room clearly belonged to Sophie. Soft pink walls, with stenciled flowers in pale green and baby blue. A flower-shaped rug. A wall of bright white cubbies brimming with dolls, dresses, and glittering ballet shoes. Tessa and Brian lived in a dorm. Little Sophie, on the other hand, inhabited a magical garden complete with bunnies running along the floorboards and butterflies painted around the windows.

It was beyond obscene, D.D. thought, to stand in the middle of such a space, and start looking for signs of blood.

Her hand was pressed to her stomach. She didn't even notice it as she
carefully began her first visual inspection of the bed.

"Luminol?" she murmured.

"No hits," Bobby responded.

Per protocol, the crime-scene techs
had sprayed Sophie Leoni's sheets with
luminol, which reacted with bodily fluids
such as blood and semen. The lack of
hits meant the sheets were clean. Which
didn't mean Sophie Leoni had never
been sexually assaulted; just meant she
hadn't been recently assaulted on this
set of linens. The crime-scene techs
would also check the laundry, even pull
bedding out of the washing machine if
necessary. Unless someone knew to
clean all items in bleach, it was amazing
what the luminol could find on "clean"
linens.

More things D.D. didn't want to know
while standing in the middle of a magical garden.

She wondered who had painted this
room. Tessa? Brian? Or maybe the three
of them working together back in the

days when the love was still new and the family felt fresh and committed to one another.

She wondered just how many nights had passed before Sophie woke up to the first sound of a distinct smack, a muffled scream. Or maybe Sophie hadn't been sleeping at all. Maybe she'd been sitting at the kitchen table, or playing with a doll in the corner.

Maybe she'd run to her mother the first time. Maybe . . .

Ah, Jesus Christ. D.D. did not want to be working this case right now.

She fisted her hands, turned toward the window, and focused on the weak March daylight.

Bobby had stilled next to the wall. He was studying her, but didn't say a word.

Once more, she was grateful.

"We should find out if there's a favorite snuggle toy," she said at last.

"Rag doll. Green dress, brown yarn hair, blue button eyes. Named Gertrude."

D.D. nodded, scanning the room slowly. She identified a night-light—

Sophie's terrified of the dark—but no snuggle toy. "I don't see it."

"Neither did the first responder. So far, we're operating under the assumption the doll is missing, too."

"Her pajamas?"

"Trooper Leoni said her daughter was wearing a long-sleeved set, pink with yellow horses. No sign of them."

D.D. had a thought. "What about her coat, hat, and snow boots?"

"Don't have that in my notes."

For the first time, D.D. felt a glimmer of hope. "Missing coat and hat means she was roused out of bed in the middle of the night. Not given the time to change, but the chance to bundle up."

"No need to bundle up a corpse," Bobby remarked.

They left the room and pounded down the stairs. Inspected the coat closet, then the bin of shoes and winter accessories tucked by the front door. No little kid coat. No little kid hat. No little kid boots.

"Sophie Leoni was bundled up!" D.D. declared triumphantly.

"Sophie Leoni left the house alive."

"Perfect. Now, all we gotta do is find her before nightfall."

They returned upstairs long enough to examine the windows for signs of forced entry. Finding none, they headed downstairs for the same drill. Both doors featured relatively new hardware and bolt locks, none of which showed signs of tampering. The windows in the sunroom, they discovered, were so old and moisture-warped they refused to budge.

All in all, the house appeared secure. To judge from the look on Bobby's face, he hadn't expected anything different and neither had D.D. Sad rule in missing kid cases—most of the time, the trouble came from inside the home, not outside it.

They toured the family room, which reminded D.D. of the bedroom. Plain walls, wooden floors topped by a beige area rug. The black leather L-shaped sofa seemed more like a his purchase than a hers. A fairly new-looking laptop computer sat at one end of the couch, still plugged into the wall. Room also boasted a flat-screen TV, mounted above a sleek entertainment unit that housed a state-of-the-art audio system, Blu-ray DVD player, and Wii gaming console.

"Boys and their toys," D.D. remarked.

"Engineer," Bobby said again.

D.D. examined a small art table set up in the corner for Sophie. On one side of the table sat a stack of blank white paper. In the middle was a caddy filled with crayons. That was it. No works in progress on the table. No displays of completed genius on the walls. Very organized, she thought, especially for a six-year-old.

The starkness of the home was starting to wig her out. People did not live like this and people with kids definitely should not live like this.

They crossed into the kitchen, where D.D. stood as far away from the outline of the corpse as she could. Bloodstain, shattered glass, and toppled chairs aside, the kitchen was as meticulous as the rest of the house. Also tired and dated. Thirty-year-old dark wood cabinets, plain white appliances, stained Formica countertop. First thing Alex would do to this house, D.D. thought, was gut and modernize the kitchen.

But not Brian Darby. He spent his money on electronics, a leather sofa, and his car. Not the house.

"They made an effort for Sophie," D.D. murmured out loud, "but not for each other."

Bobby looked at her.

"Think about it," she continued. "It's an old vintage house that's still an old vintage house. As you keep pointing out, he's an engineer, meaning he's probably got some basic skills with power tools. Combined household income is a good two hundred grand a year, plus Brian Darby has this whole sixty days of vacation thing going on. Meaning they have some expertise, some time, and some resources they could spend on the home. But they don't. Only in Sophie's room. She gets the fresh paint, new furniture, pretty bedding, etc. They made an effort for her, but not for themselves. Makes me wonder in how many other areas of their life that same rule applied."

"Most parents focus on their kids," Bobby observed mildly.

"They haven't even hung a picture."

"Trooper Leoni works long hours. Brian Darby ships out for months at a time. Maybe, when they're home, they have other priorities."

D.D. shrugged. "Like what?"

Bobby nodded. "Come on. I'll show you the garage."

The garage freaked D.D. out. The broad, two-bay space was lined on all three sides with the craziest Peg-Board system she'd ever seen. Seriously, floor to ceiling of Peg-Boards, which were then fitted with shelving brackets and bike holders and plastic bins for sporting goods and even a custom golf bag holder.

D.D. took in the space and was struck by two things at once: Brian Darby did apparently have a lot of outdoor hobbies, and he needed professional help for his anal-retentiveness.

"The floor is clean," D.D. said. "It's March, it's snowy, and the entire city has been sanded within an inch of its life. How can the floor be this clean?"

"He parked his car on the street."

"He parked his sixty thousand dollar SUV on one of the busiest streets in Boston rather than dirty his garage?"

"Trooper Leoni also parked her cruiser out front. Department likes us to keep our vehicles visible in the neighborhood—presence of a cop car is viewed as a deterrent."

"This is nuts," D.D. stated. She crossed to one wall, where she found a large broom and dustpan racked side by side. Next to them sat two plastic garbage cans and a blue bin for recycling. Recycling bin revealed half a dozen green beer bottles. Garbage cans were already empty—the bags probably having been removed by the crime-scene techs. D.D. strolled by his and her dirt bikes, plus a pink number that clearly belonged to Sophie. She found a row of backpacks and a shelf dedicated to hiking boots of various weights and sizes, including a pink pair for Sophie. Hiking, biking, golfing, she determined.

Then, on the other side of the garage, she got to add skiing to the list. Six pairs of skis, three alpine, three cross country. And three sets of snowshoes.

"If Brian Darby was home, he was moving," D.D. added to her mental profile.

"Wanting the family with him," Bobby commented, gesturing to the wife and child sets that rounded out each trio.

"But," D.D. mused, "Tessa already commented—she had work, Sophie had school. Meaning, Brian was often alone. No loving family to join him, no appreciative female audience to be dazzled by his manly prowess."

"Stereotyping," Bobby warned.

D.D. gestured around the garage. "Please. This is a stereotype. Engineer. Anal-retentive. If I stay in here much longer, my head will hurt."

"You don't iron your jeans?" he asked.

"I don't label my power tools. Seriously, check this out." She'd arrived at the workbench, where Brian Darby had arranged his power tools on a shelf bearing names for each item.

"Nice tools." Bobby was frowning. "Very nice tools. An easy grand worth."

"And yet he doesn't fix up the house," D.D. lamented. "So far, I'm siding with Tessa on this."

"Maybe it's not about the doing," Bobby said. "Maybe it's about the buying. Brian Darby likes having toys. Doesn't mean he plays with them."

D.D. considered it. Certainly an option, and would explain the pristine condition of the garage. Easy to keep it clean if you never parked in it, never worked in it, never retrieved any of the gear from it.

But then she shook her head. "Nah, he didn't gain thirty pounds in muscle sitting around all day. Speaking of which, where's the weight set?"

They looked around. Of all the toys, no dumbbells or free weight systems.

"Must belong to a gym," Bobby said.

"We'll have to check that out," D.D.

concurred. "So Brian is a doer. But his wife and child are also busy. So maybe he does some stuff on his own to pass the time. Unfortunately, he still comes home to an empty house, which leaves him restless. So first he cleans the place within an inch of its life . . ."

"Then," Bobby finished, "he tosses back a couple of beers."

D.D. was frowning. She walked toward the far corner, where the concrete floor appeared darker. She bent down, touched the spot with her fingertips. Felt damp.

"Leak?" she murmured, trying to inspect the corner wall where moisture might be penetrating, but of course, the cinder-block surface was obscured by more Peg-Board.

"Could be." Bobby crossed to where she knelt. "This whole corner is built into the hillside. Could have drainage issues, even a leak from a pipe above."

"Have to watch it, see if it grows."

"Concerned the house will fall down on your watch?"

She looked at him. "No, concerned

it's not water from a leak. Meaning, it came from something else, and I want to know what."

Unexpectedly, Bobby smiled. "I don't care what the other staties say: Trooper Leoni is lucky to have you on her case, and Sophie Leoni is even luckier."

"Oh, fuck you," D.D. told him crossly. She straightened, more discomfited by praise than she was ever riled by criticism. "Come on. We're heading out."

"The pattern of the water stain told you where Sophie is?"

"No. Given that Tessa Leoni's lawyer hasn't magically called with permission to interview her yet, we're gonna focus on Brian Darby. I want to talk to his boss. I want to know exactly what kind of man needs to color-code his closet and Peg-Board his garage."

"A control freak."

"Exactly. And when something or someone undermines that control—"

"Just how violent does he get," Bobby finished for her. They stood in the middle of the garage.

"I don't think a stranger abducted Sophie Leoni," D.D. stated quietly.

Bobby paused a heartbeat. "I don't think so either."

"Meaning it's him, or it's her."

"He's dead."

"Meaning, maybe Trooper Leoni finally wised up."

8

A woman never forgets the first time she is hit.

I was lucky. My parents never whacked me. My father never slapped my face for talking back, or spanked my behind for willful disobedience. Maybe because I was never that disobedient. Or maybe, because by the time my father got home at night, he was too tired to care. My brother died and my parents became shells of their former selves, using up all their energy just getting through the day.

By the time I was twelve, I'd come to

terms with the morbid little household that passed as my own. I got into sports—soccer, softball, track team, anything that would keep me late after school and minimize the hours I spent on the homefront. Juliana liked sports, too. We were the Bobbsey twins, always in uniform, always rushing off somewhere.

I took some hits on the playing field. A line drive to the chest that knocked me flat on my back. I realized for the first time that you really do see stars when the breath has been knocked from your lungs and your skull ricochets against the hard earth.

Then there were miscellaneous soccer injuries, a head butt to the nose, cleats to the knee, the occasional elbow to the gut. Take it from me, girls can be tough. We dish out and man up with the best of them, particularly in the heat of battle, trying to score one for our team.

But those injuries were nothing personal. Just the kind of collateral damage that happens when you and your opponent both want the ball. After the game, you shook hands, slapped each other on the butt, and meant it.

First time I really had to fight was at the Academy. I knew I would receive rigorous training in hand-to-hand combat and I was looking forward to it. A lone female living in Boston? Hand-to-hand combat was an excellent idea, whether I made it as a trooper or not.

For two weeks, we practiced drills. Basic defensive stances for protecting our face, our kidneys, and, of course, our sidearms. Never forget your weapon, we were lectured again and again. Most cops who lose their gun are then shot and killed with that gun. First line of defense, subdue the offending party before ever getting within arm's length. But in the event things go sour and you find yourself in a personal combat situation, protect your weapon, and strike hard first chance you get.

Turned out, I didn't know how to deliver a punch. Sounded easy enough. But I fisted my hand wrong, had a tendency to overuse my arm, versus throwing my whole body behind the blow by rotating at the waist. So there were a couple more weeks, teaching all of us, even the big guys, how to pack a punch.

Six weeks into it, the instructors decided we'd had enough drills. Time to practice what they'd preached.

They divvied us up into two teams. We all donned protective padding and, to start, were armed with padded bars the instructors affectionately referred to as pogo sticks. Then, they turned us loose.

Don't believe for a second I got to fight another woman of my approximate size and weight. That would be too easy. As a female officer, I was expected to handle anything and anyone. So the trainers made their picks deliberately random. I ended up across from another recruit, named Chuck, who was six one, two hundred and forty pounds, and a former football player.

He didn't even try to hit me. He just ran straight at me and knocked me flat on my ass. I went down like a ton of bricks, remembering once more that line drive to my chest as I struggled to regain my breath.

The instructor blew his whistle. Chuck

offered me a hand up, and we tried again.

This time, I was aware of my fellow recruits watching. I registered my instructor's scowl at my disappointing performance. I fixated on the fact this was supposed to be my new life. If I couldn't defend myself, if I couldn't do this, I couldn't become a trooper. Then what would I do? How would I earn enough money for Sophie and me to live? How would I provide for my daughter? What would happen to us?

Chuck rushed. This time, I stepped to the side and slammed my pogo stick into his gut. I had approximately half a second to feel good about myself. Then two hundred and forty pounds of Chuck straightened, laughed, and came back at me.

It got ugly after that. To this day, I don't recall it all. I remember starting to feel genuinely panicked. That I was blocking and moving, and putting my shoulder behind the blow, and still Chuck kept coming and Chuck kept coming. Two hundred and forty pounds of linebacker against my one hundred and twenty pounds of desperate new motherhood.

The padded end of his pogo stick connecting with my face. My head snapped back as my nose absorbed the blow. I staggered, eyes flooding with instant tears, off balance, half-blinded, wanting to fall, but realizing frantically that I couldn't go down. He'd kill me. That's how it felt. Couldn't go down or I'd be dead.

Then, at the last second, I did fall, into a tight little ball that I then sprang out of, straight into the towering giant's legs. I caught him at the knees, jerked sideways, and toppled him like a redwood.

The instructor blew the whistle. My classmates cheered.

I staggered to standing, touching gingerly at my nose.

"That's gonna leave a mark," my instructor informed me cheerfully.

I crossed to Chuck, offered him a hand up.

He accepted gratefully enough. "Sorry 'bout the face," he said, looking sheepish. Poor big guy, having to take on the girl.

I assured him it was all right. We were all doing what we had to do. Then we got to square off against new partners and do it all over again.

Later that night, curled up alone in my dorm room, I finally cradled my nose with my hand and cried. Because I didn't know if I could go through that again. Because I wasn't sure if I was really prepared for a new life where I had to hit and be hit. Where I might honestly have to fight for my life.

At that moment, I didn't want to be a trooper anymore. I just wanted to go home to my baby girl. I wanted to hold Sophie and inhale the scent of her shampoo. I wanted to feel her chubby little hands pressed against my neck. I wanted to feel my ten-month-old daughter's unconditional love.

Instead, I got pummeled the next day, and the day after that. I endured bruised ribs, whacked shins, and aching wrists. I learned to take a blow. I learned to deliver in kind. Until by the end of the twenty-five-week course, I came out of the gate swinging with the best of them, covered in purple welts but ready to rumble.

Tiny, fast, and tough.

Giant Killer, my fellow recruits called me, and I was proud of the nickname.

I remembered those days now, as the doctor examined the results from the CT scan, then gently probed the mass of swollen purple flesh around my eye.

"Fracture of the zygomatic bone," he murmured, adding for my benefit: "Your cheek is broken."

More perusing of film images, more inspection of my skull. "No sign of hematoma or contusion of the brain. Nausea? Headache?"

I murmured yes to both.

"Name and date."

I managed my name, blanked on the date.

Doctor's turn to nod. "Given the clear CT scan, it would seem you have only a concussion to go with your fractured zygomatic. And what happened here?" He finished with my head, moving to my torso, where the yellow and green remnants of a fading bruise covered half my ribs.

I didn't answer, just stared at the ceiling.

He palpitated my stomach. "Does this hurt?"

"No."

He rotated my right arm, then my left, searching for further signs of damage. He found it on my left hip, another deep purple bruise, this time in the shape of a rounded arc, like what might be formed from the toe of a work boot.

I'd seen bruises in the shape of men's rings, watch faces, even an imprint of a quarter on a female who'd been slugged by a boyfriend holding a roll of coins. Judging by the doctor's face, he'd seen it all, as well.

Dr. Raj smoothed my gown back in place, retrieved my medical chart, made some notes.

"Cheek fracture will heal best if left alone," he stated. "We'll keep you overnight to monitor the concussion. If your nausea and headache have subsided by morning, chances are you may go home."

I didn't say anything.

The doctor stepped closer, cleared his throat.

"There is a bump on your left sixth rib," he stated. "A fracture I suspect did not heal correctly."

He paused as if waiting for me to say something, perhaps a statement he could enter into my medical chart: *Patient says husband knocked her down and kicked her in the ribs. Patient says husband has a favorite baseball bat.*

I said nothing, because statements became records, and records became evidence that could be used against you.

"Did you wrap your ribs yourself?" the doctor asked.

"Yes."

The doctor grunted, my one admission filling in all his blanks.

The doctor saw me as a victim, just as the EMT had seen me as a victim. They were both wrong. I was a survivor and I was currently walking a tightrope where I absolutely, positively could not afford to fall.

Dr. Raj studied me again. "Rest is the

best medicine for healing," he said finally. "Given your concussion, I cannot
prescribe a narcotic, but I will have a
nurse bring you some ibuprofen for the
pain."

"Thank you."

"In the future," he said, "should you
injure your ribs, please come to me immediately. I would like to see them better wrapped."

"I'll be all right," I said.

Dr. Raj did not appear convinced.
"Rest," he repeated. "The pain and the
swelling will subside soon enough.
Though I have a feeling you already
know that by now."

The doctor departed.

My cheek burned. My head throbbed.
But I was satisfied.

I was awake, I was lucid. And finally, I
was alone.

Time to plan.

My fingers fisted against the sheets. I
studied the ceiling tiles with my one
good eye, and used my pain to steel my
resolve.

A woman remembers the first time
she is hit. But with any luck, she also re-

members the first time she fights back and wins.

I am the Giant Killer.

Just gotta think. Just gotta plan. Just gotta get one step ahead.

I could do this. I would do this.

All I want for Christmas is my two front teeth, my two front teeth, my two front teeth.

Then, I rolled onto my side, curled up in a ball, and wept.

9

When D.D. wasn't overseeing an interagency taskforce charged with solving a murder and rescuing a child, she led a three-man squad in Boston's homicide unit. Her first squadmate, Phil, was the quintessential family man, married to his high school sweetheart and raising four kids. Her other squadmate, Neil, was a lanky redhead who'd formerly served as an EMT before joining the BPD. He had a tendency to handle the autopsies for the team, spending so much time at the morgue that he was now dating the ME, Ben Whitley.

D.D. had a whole taskforce at her disposal; she still preferred to go with what she knew. She put Neil in charge of Brian Darby's autopsy, currently scheduled for Monday afternoon. In the meantime, Neil could start pestering the medical staff overseeing Tessa Leoni's care to determine the extent of her current injuries as well as any medical history of past "accidents." She assigned Phil, their data cruncher, to run the computer background checks on Brian Darby and Tessa Leoni. And, of course, get her the information on Brian Darby's employer, immediately.

Turned out, Brian worked for Alaska South Slope Crude, otherwise known as ASSC. Head offices were in Seattle, Washington, and not open on Sunday. This did not suit D.D. She chewed the inside of her cheek while sitting in the command van, nursing a bottle of water. The initial crush of officers had subsided. Most of the neighbors had drifted off, leaving the usual assortment of "didn't see nothing, don't know anything" mutterings in their wake. Now only the media remained, still ensconced across the street, still clamoring for a press conference.

D.D. was probably going to have to do something about that, but she wasn't ready yet. She wanted something to happen first. Maybe a breaking lead she could dangle in front of the hungry hordes. Or a new piece of information that would enable the media to work on her behalf. Something. Anything.

Crap, she was tired. Really, truly, bone deep, could curl up on the command center floor and fall asleep right now sort of tired. She couldn't get used to it. The intense bouts of nausea followed by the nearly deadening sense of fatigue. Five weeks late and her body already wasn't her own.

What was she going to do? How could she tell Alex, when she still didn't know how she felt about it herself?

What was she going to do?

Bobby, who'd been in earnest conversation with his lieutenant colonel, finally broke away and took a seat beside her. He stretched out his legs.

"Hungry?" he asked.

"What?"

"It's after two, D.D. We need lunch."

She looked at him blankly, not quite believing it was after two and definitely not ready to deal with all the current issues that surrounded mealtimes.

"You okay?" He asked it evenly.

"'Course I'm okay! Just . . . preoccupied. In case you haven't noticed, we're still missing a six-year-old girl."

"Then I have a gift for you." Bobby held out a piece of paper. "The lieutenant colonel just had this faxed over. It's from Tessa Leoni's file, and it includes an emergency contact other than her husband."

"What?"

"Mrs. Brandi Ennis. Guess she watched Sophie when Trooper Leoni was on patrol and Brian Darby out to sea."

"Hot damn." D.D. grabbed the paper, skimmed the contents, then flipped open her phone.

Brandi Ennis answered on the first ring. Yes, she'd seen the news. Yes, she wanted to talk. Immediately. At her home would be fine. She provided an address.

"Give us fifteen minutes," D.D. assured the elderly-sounding woman. Then she and Bobby were out the door.

Twelve minutes later, D.D. and Bobby pulled up in front of a squat brick apartment building. Peeling white trim around small windows. Crumbling concrete on the front stoop.

Low-income housing, D.D. decided, which was probably still a stretch for most of its inhabitants.

A couple of kids were playing in the snow out front, trying to fashion a sad-looking snowman. They spotted two cops getting out of their car and immediately bolted inside. D.D. grimaced. Countless hours of community relations later, and the next generation was still as suspicious of the police as the first. It didn't make any of their lives easier.

Mrs. Ennis lived on the second floor, Unit 2C. Bobby and D.D. took the stairs up, knocking lightly on the scarred wooden door. Mrs. Ennis opened before D.D.'s fist had even dropped down, obviously waiting for them.

She gestured them inside a small but tidy studio apartment. Kitchen cabinets to the left, kitchen table to the right, brown floral sleeper sofa straight ahead. The TV was on, blaring away on top of a cheap microwave stand. Mrs. Ennis took a second to cross the space and snap it off. Then she asked them politely if they'd like some tea or coffee.

D.D. and Bobby declined. Mrs. Ennis bustled at the cabinets anyway, putting on a pot of water, getting down a package of Nilla wafers.

She was an older woman, probably late sixties, early seventies. Steel gray hair cut no-nonsense short. Wearing a dark blue running suit over a petite, stoop-shouldered frame. Her gnarled hands shook slightly as she opened the box of cookies, but she moved briskly, a woman who knew what she was about.

D.D. took a moment to wander the space, just in case Sophie Leoni was magically sitting on the sofa with her gap-tooth smile, or maybe playing with duckies in the bath, or even tucked inside the lone closet to hide from her abusive parents.

As she closed the closet door, Mrs. Ennis said calmly, "You may sit now, Detective. I don't have the child, nor would I ever do that to her poor mother."

Sufficiently chastised, D.D. shed her heavy winter coat and took a seat. Bobby was already munching on a Nilla wafer. D.D. eyed them. When her stomach did not flip-flop in protest, she reached out carefully. Simple foods such as crackers and dry cereal had been good to her thus far. She took several experimental bites, then decided she might be in luck, because now that she thought about it, she was starving.

"How long have you known Tessa Leoni?" D.D. asked.

Mrs. Ennis had taken a seat, clutching a mug of tea. Her eyes appeared red, as if she'd been crying earlier, but she seemed composed now. Ready to talk.

"I first met Tessa seven years ago, when she moved into the building. Across the hall, apartment 2D. Also a studio, though she changed to a one bedroom not long after Sophie was born."

"You met her before Sophie was born?" D.D. asked.

"Yes. She was three, four months pregnant. Just this little thing with this little belly. I heard a crash and came out into the hallway. Tessa had been trying to carry a box filled with pots and pans up the stairs and it had broken on her. I offered to help, which she declined, but I picked up her chicken fryer anyway and that's how it began."

"You became friends?" D.D. clarified.

"I would have her over for dinner on occasion and she would return the favor. Two lone females in the building. It was nice to have some company."

"And she was already pregnant?"

"Yes, ma'am."

"She talk much about the father?"

"She never mentioned him at all."

"What about dating, social life, visits from her family?"

"No family. No boys either. She worked at a coffee shop, trying to save her money for the baby's birth. It's not an easy thing, expecting a baby all alone."

"No male companionship?" D.D.

pressed. "Maybe she went out late a couple of nights, hung out with friends . . ."

"She doesn't have friends," Mrs. Ennis said emphatically.

"She doesn't have friends?" D.D. repeated.

"It's not her way," Mrs. Ennis said.

D.D. glanced over at Bobby, who also appeared intrigued by this news.

"What is her way?" D.D. asked at last.

"Independent. Private. Her baby mattered to her. From the beginning, that's what Tessa talked about and that's what she worked for. She understood being a single mother was going to be tough. Why, it was sitting here at this very table she came up with the idea to become a cop."

"Really?" Bobby spoke up. "Why a trooper?"

"She was trying to plan ahead—she couldn't very well support a child working in a coffee shop her whole life. So we started to discuss her options. She had a GED. She couldn't see herself behind a desk, but some kind of job where she could do things, be active, appealed to her. My son had become a firefighter. We talked about that, and next thing I knew, Tessa had homed in on joining the police force. She looked up applications, did all sorts of research. Pay scale was good, she met the initial requirements. Then, of course, she found out about the Academy and the wind went out of her sails. That's when I volunteered to babysit. Hadn't even met little Sophie yet, but I said I'd take her. If Tessa could get that far into the recruitment process, I'd assist with childcare."

D.D. was looking at Bobby. "How long's the state Police Academy again?"

"Twenty-five weeks," he supplied. "Live in dorms, only allowed home on the weekends. Not easy if you're a solo parent."

"I will have you know," Mrs. Ennis said stiffly, "we all did just fine. Tessa completed her application before giving birth. She was accepted into the next recruitment class, when Sophie was nine months old. I know Tessa was nervous. I was, too. But it was also exciting." The older woman's eyes flashed.

She considered D.D. "Are you a single woman? Have any children of your own? There's something invigorating about embarking on a new chapter in your life, taking a risk that might provide a whole new future for you and your child.

"Tessa was always serious, but now she was dedicated. Diligent. She knew what she was up against, a single mother trying to become a police officer. But she also believed that becoming a state police trooper was the best shot she had for her and Sophie. She never wavered. And that woman, once she puts her mind to something . . ."

"Single, dedicated parent," D.D. murmured.

"Very."

"Loving?"

"Always!" Mrs. Ennis said emphatically.

"What about when she graduated from the Academy," Bobby spoke up. "You come to cheer her on?"

"Even bought a new dress," Mrs. Ennis confirmed.

"Anyone else there in her corner?"

"Just us girls."

"She'd have to start on patrol right away," Bobby continued. "Working the graveyard shift then coming home to a small child . . ."

"She had thought to put Sophie in daycare, but I wouldn't hear of it. Sophie and I had done just fine during our Academy days. Easy enough for me to cross the hall and sleep on Tessa's sofa instead of my own. Then when Sophie was awake, I'd bring her back over to my place until after lunch so Tessa could get some rest. It was hardly a bother to entertain Sophie for a few hours. Lord, that child . . . All smiles and giggles and kisses and hugs. We should all be so lucky to have a little Sophie in our lives."

"Happy child?" D.D. asked.

"And funny and feisty. Beautiful little girl. 'Bout broke my heart when they moved away."

"When was that?"

"When she met her husband, Brian. He swept both her and Sophie off their feet. Regular Prince Charming. Least Tessa deserved, after working so hard on her own. And Sophie, too. Every girl should have a chance to be Daddy's Little Princess."

"Did you like Brian Darby?" D.D. asked.

"Yes," Mrs. Ennis stated, though her tone was noticeably more reserved.

"How did they meet?"

"Through the job, I believe. Brian was a friend of another trooper."

D.D. looked at Bobby, who nodded and made the note.

"He spend much time here?"

Mrs. Ennis shook her head. "Too small; it was easier for them to go to his place. There was a spell when I didn't see Tessa or Sophie too much. And I was happy for them, of course, of course. Though . . ." Mrs. Ennis sighed. "I don't have grandkids of my own. Sophie, she's like my own, and I miss her."

"But you still help out?"

"When Brian ships out. Those couple of months I come over, spend the night with Sophie, just like the old days. In the morning, I get her off to school. I'm also listed as an emergency contact, because with Tessa's job, she can't always be immediately available. So snow days, maybe Sophie isn't feeling too good. I handle those days. And it's no bother. As I said, Sophie's like my own."

D.D. pursed her lips, regarded the elderly woman.

"How would you describe Trooper Leoni as a mother?" she asked.

"There isn't anything she wouldn't do for Sophie," Mrs. Ennis replied immediately.

"Trooper Leoni ever drink?"

"No, ma'am."

"Gotta be stressful, though. Working, then coming home to a child. Sounds to me she never had a moment to herself."

"Never heard her complain," Mrs. Ennis said stubbornly.

"Ever get a call just because Tessa's having a bad day, could use a little break?"

"No, ma'am. If she wasn't working, she wanted to be with her daughter. Sophie's her world."

"Until she met her husband."

Mrs. Ennis was silent for a moment. "Honestly?"

"Honestly," D.D. said.

"I think Tessa loved Brian because Sophie loved Brian. Because, at least in the beginning, Brian and Sophie got along so well."

"In the beginning," D.D. prodded.

The older woman sighed, looked down at her tea. "Marriage," she said, a weight of emotion behind the word. "It always starts out so fresh. . . ." She sighed again. "I can't tell you what goes on behind closed doors, of course."

"But . . ." D.D. prodded again.

"Brian and Tessa and Sophie made one another happy in the beginning. Tessa would come home with stories of hikes and picnics and bike rides and cookouts, all the good stuff. They played well together.

"But marriage is more than playing. It also became Brian shipping out, and now Tessa's in a house with a yard and the lawn mower is broken or the leaf blower is broken and she's gotta figure it all out because he's gone and she's here and houses have to be taken care of, just like kids and dogs and state police jobs. I saw her . . . I saw her get frazzled more. Life with Brian home was better for her, I think. But life with Brian gone grew a lot harder. She had more to deal with, more to take care of, than when it had just been her and Sophie in a little one-bedroom apartment."

D.D. nodded. She could see that. There was a reason she didn't have a yard, a plant, or a goldfish.

"And for Brian?"

"Of course, he never confided in me," Mrs. Ennis said.

"Of course."

"But, from comments Tessa made . . . He worked when he shipped out. Twenty-four/seven, apparently, no days off. So when he came home, he didn't always want to go straight to house chores or lawn tending or even child rearing."

"He wanted to play," D.D. stated.

"Man needed some time to relax. Tessa changed the schedule, so the first week he was home, I'd still come over to help Sophie in the mornings. But Brian didn't like that either—said he couldn't relax with me in the house. So we went back to the old routine. They were trying," Mrs. Ennis spoke up earnestly. "But their schedules were tough. Tessa had to work when she had to work and she didn't always come home when she was supposed to come home. Then Brian disappeared for sixty days, then reappeared for sixty days . . . I don't think it was easy on either of them."

"Ever hear them fight?" D.D. asked.

Mrs. Ennis studied her tea. "Not fight . . . I could feel the tension. Sophie sometimes . . . When Brian came home, she'd have a couple of days where she'd be unusually quiet. Then he'd leave again, and she'd perk up. A father who came and went, that's not easy for a child to understand. And the stress of the household . . . kids can feel that."

"He ever hit her?"

"Heavens no! And if I so much as suspected such a thing, I would've reported him myself."

"To whom?" D.D. asked curiously.

"Tessa, of course."

"He ever hit her?"

Mrs. Ennis hesitated. D.D. eyed the older woman with renewed interest.

"I don't know," the older woman said.

"You don't know?"

"Sometimes, I noticed some bruising. Once or twice, not so long ago, Tessa seemed to limp. But when I asked her about it—she fell down the icy steps, had a minor accident snowshoeing. They're an active family. Sometimes, active people get injured."

"But not Sophie."

"Not Sophie!" Mrs. Ennis said fiercely.

"Because you would've done something about that."

For the first time, the woman's mouth trembled. She looked away, and in that moment, D.D. could see the woman's shame.

"You did suspect he was hitting her," D.D. stated levelly. "You worried Tessa was being abused by her husband, and you did nothing about it."

"Six, eight weeks ago . . . It was clear something had happened, she wasn't moving well, but was also refusing to acknowledge it. I tried to bring it up. . . ."

"What did she say?"

"That she fell down the front steps. She'd forgotten to salt them, it was all her fault. . . ." Mrs. Ennis pursed her lips, clearly skeptical. "I couldn't figure it out," the older woman said at last. "Tessa's a police officer. She's had training, she carries a gun. I told myself, if she really needed help, she'd tell me. Or maybe another officer. She spends all day with the police. How could she not ask for help?"

Million dollar question, D.D. thought. She could tell from the look on Bobby's face he thought the same. He leaned forward, caught Mrs. Ennis's attention.

"Did Tessa ever mention Sophie's biological father? Maybe he contacted her recently, showed interest in his child?"

Mrs. Ennis shook her head. "Tessa never spoke of him. I always assumed the man didn't have any interest in being a father. He had a better offer, she said, and left it at that."

"Tessa ever mention being worried about an arrest she'd made recently?"

Mrs. Ennis shook her head.

"What about trouble on the job, maybe with another trooper? Couldn't have been easy to be the only female in the Framingham barracks."

Again, Mrs. Ennis shook her head.

"She never spoke of work. Least not to me. Tessa was proud of her job, though. I could see that, just watching her leave for patrol each night. Maybe she picked the state police because she thought it would help her child, but it helped her, too. A strong job for a strong woman."

"You think she could've shot her husband?" D.D. asked bluntly.

Mrs. Ennis wouldn't answer.

"What if he hurt her child?"

Mrs. Ennis looked up sharply. "Oh dear Lord. You can't mean . . ." She covered her mouth with her hand. "You think Brian killed Sophie? You think she's dead? But the Amber Alert . . . I thought she was just missing. Maybe run off because of the confusion . . ."

"What confusion?"

"The news said there was an incident. Left one dead. I thought maybe there was a break-in, a struggle. Maybe Sophie ran away, to be safe."

"Who would break in?" D.D. asked.

"I don't know. It's Boston. Burglars, gangsters . . . These things happen."

"There's no sign of break-in," D.D. said quietly, giving Mrs. Ennis time to let that news settle in. "Tessa has confessed to shooting her husband. What we're trying to determine is what led up to that event, and what happened to Sophie."

"Oh my Lord. Oh my . . . Oh my . . ." Mrs. Ennis's hands moved from her mouth to her eyes. Already, she had started crying. "But I never thought . . . Even if Brian had . . . lost his temper a few times, I never suspected things had gotten so bad. I mean, he went away, right? If things had gotten so bad, why didn't she and Sophie just leave him when he was away? I would've helped. Surely she knew that!"

"Excellent question," D.D. agreed softly. "Why didn't she and Sophie just leave once he'd shipped out?"

"Sophie ever talk much about school?" Bobby spoke up. "Did she seem happy there, or have any concerns?"

"Sophie loved school. First grade. Mrs. DiPace. She'd just started reading all the Junie B. Jones novels with a little help. I mean reading, just like that. She's a bright child. And a good girl, too. I can . . . I can get you the principal's name, teachers, I have the whole school list since I dropped her off half the time. Everyone only ever has wonderful things to say about her, and oh my, just . . ."

Mrs. Ennis was out of her seat, walking in a tight circle before she seemed to remember what she needed to do. She crossed to a little end table next to the sofa, opened the top drawer, and started pulling out information.

"What about after-school activities?" D.D. asked.

"They had an after-school art program. Every Monday. Sophie loved that."

"Parents volunteer as part of that?" Bobby probed.

D.D. nodded, following his train of thought. Parents who they could grind through more background checks.

Mrs. Ennis returned to them, holding several pieces of paper—a school calendar, contact information for administrative personnel, a phone tree of other parents to notify in the event of snow days.

"Can you think of anyone who might

want to harm Sophie?" D.D. asked as gently as she could.

Mrs. Ennis shook her head, her face still stricken.

"If she ran away, can you think of where she'd hide?"

"In the tree," Mrs. Ennis said immediately. "When she wanted time alone, she always climbed the big oak in the backyard. Tessa said she used to do the same thing as a child."

Bobby and D.D. nodded. They had both studied the bare limbed tree. Six-year-old Sophie had not been perched among the branches.

"How do you get to the house?" D.D. thought to ask, as she and Bobby rose out of their chairs.

"The bus."

"Has Sophie ever ridden it with you? Does she understand mass transit?"

"We have been on the bus. I don't think she would know how. . . ." Mrs. Ennis paused, her dark eyes brightening. "But she does know her coins. The last few times we rode, she counted out the money. And she's very adventurous. If she thought she needed to get on the

bus for some reason, I could see her trying it alone."

"Thank you, Mrs. Ennis. If you think of
anything else . . ." D.D. handed the
woman her card.

Bobby had opened the door. At the
last moment, just as D.D. was exiting
into the hall, Bobby turned back.

"You said another officer introduced
Tessa and Brian. Do you remember who
that was?"

"Oh, it was at a cookout. . . ." Mrs.
Ennis paused, searched her memory
banks. "Shane. That's what Tessa called
him. She'd gone to Shane's house."

Bobby thanked the woman, then followed D.D. down the stairs.

"Who's Shane?" D.D. asked, the moment they were outside, puffing out
frosty breaths of air and tugging on their
gloves.

"I'm guessing Trooper Shane Lyons,
out of the Framingham barracks."

"The union rep!" D.D. stated.

"Yep. As well as the officer who made
the initial call."

"Then that's who we'll be interviewing
next." D.D. glanced at the distant hori-

zon, noticed for the first time the rapidly fading daylight, and felt her heart sink. "Oh no. Bobby . . . It's nearly dark!"

"Then we'd better work faster."

Bobby turned down the walk. D.D. followed quickly behind him.

10

I was dreaming. In a hazy sort of way, I understood that, but didn't jolt myself awake. I recognized the fall afternoon, the golden wisps of memory, and I didn't want to leave it. I was with my husband and daughter. We were together, and we were happy.

In my dream/memory, Sophie is five years old, her dark hair pulled into a stubby ponytail beneath her helmet as she rides her pink bike with big white training wheels through the neighborhood park. Brian and I trail behind her, holding hands. Brian's face is relaxed, his shoulders down. It's a beautiful fall day in Boston, the sun is out, the leaves are bright copper, and life is good.

Sophie comes to the top of a hill. She waits for us to catch up, wanting an audience. Then, with a squeal, she kicks off against the pavement and sails her bike down the small incline, pedaling madly for maximum speed.

I shake my head at my daughter's madcap ways. Never mind that my stomach clenched the moment she took off. I know better than to let anything show on my face. My nervousness only encourages her, "scaring Mommy" a favorite game both she and Brian like to play.

"I want to go faster!" Sophie announces at the bottom.

"Find a bigger hill," Brian says.

I roll my eyes at both of them. "That was plenty fast, thank you very much."

"I want to take off my training wheels."

I pause, do a little double take. "You want to remove your training wheels?"

"Yes." Sophie is adamant. "I want to

ride like a big girl. On two wheels. Then I'll be faster."

I'm not sure what I think. When did I lose my training wheels? Five, six, I don't remember. Probably sooner versus later. I was always a tomboy. How can I blame Sophie for sharing the same trait?

Brian is already beside Sophie's bike, checking out the setup.

"Gonna need tools," he declares, and that quickly, it's settled. Brian trots home for a set of wrenches, Sophie bounds around the park, announcing to all strangers and at least half a dozen squirrels that she's going to ride on two wheels. Everyone is impressed, particularly the squirrels, who chatter at her, before scampering up trees.

Brian returns within fifteen minutes; he must have run the whole way to our house and back and I feel a rush of gratitude. That he loves Sophie that much. That he understands a five-year-old's impulsiveness so well.

Removing training wheels turns out to be remarkably easy. Within minutes, Brian has tossed the wheels into the grass, and Sophie is back on her bike, feet flat on the ground as she tightens the straps of her red helmet and regards us solemnly.

"I'm ready," she declares.

And I have a moment, my hand pressed against my stomach, thinking, *But I'm not.* I'm really not. Wasn't it just yesterday that she was this tiny little baby that fit on the curve of my shoulder? Or maybe a careening ten-month-old, taking that first wild step? How did she get this tall and where did all those years go and how do I get them back?

She's my whole world. How will I handle it if she falls?

Brian is already stepping forward. He instructs Sophie to mount her bike. He has one hand on the handlebars, keeping them straight, another hand on the back of the banana seat to hold the bike steady.

Sophie sits on the seat, both feet on the pedals. She appears both somber and fierce. She's going to do this, it's only a question of how many crashes until she gets it right.

Brian is talking to her. Murmuring

some instructions I can't hear, because it's easier if I stand back, distance myself from what is about to happen. Mothers hold close, fathers let go. Maybe that's the way of the world.

I try to remember again my first experience without training wheels. Did my father help me? Did my mother come out to witness the event? I can't remember. I want to. Any kind of memory of my father providing words of advice, my parents paying attention.

But I come up blank. My mother is dead. And my father made it clear ten years ago that he never wanted to see me again.

He doesn't know he has a granddaughter named Sophie. He doesn't know his only child became a state police officer. His son died. His daughter, he threw away.

Brian has Sophie lined up. The bike is trembling a little. Her nervousness. Maybe his. They are both wired, intent. I remain on the sidelines, unable to speak.

Sophie starts to peddle. Beside her, Brian breaks into a jog, hands on the bike, assisting with balance as Sophie gains momentum. She's going faster. Faster, faster.

I hold my breath, both hands clenched into fists. Thank God for the helmet. It's all I can think. Thank God for the helmet and why didn't I cocoon my entire child in bubble wrap before letting her mount up?

Brian lets go.

Sophie surges forward, pedaling strong. Three feet, four feet, six, eight. Then, at the last second she glances down, seems to realize that Brian is no longer beside her, that she really is on her own. In the next instant, the handlebars twist and down she goes. A startled cry, an impressive crash.

Brian is already there, on his knees beside her before I can take three steps. He untangles Sophie from her bike, gets her to standing, inspects each limb.

Sophie's not crying. Instead, she turns to me, as I hustle down the bike path toward her.

"Did you *see* me?" my wild child squeals. "Mommy, did you *see* me?"

"Yes, yes, yes," I hasten to assure her,

finally arriving at the scene and inspecting my child for damage. She's safe; I've lost twenty years off my life.

"Again!" my child demands.

Brian laughs as he straightens out her bike and helps her climb aboard. "You're crazy," he tells her, shaking his head.

Sophie simply beams.

By the end of the afternoon, she's sailing around the park, training wheels nothing but a distant memory. Brian and I can no longer stroll behind her; she's too fast for us. Instead, we climb up on a picnic table, where we can sit and watch her bike exuberant laps.

We're holding hands again, snuggled shoulder to shoulder against the late afternoon chill. I place my head on his shoulder as Sophie goes racing by.

"Thank you," I say.

"She's a nut," he answers.

"I don't think I could've done that."

"Hell, my heart's still hammering in my chest."

That surprises me enough to straighten and look at him. "She scared you?"

"Are you kidding? That first spill." He shakes his head. "No one tells you how terrifying it is to be a parent. And we're just beginning. She's gonna want a trick bike next, you know. She'll be leaping down stairs, standing on handlebars. I'm going to need that hair stuff for men, what's it called, that gets the gray out?"

"Just for Men?"

"Yep. First thing when we get home, I'm ordering a case."

I laugh. He puts his arm around my shoulders.

"She really is amazing," he says, and all I can do is nod, because he's exactly right. She's Sophie and she's the best thing that ever happened to either of us.

"I'm sorry about this weekend," Brian says, one, two minutes later.

I nod against his shoulder, accepting his words without looking at him.

"I don't know what I was thinking," he continues. "Guess I got caught up in the moment. It won't happen again."

"It's okay," I say and I mean it. At this stage of the marriage, I still accept his apologies. At this stage of the marriage, I still believe in him.

"I'm thinking of joining a gym," Brian says shortly. "Got enough time on my hands, figured I could spend it getting into shape."

"You're in good shape."

"Yeah. But I want to get back to weight lifting. Haven't done that since my college days. And let's face it." Sophie zooms past our picnic table. "At the rate she's going, I'm going to need all my strength to keep up."

"Whatever you want to do," I tell him.

"Hey, Tessa."

"What?"

"I love you."

In my dream/memory, I smile, curve my arms around my husband's waist. "Hey, Brian. Love you, too."

I woke up hard, a noise jerking me from the golden past to the sterile present. That afternoon, the solid feel of my husband's arms, the bright sound of Sophie's exuberant laugh. The lull before the storm, except I hadn't known it then.

That afternoon Brian and I had returned home with an exhausted child.

We'd put her to bed early. Then, after a leisurely dinner, we'd made love and I'd fallen asleep thinking I was the luckiest woman in the world.

It would be a year before I told my husband I loved him again. Then he would be dying on our freshly scrubbed kitchen floor, his chest plugged with the bullets from my gun, his face a sad mirror of my own regrets.

In the seconds before I ran through the house, tore apart the house, searching frantically for the daughter I hadn't found yet.

More noises penetrated my consciousness. Distant beeps, rapid footsteps, someone yelling for something. Hospital noises. Loud, insistent. Urgent. It returned me once and for all to the present. No husband. No Sophie. Just me, alone in a hospital room, wiping tears from the unbruised half of my face.

For the first time, I realized there was something in my left hand. I drew my hand up so I could inspect the find with my one good eye.

It was a button, I realized. Half an inch in diameter. Navy blue frayed thread still looped through double-holes. Could be from pants, or a blouse, maybe even a state police uniform.

But it wasn't. I recognized the button the instant I saw it. I could even picture the second button that should be sewn right beside it, twin plastic rounds forming blue eyes on my daughter's favorite doll.

And for a second, I was so angry, so filled with rage my knuckles turned white and I couldn't speak.

I hurtled the button across the room, where it smacked against the privacy curtain. Then, just as quickly, I was sorry I'd done such an impulsive thing. I wanted it back. Needed it back. It was a tie to Sophie. One of my only links to her.

I tried to sit up, intent on retrieval. Immediately, the back of my skull roared to life, my cheek throbbing in a fresh spike of pain. The room wavered, tilted sickeningly, and I could feel my heart rate skyrocket from sudden, excruciating distress.

Dammit, dammit, dammit.

I forced myself to lie down, take a

steadying breath. Eventually, the ceiling righted and I could swallow without gagging. I lay perfectly still, acutely aware of my own vulnerability, the weakness I couldn't afford.

This was why men beat women, of course. To prove their physical superiority. To demonstrate they were bigger and stronger than us, and that no amount of special training would ever change that. They were the dominant gender. We might as well submit now and surrender.

Except I didn't need to be smashed over the head with a beer bottle to understand my physical limitations. I didn't need a hairy-knuckled fist exploding in my face to realize that some battles couldn't be won. I'd already spent my whole life coming to terms with the fact that I was smaller, more vulnerable than others. I'd still survived the Academy. I'd still spent four years patrolling as one of the state's few female troopers.

And I'd still given birth, all alone, to an amazing daughter.

Like hell I would submit. Like hell I would surrender.

I was crying again. The tears shamed me. I wiped my good cheek again, careful not to touch my black eye.

Forget the fucking duty belt, our instructors had told us the first day of Academy training. Two most valuable tools an officer has are her head and her mouth. Think strategically, speak carefully, and you can control any person, any situation.

That's what I needed. To regain control, because the Boston cops would be returning soon, and then I was probably doomed.

Think strategically. Okay. Time.

Four, five o'clock?

It would be dark soon. Night falling.

Sophie . . .

My hands trembled. I supressed the weakness.

Think strategically.

Stuck in a hospital. Can't run, can't hide, can't attack, can't defend. So I had to get one step ahead. Think strategically. Speak carefully.

Sacrifice judiciously.

I remembered Brian again, the beauty of that fall afternoon, and the way you can both love a man and curse him all in one breath. I knew what I had to do.

I found the bedside phone, and I dialed.

"Ken Cargill, please. This is his client, Tessa Leoni. Please tell him I need to make arrangements for my husband's body. Immediately."

11

Trooper Shane Lyons agreed to meet Bobby and D.D. at the BPD headquarters in Roxbury after six. That gave them enough time to stop for dinner. Bobby ordered up a giant hoagie, double everything. D.D. nursed a bowl of chicken noodle soup, liberally topped with crumbled saltines.

Sub shop had a TV blaring in the corner, the five o'clock news leading with the shooting in Allston-Brighton and the disappearance of Sophie Marissa Leoni. The girl's face filled the screen, bright blue eyes, huge, gap-tooth smile. Beneath her photo ran the hotline number, as well as an offer of a twenty-five thousand dollar reward for any tips that might lead to her recovery.

D.D. couldn't watch the newscast. It depressed her too much.

Eight hours after the first call out, they weren't making sufficient progress. One neighbor had reported seeing Brian Darby driving away in his white GMC Denali shortly after four p.m. yesterday. After that, nothing. No visual sightings. No phone calls logged on the landline or messages on his cell. Where Brian Darby had gone, what he'd done, who he might have seen, no one had any idea.

Which brought them to six-year-old Sophie. Yesterday had been a Saturday. No school, no playdates, no appearances in the yard, no sightings in local cameras or magical tips pouring in through the hotline. Friday, she'd been picked up from school at three p.m. After that, it was anybody's guess.

Tessa Leoni had reported in for her eleven p.m. graveyard shift on Saturday night. Three neighbors had noticed her cruiser departing; one had noticed its reappearance after nine the next morning. Dispatch had a full roster of duty calls, verifying Trooper Leoni had worked her shift, turning in the last batch of paperwork shortly after eight a.m. Sunday morning.

At which point, the entire family fell off the grid. Neighbors didn't see anything. Neighbors didn't hear anything. No fighting, no screaming, not even gunshots, though that made D.D. suspicious because how you could *not* hear a 9mm fire off three rounds was beyond her. Maybe people just didn't want to hear what they didn't want to hear. That seemed more likely.

Sophie Leoni had now been declared missing since ten this morning. Sun was down, thermostat was plunging, and four to six inches of snow were reportedly on their way.

The day had been bad. The night would be worse.

"I gotta make a call," Bobby said. He'd finished his sandwich, was balling up the wrapping.

"Gonna tell Annabelle you're working late?"

He gestured outside the sub shop window, where the first flakes had started to fall. "Am I wrong?"

"She okay with your schedule?" D.D. asked.

He shrugged. "What can she do? The job's the job."

"What about Carina? Soon she'll figure out Daddy disappears and doesn't always return home to play. Then there's the missed recitals, school plays, soccer games. *I scored one for the team, Dad! Except you weren't there.*"

Bobby regarded her curiously. "The job's the job," he repeated. "Yeah, there are times it sucks, but then, most jobs do."

D.D. scowled. She looked down, poked at her soup. The saltines had absorbed the broth, creating a lumpy mess. She didn't feel like eating anymore. She was tired. Discouraged. She was thinking of a little girl they probably wouldn't find alive. She was thinking of elderly Mrs. Ennis's comments on how hard it was for Trooper Leoni to juggle her job, a house, and a kid.

Maybe female law enforcement officers weren't meant to lead lives of domestic bliss. Maybe if Trooper Leoni hadn't tried for the whole husband and white picket fence, D.D. wouldn't have been called out this morning and a cute, innocent child wouldn't now be missing.

Good Lord, what was D.D. supposed to tell Alex? How was she, a career detective and self-admitted workaholic, supposed to *feel* about this?

She poked at her soup one last time, then pushed it away. Bobby was still standing there, apparently waiting for her to say something.

"You ever picture me as a mom?" she asked him.

"No."

"You didn't even have to think about that."

"Don't ask the question if you don't want the answer."

She shook her head. "I've never pictured myself as a mom. Moms . . . sing lullabies and carry around Cheerios and make funny faces just to get their babies to smile. I only know how to make my squad smile and that involves fresh coffee and maple-frosted donuts."

"Carina likes peekaboo," Bobby said.

"Really?"

"Yeah. I put my hand over my eyes, then jerk it away and cry, *'Peekaboo!'* She can do that for hours. Turns out I can do that for hours, too. Who knew?"

D.D. covered her eyes with her palm, then whipped her hand away. Bobby disappeared. Bobby reappeared. Other than that, it didn't do much for her.

"I'm not your baby," Bobby said by way of explanation. "We're genetically programmed to want to make our children happy. Carina beams, and . . . I can't even describe it. But my whole day has been worth it, and whatever silly thing makes her look like that, I'm gonna do it again. What can I tell you? It's crazier than love. Deeper than love. It's . . . being a parent."

"I think Brian Darby murdered his stepdaughter. I think he killed Sophie, then Tessa Leoni returned home and shot him."

"I know."

"If we're genetically programmed to want to make our offspring happy, how come so many parents hurt their own kids?"

"People suck," Bobby said.

"And that thought gets you out of bed each morning?"

"I don't have to hang out with people. I have Annabelle, Carina, my family, and my friends. That's enough."

"Gonna have a second Carina?"

"Hope so."

"Why, you're an optimist, Bobby Dodge."

"In my own way. I take it you and Alex are getting serious?"

"Guess that's the question."

"Does he make you happy?"

"I'm not someone who gets happy."

"Then does he make you content?"

She thought of her morning, wearing Alex's shirt, sitting at Alex's table. "I could spend more time with him."

"It's a start. Now, if you'll excuse me, I'm gonna call my wife and probably make some goo-goo noises for my daughter."

Bobby stepped away from the table. "Can I listen in?" D.D. called after him.

"Absolutely not," he called back.

Which was just as well, because her stomach was cramping uneasily again and she was thinking of a little bundle in blue or maybe a little bundle in pink and wondering what a little Alex or little D.D. might look like, and if she could love a child as much as Bobby obviously loved Carina, and if that love alone could be enough.

Because domestic bliss rarely worked out for female cops. Just ask Tessa Leoni.

By the time Bobby finished his call, the early evening snow had turned the roads into a snarled mess. They used lights and sirens all the way, but it still took them over forty minutes to hit Roxbury. Another five minutes to find parking, and Trooper Shane Lyons had been cooling his heels for at least a quarter of an hour by the time they entered the lobby of BPD headquarters. The burly officer stood as they walked in, still dressed in full uniform, hat pulled low on his brow, black leather gloves encasing both hands.

Bobby greeted the officer first, then D.D. An interrogation room would appear disrespectful, so D.D. found an unoccupied conference room for them to use. Lyons took a seat, removing his hat, but leaving on his coat and gloves. Apparently, he was planning on a short conversation.

Bobby offered him a Coke, which he accepted. D.D. stuck to water, while Bobby nursed a black coffee. Preliminaries settled, they got down to business.

"You didn't seem surprised to hear from us," D.D. started off.

Lyons shrugged, twirled his Coke can between his gloved fingers. "I knew my name would come up. Had to complete my duties as union rep, first, however, which was my primary responsibility at the scene."

"How long have you known Trooper Leoni?" Bobby asked.

"Four years. Since she started at the barracks. I was her senior officer, over-

seeing her first twelve weeks of patrol."
Lyons took a sip of his soda. He appeared uncomfortable, every inch the
reluctant witness.

"You worked closely with Trooper
Leoni?" D.D. prodded.

"First twelve weeks, yes. But after
that, no. Troopers patrol alone."

"Socialize much?"

"Maybe once a week. On duty officers will try to meet up for coffee or
breakfast. Breaks up our shifts, main-
tains camaraderie." He looked at D.D.
"Sometimes, the Boston cops even join
us."

"Really?" D.D. did her best to sound
horrified.

Lyons finally smiled. "Gotta back
each other up, right? So good to keep
the lines of communication open. But
having said that, most of a trooper's
shift is spent alone. Especially graveyard. It's you, the radar gun, and a highway full of drunks."

"What about at the barracks?" D.D.
wanted to know. "You and Tessa hang
out, grab a bite to eat after work?"

Lyons shook his head. "Nah. A

trooper's cruiser is his—or her—office. We only return to the barracks if we make an arrest, need to process an OUI, that kind of thing. Again, most of our time is on the road."

"But you assist one another," Bobby spoke up. "Especially if there's an incident."

"Sure. Last week, Trooper Leoni pinched a guy for operating under the influence on the Pike, so I arrived to help. She took the guy to the barracks to administer the breathalyzer and read him his rights. I stayed with his vehicle until the truck came to tow it away. We backed each other up, but we hardly stood around talking about our spouses and kids while she stuffed a drunk in the back of her cruiser." Lyons pinned Bobby with a look. "You must remember how it is."

"Tell us about Brian Darby," D.D. spoke up again, redirecting Lyons's stare.

The state trooper didn't answer right away, but thinned his lips, appearing to be wrestling with something inside himself.

"I'm damned if I do, damned if I don't," he muttered abruptly.

"Damned for what, Trooper?" Bobby asked evenly.

"Look." Lyons set down his soda. "I know I'm screwed here. I'm supposed to be an excellent judge of character, goes with the job. But then, this situation with Tessa and Brian. Hell, either I'm a total idiot who didn't know my neighbor had rage management issues, or I'm an asshole who set up a fellow officer with a wife beater. Honest to God . . . If I'd known, if I'd suspected . . ."

"Let's start with Brian Darby," D.D. said. "What did you know about him?"

"Met him eight years ago. We were both in a neighborhood hockey league. Played together every other Friday night; he seemed like a nice guy. Had him over a couple of times for dinner and beer. Still seemed like a nice guy. Worked a crazy schedule as a merchant marine, so he got my job, too. When he was around, we'd get together—play hockey, go skiing, maybe a day hike. He liked sports and I do, too."

"Brian was an active guy," Bobby said.

"Yeah. He liked to keep moving. Tessa did, too. Frankly, I thought they'd be a good fit. That's why I set them up. Figured even if they didn't end up dating, they could be hiking buddies, something."

"You set them up," D.D. repeated.

"Invited them both to a summer cookout. Let them take it from there. Come on, I'm a guy. That's as involved as a guy gets."

"They leave the party together?" Bobby asked.

Lyons had to think about it. "Nah. They met later for drinks, something like that. I don't know. But next thing I knew, Tessa and her daughter were moving in with him, so I guess it worked."

"You attend the wedding?"

"No. Didn't even hear about it until it was all over. I think I noticed Tessa was suddenly wearing a ring. When I asked, she said they'd gotten married. I was a little startled, thought it was kind of quick, and okay, maybe I was surprised they didn't invite me, but . . ." Lyons shrugged. "It's not like we were that close or I was that involved."

It seemed important for him to establish the point. He wasn't *that* close to the couple, not *that* involved in their lives.

"Tessa ever talk about the marriage?" D.D. asked.

"Not to me."

"So to others?"

"I can only speak for myself."

"And you're not even doing that," D.D. stated bluntly.

"Hey. I'm trying to tell you the truth. I don't spend my Sundays dining at Brian and Tessa's house or having them over to my place after church. We're friends, sure. But, we got our own lives. Hell, Brian wasn't even in town half the year."

"So," D.D. said slowly. "Your hockey buddy Brian Darby ships out half the year, leaving behind a fellow trooper to juggle the house, the yard, and a small child, all by herself, and you just go your own way. Have your own life, don't need to get bogged down with theirs?"

Trooper Lyons flushed. He looked at

his Coke, his square jaw noticeably clenched.

Good-looking guy, D.D. thought, in a ruddy face sort of way. Which made her wonder: Did Brian Darby start bulking up because his wife carried a gun? Or because his wife started calling a hunky fellow trooper for help around the house?

"I might have fixed the lawn mower," Lyons muttered.

D.D. and Bobby waited.

"Kitchen faucet leaked. Took a look at that, but out of my league, so I gave her the name of a good plumber."

"Where were you last night?" Bobby asked quietly.

"Patrolling!" Lyons looked up sharply. "For chrissake, I haven't been home since eleven last night. I got three kids of my own, you know, and if you don't think I'm not picturing them every time Sophie's photo flashes across the news . . . Shit. Sophie's just a kid! I still remember her rolling down the hill in my backyard. Then last year, climbing the old oak. Not even my eight-year-old son could catch up with her. She's half monkey, that one. And that smile, and ah . . . Dammit."

Trooper Lyons covered his face with his hand. He appeared unable to speak, so Bobby and D.D. gave him a moment.

When he finally got himself together, he lowered his hand, grimacing. "You know what we called Brian?" he said abruptly. "His nickname on the hockey team?"

"No."

"Mr. Sensitive. The man's favorite movie is *Pretty Woman.* When his dog, Duke, died, he wrote a poem and ran it in the local paper. He was that kind of guy. So no, I didn't think twice about introducing him to a fellow officer with a small child. Hell, I thought I was doing Tessa a favor."

"You and Brian still play hockey together?" Bobby asked.

"Not so much. My schedule changed; I work most Friday nights."

"Brian looks bigger now than when he got married. Like he's bulked up."

"I think he joined a gym, something like that. He talked about lifting weights."

"You ever work out with him?"

Lyons shook his head.

D.D.'s pager went off. She glanced at the display, saw it was the crime-scene lab and excused herself. When she left the conference room, Bobby was grilling Trooper Lyons on Brian Darby's exercise regimen and/or possible supplements.

D.D. got out her cellphone and dialed the crime lab. Turned out they had some initial findings from Brian's white GMC Denali. She listened, nodded, then ended the call in time to bolt for the ladies' room, where she managed to keep the soup down, but only after splashing a great deal of cold water on her face.

She rinsed her mouth. Ran more cold water over the back of her hands. Then she studied her pale reflection and informed herself that like it or not, she would get this done.

She would survive this evening. She would find Sophie Leoni.

Then she would go home to Alex, because they had a couple of things to talk about.

D.D. marched back into the conference room. She didn't wait, but led with the big guns because Trooper Lyons was stonewalling them, and frankly, she didn't have time for this bullshit anymore.

"Preliminary report on Brian Darby's vehicle," she said sharply.

She flattened her hands on the table in front of Trooper Lyons and leaned down, till she was mere inches from his face.

"They found a collapsible shovel tucked into a rear compartment, still covered in dirt and bits of leaves."

Lyons didn't say anything.

"Found a brand-new air freshener as well, melon scented, the kind that plugs into a socket. Lab geeks thought that was strange, so they took it out."

Lyons didn't say anything.

"Odor became apparent in less than fifteen minutes. Very strong, they said. Very distinct. But being geeks, they call in a cadaver dog just to be sure."

The officer paled.

"Decomp, Trooper Lyons. As in, the lab gurus are pretty damn certain a dead body was placed in the back of Brian Darby's vehicle in the past twenty-four hours. Given the presence of the shovel, they further surmise the body was driven to an unknown location and buried. Brian got a second home? Lake house, hunting lodge, ski cabin? Maybe if you finally start talking to us, we can at least bring home Sophie's body."

"Ah no . . ." Lyons paled further.

"Where did Brian take his stepdaughter?"

"I don't know! He doesn't have a second home. Least nothing he ever told me about!"

"You failed them. You introduced Brian Darby to Tessa and Sophie, and now Tessa is in a hospital beaten to a pulp and little Sophie's most likely dead. *You* set these wheels in motion. Now man up, and help us find Sophie's body. Where would he take her? What would he do? Tell us all of Brian Darby's secrets."

"He didn't have secrets! I swear . . . Brian was a stand-up guy. Sailed the ocean blue, then returned home to his wife and stepdaughter. Never heard him raise his voice. Certainly, never saw him raise a fist."

"Then what the hell happened?"

A heartbeat pause. Another long, shuddering breath.

"There is . . . There is another option," Lyons said abruptly. He looked at both of them, face still ashen, hands flexing and unflexing around his Coke. "Not really talking out of school," he babbled. "I mean, you'll find out sooner or later from Lieutenant Colonel Hamilton. He's the one who told me. Plus, it's a matter of record."

"Trooper Lyons! Spit it out!" D.D. yelled.

So he did. "What happened this morning . . . Well, let's just say, this wasn't the first time Trooper Leoni has killed a man."

12

First thing I learned as a female police officer was that men were not the enemy I feared them to be.

A bunch of drunken rednecks at a bar? If my senior officer, Trooper Lyons, got out of the cruiser, they escalated immediately to more aggressive acts of machismo. If I appeared on the scene, however, they dropped their posturing and began to study their boots, a bunch of sheepish boys caught in the act by Mom. Rough-looking long-haul truckers? Can't say *yes, ma'am,* or *no, ma'am* fast enough if I'm standing beside their rigs with a citation book. Pretty college boys who've tossed back a few too many brews? They stammer, hem and haw, then almost always end up asking me out on a date.

Most men have been trained since birth to respond to a female authority figure. They view someone like me either as the mom they have been prepped to obey, or maybe, given my age and appearance, as a desirable woman worthy of being pleased. Either way, I'm not a direct challenge. Thus, the most belligerent male can afford to step down in front of his buddies. And in situations overloaded with testosterone, my fellow troopers often called me directly for backup, counting on my woman's touch to defuse the situation, as it generally did.

Male parties might flirt a little, fluster a little, or both. But inevitably, they did what I said.

Females on the other hand . . .

Pull over the soccer mom doing ninety-five in her Lexus, and she'll instantly become verbally combative, screeching shrilly about her need for speed in front of her equally entitled-looking two-point-two kids. Doing a civil standby, assisting while a guy under a restraining order fetches his last few things from the apartment, and the battered girlfriend will inevitably come flying at me, demanding to know why I'm letting him pack his own underwear and cursing and screaming at me as if I'm the one responsible for every bad thing that's ever happened in her life.

Men are not a problem for a female trooper.

It's the women who will try to take you out, first chance they get.

My lawyer had been prattling away at my bedside for twenty minutes when Sergeant Detective D. D. Warren yanked back the privacy curtain. The state police liason, Detective Bobby Dodge, was directly behind her. His face was impossible to read. Detective Warren, however, wore the hungry look of a jungle cat.

My lawyer's voice trailed off. He appeared unhappy with the sudden appearance of two homicide detectives, but not surprised. He'd been trying to explain to me my full legal predicament. It wasn't good, and the fact I had yet to give a full statement to the police, in his expert opinion, made it worse.

Currently, my husband's death was listed as a questionable homicide. Next course of action would be for the Suffolk County DA, working in conjunction with the Boston police, to determine an appropriate charge. If they thought I was a credible victim, a poor battered wife with a corroborating history of visits to the emergency room, they could view Brian's death as justifiable homicide. I shot him, as I claimed, in self-defense.

But murder was a complicated business. Brian had attacked with a broken bottle; I had retaliated with a gun. The DA could argue that while I was clearly defending myself, I'd still used unnecessary force. The pepper spray, steel baton, and Taser I carried on my duty belt all would've been better choices, and for my trigger-happy ways, I'd be charged with manslaughter.

Or, maybe they didn't believe I'd feared for my life. Maybe they believed Brian and I had been fighting and I'd shot and killed my husband in the heat of the moment. Homicide without premeditation, or Murder 2.

Those were the best-case scenarios. There was, of course, another scenario. One where the police determined my husband was not a violent wife beater, but instead, found me to be a master manipulator who shot my husband with premeditated malice and forethought. Murder 1.

Otherwise known as the rest of my life behind bars. Game over.

These were the concerns that had brought my lawyer to my bedside. He didn't want me fighting the police for my husband's remains. He wanted me to issue a statement to the press, a victimized wife extolling her innocence, a desperate mother pleading for her young daughter's safe return. He also wanted me to start playing nicely with the detectives handling my case. As he pointed out, battered woman's syndrome was an affirmative defense, meaning the burden of proof rested on my bruised shoulders.

Marriage, it turned out, boiled down to he said, she said, long after one of the spouses was dead.

Now the homicide detectives were back and my lawyer rose awkwardly to assume a defensive stance beside my bed.

"As you can see," he began, "my client is still recovering from a concussion, not to mention a fractured cheekbone. Her doctor has ordered her to remain overnight for observation, and to get plenty of rest."

"Sophie?" I asked. My voice came out strained. Detective Warren appeared too harsh to be approaching a mother with bad news. But then again . . .

"No word," she said curtly.

"What time is it?"

"Seven thirty-two."

"After dark," I murmured.

The blonde detective stared at me. No compassion, no sympathy. I wasn't surprised. There were so few women in blue, you'd think we'd help each other out. But women were funny that way. So willing to turn on one of their own, especially a female perceived as weak, such as one who served as her husband's personal punching bag.

I couldn't imagine Detective Warren ever tolerating domestic abuse. If a man hit her, I bet she'd hit back twice as hard. Or taser him in the balls.

Detective Dodge was on the move. He'd commandeered two low-slung chairs and positioned them next to the bed. He gestured for D.D. to take a seat, both of them pulling up close. Cargill took the hint and perched on the edge of his own chair, still looking uncomfortable.

"My client isn't up to answering a lot of questions, just yet," he said. "Of course, she wants to do anything she can to assist in the search for her daughter. Is there information you need relevant to that investigation?"

"Who is Sophie's biological father?" Detective Warren asked. "And where is he?"

I shook my head, a motion that immediately caused me to wince.

"I need a name," Warren said impatiently.

I licked my dry lips, tried again. "She doesn't have a father."

"Impossible."

"Not if you're a slut and an alcoholic," I said.

Cargill shot me a startled glance. The detectives, however, appeared intrigued.

"You're an alcoholic?" Bobby Dodge asked evenly.

"Yes."

"Who knows?"

"Lieutenant Colonel Hamilton, some of the guys." I shrugged, trying not to move my bruised cheek. "I sobered up seven years ago, before I joined the force. It hasn't been an issue."

"Seven years ago?" D.D. repeated. "When you were pregnant with your daughter?"

"That's right."

"How old were you when you got pregnant with Sophie?"

"Twenty-one. Young and stupid. I drank too much, partied too hard. Then one day, I was pregnant and it turned out the people I thought were my friends only hung out with me because I was part of the circus. Minute I left the show, I never saw any of them again."

"Male associates?" D.D. asked.

"Won't help you. I didn't sleep with men I knew. I slept with men I didn't know. Generally older men who were interested in buying a young stupid girl plenty of alcohol. I got drunk. They got laid. Then we each went our own way."

"Tessa," my lawyer began.

I held up a hand. "It's old news, and nothing that matters. I don't know Sophie's dad. I couldn't have worked it out if I tried, and I didn't want to try. I got pregnant. Then I grew up, wised up, and sobered up. That's what matters."

"Sophie ever ask?" Bobby asked.

"No. She was three when I met Brian. She started calling him Daddy within a matter of weeks. I don't think she remembers anymore that we ever lived without him."

"When did he first hit you?" D.D. asked. "One month into the marriage? Six? Maybe a whole year?"

I didn't say anything, just stared up at

the ceiling. I had my right hand under the thin green hospital blanket, gripping the blue button a nurse had retrieved for me.

"We're going to need to see your medical records," D.D. stated. She was staring at my lawyer, challenging him.

"I fell down the stairs," I said, my lips twisting into a funny smile, because it was actually the truth, but they, of course, would interpret it as the appropriate lie. Irony. God save me from irony.

"Excuse me?"

"The bruise on my ribs . . . Should've de-iced the outdoor steps. Oops."

Detective Warren gave me an incredulous look. "Sure. You fell. What, three, four times?"

"I think it was only twice."

She didn't appreciate my sense of humor. "Ever report your husband for battery?" she pressed.

I shook my head. Made the back of my skull ping-pong with pain while filling my good eye with tears.

"What about to a fellow trooper? Say, Trooper Lyons. Sounds like he's good at helping out around the house."

I didn't say anything.

"Female friend?" Bobby spoke up. "What about a minister, or a call to a hotline? We are asking these things to help you, Tessa."

The tears built up more. I blinked them away.

"Wasn't that bad," I said finally, staring up at the white ceiling tiles. "Not in the beginning. I thought . . . I thought I could control him. Get things back on track."

"When did your husband start lifting weights?" Bobby asked.

"Nine months ago."

"Looks like he packed on some pounds. Thirty pounds over nine months. Was he using supplements?"

"He wouldn't say."

"But he was bulking up. Actively working on increasing muscle mass?"

Miserably, I nodded my head. All the times I told him he didn't need to work out that hard. That he already looked good, was plenty strong. I should've known better, his obsessive need for tidiness, his compulsive drive to organize even the soup cans. I should've

read the signs. But I hadn't. As the saying goes, the wife is always the last to
know.

"When did he first hit Sophie?" D.D.
asked.

"He did not!" I fired to life.

"Really? You're seriously gonna tell
me, with your bashed-up skull and shattered cheek, that your brute of a dead
husband hit you and only you, for as
long as you both shall live?"

"He loved Sophie!"

"But he didn't love you. That was the
problem."

"Maybe he was on steroids." It was
something. I looked at Bobby.

"'Roid rage doesn't discriminate,"
D.D. drawled. "Then he'd definitely
whack both of you."

"I'm just saying . . . He'd only been
home from his last tour a couple of
weeks, and this time . . . this time something had definitely changed." That
much wasn't a lie. In fact, I hoped they
would trace that thread. I could use a
couple of crack detectives on my side.
Certainly, Sophie deserved investigators
smarter than me coming to the rescue.

"He was more violent," Bobby stated carefully.

"Angry. All the time. I was trying to understand, hoping he'd settle back in. But it wasn't working." I twisted the top blanket with one hand, squeezed the button beneath the blanket with the other. "I just . . . I don't know how it got to this. And that's the truth. We loved each other. He was a good husband and a good father. Then . . ." More tears. Honest ones this time. I let a single drop trace down my cheek. "I don't know how it got to this."

The detectives fell quiet. My lawyer had relaxed beside me. I think he liked the tears, and probably the mention of possible steroid abuse, as well. That was a good angle.

"Where's Sophie?" D.D. asked, less hostile now, more intent.

"Don't know." Another honest answer.

"Her boots are gone. Coat, too. Like someone bundled her up, took her away."

"Mrs. Ennis?" I spoke up hopefully. "She's Sophie's caretaker—"

"We know who she is," D.D. inter-jected. "She doesn't have your child."

"Oh."

"Does Brian have a second home? Old ski lodge, fishing shack, anything like that?" Bobby this time.

I shook my head. I was getting tired, feeling my fatigue in spite of myself. I needed to get my endurance up. Build up my strength for the days and nights to come.

"Who else might know Sophie, re-move her from your home?" D.D. insis-tent, not letting it go.

"I don't know—"

"Brian's family?" she persisted.

"He has a mother, four sisters. The sisters are scattered, his mother lives in New Hampshire. You'd have to ask, but we never saw them that much. His schedule, mine."

"Your family?"

"I don't have a family," I said automat-ically.

"That's not what the police file said."

"What?"

"What?" my lawyer echoed.

Neither detective looked at him. "Ten

years ago. When you were questioned by the police for the death of nineteen-year-old Thomas Howe. According to the paperwork, it was your own father who supplied the gun."

I stared at D. D. Warren. Just stared and stared and stared.

"Those records are sealed," I said softly.

"Tessa . . ." my lawyer began again, not sounding happy.

"But I told Lieutenant Colonel Hamilton about the incident when I first started on the force," I stated levelly. "I didn't want there to be any misunderstandings."

"You mean, like one of your fellow officers discovering you'd shot and killed a kid?"

"Shot and killed a kid?" I mimicked. "I was sixteen. *I* was the kid! Why the hell do you think they sealed the records? Anyway, the DA never brought charges, ruling it justifiable homicide. Thomas assaulted me. I was just trying to get away."

"Shot him with a twenty-two," Detective Warren continued as if I'd never spoken. "Which you just so happened to have on you. Also, no signs of physical assault—"

"You have been speaking to my father," I said bitterly. I couldn't help myself.

D.D. tilted her head, eyeing me coolly. "He never believed you."

I didn't say anything. Which was answer enough.

"What happened that night, Tessa? Help us understand, because this really doesn't look good for you."

I clutched the button tighter. Ten years was a long time. And yet, not long enough.

"I was spending the night at my best friend's house," I said at last. "Juliana Howe. Thomas was her older brother. The last few times I'd been over, he'd made some comments. If we were alone in a room together, he stood too close, made me feel uncomfortable. But I was sixteen. Boys, particularly older boys, made me uncomfortable."

"Then why'd you spend the night?" D.D. wanted to know.

"Juliana was my best friend," I said

quietly, and in that moment I felt it all again. The terror. Her tears. My loss.

"You brought a gun," the detective continued.

"My father gave me the gun," I corrected. "I'd gotten a job in the food court at the mall. I often worked till eleven, then had to walk out to my car in the dark. He wanted me to have some protection."

"So he gave you a gun?" D.D. sounded incredulous.

I smiled. "You'd have to know my father. Picking me up in person would have meant getting involved. Handing me a twenty-two semiauto I had no idea how to use, on the other hand, got him off the hook. So that's what he did."

"Describe that night." Bobby spoke up quietly.

"I went to Juliana's house. Her brother was out; I was happy. We made popcorn and had a Molly Ringwald movie marathon—*Sixteen Candles*, followed by *Breakfast Club*. I fell asleep on the sofa. When I woke up all the lights were off and someone had put a blanket over me. I assumed Juliana had headed up to bed. I was just going to follow when her brother walked through the front door. Thomas was drunk. He spotted me. He . . ."

Both detectives and my lawyer waited.

"I tried to get around him," I said finally. "He cornered me against the sofa, pressed me down into it. He was bigger, stronger. I was sixteen. He was nineteen. What could I do?"

My voice trailed off again. I swallowed.

"May I have some water?" I asked.

My lawyer found the pitcher bedside, poured me a glass. My hand was shaking when I raised the plastic cup. I figured they couldn't blame me for the show of nerves. I drank the whole cup, then set it down again. Given how long it had been since I'd last given a statement, I had to think this through. Consistency was everything, and I couldn't afford a mistake this late in the game.

Three pairs of eyes waited for me.

I took another deep breath. Gripped the blue button and thought about life, the patterns we made, the cycles we couldn't escape.

Sacrifice judiciously.

"Just about when . . . Thomas was going to do what he was going to do, I felt my purse, against my hip. He had me pinned with the weight of his body while he worked on the zipper of his jeans. So I reached down with my right hand. I found my purse. I got the gun. And when he wouldn't get off me, I pulled the trigger."

"In the living room of your best friend's house?" Detective Warren said.

"Yes."

"Must've made a helluva mess."

"Twenty-two's not that big of a gun," I said.

"What about your best friend? How'd she take all this?"

I kept my gaze on the ceiling. "He was her brother. Of course she loved him."

"So . . . DA clears you. Court seals the records. But your father, your best friend. They never forgave you, did they."

She made it a statement, not a question, so I didn't answer.

"Is that when you started drinking?" Detective Dodge asked.

I nodded wordlessly.

"Left home, dropped out of school . . ." he continued.

"I'm hardly the first officer with a misspent youth," I retorted stiffly.

"You got pregnant," Detective Warren said. "Grew up, wised up, and sobered up. That's a lotta sacrifice for a kid," she commented.

"No. That's love for my daughter."

"Best thing that ever happened to you. Only family you have left."

D.D. still sounded skeptical, which I guess was warning enough.

"You ever hear of decomposition odor analysis?" the detective continued, her voice picking up. "Arpad Vass, a research chemist and forensic anthropologist, has developed a technique for identifying the more than four hundred body vapors that emanate from decaying flesh. Turns out, these vapors get trapped in soil, fabrics—even, say, the carpet in the back of a vehicle. With the use of an electronic body sniffer, Dr.

Vass can identify the molecular signature of body decomp left behind. For example, he can scan carpet that has been removed from a vehicle and actually see the vapors formed into the shape of a child's dead body."

I made a noise. Might have been a gasp. Might have been a moan. Beneath the sheet, my hand tightened.

"We just sent Dr. Vass the carpet from your husband's SUV. What's he gonna find, Tessa? Is this going to be your last glimpse of your daughter's body?"

"Stop. That is insensitive and inappropriate!" My lawyer was already on his feet.

I didn't really hear him. I was remembering pulling back the covers, gazing, horrified, at Sophie's empty bed.

All I want for Christmas is my two front teeth. . . .

"What happened to your daughter!" Detective Warren demanded to know.

"He wouldn't tell me."

"You came home? She was already gone?"

"I searched the house," I whispered. "The garage, sunroom, attic, yard. I searched and searched and searched. I demanded that he tell me what he did."

"What happened, Tessa? What did your husband do to Sophie?"

"I don't know! She was gone. Gone! I went to work and when I came home . . ." I stared at D.D. and Bobby, feeling my heart beat wildly again. Sophie. Vanished. Just like that.

All I want for Christmas is my two front teeth, my two front teeth. . . .

"What did he do, Trooper Leoni? Tell us what Brian did."

"He ruined our family. He lied to me. He betrayed us. He destroyed . . . everything."

Another deep breath. I looked both detectives in the eye: "And that's when I knew he had to die."

13

"What do you think of Tessa Leoni?" Bobby asked five minutes later, as they headed back to HQ.

"Liar, liar, pants on fire," D.D. said crossly.

"She seems deliberate with her replies."

"Please. If I didn't know any better, I'd say she doesn't trust cops."

"Well, advanced rates of alcoholism, suicide, and domestic violence aside, what's not to love?"

D.D. grimaced, but got his point. Law enforcement officers weren't exactly walking advertisements for well-adjusted human beings. Lotta cops graduated from the school of hard knocks. And most of them swore that's what it took to work these streets.

"She changed her story," D.D. said.

"Noticed that myself."

"We've gone from her shooting her husband first, then discovering that her daughter was missing, to she discovered Sophie was missing first, then ended up killing her husband."

"Different timelines, same results. Either way Trooper Leoni was beaten to a pulp, and either way, six-year-old Sophie is gone."

D.D. shook her head. "Inconsistency about one detail makes you have to question all details. If she lied about the timeline, what other pieces of her story are false?"

"A liar is a liar is a liar," Bobby said softly.

She glanced over at him, then tightened her hands on the wheel. Tessa's sob story had gotten to him. Bobby had always had a weakness for damsels in distress. Whereas D.D. had been spot-on with her first impression of Tessa Leoni: pretty and vulnerable, which was trying D.D.'s nerves.

D.D. was tired. It was after eleven and her new, high maintenance body was begging for sleep. Instead, she and Bobby were returning to Roxbury for the first taskforce meeting. Clock was still ticking. Media needed a statement. DA demanded an update. Brass just wanted the homicide case closed and the missing child found, right now.

In the old days, D.D. would be brewing six pots of coffee and eating half a dozen donuts to get through the night. Now, instead, she was armed with a fresh bottle of water and a package of saltines. They weren't getting the job done.

She'd texted Alex as they were leaving the hospital: *Won't see you tonight, sorry bout tomorrow.* He'd texted back: *Saw the news. Good luck.*

No guilt, no whining, no recriminations. Just genuine support.

His text made her weepy, which she blamed squarely on her condition, because no man had made D. D. Warren cry in at least twenty years and like hell she'd start now.

Bobby kept looking at her ubiquitous water bottle, then at her, then at her water bottle. If he did it again, she was going to dump the contents of said bottle over his head. The thought cheered her up, and she'd almost pulled herself together by the time they found parking.

Bobby grabbed a fresh cup of black coffee, then they headed upstairs to the homicide unit. D.D. and her fellow detectives were lucky. BPD headquarters had been built only fifteen years ago, and while the location was still subject to debate, the building itself was modern and well maintained. The homicide unit appeared less *NYPD Blue* and more MetLife Insurance Company. Sensible dividers carved out brightly lit work spaces. Broad expanses of gray metal files were covered in green plants, family photos, and personal knickknacks. A Red Sox foam finger was mounted here, a Go Pats banner hung there.

The secretary had a thing for cinnamon potpourri, while the detectives had a fetish for coffee, so the space even smelled nice—a cinnamon, coffee blend that made one of the newer guys nickname the reception area Starbucks. In typical cop fashion, the nickname stuck and now the secretary had Starbucks stickers, napkins, and paper cups all positioned on the front counter, which had confused more than one witness arriving to make a statement.

D.D. found her squad and a leader from each investigative team already gathered in the conference room. She moved to the head of the table, next to the large white board that would become their case bible for the coming days. She set down her water, picked up a black marker, and they were off and running.

The search for Sophie Leoni was highest priority. Hotline was ringing nonstop and had generated two dozen tips which officers were chasing down as they spoke. Nothing significant as of yet. Canvassing of neighbors, local businesses, and community medical centers was proceeding along the same lines—some leads, but nothing significant as of yet.

Phil had run background on Sophie's caretaker, Brandi Ennis, which had come back clean. Coupled with D.D. and Bobby's personal interview, they felt they could rule her out as a suspect. Initial backgrounds on the school administration and Sophie's teacher raised no red flags. They were starting on parents next.

The video team had studied seventy-five percent of the outtakes from various cameras within a two-mile radius of the Leoni residence. They had yet to see any sign of Sophie, Brian Darby, or Tessa Leoni. Their search had broadened to include any visual of Brian Darby's white GMC Denali.

Given the crime lab's findings that a body had most likely been placed in the back of Darby's vehicle, retracing the last twenty-four hours of the Denali was their best lead. D.D. assigned two detectives to pore through credit card records to see if they could determine the last time the Denali had been fueled up. Based on that date and how many gallons were currently left in the tank, they could work out the largest possible distance Brian Darby would've been able to drive with a body in the back of his vehicle. Also, the same two detectives would check for any parking tickets, speeding citations, or Fast Lane/E-Z Pass (toll booth) records that might help place the Denali Friday night through Sunday morning.

Finally, D.D. would leak details about the Denali to the press, encouraging eye witnesses to phone in with new details.

Phil agreed to search for any properties that might be owned by Brian Darby or a family member. His initial background reports on the family hadn't revealed any red flags. Brian Darby had no arrests or warrants under his name. Couple of speeding tickets scattered over the past fifteen years, other than that he appeared to be a law-abiding citizen. He'd worked the past fifteen years for the same company, ASSC, as a merchant marine. He had a two hundred thousand dollar mortgage on the home, a thirty-four thousand dollar loan on the Denali, four grand in consumer debt, and over fifty grand in the bank, so not a bad financial picture.

Phil had also made initial contact with Brian Darby's boss, who agreed to a phone interview tomorrow morning at eleven a.m. By phone, Scott Hale had expressed shock at Darby's death, and total disbelief the man had beat his wife. Hale had also been dismayed by Sophie's disappearance and was going to ask ASSC to increase the amount of money currently being offered as a reward.

D.D., who'd written across the top of the board, *Did Brian Darby Beat His Wife?* added a check to the No column.

Which made her other squadmate, Neil, raise his hand for the Yes column. Neil had spent the day at the hospital, where he'd subpoenaed Tessa Leoni's medical records. While there wasn't a long history of "accidents," today's admittance alone had revealed multiple injuries from multiple time frames. Tessa Leoni presented with bruised ribs, probably from an incident at least one week ago (the fall down the front steps, D.D. had retorted, already rolling her eyes). The doctor had also made a notation he was concerned that one fractured rib had healed improperly due to "inadequate medical attention," which would support Tessa's assertion that she didn't seek outside assistance, but dealt with the consequences of each beating on her own.

In addition to her concussion and fractured cheekbone, her medical chart listed a multitude of contusions, including a bruise in the shape of a rounded work boot.

"Does Brian Darby have steel-toed work boots?" D.D. asked excitedly.

"Went back to the house and retrieved one pair," Neil said. "Asked the lawyer if we could match the boots against the bruise on Leoni's hip. He considered that an invasion of privacy and requested we get a warrant."

"Invasion of privacy!" D.D. snorted. "This is the sort of discovery that helps her. Establishes pattern of abuse, meaning she won't end up in jail for twenty to life."

"He didn't argue that. Just said she was under doctor's orders to rest, so he wanted to wait until she's recovered from her concussion."

"Please! Then the bruise is faded and we've lost our match and she's lost her corroboration. Screw the lawyer. Get a warrant. Get it done."

Neil agreed, though it would have to wait till midmorning, as he'd be starting his day at the ME's office with the autopsy of Brian Darby. The autopsy was now scheduled for seven a.m., given that Tessa Leoni was requesting the return of her husband's remains ASAP, in order to plan an appropriate funeral.

"What?" D.D. exclaimed.

"Not kidding," Neil said. "Her lawyer called the ME this afternoon, wanting to know how soon Tessa could get the body back. Don't ask me."

But D.D. stared at the lanky redhead anyway. "Brian Darby's shooting is a questionable death. Of course his body must be autopsied, which Tessa knows as well as anyone." She turned her gaze to Bobby. "State Troopers learn homicide one-oh-one right?"

Bobby made a show of scratching his head. "What? They cram ninety classes into twenty-five weeks of Academy

training, and we're supposed to graduate knowing basic investigative steps?"

"So why would she ask for the body
back?" D.D. asked him. "Why even
make that call?"

Bobby shrugged. "Maybe she
thought the autopsy had already been
performed."

"Maybe she thought she'd get lucky,"
Neil spoke up. "She's a fellow member
of law enforcement. Maybe she thought
the ME would honor her request and return her husband's body without the basic post-mortem."

D.D. chewed her lower lip. She didn't
like it. Pretty and vulnerable aside,
Tessa Leoni was a cool customer, amaz-
ingly lucid when she needed to be. If
Tessa had made the call, there had to be
a reason.

D.D. turned back to Neil. "What did
the ME tell her?"

"Nothing. The ME was speaking to
her lawyer, not Trooper Leoni. Ben reminded the lawyer that an autopsy had
to be performed, which Cargill didn't refute. My understanding is that they settled on a compromise—Ben would per-

form the autopsy first thing, to speed up the return of Darby's body to his family."

"So autopsy is happening sooner," D.D. mused, "and body is being returned sooner. When will Darby's body be released?"

Neil shrugged. "After the autopsy, an assistant will need to suture and clean up the corpse. Maybe as soon as end of day Monday, or Tuesday afternoon."

D.D. nodded, still turning the matter around in her head, but not seeing the angle. For some reason, Tessa Leoni wanted her husband's body sooner versus later. They would have to come back to that, as there must be a reason. There was always a reason.

D.D. returned to her taskforce. She demanded some good news. Nobody had any. She demanded some fresh leads. Nobody had any.

She and Bobby volunteered what they'd learned about Tessa Leoni's misspent youth. Having to shoot to kill once in self-defense was bad luck. Twice seemed dangerously close to a pattern of behavior, though from a legal perspective, it would take three times to be the charm.

D.D. wanted to learn more about the shooting of Thomas Howe. First thing in the morning, she and Bobby would track down the officer in charge of the investigation. If possible, they'd also contact the Howe family and Tessa's father. Last but not least, they wanted to identify Brian Darby's gym and check out his exercise regimen and the possibility of steroid abuse. Man had bulked up relatively quickly, Mr. Sensitive becoming Mr. Tempermental. It was worth checking out.

With that, D.D. jotted down the next steps and handed out homework. Video team needed to complete their marathon viewing of Boston cameras. Phil needed to complete background reports, conduct property searches, and interview Brian Darby's boss. Neil had autopsy duty as well as securing a warrant for matching Brian Darby's boot against Tessa Leoni's bruised hip.

Fuel squad got to play with gas consumption and Boston maps, creating a maximum search area for Sophie Leoni, while the hotline officers would continue running down old leads and mining for fresh information.

D.D. needed reports from today's interviews on her desk within the hour. Get to documenting, she ordered her team, then return for duty at oh-dark-thirty. Sophie Leoni remained missing, which meant no rest for the weary.

The detectives filed out.

D.D. and Bobby stayed behind to brief the superintendent of homicide, then consult with the Suffolk County DA. Neither man was interested in details, as much as they wanted results. It was D.D.'s fun-filled job as lead detective to inform them she had not determined the events leading up to Brian Darby's shooting, nor located six-year-old Sophie Leoni. But hey, pretty much every cop in Boston was currently working the case, so the taskforce was bound to have something . . . sometime.

The DA, who'd gone positively bug-eyed at the revelation that Tessa Leoni had already pleaded self-defense once before, agreed to D.D.'s request for more time before determining criminal charges. Given the differences between building a case for manslaughter versus Murder 1, additional information would be ideal and a deep bore into Tessa Leoni's misspent youth a necessity.

They'd keep the media focused on the search for Sophie, and away from the particulars of Brian Darby's death.

Twelve thirty-three in the morning, D.D. finally slunk back to her own office. Her boss was satisfied, the DA appeased, her taskforce engaged. And so it went, another day in another high profile case. The cogs of the criminal justice system churning round and round.

Bobby took the seat across from her. Without a word, he picked up the first typed report from the pile on her desk and began to read.

After another moment, D.D. joined him.

14

When Sophie was almost three, she locked herself in the trunk of my police cruiser. This happened before I ever met Brian, so I had only myself to blame.

We were living across the hall from Mrs. Ennis at the time. It was late fall, when the sun faded earlier and the nights were growing colder. Sophie and I had been outside, where we'd walked to the park and back. Now it was dinnertime, and I was fussing in the kitchen while assuming she was playing in the family room, where the TV was blaring *Curious George*.

I'd made a small salad, part of my program to introduce more vegetables into my child's diet. Then I'd grilled two chicken breasts and baked Ore-Ida French fries—my compromise, Sophie could have her beloved fries as long as she ate some salad first.

This project took me twenty, twenty-five minutes. But a busy twenty-five minutes. I was occupied and apparently not paying attention to my toddler because when I walked into the family room to announce it was time for dinner, my child wasn't there.

I didn't panic right away. I'd like to say it was because I was a trained police officer, but it had more to do with being Sophie's mom. Sophie started running at thirteen months and hadn't slowed down since. She was the child who disappeared in grocery stores, bolted away from park swing sets, and made a quick beeline through a sea of legs in a crowded mall, whether I was following or not. In the past six months, I'd already lost Sophie several times. In a matter of minutes, however, we always found each other again.

I started with the basics—a quick walk through our tiny one bedroom. I called her name, then for good measure, checked the cupboards in the bathroom, both closets, and under the bed. She wasn't in the apartment.

I checked the front door, which, sure enough, I'd forgotten to bolt, meaning the entire apartment complex had just become fair game. I crossed the hall, cursing myself silently and feeling the growing frustration that comes from being an overstretched single parent, responsible for all things at all times, whether I was up to the challenge or not.

I knocked on Mrs. Ennis's door. No, Sophie wasn't there, but she swore she'd just seen Sophie playing outside.

Outside I went. Sun had gone down. Streetlights blazed, as well as the spotlights on the front of the apartment building. It was never truly dark in a city like Boston. I took that to heart as I walked around the squat brick complex, calling my daughter's name. When no laughing child came running around the corner, no high-pitched giggles erupted from a nearby bush, I grew more concerned.

I started to shiver. It was cold, I didn't have a jacket, and given that I remembered seeing Sophie's raspberry-colored fleece hanging next to the door in our apartment, she didn't have a coat either.

My heart accelerated. I took a deep, steadying breath, trying to fight a growing well of dread. The whole time I'd been pregnant with Sophie, I'd lived in a state of fear. I hadn't felt the miracle of life growing in my body. Instead, I saw the photo of my dead baby brother, a marble white newborn with bright red lips.

When I'd gone into labor, I didn't think I'd be able to breathe through the terror clutching my throat. I would fail, my baby would die, there was no hope, no hope, no hope.

Except, then there was Sophie. Perfect, mottled red, screaming loudly Sophie. Warm and slippery and achingly beautiful as I cradled her against my breast.

My daughter was tough. And fearless and impulsive.

You didn't panic with a kid like Sophie. You strategized: What would Sophie do?

I returned to the apartment complex, performed a quick door-to-door canvass. Most of my neighbors weren't home from work yet; the few that answered hadn't seen Sophie. I moved fast now, footsteps with purpose.

Sophie liked the park and might head there, except we'd already spent an afternoon playing on the swings and even she'd been ready to leave at the end. She liked the corner store and was positively fascinated by the Laundromat— she loved to watch the clothes spin.

I decided to head back upstairs. Another quick walk-through of our apartment to determine if anything else might be missing—a special toy, her favorite purse. Then I'd grab my car keys and tour the block.

I made it just inside the door, then discovered what she'd taken: The keys to my police cruiser were no longer sitting in the change dish.

This time, I hauled ass out of the apartment and down the front steps. Toddlers and police cruisers didn't mix. Forget the radio, lights, and sirens in the front. I had a shotgun in the trunk.

I ran to the passenger's side, peering in from the sidewalk. The interior of the cruiser appeared empty. I tried the door, but it was locked. I walked around more carefully, heart pounding, breathing shallow as I inspected each door and window. No sign of activity. Locked, locked, locked.

But she'd taken the keys. Think like Sophie. What button might she have hit on the key fob? What might she have done?

Then I heard her. A *thump, thump, thump* from the trunk. She was inside, banging against the lid.

"Sophie?" I called out.

The thumping stopped.

"Mommy?"

"Yes, Sophie. Mommy's here. Honey," my voice had risen shrilly, despite my best intentions. "Are you all right?"

"Mommy," my child replied calmly

from inside the locked trunk. "Stuck, Mommy. Stuck."

I closed my eyes, exhaling my pent-up breath. "Sophie, honey," I said as firmly as I could. "I need you to listen to Mommy. Don't touch anything."

"'Kay."

"Do you still have the keys?"

"Mmm-hmm."

"Are they in your hand?"

"No touching!"

"Well, you can touch the keys, honey. Hold the keys, just don't touch anything else."

"Stuck, Mommy. Stuck."

"I understand, honey. Would you like to get out?"

"Yes!"

"Okay. Hold the keys. Find a button with your thumb. Push it."

I heard a click as Sophie did as she was told. I ran to the front door to check. Of course, she'd hit the lock key.

"Sophie, honey," I called back. "Button next to it! Hit that one!"

Another click, and the front door unlocked. Expelling another breath, I opened the door, found the latch for the trunk and released it. Seconds later, I was standing above my daughter, who was curled up as a pink puddle in the middle of the metal locker holding my backup shotgun and a black duffel bag filled with ammo and additional policing gear.

"Are you all right?" I demanded to know.

My daughter yawned, held out her arms to me. "Hungry!"

I scooped her out of the trunk, placed her on her feet on the sidewalk, where she promptly shivered from the chill.

"Mommy," she started to whine.

"Sophie!" I interrupted firmly, feeling the first edge of anger now that my child was out of immediate danger. "Listen to me." I took the keys from her, held them up, shook them hard. "These are *not* yours. You *never* touch these keys. Do you understand? No touching!"

Sophie's lower lip jutted out. "No touching," she warbled. The full extent of what she'd done seemed to penetrate. Her face fell, she stared at the sidewalk.

"You do not leave the apartment without telling me! Look me in the eye. Repeat that. Tell Mommy."

She looked up at me with liquid blue eyes. "No leave. Tell Mommy," she whispered.

Reprimand delivered, I gave in to the past ten minutes of terror, scooped her back into my arms, and held her tight. "Don't scare Mommy like that," I whispered against the top of her head. "Seriously, Sophie. I love you. I never want to lose you. You are my Sophie."

In response her tiny fingers dug into my shoulders, clutched me back.

After another moment, I set her down. I should've set the bolt lock, I reminded myself. And I'd have to move my keys to the top of a cabinet, or perhaps add them to the gun safe. More things to remember. More management in an already overstretched life.

My eyes stung a little, but I didn't cry. She was my Sophie. And I loved her.

"Weren't you scared?" I asked as I took her hand and led her back to the apartment for our now cold dinner.

"No, Mommy."

"Not even locked in the dark?"

"No, Mommy."

"Really? You're a brave girl, Sophie Leoni."

She squeezed my hand. "Mommy come," she said simply. "I know. Mommy come for me."

I reminded myself of that evening now, as I lay trapped in a hospital room, surrounded by beeping monitors and the constant hum of a busy medical center. Sophie was tough. Sophie was brave. My daughter was not terrified of the dark, as I'd let the detectives believe. I wanted them to fear for her, and I wanted them to feel for her. Anything that would make them work that much harder, bring her home that much sooner.

I needed Bobby and D.D., whether they believed me or not. My daughter needed them, especially given that her superhero mother currently couldn't stand without vomiting.

It went against the grain, but there it was: My daughter was in jeopardy, lost in the dark. And there wasn't a damn thing I could do about it.

One a.m.

I fisted my hand around the blue button, held it tight.

"Sophie, be brave," I whispered in the semi-darkened room, willing my body to heal faster. "Mommy's coming. Mommy will always come for you."

Then I forced myself to review the past thirty-six hours. I considered the full tragedy of the days behind. Then I contemplated the full danger of the days ahead.

Work the angles, anticipate the obstacles, get one step ahead.

Brian's autopsy had been moved to first thing in the morning. A Pyrrhic victory—I had gotten my way, and in doing so, had certainly stuck my own head in the noose.

But it also fast-forwarded the timeline, took some of the control from them and gave it back to me.

Nine hours, I figured. Nine hours to physically recover, then ready or not, the games began.

I thought of Brian, dying on the

kitchen floor. I thought of Sophie, snatched from our home.

Then I allowed myself one last moment to mourn my husband. Because once upon a time, we'd been happy.

Once upon a time, we'd been a family.

15

D.D. made it back to her North End condo at two-thirty in the morning. She collapsed on her bed, fully clothed, and set her alarm for four hours' sleep. She woke up six hours later, glanced at the clock, and immediately panicked.

Eight-thirty in the morning? She never overslept. Never!

She bolted out of bed, gazed wild-eyed around her room, then grabbed her cellphone and dialed. Bobby answered after the second ring, and she expelled in a breathless rush: "I'm coming I'm coming I'm coming. I just need forty minutes."

"Okay."

"Must have screwed up the alarm. Just gotta shower, change, breakfast. I'm on my way."

"Okay."

"Fuck! The traffic!"

"D.D.," Bobby said, more firmly. "It's okay."

"It's eight-thirty!" she shouted back, and to her horror realized she was about to cry. She plopped back on the edge of her bed. Good God, she was a mess. What was happening to her?

"I'm still home," Bobby said now. "Annabelle's sleeping, I'm feeding the baby. Tell you what. I'll call the lead detective from the Thomas Howe shooting. With any luck, we can meet in Framingham in two hours. Sound like a plan?"

D.D., sounding meek: "Okay."

"Call you back in thirty. Enjoy the shower."

D.D. should say something. In the old days, she would've definitely said something. Instead, she clicked off her cell and sat there, feeling like a balloon that had abruptly deflated.

After another minute, she trudged to the sleek master bath, where she stripped off yesterday's clothes and stood in a sea of white ceramic tiles, staring at her naked body in the mirror.

She touched her stomach with her fingers, brushed her palms across the smooth expanse of her skin, tried to feel some sign of what was happening to her. Five weeks late, she didn't detect any baby bump or gentle mound. If anything, her stomach appeared flatter, her body thinner. Then again, going from all you can eat buffets to broth and crackers could do that to a girl.

She switched her inspection to her face, where her rumpled blonde curls framed gaunt cheeks and bruised eyes. She hadn't taken a pregnancy test yet. Given her missed cycle, then the intense fatigue interspersed with relentless nausea, her condition seemed obvious. Just her luck to end a three-year sex drought by getting knocked up.

Maybe she wasn't pregnant, she

thought now. Maybe she was dying instead.

"Wishful thinking," she muttered darkly.

But the words brought her up short. She didn't mean that. She couldn't mean that.

She felt her stomach again. Maybe her waist was thicker. Maybe, right over here, she could feel a hint of round. . . . Her fingers lingered, cradled the spot gently. And for a second, she pictured a newborn, puffy red face, dark slitted eyes, rosebud lips. Boy? Girl? It didn't matter. Just a baby. An honest to God baby.

"I won't hurt you," she whispered in the quiet of the bathroom. "I'm not mommy material. I'm gonna suck at this. But I won't hurt you. I'd never intentionally hurt you."

She paused, sighed heavily, felt her denial take the first delicate step toward acceptance.

"But you're gonna have to work with me on this. Okay? You're not winning the mommy lottery here. So it's gonna take some compromise on both our parts. Like maybe you could start letting me eat again, and in return, I'll try to get to bed before midnight. It's the best I can do. If you want a better offer, you need to return to the procreation pot and start over.

"Your mommy's trying to find a little girl. And maybe you don't care about that, but I do. Can't help myself. This job's in my blood."

Another pause. She sighed heavily again, her fingers still stroking her stomach. "So I gotta do what I gotta do," she whispered. "Because the world is a mess, and someone has to clean it up. Or girls like Sophie Leoni will never stand a chance. I don't want to live in a world like that. And I don't want you to grow up in a world like that. So let's do this together. I'm going to shower, then I'm going to eat. How about some cereal?"

Her stomach didn't immediately sour, which she took as a yes. "Cereal it is. Then back to work for both of us. Sooner we find Sophie, sooner I can take you home to your daddy. Who, at least once upon a time, mentioned wanting kids. Hope that's still true. Ah geez. We're all gonna need a little faith here. All right, let's get this done."

D.D. turned on the shower spray.

Later, she ate Cheerios, then left her condo without throwing up.

Good enough, she decided. Good enough.

Detective Butch Walthers lived up to his name. Heavyset face, massive shoulders, barrel gut of a former linebacker now gone to seed. He agreed to meet Bobby and D.D. at a small breakfast spot around the corner from his house, because it was his day off and as long as he was talking shop, he wanted a meal out of it.

D.D. walked in, hit a solid wall of cooked eggs and fried bacon and nearly walked back out. She'd always loved diners. She'd always loved eggs and bacon. To be reduced to instant nausea now was beyond cruel.

She took several steadying breaths through her open mouth. Then in a fit of inspiration, she fished peppermint gum out of her shoulder bag. Old trick learned from working countless homicide scenes—chewing minty gum overwhelms one's sense of smell. She stuck three sticks into her mouth, felt the sharp peppermint flavor flood the back of her throat, and managed to make it to the rear of the diner, where Bobby was already sitting across from Detective Walthers in a side booth.

Both men stood as she approached. She introduced herself to Walthers, nodded at Bobby, then slid into the booth first, so she could be closest to the window. She was in luck, the double-hung appeared to actually open. She immediately went to work on the latches.

"Little hot," she commented. "Hope you don't mind."

Both men watched her curiously, but said nothing. The diner was hot, D.D. thought defensively, and the rush of crisp March air smelled of snow and nothing else. She leaned closer to the narrow opening.

"Coffee?" Bobby asked.

"Water," D.D. said.

He arched a brow.

"Already had java," she lied. "Don't want the jitters."

Bobby wasn't buying it. She should've known. She turned to Walthers before Bobby could ask about breakfast. D.D. turning down a meal probably signaled the end of the universe as he knew it.

"Thanks for meeting with us," D.D. said. "Especially on your day off."

Walthers nodded accommodatingly. His bulbous nose was lined with broken red capillaries. Drinker, D.D. deduced. One of the old-time veterans nearing the end of his policing career. If he thought life was hard now, she thought with a trace of sympathy, wait till he tried retirement. So many empty hours to fill with memories of the good old days, and regrets over the ones that got away.

"Surprised to get a call 'bout the Howe shooting," Walthers said now. "Worked a lotta cases in my time. Never considered that investigation to be an interesting one."

"Seemed pretty clear-cut?"

Walthers shrugged. "Yes and no.

Physical evidence was FUBAR, but background on Tommy Howe was straightforward—Tessa Leoni wasn't the first girl he'd attacked; just the first who'd fought back."

"Really?" D.D. was intrigued.

The waitress appeared, gazing at them expectantly. Walthers ordered the Trailblazer Special with four links of sausage, two fried eggs, and half a plate of home fries. Bobby seconded the order. D.D., feeling brave, went with orange juice.

Now Bobby was definitely staring at her.

"So walk us through the case," D.D. said to Walthers, the moment the waitress left.

"Call came into nine-one-one. The mom, that's my memory, quite hysterical. First responder found Tommy Howe dead from a single gunshot wound in the family room, the parents and his sister gathered round in their bathrobes. The mother was sobbing, father trying to console, younger sister shell-shocked. Parents didn't know nothing 'bout anything. They'd woken up to a noise, father had gone downstairs, found Tommy's body, and that had been that.

"Sister, Juliana, was the one with the answers, but it took a bit to get them. She'd had a friend sleeping over—"

"Tessa Leoni," D.D. supplied.

"Exactly. Tessa had fallen asleep on the couch while they were watching movies. Juliana had gone upstairs to bed. Shortly after one a.m., she'd also heard a noise. She'd come downstairs and saw her brother and Tessa on the couch. In her own words, she wasn't sure what was going on, but then she heard a gunshot and Tommy staggered back. He fell to the floor, and Tessa got off the sofa, still holding the gun."

"Juliana saw Tessa shoot her brother?" D.D. asked.

"Yep. Juliana was pretty messed up. She said Tessa claimed Tommy had attacked her. Juliana didn't know what to do. Tommy was bleeding everywhere, she could hear her father coming down the stairs. She panicked, told Tessa to go home, which Tessa did."

"Tessa ran home in the middle of the night?" Bobby spoke up with a frown.

"Tessa lived on the same street, five houses down. Not a big distance to cover. When the dad made it downstairs, he yelled at Juliana to have her mom call nine-one-one. Which is the scene I walked into. Bloody family room, dead teenager, missing shooter."

"Where was Tommy shot?"

"Upper left thigh. Bullet nicked his femoral artery and he bled out. Bad luck, if you think about it—dying from a single GSW to the leg."

"Only one shot?"

"That's all it took."

Interesting, D.D. thought. At least Brian Darby had earned three in the chest. What a difference twenty-five weeks of intensive firearms training could make.

"So where was Tessa?" D.D. asked.

"After Juliana's statement, I proceeded to the Leoni residence, where Tessa answered on the first knock. She'd showered—"

"No way!"

"Told you the physical evidence was FUBAR. Then again"—Walthers shrugged his burly shoulders—"she

was sixteen years old. By her own admission, she'd been sexually assaulted,
before shooting her attacker. Heading
straight for the shower—can you blame
her?"

D.D. still didn't like it. "What physical
evidence could you recover?"

"The twenty-two. Tessa handed it
right over. Her prints were on the handle
and ballistics matched the slug that
killed Tommy Howe to the gun. We
bagged and tagged her discarded
clothes. No semen on the underwear—
she claimed he didn't, ahem, get to finish what he'd started. But some blood
on her clothing, same type as Tommy
Howe."

"Test her hands for powder?"

"Negative—but then, she'd showered."

"Rape kit?"

"She declined."

"She declined?"

"She said she'd been through
enough. I tried to convince her to let a
nurse examine her for bruising, tried to
explain it would be in her own best interest, but she wasn't buying it. Girl was

shaking like a leaf. You could see—she was done."

"Where's the father through all this?" Bobby wanted to know.

"He woke up when we entered the home. Apparently figuring out for the first time that his daughter had returned early from her sleepover and that there'd been an incident. He seemed a little . . . checked out. Stood in the kitchen in his boxers and wife-beater T-shirt, arms crossed over his chest, not saying a word. I mean, here's his sixteen-year-old daughter talking about being attacked by a boy, and he's just standing there like a goddamn statue. Donnie," Walthers snapped his fingers as the name came to him, "Donnie Leoni. Owned his own garage. Never could figure him out. I was guessing drinking, but never confirmed it."

"Mother?" D.D. asked.

"Dead. Six months earlier, heart failure. Not a happy household, but . . ." Again, Walthers shrugged. "Most of them aren't."

"So," D.D. replayed the events in her mind, "Tommy Howe is dead from a sin-

gle GSW in his family room. Tessa con-
fesses to the crime, all cleaned up and
unwilling to submit to a physical exam. I
don't get it. The DA simply took her
word for it? Poor traumatized sixteen-
year-old girl must be telling the truth?"

Walthers shook his head. "Between
you and me?"

"By all means," D.D. assured him.
"Between friends."

"I couldn't make heads or tails of
Tessa Leoni. I mean, on the one hand,
she was sitting in her kitchen trembling
uncontrollably. On the other hand . . .
she delivered a precise recounting of
every minute of the evening. In all my
years, never had a victim recount so
many details with such clarity, especially
a victim of sexual assault. It bothered
me, but what could I say: *Honey, your
memory is too good for me to take you
seriously*?" Walthers shook his head. "In
this day and age, those kinds of statements can cost a detective his shield,
and trust me—I got two ex-wives to
support—I need my pension."

"So why let her off with self-defense?

Why not press charges?" Bobby asked, clearly as perplexed as D.D.

"Because Tessa Leoni might have been a questionable victim, but Tommy Howe was the perfect perpetrator. Within twenty-four hours, three different girls phoned in with accounts of being sexually assaulted by him. None of them wanted to make a formal statement, mind you, but the more we dug, the more we discovered Tommy had a clear reputation with the ladies: He didn't take no for an answer. He didn't necessarily use brute force, which is why so many of the girls were reluctant to testify. Instead, sounded like he would ply them with alcohol, maybe even spike their drinks. But a couple of the girls remembered clearly *not* being interested in Tommy Howe, and waking up in his bed anyway."

"Rohypnol," D.D. said.

"Probably. We never found any trace of it in his dorm room, but even his buddies agreed that what Tommy wanted, Tommy got, and the girl's feelings on the subject weren't of much interest to him."

"Nice guy," Bobby muttered darkly.

"His parents certainly thought so," Walthers remarked. "When the DA announced he wasn't pressing charges, tried to explain the mitigating circumstances . . . You would've thought we were claiming the Pope was an atheist. The father—James, James Howe—hit the roof. Screamed at the DA, called my lieutenant to rant how my shitty police work was allowing a cold-blooded murderer to go free. Jim had contacts, he'd get us all in the end."

"Did he?" D.D. asked curiously.

Walthers rolled his eyes. "Please, he was corporate middle management for Polaroid. Contacts? He made a decent living, and I'm sure his underlings feared him. But he was only a king of an eight-by-eight cubicle and a two thousand square foot house. Parents." Walthers shook his head.

"Mr. and Mrs. Howe never believed Tommy attacked Tessa Leoni?"

"Nope. They could never see their son's guilt, which was interesting, 'cause Donnie Leoni could never see his daughter's innocence. I heard through the grapevine that he kicked her out. Apparently, he's one of those guys who believes the girl must be asking for it." Walthers shook his head again. "What can you do?"

The waitress reappeared, bearing platters of food. She slid plates in front of Walthers and Bobby, then handed D.D. her glass of juice.

"Anything else?" the waitress asked.

They shook their heads; she departed.

The men dug in. D.D. leaned closer to the cracked window to escape the greasy odor of sausage. She removed her gum, attempted the orange juice.

So Tessa Leoni had shot Tommy Howe once in the leg. If D.D. pictured the scene in her mind, the choreography made sense. Tessa, sixteen years old, terrified, pressed down into the sofa cushions by the weight of a bigger, stronger male. Her right hand fumbling beside her, feeling the lump of her purse digging into her hip. Fishing for her father's twenty-two, finally getting her hand around the grip, wedging it between their bodies . . .

Walthers had been right—damned unlucky for Tommy that he'd died from such a wound. All things considered, unlucky for Tessa, too, as she'd lost her father and her best friend over it.

It sounded like justifiable homicide, given the number of other women willing to corroborate Tommy's history of sexual assault. And yet, for one woman to have now been involved in two fatal shootings . . . First one involving an aggressive teenage boy. Second one involving an abusive husband. First incident a single shot to the leg that just happened to prove fatal. Second incident three shots to the chest, center of the kill zone.

Two shootings. Two incidents of self-defense. Bad luck, D.D. mused, taking a second small sip of orange juice. Or learning curve?

Walthers and Bobby finished up their meals. Bobby grabbed the check, Walthers grunted his thanks. They exchanged cards, then Walthers went his way, leaving Bobby and D.D. standing alone on the sidewalk.

Bobby turned to her the second

Walthers disappeared around the corner. "Something you want to tell me, D.D.?"

"No."

He clenched his jaw, looked like he might press the matter, then didn't. He turned away, studying the front awning of the diner. If D.D. didn't know better, she'd think his feelings were hurt.

"Got a question for you," D.D. said, to change the subject and ease the tension. "I keep coming back to Tessa Leoni, forced to kill two men in two separate incidents of self-defense. I'm wondering, is she that unlucky, or is she that smart?"

That caught Bobby's attention. He turned back to her, expression intent.

"Think about it," D.D. continued. "Tessa's hung out to dry at sixteen, ends up pregnant and alone at twenty-one. But then, in her own words, she rebuilds her life. Sobers up. Gives birth to a beautiful daughter, becomes a respectable police officer, even meets a great guy. Until the first time he drinks too much and whacks her. Now what does she do?"

"Cops don't confide in other cops," Bobby said stiffly.

"Exactly," D.D. agreed. "Violates the code of the patrol officer, who's expected to handle all situations alone. Now, Tessa could leave her husband. Next time Brian shipped out, Tessa and Sophie would have a sixty-day window to get settled into their own place. Except, maybe having lived in a cute little house, Tessa doesn't want to return to one-bedroom living. Maybe she likes the house, the yard, the expensive SUV, the fifty grand in the bank."

"Maybe she doesn't believe moving out will be enough," Bobby countered levelly. "Not all abusive husbands are willing to take the hint."

"All right," D.D. granted him. "That, too. Tessa decides she needs a more permanent solution. One that removes Brian Darby from her and Sophie's life forever, while preserving prime Boston real estate. So what does she do?"

Bobby stared at her. "You're saying that based on her experience with Tommy Howe, Tessa decides to stage an attack where she can shoot her husband in self-defense?"

"I'm thinking that thought should've crossed her mind."

"Yeah. Except Tessa's injuries aren't staged. Concussion, fractured cheekbone, multiple contusions. Woman can't even stand up."

"Maybe Tessa goaded her husband into attacking. Not too hard to do. She knew he'd been drinking. Now all she has to do is incite him into whacking her a few times, and she's safe to open fire. Brian gives in to his inner demon, and Tessa takes advantage."

Bobby frowned, shook his head. "That's cold. And still doesn't hold water."

"Why not?"

"Because of Sophie. So Tessa gets her husband to hit her. And Tessa shoots her husband. As you put it yesterday, that explains his body in the kitchen, and her visit with the EMTs in the sunroom. But what about Sophie? Where's Sophie?"

D.D. scowled. Her arm rested across her stomach. "Maybe she wanted Sophie out of the house in case she witnessed the event."

"Then she arranges for Sophie to stay with Mrs. Ennis."

"Wait—maybe that's the problem. She didn't arrange for Sophie to stay with Mrs. Ennis. Sophie saw too much, then Tessa had to squirrel her away so we couldn't question her."

"Tessa has Sophie in hiding?"

D.D. thought about it. "It would explain why she was so slow to cooperate. She's not worried about her child—she knows Sophie is safe."

But Bobby was already shaking his head. "Come on, Tessa's a trained police officer. She knows the minute she declares her child missing, the whole state goes on Amber Alert. What are the chances of successfully hiding a child whose photo is being beamed over every major news medium in the free world? Who would she even trust with that kind of request—*It's nine a.m. Sunday morning, I just shot my husband, so hey, want to run away with my six-year-old for a bit?* This is a woman we've already established doesn't have close family or friends. Her options would be Mrs. Ennis or Mrs. Ennis, and Mrs. Ennis doesn't have Sophie.

"Furthermore," Bobby continued relentlessly, "there's no endgame there. Sooner or later, we're gonna find Sophie. And when we do, we're gonna ask her what she saw that morning. If Sophie did witness Tessa and Brian's confrontation, a few days' delay isn't going to change anything. So why take such a risk with your own kid?"

D.D. pursed her lips. "Well, when you put it like that . . ." she muttered.

"Why is this so hard for you?" Bobby asked suddenly. "A fellow officer is hospitalized. Her young daughter is missing. Most of the detectives are happy to help her out, while you seem hell-bent on finding a reason to string her up."

"I am not—"

"Is it because she's young and pretty? Are you really so petty?"

"Bobby Dodge!" D.D. exploded.

"We need to find Sophie Leoni!" Bobby yelled right back. In all their years together, D.D. wasn't sure she'd ever heard Bobby yell, but that was okay, because she was shouting, too.

"I know!"

"It's been over twenty-four hours. My daughter was crying at three a.m., and all I could wonder was if somewhere little Sophie was doing the same."

"I know!"

"I hate this case, D.D.!"

"Me, too!"

Bobby stopped yelling. He breathed heavily instead. D.D. took a moment to expel a frustrated breath. Bobby ran a hand through his short hair. D.D. mopped back her blonde curls.

"We need to talk to Brian Darby's boss," Bobby stated after another minute. "We need a list of any friends, associates who might know what he'd do with his stepdaughter."

D.D. glanced at her watch. Ten a.m. Phil had scheduled the call with Scott Hale for eleven. "We gotta wait another hour."

"Fine. Let's start calling gyms. Maybe Brian had a personal trainer. People confess everything to their personal trainers, and we need a confession right about now."

"You call gyms," she said.

Bobby eyed her warily. "Why? What are you going to do?"

"Locate Juliana Howe."

"D.D.—"

"Divide and conquer," she interjected crisply. "Cover twice the ground, get results twice as fast."

"Jesus. You really are a hard-ass."

"Used to be what you loved about me."

D.D. headed for her vehicle. Bobby didn't follow her.

16

Brian and I had our first big fight four months after getting married. Second week in April, an unexpected snowstorm had blanketed New England. I'd been on duty the night before, and by seven a.m. the Mass Pike was a tangled mess of multiple auto accidents, abandoned vehicles, and panicked pedestrians. We were up to our ears in it, graveyard shift swinging into day shift even as additional officers were being summoned and most emergency personnel activated. Welcome to the day in the life of a uniformed officer during a wintry Nor'easter.

At eleven a.m., four hours after I would've normally ended my shift, I managed to call home. No one answered. I didn't worry. Figured Brian and Sophie were outside playing in the snow. Maybe sledding, or building a snowman or digging for giant purple crocuses beneath the crystal blue April snow.

By one, my fellow officers and I had managed to get the worst of the accidents cleared, about three dozen disabled vehicles relocated, and at least two dozen stranded drivers on their way. Clearing the Pike allowed the plows and sand and gravel trucks to finally do their job, which in turn eased our job.

I finally returned to my cruiser long enough to take a sip of cold coffee and check my cellphone, which had buzzed several times at my waist. I was just noticing the long string of calls from Mrs. Ennis when my pager went off at my shoulder. It was dispatch, trying to reach me. I had an emergency phone call they were trying to patch through.

My heart rate spiked. I reached reflexively for the steering wheel of my parked cruiser, as if that would ground me. I had a vague memory of granting permission, of picking up the radio to hear Mrs. Ennis's panicked voice. She'd been waiting for over five hours now. Where was Sophie? Where was Brian?

At first, I didn't understand, but then the pieces of the story emerged. Brian had called Mrs. Ennis at six a.m., when the snow had first started falling. He'd been watching the weather and, in his adrenaline junkie way, had determined this would be a perfect powder ski day. Sophie's daycare was bound to be canceled. Could Mrs. Ennis watch her instead?

Mrs. Ennis had agreed, but she'd need at least an hour or two to get to the house. Brian hadn't been thrilled. Roads would be getting worse, yada yada yada. So instead, he offered to drop Sophie at Mrs. Ennis's apartment on his way to the mountains. Mrs. Ennis had liked that idea better, as it kept her off the bus. Brian would be there by eight. She agreed to have breakfast waiting for Sophie.

Except, it was now one-thirty. No Brian. No Sophie. And no one answering the phone at the house. What had happened?

I didn't know. Couldn't know. Refused to picture the possibilities that immediately leapt into my mind. The way a teenager's body could eject from a car and wrap around a telephone pole. Or the way the steering column of an older, pre–air bag vehicle could cave in a grown adult's chest, leaving a man sitting perfectly still, almost appearing asleep in the driver's seat until you noticed the trickle of blood at the corner of his mouth. Or the eight-year-old girl, who'd just three months ago had to be cut out of the crushed front end of a four-door sedan, her relatively uninjured mother standing there, screaming how the baby had been crying, she'd just turned around to check the baby. . . .

These are the things I know. These are the scenes I remembered as I slammed my cruiser into gear, flipped on lights and sirens and fishtailed my way toward my home, thirty minutes away.

My hands were shaking when I finally careened to a halt in front of our brick garage, front end of my cruiser on the sidewalk; back half in the street. I left on my lights, bolting out of the cruiser and up the snow-buried stairs toward the dark home above. My boot hit the first patch of ice and I grabbed the metal railing just in time to keep from plummeting to the street below. Then I crested the hill and was pulling on my front door, working my keys with one hand, banging on the door with the other, even as the dark-eyed windows told me everything I didn't want to know.

Finally, with a sharp wrench of my hand, I twisted the key in the lock, shoved open the door. . . .

Nothing. Empty kitchen, vacant family room. I rushed upstairs; both bedrooms unoccupied.

My duty belt jingled loudly at my waist as I rat-tat-tatted back down the stairs into the kitchen. There, I finally paused,

took several steadying breaths, and reminded myself I was a trained police officer. Less adrenaline, more intelligence.
That's how one solved problems. That's
how one stayed in control.

"Mommy? Mommy, you're home!"

My heart practically leapt out of my
chest. I turned just in time to catch Sophie as she hurtled herself into my arms,
hugged me half a dozen times, and
started prattling about her exciting
snow day in one long breathless rush
that left me dazed and confused all over
again.

Then I realized Sophie hadn't returned alone, but that a neighborhood
girl was standing in the doorway. She
raised her hand in greeting.

"Mrs. Leoni?" she asked, then immediately flushed. "I mean, Officer Leoni."

It took a bit, but I managed to sort it
out. Brian had definitely gone skiing. But
he'd never taken Sophie to Mrs. Ennis's
house. Instead, while loading his gear,
he'd run across fifteen-year-old Sarah
Clemons, who lived in the apartment
building next door. She'd been shoveling the front walk, he'd started talking to

her, and next thing she knew, she'd agreed to watch Sophie until I got home, so Brian could get out of town faster.

Sophie, who was enamored with teenage girls, had thought this was an exciting change of plans. Apparently, she and Sarah had spent the morning sledding down the street, having a snowball fight, and watching episodes of *Gossip Girl,* which Sarah had TiVo'd.

Brian had never clarified his return, but had informed Sarah that I'd appear home sooner or later. Sophie had caught sight of my cruiser coming down the street and that had been that.

I was home. Sophie was happy, and Sarah was relieved to turn over her unexpected charge. I managed to scrounge up fifty bucks. Then I called Mrs. Ennis, reported back to dispatch, and sent my daughter, who was hopped up on hot chocolate and teenage television shows, outside to build a snowman. I stood on the back deck to supervise, still in uniform, while I placed the first phone call to Brian's cell.

He didn't answer.

After that, I forced myself to return my duty belt to the gun safe in the master bedroom, and carefully turn the combo lock. There are other things I remember. Other things I know.

Sophie and I made it through the evening. I discovered you can want to kill your spouse and still be an effective parent. We ate macaroni and cheese for dinner, played several games of Candy Land, then I stuck Sophie in the tub for her nightly bath.

Eighty-thirty p.m., she was sound asleep in bed. I paced the kitchen, the family room, the freezing cold sunroom. Then I returned outside, hoping to burn off my growing rage by raking the snow from the roof and shoveling the side steps and back deck.

At ten p.m., I took a hot shower and changed into a clean uniform. Did not remove the duty belt from the safe. Did not trust myself with my state-issued Sig Sauer.

At ten-fifteen, my husband finally walked through the front door, carrying a giant bag and his downhill skis. He was whistling, moving with the kind of loose-limbed grace that comes from spending an entire day engaged in intense physical activity.

He leaned his skis against the wall. Set down his ski bag. Tossed his keys on the kitchen table, then was just starting to remove his boots when he spotted me. He seemed to notice my uniform first, his gaze going automatically to the clock on the wall.

"It's that late? Crap, sorry. I must've lost track of time."

I stared at him, hands on my hips, the epitome of the nagging fishwife. I didn't fucking care.

"Where. Were. You."

The words came out hard and clipped. Brian looked up, appeared genuinely surprised. "Skiing. Didn't Sarah tell you that? The girl next door. She brought Sophie home, right?"

"Funny question to ask now, don't you think?"

He hesitated, less certain. "Is Sophie home?"

"Yes."

"Did Sarah do okay? I mean, Sophie's okay?"

"Best I can tell."

Brian nodded, seemed to be considering. "So . . . why am I in so much trouble?"

"Mrs. Ennis—" I started.

"Shit!" he exploded, jumping immediately to standing. "I was supposed to call her. While driving. Except the roads really were crap, and I needed two hands on the wheel, and by the time I got to the highway and better conditions . . . Oh no . . ." He groaned. Slumped back down in his seat. "I screwed that up."

"You left my child with a stranger! You took off to play, when I needed you here. And you panicked a perfectly wonderful old woman who will probably have to double her heart medicine for the next week!"

"Yeah," my husband agreed, mumbling. "I messed up. I should've called her. I'm sorry."

"How could you?" I heard myself say.

He went back to work on the laces of his boots. "I forgot. I was going to drop Sophie off at Mrs. Ennis's house, but then I met Sarah and she's right next door—"

"You left Sophie with a stranger for the entire day—"

"Whoa, whoa, whoa. It was already eight. I figured you'd be home at any time."

"I worked till after one. And I'd still be working, except Mrs. Ennis called dispatch and had them emergency page me."

Brian paled and stopped fiddling with his boots. "Uh-oh."

"No kidding!"

"Okay. Okay. Yes. Definitely. Not calling Mrs. Ennis was a first-class fuckup. I'm sorry, Tessa. I'll call Mrs. Ennis in the morning and apologize."

"You don't know how scared I was," I had to state.

He didn't speak.

"The whole way . . . driving here. Have you ever held an infant's skull in your hands, Brian?"

He didn't speak.

"It's like cradling rose petals. The unfused segments are so paper thin you can see through them, so light that if you exhale, they'll blow out of your cupped hands. These are the things I know, Brian. These are the things I can't forget. Which means, you *don't* screw up with a woman like me, Brian. You *don't* hand over my kid to a stranger, you *don't* ditch my daughter just so you can get out to play. You guard Sophie. Or you get the hell out of our lives. Are we clear on that?"

"I screwed up," he replied levelly. "I get that. Is Sophie all right?"

"Yes—"

"Did she like Sarah?"

"Apparently—"

"And you called Mrs. Ennis?"

"Of course!"

"Then at least things turned out all right in the end." He returned to his boots.

I crossed the kitchen so fast I nearly caught flight. "You *married* me!" I screamed at my new husband. "You *chose* me. You *chose* Sophie. How dare you *fail* us!"

"It was a phone call, Tessa. And yes, I will try to do better next time."

"I thought you'd died! I thought Sophie had died!"

"Well, yeah, then isn't it good that I'm finally home?"

"Brian!"

"I know I screwed up!" He finally gave up on his boots, throwing his hands in the air. "I'm new at this! I've never had a wife and daughter before, and just because I love you doesn't mean I'm not sometimes stupid. For chrissake, Tessa . . . I'm about to ship out again. I just wanted one last day of fun. Fresh snow. Powder skiing . . ." He inhaled. Exhaled. Stood up.

"Tessa," he said more quietly. "I would never intentionally hurt you or Sophie. I love you both. And I promise to do better next time. Have a little faith, okay? We're both new at this and we're bound to make some mistakes, so please . . . Have a little faith."

My shoulders sagged. The fight left me. I let go of my anger long enough to feel the relief that my daughter was okay, my husband was safe, and the afternoon had worked out in the end.

Brian pulled me against his chest. I allowed his embrace. I even slid my arms around his waist.

"Be careful, Brian," I whispered against his shoulder. "Remember, I'm not like other women."

For a change, he didn't argue.

I remembered this moment of my marriage, and others, as the nurse stood back and gestured for me to take my first awkward step. I'd managed to eat dry toast at six a.m. without throwing up. At seven-thirty, they'd moved me to the chair next to my bed to see how I'd do sitting up.

The pain inside my skull had flared the first few minutes, then settled into a dull roar. Half of my face remained swollen and tender, my legs felt shaky, but overall, I'd made progress in the past twelve hours. I could stand, sit, and eat dry toast. World, look out.

I wanted to run, madly, desperately, out of the hospital, where by some miracle I would find Sophie standing on the sidewalk waiting for me. I would swing her into my arms. *Mommy* she would cry happily. And I would hug her and kiss her and tell her how sorry I was for everything and never let her go.

"All right," the nurse said crisply. "First step, let's give it a whirl."

She offered her arm for balance. My knees trembled violently, and I placed a grateful hand on her arm.

That first shuffling step made my head swim. I blinked my eyes several times, and the disorientation passed. Up was up, down was down. Progress.

I inched forward, tiny little hiccups of my feet that slowly but surely took me across the gray linoleum, closer and closer to the bathroom. Then I was inside, gently shutting the door behind me. The nurse had supplied toiletries for showering. Second test of the day— seeing if I could pee and shower on my own. Then the doctor would examine me again.

Then, maybe, just maybe, I could go home.

Sophie. Sitting on the floor of her room, surrounded by painted bunnies and bright orange flowers, playing with her favorite raggedy-haired doll.

Mommy, you're home! Mommy, I love you!

I stood at the sink and stared at my reflection in the mirror.

The flesh around my eye was so black and engorged with blood, it looked like an eggplant. I could barely make out the bridge of my nose, or the top line of my eyebrow. I thought of those scenes in the early Rocky movies, where they'd razor-opened his swollen flesh just so he could see. I might have to give it a try. Day was still young.

My fingers traveled from my black eye, to the laceration two inches above it, the scab just now forming, pulling at the roots of my hair. Then I reached around to the prominent lump still protruding from the back of my skull. It felt hot and tender to the touch. I let my hand fall away, holding on to the edge of the sink instead.

Eight a.m. Monday morning.

The autopsy would've started an hour ago. The Y-incision down my husband's chest. Cracking apart his ribs. Fishing out three slugs fired from the 9mm Sig Sauer bearing my fingerprints. Then the

sound of the saw as they began to remove the top of his skull.

Eight a.m. Monday morning . . .

I thought again of all the moments I'd
like to have back. Places I should've
said yes, times I should've said no. Then
Brian would be alive, maybe waxing his
skis for his next big adventure. And Sophie would be home, playing on the
floor of her room, Gertrude nestled beside her, waiting for me.

Eight a.m. Monday morning . . .

"Hurry up, D.D. and Bobby," I murmured. "My daughter needs you."

17

Thanks to the wonder of GPS, Bobby identified Brian Darby's gym on his second try. He simply put in Darby's address, then searched for nearby gyms. Half a dozen popped up. Bobby started with the location closest to Brian's house and worked his way out. A national chain turned out to be the winner. Bobby drove there in thirty minutes, and was meeting with Brian's personal trainer eight minutes after that.

"Saw the news," the petite, dark-haired woman said, already looking worried. Bobby was trying to size her up. She appeared about five feet tall and ninety pounds, more gymnast than trainer. Then she twisted both her hands in an anxious gesture, and half a dozen tendons snaked to life in her forearms.

He revised his initial opinion of Jessica Ryan—tiny, but dangerous. Minihulk.

She'd been working out with some middle-aged man sporting a hundred dollar workout shirt and four hundred dollar haircut when Bobby had arrived. When Bobby first approached, Jessica had pointedly given him a cold shoulder, focusing on her obviously well-paying customer. Bobby had flashed his creds, however, and that quickly, Jessica with the tight pink T-shirt and sparkling purple nails was his.

Her disappointed client got to finish his workout with some kid whose neck was bigger than Bobby's thigh. Bobby and Jessica retreated to the employee break room, where Jessica quickly shut the door.

"Is he really dead?" Jessica asked now, biting her lower lip.

"I'm here regarding Brian Darby's death," Bobby stated.

"And his little girl? They've been showing her picture all over the news. Sophie, right? Have you found her yet?"

"No, ma'am."

Jessica's big brown eyes welled up. For the second time in the past hour, Bobby was happy he'd left D.D. to work on his own. The first time, because it was either walk away from her or strangle her. Now because there was no way D.D. would've played well with a doe-eyed female trainer prone to glistening tears and hot pink micro-shorts.

Being a happily married man, Bobby was making it a point not to study the micro-shorts or the tight T-shirt. So far, that left him staring at the personal trainer's extremely well-sculpted bicep.

"What do you bench-press?" he heard himself ask.

"One thirty-five," Jessica replied easily, still dabbing at the corners of her eyes.

"What's that? Twice your weight?"

She blushed.

He realized he'd basically just flirted

and shut up. Maybe he shouldn't have left D.D. Maybe no man, happily married or not, should be sequestered alone with a woman like Jessica Ryan. Which made him wonder if Tessa Leoni had ever met Jessica Ryan. Which made him wonder how Brian Darby had ever lived past the first week of fitness training.

Bobby cleared his throat, took out his spiral notepad and a mini-recorder. He turned on the recorder and placed it on the counter next to the microwave.

"Have you met Sophie?" he asked his interview subject.

"Once. School was canceled so Brian brought her in with him for his workout. She seemed really sweet; she found a set of one pound hand weights and carried them around, mimicking all of Brian's exercises."

"Brian works out solely with you?"

"I'm his primary personal trainer," Jessica said with a touch of pride. "Sometimes, however, our schedules don't mix, then another trainer might fill in for me."

"And how long has Brian been working out with you?"

"Oh, nearly a year. Well, maybe closer to nine months."

"Nine months?" Bobby made a note.

"He's done great!" Jessica gushed. "One of my best clients. His goal was to bulk up. So the first three months I put him on this wicked hard diet. Eliminated his fats and salts and carbs—and he's one of those guys that really loves his refined carbs, too. French toast for breakfast, hoagies for lunch, mashed potatoes for dinner, and a bag of cookies for dessert. Let me tell you, I didn't think he was going to make it through the first two weeks. But once he got his system cleaned out and reset, then we started the next stage: For the past six months, he's been following this regimen I developed from my fitness competitions—"

"Fitness competitions?"

"Yes. Miss Fit New England, four years running." Jessica flashed him a white smile. "It's my passion."

Bobby tore his gaze away from her

tanned, toned bicep and returned it to his notebook.

"So I gave Brian a week by week diet of six high-protein meals a day," Jessica continued perkily. "We're talking thirty grams of protein per meal, consumed every two to three hours. It's a big commitment of time and resources, but he did awesome! Then I added in a fitness regimen of sixty minutes of cardio followed by sixty minutes of heavy weights."

"Every day?" Bobby ran. Or had run, before Carina was born. He shifted his notepad two inches lower, in front of his waistline, which come to think about it, had been a bit tight this morning.

"Cardio five to seven times a week, strength training five times a week. And I introduced him to hundreds. He was great at hundreds!"

"Hundreds?"

"Lower weight, but higher rep, to see if you can hit a hundred. If we do it right, you can't on the first try, but continue training, then four weeks later, try again. In the first two months, Brian nailed all his hundreds, forcing me to bump up his weights. Really, amazing results. I mean, not for nothing, but most of my clients talk a good game. Brian was delivering the goods."

"He appeared to have put on a fair amount of weight in the past year," Bobby commented.

"He put on a fair amount of *muscle*," Jessica corrected immediately. "Three inches to his arms alone. We took measurements every two weeks if you want them. Of course, his work sched-ule means we missed months at a time, but he kept on track."

"You mean when he shipped out as a merchant marine?"

"Yeah. He'd disappear for two months at a time. First trip out, totally wrecked him. Lost most of what we'd done. Second time, I prepared an entire program for him to follow, including diet, cardio, and weights. I got a list of all the equipment available on the ship, and tailored it perfectly, so he'd have no ex-cuses. He did much better."

"So Brian was working hard with you when he was here and hard on the ship when he went away. Any reason he was working so hard?"

Jessica shrugged. "To look better. To feel better. He was an active guy. When we first started, he wanted to improve his fitness so he could tackle some bigger mountains skiing, biking, that sort of thing. He was active, but thought he should be stronger. We took it from there."

Bobby set down his notepad, regarded her for a moment. "So Brian wants to improve his skiing and biking. And in order to do that, he's spending how much money a week...?" He waved his hand around the well-kept room in an obviously well-equipped gym.

"Couple hundred," Jessica said. "But there's no price tag for good health!"

"Two hundred a week. And how many hours of training, grocery shopping, food prep..."

"You gotta commit if you want results," Jessica informed him.

"Brian committed. Brian got results. Brian was still following the program. Why? What's he looking for? Forty pounds of muscle later, what was he lacking?"

Jessica regarded him curiously. "He wasn't still trying to bulk up. However, Brian's not naturally a big guy. When a . . . smaller man . . ."

On behalf of men everywhere, Bobby winced.

"When a smaller man wants to maintain bigger results, he has to keep working. That's the truth. High protein, big weights, day after day. Otherwise, his body is going to return to its preferred size, which in Brian's case was closer to one eighty, not two twenty."

Bobby considered that information, which, as a smaller guy, wasn't great to hear.

"Sounds like a lot of work," he said at last. "Not easy for anyone to maintain, let alone a working parent. Time to time, I bet Brian's schedule got a little busy, his hours squeezed. He ever . . . seek additional assistance?"

Jessica furrowed her brow. "What do you mean?"

"Products to aid his speed/ability to add muscle?"

Jessica frowned harder; then, she got it. "You mean steroids."

"I'm curious."

Immediately, she shook her head. "I'm not down with that. If I thought he was juicing up, I'd quit. Screw the two hundred a week. I dated a guy into 'roids. No way I'd go down that road again."

"You were dating Brian?"

"No! I didn't mean *that*. I mean associating with someone abusing steroids. It makes people crazy. The stuff you see on the news—it's not a lie."

Bobby regarded her levelly. "And for your own training?"

She met his gaze just as levelly. "Sweat and tears, baby. Sweat and tears."

Bobby nodded. "So you're not a proponent of steroids—"

"No!"

"But what about other trainers in the gym? Or even outside the gym. Brian got some great results very fast. How sure are you that it was all his sweat and tears?"

Jessica didn't answer right away. She

chewed her lower lip again, crossing her arms over her chest.

"I don't think so," she said at last. "But I couldn't swear to it. Something was going on with Brian. He just got back into town three weeks ago, and this time around . . . He was moody. Dark. Something was on his mind."

"You ever meet his wife?"

"The state trooper? No."

"But he talked about her."

Jessica shrugged. "They all do."

"They?"

"Clients. I don't know, being a trainer is like being a hairdresser. The ministers of the grooming services sector. Clients talk. We listen. It's half our job."

"So what did Brian say?"

Jessica shrugged, obviously uncomfortable again.

"He's dead, Jessica. Killed in his own home. Help me understand why Brian Darby embarked on a major self-improvement program and it still wasn't enough to save him."

"He loved her," Jessica whispered.

"Who?"

"Brian loved his wife. Genuinely,

deeply, soulfully. I'd kill for a man to love me like that."

"Brian loved Tessa."

"Yeah. And he wanted to be stronger for her. For her and Sophie. He needed to be a big man, he used to joke, because guarding two females was four times the work."

"Guarding?" Bobby asked with a frown.

"Yeah. That's the word he'd used. Guess he'd screwed up once and Tessa had gotten on his case. Sophie was to be guarded. He took it seriously."

"You ever sleep with Brian?" Bobby asked suddenly.

"No. I don't screw around with my clients." She shot him a look. "Asshole," she muttered.

Bobby flashed his creds again. "That would be 'Detective Asshole' to you."

Jessica merely shrugged.

"Tessa screw around on Brian? Maybe he discovered something, helped spark his quest to become a bigger man."

"Not that he ever said. Though . . ." She paused. "No guy is gonna admit that to a girl. Especially a pretty one like me. Come on, that's like saying, *I'm a miserable weenie,* up front. Guys make you find that out for yourself."

Bobby couldn't argue with that logic. "But Brian didn't think his wife loved him."

That hesitation again. "I don't know. I got the impression . . . Tessa's a state trooper, right? A police officer. Kind of sounded like she was tough. Things were her way or the highway. Brian jumped through a lot of hoops. Didn't mean, however, she thought he was the greatest guy on God's green earth. Just meant she expected him to jump through a lot of hoops, especially when it came to Sophie."

"She had a lot of rules regarding her daughter?"

"Brian worked hard. When he was home, he wanted to play. Tessa, however, wanted him to babysit. Sounds like sometimes they went round and round a bit. But he never said anything bad about her," Jessica added hastily. "He wasn't that kind of guy."

"What kind of guy?"

"Guy who rags on his wife. Trust me"—she rolled her eyes—"we have plenty of those around here."

"So why was Brian moody?" Bobby cycled back. "What happened this last time he was on tour?"

"I don't know. He never said. He just seemed . . . miserable."

"You think he beat his wife?"

"No!" Jessica appeared horrified.

"She has a medical history consistent with abuse," Bobby added, just for the sake of argument.

Jessica, however, stood by her man. "No fucking way."

"Really?"

"Really."

"How would you know?"

"Because he was sweet. And sweet guys don't whack their wives."

"Again, how would you know?"

She stared at him. "Because I managed to find a wife beater all by myself. Married him for five long years. Till I got smart, got fit, and kicked his ass to the curb."

She flexed her arms pointedly. Miss Fit New England four times running, indeed. "Brian loved his wife. He didn't hit her, and he didn't deserve to die. Are we done?"

Bobby reached into his pocket, fished out his card. "Think about why Brian might have been 'moody' since his last return. And if anything comes to you, give me a call."

Jessica took his card, while regarding his outstretched arm, which did not look nearly as toned as her own.

"I could help you with that," she said.

"No."

"Why not? Cost? You're a detective. I could cut you a deal."

"You haven't met my wife," Bobby said.

"She also a cop?"

"Nope. But she's very good with a gun."

Bobby got his mini-recorder, got his notepad, and got out of there.

18

D.D. didn't have any trouble tracking down Tessa's childhood friend Juliana MacDougall, nee Howe, wife of three years, mother of one, living in a seventeen hundred square foot cape in Arlington. D.D. might have lied a little. Said she was from the high school, tracking down alumnae for an upcoming reunion.

Hey, not everyone wanted to take calls from their local detectives, and even fewer probably wanted to answer yet more questions regarding the shooting that had killed a brother ten years ago.

D.D. got Juliana's address, established she was home, and took a ride over. On the way there, she checked her voice messages, including a cheery morning greeting from Alex wishing her the best with the missing persons case and letting her know he was in the mood to cook homemade alfredo, if she was in the mood to eat it.

Her stomach growled. Then spasmed. Then growled again. Leave it to her to be carrying a baby as contrarian as she was.

She should call Alex. She should make some time this evening, even thirty minutes to sit and talk. She tried to picture the conversation in her mind, but still wasn't sure how it would go.

HER: So remember how you said you and your first wife tried to have a baby a few years ago, but it didn't work out? Turns out, you were *not* the problem in that equation.
HIM:
HER:
HIM:
HER:

It wasn't much of a conversation. Maybe because she didn't have much of an imagination, or any experience with these things. Personally, she was more adept at the "Don't call me, I'll call you" conversation.

Would he offer to marry her? Should she accept that kind of deal, if not for her sake, then for the baby's? Or did it matter in this day and age? Did she just assume he would help her? Or would he just assume she'd never let him?

Her stomach hurt again. She didn't want to be pregnant anymore. It was too confusing and she wasn't great with big life questions. She preferred more elemental debates, such as why did Tessa Leoni kill her husband, and what did it have to do with her shooting Thomas Howe ten years ago?

Now, there was a question for the ages.

D.D. followed her guidance system into a maze of tiny side streets in Arlington. A left here, two rights there, and she arrived in front of a cheerful red-painted house with white trim and a snow-covered front yard the size of D.D.'s car.

D.D. parked by the curb, grabbed her heavy coat, and headed for the door.

Juliana MacDougall answered after the first ring. She had long, dishwater blonde hair pulled back into a messy ponytail and a fat, drooling baby balanced on her denim-clad hip. She regarded D.D. curiously, then blanked her face completely when D.D. flashed her creds.

"Sergeant Detective D. D. Warren, Boston PD. May I come in?"

"What is this regarding?"

"Please." D.D. gestured to the inside of the toy-strewn house. "It's cold out here. I think we'd all be more comfortable talking inside."

Juliana thinned her lips, then silently held the door open for D.D. to enter. The home boasted a tiny, tiled entryway, opening to a small family room with nice windows and recently refinished hardwood floors. The house smelled like fresh paint and baby powder, a new little family settling into a new little home.

A laundry basket occupied the single dark green sofa. Juliana flushed, then lowered the plastic bin to the floor without ever releasing her grip on her baby. When she finally sat, she perched on the edge of the cushion, her child held in the middle of her lap as the first line of defense.

D.D. sat on the other end of the sofa. She regarded the drooling baby. The drooling baby stared back at her, then shoved its whole fist in its mouth and made a sound that might have been "Gaa."

"Cute," D.D. said, in a voice that was clearly skeptical. "How old?"

"Nathaniel is nine months."

"Boy."

"Yes."

"Walking?"

"Just learned to crawl," Juliana said proudly.

"Good boy," D.D. said, and that quickly was out of baby prattle. Good Lord, how was she ever going to be a mom, when she couldn't even talk to one?

"Do you have a job?" D.D. asked.

"Yes," Juliana said proudly, "I'm raising my child."

D.D. accepted that answer, moved

on. "So," she announced curtly. "I imagine you've seen the news. The missing girl in Allston-Brighton."

Juliana regarded her blankly. "What?"

"The Amber Alert? Six-year-old Sophie Leoni, missing from her home in Allston-Brighton?"

Juliana frowned, held her baby a little closer. "What does that have to do with me? I don't know any child from Allston-Brighton. I live in Arlington."

"When was the last time you saw Tessa Leoni?" D.D. asked.

Juliana's reaction was immediate. She stiffened and looked away from D.D., her blue gaze dropping to the hardwood floor. A square block with the letter "E" and a picture of an elephant was by her slippered foot. She retrieved the block and offered it to the baby, who took it from her, then tried to cram the whole thing in his mouth.

"He's teething," she murmured absently, stroking her child's red-flushed cheek. "Poor little guy hasn't slept in nights, and whimpers to be held all day long. I know all babies go through it, but I didn't think it would be so hard. Seeing my own child in pain. Knowing there's nothing I can do but wait."

D.D. didn't say anything.

"Sometimes, at night, when he's crying, I rock and cry with him. I know it sounds corny, but it seems to help him. Maybe no one, not even babies, likes to cry alone."

D.D. didn't say anything.

"Oh my God," Juliana MacDougall exclaimed abruptly. "Sophie Leoni. *Sophia* Leoni. She's Tessa's daughter. Tessa had a little girl. Oh. My. God."

Then Juliana Howe shut up completely, just sitting there with her baby boy, who was still chewing the wooden block.

"What did you see that night?" D.D. asked the young mother gently. No need to define which night. Most likely, Juliana's entire life circled back to that one moment in time.

"I didn't. Not really. I was half asleep, heard a noise, came downstairs. Tessa and Tommy . . . They were on the couch. Then there was a noise, and Tommy stood up, kind of stepped back, then fell down. Then Tessa stood up, saw me, and started crying. She held out her hand, and she was holding a gun. That was the first thing I really noticed. Tessa had a gun. The rest sunk in from there."

"What did you do?"

Juliana was quiet. "It's been a long time."

D.D. waited.

"I don't understand. Why these questions now? I told everything to the police. Last I knew, it was an open-and-shut case. Tommy had a reputation . . . The detective said Tessa wasn't the first girl he'd hurt."

"What do you think?"

Juliana shrugged. "He was my brother," she whispered. "Honestly, I try not to think about it."

"Did you believe Tessa that night? That your friend was protecting herself?"

"I don't know."

"She ever show any interest in Tommy before? Ask about his schedule? Bat her eyelashes in his direction?"

Juliana shook her head, still not looking at D.D.

"But you never spoke to her afterward. You cast her out. Like her father."

Now Juliana flushed. Her grip tightened on her baby. He whimpered and immediately she let go.

"Something was wrong with Tommy," she said abruptly.

D.D. waited.

"My parents couldn't see it. But he was . . . mean. If he wanted something, he took it. Even when we were little, if I had a toy and he wanted that toy . . ." She shrugged again. "He'd break something, rather than let me keep it. My father would say boys will be boys, and let it go. But I learned. Tommy wanted what he wanted and you didn't get in his way."

"You think he attacked Tessa."

"I think when Detective Walthers told us other girls had called about Tommy, I wasn't surprised. My parents were horrified. My father . . . he still doesn't believe. But I could. Tommy wanted what he wanted and you didn't get in his way."

"Did you ever tell that to Tessa?"

"I haven't spoken to Tessa Leoni in ten years."

"Why not?"

"Because." The ubiquitous shrug again. "Tommy wasn't just my brother—he was my parents' son. And when he died . . . My parents burned up their savings on Tommy's funeral. Then, when my father couldn't go back to work, we lost our house. My parents had to declare bankruptcy. Eventually, they divorced. My mother and I moved in with my aunt. My father had a nervous breakdown. He lives in an institution, where he spends his days going through Tommy's scrapbook. He can't get over it. He just can't. The world is a terrible place, where your child can be killed and the police cover it up."

Juliana stroked her own baby's cheek. "It's funny," she murmured. "I used to think my family was perfect. That's even what Tessa loved best about me. I came from this great family, not like her family at all. Then, in one night, we turned into them. It wasn't just that I lost my brother, but that my parents lost their son."

"She ever try to contact you?"

"The last words I spoke to Tessa Leoni were, 'You need to go home right now!' And that's what she did. She took her gun and she ran out of my house."

"What about seeing her around the neighborhood?"

"Her father kicked her out. Then she was no longer around the neighborhood."

"You never wondered about her? Never worried about your best friend in the whole wide world, who had to fight off your own brother? You invited her over that night. According to her initial statement, Tessa had asked if Tommy would be home for the evening."

"I don't remember."

"Did you tell Tommy she was coming?"

Juliana's lips thinned. Abruptly, she set the baby on the floor, stood up. "You should go now, Detective. I haven't spoken to Tessa in ten years. I didn't know she had a daughter, and I certainly don't know where she is."

But D.D. stayed put, sitting on the

edge of the sofa, peering up at Tessa's former best friend.

"Why did you leave Tessa in the family room that night?" D.D. pushed. "If it was a sleepover, why didn't you rouse your best friend to come up to your room? What did Tommy tell you to do?"

"Stop it!"

"You suspected, didn't you? You knew what he was up to, and that's why you came downstairs. You feared your brother, you worried about your friend. Did you warn Tessa, Juliana? Is that why she brought the gun?"

"No!"

"You knew your father wouldn't listen. Boys will be boys. Sounds like your mom had already internalized the message. That left you and Tessa. Two sixteen-year-old girls, trying to stand up to one brute of an older brother. Did she think she'd simply scare him off? Wave the gun, and that would be the end of things?"

Juliana didn't respond. Her face was ashen.

"Except the gun went off," D.D. continued conversationally. "And Tommy got hit. Tommy *died*. Your entire family fell apart. All because you and Tessa didn't really know what you were doing. Whose idea was it to bring the gun that night?"

"Get out."

"Yours? Hers? What were the two of you *thinking*?"

"Get out!"

"I'm going to check your phone records. One call. That's all I need. One call placed from Tessa to you and your new little family is going to fall apart, too, Juliana. I'm gonna rip it apart, if I learn you've been holding out on me."

"Get out!" Juliana screamed. On the floor, the baby responded to his mother's tone and started to wail.

D.D. climbed off the sofa. She kept her eyes on Juliana MacDougall, the woman's pale face, heaving shoulders, wild gaze. She looked like a deer caught in the headlights. She looked like a woman trapped by a ten-year-old lie.

D.D. gave one last try: "What happened that night, Juliana? What aren't you telling me?"

"I loved her," the woman said suddenly. "Tessa was my best friend in the whole world, and I loved her. Then my brother died, my family shattered, and my world went to shit. I'm not going back. Not for her, not for you, not for anyone. Whatever happened to Tessa this time around, I don't know and I don't care. Now get out of my home, Detective, and don't bother me or my family again."

Juliana held open the door. Her baby was still sobbing on the floor. D.D. took the hint and finally departed. The door slammed shut behind her, the dead bolt turning for good measure.

When D.D. turned, however, she could see Juliana through the front window. The woman had picked up her crying son, cradling the baby against her chest. Soothing the child or letting the child soothe her?

Maybe it didn't matter. Maybe that's the way these things worked.

Juliana MacDougall loved her son. As her parents had loved her brother. As Tessa Leoni loved her daughter.

Cycles, D.D. thought. Pieces of a

larger pattern. Except she couldn't quite pull it apart, or put it back together.

Parents loved their children. Some parents would go to any length to protect them. And other parents . . .

D.D. started to get a bad feeling.

Then her cellphone rang.

19

Sergeant Detective D. D. Warren and Detective Bobby Dodge came for me at 11:43 a.m. I heard their footsteps in the corridor, fast and focused. I had a split second; I used it to stash the blue button in the back part of the lowest drawer in the hospital bed stand.

My only link to Sophie.

My final unnecessary reminder to play by the rules.

Maybe, one day I could return and retrieve the button. If I was lucky, maybe Sophie and I could do it together, reclaiming Gertrude's missing eye and reattaching it to her dispassionate doll's face.

If I was lucky.

I'd just sat down on the edge of my hospital bed when the privacy curtain was ripped back and D.D. strode into the room. I knew what was coming next and still had to bite my lower lip to hold back my scream of protest.

"All I want for Christmas is my two front teeth, my two front teeth, my . . ."

I realized belatedly I was humming the song under my breath. Fortunately, neither of the detectives seemed to notice.

"Tessa Marie Leoni," D.D. began and I steeled my spine. "You are under arrest for the murder of Brian Anthony Darby. Please rise."

More footsteps in the corridor. Most likely the DA and his assistant, not wanting to miss the big moment. Or maybe some muckety-mucks from the BPD, always attuned to high profile photo ops. Probably some brass from the state police, as well. They wouldn't abandon me just yet, a young, abused female officer. They couldn't afford to appear so insensitive.

The press would be amassing in the parking lot, I realized, impressed by my own detachment as I rose to my feet, presenting both wrists to my colleagues. Shane would arrive shortly, as union rep. Also my lawyer. Or maybe they would meet me at the courthouse, where I would be formally charged with killing my own husband.

I had a flashback to another moment in time, sitting at a kitchen table, my freshly showered hair dripping down my back as a heavyset detective asked over and over again, *"Where'd ya get the gun, why'd ya bring the gun, what made ya fire the gun. . . ."*

My father, standing impassively in the doorway, his arms crossed over his dirty white T-shirt. And me, understanding even then that I'd lost him. That my answers didn't matter anymore. I was guilty, I would always be guilty.

Sometimes, that's the price you paid for love.

Detective Warren read me my rights. I didn't speak; what was left to say? She cuffed my wrists, prepared to lead me away, then encountered the first logistical issue. I had no clothes. My uniform had been bagged and tagged as evidence upon my admittance, delivered to the crime lab yesterday afternoon. That left me in a hospital Johnny, and even D.D. understood the political dangers of a Boston cop being photographed dragging away a battered state trooper who was wearing nothing but a hospital gown.

She and Detective Dodge had a quick conference, off to one side of the room. I sat back down on the edge of the bed. A nurse had entered and was watching the proceedings with concern. Now she crossed to me.

"Head?" she asked crisply.

"Hurts."

She took my pulse, made me track her finger with my eyes, then nodded in satisfaction. Apparently, I was merely in pain, not in crisis. Having assured herself that her patient was in no immediate danger, the nurse retreated out the door.

"Can't use a prison jumpsuit," D.D.

was arguing in low tones with Bobby. "Her lawyer will argue we biased the judge, bringing her before him in jail-house orange. Hospital gown presents the same issue, except this time we look like insensitive jerks. We need clothes. Simple nondescript blue jeans, sweater. That sort of thing."

"Get an officer to swing by her house," Bobby muttered back.

D.D. regarded him for a second, then turned to study me.

"Got a favorite outfit?" D.D. asked.

"Wal-Mart," I said, standing up.

"What?"

"Couple blocks over. Size 6 jeans, medium sweater. I'd appreciate under-clothes, too, plus socks and shoes."

"I'm not buying you clothes," D.D. said crossly. "We'll get some from your house."

"No," I said, and sat back down.

D.D. glared at me. I let her. She was arresting me, after all, what did she have to be so angry about? I didn't want clothing from home, personal articles the Suffolk County Jail would seize from me and lock away for the duration of my incarceration. I would rather arrive in a hospital gown. Why not? The look bought me sympathy, and I would take all the help I could get.

Apparently, D.D. figured that out, as well. A uniformed officer was summoned, instructions given. The patrol officer didn't even bat an eye at being told to buy women's clothing. He disappeared out the door, which left me alone with D.D. and Bobby again.

Others must be staying out in the hall. Hospital rooms weren't that big. They might as well wait in the corridor for the show.

I was counting down, though I didn't know to what.

"What did you use?" D.D. asked abruptly. "Bags of ice? Snow? Funny, you know. I noticed the damp spot on the basement floor, yesterday. I wondered about it."

I said nothing.

She walked toward me, eyes narrowed, as if studying a particular species of wildlife. I noticed when she walked, she kept one hand splayed over her stomach, the other on her hip. I also noticed that her face was pale with dark circles under her eyes. Apparently, I was keeping the good detective up at night. Score one for me.

I regarded her with my good eye. Dared her to look at the swollen, eggplant purple mess of my face, and pass judgment.

"You ever meet the ME?" she asked now, switching gears, becoming more conversational. She halted in front of me. From my vantage point, perched on the edge of the hospital bed, I had to look up at her.

I didn't speak.

"Ben's good. One of the best we've ever had," she continued. "Maybe another ME wouldn't have noticed it. But Ben loves the details. Apparently, the human body is like any other meat. You can freeze it and thaw it, but not without some changes in—how did he put it?—consistency. The flesh on your husband's extremities felt wrong to him. So he took a few samples, stuck them under a microscope, and hell if I understand all the science, but basically determined damage at a cellular level consistent with the freezing of human tissue. You shot your husband, Tessa. Then, you put him on ice."

I didn't speak.

D.D. leaned closer. "This is what I don't get, though. Obviously, you were buying time. You needed to get something done. What, Tessa? What were you doing while your husband's corpse lay frozen in the basement?"

I didn't speak. I listened to a song instead, playing in the back of my mind. *All I want for Christmas is my two front teeth, my two front teeth, my two front teeth. . . .*

"Where is she?" D.D. whispered, as if reading my mind. "Tessa, what did you do with your little girl? Where's Sophie?"

"When are you due?" I asked, and D.D. recoiled as if shot, while five feet away, Bobby inhaled sharply.

He hadn't known, I determined. Or maybe he'd known, but not known, in that way men sometimes do. I found this interesting.

"Is he the father?" I asked.

"Shut up," D.D. said curtly.

Then I remembered. "No," I corrected

myself, as if she'd never spoken. I looked over at Bobby. "You're married to another woman, from the state mental institute case, couple years back. And you have a baby now, don't you? Not that long ago. I heard about that."

He didn't say anything. Just stared at me with cool gray eyes. Did he think I was threatening his family? Was I?

Maybe I just needed to make conversation, because otherwise I might say all the wrong things. For example, I used snow, because it was easy enough to shovel and didn't leave behind trace evidence such as a dozen empty ice bags. And Brian was heavy, heavier than I'd imagined. All that working out, all that pumping up, just so myself and a hit man could lug an extra forty pounds down the stairs and into his precious, never-any-tool-out-of-place garage.

I'd cried when I scooped the snow on top of my husband's dead body. The hot tears formed little holes in the white snow, then I had to pile on more snow and all the while my hands were shaking uncontrollably. I kept myself focused.

One shovel full of snow, then a second, then a third. It took twenty-three.

Twenty-three scoops of snow to bury a grown man.

I'd warned Brian. I'd told him in the beginning that I was a woman who knew too much. You don't mess with a woman who knows the kind of things I know.

Three tampons to plug the bullet holes. Twenty-three scoops of snow to hide the body.

All I want for Christmas is my two front teeth, my two front teeth, my two front teeth. . . .

Love you more, he'd told me as he died.

Stupid, sorry son of a bitch.

I didn't speak anymore. D.D. and Bobby also sat in silence for a good ten, fifteen minutes. Three members of law enforcement not making eye contact. Finally, the door banged open and Ken Cargill barged in, black wool coat flapping around him, thinning brown hair mussed. He drew to a halt, then noticed my shackled wrists and turned on D.D.

with all the fury of a good defense lawyer.

"What is this!" he cried.

"Your client, Tessa Marie Leoni, has
been charged in the death of her husband, Brian Anthony Darby. We have
read her her rights, and are now awaiting transport to the courthouse."

"What are the charges?" Cargill demanded to know, sounding appropriately indignant.

"Murder one."

His eyes widened. "Murder with premeditated malice and forethought? Are
you out of your mind? Who authorized
these charges? Have you even *looked*
at my client lately? The black eye, the
fractured cheek, and oh yes, the *concussion*?"

D.D. simply stared at him, then turned
back to me. "Ice or snow, Tessa? Come
on, if not for us, then for your lawyer's
sake, tell him how you froze the body."

"What?"

I wondered if all lawyers went to acting school, or if they just came by it naturally, the way cops did.

The first uniformed officer was back, breathing hard; apparently he'd run all the way through the hospital with the oversized Wal-Mart bag. He thrust it at D.D., who did the honors of explaining my new wardrobe to Cargill.

D.D. unshackled my wrists. I was handed the pile of new clothes, hangers and other sharp objects removed, then allowed to disappear into the bathroom to change. The Boston patrol officer had done a decent job. Wide-leg jeans, stiff as boards with their newness. A green crewneck sweater. A sports bra, plain underwear, plain socks, bright white tennis shoes.

I moved slowly, dragging the bra, then the sweater, over my battered head. The jeans were easier, but tying my shoelaces proved impossible. My fingers were shaking too hard.

Do you know what had been the hardest part about burying my husband?

Waiting for him to bleed out. Waiting for his heart to stop and the last ounce of blood to still and cool in his chest, because otherwise he would drip. He would leave a trail, and even if it was small and I cleaned it up with bleach, the luminol would give it away.

So I sat, on a hard chair in the kitchen, holding a vigil I never thought I'd have to hold. And the whole time, I just couldn't decide, which was worse? Shooting a boy, and running away with the blood still fresh on my hands? Or shooting a man, and sitting there, waiting for his blood to dry so I could clean up properly?

I'd placed three tampons in the holes in the back of Brian's chest, as a safety measure.

"What are you doing?" the man had demanded.

"Can't leave a blood trail," I'd said calmly.

"Oh," he'd said, and let me go.

Three bloody tampons. Two front teeth. It's funny, the talismans that can bring you strength.

I hummed the song. I tied my shoes. Then, I stood up, and took one last minute to study myself in the mirror. I didn't recognize my own reflection. That distorted face, hollowed-out cheeks, lank brown hair.

It was good, I thought, to feel like a stranger to myself. It suited all the things about to happen next.

"Sophie," I murmured, because I needed to hear my daughter's name. "Sophie, love you more."

Then I opened the bathroom door and once more presented my wrists.

The cuffs were cool; they slid on with a click.

It was time. D.D. on one side. Bobby on the other. My lawyer bringing up the rear.

We strode into the bright white corridor, the DA pushing away from the wall, ready to lead the parade in triumphant glory. I saw the lieutenant colonel, his gaze steady as he regarded his shackled officer, his face impossible to read. I saw other men in uniform, names I knew, hands I had shook.

They did not look at me, so I returned the favor.

We headed down the corridor, toward the big glass doors and the screaming mob of reporters waiting on the other side.

Command presence. Never let them see you sweat.

The glass doors slid open, and the world exploded in flashing white lights.

20

"We gotta start over," D.D. was saying an hour and a half later. They'd handed Tessa over to the Suffolk County Sheriff's Department at the courthouse. The DA would present the charges. Her lawyer would enter a plea, bail would be set, and a mittimus prepared by the court, legally granting the county permission to hold Tessa Leoni until the requirements of her bail were met. At which point, Tessa would be either bailed out or transported to the Suffolk County Jail. Given that the DA was going to argue Tessa was a flight risk and request no bail, there was a good chance she was already on her way to the women's detainee unit as they spoke.

That still didn't solve all their problems.

"Our timeline was set by Tessa's initial statement to police," D.D. was saying now, back at BPD headquarters, where she'd hastily summoned all members of the taskforce. "We assumed, based upon her accounting of events, that Brian Darby was shot and killed Sunday morning, after a physical altercation with her. According to the ME, however, Darby's body was frozen prior to Sunday morning, and most likely, *unthawed* for Tessa's star-making performance."

"Can he tell how long it was frozen?" Phil spoke up from the front row.

D.D. let their third squadmate, Neil, answer the question, as he'd been the one attending the autopsy.

"Probably less than twenty-four hours," Neil provided for the room. "Ben said he can see cellular damage consistent with freezing in the extremities, but not the internal organs. Meaning the body was on ice, but not long enough to freeze all the way through. Limbs, face, fingers, toes, yes. Deep torso, no. So probably put on ice twelve to twenty-four hours. He can only estimate because the timeline would be affected by room temperature. Then you must factor in at least a few hours for the body to return to room temperature. . . . He's guessing—stress guessing—Brian Darby was actually killed Friday night or Saturday morning."

"So," D.D. stated, redirecting attention to her. "We're going to have to re-canvass all the neighbors, friends, and family—when was the last time someone saw or spoke to Brian Darby alive? Are we looking at Friday night or Saturday morning?"

"Had a call on his cellphone Friday evening," another detective, Jake Owens, commented. "Saw that when I was going through the records yesterday."

"Long call? Like he talked to someone?"

"Eight or nine minutes, so not just

leaving a message. I'll trace the number, have a chat with the recipient."

"Make sure the person spoke to Brian," D.D. ordered crisply, "and it wasn't Tessa, using his phone."

"I don't get it." Phil had been doing all the background checks and in many ways knew more about the details of the case than anyone. "We're thinking Tessa shot her husband, then froze the body—then staged a whole scene for Sunday morning. Why?"

D.D. shrugged. "Interestingly enough, she wouldn't tell us that."

"Buying time," Bobby said, from his place, leaning against the front wall. "No other good reason. She was buying time."

"For what?" Phil asked.

"Most likely, to deal with her daughter."

That brought the room up short. D.D. frowned at him. Obviously, she wasn't happy with his conjecture. That was okay. He wasn't happy to learn she was pregnant from a suspect in a murder investigation. Call him old-fashioned, but that stuck in his craw, and he was feeling pissy about it.

"You think she hurt the daughter?" Phil asked now, his voice wary. He had four kids at home.

"A neighbor saw Brian's Denali leave the house Saturday afternoon," Bobby said. "Initially, we assumed Brian was driving the SUV. Given that the lab techs believe a dead body was in the back of the vehicle, we further assumed that Brian had killed his stepdaughter, and was disposing of the evidence. Except, Brian Darby was most likely dead by Saturday afternoon. Meaning he wasn't the one transporting a corpse."

D.D. thinned her lips, but nodded curtly. "I think we have to consider the notion that Tessa Leoni killed her entire family. Given that Sophie was at school on Friday, my guess is either Friday night, before Tessa's patrol shift, or Saturday morning after her patrol shift, something terrible happened in the household. Brian's body was put on ice in the garage, while Sophie's body was driven to an undisclosed location and dumped. Tessa reported to work once again Saturday evening. Then Sunday morning, it was showtime."

"She staged it," Phil muttered. "Made it look like her husband had done something to Sophie. Then she and Brian fought and she killed him in self-defense."

D.D. nodded; Bobby, too.

"What about the facial injuries, though?" Neil spoke up from the back. "No way she made it through Saturday night patrol with a concussion and fractured face. She couldn't stand yesterday, let alone operate a motor vehicle."

"Good point," D.D. concurred. She moved in front of the whiteboard, where she'd written: *Timeline.* Now, she added one bullet—*Tessa Leoni Injuries: Sunday Morning*. "Wounds gotta be fresh. Can a doctor verify that?" she asked Neil, a former EMT and their resident medical expert.

"Tough with contusions," Neil answered. "Everyone heals at a different rate. But I'm gonna guess the severity of the injuries dictates they happened sooner versus later. She wouldn't have been terribly functional after taking such massive blows to the head."

"Who beat her up?" another officer asked.

"Accomplice," Phil muttered up front.

D.D. nodded. "In addition to revamping our timeline, this new information also means we need to reconsider the scope of the case. If Brian Darby didn't beat his wife, who did, and why?"

"Lover," Bobby said quietly. "Most logical explanation. Why did Tessa Leoni kill her husband and daughter? Because she didn't want to be with them anymore. Why didn't she want to be with them anymore? Because she had met someone new."

"Hear anything through the grapevine?" D.D. asked him. "Rumors from the barracks, that sort of thing."

Bobby shook his head. "Not that plugged in, though. I'm a detective, not a trooper. We'll need to interview the LT."

"First thing this afternoon," D.D. assured him.

"Gotta say," Phil spoke up, "this theory fits better with what Darby's boss,

Scott Hale, reported. I talked to him at eleven, and he swore up and down that Darby didn't have a violent bone in his body. A tanker crew is pretty tight. You see people sleep deprived, homesick, and stressed out, while maintaining a twenty-four/seven work schedule. As an engineer, Darby got to deal with all the technical crises, and apparently big things go wrong on big ships—water in the fuel, fried electrical systems, glitches in the control software. Still, Hale never saw Darby lose his composure. In fact, the bigger the problem, the more jazzed Darby was about finding a solution. Hale certainly doesn't believe a guy like that goes home and beats up his wife."

"Darby was a model employee," D.D. said.

"Darby was everyone's favorite engineer. And apparently, quite good at Guitar Hero—they have a rec room on board."

D.D. sighed, crossed her arms over her chest. She glanced over at Bobby, not quite meeting his eye, but looking in his general direction. "What'd you learn at the gym?" she asked.

"Brian had spent the past nine months following a vigorous exercise regimen designed to bulk up. Personal trainer swore he wasn't doing steroids, just putting in blood, sweat, and tears. She only heard him say good things about his wife, but thought that having a state trooper for a spouse was tough on the guy. Oh, and in the past three weeks, since returning home from his last tour, Darby was definitely in a mood, but not willing to talk about it."

"What do you mean by 'in a mood'?"

"Personal trainer said he seemed darker, temperamental. She'd asked a couple of times, guessing trouble on the home front, but he wouldn't comment. For what it's worth, that makes him something of a novelty. Apparently, most clients pour out their souls while working out. Go to a gym, enter a confessional."

D.D. perked up. "So something was on his mind, but Darby wasn't talking about it."

"Maybe he discovered his wife was

having an affair," Neil commented from the back. "You said when he returned, meaning, he'd just left his wife all alone for sixty days. . . ."

"In addition to the rec room on the ship," Phil spoke up, "there's a computer room for the crew. I'm working on the warrant now to get copies of all of Darby's ingoing and outgoing e-mail. Might find something there."

"So Tessa meets another man," D.D. mused, "decides to off her husband. Why homicide? Why not divorce?"

She posed the question generally, a challenge to the room.

"Life insurance," an officer spoke up.

"Expediency," said another. "Maybe he threatened to fight a divorce."

"Maybe Darby had something on her, threatened to make trouble if she divorced him."

D.D. wrote down each comment, seeming particularly interested in the third bulletin. "By her own admission, Tessa Leoni is an alcoholic, who'd already killed once when she was sixteen. Figure if that's what she's willing to admit to, what *isn't* she willing to say?"

D.D. turned back to the group. "Okay, then why kill her daughter? Brian's a stepdad, so he doesn't have grounds to challenge for custody. It's one thing to end a marriage. Why kill her own kid?"

Room was slower with this one. Of all people, it was Phil who finally ventured an answer: "Because her lover doesn't want kids. Isn't that how these things work? Diane Downs, etc., etc. Women kill their children when their children are inconvenient for them. Tessa was looking to start a new life. Sophie could not be part of that life, so Sophie had to die."

No one had anything to add to that.

"We need to identify the lover," Bobby murmured.

"We need to find Sophie's body," D.D. sighed more heavily. "Prove once and for all just what Tessa Leoni is capable of."

She set down her marker, looked over the whiteboard.

"All right, people. These are our assumptions: Tessa Leoni killed her husband and child, most likely sometime Friday evening or Saturday morning.

She froze her husband's body in the garage. She disposed of her daughter during a Saturday afternoon drive. Then she reported to work—most likely while unthawing her husband's body in the kitchen—before returning home, letting her lover beat the shit out of her, and calling her fellow state troopers. It's some story. Now get out there, and find me some *facts*. I want e-mails and phone messages between her and her lover. I want a neighbor who noticed her unloading ice or shoveling snow. I want to know exactly where Brian Darby's white Denali traveled to on Saturday afternoon. I want Sophie's body. And if this is indeed what happened, I want Tessa Leoni locked up for life. Any questions?"

"Amber Alert?" Phil asked, as he rose to his feet.

"We keep it active until we find Sophie Leoni, one way or the other."

The taskforce understood what she meant: until they found the child, or until they recovered the child's body. The detectives filed out of the room. Then it

was just Bobby and D.D., standing together, alone.

He pushed away from the wall first
and headed for the door.

"Bobby."

There was just enough uncertainty in
her voice to make him turn.

"I haven't even told Alex," she said.
"All right? I haven't even told Alex."

"Why not?"

"Because . . ." She shrugged. "Because."

"Are you going to keep the baby?"

Her eyes widened. She motioned
frantically to the open door, so he hu-
mored her by closing it. "Now see, this
is why I didn't say anything," she exploded. "This is precisely the kind of
conversation I didn't want to have!"

He remained standing there, staring
at her. She had one hand splayed
across her lower abdomen. How had he
never noticed that before, he the former
sniper? The way she cradled her belly,
almost protectively. He felt stupid, and
realized now he'd never needed to ask
the question. He knew the answer just

by looking at the way she was standing: She was keeping the baby. That's what had her so terrified.

Sergeant Detective D. D. Warren was going to be a mom.

"It's going to be okay," he said.

"Oh God!"

"D.D., you have been great at everything you've ever wanted to do. Why should this be any different?"

"Oh God," she said again, eyes wilder.

"Can I get you anything? Water? A pickle? How about ginger chews? Annabelle lived on ginger chews. Said they settled her stomach."

"Ginger chews?" She paused. Appeared a little less frantic, a little more curious. "Really?"

Bobby smiled at her, crossed the room, and because it felt like the right thing to do, he gave her a hug. "Congratulations," he whispered in her ear. "Seriously, D.D. Welcome to the ride of your life."

"You think?" She looked a little misty-eyed, then surprised them both by hugging him back. "Thanks, Bobby."

He patted her shoulder. She leaned her head into his chest. Then they both straightened, turned to the whiteboard, and got back to work.

21

I stood, my hands shackled at my waist, as the district attorney read off the charges. According to the DA, I had deliberately and willfully shot my own husband. Furthermore, they had reason to believe I may have also killed my own daughter. At this time, they were entering charges of Murder 1, and requesting I be held without bail, given the severity of the charges.

My lawyer, Cargill, blustered his protest. I was an upstanding state police trooper, with a long and distinguished career (four years?). The DA had insufficient evidence against me, and to believe such a reputable officer and dedicated mother would turn on her entire family was preposterous.

The DA pointed out ballistics had already matched the bullets in my husband's chest to my state-issued Sig Sauer.

Cargill argued my black eye, fractured face, and concussed brain. Obviously, I'd been driven to it.

The DA pointed out that might have made sense, if my husband's body hadn't been frozen after death.

This clearly perplexed the judge, who shot me a startled glance.

Welcome to my world, I wanted to tell him. But I said nothing, showed nothing, because even the smallest gesture, happy, angry, or sad, would lead to the same place: hysteria.

Sophie, Sophie, Sophie.

All I want for Christmas is my two front teeth, my two front teeth, my two front teeth.

I was going to burst into song. Then I would simply scream because that's what a mother wanted to do when she pulled back the covers of her child's empty bed. She wanted to scream, except I'd never had a chance.

There had been a noise downstairs. Sophie, I'd thought again. And I'd sprinted out of her bedroom, running downstairs, racing straight into the kitchen, and there had been my husband, and there had been a man holding a gun against my husband's temple.

"Who do you love?" he'd said, and that quickly, my choices had been laid out for me. I could do what I was told and save my daughter. Or I could fight back, and lose my entire family.

Brian, staring at me, using his gaze to tell me what I needed to do. Because even if he was a miserable fuckup, he was still my husband and, more importantly, he was Sophie's father. The only man she'd ever called Daddy.

He loved her. For all his faults, he loved us both.

Funny, the things you don't fully appreciate until it's too late.

I'd placed my duty belt on the kitchen table.

And the man had stepped forward,

ripped my Sig Sauer from the holster, and shot Brian three times in the chest.

Boom, boom, boom.

My husband died. My daughter had disappeared. And me, the trained police officer, stood there, completely shell-shocked, scream still locked in my lungs.

A gavel came down.

The sharp jolt jerked me back to attention. My gaze went instinctively to the clock: 2:43 p.m. Did the time still matter? I hoped it did.

"Bail is set at one million dollars," the judge declared crisply.

The DA smiled. Cargill grimaced.

"Hold steady," Shane muttered behind me. "Everything'll be okay. Hold steady."

I didn't dignify his empty platitudes with a response. The troopers' union had money set aside for bail, of course, just as it assisted with the hiring of a lawyer for any officer needing legal assistance. Unfortunately, the union's nest egg was hardly a million bucks. That kind of funding would take time, not to mention a special vote. Which probably meant I was out of luck.

Like the union was going to get further involved with a female officer accused of murdering her husband and child. Like my sixteen hundred male colleagues were going to vote affirmative on that one.

I said nothing, I showed nothing, because the scream was bubbling up again, a tightness in my chest that built and built. I wished I had the blue button, wished I'd been able to keep it, because holding it, in a perverse way, had kept me sane. The button meant Sophie. The button meant Sophie was out there, and I just had to find her again.

The court guard approached, placing his hand on my elbow. He jerked me forward and I started to walk, one foot in front of the other, because that's what you did, what you had to do.

Cargill was beside me. "Family?" he asked quietly.

I understood what he meant. Did I have family to bail me out? I thought of my father, felt the scream rise from my chest into my throat. I shook my head.

"I'll talk to Shane, present your case to the union," he said, but I could already feel his skepticism.

I remembered my superior officers, not meeting my gaze as I passed down the hospital corridor. The walk of shame. The first of many.

"I can request special treatment at the jail," Cargill said, speaking rapidly now, for we were approaching the doorway that led to the holding cell, where I would be officially led away. "You're a state police officer. They'll grant you segregation if you want it."

I shook my head. I'd been to the Suffolk County Jail; the segregation unit was the most depressing one in the place. I'd get my own cell, but I'd also be locked inside twenty-three hours a day. No privileges such as a gym pass or library hour, and no commons area boasting a finicky TV and world's oldest exercise bike to help pass the time. Funny, the things I was about to consider luxury items.

"Medical eval," he suggested urgently, meaning I could also request medical time, placing me in the hospital ward.

"With all the other psychos," I muttered back, because last time I'd toured the prison, all the screamers had been down in Medical, yelling 24/7 to themselves, the guards, the other inmates. Anything, I suppose, to drown out the voices in their heads.

We'd arrived outside the holding cell, the guard giving Cargill a pointed look. For a moment, my frazzled attorney hesitated. He gazed at me with something that might have been sympathy and I wished he hadn't, because it merely made the scream rise from my throat to the dark hollow of my mouth. I had to thin my lips, clench my jaw to keep it from escaping.

I was strong, I was tough. Nothing here I hadn't seen before. Usually I was the one on the other side of the bars, but details, details.

Cargill grabbed hold of my cuffed hands. He squeezed my fingers.

"Ask for me, Tessa," he murmured. "You have the legal right to confer with your lawyer at any time. Call, and I will come."

Then he was gone. The holding-cell door opened. I stumbled inside, joining five other women with faces as pale and detached as my own. As I watched, one drifted over to the stainless steel toilet, pulled up her black spandex miniskirt, and peed.

"What'ya staring at, bitch?" she asked, yawning.

The cell door banged shut behind me.

Introducing the South Bay shuffle: To execute this time-honored jail transport maneuver, a detainee must link each of her arms through the arm of the person on either side, then clasp her hands at her waist, where her wrists will be cuffed. Once each detainee has been "pretzeled" with the inmates on either side, ankles are also shackled together and a line of six females can shamble their way to the sheriff's van.

Females sit on one side of the van. Males sit on the other. A clear Plexiglas sheet separates the two. The bleach blonde beside me spent most of the journey making suggestive motions with her tongue. The two hundred and fifty pound, heavily tattooed black male across from us urged her on with his hips.

Three more minutes, and I think they could've completed their transaction. Sadly for their sake, we arrived at the Suffolk County Jail.

The sheriff's van pulled into the unloading bay. A massive metal garage door clanged down and locked tight, sealing in the place. Then the vehicle doors finally opened.

Males disembarked first, exiting the van as a shackled line and entering the sally port. After a few moments, it was our turn.

Stepping out of the van was the hardest. I felt the peer pressure not to stumble or fall, as I would take down the entire line. The fact I was white and wearing new clothes already made me stand out, as most of my fellow detainees appeared to be members of the sex and drugs trade. The cleaner ones probably worked for money. The not so clean ones worked for product.

Most of them had been up all night, and to judge by the various smells, they'd been busy.

Interestingly enough, the orange-haired woman to my right crinkled her nose at my particular odor of hospital antiseptic and brand-new blue jeans. While the girl to my left (eighteen, nineteen years old?) took in my bashed-in face, and said, "Oh honey, next time, just give him the money, and he'll go easier on you."

Doors opened. We shuffled our way into the sally port. The doors behind us shut. The doors to the left clanged open.

I could see command central directly ahead of me, staffed by two COs in dark blue BDUs. I kept my head down, afraid of spotting a familiar face.

More hobbling steps, inching our way shoulder to shoulder, hip to hip down a long corridor, past cinder-block walls painted a dirty yellow, inhaling the astringent smell of government institutions everywhere—a mix of sweat, bleach, and human apathy.

We arrived at the "dirty hold," another large cell, much like the one at the courthouse. Hard wooden bench lining one wall. Single metal toilet and sink. Two public pay phones. All calls had to be made collect, we were informed, while an automated message would inform the receiver the call originated from the Suffolk County Jail.

We were unshackled. The CO exited. The metal door clanged shut, and that was that.

I rubbed my wrists, then noticed I was the only one who did so. Everyone else was already lining up for the phone. Ready to call whomever to bail them out.

I didn't line up. I sat on the hard wooden bench and watched the hookers and drug dealers, who still had more people who loved them than I did.

The CO called my name first. Even knowing it was coming, I had a moment of panic. My hands gripped the edge of the bench. I wasn't sure I could let go.

I'd handled it so far. I'd handled so

much thus far. But now, the processing. Officer Tessa Leoni would officially cease to exist. Inmate #55669021 would take her place.

I couldn't do it. I wouldn't do it.

The CO called my name again. He stood outside the metal door, staring straight at me through the window. And I knew he knew. Of course he knew. They were admitting a female state police officer. Had to be the juiciest scuttlebutt around. A woman charged with killing her husband and suspected of murdering her six-year-old daughter. Exactly the kind of inmate COs loved to hate.

I forced myself to let go of the bench. I drew myself to standing.

Command presence, I thought, a little wildly. Never let them see you sweat.

I made it to the door. The CO snapped on the bracelets, placing his hand upon my elbow. His grip was firm, his face impassive.

"This way," the CO said, and jerked my arm to the left.

We returned to command central, where I was grilled for basic information:

height, weight, DOB, closest relative, contact information, addresses, phone numbers, distinguishing tattoos, etc. Then they took my picture standing in front of the cinder-block wall, holding a sign covered in the number that would be my new identity. The finished product became my new ID card, which I would be required to wear at all times.

Back down the corridor. New room, where they took away my clothing, and I got to squat naked while a female officer pointed a flashlight into all of my orifices. I received a drab brown prison suit—one pair of pants, one shirt—a single pair of flat white sneakers, nicknamed "Air Cabrals" in deference to the sheriff, Andrea Cabral, and a clear plastic hooter bag. The hooter bag contained a clear toothbrush the size of a pinky, a small clear deodorant, clear shampoo, and white toothpaste. The toiletries were clear to make it harder for inmates to conceal drugs in the containers. The toothbrush was small so it would be less effective when inevitably made into a shiv.

If I desired additional toiletries, say

conditioner, hand lotion, lip balm, I had to purchase them from the commissary. Chapstick ran $1.10. Lotion $2.21. I could also buy better tennis shoes, ranging from $28 to $47.

Next, the nurse's office. She checked out my black eye, swollen cheek, and gashed head. Then I got to answer routine medical questions, while being inoculated for TB, always a major consideration for prison populations. The nurse lingered on the psych eval, perhaps trying to determine if I was the kind of woman who might do something rash, like hang myself with over-bleached sheets.

The nurse signed off on my medical eval. Then the CO escorted me down the cinder-block hall to the elevator banks. He punched the ninth floor, which held pretrial women. I had two choices, Unit 1-9-1 or Unit 1-9-2. I got 1-9-2.

Sixty to eighty women held at a time in the pretrial units. Sixteen cells to a unit. Two to three women to a cell.

I was led to a cell with only one other female. Her name was Erica Reed. She currently slept on the top bunk, kept her personal possessions on the bottom. I could make myself at home on the butcher block that also served as a desk.

Second the metal door shut behind me, Erica started chewing her discolored fingernails, revealing a row of blackened teeth. Meth addict. Which explained her pale sunken face and lank brown hair.

"Are you the cop?" she asked immediately, sounding very excited. "Everyone said we were getting a cop! I *hope* you're the cop!"

I realized then that I was in even bigger trouble than I'd thought.

22

Lieutenant Colonel Gerard Hamilton didn't sound thrilled to talk to D.D. and Bobby; more like resigned to his fate. One of his troopers was involved in an "unfortunate incident." Of course the investigative team needed to interview him.

As a matter of courtesy, D.D. and Bobby met him in his office. He shook D.D.'s hand, then greeted Bobby with a more familiar hand clasp to the shoulder. It was obvious the men knew each other, and D.D. was grateful for Bobby's presence—Hamilton probably wouldn't have been so collegial otherwise.

She let Bobby take the lead while she studied Hamilton's office. The Massachusetts State Police were notoriously fond of their military-like hierarchy. If D.D. worked in a modest office space decorated as Business-R-Us, then Hamilton's space reminded her of an up-and-coming political candidate's. The wood-paneled walls held black-framed photos of Hamilton with every major Massachusetts politician, including a particularly large snapshot of Hamilton and Mass.'s Republican senator, Scott Brown. She spotted a diploma from UMass Amherst, another certificate from the FBI Academy. The impressive rack of antlers mounted above the LT's desk showcased his hunting prowess, and in case that didn't do the trick, another photo showed Hamilton in green fatigues and an orange hunting vest standing next to the fresh kill.

D.D. didn't dwell on the photo too long. She was getting the impression that Baby Warren was a vegetarian. Red meat bad. Dry cereal, on the other hand, was starting to sound good.

"Of course I know Trooper Leoni," Hamilton was saying now. He was a distinguished-looking senior officer. Trim, athletic build, dark hair graying at the temples, permanently tanned face from years of outdoor living. D.D. bet the young male officers openly admired him, while the young female officers secretly found him sexy. Was Tessa Leoni one of those officers? And did Hamilton return the sentiment?

"Fine officer," he continued evenly. "Young, but competent. No history of incidents or complaints."

Hamilton had Tessa's file open on his desk. He confirmed Tessa had worked graveyard Friday and Saturday nights. Then he and Bobby reviewed her duty logs, much of which made no sense to D.D. Detectives tracked active cases, cleared cases, warrants, interviews, etc., etc. Troopers tracked, among other things, vehicle stops, traffic citations, call outs, warrants served, property seized, and a whole slew of assists. It sounded less like policing to D.D. and more like basketball. Apparently, troopers were either making calls or assisting other troopers making calls.

Either way, Tessa had particularly robust duty logs, even Friday and Saturday night. On Saturday's graveyard shift alone, she'd issued two citations for operating under the influence—OUI—which in the second case involved not just taking the driver into custody, but arranging for the suspect's vehicle to be towed.

Bobby grimaced. "Seen the paperwork yet?" he said, tapping the two OUIs.

"Got it from the captain a couple of hours ago. It's good."

Bobby looked at D.D. "Then she definitely didn't have a concussion Saturday night. I can barely complete those forms stone-sober, let alone suffering from a massive head trauma."

"Take any personal calls Saturday night?" D.D. asked the LT.

Hamilton shrugged. "Troopers patrol with their personal mobiles, not just their department-issued pager. It's possible she took all sorts of personal calls.

Nothing, however, through official channels."

D.D. nodded. She was surprised troopers were still allowed their cellphones. Many law enforcement agencies were banning them, as uniformed officers, often the first responders to crime scenes, had a tendency to snap personal photos using their mobiles. Maybe they thought the guy who blew his head off looked funny. Or they wanted to share that particular blood spatter with a buddy they had in a different field office. From a legal perspective, however, any crime-scene photo was evidence and subject to full disclosure to the defense. Meaning that if any such photos surfaced *after* the case had been adjudicated, their mere presence would be grounds for a mistrial.

The DA didn't like it very much when that happened. Had a tendency to get downright nasty on the subject.

"Leoni ever reprimanded?" D.D. asked now.

Hamilton shook his head.

"Take a lot of days off, maybe personal time? She's a young mom, spending half her year alone with a kid."

Hamilton flipped through the file, shook his head. "Admirable," he commented. "Not easy meeting both the demands of the job and the needs of a family."

"Amen," Bobby murmured.

They both sounded sincere. D.D. chewed her lower lip. "How well did you know her?" she asked the LT abruptly. "Group bonding activities, the gang meeting for drinks, that sort of thing?"

Hamilton finally hesitated. "I didn't really know her," he said at last. "Trooper Leoni had a reputation for being distant. Couple of her performance reviews touched on the subject. Solid officer. Very reliable. Showed good judgment. But on the social front, remained aloof. It was a source of some concern. Even troopers, who primarily patrol alone, need to feel the cohesiveness of the group. The reassurance that your fellow officer always has your back. Trooper Leoni's fellow troopers respected her professionally. But no one really felt they knew her personally. And in this job, where the lines between professional and personal life easily blur . . ."

Hamilton's voice trailed off. D.D. got his point and was intrigued. Law enforcement wasn't a day job. You didn't just punch a clock, perform your duties, and hand off to your coworkers. Law enforcement was a calling. You committed to your work, you committed to your team, and you resigned yourself to the life.

D.D. had wondered if Tessa had been too close to a fellow officer, or even a commanding officer, such as the LT. In fact, it sounded as if she wasn't close enough.

"Can I ask you a question?" Hamilton asked suddenly.

"Me?" Startled, D.D. blinked at the lieutenant colonel, then nodded.

"Do you fraternize with your fellow detectives? Grab a beer, share cold pizza, catch the game at one another's homes?"

"Sure. But I don't have a family," D.D. pointed out. "And I'm older. Tessa Leoni . . . you're talking about a young, pretty mom dealing with a barrack of entirely male officers. She's your only female trooper, right?"

"In Framingham, yes."

D.D. shrugged. "Not a lot of women in blue. If Trooper Leoni wasn't feeling the brotherly love, can't say I blame her."

"We never had any complaints of sexual harassment," Hamilton stated immediately.

"Not all women feel like doing the paperwork."

Hamilton didn't like this assertion. His face shuttered up, he looked intimidating, harsh even.

"At the barracks level," he stated crisply, "we encouraged Leoni's commanding officer to create more opportunities for her to feel included. Let's just say it met with mixed results. No doubt it is difficult to be the lone female in a dominantly male organization. On the other hand, Leoni herself did not appear inclined to bridge the divide. To be blunt, she was perceived as a loner. And even officers who made an effort to befriend her—"

"Such as Trooper Lyons?" D.D. interrupted.

"Such as Trooper Lyons," Hamilton agreed. "They tried and failed. Teamwork is about winning the hearts and minds of your fellow officers. In that regard, Trooper Leoni got it half right."

"Speaking of hearts and minds." Bobby sounded apologetic, as if sorry to reduce the LT down to the level of gossipmonger. "Any reports of Leoni being involved with another officer? Or perhaps an officer who was interested in her, whether she returned the interest or not?"

"I did some asking. Trooper Leoni's closest associate seems to be Trooper Shane Lyons, though that relationship is more through the husband than Leoni."

"Did you know him?" D.D. asked curiously. "The husband, Brian Darby? Or her daughter, Sophie?"

"I knew them both," Hamilton answered gravely, surprising her. "At various cookouts and family functions over the years. Sophie is a pretty little girl. Very precocious, that's my memory." He frowned, seemed to be wrestling with something inside himself. "You could tell Trooper Leoni loved her very much," he said abruptly. "At least, that's what I always thought when I saw them together. The way Tessa held her daughter, doted on her. The thought . . ."

Hamilton looked away. He cleared his throat, then clasped his hands on the desk before him. "Sad, sad business," the LT murmured to no one in particular.

"What about Brian Darby?" Bobby asked.

"Knew him even longer than Tessa. Brian was a good friend of Trooper Lyons. He started appearing at cookouts a good eight, nine years ago. Even joined us a couple of times to see the Boston Bruins, attended poker night every now and then."

"Didn't know you and Trooper Lyons were so close," D.D. stated, arching a brow.

Hamilton gave her a stern look. "If my troopers invite me to a function, I always try to attend. Camaraderie is important, not to mention that informal gatherings are invaluable for keeping the lines of communication open between troopers and the chain of command. Having said that, I probably join Trooper Lyons and his 'posse,' as he calls them, three or four times a year."

"What did you think of Brian?" Bobby asked.

"Followed hockey, also liked the Red Sox. Made him a stand-up guy in my book."

"Talk to him much?"

"Hardly at all. Most of our outings were of the male-bonding variety—catching a game, playing a game, or betting on a game. And yes," he turned to D.D. as if already anticipating her complaint, "it's possible such activities made Trooper Leoni feel excluded. Though from what I remember, she also follows the Red Sox, with the whole family attending many of the games."

D.D. scowled. She hated it when she was so transparent.

"And Trooper Leoni's alcoholism," Bobby asked quietly. "That ever come up?"

"I was aware of the situation," Hamilton replied just as evenly. "To the best of my knowledge, Leoni had successfully completed a twelve-step program and remained on track. Again, no history of incidents or complaints."

"What about that whole matter of her shooting and killing someone when she was sixteen?" D.D. asked.

"That," Hamilton said heavily, "is gonna bite us on the ass."

The bluntness of his statement took D.D. by surprise. She had a moment, then got it. The press digging deeper into Boston's latest femme fatale, demanding to know what the state police were thinking, hiring a trooper who already had a history of violence . . .

Yep, the LT would have a lot of explaining to do.

"Look," the commanding officer said now. "Trooper Leoni was never charged with a crime. She met all of our candidacy requirements. To refuse her application—that would've been discrimination. And for the record, she passed the Academy with flying colors and has performed exemplary in the line of duty. We had no way of knowing, no way of anticipating. . . ."

"You think she did it?" D.D. asked.

"You knew her husband, her child. Think Tessa killed them both?"

"I think the longer I stay in this job, the less I'm surprised by all the things that should surprise me."

"Any talk of marital problems between her and Brian?" Bobby asked.

"I would be the last to know," Hamilton assured him.

"Noticeable changes in behavior, particularly the past three weeks?"

Hamilton tilted his head to the side. "Why the past three weeks?"

Bobby merely studied his superior officer. But D.D. understood. Because Brian Darby had only been home for the past three weeks, and according to his personal trainer, he'd returned from his last tour of duty not very happy with life.

"There was one situation that comes to mind," Hamilton said abruptly. "Not involving Trooper Leoni, but her husband."

D.D. and Bobby exchanged a glance.

"Probably six months ago," Hamilton continued, not really looking at them. "Let's see . . . November. That sounds right. Trooper Lyons arranged an outing to Foxwoods. Many of us attended, including Brian Darby. Personally, I took in a show, blew my fifty bucks in the casino, and called it a night. But Brian . . . When the time came, we couldn't get him to leave. One more round, one more round, this would be the one. He and Shane ended up in an argument, with Shane physically pulling him off the casino floor. The other guys laughed it off. But . . . It seemed pretty clear to me that Brian Darby should not return to Foxwoods."

"He had a gambling problem?" Bobby asked with a frown.

"I'd say his interest in gaming appeared higher than average. I'd say that if Shane hadn't yanked him away from the roulette table, Brian would still be sitting there, watching the numbers spin around."

Bobby and D.D. exchanged glances. D.D. would like this story better if Brian didn't have fifty grand sitting in the bank. Gambling addicts didn't normally leave fifty grand in savings. Still, they studied the lieutenant colonel.

"Have Shane and Brian returned to Foxwoods lately?" Bobby asked.

"You would have to ask Trooper Lyons."

"Trooper Leoni ever mention any financial stress? Ask for extra shifts, more OT hours, that sort of thing?"

"To judge by the duty logs," Hamilton said slowly, "she's been working more hours lately."

But fifty grand in the bank, D.D. thought. Who needed OT when you had fifty grand in the bank?

"There is something else you probably should know," Hamilton said quietly. "I need you to understand, this is strictly off the record. And it may have nothing to do with Trooper Leoni. But . . . You said the past three weeks, and as a matter of fact, we launched an internal investigation exactly two weeks ago: An outside auditor discovered funds had been improperly moved from the union's account. The auditor believes the funds were embezzled, most likely from an inside source. We are trying to locate those monies now."

D.D. went wide-eyed. "How nice of you to mention that. And to volunteer it so readily, too."

Bobby shot her a warning glance.

"How much are we talking?" he asked in a more reasonable tone.

"Two hundred and fifty thousand."

"Missing as of two weeks ago?"

"Yes. But the embezzlement started twelve months prior, a series of payments made to an insurance company, which it turns out, doesn't exist."

"But the checks have been cashed," Bobby stated.

"Each and every one," Hamilton replied.

"Who signed for them?"

"Hard to make out. But all were deposited into the same bank account in Connecticut, which four weeks ago was closed out."

"The fake insurance company was a shell," D.D. determined. "Set up to receive payments, a quarter of a million dollars' worth, then shut down."

"That's what the investigators believe."

"Bank's gotta have information for

you," Bobby said. "Same bank for all transactions?"

"The bank has been cooperating fully. It supplied us with video footage of a woman in a red baseball cap and dark sunglasses closing out the account. That has become internal affair's biggest lead—they are pursuing a female with inside information on the troopers' union."

"Such as Tessa Leoni," D.D. murmured.

The lieutenant colonel didn't argue.

23

If you want someone dead, prison is the perfect place to do it. Just because the Suffolk County Jail was minimum security didn't mean it wasn't filled with violent offenders. The convicted murderer who'd just served twenty years at the state maximum security prison might finish up his or her county sentence here, completing eighteen months for burglary or simple assault that had been in addition to the homicide charge. Maybe my roommate Erica was locked up for dealing drugs, or turning tricks, or petty theft. Or maybe she'd killed the

last three women who'd tried to get between her and her meth.

When I asked the question, she just
smiled, showing off twin rows of black
teeth.

Unit 1-9-2 held thirty-four other
women just like her.

As pretrial detainees, we were kept
separate from the general inmate population, in a locked-down unit where food
came to us, the nurse came to us, and
programming came to us. But within the
unit, there was plenty of intermingling,
creating multiple opportunities for violence.

Erica walked me through the daily
schedule. Morning started at seven
a.m., with "count time," when the CO
would conduct head count. Then we
would be served breakfast in our cells,
followed by a couple of hours "rec
time"—we could leave our cells and
roam unshackled around the unit,
maybe hang out in the commons area
watching TV, maybe shower (three
showers located right off the commons
area, where everyone could also enjoy
that show), or ride the squeaky exercise

bike (verbal insults from your fellow detainees not included).

Most women, I quickly realized, spent their time playing cards or gossiping at the round stainless steel tables in the center of the unit. A woman would join a table, pick up one rumor, share two more, then visit a neighbor's cell, where she could be the first to provide the big scoop. And around and around the women went, table to table, cell to cell. The whole atmosphere reminded me of summer camp, where everyone wore the same clothes, slept in bunks, and obsessed over boys.

Eleven a.m., everyone returned to their assigned cell for the second session of count time, followed by lunch. More rec time. Count time again at three. Dinner around five. Final count time at eleven, followed by lights out, which was not to be confused with quiet time. In prison, there was no such thing as quiet time, and in a corrections facility that housed both men and women, there was definitely no such thing as quiet time.

The females, I quickly learned, occupied the top three floors of the Suffolk County "tower." Some enterprising woman (or man, I suppose) determined that the plumbing pipes from the upper floors connected to the lower floors. Meaning that a female detainee—say, my roommate Erica—could stick her head inside the white porcelain toilet bowl and proceed to "talk" to a random male on the lower floor. Though, talking isn't really what any man wants to do. Think of it more as the prison version of sexting.

Erica would make lewd comments. Nine floors beneath us, a faceless man would groan. Erica would make more lewd comments: *Harder, faster, come on, baby, I'm rubbing my tits for you, can you feel me rubbing my tits for you?* (I made that up: Erica didn't have tits. Meth had dissolved all the fat and tissue from her bones, including her breasts. Black teeth, black nails, no boobs. Erica should be starring in a public service announcement targeting teenage girls: This is your body on meth.)

Faceless man nine floors below us, however, wouldn't know that. In his mind, Erica was probably some buxom blonde, or maybe the hot Latina chick he'd spotted once in Medical. He would whack off happily. Erica would start round two.

As would the woman in the cell beside us, and the cell beside her and the cell beside her. All. Night. Long.

Prison is a social place.

The Suffolk County Jail involves multiple buildings. Sadly, only males in the lower floors of the tower could communicate via the toilets with the females on the top three levels. Obviously, this posed a great hardship for the men in other buildings.

The enterprising males in Building 3, however, figured out that we could peer down at their windows from our cells. As Erica explained to me, first thing in the morning our job was to check for messages posted in the windows of Building 3—say, an artful arrangement of socks, underwear, and T-shirts forming a series of numbers or letters. Only so much could be spelled out with socks, obviously, so a code had been developed. We would write down the code, which would direct the women of 1-9-2 to various books during library time, where a more complete message could be recovered (*fuck me, fuck me, do me, do me, oh you're so pretty can you feel me get so hard . . .*).

Prison poetry, Erica told me with a sigh. Spelling wasn't her strong suit, she confessed, but she always did her best to write back, leaving behind a fresh note (*yes, yes, YES!*) in the same novel.

In other words, inmates could communicate between units, female pretrial detainees to males in general pop and vice versa. Most likely, then, the entire prison population knew of my presence, and an inexperienced detainee in one unit could gain assistance from a more hardened inmate from another.

I wondered how it would happen.

Say, when my entire unit was escorted down nine floors to the lower-level library. Or the couple of times we'd go to the gym. Or during visitation, which was also a group activity, one huge room filled with a dozen tables where everyone intermingled.

Easy enough for a fellow inmate to

saddle up beside me, drive a shiv through my ribs, and disappear.

Accidents happen, right? Especially in prison.

I did my best to think it through. If it were me, a female detainee trying to get at a trained police officer, how would I do it? On second thought, maybe not overt violence. One, a cop should be able to fend off an attack. Two, the few times the unit was on the move—walking to the library or the gym or visitation—we were escorted by the SERT team, a bunch of hulking COs prepared to pounce at a moment's notice.

No, if it were me, I'd go with poison.

Time-honored female weapon of choice. Not hard to smuggle in. Each detainee was allowed to spend fifty bucks a week at the canteen. Most seemed to blow their wad on Ramen noodles, tennis shoes, and toiletries. With outside help, no problem stashing a little rat poison in the seasoning packet of the Ramen noodles, the cap of the newly purchased hand lotion, etc., etc.

A moment's distraction and Erica

could stir it into my dinner. Or later, out in the commons area when another detainee, Sheera, offered me peanut butter on toast.

Arsenic could be combined into lotions, hair products, toothpaste. Every time I moisturized my skin, washed my hair, brushed my teeth . . .

Is this how you go crazy? Realizing all the ways you could die?

And if you did, how few people would care?

Eight twenty-three p.m. Sitting alone on a thin mattress in front of a thickly barred window. Sun long gone. Gazing out at the frigid darkness beyond the glass, while behind me, the relentless fluorescent lights burned too bright.

And wishing for just an instant that I could bend back those bars, open up the high window and, nine stories above the churning city of Boston, step out into the brisk March night and see if I could fly.

Let it all go. Fall into the darkness there.

I pressed my hand against the glass. Stared into the deep dark night. And wondered if somewhere Sophie was gazing out at the same darkness. If she could feel me trying to reach her. If she knew that I was still here and that I loved her and I was going to find her. She was my Sophie and I would save her, just as I had done when she'd locked herself in the trunk.

But first, we both had to be brave.

Brian had to die. That's what the man had told me, Saturday morning in my kitchen. Brian had been a very bad boy and he had to die. But Sophie and I might live. I just had to do as I was told.

They had Sophie. To get her back, I would take the blame for killing my husband. They even had a few ideas on the subject. I could set things up, argue self-defense. Brian would still be dead, but I'd get off and Sophie would be miraculously found and returned to me. I'd probably have to quit the force, but hey, I'd have my daughter.

Standing in the middle of the kitchen, my ears ringing from gunfire, my nostrils still flared with the scent of gunpowder and blood, this had seemed a good deal. I'd said yes, to anything, to everything.

I'd just wanted Sophie.

"Please," I'd begged, *begged* in my own home. "Don't hurt my daughter. I'll do it. Just keep her safe."

Now, of course, I was starting to realize how foolish I'd been. Brian had to die and someone *else* take the blame for his death? If Brian had to die, why not tamper with his brakes, or cause an "accident" next time he went skiing? Brian was alone most of the time, plenty of things the man in black could've done other than shoot Brian and order his wife to take the blame. Why that? Why me?

Sophie would be miraculously found? How? Wandering in a major department store, or maybe waking up at a highway rest stop? Obviously the police would question her, and children were notoriously unreliable witnesses. Maybe the man could scare her into saying nothing, but why take that risk?

Not to mention once my daughter was returned to me, what incentive did I have to stay quiet? Maybe I'd go to the police then. Why take that risk?

I was thinking more and more that the kind of person who could shoot a man three times in cold blood probably didn't take unnecessary risks.

I was thinking more and more that the kind of person who could shoot a man three times in cold blood had a lot more going on than he was admitting.

What had Brian done? Why did he need to die?

And did he realize, in the last second of his life, that he'd almost certainly doomed me and Sophie, as well?

I felt the metal bars press against either side of my hand, not round as I'd assumed, but fashioned in a shape similar to the slats in vertical blinds.

The man wanted me in prison, I realized now. He, and the people he no doubt worked for, wanted me out of the way.

For the first time in three days, I smiled.

Turned out, they had a little surprise coming. Because in the bloody aftermath, my ears still ringing, my eyes wide with horror, I'd latched onto one thought. I needed to buy time, I needed to slow things down.

Fifty thousand dollars, I'd offered the man who'd just killed my husband. Fifty thousand dollars if he'd give me twenty-four hours to "get my affairs in order." If I was going to take the blame for my husband's death, end up in jail, I had to make arrangements for my daughter. That's what I'd told him.

And maybe he didn't trust me, and maybe he had been suspicious, but fifty grand was fifty grand, and once I explained to him that I could put Brian's body on ice . . .

He'd been impressed. Not shocked. Impressed. A woman who could preserve her husband's body with snow was apparently his kind of gal.

So the nameless hit man had accepted fifty grand, and in return I had twenty-four hours to "get my story straight."

Turns out, there's a lot you can do in twenty-four hours. Especially when you're the kind of woman who can dispassionately shovel snow over the man who'd once promised to love her, to take care of her, to never leave her.

I didn't think of Brian now. I wasn't ready, couldn't afford to go to that place. So I focused on what mattered most.

Who do you love?

The hit man was right. That's what life comes down to in the end. Who do you love?

Sophie. Somewhere out there in that same darkness, my daughter. Six years old, heart-shaped face, big blue eyes, and a toothless smile that could power the sun. Sophie.

Brian had died for her. Now I would survive for her.

Anything to get my daughter back.

"I'm coming," I whispered. "Be brave, sweetheart. Be brave."

"What?" Erica said, from the top bunk where she was mindlessly flipping cards.

"Nothing."

"Window won't break," she stated. "No escaping that way!" Erica cackled as if she'd told a great joke.

I turned toward my roommate. "Erica,

the pay phone in the commons area—
can I use that to make a call?"

She stopped playing her cards.

"Who you gonna call?" she asked
with interest.

"Ghostbusters," I said, straight-faced.

Erica cackled again. Then she told me
what I needed to know.

24

Bobby wanted to stop for dinner. D.D. did not.

"You need to take better care of yourself," Bobby informed her.

"And you need to stop fussing over me!" she snapped back, as they drove through the streets of Boston. "I never liked it before and I don't like it now."

"No."

"Excuse me?"

"I said no. And you can't make me."

D.D. twisted in the passenger's seat until she could glare straight at him. "You do realize pregnant women are expected to be hormonal and crazy. Meaning I could kill you now, and as long as there's one mother on the jury, I'd get away with it."

Bobby smiled. "Ahh, Annabelle used to say the same thing!"

"Oh, for Pete's sake—"

"You're pregnant," he interrupted her. "Men like to fuss over pregnant women. It gives us something to do. We also, secretly, love to fuss over babies. Why, the first time you bring in the infant to meet your squad . . . I bet Phil will knit a pair of booties. Neil . . . I'm guessing he'll provide Looney Tunes Band-Aids and the baby's first bike helmet."

D.D. stared at him. She hadn't thought of booties, Band-Aids, or bringing the kid to work. She was still working on baby, let alone Life with Baby.

She had a text from Alex: *Heard about the arrest, how goes the rest of the battle?*

She hadn't answered. She didn't know what to say. Sure, they'd arrested Tessa Leoni, but they'd also failed to find six-year-old Sophie. And the sun had gone down for the second time, now thirty-six hours since the initial Amber Alert, but probably two full days since Sophie had gone missing. Except, most likely the Amber Alert didn't matter. Most likely Tessa Leoni had killed her entire family, including Sophie.

D.D. wasn't working a missing persons case; she was leading a murder investigation to recover a child's body.

She wasn't ready to think about that yet. Not prepared for Alex's gentle, but always probing questions. Nor did she know how to segue from that conversation to *Oh yes, and I'm pregnant, which you haven't heard yet, but Bobby Dodge knows all about, having been informed by a female murder suspect.*

These were exactly the kind of situations that made D.D. a workaholic. Because finding Sophie and nailing Tessa would make her feel better. While talking to Alex about the new world order would only be falling deeper and deeper down the rabbit's hole.

"What you need is a falafel," Bobby said now.

"Gesundheit," D.D. answered.

"Annabelle loved them when she was

pregnant. It's meat, isn't it? You can't stand the smell of meat."

D.D. nodded. "Eggs don't do wonders for me either."

"Hence, Mediterranean food, with its many and varied vegetarian dishes."

"Do you like falafels?" D.D. asked suspiciously.

"No, I like Big Macs, but that's probably not going to work for you right now—"

D.D. shook her head.

"So falafels it is."

Bobby knew a place. Apparently a favorite of Annabelle's. He went inside to order, D.D. stayed in the car to avoid kitchen odors and catch up on voice mail. She started by returning Phil's call, asking him to rerun Brian Darby's financials, while digging deeper for other accounts or transactions, possibly under a family name or an alias. If Darby had a gambling habit, they should be able to see its impact on his bank account, with large sums of money coming and going, or perhaps a series of cash withdrawals from ATMs at Foxwoods, Mohegan Sun, or other casinos.

Then she transferred to Neil, who'd been working the hospital beat. Neil had been asking about Tessa's medical history. Now D.D. wanted to know about Brian's. In the past twelve months, any incidents of broken kneecaps (maybe a ski injury, D.D. mused)—or, say, a fall down a long flight of stairs. Neil was intrigued, saying he'd start right on it.

The hotline was receiving fewer Sophie sightings, but more calls concerning the white Denali. Turned out the city was filled with white SUVs, meaning the taskforce needed additional manpower to chase down all leads. D.D. suggested that the hotline squad pass all vehicle sightings to the three-man team currently tracing the truck's final hours. Which, she informed them, should be working 24/7, all OT requests automatically approved and if they needed more bodies, then snag more officers.

Tracking down the final drive of Brian Darby's SUV was a clear priority—pinpoint where the Denali had gone Saturday afternoon, find Sophie's body.

The thought depressed D.D. She

ended her calls and stared out the window instead.

Chilly night. Pedestrians hustled by on the sidewalk, collars turned up tight around their ears, gloved hands thrust deep into coat pockets. No snow yet, but it felt like it was coming. A cold raw night, which fit D.D.'s mood.

She didn't feel good about arresting Tessa Leoni. She wanted to. The female trooper bothered her. Both too young and too composed. Too pretty and too vulnerable. All bad combinations in D.D.'s mind.

Tessa was lying to them. About her husband, her daughter, and if Hamilton's theory was correct, about two hundred and fifty thousand dollars currently missing from the troopers' union. Had Tessa stolen the money? Was this part of her "new life"? Steal a quarter of a million, eliminate the family, and ride off into the sunset, young, pretty, and rich?

Or did it come back to the husband? Had he accrued gambling debts no honest man could pay? Maybe embezzling state police monies was his idea and she'd been pressured into going along. Stand behind your man. Except then, once she had the cash, realized the full risk she'd taken, and considered the lure of total freedom . . . Why hand over the ill-gotten gains if you could keep them all for yourself?

She'd had a pretty good plan, too. Set up her husband as a child murderer and wife beater. Then off him in self-defense. Once the dust settled, Tessa could quietly resign from the police and move to another state, where she could be a widow who'd inherited two hundred and fifty thousand in life insurance.

Plan would've worked, D.D. thought, if the ME hadn't noticed the cellular damage caused by freezing.

Maybe that's why Tessa had been putting pressure on Ben to release her husband's body. To try to avoid the autopsy altogether, or if it did happen, for it to be rushed. Ben would get in, out, done, and nobody would be the wiser.

Way to go, Ben, D.D. thought, then realized she was exhausted. She hadn't eaten today, she hadn't slept much last night. Her body was shutting down on her. She needed a nap. She needed to call Alex.

Dear God, what was she ever going to say to Alex?

Car door popped open. Bobby climbed in. He was holding a brown paper bag that wafted all sorts of curious scents. D.D. inhaled, and for once, her stomach didn't rebel. She breathed in deeper, and just like that, she was starving.

"Falafel!" she ordered.

Bobby patted her hand, already digging out the wrap. "Now, who was saying men shouldn't fuss. . . ."

"Gimme, gimme, gimme!"

"Love you, too, D.D. Love you, too."

They ate. Food was good. Food was energy. Food was power.

When they were done, D.D. demurely wiped her mouth, cleaned her hands, and returned the trash to the brown paper bag.

"I have a plan," she said.

"Does it involve me going home to my wife and baby?"

"No. It involves going to Trooper Lyons's house, and questioning him in front of his wife and children."

"I'm in."

She patted his hand. "Love you, too, Bobby. Love you, too."

Lyons lived in a modest 1950s raised ranch, seven blocks over from Brian Darby. From the street, the house appeared dated but well maintained. Tiny front yard, currently cluttered with a collection of plastic snow shovels and sleek sleds. The remains of a snowman and what appeared to be a snow fort lined the driveway, where Lyons's cruiser was parked at attention.

Bobby had to circle the block a couple of times for parking. When no spots became available, he parked illegally behind Lyons's cruiser. What was the point of being a cop if you couldn't bend a few rules?

By the time D.D. and Bobby got out of the car, Lyons was standing on the front porch. The burly trooper wore faded jeans, a heavy flannel shirt, and an un-welcoming scowl.

"What?" he asked by way of greeting.

"Got a couple of questions," D.D. said.

"Not at my house you don't."

D.D. eased back, let Bobby take the lead. He was a fellow state officer, not to mention better at playing good cop.

"Not intruding," Bobby said immediately, tone placating. "We were at the Darby house," he lied, "thought of a couple of things, and since you're right around the corner . . ."

"I don't bring work home." Lyons's ruddy face was still guarded, but not as hostile. "I got three kids. They don't need to be hearing about Sophie. They're freaked out enough as it is."

"They know she's missing," D.D. spoke up. He shot her a look.

"Heard it on the radio when their mother was driving them to school. Amber Alerts." He shrugged his massive shoulders. "Can't avoid 'em. Guess that's the whole point. But they know Sophie. They don't understand what could've happened to her." His voice grew rougher. "They don't understand why their father, the super-cop, hasn't brought her home yet."

"Then we're all on the same page," Bobby said. He and D.D. had made it to the front stoop. "We want to find Sophie, bring her home."

Lyons's shoulders came down. He seemed to finally relent. After another moment, he opened the door, gestured them inside.

They entered into a small mudroom, wood-paneled walls covered in coats, ceramic-tiled floor overrun with boots. House was small, and it only took D.D. a minute to figure out who ran the roost, three young boys, ages five to nine, who rushed into the crowded space to greet the newcomers, talking over one another in their excitement, before their mother, a pretty thirty-something woman with shoulder-length brown curls, tracked them down, looking exasperated.

"Bedtime!" she informed the boys. "To your rooms. I don't want to see you again until you've brushed your teeth and changed into pajamas!"

Three boys stared at her, didn't budge a muscle.

"Last one to the top of the stairs is a rotten egg!" the oldest boy suddenly yelled, and the three roared off like rockets, piling over one another in their haste to get to the stairs first.

Their mother sighed.

Shane shook his head.

"This is my wife, Tina," he offered, making the introduction. Tina shook their hands, smiling politely, but D.D. could read tension in the fine lines bracketing the woman's mouth, the way she looked instinctively at her husband, as if for assurance.

"Sophie?" she whispered, the name hitching in her throat.

"No news," Shane said softly, and he laid his hands on his wife's shoulders in a gesture D.D. found genuinely touching. "Got some work to do here, okay? I know I said I'd put the boys to bed. . . ."

"It's okay," Tina said automatically.

"We'll be in the front room."

Tina nodded again. D.D. could feel her eyes on them as they followed Shane from the mudroom into the kitchen. She thought the woman still looked worried.

Off the kitchen was a small front room. Looked like it had once been a three-season porch that Lyons had finished off with windows, installing a small gas-burning stove for heat. The room was decorated Rugged Male, with a big-screen TV, two oversized brown recliners, and a plethora of sports memorabilia. The Man Cave, D.D. deduced, where the stressed-out state trooper could retreat to recover from his day.

She wondered if the wife had an equivalent Crafts Room or Day Spa, because personally, she was betting life with three boys topped eight hours on patrol any day of the week.

Room didn't really offer seating for three, unless you counted the beanbags piled in the corner, so they stood.

"Nice home," Bobby said, once again good cop.

Lyons shrugged. "We bought it for the location. You can't see it right now, but the back lawn rolls down into a park, giving us plenty of green space. Great for barbecues. Essential for three boys."

"That's right," D.D. spoke up. "You're known for your cookouts. That's how Tessa and Brian met."

Lyons nodded, didn't say anything. He had his arms crossed over his chest, a defensive stance, D.D. thought. Or maybe an aggressive stance, given how it bulged the muscles of his shoulders and chest.

"We talked to Lieutenant Colonel Hamilton," Bobby commented.

Was it D.D.'s imagination, or did Lyons just tense?

"He mentioned several of the outings you've organized, you know—boys' night out to Red Sox games, Foxwoods."

Lyons nodded.

"Sounds like Brian Darby often joined."

"If he was around," Lyons said. Another noncommittal shrug.

"Tell us about Foxwoods," D.D. said.

Lyons stared at her, then returned his gaze to Bobby. "Why don't you just ask me the question."

"All right. To your knowledge did Brian Darby have a gambling problem?"

"To my knowledge . . ." The trooper suddenly sighed, uncrossed his arms, shook them out. "Goddammit," he said.

D.D. took that as a yes.

"How bad?" she asked.

"Don't know. He wouldn't talk about it with me. He knew I disapproved. But Tessa called me, 'bout six months ago. Brian was on tour, upstairs bathtub had sprung a leak. I gave her the name of a plumber, which she then contacted. Couple of pipes had to be replaced, some drywall patched. When all was said and done, guess it cost a good eight hundred, nine hundred bucks. Except when she went to withdraw it from savings, the money wasn't there."

"It wasn't there?" D.D. repeated.

Lyons shrugged. "According to Tessa, they should've had thirty grand in savings, except they didn't. I ended up loaning her the money to pay the contractors. Then, when Brian got back . . ."

"What happened?"

"We confronted him. Both of us. Tessa wanted me there. She said, if it was just her, it would sound like a nagging wife. But if it was both of us, Brian's wife and best friend, he'd have to pay attention."

"You ran a gambling addiction 'intervention,'" Bobby said. "Did it work?"

Lyons barked hollowly. "Did it work? Hell, not only did Brian refuse to acknowledge he had a problem, he actually accused us of having an affair. We were in cahoots against him. Whole world out to get him." Lyons shook his head. "I mean . . . you think you know a guy. We'd been friends for how long? And then one day, he just goes off. It's easier for him to believe his best friend is fucking his wife than to accept that he has a gambling problem, and that liquidating his life savings to pay off loan sharks isn't a good way to live."

"He took money from loan sharks?" D.D. asked sharply.

Lyons gave her a look. "Not according to him. He said he'd taken the money to pay off the Denali. So, while we're all sitting there, Tessa, cool as a cucumber, picks up the phone and dials their bank. It's all automated systems these days, and sure enough, their vehicle loan still has a $34,000 balance due.

Which is when he started yelling that we were obviously sleeping together. Go figure."

"What did Tessa do?"

"Pleaded with him. Begged him to get help before he got in too deep. Which he refused to acknowledge. So finally she said, if he didn't have a problem, then it should be easy for him to agree not to gamble. At all. He'd stay out of Foxwoods, Mohegan Sun, everywhere. He agreed, after making her promise never to see me again."

D.D. raised a brow, looked at him. "Sounds like he really believed you and Tessa were too close."

"Addicts blame everyone else for their problems," Lyons replied evenly. "Ask my wife. I told her all about it, and she can vouch for my time, both when Brian is home and when he's not home. We don't have secrets between us."

"Really? Then why didn't you tell us this sooner?" D.D. said. "Instead, I recall this whole little spiel on how you weren't too involved with Brian and Tessa's marriage. Now, twenty-four hours later,

you're their personal intervention specialist."

Lyons flushed. His fists were clenched
at his side. D.D. glanced down, then . . .

"Son of a bitch!"

She grabbed his right hand, yanking it
toward the light. Immediately, Lyons
raised his left as if to shove her back,
and in the next instant he had a loaded
Sig Sauer dug into his temple.

"Touch her and die," Bobby said.

Both men were breathing hard, D.D.
sandwiched between them.

The state trooper had a solid fifty
pounds on Bobby. He was stronger, and
as a patrol officer, more experienced in
a street fight. Maybe, if it had been any
other officer, he would've been tempted
to make a move, call the officer's bluff.

But Bobby had already earned his
battle stripes—one shot, one kill. Other
officers didn't ignore that kind of thing.

Lyons eased back, standing passively
as D.D. jerked his bruised and battered
fist under the overhead light. The knuckles on his right hand were purple and
swollen, the skin abraded in several areas.

As Bobby slowly moved his firearm to his side, D.D.'s gaze went to the steel-toed boots on Lyons's feet. The rounded tip of the boot. The bruise on Tessa's hip her lawyer wouldn't let them examine.

"Son of a bitch," D.D. repeated. "You hit her. *You're* the one who beat the shit out of Tessa Leoni."

"Had to," Lyons replied in a clipped tone.

"Why?"

"Because she begged me to."

In Lyons's new and improved story, Tessa had phoned him, hysterical, at nine a.m. Sunday morning. Sophie was missing, Brian was dead, some mystery man had done it all. She needed help. She wanted Lyons to come, alone, now, now, now.

Lyons had literally run to her place, as his cruiser would be too conspicuous.

When he'd arrived, he'd discovered Brian dead in the kitchen and Tessa, still in her uniform, weeping beside the corpse.

Tessa had told him some preposterous story. She'd arrived home from patrol, depositing her belt on the kitchen table, then walking upstairs to check on Sophie. Sophie's room had been empty. Tessa had just started getting nervous, when she heard a sound from the kitchen. She'd raced back down, where she'd discovered a man in a black wool trench coat holding Brian at gunpoint.

The man had told Tessa that he'd taken Sophie. The only way to get her back was to do as he said. Then he'd shot Brian three times in the chest with Tessa's gun and left.

"You believed this story?" D.D. asked Lyons incredulously. They were now sitting in the beanbags. It would almost appear cordial, except Bobby had his Sig Sauer on his lap.

"Not at first," Lyons admitted, "which became Tessa's point. If I didn't believe her story, then who would?"

"You think the man in black was an enforcer?" Bobby asked with a frown, "sent by someone Brian owed money to?"

Lyons sighed, looked at Bobby. "Brian muscled up," he said abruptly.

"You asked about it, yesterday. Why'd Brian bulk up?"

Bobby nodded.

"Brian's gambling started a year ago. Three months into it, he has his first little 'episode.' Ran up a bit too much on tab, got roughed up by some casino goons till he worked out a payment plan. Next week, he joined the gym. I think Brian's bulking up was his own self-protection plan. Let's just say, *after* Tessa and I confronted him, he didn't quit the gym."

"He was still gambling," Bobby said.

"That's my guess. Meaning, he could've run up more debt. And the gunman came to collect."

D.D. frowned at him. "But he killed Brian. Last I knew, killing the mark made it difficult for him to pay up."

"I think Brian was past that point. Sounds to me like he pissed off the wrong people. They didn't want his money, they wanted him dead. But he's the husband of a state police officer. Those kinds of murders can cause unwanted attention. So they came up with a scenario where Tessa herself became the suspect. Keeps all eyes off them, while getting the job done."

"Brian's a bad boy," D.D. repeated slowly. "Brian is killed. Sophie is kidnapped, to keep Tessa in line."

"Yeah."

"This is what Tessa told you."

"I already explained—"

D.D. held up a silencing hand. She'd already heard the story, she just didn't believe it. And the fact it came from a fellow police officer who'd already lied to them once wasn't helping.

"So," D.D. reviewed, "Tessa is in a panic. Her husband has been shot with her gun, her daughter kidnapped, and her only hope of seeing her daughter alive is to plead guilty to her husband's murder."

"Yes." Lyons nodded enthusiastically.

"Tessa hatches a master plan: You'll beat the shit out of her. Then she'll claim Brian did it, and she shot him in self-defense. That way she can plead guilty—meeting the terms of her daughter's kidnappers—while keeping out of prison." This part actually made some sense to D.D. Given past experience,

Tessa Leoni had played to her strengths. Smart woman.

Bobby, however, had a question for Lyons. "But you really, I mean *really* beat the shit out of her. Why?"

The trooper flushed, stared down at his mangled fist. "I couldn't hit her," he said in a muffled voice.

"Then how do you explain the fractured cheek?" D.D. asked.

"She's a girl. I don't hit girls. And she knew it. So she started . . . At the Academy, we had to pound one another. It was part of the self-defense training. And big guys like me struggled. We're interested in becoming cops because we have a sense of fair play—we don't hit women or pick on the little guy." He eyed Bobby. "Except at the Academy, where all of a sudden you had to."

Bobby nodded, as if he understood.

"So, we trash-talked each other, right? Goaded each other into action, because the big guys had to start seriously hitting, if the little guys were going to seriously learn to defend."

Bobby nodded again.

"Let's just say, Tessa was really good

at goading. It had to be convincing, she said. Spousal abuse is an affirmative defense, meaning the burden of proof would be on her. I had to hit her *hard*. I had to make her . . . *fear.* So she started goading, and kept needling and needling and by the time she was done . . . Damn . . ." Lyons looked off at something only he could see. "I had a moment. I really did want her dead."

"But you stopped yourself," Bobby said quietly.

He drew himself upright. "Yes."

"Bully for you," D.D. said dryly, and the state trooper flushed again.

"You did this on Sunday morning?" Bobby inquired.

"Nine a.m. You'll find a record of her call on my cell. I ran over, we did our thing. . . . I don't know. It must've been ten-thirty. I returned home. She made the official call in, and the rest is what you already know. Other troopers arriving, the lieutenant colonel. That's all true. I think Tessa and I were both hoping the Amber Alert might shake things loose. Whole state's looking for Sophie. Brian's dead, Tessa's arrested. So the man can let Sophie go now, right? Just leave her at a bus stop or something. Tessa did what they asked of her. Sophie should be all right."

Lyons sounded a little desperate. D.D. didn't blame him. The story didn't make much sense, and as hour passed into hour, she was guessing Lyons was also coming to that realization.

"Hey, Lyons," she said now. "If you came to Tessa's house on Sunday morning, how come Brian's body was frozen before that?"

"What?"

"Brian's body. The ME ruled he was killed prior to Sunday morning, and put on ice."

"I heard the DA . . . some comment . . ." Lyons's voice trailed off. He gazed at them dully. "I don't understand."

"She played you."

"No . . ."

"There wasn't any mystery man at Tessa's house Sunday morning, Shane. In fact, Brian was most likely killed Friday night or Saturday morning. And as for Sophie . . ."

The burly trooper closed his eyes, didn't seem to be able to swallow. "But she said . . . For Sophie. We were doing this . . . Had to hit her . . . To save Sophie . . ."

"Do you know where Sophie is?" Bobby asked gently. "Have any idea where Tessa might've taken her?"

Lyons shook his head. "No. She wouldn't harm Sophie. You don't understand. There's no way Tessa would harm Sophie. She loves her. It's just . . . not possible."

D.D. regarded him gravely. "Then you're an even bigger fool than we thought. Sophie's gone, and given that you're now an accomplice to murder, looks to me like Tessa Leoni screwed you over good."

25

Bobby and D.D. didn't arrest Lyons. Bobby felt it was more appropriate to let internal affairs kick into gear as state investigators could squeeze Lyons more effectively than the Boston police could. Plus internal affairs was in a better position to identify any links between Lyons's actions and their other major investigation—the missing funds from the troopers' union.

Instead, Bobby and D.D. returned to BPD headquarters, for the eleven p.m. debrief with the taskforce.

The falafel had done D.D. a world of

good. She had that gleam in her eye and hitch in her step as they pounded up the stairs to the homicide unit.

They were closing in now. Bobby could feel the case building momentum, rolling them toward an inevitable conclusion: Tessa Leoni had murdered her husband and child.

All that remained was putting a few last pieces of the case in place—including locating Sophie's body.

The other taskforce officers were already seated by the time D.D. and Bobby walked through the door. Phil looked as jazzed as D.D., and sure enough, he went first.

"You were right," he burst out as D.D. strode to the front of the room. "They don't have fifty grand in savings—the entire sum was withdrawn Saturday morning. The transaction hadn't been posted when I got the initial report. And get this—the money had also been withdrawn twelve days prior, then returned six days after that. That's a lot of activity on fifty grand."

"How was it finally taken out?" D.D. asked.

"Bank check, made out to cash."

Bobby whistled low. "Couple of pennies, available as hard currency."

"Male or female closed the account?" D.D. asked.

"Tessa Leoni," Phil supplied. "Teller recognized her. She was still in uniform when she made the transaction."

"Setting up her new life," D.D. said immediately. "If she ends up under investigation for killing her husband, joint assets might be frozen. So she got out the big money first, squirreled it away. Now, how much do you want to bet that if we find that fifty grand, there will be another quarter million sitting with it?"

Phil was intrigued, so Bobby related the state police's current investigation into embezzled funds. Best lead—the account had been closed out by a female wearing a red baseball cap and dark sunglasses.

"They needed the money," Phil stated. "Did a little more digging, and while Brian Darby and Tessa Leoni look good on paper, you won't believe the credit card debt six-year-old Sophie has run up."

"What?" D.D. asked.

"Exactly. It would appear Brian Darby opened half a dozen credit cards in Sophie's name, using a separate PO box. I found over forty-two grand in consumer debt, run up over the past nine months. Some evidence of lump sum payments, but inevitably followed by significant cash advances, most of which were at Foxwoods."

"So Brian Darby does have a gambling problem. Putz."

Phil grinned. "Just to amuse myself, I correlated the dates of the cash advances with Brian's work schedule, and sure enough, Sophie only withdrew large sums of money when Brian was in port. So yeah, I'm guessing Brian Darby was gambling away his stepdaughter's future."

"Last transaction?" Bobby asked.

"Six days ago. He made a payment before that—maybe the first time the fifty grand was taken out of savings. He paid off the credit cards, then he returned to the tables and either won big, or borrowed big, because he was able to replace the entire fifty grand to savings in six days. Wait a minute . . ." Phil frowned.

"No," the detective corrected himself. "He borrowed big, because the latest credit card statements show significant cash advances, meaning in the past six days, Brian went deeper into debt, yet was able to replace fifty grand to his savings. Gotta be he took out a personal loan. Maybe to cover his tracks with his wife."

Bobby looked at D.D. "You know, if Darby was into it big with loan sharks, it's possible an enforcer might have been sent to the house."

D.D. shrugged. She filled the task-force in on Trooper Lyons's revised statement—that Tessa Leoni had called him Sunday morning, claiming a mysterious hit man had kidnapped her child and killed her husband. She was to take the blame in order to get her child back. Shane Lyons had then agreed to assist her efforts by beating her to a pulp.

When she finished, most of her fellow investigators wore similar frowns.

"Wait a minute," Neil spoke up. "She called Lyons on Sunday? But Brian was dead at least twenty-four hours before then."

"Something she neglected to tell him, and yet more evidence she's a compulsive liar."

"I traced Darby's Friday night call," Detective Jake Owens spoke up. "Unfortunately, it went to a prepaid cellphone. No way to determine the caller, though a prepaid cellphone suggests someone who doesn't want his calls monitored—such as a loan shark."

"And it turns out Brian suffered two recent 'accidents,'" Neil offered. "In August, he received treatment for multiple contusions to his face, which he attributed to a hiking mishap. Let's see . . ." Neil flipped through his notes. "Worked with Phil on this one—yep, Brian shipped out September through October. Returned November three and November sixteen was in the ER again, this time with cracked ribs, which he said he received after falling from a ladder while patching a leak on his roof."

"For the record," Phil spoke up, "Sophie Leoni's credit cards were all maxed out in November, meaning if Brian had accrued debt, he couldn't use her lines of credit to pay it off."

"Any withdrawals from the personal accounts?" D.D. asked.

"I found a major one in July—forty-two grand. But that money was replaced right before Brian shipped out in September, and after that, I don't see any more significant lump sum transactions until the past two weeks."

"The intervention," Bobby commented. "Six months ago, Tessa and Shane confronted Brian about his gambling, which Tessa had figured out due to the sudden loss of thirty grand. He replaced the money—"

"Winning big, or borrowing large?" D.D. muttered.

Bobby shrugged. "Then he moved his habit underground, using a bunch of phony credit cards, with the statements mailed to a separate PO box, so Tessa would never see them. Until two weeks ago, when apparently Brian Darby fell off the wagon, this time withdrawing fifty grand. Which maybe Tessa found out about, which would explain its rapid re-placement six days later."

"And why she might have withdrawn it Saturday morning," Phil pointed out. "Forget starting a new life; seems to me Tessa Leoni was working pretty hard to save the old one."

"All the more reason to kill her spouse," D.D. declared. She moved to the whiteboard. "All right. Who thinks Brian Darby had a gambling problem?"

Her entire taskforce raised their hands. She agreed, added the detail to their murder board.

"Okay. Brian Darby gambled. Apparently, not successfully. He was in deep enough to run up debt, commit credit card fraud, and perhaps receive some poundings from the local goons. Then what?"

Her investigators stared at her. She stared back at them.

"Hey, don't let me have all the fun. We assumed Tessa Leoni's lover beat the crap out of her. Instead, it turns out it was a fellow police officer, who felt he was doing her a favor. Now we can cor-roborate half that story—Brian Darby did gamble. Brian Darby may have had debt worth an enforcer paying him a visit. So where does that leave us?"

D.D. wrote a fresh header: *Motive.*

"If I were Tessa Leoni," she stated, "and I discovered my husband was not only still gambling, but that the sorry son of a bitch had run up tens of thousands in credit card debt in my daughter's name, I'd kill him for that alone. Interestingly enough, my-husband-is-a-worthless-asshole is not an affirmative defense, meaning Tessa's still better off arguing battery and getting Lyons to beat the shit out of her."

Several officers nodded agreeably. Bobby, of course, poked the first hole in the argument.

"So she loves her daughter enough to be offended by the credit card scam, but then kills her anyway?"

D.D. pursed her lips. "Point taken." She looked at the room. "Anyone?"

"Maybe she didn't kill Sophie on purpose," Phil suggested. "Maybe, it was an accident. She and Brian were having a fight, Sophie got in the way. Maybe,

Sophie's death became one more reason to kill Brian. Except now her family's
dead, her husband shot by her service
weapon—automatic investigation right
there," Phil added, "so Tessa panics.
Gotta figure out a plausible scenario—"

"Self-defense worked for her once before," Bobby commented. "The Tommy
Howe shooting."

"She freezes her husband's body to
buy her time, takes Sophie's body for a
drive, and the next morning concocts a
story to manipulate both Shane Lyons
and us into believing what she needs
us to believe," D.D. finished. "Sunday
morning becomes showtime."

"What if she withdrew the fifty grand
Saturday morning because she discovered Brian was gambling again?" another officer spoke up. "Brian found out,
or she confronted him. Events escalated
from there."

D.D. nodded, wrote a new note on the
board: *Where's the $$$?*

"Gonna be hard to trace," Phil
warned. "Check's made out to cash,
meaning it can be deposited at any

bank under any name, or taken to a dealer and cashed."

"Big check for most dealers," Bobby said.

"Guaranteed percentage," Phil countered. "Especially if she called ahead, there are several check cashers who'd make that deal. Bank checks are good as gold and it's a tight financial market out there."

"What if Tessa needed the money?" D.D. asked abruptly. "What if she had a payment to make?"

Thirty pairs of eyes looked at her.

"It's another possibility," she thought out loud. "Brian Darby had a gambling problem. He couldn't control it, and like a sinking ship was taking Tessa and Sophie down with him. Now, Tessa is a woman who's already hit bottom once before. She knows better. In fact, she's worked doubly hard to rebuild a life, particularly for her daughter's sake. So what can she do? Divorce takes time, and God knows how much Brian will destroy their financials until it goes through.

"Maybe," D.D. mused, "maybe there

was an enforcer. Maybe, Tessa Leoni *hired* him—a hit man to finally put her husband out of his misery. Except the man in black took out his own insurance policy—Sophie Leoni—so Tessa couldn't turn around and arrest him."

Bobby looked at her. "I thought you were convinced she'd killed her own daughter?"

D.D.'s hand was resting unconsciously across her stomach. "What can I tell you? I'm getting soft in my old age. Besides, a jury will buy a wife killing her gambling-addicted husband. A mother killing her child, however, is a tougher sell."

She glanced at Phil. "We need to follow the money. Nail down that Tessa definitely took it out. See what else you can find in the financials. And tomorrow, we'll give Tessa's lawyer a call, see if we can arrange for a fresh chat. Twenty-four hours in jail has a tendency to make most people more talkative.

"Any other news from the hotline?" she asked.

Nothing, her taskforce agreed.

"Final drive of the white Denali?" she tried hopefully.

"Based on fuel mileage, it remained within a hundred miles of Boston," the lead detective reported.

"Excellent. So we've narrowed it to, what, a quarter of the state?"

"Pretty much."

D.D. rolled her eyes, set down the marker. "Anything else we should know?"

"Gun," spoke up a voice from the back of the room. Detective John Little.

"What about it?" D.D. asked. "Last I knew, the firearms discharge investigation team had turned it over for processing."

"Not Tessa's gun," Little said. "Brian's gun."

"Brian had a gun?" D.D. asked in surprise.

"Took out a permit two weeks ago. Glock forty. I couldn't find it on the evidence logs as seized from either the house or his car."

The detective gazed at her expectantly. D.D. returned his stare.

"You're telling me Brian Darby had a gun," she said.

"Yes. Applied for the permit two weeks ago."

"Maybe bulking up wasn't getting the job done anymore," Bobby murmured.

D.D. waved her hand at him. "Hello. Bigger picture here. Brian Darby had a Glock forty, *and we have no idea where it is.* Detective, that's not a small thing."

"Gun permit just went through," Detective Little countered defensively. "We're a little backed up these days. Haven't you been reading the papers? Armageddon is coming and, apparently, half the city intends to be armed for it."

"We need that gun," D.D. said in a clipped voice. "For starters, what if that's the weapon that killed Sophie Leoni?"

The room went silent.

"Yeah," she said. "No more talk. No more theories. We have a dead husband of a state police officer, and a missing six-year-old. I want Sophie Leoni. I want Brian Darby's gun. And if that evidence leads us where we think it's probably going to lead us, then I want us to build a case so fucking airtight, Tessa Leoni goes away for the rest of her miserable life. Get out. Get it done."

Eleven o'clock Monday night, the detectives scrambled.

26

Every woman has a moment in her life when she realizes she genuinely loves a guy, and he's just not worth it.

It took me nearly three years to reach that point with Brian. Maybe there were signs along the way. Maybe, in the beginning, I was just so happy to have a man love me and my daughter as much as Brian seemed to love me and Sophie, I ignored them. Yes, he could be moody. After the initial six-month honeymoon, the house became his anal-retentive domain, Sophie and I receiving daily lectures if we left a dish on the counter, a toothbrush out of its holder, a crayon on the table.

Brian liked precision, needed it.

"I'm an engineer," he'd remind me. "Trust me, you don't want a dam built by a sloppy engineer."

Sophie and I did our best. Compromise, I told myself. The price of family; you gave up some of your individual preferences for the greater good. Plus, Brian would leave again and Sophie and I would spend a giddy eight weeks dumping our junk all over the place. Coats draped over the back of kitchen chairs. Art projects piled on the corner of the counter. Yes, we were regular Girls Gone Wild when Brian shipped out.

Then, one day I went to pay the plumber and discovered our life savings was gone.

It's a tough moment when you have to confront the level of your own complacency. I knew Brian had been going to Foxwoods. More to the point, I knew the evenings he came home reeking of booze and cigarettes, but claimed he'd been hiking. He'd lied to me, on several occasions, and I'd let it go. To pry would involve being told an answer I didn't want to hear. So I didn't pry.

While my husband, apparently, gave in to his inner demons and gambled away our savings account.

Shane and I confronted him. He denied it. Not very plausibly. But at a certain point, there wasn't much more I could do or say. The money magically returned, and again, I didn't ask many questions, not wanting to know what I didn't want to know.

I thought of my husband as two people after that. There was Good Brian, the man I fell in love with, who picked up Sophie after school and took her sledding until they were both pink-cheeked from laughter. Good Brian fixed me pancakes and maple syrup when I got home from graveyard shift. He would rub my back, strained from the weight of carrying body armor. He would hold me while I slept.

Then there was Bad Brian. Bad Brian yelled at me when I forgot to wipe down the counter after doing the dishes. Bad Brian was curt and distant, not only turning the TV to whatever testosterone-bound show he could find, but turning up the volume if Sophie or I tried to protest.

Bad Brian smelled like cigarettes, booze, and sweat. He worked out compulsively, with the demons of a man with something to fear. Then he'd disappear for a couple of days at a time—time with *the guys,* Bad Brian would say, when we both knew he was going off alone, his friends having long since given up on him.

But that was Bad Brian for you. He could look his state police officer wife in the eye, and tell a lie.

It always made me wonder: Would he be a different kind of husband if I were a different kind of wife?

Bad Brian broke my heart. Then Good Brian would reappear long enough to patch it back together again. And around and around we would go, plummeting through the roller coaster ride of our lives.

Except all rides have to end.

Good Brian and Bad Brian's ride

ended at exactly the same moment, on our kitchen's spotlessly clean floor.

Bad Brian can't hurt me or Sophie anymore.

Good Brian is going to take me a while to let go.

Tuesday morning, seven a.m.

The female CO started head count and the unit officially stirred to life. My roommate, Erica, had already been awake for an hour, curled up in the fetal position, rocking back and forth, eyes pinned on something only she could see, while muttering beneath her breath.

I would guess she'd retired to her bunk shortly after midnight. No watch on my wrist, no clock in the cell, so I had to gauge the time in my head. It gave me something to do all night long—I think it's . . . two a.m., three a.m., four twenty-one a.m.

I fell asleep once. I dreamt of Sophie. She and I were in a vast, churning ocean, paddling for all we were worth against steadily climbing waves.

"Stay with me," I screamed at her. "Stay with me, I'll keep you safe!"

But her head disappeared beneath the black water, and I dove and I dove and I dove, but I couldn't find my daughter again.

I woke up, tasting salt on my lips. I didn't sleep again.

The tower made noises in the night. Nameless women, goading nameless groaning men. The rattle of pipes. The hum of a huge facility, trying to settle its bones. It felt as if I were inside some giant beast, swallowed up whole. I kept touching the walls, as if the rough feel of cinder blocks would keep me grounded. Then I would get up and pee, as the cover of night was the closest to privacy I could get.

The female CO had reached our cell. She glanced at rocking Erica, then at me, and our eyes met, a flicker of recognition, before she turned away.

Kim Watters. Dated one of the guys in the barracks, had attended a couple of the group dinners. 'Course. CO at the Suffolk County Jail. Now I remembered.

She moved to the next cell. Erica

rocked harder. I peered out the barred window and tried to convince myself that personally knowing my own prison guard didn't make things worse.

Seven-thirty. Breakfast.

Erica was up. Still muttering, not looking at me. Agitated. Meth had fried her brain. She needed rehab, and mental health services more than a jail sentence. Then again, welcome to most of the prison population.

We got limp pancakes, applesauce, and milk. Erica put the applesauce on her pancakes, rolled it all together, and ate it in three giant mouthfuls. Four gulps took care of the milk. Then she eyed my tray.

I had no appetite. The pancakes tasted like wet tissue on my tongue. I stared at her and slowly ate them anyway.

Erica sat on the toilet. I turned around to give her privacy.

She laughed.

Later, I used my hooter bag to brush my teeth and apply deodorant. Then . . . Then I didn't really know what to do. Welcome to my first full day in prison.

Rec time arrived. The CO opened our cell. Some women drifted out, some stayed inside. I couldn't take it anymore. The ten foot ceilings and yawning windows gave the illusion of space, but a jail cell was a jail cell. I already felt over-flouresced, pining for natural sunlight.

I paced over to the sitting area at one end of the commons, where six ladies had gathered to watch *GMA.* The show was too happy for me. Next, I tried the tables, four silver rounds where two women currently played hearts, while one more sat and cackled at something only she understood.

A shower went on. I didn't look. I didn't want to know.

Then I heard a funny sound, like a shivery gasp, someone trying to inhale and exhale at the same time.

I turned around. The CO, Kim Watters, looked like she was doing a funny dance. Her body was up in the air, her feet twitching as if reaching for the floor, except they couldn't find it. A giant black female with long dark hair stood directly behind her, heavily muscled arm cocked around Kim's windpipe, squeezing tight even as Kim's fingers scraped frantically at the massive forearm.

I stepped forward and in the next instant, my roommate, Erica, screamed, "Get the fucking pig!" and half a dozen detainees rushed toward me.

I took the first blow in the stomach. I tightened my abs reflexively, rocked left and drove my fist into a soft, oomphing middle. Another careening blow. Ducking low, moving on instinct now, because that's why recruits trained. Do the impossible over and over and it becomes the possible. Better yet, it becomes routine, meaning one day, when you least expect it, months and years of training can suddenly save your life.

Another hard crack to my shoulder. They were aiming for my face, my swollen eye and shattered cheek. I brought up both hands in the classic pugilist stance, blocking my head, while driving myself toward the closest attacker. I caught her around the waist and flung her back at the rushing stampede, toppling two in a tangle of limbs.

Cries. Pain, rage, theirs, mine, didn't really matter. Moving, moving, moving, had to stay on my feet, confront the on-slaught or be crushed by sheer num-bers.

Sharp sting. Something cutting my forearm, while another fist connected with my shoulder. I sidestepped again, drove my elbow into the stomach of the attacker, then the side of my hand sharp into her throat. She went down and stayed there.

The remaining four finally backed up. I kept my gaze on them, trying to process many things at once. Other de-tainees, where? Back in their cells? Self-imposed confinement so they wouldn't be busted later?

And Kim? Gasping scuffle behind me. Officer down, officer down, officer down.

Panic button. Had to be one some-where—

Fresh slice to my arm. I slapped at it, kicking out and catching the woman in the knee.

Then I screamed. I screamed and screamed and *screamed,* days' worth of rage and helplessness and frustration fi-nally erupting from my throat, because Kim was dying and my daughter was probably already dead and my husband had died, right in front of my eyes, taking Good Brian with him, and the man in black had taken my daughter and left behind only the blue button eye from her favorite doll and *I would get them. I would make them all pay.*

Then I moved. I was probably still screaming. A lot. And I don't think it was a sane sound because my attackers retreated until I was the one falling upon them, lips peeled back, hands fisted into hard balls.

I moved, I kicked, I jabbed, and I punched. I was twenty-three years old again. Behold the Giant Killer. Behold the Giant Killer really truly *pissed off.*

And my face dripped with sweat and my hands dripped with blood and the first two females were down and the third was running now, ironically toward the safety of her cell, but the fourth had a shank and she thought that would keep her safe. She'd probably fought off aggressive johns and pissed-off pimps. I was just a prissy white girl and no match for a genuine graduate of the school of hard knocks.

Rattling gasp from the CO's desk. The sound of a woman dying.

"Do it!" I snarled at her. "Come on, bitch. Show me what you got."

She charged. Stupid shit. I moved left, and straight-armed her in the throat. She dropped the shank and clutched at her crushed windpipe. I picked up the shank, and jumped over her body for central command.

Kim's toes weren't dancing anymore. She remained suspended in the air, black arm still twisted around her throat as her eyes glazed over.

I stepped around her.

I looked up at the large black female who turned out not to be a female at all, but a long-haired male who'd somehow infiltrated the unit.

He appeared startled to see me.

So I smiled at him. Then drove the shank through his ribs.

Kim's body dropped to the floor. The inmate staggered back, grabbing his side. I advanced upon him. He scrambled, twisting around, trying to run for the unit door. I kicked him in the back of his right knee. He stumbled. I kicked him in the back of the left knee. He went down, then rolled over, hands coming up defensively.

I stood over him, holding the bloody shank. I must have looked fearsome, with my dripping hands, battered face, and one good eye, because large black male peed his orange prison jumpsuit.

I raised the shank.

"No," he whispered hoarsely.

I brought it down into the meat of his thigh. He screamed. I twisted.

Then I sang for the entire unit to hear: *"All I want for Christmas is my two front teeth, my two front teeth, two front teeth. . . ."*

The inmate cried, as I leaned over, brushed back the long dark locks of his hair, and whispered like a lover in his ear: "Tell the man in black I'm coming for him. Tell him he's next."

I twisted the shank again.

Then I stood up, wiped the shank on my pant leg, and hit the panic button.

Do you mourn when your world has ended? When you have arrived at a des-

LISA GARDNER

tination from where there is no going back?

The SERT team descended as a stampede. The entire facility went to lockdown. I was shackled where I stood, legs swaying, arms lacerated, fresh bruises blooming down my sides and across my back.

They removed Kim on a stretcher, unconscious but breathing.

My fourth attacker, the one who'd brought the shank, left in a body bag. I watched them zip it up. I felt nothing at all.

Erica sobbed. Screamed and wailed and carried on to such an extent, they finally carted her off to Medical, where she would be heavily sedated and put under suicide watch. Others were questioned, but in the way these things worked, they had no idea what had just taken place.

"In my cell the whole time . . ."

"Never looked out . . ."

"Heard some noises, though . . ."

"Sounded like a lot of ass-whooping . . ."

"I slept through the whole thing, Officer. Really, I did."

The male inmate, however, told anyone who would listen that I was the angel of death, and please God, please God, please God, keep me away from him.

The assistant deputy superintendent finally halted in front of me. He studied me for a long time, his expression judging me more trouble than I was worth.

He delivered my punishment as a single word. "Segregation."

"I want my lawyer."

"Who attacked the CO, *detainee*?"

"Mrs. Doubtfire."

"Mrs. Doubtfire, *sir*. Now, why did the inmate attack CO Watters?"

"Don't know, *sir*."

"You've been in prison less than twenty-four hours. How'd you get a shank?"

"Took it off the ho' trying to kill me." I paused. *"Sir."*

"All six of them?"

"Don't fuck with the state police. *Sir.*"

He almost smiled. Instead, he jerked his thumb toward the ceiling and the multiple mounted cameras. "Here's the thing about prison: Big Brother's always watching. So last time, *detainee,* anything you want to tell me?"

"Officer Watters owes me a thank you card."

He didn't argue, so maybe he already knew more than he was letting on. "Medical," he said now, gesturing to my sliced-up forearms.

"Lawyer," I repeated.

"The request will be sent through proper channels."

"Don't have time." I looked the assistant deputy superintendent in the eye. "I have decided to cooperate fully with the Boston police," I declared for all to hear. "Call Detective D. D. Warren. Tell her I will take her to my daughter's body."

27

"Fuck that!" D.D. exploded two hours later. She was at BDP headquarters, in a conference room with Bobby, the deputy superintendent of homicide, and Tessa Leoni's lawyer, Ken Cargill. Cargill had called the meeting twenty minutes ago. Had a limited-time offer, he'd told them. Needed D.D.'s boss in the room, because if a decision was going to be made, it had to be made fast. Meaning, he was planning on negotiating for something above D.D.'s paygrade. Meaning, she should be letting the deputy superintendent, Cal Horgan, respond to his preposterous demand.

D.D. had never been good at keeping silent.

"We don't give guided tours!" she continued hotly now. "Tessa wants to finally do the right thing? Good for her. Bobby and I can be cell-side in twenty minutes, and she can draw us a map."

Horgan said nothing, so maybe he agreed with her.

"She can't draw you a map," Cargill answered steadily. "She doesn't remember the precise location. She'd been driving for a bit before she pulled over. As it is, she may not be able to get you to the exact spot, but figures she can get fairly close, by looking for familiar landmarks."

"Can't even get us to the exact spot?" Bobby spoke up, sounding as skeptical as D.D. felt.

"I would arrange for a dog team to assist," Cargill replied.

"Cadaver team, you mean," D.D. said bitterly. She sank back down in her chair, both arms crossed over her stomach. She had known, after the first twenty-four hours, that little Sophie Leoni with the curly brown hair, big blue eyes, and heart-shaped face was most likely dead. Still, to hear it said out loud, from Tessa's lawyer of all people, that it was time to recover the body . . .

There were days this job was just too hard.

"How did she say Sophie died again?" Bobby asked.

Cargill skewered him with a glance. "She didn't."

"That's right," Bobby continued. "She's not really telling us anything, is she? She's just demanding that we spring her from prison and take her for a drive. Imagine that."

"She almost died this morning," Cargill argued. "Coordinated attack, six female detainees going after her, while a male inmate took out the CO. If not for the quick response by Trooper Leoni, Officer Watters would be dead and probably Tessa, as well."

"Self-preservation," Bobby said.

"Another fanciful story," D.D. added harshly.

Cargill looked at her. "Not fanciful.

Caught on tape. I've watched the video myself. Male inmate attacked the CO first, then six females rushed Tessa. She's lucky to be alive. And you're lucky that the shock of said events has led her to want to cooperate."

"Cooperate," D.D. stated. "There's that word again. 'Cooperate,' to me, means to assist others. For example, she could draw us a map, perhaps one based on recalled landmarks. That would be cooperating. She could tell us how Sophie died. That would be cooperating. She could also tell us, once and for all, what happened to her husband and child, yet another form of cooperation. Somehow, she doesn't seem to be getting it."

Cargill shrugged. He stopped studying Bobby and D.D. and turned his attention to the deputy superintendent instead. "Like it or not, I don't know how long my client is going to continue to want to *cooperate.* This morning she suffered a traumatic experience. By this afternoon, certainly by tomorrow morning, I can't guarantee the impulse will remain. In the meantime, while my client may not feel like answering all your questions, I would imagine that the recovery of Sophie Leoni's body would answer a great deal of them for you. You know—by supplying evidence. Or are you people still in the business of gathering evidence?"

"She goes back to jail," Horgan said.

"Oh please." D.D. blew out a puff of breath. "Never negotiate with terrorists."

Cargill ignored her, attention still on Horgan. "Understood."

"Shackled at all times."

"Never assumed otherwise." Short pause. "You might, however, want to coordinate with the Suffolk County Sheriff's Department. From a legal perspective, she is under their custody, meaning they may want to be the ones providing escort."

Horgan rolled his eyes. Multiple law enforcement agencies, just what they needed.

"How long a drive to the site?" Horgan asked.

"No more than one hour."

D.D. glanced at the clock on the wall. It was ten-thirty a.m. Sun set by five-thirty. Meaning time was already of the essence. She stared at her boss, not sure what she wanted anymore. Hating to give in to a suspect's demands, and yet . . . She wanted to bring Sophie home. Yearned for that small piece of closure. As if it might ease some of the ache in her heart.

"Pick her up at noon," Horgan said abruptly. He turned to regard D.D. "Get a dog team. Now."

"Yes, sir."

Horgan, turning back to Cargill. "No runarounds. Your client cooperates, or all her existing prison privileges vanish. She'll not only return to jail, but it'll be hard time now. Understood?"

Cargill smiled thinly. "My client is a decorated member of law enforcement. She understands. And may I congratulate you on getting her out of jail, while she's still alive to assist in your efforts."

There were a lot of things D.D. wanted to do right now—kick, storm, rage. Given the day's tight time frame, however, she restrained herself and contacted the Northern Massachusetts Search & Recovery Canine Team.

Like most canine teams, the Mass. group was comprised of all volunteers. They had eleven members, including Nelson Bradley and his German shepherd, Quizo, who was one of only several hundred trained cadaver dogs in the world.

D.D. needed Nelson and Quizo and she needed them now. Good news, team president Cassondra Murray agreed to have the whole crew mobilized within ninety minutes. Murray and possibly Nelson would meet the police in Boston, and follow caravan style. Other members of the team would arrive once they had a location, as they lived too far outside the city to make it downtown in a timely manner.

That worked for D.D.

"What d'ya need?" D.D. asked by phone. She hadn't worked with a dog team in years and then it'd been a live rescue, not a body recovery. "I can get you clothing from the child, that sort of thing."

"Not necessary."

LISA GARDNER

"'Cause it's a body," D.D. filled in.

"Nope. Doesn't matter. Dogs are trained to identify human scent if it's a rescue and cadaver scent if it's a recovery. Mostly, we need you and your team to stay out of our way."

"Okay," D.D. drawled, a bit testily.

"One search dog equals a hundred and fifty human volunteers," Murray recited firmly.

"Will the snow be an issue?"

"Nope. Heat makes scent rise, cold keeps it lower to the ground. As handlers, we adjust our search strategy accordingly. From our dogs' perspectives, however, scent is scent."

"How about time frame?"

"If the terrain's not too difficult, dogs should be able to work two hours, then they'll need a twenty-minute break. Depends on the conditions, of course."

"How many dogs are you going to bring?"

"Three. Quizo's the best, but they're all SAR dogs."

"Wait—I thought Quizo was the only cadaver dog."

"Not anymore. As of two years ago,

all our dogs are trained for live, cadaver, and water. We start with live searches first, as that's the easiest to teach a puppy. But once the dogs master that, we train them for cadaver recovery, then, water searches."

"Do I want to know how you train for cadaver?" D.D. asked.

Murray laughed. "Actually, we're lucky. The ME, Ben—"

"I know Ben."

"He's a big supporter. We give him tennis balls to place inside the body bags. Once the scent of decomp has transferred to the tennis balls, he seals them in airtight containers for us. That's what we use to train. It's a good compromise, as the fine state of Massachusetts frowns on private ownership of cadavers, and I don't believe in synthetic 'cadaver scent.' Best scientists in the world agree that decomp is one of the most complicated scents on earth. God knows what the dogs are honing in on, meaning man shouldn't tamper with it."

"Okay," D.D. said.

"Do you anticipate a water search?" Murray asked, "because that poses a couple of challenges this time of year. We take the dogs out in boats, of course, but given the temperatures, I'd still want them in special insulated gear in case they fall in."

"Your dogs work in boats?"

"Yep. Catch the scent in the current of water, just like the drift of the wind. Quizo has found bodies in water a hundred feet deep. It does seem like voodoo, which again, is why I don't like synthetic scent. Dogs are too damn smart to train by lab experiment. Do you anticipate water?"

"Can't rule anything out," D.D. said honestly.

"Then we'll bring full gear. You said search area was probably within an hour drive of Boston?"

"Best guess."

"Then I'll bring my book of Mass. topographic maps. Topography is *everything* when working scents."

"Okay," D.D. said again.

"Is the ME or a forensic anthropologist gonna be on-site?"

"Why?"

"Sometimes the dogs hit on other remains. Good to have someone there who can make the call right away that it's human."

"These remains . . . less than forty-eight hours old," D.D. said. "In below freezing conditions."

A moment of silence. "Well, guess that rules out the anthropologist," Murray said. "See you in ninety."

Murray hung up. D.D. went to work on assembling the rest of the team.

28

Tuesday, twelve p.m. I stood shackled in the processing area of the Suffolk County Jail. No sheriff's van parked in the garage this time. Instead, a Boston detective's Crown Vic had rolled into the secured loading bay. Despite myself, I was impressed. I had assumed the Suffolk County Sheriff's Department would be in charge of transport. I wonder how many heads had rolled and markers had been called in to place me in Detective D. D. Warren's custody.

She got out of the car first. Derisive glance flicked my way, then she approached the command center, handing over paperwork to the waiting COs. Detective Bobby Dodge had opened the passenger's door. He came around the vehicle toward me, his face impossible to read. Still waters that ran deep.

No pedestrian clothes for my road trip. Instead, my previously issued pants and top had been replaced with the traditional orange prison jumpsuit, marking my status for the world to see. I'd asked for a coat, hat, and gloves. I'd been granted none of the above. Apparently, the sheriff's department worried less about frostbite and more about escape. I would be shackled for the full length of my sojourn into society. I would also be under direct supervision of a law enforcement officer at all times.

I didn't fight these conditions. I was tense enough as it was. Keyed up for the afternoon events to come, while simultaneously crashing from the morning's misadventures. I kept my gaze forward and my head down.

The key to any strategy is not to overplay your hand.

Bobby arrived at my side. The female

CO who'd been standing guard relinquished my arm. He seized it, leading me back to the Crown Vic.

D.D. had finished the paperwork. She arrived at the cruiser, staring at me balefully as Bobby opened the back door and I struggled to slide gracefully into the backseat with my hands and legs tied. I tilted back too far, got stuck like a beetle with its legs in the air. Bobby had to reach down, place one hand on my hip, and shove me over.

D.D. shook her head, then took her place behind the steering wheel.

Another minute and the massive garage door slowly creaked up. We backed up, onto the streets of Boston.

I turned my face to the gray March sky and blinked my eyes against the light.

Looks like snow, I thought, but didn't say a word.

D.D. drove to the nearby hospital parking lot. There, a dozen other vehicles, from white SUVS to black-and-white police cruisers were waiting. She pulled in and they formed a line behind us. D.D. looked at me in the rearview mirror.

"Start talking," she said.

"I'd like a coffee."

"Fuck you."

I smiled then, couldn't help myself. I had become my husband, with a Good Tessa and a Bad Tessa. Good Tessa had saved Kim Watters's life. Good Tessa had fought off evil attacking inmates and had felt, for just one moment, like a proud member of law enforcement.

Bad Tessa wore prison orange and sat in the back of a police cruiser. Bad Tessa . . . Well, for Bad Tessa, the day was very young.

"Search dogs?" I asked.

"*Cadaver* dogs," D.D. emphasized.

I smiled again, but it was sad this time, and for a second, I felt my composure crack. A yawning emptiness bloomed inside. All the things I had lost. And more I could still lose.

All I want for Christmas is my two front teeth. . . .

"You should've found her," I murmured. "I was counting on you to find her."

"Where?" D.D. snapped.

"Route two. Westbound, toward Lexington."

D.D. drove.

"We know about Trooper Lyons," D.D. said curtly, talking from the front seat. We'd taken Route 2 past Arlington, exchanging urban jungle for suburban pipe dreams. Next up, the old money of Lexington and Concord, to be followed by the quaint, country charm of Harvard, Mass.

"What do you know?" I asked. I was genuinely curious.

"That he beat you up, in order to substantiate your claim of spousal abuse."

"Have you ever hit a girl?" I asked Detective Dodge.

Bobby Dodge twisted in his seat. "Tell me about the hit man, Tessa. Find out how much I'm willing to believe."

"Can't."

"Can't?"

I leaned forward, best I could with my hands tied. "I'm going to kill him," I said somberly. "And it's not nice to speak ill of the dead."

"Oh please," D.D. interjected crossly. "You sound like a Looney Tune."

"Well, I have taken some blows to the head."

The eye roll again. "You're no more crazy than I'm kindhearted," D.D. snapped. "We know all about you, Tessa. The gambling-addicted husband who cleaned out your savings accounts. The horny teenage brother of your best friend, who figured he might get lucky one night. You seem to have a history of attracting the wrong men, then shooting them."

I didn't say anything. The good detective did have a way of cutting to the heart of the matter.

"But why your daughter?" she asked relentlessly. "Trust me, I don't fault you for plugging Brian with three in the chest. But what the hell made you turn on your own kid?"

"What did Shane have to say?" I asked.

D.D. frowned at me. "You mean before or after your loser friend tried to deck me?"

I whistled low. "See, this is what happens. You hit your first woman, and it gets easier after that."

"Were you and Brian arguing?" Bobby spoke up now. "Maybe the fight turned physical. Sophie got in the way."

"I reported for duty Friday night," I said, looking out the window. Fewer houses, more woods. We were getting close. "I haven't seen my daughter alive since."

"So Brian did it? Why not just blame him? Why cover it up, concoct such an elaborate story?"

"Shane didn't believe me. If he couldn't, then who would?"

Red-painted apple stand, off to the left. Empty now, but sold the best glasses of cider in the fall. We had come here just seven months ago, drinking apple cider, going on a hay ride, then visiting the pumpkin patch. Is that what had brought me back, Saturday afternoon when my heart had been pounding and the daylight fading and I *had* felt like a Looney Tune, crazed by grief and panic and sheer desperation? I'd had to move, fast, fast, fast. Less thinking. More doing.

Which had brought me here, to the place of our last family outing before Brian shipped out for the fall. One of my last happy memories.

Sophie had loved this apple stand. She'd consumed three cups of cider and then, hopped up on fermented sugar, had run laps in the pumpkin patch before picking out not one pumpkin, but three. A daddy pumpkin, a mommy pumpkin, and a girl pumpkin, she'd declared. A whole entire pumpkin *family.*

"Can we, Mommy? Can we can we can we? Please, please, please."

"Sure, sweetheart, you're absolutely right. It would be a shame to separate them. Let's save the whole family."

"Yippee! Daddy, Daddy, Daddy, we're gonna buy a pumpkin family! Yippee!"

"Turn right up ahead," I murmured.

"Right?" D.D. braked hard, made the turn.

"Quarter mile up, next left, onto a rural road. . . ."

"Three pumpkins?" Brian shaking his head at me. "Softy."

"You bought her the donuts to go with the cider."

"So three donuts equals three pumpkins?"

"Apparently."

"Okay, but dibs on carving the daddy pumpkin . . ."

"The tree! Turn here. Left, left. Now, thirty yards, road on the right."

"Sure you couldn't have drawn a map?" D.D. scowled at me.

"I'm sure."

D.D. turned right onto the smaller, rural road, tires spinning on the hard-packed snow. Behind us, one, two, three, four cars labored to follow suit, then a couple of white SUVs, then the line of police cruisers.

Definitely going to snow, I decided.

But I didn't mind anymore. Civilization was long gone. This was the land of skeletal trees, frozen ponds, and white barren fields. The kind of place lots of things could happen before the general population noticed. The kind of place a desperate woman might use for her last stand.

Bad Tessa, rising.

"We're here," I said.

And Detective D. D. Warren, heaven help her, pulled over.

"Get out," she said crossly.

I smiled. I couldn't help myself. I looked the fine detective in the eye and I said, "Words I've been waiting to hear all day."

29

"I don't want her walking the woods!" D.D. was arguing with Bobby ten minutes later, off to one side of the stacked-up vehicles. "Her job was to get us here. Now her job is done, and our job is beginning."

"The canine team wants her help," Bobby countered. "There's no wind, meaning it'll be hard for the dogs to catch the open cone of the scent."

D.D. stared at him blankly.

"Scent," he tried again, forming a triangular shape with his hands, "radiates from the target in the shape of an expanding cone. For the dog to catch the scent, it has to be downwind, in the opening of the cone, or the dog can be two feet from the target and still miss it."

"When did you learn about dogs?" D.D. demanded.

"Thirty seconds ago, when I asked Nelson and Cassondra what they needed us to do. They're concerned about the conditions. Terrain's flat, which I guess is good, but it's open, which is more complicated—"

"Why?"

"Scent pools when it hits a barrier. So if this were a fenced-in field or brush-lined canyon, they'd start at the edges. But no fence or brush. Just big open . . . this . . ."

Bobby waved his hand around them. D.D. sighed heavily.

Tessa Leoni had brought them to one of the few half-forested, half-fielded, all-in-the-middle-of-nowhere places left in Massachusetts. Given Sunday night's fresh snowfall, the fields were a flat white expanse of sheer nothingness— no footprints, no tire tracks, no drag marks, interspersed with dark patches of skeletal trees and shaggy bushes.

They were lucky they'd been able to drive in, and D.D. still wasn't sure they'd be able to get back out. Snowshoes would be a good idea. A vacation even better.

"Dogs are gonna tire faster," Bobby was saying, "trudging through fresh snowfall. So the team wants to start with the smallest search area possible. Which means having Tessa get us as close to the target as possible."

"Maybe she can point us in the right direction," D.D. muttered.

Bobby rolled his eyes. "Tessa's shackled and trying to walk through four inches of powder. Woman's not running away any time soon."

"She doesn't have a jacket."

"I'm sure someone has a spare."

"She's playing us," D.D. said abruptly.

"I know."

"Notice how she answered none of our questions."

"I noticed."

"While doing her best to milk us for in-formation."

"Yep."

"Did you hear what she did to the male inmate who attacked the CO? She didn't just take him out. She drove a shank into his thigh and twisted it. Twice. That's a little beyond professional training. That's personal satisfaction."

"She seems . . . edgy," Bobby agreed. "I'm thinking life hasn't gone too well for her the past few days."

"And yet here we are," D.D. said, "dancing to the beat of her different drummer. I don't like it."

Bobby thought about it. "Maybe you should stay in the car," he said at last. "Just to be safe . . ."

D.D. fisted her hands to keep from hitting him. Then she sighed and rubbed her forehead. She hadn't slept last night, hadn't eaten this morning. Meaning she'd been tired and cranky even *before* receiving the news that Tessa Leoni was willing to take them to her daughter's body.

D.D. didn't want to be here. She didn't want to be trudging through snow. She didn't want to come to a faint mound and brush it back to find the frozen features of a six-year-old girl. Would it look like Sophie was sleeping? Wrapped up in her pink winter coat, clutching her favorite doll?

Or would there be bullet holes, red droplets giving testimony to a last moment filled with violence?

D.D. was a professional who didn't feel professional anymore. She wanted to crawl into the backseat and wrap her hands around Tessa Leoni's throat. She wanted to squeeze and shake and scream, *How could you do such a thing! To the little girl who* loved *you!*

D.D. probably should stay behind. Which meant, of course, that she wouldn't.

"The SAR team is requesting further assistance," Bobby was stating quietly. "We have four hours of daylight left, in less than ideal conditions. Dogs can only walk so fast. Same with the handlers. What do you suggest?"

"Shit," D.D. murmured.

"My thoughts exactly."

"Any funny business, I'm going to

have to kill her," D.D. said after another moment.

Bobby shrugged. "Don't think too many people out here will argue with that."

"Bobby . . . if we find the body . . . If I can't handle it . . ."

"I'll cover for you," he said quietly.

She nodded. Tried to thank him, but her throat had grown too tight. She nodded again. He clasped her shoulder with his hand.

Then they returned to Tessa Leoni.

Tessa had left the Crown Vic. No coat, shackled at the wrists and ankles, she'd still managed to make it over to one of the SAR trucks, where she was watching Nelson unload his canines.

First two pet carriers contained smaller dogs, who were twirling in excited circles while barking maniacally.

"Those are search dogs?" Tessa was asking skeptically, as Bobby and D.D. approached.

"Nope," Nelson said, opening a third,

much larger carrier to reveal a German shepherd. "Those are the reward."

"What?"

Having released the German shepherd, who loped around him in a tight circle, Nelson bent down to open the other two carriers. The smaller, shaggier dogs were out like twin shots, leaping at the German shepherd, Nelson, Tessa, Bobby, D.D., and everyone else in a twenty foot square radius.

"Meet Kelli and Skyler," Nelson drawled. "Soft Coated Wheaten Terriers. Definitely smart as whips, but a little high strung for SAR work. On the other hand, Quizo thinks they're the best playmates in the whole world, and I'll be damned if he didn't choose them for his reward."

"He doesn't eat them, does he?" Tessa asked skeptically. She appeared as a stain of orange against bright white snow, shivering from the cold.

Nelson was grinning at her, obviously amused by her statement. If talking to a murder suspect bothered him, D.D. thought, he didn't show it. "Most important part of training a dog," he said now, unloading more supplies from the back of his covered truck bed, "is learning the dog's motivation. Each pup is different. Some want food. Some affection. Most hone in on a particular toy that becomes *the* toy. As a handler, you gotta pick up on those signals. When you finally figure out what the reward is, the single item that truly motivates your dog, that's when the serious training begins.

"Now, Quizo, here"—he gave the shepherd a quick pat on the head— "was a tough nut to crack. Smartest damn dog I ever saw, but only when he felt like it. 'Course, that doesn't work. I need a dog who searches on command, not when he's in the mood. Then one day, these two"—he flicked a hand toward the bouncing, barking terriers— "showed up. Had a friend who couldn't keep 'em anymore. Said I'd help out for a bit, till he could make better arrangements. Well, damned if it wasn't love at first sight. Miss Kelli and Mr. Skyler ran all over Quizo like twin rugrats and he chased them right back. Which got me to thinking. Maybe playtime with his

LISA GARDNER

best buds could be a reward. Tried it out a few times, and bingo. Turns out, Quizo is a bit of a show-off. He doesn't mind working, he just wants the right audience.

"Now when we arrive on-scene, I bring all three. I'm giving Quizo a moment here to interact with his buds, know they're on-site. Then Kelli and Skyler will have to be put away—or they'll be underfoot the entire time, let me tell you—and I'll give Quizo the command to work. He'll get right to it, as he understands the sooner he's completed his mission, the sooner he gets to return to his friends."

Nelson looked up, regarded Tessa squarely in the eye. "Skyler and Kelli will also help cheer him up," the canine handler said levelly. "Even SAR dogs don't like finding bodies. Depresses 'em, making it doubly important for Skyler and Kelli to be here today."

Was it D.D.'s imagination, or did Tessa finally flinch? Maybe a heart still beat under that façade after all.

D.D. stepped forward, Bobby beside

her. She addressed Nelson first. "How much more time do you need?"

He glanced at his dogs, then the rest of the SAR team, unloading in the vehicles strung out behind his. "Fifteen more minutes."

"Anything more you need from us?" D.D. asked.

Nelson cracked a thin smile. "An X to mark the spot?"

"How do you know when the dogs have found it, made a hit?" D.D. asked curiously. "Quizo will bark . . . louder?"

"Three-minute sustained bark," Nelson supplied. "All SAR dogs are trained a little different—some sit to indicate a hit, others have a particular woofing pitch. But given our team specializes in search and rescue, we've gone with a three-minute sustained bark, assuming our dogs might be out of sight, behind a tree or boulder, and we might need three minutes to catch up. Works for us."

"Well, I can't supply a marked X," D.D. said, "but we do have one way of getting started."

D.D. turned to Tessa. "So let's take a

trip down memory lane. You drove this far?"

Tessa's expression had gone blank. She nodded.

"Park here?"

"Don't know. The road was better formed, packed down. I drove to the end."

D.D. gestured around. "Trees, fields, anything look familiar?"

Tessa hesitated, shivering again. "Maybe that copse of trees over there," she said at last, pointing vaguely with two hands bound on the wrists. "Not sure. The fresh snowfall . . . it's like someone wiped the chalkboard clean. Everything is both the same and different."

"Four hours," D.D. said crisply. "Then one way or another, you're back behind bars. So I suggest you start studying the landscape, because if you really want to bring your daughter home, this is the only chance you're gonna get."

Something finally moved in Tessa's face, a spasm of emotion that was hard to read, but might have included regret.

It bothered D.D. She turned away, both arms wrapped around her middle now.

"Get her a coat," she muttered to Bobby.

He was already holding an extra jacket in his hands. He held it out and D.D. almost laughed. It was a down-filled black coat emblazoned *Boston PD,* no doubt from the trunk of one of the patrol officers. He draped it around Tessa's shoulders, as she could not slide her shackled arms into the sleeves, then zippered up the front to hold it in place.

"What's more incongruous?" D.D. murmured out loud. "A state trooper in a Boston PD field coat, or a Suffolk County Jail inmate in a Boston PD field coat? Either way," her voice dropped, sounding dark, even nasty, "it just doesn't fit."

D.D. stalked back to her car. She stood alone, huddled against the cold and her own feeling of impending doom. Dark gray clouds gathered on the horizon.

Snow's coming, she thought, and

wished again that none of them were here.

They set out twelve minutes later, a shackled Tessa in the lead, Bobby and D.D. on either side, with the canine team and an assortment of officers bringing up the rear. The dogs remained leashed. They hadn't been given the work command yet, but strained against their leads, clearly anxious.

They'd made it only twenty feet before having to stop for the first time. No matter how vindictive D.D. was feeling, Tessa couldn't walk shackled in four inches of fresh snow. They released the binds at her ankles, then finally made some progress.

Tessa led the group to a first copse of trees. She walked around it, frowning as if studying hard. Then she entered the cluster of bare-branched trees, making it ten feet before shaking her head and withdrawing again. They explored three more patches of woods in a similar fashion, before the fourth spot appeared to be the charm.

Tessa entered and kept on walking, her footsteps growing faster, surer now. She came to a massive gray boulder jutting up from the landscape and seemed to nod to herself. They veered left around the rock, Quizo whining low in his throat, as if already on-scent.

No one spoke. Just the squeaky crunch of footsteps trampling snow, the panting of dogs, the muffled exhalations of their handlers and officers, bundled up in neck warmers and wool scarves.

They exited the copse of trees. D.D. paused, thinking that must be a mistake, but Tess kept moving forward, crossing an open expanse of snow, fording a small, trickling stream just visible between fluffy white banks, before disappearing into a more serious line of woods.

"Awfully far to walk with a body," D.D. muttered.

Bobby shot her a glance, seeming to think the same thing.

But Tessa didn't say a word. She was walking faster now, with purpose. There was a look on her face that was almost uncanny to see. Grim determination rimmed with ragged desperation.

Did Tessa even register the dog team, her entourage of law enforcement handlers? Or had she gone back somewhere in her mind, to a cold Saturday afternoon. Neighbors had seen the Denali depart around four p.m., meaning there hadn't been much daylight left by the time she made it all the way out here.

What had Tessa Leoni been thinking in those last thirty minutes of twilight? Struggling with the weight of her daughter's body as she careened through the woods, across flat white fields, heading deeper and deeper into the dense underbrush.

When you buried your child, was it like imparting your greatest treasure into the sanctity of nature? Or was it like hiding your greatest sin, instinctively seeking out the darkest bowels of the forest to cover your crime?

They came to another collection of moss-covered rocks, this time with a vague man-made shape. Rock walls, old foundations, the remnants of chimneys. In a state that had been inhabited as long as Massachusetts, even the woods were never totally without remnants of civilization.

The trees gave way to a smaller clearing and Tessa stopped.

Her throat worked. It took her a couple of times, then the word came out as a whisper: "Here," Tessa said.

"Where?" D.D. asked.

"There was a fallen tree. Snow had collected in front of it, forming a snowbank. Seemed . . . like an easy place to dig."

D.D. didn't say anything right away. She peered at the clearing, smothered with fresh white flakes. Over to her left, there appeared to be a gentle rise, like what might be formed by a toppled tree. Of course, there was another such rise a few feet in front of that, while she made a third on the other side of the clearing, next to a patch of stray trees. Still, she was gazing at three hundred square yards of space, give or take. Given a team of three experienced SAR dogs, the search area was highly manageable.

Bobby was studying the landscape as well, going over it with his fine sniper's eye. He looked at D.D., pointed out the first couple of swells, then an even broader rise next to the far edges of the woods. D.D. nodded.

Time to release the hounds.

"You will return to the car now," D.D. said, not looking at Tessa.

"But—"

"You will return to the car!"

Tessa shut up. D.D. turned back to the assembled team. She spotted an officer in the back, same one who'd worked the murder book at the original crime scene. She waved him over. "Officer Fiske?"

"Yes, ma'am."

"You will escort Inmate Leoni back to your cruiser and wait with her there."

The kid's face fell. From active search to passive babysitting. "Yes, ma'am," he said.

"It's a big responsibility, escorting a prisoner alone."

He perked up a little, taking up position at Tessa's side, one hand on his holster.

Tessa didn't say anything, just stood there, her face expressionless once more. A cop's face, D.D. thought suddenly, and for some reason, that made her shiver.

"Thank you," D.D. said abruptly.

"For what?" Tessa asked.

"Your daughter deserves this. Children shouldn't be lost in the woods. Now we can bring her home."

Tessa's expression cracked. Her eyes went wide, endlessly stark, and she swayed on her feet, might have even gone down, except she shifted her stance and caught herself.

"I love my daughter."

"We'll treat her with respect," D.D. replied, already gesturing to the SAR team, which was starting to re-form itself into a search line at the closest edge of the woods.

"I love my daughter," Tessa repeated, her tone more urgent. "You think you understand that now, but it's just the beginning for you. Nine months from now, you'll be amazed by how little you loved before that, and then a year after that, and then a year after that. Imagine six years. Six whole years of that kind of love . . ."

D.D. looked at the woman. "Didn't save her in the end, did it?"

D.D. deliberately turned away from Tessa Leoni and joined the cadaver dogs.

30

Who do you love?

That was the question, of course. Had been from the very beginning—but, of course, Detective D.D. didn't know that. She thought she was dealing with a typical case of child abuse and homicide. Can't say that I blame her. God knows, I was called out to enough houses where wan-faced five-year-olds tended their passed-out mothers. I've watched a mother slap her son with no more expression than swatting a fly. Seen children bandage their own scrapes because they already knew their mothers didn't care enough to do it for them.

But I'd tried to warn D.D. I'd rebuilt my life for Sophie. She wasn't just my daughter, she was the love that finally saved me. She was giggles and joy and pure, distilled enthusiasm. She was anything that was good in my world, and everything worth coming home to.

Who do you love?

Sophie. It has always been Sophie.

D.D. assumed she was seeing the worst a mother could do. She hadn't realized yet that she was actually witnessing the true lengths a mother would go to for love.

What can I tell you? Mistakes in this business are costly.

I'd returned to Officer Fiske's police cruiser. Hands shackled at my waist, but legs still free. He seemed to have forgotten that detail, and I didn't feel compelled to remind him. I sat in the back, working on keeping my body language perfectly still, nonthreatening.

Both doors were open, his and mine. I needed air, I'd told him. I felt sick, like I might vomit. Officer Fiske had given me a look, but had consented, even helped unzip the heavy BPD coat that pinned my arms to my torso.

Now, he sat in the front seat, obviously frustrated and bored. People became cops because they wanted to play ball, not sit on the bench. But here he was, relegated to listening to the game in the distance. The echoing whines of the search dogs, the faint hum of voices in the woods.

"Drew the short straw," I commented.

Officer Fiske kept his eyes straight ahead.

"Ever done a cadaver recovery?"

He refused to speak; no consorting with the enemy.

"I did a couple," I continued. "Meticulous work, holding the line. Inch by inch, foot by foot, clearing each area of the grid before moving to the next, then moving to the next. Rescue work is better. I got called up to help locate a three-year-old boy lost by Walden's Pond. A pair of volunteers finally found him. Unbelievable moment. Everyone cried, except the boy. He just wanted another chocolate bar."

Officer Fiske still didn't say anything.

I shifted on the hard plastic bench, straining my ears. Did I hear it yet? Not yet.

"Got kids?" I asked.

"Shut up," Officer Fiske growled.

"Wrong strategy," I informed him. "As long as you're stuck with me, you should engage in conversation. Maybe you're the lucky one who will finally earn my trust. Next thing you know, I'll confide to you what actually happened to my husband and child, turning you into an overnight hero. Something to think about."

Officer Fiske finally looked at me.

"I hope they bring back the death penalty, just for you," he said.

I smiled at him. "Then you're an idiot, because death, at this point, would be the easy way out."

He twisted around till he was staring out the front of the parked cruiser, falling silent once more.

I started humming. Couldn't help myself. Bad Tessa rising.

"All I want for Christmas is my two

front teeth, my two front teeth, my two front teeth."

"Shut up," Officer Fiske snapped again.

Then we both heard it: The sudden excited barks of a dog catching scent. The cry of the handler, the corresponding rush of the search team, closing in on target. Officer Fiske sat up straighter, leaned over the steering wheel.

I could feel his tension, the barely repressed urge to abandon the cruiser and join the fray.

"You should thank me," I said from the back.

"Shut up."

The dog, barking even louder now, honing in. I could picture Quizo's path, across the small clearing, circling the gentle rise of snow. The fallen tree had created a natural hollow, filled with lighter, fluffier flakes, not too big, not too small. I'd been staggering under the weight of my burden by the time I'd found it, literally swaying on my feet from exhaustion.

Setting down the body. Taking out the collapsible shovel strapped around my waist. My gloved hands shaking as I snapped the pieces of handle together. My back aching as I bent over, punching my way through the thin outer layer of ice to the softer snow underneath. Digging, digging, digging. My breath in short, frosty pants. The hot tears that froze almost instantaneously on my cheeks.

As I carved out the hollow, then gently placed the body inside. Moving slower now as I replaced scoop after scoop of snow, then carefully patted it all back into place.

Twenty-three scoops of snow to bury a grown man. Not nearly so many for this precious cargo.

"You should thank me," I said again, slowly sitting up straight, uncoiling my body. Bad Tessa rising.

Dog was on it. Quizo had done his job and was letting his handler know it with his sustained bark.

Let him go play with his friends, I thought, tense now in spite of myself. Reward the dog. Take him away to Kelli and Skyler. Please.

Officer Fiske was finally staring at me.

"What's your problem?" he asked crossly.

"What's *your* problem? After all, I'm the one who just saved your life."

"Saved my life? What the hell—"

Then, staring at my impassive face, he finally connected the dots.

Officer Fiske jumped from the car. Officer Fiske scrambled for the radio on his duty belt. Officer Fiske turned his back to me.

What can I tell you? Mistakes in this business are costly.

I sprang from the rear of the cruiser, fisted both of my shackled hands together and cracked him over the skull. Officer Fiske stumbled forward. I got my arms over his head, around his neck, and yanked hard.

Officer Fiske gasped, made a funny rattling hum, which come to think of it was a lot like CO Kim Watters. Or maybe Brian, dying on the spotless kitchen floor.

I am not sane. That was my last thought. *I can't possibly be sane anymore*.

Officer Fiske's knees buckled. We

both went down, while a quarter mile ahead, the snow blew up and screams split the sky and the first dog began to howl.

When Officer Fiske's legs finally stopped churning, I gasped three times, inhaling shocks of cold air that forced me back to the present. So much to do, so little time to do it.

Don't think, don't think, don't think.

I unwrapped my hands, fumbling with the keys at Officer Fiske's waist, then remembered to snatch his cellphone. Had a very important call to make in the next thirty seconds.

I could hear cries in the distance. More dogs howling. Four vehicles over, Kelli and Skyler picked up the message of distress, their higher-pitched barks joining the fray.

Don't think, don't think, don't think.

I glanced at the sky, calculating remaining hours of daylight.

Looks like snow, I thought again.

Then, clutching keys and cellphone, I ran for it.

31

When the first explosion rocked the sky, D.D. was halfway across the clearing, striding toward the snowy mound where Quizo barked with excited intent. Then the world went white.

Snow sprayed up and out in a giant concussive boom. D.D. just got her arms up and it still felt like being hit by a thousand stinging needles. Quizo's deep bark turned into an immediate bay of distress. Someone screamed.

Then, another rocking explosion and several more cries, while D.D. was knocked back on her ass, head buried behind both arms to shield herself.

"Quizo, Quizo," someone was crying. Probably Nelson.

"D.D., D.D., D.D.," someone else was crying. Probably Bobby.

She got her eyes open in time to see Bobby charging across the clearing, legs plunging through the snow, face ashen with panic. "Are you all right? Talk to me, D.D. Talk to me, dammit."

"What, what, what?" She blinked. Shook ice and snow from her hair. Blinked again. Her ears were ringing, filled with a sense of pressure. She cracked her jaw, trying to release it.

Bobby had reached her side, clutching her shoulders.

"Are you okay are you okay are you okay?" His lips moved. It took another second for his words to penetrate the buzz in her head.

She nodded weakly, pushing him back so she could inventory her arms, legs, and most importantly, her torso. By and large, she appeared to be in one piece. She'd been far enough away and the snow had cushioned her fall. She wasn't hurt, just dazed and confused.

She let Bobby help her to her feet, then triaged the rest of the damage.

The snowy rise targeted by Quizo's keen nose had disintegrated. In its place was a brown hollow of earth, covered in shredded bits of tree, leaves, and— heaven help them—pink fabric.

Quizo was off to one side, muzzle buried in the snow, whimpering and panting. Nelson stood over his dog, hands gently holding the shepherd's ears as he whispered low, soothing sounds to his distressed pet.

The other search dogs had halted in their tracks and were howling at the sky.

Officer down, D.D. thought. The dogs were telling the world. She wanted to bay with them, until this terrible feeling of rage and helplessness eased in her chest.

Cassondra Murray, team leader, already had her cellphone out and in clipped tones was summoning a vet. Other BPD officers were swarming the scene, hands on holsters, searching for signs of immediate threat.

"Stop!" Bobby yelled suddenly.

The officers stopped. The dog handlers froze.

He was looking around them in the snow. D.D., still cracking her jaw against the ringing in her ears, did the same.

She saw pieces of hot pink fabric, a shred of blue jeans, what might have been a child's tennis shoe. She saw red and brown and green. She saw . . . Pieces. That was the only word for it. Where there had once been the buried remains of a body, there were now pieces, sprayed in all directions.

The entire clearing had just become a body recovery site. Meaning every single person needed to evacuate in order to limit cross-contamination. They needed to contain, they needed to control. And they needed to immediately contact the ME's department, let alone busloads of crime-scene techs. They had bits of human remains, they had hair and fiber, they had . . . they had so much work to do.

Dear God, D.D. thought vaguely, her ears still ringing, her arms still stinging.

The dogs howling, howling, and howling.

She couldn't . . . It couldn't . . .

She looked down and realized there
was a puff of pink now stuck to her
boot. Part of a coat maybe, or a girl's favorite blanket.

Sophie Leoni with big blue eyes and a
heart-shaped face. Sophie Leoni with
brown hair and a gap-tooth smile who
loved to climb trees and hated to sleep
in the dark.

Sophie Leoni.

I love my daughter, Tessa had stood
here and said. *I love my daughter.*

What kind of mother could do such a
thing?

Then, all of a sudden, D.D.'s brain
fired to life and she realized the next
piece of the puzzle:

"Officer Fiske," she yelled urgently,
grabbing Bobby's arm. "We need to
alert Officer Fiske. Get him on the radio,
now!"

Bobby already had his radio out, hit
the button to transmit. "Officer Fiske.
Come in, Officer Fiske. Officer Fiske."

But there was no reply. Of course

there was no reply. Why else would Tessa Leoni demand to personally escort them to the body? Why else rig her own child with explosives?

D.D. turned to her fellow investigators.

"Officer down!" she shouted, and as a group they plunged back through the woods.

Afterward, it all seemed so obvious, D.D. couldn't believe she hadn't seen it coming. Tessa Leoni had frozen her husband's body for at least twenty-four hours. Why so long? Why such an elaborate plan to dispose of her daughter's remains?

Because Tessa Leoni hadn't been just dumping a corpse. She'd been planting her get-out-of-jail-free card.

And D.D. had played right into her hand.

She'd personally checked Tessa Leoni out of the Suffolk County Jail. She'd personally driven a suspected double-murderer to a remote location in central Mass. Then she'd personally escorted a canine team to a body rigged with explosives, allowing Tessa Leoni to disappear into the wild blue yonder.

"I am such a fucking idiot!" D.D. exclaimed two hours later. They remained at the wilderness site, Boston police and local sheriff's department vehicles stacked up for a good three hundred yards.

Ambulance had arrived first, EMTs attempting to treat Officer Fiske, but then, when he waved them off, embarrassed, ashamed, and otherwise not ready to play well with others, they'd tended to Quizo instead. Poor dog had suffered a ruptured eardrum and singeing to the muzzle from being closest to the blast. Eardrum would heal naturally, just as it would in humans, the EMTs assured Nelson.

In the meantime, they'd be happy to drive the dog to his vet. Nelson had taken them up on that deal, obviously very shaken. The rest of the SAR team packed up his truck, including the mournful Kelli and Skyler. They would debrief with D.D. in the morning, team leader Cassondra had assured her. But for now, they needed to regroup and decompress. They were accustomed to searches that ended in tangible discoveries, not homemade explosives.

With the SAR team departing, D.D. got on the phone to Ben, the state medical examiner. Had body parts, definitely needed assistance.

So it went. Officers had withdrawn. Evidence techs had advanced.

And the search for former state police trooper Tessa Leoni, now officially a fugitive from justice, kicked into high gear.

According to Fiske, he'd forgotten to reshackle her ankles (another shamefaced admission that would no doubt lead to a pint of whiskey later tonight). Tessa had also grabbed his keys, meaning there was a good chance she'd freed her wrists.

She'd taken his cellphone, but not his sidearm, which was good news for the fugitive recovery team, and probably a narrow escape from death for Fiske (a second pint of whiskey, probably tomorrow night). Tessa was last seen in an unzippered black BPD jacket, and a thin orange jumpsuit. On foot, no supplies, no hat or gloves, and in the middle of nowhere to boot, no one expected the woman to get far.

Adrenaline would carry her over the first mile or two, but soft snowfall made for exhaustive running, while providing a trail a blind man could follow.

Fugitive recovery team geared up, headed out. An hour of daylight left. They expected it to be enough, but were armed with searchlights in case it was not. Twenty officers against one desperate escapee.

They would get the job done, the lead officer had promised D.D. No child killer would be running on his watch.

D.D.'s turn to be shamefaced, but no pint of whiskey for her later tonight. Just another crime scene to process and a taskforce to debrief and a boss to update, who was probably going to be very unhappy with her, which was okay, because currently, she was very unhappy with herself, as well.

So she did what she always did: headed back to the scene of the crime, with Bobby at her side.

The ME had his staff on-site, suited up and delicately depositing body parts into red-marked biohazard bags. Evidence techs followed in their wake, collecting other detritus, which hopefully included pieces of the incendiary device. Not too hard to rig homemade explosives in this day and age. Took about ten minutes on the Internet and a quick trip to the local hardware store. Tessa was a bright woman. Assemble a couple of pressure-sensitive devices, then place them in the snowy hollow with the body. Cover and wait.

Dogs and police arrive. Tessa retreats. Bombs go ka-boom. Her guard goes Say What? And Tessa seizes the opportunity to take down a fellow officer and hit the road.

Hello, injured search party. Goodbye, BPD.

As far as D.D. was concerned, each piece of evidence now recovered was another nail in Tessa Leoni's coffin, and she wanted them all. She wanted them *all*.

Ben looked up at Bobby and D.D.'s approach. He handed over his bag to one of his assistants, then crossed to them.

"Well?" D.D. asked immediately.

The ME, mid-forties, stoutly built, with buzz-cut steel gray hair, hesitated. He crossed his arms over his burly chest. "We have recovered organic matter and bone consistent with a body," he granted.

"Sophie Leoni?"

In answer, the ME held out his gloved hand, revealing a slender fragment of white bone, approximately two inches long and smeared with dirt and bits of leaves. "Rib bone segment," he said. "Full length would be consistent with a six-year-old."

D.D. swallowed, forced herself to briskly nod her head. Bone was smaller than she would've imagined. Impossibly delicate.

"Found a clothing tag, size 6T," Ben continued. "Fabric remnants are mostly pink. Also consistent with a female child."

D.D. nodded again, still eyeing the rib bone.

Ben moved it to one side of his palm,

revealing a smaller, corn-sized kernel. "Tooth. Also consistent with a prepubescent girl. Except . . . no root." The ME sounded puzzled. "Generally when you recover a tooth from remains, the root is still attached. Unless, it was already loose." The ME seemed to be talking more to himself than to D.D. and Bobby. "Which I suppose would be right for a first-grader. A loose tooth, coupled with the force of the blast . . . Yes, I could see that."

"So the tooth most likely came from Sophie Leoni?" D.D. pressed.

"Tooth most likely came from a prepubescent girl," Ben corrected. "Best I can say at this time. I need to get the remains back to my lab. Dental X-ray would be most helpful, though we have yet to recover a skull or jawbone. Bit of work still to be done."

In other words, D.D. thought, Tessa Leoni had rigged an explosive powerful enough to blow a tooth right out of her daughter's skull.

A flake of snow drifted down, followed by another, then another.

They all peered up at the sky, where

the looming gray snow clouds had finally arrived.

"Tarp," Ben said immediately, hurrying toward his assistant. "Protect the remains, now, now, *now.*"

Ben rushed away. D.D. retreated from the clearing, ducking behind a particularly dense bush, where she leaned over and promptly dry-heaved.

What had Tessa said? The love D.D. currently felt for her unborn child was nothing compared to the love she'd feel a year from now, or a year after that or a year after that. Six years of that love. Six years . . .

How could a woman . . . How could a mother . . .

How did you tuck in your child one moment, then search out the perfect place to bury her the next? How did you hug your six-year-old good night, then rig her body with explosives?

I love my daughter, Tessa said. *I love my daughter.*

What a fucking bitch.

D.D. dry-heaved again. Bobby was beside her. She felt him draw her hair back from her cheeks. He handed her a bottle of water. She used it to rinse her mouth, then turned her flushed face to the sky, trying to feel the snow upon her cheeks.

"Come on," he said quietly. "Let's get you to the car. Time for a little rest, D.D. It's going to be okay. Really. It will be."

He took her hand, pulling her through the woods. She trod dispiritedly behind him, thinking that he was a liar. That once you saw the body of a little girl blow up in front of your eyes, the world was never okay again.

They should head for HQ, get out before the rural road became impassable. She needed to prepare for the inevitable press conference. *Good news, we probably found the body of Sophie Leoni. Bad news, we lost her mother, a distinguished state police officer who most likely murdered her entire family.*

They reached the car. Bobby opened the passenger-side door. She slid in, feeling jumbled and restless and almost desperate to escape her own skin. She didn't want to be a detective anymore. Sergeant Detective D. D. Warren hadn't gotten her man. Sergeant Detective

D. D. Warren hadn't rescued the child.
Sergeant Detective D. D. Warren was
about to become a mother herself, and
look at Tessa Leoni, trooper extraordi-
naire who'd killed, buried, and then
blown up her own kid, and what did that
say about female police officers becoming parental units, and what the hell was
D.D. thinking?

She shouldn't be pregnant. She
wasn't strong enough. Her tough veneer
was cracking and beneath it was simply
a vast well of sadness. All the dead bodies she'd studied through the years.
Other children who'd never made it
home. The unrepentant faces of parents, uncles, grandparents, even next
door neighbors who'd done the deed.

The world was a terrible place. She
solved each murder only to move on to
the next. Put away a child abuser, watch
a wife beater get released the next day.
And on and on it went. D.D., sentenced
to spend the rest of her career roaming
backwoods for small lifeless bodies
who'd never been loved or wanted in
the first place.

She'd just wanted to bring Sophie

home. Rescue this one child. Make this one drop of difference in the universe, and now . . . Now . . .

"Shhh." Bobby was stroking her hair.

Was she crying? Maybe, but it wasn't enough. She pressed her tearstained cheek into the curve of his shoulder. Felt the shuddering heat of him. Her lips found his neck, tasting salt. Then it seemed the most natural thing in the world to lean back and find his lips with her own. He didn't pull back. Instead, she felt his hands grip her shoulders. So she kissed him again, the man who'd once been her lover and one of the few people she regarded as a pillar of strength.

Time suspended, a heartbeat or two when she didn't have to think, she only had to feel.

Then, Bobby's hands tightened again. He lifted her up and gently set her back, until she sat squarely in the passenger seat and he sat in the driver's seat and at least two feet loomed between them.

"No," he said.

D.D. couldn't speak. The enormity of what she'd just done started to penetrate. She glanced around the small car, desperate for escape.

"It was a moment," Bobby continued. His voice sounded rough. He paused, cleared his throat, said again: "A moment. But I have Annabelle and you have Alex. You and I both know better than to mess with success."

D.D. nodded.

"D.D.—"

Immediately, she shook her head. She didn't want to hear anything more. She'd fucked this up enough. A moment. Like he said. A moment. Life was filled with moments.

Except she'd always had a weakness for Bobby Dodge. She'd let him go, then never gotten over him. And if she spoke now, she was going to cry and that was stupid. Bobby deserved better. Alex deserved better. They all did.

Then, she found herself thinking of Tessa Leoni and she couldn't help but feel the connection again. Two women, so capable in their professional lives, and such total fuckups in their personal ones.

The radio on the dash crackled to life.

D.D. snatched it up, hoping for good news.

It was the search team, Officer Landley reporting in. They'd followed Tessa's trail for two and half miles, as she'd run down the snow-packed rural road to the larger intersecting street. Then her footsteps had ended and fresh tire tracks had begun.

Best guess: Tessa Leoni was no longer alone and on foot.

She had an accomplice and a vehicle.

She had disappeared.

32

When Juliana and I were twelve years old, we developed a catchphrase: "What are friends for?" We used it like a code—it meant that if one of us needed a favor, most likely something embarrassing or desperate, then the other had to say yes, because that's what friends were for.

Juliana forgot her math homework. What are friends for, she'd announce at our lockers, and I'd hastily share my answers. My father was being an asshole about letting me stay after school for track. What are friends for, I'd say, and

Juliana would have her mother notify my father that she'd bring me home, because my father would never argue with Juliana's mom. Juliana developed a crush on the cute boy in our biology class. What are friends for? I'd sidle up to him during lunch and find out if my friend stood a chance.

Get arrested for murdering your husband. What are friends for?

I looked up Juliana's number Saturday afternoon, as my world was imploding and it occurred to me that I needed help. Ten years later, there was still only one person I could trust. So after the man in black finally departed, leaving my husband's body down in the garage, buried in snow, I looked up the married name, address, and phone number of my former best friend. I committed the information to memory, in order to eliminate the paper trail.

Shortly thereafter I built two small explosive devices, then loaded up the Denali and went for a drive.

My last acts as a free woman. I knew it even then. Brian had done something bad, but Sophie and I were going to be the ones punished. So I paid my own husband's murderer fifty thousand dollars in order to gain twenty-four hours' lead time. Then I used that time to desperately get two steps ahead.

Sunday morning, Shane had arrived and the games had begun. One hour later, beat within an inch of my life, head concussed, cheek fractured, I went from brilliant strategist to genuinely battered woman, dazed, confused, and somewhere in the back of my scrambled head, still dimly hoping that I'd been wrong about everything. Maybe Brian hadn't died in front of my eyes. Maybe Sophie hadn't been snatched out of her bed. Maybe next time I woke up, my world would be magically whole again and my husband and daughter would be by my side, holding my hands.

I never got that lucky.

Instead, I was confined to a hospital bed until Monday morning, when the police arrested me, and plan B kicked into gear.

All prison calls start with a recorded message to the receiver that the collect call has originated from a correctional institute. Would the other party accept the charges?

Million dollar question, I thought Monday night, as I stood in the commons area of the detainee unit and dialed Juliana's number with shaking fingers. I was as surprised as anyone when Juliana said yes. Bet she surprised herself, too. And bet she wished, within thirty seconds, that she'd said no instead.

Given that all outgoing calls are recorded, I kept the conversation simple.

"What are friends for?" I stated, heart hammering. I heard Juliana suck in her breath.

"Tessa?"

"I could use a friend," I continued, quickly now, before Juliana did something sensible, such as hang up. "Tomorrow afternoon. I'll call again. What are friends for."

Then I hung up, because the sound of Juliana's voice had brought tears to my eyes, and you can't afford to cry in prison.

Now, having just taken out Officer Fiske, I snatched his cellphone. Then I sprinted one hundred yards down the hardpacked snow of the rural road until I came to an enormous fir tree. Ducking underneath its canopy of green branches I quickly dialed Juliana's number while withdrawing a small waterproof bag I'd previously tucked beneath the branches.

"Hello?"

I talked fast. Directions, GPS coordinates, and a list of supplies. I'd had twenty-four hours in prison to plan my breakout, and I'd put it to good use.

On the other end of the cellphone, Juliana didn't argue. What are friends for?

Maybe she would call the cops the second she hung up. But I didn't think so. Because the last time that phrase was spoken between us, Juliana had uttered the words, while handing me the gun that had just taken her brother's life.

I put down Officer Fiske's cellphone and opened up the waterproof bag. Inside was Brian's Glock .40, which I'd removed from our gun safe.

He didn't need it anymore. But I did.

By the time the silver SUV slowed to a halt on the main road, my confidence had fled and I was jumpy with nerves. Gun tucked into the pocket of my black coat, arms wrapped tight around me, I kept to the fringes of the bordering woods, feeling conspicuous. Any second now, a police car would roar by. If I didn't duck for cover in time, the alert officer would spot me, execute a tight one-eighty and that would be that.

Had to pay attention. Gotta run. Gotta hide.

Then, another vehicle looming in the distance, headlights bright against the thickening gloom. Vehicle was moving slower, more uncertainly, as if the driver was looking for something. No roof rack bearing sirens, meaning a pedestrian vehicle versus a cop car. Now or never.

I took a deep breath, stepped toward the asphalt. The headlights swept across my face, then the SUV braked hard.

Juliana had arrived.

I clambered quickly into the backseat. Second I closed the door, she was off like a shot. I hit the floor and stayed there.

Car seat. Empty, but half-covered in a baby blanket, so recently occupied. Don't know why that surprised me. I had a child. Why not Juliana?

When we were girls we planned to marry twin brothers. We would live in houses side by side and raise our kids together. Juliana wanted three children, two boys and one girl. I planned on having one of each. She was going to stay home with her kids, like her mom. I was going to own a toy store, where of course her kids would receive a family discount.

Next to the car seat was a dark green duffel bag. I got on my knees, keeping out of sight of the windows, and unzipped the bag. Inside I found everything I'd requested—a change of clothes, all black. Fresh pair of underwear, two additional tops. Scissors, makeup, black cap and gloves.

Hundred and fifty in cash, small bills. Probably the best she could scrounge up on short notice.

I wondered if that was a lot of money

for Juliana these days. I only knew the girl she'd been, not the wife and mother she'd become.

I started by taking out all items in black and laying them on the backseat. It took a bit of wiggling, but I finally managed to shed the orange jumpsuit and redress in the black jeans and a black turtleneck. I twisted my hair up onto the top of my head and covered it with the dark baseball cap.

Then I turned around to study myself in the rearview mirror.

Juliana was staring at me. Her lips were pressed into a thin line, her hands white-knuckled on the steering wheel.

Newborn, I thought immediately. She had that look about her—the frazzled new mom, still not sleeping at night and frayed around the edges. Knowing the first year would be difficult, surprised to discover it was even harder than that. She glanced away, eyes on the road.

I sat down on the rear bench seat.

"Thank you," I said at last.

She never answered.

We drove in silence for another forty minutes. The snow had finally started, lightly at first, then falling heavily enough that Juliana had to reduce her speed.

At my request, she turned the radio to the news. No word of any officers involved in a situation, so apparently D. D. Warren and her team had survived my little surprise, and had chosen to keep a lid on things.

Made sense. No cop wanted to admit she'd lost a prisoner, especially if she believed she would recapture the inmate shortly. Last Detective Warren knew, I was alone and on foot, meaning D.D. probably had believed she'd round me up within an hour.

Not sorry to disappoint her, but relieved everyone was okay. I'd done my best to rig the twin pressure-sensitive devices to blow back, away from the recovery team and into the relative shelter of the fallen tree. But given that it was a rookie effort, I had no way of knowing how successful I'd be.

I'd sat behind Officer Fiske, both hoping and dreading what would happen next.

SUV slowed again. Juliana had her blinker on, was preparing to exit the highway for Route 9. She'd driven under the speed limit the entire way, eyes straight ahead, two hands on the wheel. The conscientious getaway driver.

Now our adventure was almost over, and I could see her lower lip trembling. She was scared.

I wondered if she thought I'd killed my husband. I wondered if she thought I'd murdered my own daughter. I should protest my innocence, but I didn't.

I thought she of all people should know better.

Twelve more minutes. All it took to travel back in time, to return to the old neighborhood. Past her old house, past my parents' shabby home.

Juliana didn't look at any of the buildings. Didn't sigh, wax nostalgic, say a single word.

Two final turns and we were there, at my father's garage.

She pulled over, killed the lights.

Snow was falling heavily now, blanketing the dark world in white.

I gathered up the last of my things, tucked them into the duffel bag, which I would take with me. Leave no evidence behind.

"When you get home," I said now, my voice surprisingly loud in the silence, "mix ammonia with warm water, and use it to wipe down the car. That will erase any fingerprints."

Juliana looked at me in the review mirror again, but remained silent.

"The police are going to find you," I continued. "They'll hone in on the call I placed to you last night from jail. It's one of the only leads they have, so they're going to follow up on it. Just tell the truth. What I said, what you said. The whole conversation was recorded, so you're not telling them anything they don't already know, and it's not like we said anything incriminating."

Juliana looked at me, remained silent.

"They shouldn't be able to trace today's call," I told her. "Our only point of contact has been someone else's cellphone, and I'm about to take an acetylene torch to it. Once I've melted its circuits, there's nothing it can give away. So you went for a drive this afternoon. I deliberately chose a location that didn't involve any toll roads, meaning there's no way for them to trace where you went. You could've gone anywhere and done anything. Make them work for it."

It went without saying that she would hold up under police questioning. She had before.

"We're even." She spoke up suddenly, her voice flat. "Don't call again. We're even."

I smiled, sadly, with genuine regret. For ten years, we'd kept our distance. And would've continued if not for Saturday morning and my stupid husband dying on our stupid kitchen floor.

Blood is thicker than water. Actually, friendship was, and so I had honored what I'd known Juliana had needed. Even when it hurt me.

"I would do it again," I murmured, my eyes locking on hers in the rearview mirror. "You were my best friend, and I loved you and I would do it again."

"Did you really name her Sophie?"

"Yeah."

Juliana Sophia MacDougall nee Howe covered her mouth. She started to cry.

I slung the duffel bag over my shoulder and stepped out into the snowy night. Another moment, the engine started up. Then the headlights flicked on and Juliana drove away.

I headed toward my father's shop. I could tell from the light burning inside that he was already waiting.

33

Bobby and D.D. headed back to HQ in silence. Bobby drove. D.D. sat in the passenger's seat. She had her hands fisted on her lap, trying not to think, her mind racing anyway.

She hadn't eaten all day and last night her sleep had been marginal at best. Combine that with the all-time shittiest day of her career and she was entitled to go a little nuts and kiss a married man while carrying another man's baby. Made total sense.

She leaned her forehead against the cool window, stared at the snow. The frozen flakes were falling heavily now. Obliterating Tessa Leoni's trail. Snarling traffic. Complicating an already complicated investigative operation.

She'd contacted her boss before leaving the crime scene. Better Horgan hear the news from her than the latest media report, where it was bound to break at any time. D.D. had lost a suspected double-murderer. Taken her out to middle-of-nowhere Mass., where her entire team had fallen victim to a rookie booby trap.

The BPD looked like a bunch of idiots. Not to mention, the violent fugitive apprehension unit—a state operation—was most likely going to take the entire case from them, given the steadily growing size of the search operation. So the BPD would appear incompetent and be denied any chance to redeem themselves. Talk about a one-way ticket to Asshole Avenue. Let alone a punch line in all future media reports—*suspected double-murderer Tessa Leoni, who escaped while in the custody of the Boston police . . .*

She'd better hope she was pregnant,

D.D. thought. Then, instead of getting fired, she could take maternity leave.

She ached.

She did. Her head hurt. Her chest, as well. She mourned for Sophie Leoni, a sweet-faced child who'd deserved better. Had she looked forward to her mommy coming home from work each morning? Hugs and kisses, while snuggling close for stories or showing off her latest homework? D.D. would think so. That's what children did. They loved and loved and loved. With their entire hearts. With every fiber of their being.

Then the adults in their lives failed them.

And the police failed them.

And so it went.

I love my daughter.

"Gonna stop ahead," Bobby spoke up, flipping on the right turn signal. "Need food. Want anything?"

D.D. shook her head.

"How about some dry cereal? Gotta eat something, D.D. Low blood sugar has never been your strong suit."

"Why do you do that?"

"Do what?"

"Take care of me."

Bobby took his eyes off the road long enough to regard her evenly. "Bet Alex would, too. If you'd let him."

She scowled. Bobby shrugged off the glare, attention back on the treacherous highway. It took a bit to ease the Crown Vic over, find the exit, then work their way into the parking lot of a small shopping plaza. D.D. noted a dry cleaner's, a pet supply store, and a mid-sized grocery store.

The grocery store appeared to be Bobby's target. They parked up front, most customers scared off by the wintry conditions. When D.D. got out of the car, she was surprised to see how much snow had already accumulated. Bobby came around the vehicle, wordlessly offering his arm.

She accepted his help, making her way gingerly along the snow-covered sidewalk into the brightly lit store. Bobby headed for the deli. She lasted five seconds before the smell of rotisserie chicken proved too much. She left him to wander on her own, commandeering an apple from produce, then a box of Cheerios from the cereal aisle. Maybe one of those fancy organic fruit drinks, she thought, or a premade protein shake. She could live on Ensure, next logical stage of the life cycle.

She found herself in the small pharmacy section, and that quickly knew what she was going to do.

Fast, before she could change her mind, before Bobby could appear: family planning section, condoms, condoms, and of course, when the condoms broke, home pregnancy kits. She snatched the first box she found. Pee on a stick, wait to see what it tells you. How hard could it be?

No time to pay. Bobby would spot her for sure. So she high-tailed it for the restroom, apple, cereal box, and home pregnancy test clutched tight against her chest.

A green sign declared that no merchandise was allowed in the restroom.

Tough shit, D.D. thought, and pushed through the door.

She commandeered the handicap stall. Turned out it had a changing station bolted to the wall. She unfolded the plastic table and used it as a work-bench. Apple, Cheerios, pregnancy kit.

Her fingers were shaking. Violently. To the point she couldn't hold the box and read the words. So she flipped the box over on the changing table, reading the directions as she worked the button on her pants, finally shoving her jeans down to her knees.

Probably this was the kind of thing women did at home. Surrounded by the cozy comfort of their favorite towels, peach-painted walls, maybe some floral potpourri. She squatted in an industrial gray tiled public restroom and did the deed, fingers still shaking as she tried to position the stick and pee on command.

Took her three tries to get it done. She set the stick on the changing table, re-fusing to look at it. She finished peeing. She pulled up her pants. She washed her hands at the sink.

Then she returned to the stall. Out-side, she could hear the bathroom door opening. Footsteps as another woman entered, headed for the neighboring stall. D.D. closed her eyes, held her breath.

She felt naughty, the bad schoolgirl caught smoking in the loo.

She couldn't be seen, couldn't be discovered. For her to look at the stick, she needed absolute privacy.

Toilet flushing. Stall door opening. Sound of water running at the sink, then the blast from the automatic hand dryer.

Outside door opened. Outside door closed.

D.D. was alone again.

Slowly she cracked one eye. Then the other. She stared at the stick.

Pink plus sign.

Sergeant Detective D. D. Warren was officially pregnant.

She sat back down on the toilet, put her head in her hands, and wept.

Later, still sitting on the edge of the toilet, she ate the apple. The rush of sugary fruit hit her bloodstream, and suddenly, she was ravenous. She consumed half a box of Cheerios, then abandoned the bathroom in search of a protein bar, mixed nuts, potato chips, yogurt, and bananas.

When Bobby finally caught up with her, she was standing in the checkout line with her apple core, opened Cheerios box, opened pregnancy kit box, and half a dozen other groceries. The checkout girl, who sported three facial piercings and a constellation of star tattoos, was regarding her with clear disapproval.

"Where'd you go?" Bobby asked with a frown. "Thought I'd lost you."

Then his gaze fell upon the pregnancy test kit. His eyes widened. He didn't say another word.

D.D. handed over her credit card, accepted her grocery bags. She didn't say a word either.

They'd just made it out to the car when her cellphone rang. She checked the caller ID—Phil from headquarters.

Work. Just what she needed.

She punched Talk, listened to what Phil had to say, and whether from his news or her feeding frenzy, she finally felt better about the day.

She put away her phone, turned back to Bobby, who stood beside his car in the snow.

"Guess what? Tessa Leoni placed a phone call while under the fine care of the Suffolk County Sheriff's Department. Nine p.m. last night, she contacted her childhood BFF, Juliana Sophia Howe."

"Sister of the guy she shot?"

"Exactly. Now, if you were arrested for murdering your spouse, what are the odds you'd call a family member of the last person you killed?"

Bobby frowned. "Don't like it."

"Me either." D.D.'s face lit up. "Let's go get her!"

"Deal." Bobby opened his door, then paused. "D.D. . . ." His gaze flickered to her grocery bags. "Happy?"

"Yeah," she said, nodding slowly. "I think I am."

When Bobby and D.D. finally completed the treacherous drive to Juliana's house, they discovered the small home lit up bright as day against fat, slow falling snowflakes. A silver SUV and darker sedan were parked in the driveway.

As Bobby and D.D. approached, the front door opened and a man appeared.

He wore a suit, still dressed for his workday, but now lugging a baby and a diaper bag. He met Bobby and D.D.'s gaze as they stepped onto the front porch.

"I already told her to call a lawyer," he said.

The caring husband, D.D. deduced. "She need one?"

"She's a good person and a great mother. You want someone to prosecute, go back and shoot her brother again. He deserves this abuse. Not her."

Having said his piece, Juliana's husband pushed past both of them and strode through the snow for the dark blue sedan. Another minute to strap the baby in the back, then Juliana's family was out of the way.

"Definitely expecting our visit," Bobby murmured.

"Let's go get her!" D.D. said again.

Caring husband hadn't fully closed the door behind him, so Bobby finished pushing it open. Juliana was sitting on the couch directly across from the door. She didn't get up, but regarded them evenly.

D.D. entered first. She flashed her creds, then introduced Bobby. Juliana didn't rise. Bobby and D.D. didn't sit. The room was already humming with tension, and it made it easy for D.D. to reach the next logical conclusion:

"You helped her out, didn't you? You picked up Tessa Leoni this afternoon and drove her away from her daughter's burial site. You aided and abetted a fugitive. Why? I mean seriously." D.D. gestured around the cute home with its fresh paint and cheerful collection of baby toys. "Why the hell would you risk all this?"

"She didn't do it," Juliana said.

D.D. arched a brow. "Exactly when did you take the stupid pill and how long before it wears off?"

Juliana's chin came up. "I'm not the idiot here. You are!"

"Why?"

"It's what you do," Juliana burst out in a bitter rush. "Police. Cops. Looking but never seeing. Asking but never hearing. Ten years ago they fucked up everything. Why should now be any different?"

D.D. stared at the young mom, startled by the violence of the outburst. At that moment, it came to D.D. What the husband had said outside. Juliana's inexplicable agreement to aid the woman who'd destroyed her family ten years ago. Her lingering rage with the police.

D.D. took the first step forward, then another. She squatted down until she was eye level with Juliana, seeing the tear tracks on the woman's cheeks.

"Tell us, Juliana. Who shot your brother that night? It's time to unload. So you talk, and I promise, we'll listen."

"Tessa didn't have the gun," Juliana Howe whispered. "She brought it for me. Because I asked her to. She didn't have the gun. She never had the gun."

"Who shot Tommy, Juliana?"

"I did. I shot my brother. And I'm sorry, but I'd do it all over again!"

Now that the dam had finally broken, Juliana confessed the rest of the story in a sobbing rush. The first night her brother had come home and sexually assaulted her. How he'd cried the next morning and begged her forgiveness. He'd been drunk, hadn't known what he was doing. Of course he'd never do it again . . . please just don't tell Mom and Dad.

She'd agreed to keep his secret, except after that he'd raped her again and again. Until it'd been half a dozen times, and he was no longer drunk and he no longer apologized. He told her it was her fault. If she didn't wear those kind of clothes, if she wouldn't flaunt herself right under his nose . . .

So she started to wear baggier clothes and stopped doing her hair and makeup. And maybe that helped, or maybe it was just because he went away to college, where it turned out he'd found lots of other girls to rape. Mostly, however, he left her alone. Except for the weekends.

She lost her ability to concentrate at school, always had dark shadows under her eyes, because if it was Friday, then Tommy might come home so she had to be vigilant. She added a lock to her room. Two weeks later, she came home to find her entire bedroom door splintered into bits.

"Terribly sorry," Tommy had said over

dinner. "Shouldn't have been running in the hall like that." And her parents had beamed at him because he was their oldest son and they adored him.

One Monday morning Juliana broke. Went to school, started to cry, couldn't stop. Tessa tugged her into the end stall of the girl's restroom, then stood there until Juliana stopped weeping and started talking.

Together, the two girls had devised a plan. Tessa's father had a gun. She would get it.

"Not like he's ever paying attention," Tessa had said with a shrug. "How hard can it be?"

So Tessa would get the gun and bring it over on Friday night. They would have a sleepover. Tessa would stand guard. When Tommy showed up, Juliana would produce the weapon. She'd point the gun at him and tell him if he ever touched her again, she would shoot off his balls.

The girls practiced the phrase several times. They liked it.

It had made sense, huddled in a bathroom stall. Tommy, like any bully, needed to be confronted, Then he would back down, and Juliana would be safe again.

It had all made perfect sense.

By Thursday, Tessa had the gun. Friday night, she came over to the house and gave it to Juliana.

Then they sat together on the sofa and, a bit nervously, started their movie marathon.

Tessa had fallen asleep on the floor. Juliana on the couch. But both had woken up when Tommy came home.

For a change, he didn't look at his sister. Instead, he'd kept his eyes glued on Tessa's chest.

"Like ripe apples," he'd said, already lurching for her when Juliana triumphantly whipped out the handgun.

She pointed it at her brother. Screamed at him to go away. Leave her and Tessa alone, *or else.*

Except Tommy had looked right at her and started laughing. "Or else *what*? Do you even know how to shoot that thing? I'd check the safety if I were you."

Juliana had immediately raised the gun to check the safety. At that moment

Tommy had lunged for her, going after the weapon.

Tessa was screaming. Juliana was screaming. Tommy was snarling and pulling Juliana's hair and making grabby grabby.

The gun, squished between them. The gun, going off.

Tommy staggering back, gaping at his leg.

"You bitch," her brother had said. Those were the last words he'd spoken to her. "You bitch," he'd said again, then he'd fallen down and, slowly but surely, died.

Juliana had panicked. She hadn't meant . . . Her parents, dear God her parents . . .

She'd thrust the gun at Tessa. Tessa had to take it. Tessa had to . . . run . . . just get out. *Get out get out get out.*

So Tessa did. And those words were the last Juliana had spoken to her best friend. *Get out get out get out.*

By the time Tessa had arrived at her house, the police were arriving at Juliana's. Juliana could've admitted what she'd done. She could've confessed what her brother was really like. But her mother was screaming hysterically and her father was shell-shocked and she couldn't do it. She just couldn't do it.

Juliana had whispered Tessa's name to the police and, that quickly, fiction became fact. Tessa had shot her brother.

And Tessa never said otherwise.

"I would have confessed," Juliana said now. "If it had gone to trial, if it looked like Tessa was really going to get into trouble . . . I would've confessed. Except the other women started coming forward and it became clear that Tessa would never face charges. The DA himself said he felt it was justifiable use of force.

"I figured she'd be okay. And my father . . . by then, he was a wreck. If he couldn't accept Tommy had ever assaulted other women, how could he believe what Tommy had done to *me*? It seemed better to just keep my mouth shut. Except . . . the longer you go without speaking, the harder it becomes. I wanted to see Tessa, but I didn't know what to say. I wanted my parents to know what happened, but I didn't know how to tell them.

"I stopped speaking. Literally. For an entire year. And my parents never even noticed. They were too busy with their own nervous breakdowns to bother with mine. Then Tessa disappeared—I heard her father had kicked her out. She never told me. Never stopped by to say good-bye. Maybe she couldn't speak either. I never knew. Until you showed up yesterday morning, I didn't know she'd become a cop, I didn't know she'd gotten married, and I didn't know she had a little girl named Sophie. That's my middle name, you know. She named her daughter for me. After everything I did to her, she still named her daughter for me. . . ."

"The daughter who's now dead," D.D. said bluntly.

"You're wrong!" Juliana shook her head.

"You're wrong, Juliana: We saw the body. Or at least the pieces after she blew it up."

Juliana paled, then shook her head again. "You're wrong," the young woman insisted stubbornly.

"Once again, from the woman whose family could give lessons in denial . . ."

"You don't know Tessa."

"For the past ten years, neither have you."

"She's clever. Self-sufficient. But she wouldn't harm a child, not after what happened to her brother."

Bobby and D.D. exchanged glances. "Brother?" D.D. said.

"Stillborn baby. That's what tore her family apart, years before I knew her. Her mother fell into a deep depression, probably should've been institutionalized, except what did people know back then? Her mom lived in the bedroom. Never came out, certainly never cared for Tessa. Her father did the best he could, but he was not exactly nurturing. But Tessa loved them. She tried to take care of them, in her own way. And she loved her baby brother, too. One day, we had a funeral for him, just she and I. And she cried, she truly cried, because that's the one thing in her house you were never allowed to do."

D.D. stared at Juliana. "You know, you could've told me this sooner."

"Well, you could've figured it out sooner. Cops. Must the victims do all the work for you?"

D.D. bristled. Bobby promptly placed a settling hand on her arm.

"Where did you take her?" he asked quietly.

"I don't know what you're talking about," Juliana said primly.

"You picked Tessa up. You already admitted that."

"No. I did not. Your partner stated I picked her up. I never said any such thing."

D.D. ground her teeth. "So that's the way you want to play it?" She swept her arm across the toy-strewn floor. "We can take you down to HQ. Seize your car. We'll tear it apart while you rot behind bars. How old's your kid again? Because I don't know if babies are even allowed to visit prison."

"Tessa called me Monday evening shortly after nine p.m.," Juliana stated defiantly. "She said, what are friends for? I said, Tessa? Because I was surprised to hear her voice after all these years. She said she wanted to call me again. Then she hung up. That's what we said, and the only interaction I have had in the past ten years with Tessa Leoni. If you want to know why she called, what she meant, or if she intended any further contact, you'll have to ask her."

D.D. was flabbergasted, honestly flabbergasted. Who knew Tessa's suburbanite playmate had it in her?

"One hair in your car, and you're screwed," D.D. said.

Juliana made a show of slapping her cheeks. "OhmyGod, so sorry. Did I mention that I vacuumed? Oh, and just the other day, I read the best trick for washing your car. It involves ammonia. . . ."

D.D. stared at the housewife. "I'm going to arrest you for that alone," she said finally.

"Then do it."

"Tessa shot her husband. She dragged his body down into the garage, and she buried it in snow," D.D. snapped angrily. "Tessa killed her daughter, drove her body out to the woods, and rigged it with enough explosives to take out the recovery team. This is the woman you're trying to protect."

"This is the woman you *thought* killed my brother," Juliana corrected. "You were wrong about that. Not so hard to believe you're wrong about the rest of it, too."

"We are not wrong—" D.D. started, but then she stopped. She frowned. Something occurred to her, the niggling doubt from earlier in the woods. Oh, crap.

"I've gotta make a phone call," she said abruptly. "You. Sit. Take even one step from that sofa and I'll arrest your sorry ass."

Then she nodded at Bobby and led him to the front porch, where she whipped out her cellphone.

"What—" he started, but she held up a silencing hand.

"Medical examiner's office?" she spoke into the receiver. "Get Ben. I know he's working. What the hell do you think I'm calling about? Tell him it's Sergeant Warren, because I bet you a hundred bucks he's standing over a microscope right now, thinking *Oh shit.*"

34

My father's garage had never been very impressive, and ten years hadn't improved it any. A squat, cinder-block building, the exterior paint was the color of nicotine and peeling off in giant flakes. Heating had always been unreliable; in the winter, my father would work under cars in full snow gear. Plumbing wasn't any better. Once upon a time, there'd been a working toilet. Mostly, my father and his male friends peed on the fence line—men, marking turf.

Two advantages of my father's shop, however: first, a bullpen of used cars awaiting repair and resell; second, an acetylene torch, perfect for cutting through metal and, coincidentally, melting cellphones.

The heavy front door was locked. Ditto with the garage bay. Back door, however, was open. I followed the glow of the bare bulb to the rear of the garage, where my father sat on a stool, smoking a cigarette and watching my approach.

A half-empty bottle of Jack sat on the workbench behind him. It'd taken me years to realize the full extent of my father's drinking. That we didn't go to bed by nine p.m. just because my father got up so early in the morning, but because he was too drunk to continue on with his day.

When I gave birth to Sophie, I'd hoped it would help me understand my parents and their endless grief. But it didn't. Even mourning the loss of an infant, how could they fail to feel the love of their remaining child? How could they simply stop seeing me?

My father inhaled one last time, then stubbed out his cigarette. He didn't use an ashtray; his scarred workbench got the job done.

"Knew you'd come," he said, speaking with the rasp of a lifetime smoker. "News just announced your escape. Figured you'd head here."

So Sergeant Warren had copped to her mistake. Good for her.

I ignored my father, heading for the acetylene torch.

My father was still dressed in his oil-stained coveralls. Even from this distance I could tell his shoulders remained broad, his chest thickly muscled. Spending all day with your arms working above your head will do that to a man.

If he wanted to stop me, he had brute strength on his side.

The realization made my hands tremble as I arrived at the twin tanks of the acetylene torch. I took the safety goggles down from their nearby hook and set about prepping for business. I wore the dark gloves Juliana had supplied for me. I had to take them off long enough to dismantle the cellphone—slide off the cover, remove the battery.

Then I slipped the black gloves back on, topping them with a heavy-duty pair of work gloves. I set the duffel bag next to the wall, then placed the cellphone in the middle of the cement floor, the best surface when working with a torch that can cut through steel like a knife through butter.

When I was fourteen, I'd spent an entire summer working at my father's shop. Helped change oil, replace spark plugs, rotate tires. One of my misguided notions, that if my father wouldn't take an interest in my world, maybe I should take an interest in his.

We worked side by side all summer, him barking out orders in his deep, rumbling voice. Then, come break time, he'd retreat to his dust-covered office, leaving me alone in the garage to eat. No random moments of comfortable silence between father and daughter, no spare words of praise. He told me what to do. I did what he said. That was it.

By the end of the summer, I'd realized my father wasn't a talker and probably never would love me.

Good thing I had Juliana instead.

My father remained on the stool. Cigarette done, he'd moved on to the Jack Daniel's, sipping from an ancient-looking plastic cup.

I lowered my safety goggles, lit the torch, and melted Officer Fiske's cellphone into a small, black lump of useless plastic.

Hated to see the thing go—never knew when the ability to make a call might come in handy. But I couldn't trust it. Some phones had GPS, meaning it could be used to track me. Or if I did make a call, they could triangulate the signal. On the other hand, I couldn't risk just tossing it either—if the police recovered it, they would trace my call to Juliana.

Hence, the acetylene torch, which, I have to say, got the job done.

I turned it off. Closed the tanks, rewrapped the hose, and hung up the work gloves and safety goggles.

I tossed the melted cellphone, now cooled, inside my duffel bag to reduce my evidence trail. Police would be here soon enough. When chasing fugitives you always visited all past haunts and known acquaintances, which would include my father.

I straightened and, my first order of business completed, finally faced my dad.

The years were catching up with him. I could see that now. His cheeks were turning into jowls, heavy lines creasing his forehead. He looked defeated. A formerly strong young man, deflated by life and all the dreams that never came true.

I wanted to hate him, but couldn't. This was the pattern of my life: to love men who didn't deserve me, and, knowing that, to yearn for their love anyway.

My father spoke. "They say you killed your husband." He started to cough, and it immediately turned phlegmy.

"So I've heard."

"And my granddaughter." He said this accusingly.

That made me smile. "You have a granddaughter? That's funny, because I don't remember my daughter ever receiving a visit from her grandfather. Or a gift on her birthday, or a stocking stuffer at Christmas. So don't talk to me about grandchildren, old man. You reap what you sow."

"Hard-ass," he said.

"I get it from you."

He slammed down his cup. Amber liquid sloshed. I caught a whiff of whiskey and my mouth watered. Forget a circular argument that would get us nowhere. I could pull up a chair and drink with my father instead. Maybe that's what he'd been waiting for the summer I'd been fourteen. He hadn't needed a child to work for him, he'd needed a daughter to drink with him.

Two alcoholics, side by side in the dim lighting of a run-down garage.

Then we would've both failed our children.

"I'm taking a car," I said now.

"I'll turn you in."

"Do what you need to do."

I turned toward the Peg-Board on the left side of the workbench, dotted with little hooks bearing keys. My father climbed off his stool, standing to his full height before me.

Tough guy, filled with the false bravado of his liquid buddy Jack. My father had never hit me. As I waited for him to start now, I wasn't afraid, just tired. I knew this man, not just as my dad, but as half a dozen jerks I confronted and talked down five nights a week.

"Dad," I heard myself say softly. "I'm not a little girl anymore. I'm a trained police officer, and if you want to stop me, you're going to have to do better than this."

"I didn't raise no baby killer," he growled.

"No. You didn't."

His brow furrowed. In his fuzzy state, he was having problems working this out.

"Do you want me to plead my innocence?" I continued. "I tried that once before. It didn't work."

"You killed that Howe boy."

"No."

"Police said so."

"Police make mistakes, as much as it pains me to say that."

"Then why'd you become a cop, if they're no good?"

"Because." I shrugged. "I want to serve. And I'm good at my job."

"Till you killed your husband and little girl."

"No."

"Police said so."

"And round and round we go."

His brow furrowed again.

"I'm going to take a car," I repeated. "I'm going to use it to hunt down the man who has my daughter. You can argue with me, or you can tell me which of these clunkers is most prepared to log a few miles. Oh, and fuel would help. Stopping at a gas station isn't gonna work for me right now."

"I got a granddaughter," he said roughly.

"Yes. She's six years old, her name is Sophie and she's counting on me to rescue her. So help me, Dad. Help me save her."

"She as tough as her mom?"

"God, I hope so."

"Who took her?"

"First thing I have to figure out."

"How you gonna do that?"

I smiled, grimly this time. "Let's just say, the Commonwealth of Massachusetts invested a lot of resources into my training, and they're about to get their money's worth. Vehicle, Dad. I don't have much time, and neither does Sophie."

He didn't move, just crossed his arms and peered down at me. "You lying to me?"

I didn't feel like arguing anymore. Instead, I stepped forward, wrapped my arms around his waist, and leaned my head against the bulk of his chest. He smelled of cigarettes, motor oil, and whiskey. He smelled of my childhood, and the home and mother I still missed.

"Love you, Dad. Always have. Always will."

His frame shook. A slight tremor. I chose to believe that was his way of saying he loved me, too. Mostly because the alternative hurt too much.

I stepped back. He unfolded his arms, crossed to the Peg-Board, and handed me a single key.

"Blue Ford truck, out back. Gotta lotta miles, but its heart's good. Four-wheel drive. You're gonna need that."

For navigating the snowy road. Perfect.

"Gas cans are against the outside wall. Help yourself."

"Thank you."

"Bring her," he said suddenly. "When you find her, when you . . . get her back. I want . . . I want to meet my grand-daughter."

"Maybe," I said.

He startled at my hesitation, glared at me.

I took the key, returning his look calmly. "From one alcoholic to another—gotta stop drinking, Dad. Then we'll see."

"Hard-ass," he muttered.

I smiled one last time, then kissed him on his leathery cheek. "Get it from you," I whispered.

I palmed the key, picked up my duffel bag, then I was gone.

35

"Why was the scene in the woods so horrific?" D.D. was saying fifteen minutes later. She answered her own question: "Because what kind of mom would kill her own child, then blow up the body? What kind of woman could do such a thing?"

Bobby, standing beside her on Juliana Howe's front porch, nodded. "Diversion. She needed to buy time to escape."

D.D. shrugged. "Except not really. She was already alone with Officer Fiske and they were a quarter of a mile away from the search team. She could've easily jumped Fiske without the diversion, and still had a solid thirty minutes head start. Which is why exploding the child's remains seems so horrifying— it's gratuitous. Why do such a terrible thing?"

"Okay, I'll bite: Why do such a thing?"

"Because she needed the bones fragmented. She couldn't afford for us to find the remains *in situ*. Then it would've been obvious the body didn't belong to a child."

Bobby stared at her. "Excuse me? The pink bits of clothing, blue jeans, rib bone, tooth . . ."

"Clothing was planted with the body. Rib bone is approximately the right size for a six-year-old—or a large breed of dog. Ben just finished spending some quality time studying bone fragments in the lab. Those bones aren't human. They're canine. Right size. Wrong species."

Bobby did a little double-take. "Fuck me," he said, a man who hardly ever swore. "The German shepherd. Brian

Darby's old dog that passed away. Tessa buried *that* body?"

"Apparently. Hence the strong scent of decomp in the white Denali. Again, according to Ben, the size and length of many bones in a large dog would match a six-year-old human. Of course, the skull would be all wrong, as well as minor details like tail and paws. An intact canine skeleton, therefore, would never get confused for a human one. Scrambled pieces of bone fragments, however . . . Ben apologizes for his error. He's a bit embarrassed to tell you the truth. It's been a while since he's had a crime scene mess this much with his head."

"Wait a second." Bobby held up a cautioning hand. "The cadaver dogs, remember? They wouldn't hit on nonhuman remains. Their noses and training are better than that."

D.D. suddenly smiled. "Fucking clever," she muttered. "Isn't that what Juliana said? Tessa Leoni is very clever, gotta give her that.

"Two front teeth," she filled in for Bobby. "Also three bloody tampons, recovered from the scene after we left. Ben supplies some of the training materials used by the SAR teams. According to him, dog handlers are fairly creative at finding sources of 'cadaver,' since owning actual dead people is illegal. Turns out, teeth are like bone. So search handlers get teeth from a local dentist's office, and use them to train the dogs. Same with used tampons. Tessa hid a dog body, but scattered the site with 'human cadaver'—her daughter's baby teeth topped with a dash of feminine hygiene."

"That's disgusting," Bobby said.

"That's ingenious," D.D. countered.

"But why?"

D.D. had to think about it. "Because she knew we'd blame her. That's been her experience, right? She didn't shoot Tommy Howe, but the cops assumed she did. Meaning we were right before—the first experience ten years ago has informed her experience now. Another terrible thing happened in Tessa Leoni's world. Her first instinct is that she will be blamed. Except this time she'll probably be arrested. So she stages an elaborate scheme to get out of jail."

"But why?" Bobby repeated. "If she didn't do anything, why not tell us the truth? Why ... such a complicated ruse? She's a cop now. Shouldn't she have more faith in the system?"

D.D. arched a brow.

He sighed. "You're right. We're born cynics."

"But why not talk to us?" D.D. was continuing. "Let's think about that. We assumed Tessa shot Tommy Howe ten years ago. We were wrong. We assumed she shot her husband, Brian, Saturday morning. Well, maybe we're wrong about that, too. Meaning, someone else did it. That person shot Brian, took Sophie."

"Why kill the husband, but kidnap the child?" Bobby asked.

"Leverage," D.D. supplied immediately. "This does go back to gambling. Brian owed too much. Instead of shaking him down, however—the weak link—they're going after Tessa instead. They shoot Brian to show they mean business, then grab Sophie. Tessa can have her daughter back if she pays up. So Tessa heads to the bank, takes out fifty grand—"

"Clearly not enough," Bobby commented.

"Exactly. She needs more money, but also has to deal with the fact that her husband's dead, shot by her gun, as ballistics was a match."

Bobby's eyes widened. "She was home," he said suddenly. "Only way they could've shot Brian with her gun. Tessa was home. Maybe even walked into the situation. Someone's already holding her child. What can she do? Man demands that she turn over her Sig Sauer, then . . ."

"Shoots Brian," D.D. said softly.

"She's screwed," Bobby continued quietly. "She knows she's screwed. Her husband is dead by her service weapon, her child has been kidnapped, and she already has a previous history of shooting to kill. What are the odds of anyone believing her? Even if she said, *Hey, some mobster offed my gambling-addicted husband with my state side-*

arm, and now I need your help to rescue my kid . . ."

"I wouldn't buy it," D.D. said flaty.

"Cops are born cynics," Bobby repeated.

"So she starts thinking," D.D. continued. "Only way to get Sophie back is to get the money, and only way to get the money is to stay out of jail."

"Meaning, she needs to start planning ahead," Bobby filled in.

D.D. frowned. "So, based on the Tommy shooting, option A is to plead self-defense. That can be tricky, however, as spousal abuse is an affirmative defense, so she decides she needs a safety net, as well. Option A will be self-defense, and option B will be to hide dog bones in the woods, which she'll claim are her daughter's remains. If self-defense doesn't work and she ends up arrested, then she can escape utilizing plan B."

"Clever," Bobby commented. "As Juliana said, self-sufficient."

"Complicated." D.D. was scowling. "Especially given that she's now on the run, making it that much harder for her to get money and rescue Sophie. Would you risk that much when it's your daughter's life at stake? Wouldn't it still be cleaner to fall on her sword and beg for our help? Get us tracking mobsters, get us to rescue Sophie, even if we arrest her first?"

Bobby shrugged. "Maybe, like Juliana, she's not impressed by other cops."

But D.D. suddenly had another thought. "Maybe," she said slowly, "because another cop is part of the problem."

Bobby stared at her, then she could see him connect the dots.

"Who beat her up?" D.D. asked now. "Who hit her so hard that for the first twenty hours she couldn't even stand? Who was present the entire time we were at her house on Sunday morning, his hand on her shoulder? I thought he was showing his support. But maybe, he was reminding her to shut up."

"Trooper Lyons."

"The helpful 'friend' who fractured her cheekbone, and got her husband hooked on gambling in the first place.

Maybe because Lyons was already spending a lot of quality time at Foxwoods."

"Trooper Lyons isn't part of the solution," Bobby muttered. "Trooper Lyons is the heart of the problem."

"Let's get him!" D.D. said.

She was already taking the first step off the front porch when Bobby grabbed her arm, drawing her up short.

"D.D., you know what this means?"

"I finally get to break Trooper Lyons?"

"No, D.D. Sophie Leoni. She could still be alive. And Trooper Lyons knows where she's at."

D.D. stilled. She felt a flare of emotion. "Then listen to me, Bobby. We need to do this right, and I have a plan."

36

The old Ford didn't like to shift or brake. Thankfully, given the winter storm alert and the late hour, the roads were mostly empty. I passed several snowplows, a couple of emergency vehicles, and various police cruisers tending to business. I kept my eyes forward and the speedometer at the exact speed limit. Dressed in black, baseball cap pulled low over my brow, I still felt conspicuous heading back into Boston, toward my home.

I drove slowly by my house. Watched my headlights flash across the yellow crime-scene tape, which stood out garishly against the clean white snow.

The house looked and felt empty. A walking advertisement for Something Bad Happened Here.

I kept going until I found parking in an empty convenience store parking lot.

Shouldering my bag, I set out the rest of the way on foot.

Moving quickly now. Wanting the cover of darkness and finding little in a busy city liberally sprinkled with streetlights and brightly lit signs. One block right, one block left, then I was honing in on target.

Shane's police cruiser was parked outside his house. It was five till eleven, meaning he'd be appearing any time for duty.

I took up position, crouched low behind the trunk, where I could blend into the shadow cast by the Crown Vic in the pool of streetlight.

My hands were cold, even with gloves. I blew on my fingers to keep them warm; I couldn't afford for them to be sluggish. I was going to get only one shot at this. I would either win, or I wouldn't.

My heart pounded. I felt a little dizzy and it suddenly occurred to me I hadn't eaten in at least twelve hours. Too late now. Front door opened. Patio light came on. Shane appeared.

His wife, Tina, stood behind him in a fluffy pink bathrobe. Quick kiss to the cheek, sending her man off for duty. I felt a pang. I squashed it.

Shane came down the first step, then the second. Door closed behind him, Tina not waiting for the full departure.

I released the breath I didn't realize I'd been holding and started the count-down in my head.

Shane descended all the steps, crossing the driveway, keys jingling in his hand. Arriving at his cruiser, inserting the key in the lock, twisting, popping open the driver-side door.

I sprung out from behind the cruiser and rammed my Glock .40 into the side of his neck.

"One word and you're dead."

Shane remained silent.

I took his duty weapon. Then we both climbed into his police cruiser.

I made him sit in the back, away from the radio and the instrument panel. I took the driver's seat, the sliding security panel open between us. I kept the Glock on this side of the bulletproof barrier, away from Shane's lunging reach, while pointing squarely on target. Normally, officers aimed for the subject's chest—the largest mass. Given that Shane was already wearing body armor, I trained on the solid block of his head.

At my command, he passed me his cellphone, his duty belt, then his pager. I piled it all in the passenger's seat, helping myself to the metal bracelets, which I then passed back and had him place around his own wrists.

Subject secured, I pulled my gaze from him long enough to start the car engine. I could feel his body tense, preparing for some kind of action.

"Don't be stupid," I said crisply. "I owe you, remember?" I gestured to my battered face. He sagged again, cuffed hands flopping back down onto his lap.

Car engine roared to life. If Shane's wife happened to glance out the window, she would see her husband warming up his cruiser while checking in with dispatch, maybe tending to a few messages.

A five- to ten-minute delay wouldn't be too unusual. Anything more than that, she might grow concerned, might even come out to investigate. Meaning, I didn't have much time for this conversation.

Still had to get a few digs in.

"Shoulda hit me harder," I said, turning back around, giving my former fellow officer my full attention. "Did you really think a concussion would be enough to keep me down?"

Shane didn't say anything. His eyes were on the Glock, not my bruised face.

I felt myself growing angry. Like I wanted to crawl through the narrow opening in the security shield and pistol-whip this man half a dozen times, before beating him senseless with my bare hands.

I had trusted Shane, a fellow officer. Brian had trusted him, a best friend. And he had betrayed us both.

I'd called him Saturday afternoon, after paying off the hit man. My last hope in a rapidly disintegrating world, I'd thought. Of course I'd been told not to contact the police. Of course I'd been told to keep quiet *or else.* But Shane wasn't just a fellow officer. He was my friend, he was Brian's closest friend. He'd help me save Sophie.

Instead, his voice cold, totally devoid of emotion on the other end of the phone: "You don't take instruction too well, do you, Tessa? When these boys tell you to shut up, you *shut up.* Now stop trying to get us all killed, and do what they told you to do."

Turned out, Shane already knew Brian was dead. He'd received some instructions of his own over the matter, and now he spelled it all out for me: Brian was a wife beater. In the heat of the moment, he'd gone too far and I'd discharged my weapon in self-defense. No evidence of physical assault? Don't worry, Shane would assist with that. I babbled that I'd been granted twenty-four hours to prepare for Sophie's return. Fine, he'd said curtly. He'd be over first thing in the morning. A minor pummeling, then we'd contact the authorities together, Shane by my side every step of the way. Shane, keeping watch and reporting back.

Of course, I'd realized then. Shane wasn't just Brian's friend, he was his partner in crime. And now he had to protect his own hide at any cost. Even if that involved sacrificing Brian, me, and Sophie.

I was screwed and my daughter's life hung in the balance. It's amazing how clear-eyed you can suddenly become when your child needs you. How covering your husband's dead body with snow makes all the sense in the world. As well as fetching Duke's corpse from underneath the back deck, where Brian had stored the body while waiting for the spring thaw. And looking up bombs on the Internet . . .

I let go of my denial. I embraced the chaos. And I learned that I was a much more ruthless person than I'd ever believed.

"I know about the money," I told Shane now. Despite my best intentions for calm, I could feel my rage bubble up again. I remembered the first eye-shattering impact of Shane's fist connecting with my face. The way he'd towered above me as I went down on the bloody kitchen floor. The endless minute, when I'd realized he could kill me, and then there would be no one to save Sophie. I'd cried. I'd begged. That's what my "friend" had done to me.

Now Shane's gaze flickered to mine, his eyes rounding in surprise.

"Did you think I'd never connect the dots?" I said. "Why did you demand this whole farce that I claim to have killed my own husband? Because you and your partners wanted me out of the way. You wanted to destroy my credibility, then frame me for the theft. Your mobster friends aren't interested in shaking me down for money. You're using me to cover your tracks, letting me take the fall for all the money *you* stole from the troopers' union. You were gonna blame me for everything. *Everything!*"

He didn't say a word.

"You goddamn bastard!" I exploded. "If I went to prison, what would happen to Sophie? You signed her death warrant, you prick. You basically killed my daughter!"

Shane blanched. "I didn't . . . I wouldn't. It never would've gone that far!"

"*That far?* You *stole* from the troopers' union. You screwed your friends, your career, and your family. That wasn't letting things go too far?"

"It was Brian's idea," Shane said automatically. "He needed the money. He'd lost a little too much . . . They'd kill him, he said. I was just trying to help. Honest, Tessa. You know how Brian can be. I was just trying to help."

In response, I grabbed his duty belt with my left hand, unclipped the Taser, and held it up.

"One more lie, and you're gonna dance. Do you understand me, Shane? Stop *lying!*"

He swallowed, tongue darting out

nervously to lick the corner of his mouth.

"I don't . . . Ah Christ," he blurted out suddenly. "I'm sorry, Tessa. I don't know how it came to this. At first, I'd go with Brian to Foxwoods to keep *him* under control. Which meant, of course, that sometimes I'd play, too. Then, coupla of times, I won. I mean, I *won.* Five grand, just like that. Bought Tina a new ring. She cried. And it felt . . . great. Wonderful. Like I was Superman. So, of course, I had to play again, except we didn't always win. So then you play more because now you're due. It's your turn. One good hand, that's all you need, one good hand.

"That's what we told ourselves, these past few weeks. One solid afternoon at the tables and it would all turn around. We'd be okay. Couple of hours even. Just the right coupla hours and we would've been fine."

"You embezzled money from the troopers' union. You sold your soul to mobsters."

Shane looked at me. "Gotta have money to make money," he said simply, as if this were the most logical explanation in the world.

Maybe to a gambler, it was.

"Who did you borrow the money from? Who shot Brian? Who took my daughter?"

Shrug.

"Fuck you, Shane! They have my little girl. You will talk or I will blow off your head!"

"They'll kill me anyway!" he fired back, eyes finally blazing to life. "You don't mess with these guys. They already sent me pictures—Tina in the grocery store, Tina going to yoga, Tina picking up the boys. I'm sorry about Brian. I'm sorry about Sophie. But I gotta protect my own family. I might be a fuckup, but I'm not a total failure."

"Shane," I said crisply. "You're not getting it yet. I'm going to kill you. Then I'm going to pin the word 'snitch' to your chest. I give Tina and the boys about forty-eight hours to live beyond that. Probably less."

He blinked. "You wouldn't. . . ."

"Think of how far you'd go for your sons, and know that I would, too."

Shane exhaled sharply. He stared at me, and I could tell in his gaze he'd finally figured out how this was all going to go down. Maybe, like me, he'd spent the last few days figuring out there really were multiple layers of Hell, and no matter how deep you'd thought you'd fallen, there was still someplace deeper and darker to go.

"If I give you a name," he said abruptly, "you gotta kill him. Tonight. Swear to me, Tessa. You'll get him, before he gets my family."

"Done."

"I love them," Shane whispered. "I'm a fuckup, but I love my family. I just want them to be okay."

My turn not to talk.

"I'm sorry about Brian, Tessa. Really, didn't think they'd do that. Didn't think they'd harm him. Or go after Sophie. I never shoulda gambled. Never shoulda picked up one fucking card."

"The name, Shane. Who killed Brian? Who took my daughter?"

He studied my battered face, finally seemed to wince. Then he nodded, sat up a little straighter, squared his shoulders. Once, Shane had been a good cop. Once, he'd been a good friend. Maybe he was trying to find that person again.

"John Stephen Purcell," he told me. "An enforcer. A guy who works for guys. Find Purcell, and he'll have Sophie. Or at least know where she is."

"His address?"

Slight hesitation. "Take off the cuffs and I'll get it."

His pause was enough warning for me. I shook my head. "You never should've harmed my daughter," I said softly, bringing up the Glock.

"Tessa, come on. I told you what you needed to know." He rattled his cuffed wrists. "Jesus Christ, this is crazy. Let me go. I'll help you get your daughter back. We'll find Purcell together. Come on . . ."

I smiled, but it was sad. Shane made it all sound so easy. Of course, he could've made that offer on Saturday. Instead, he'd informed me to sit down, shut up, and oh yeah, he'd be by in the morning for my beating.

Good Brian. Bad Brian.

Good Shane. Bad Shane.

Good Tessa. Bad Tessa.

Maybe for all of us, that line between good and bad is thinner than it ought to be. And maybe for all of us, once that line's been crossed, there's no going back. You were who you were, and now you are who you are.

"Shane," I murmured. "Think of your sons."

He appeared confused, then I saw him connect the dots. Such as cops who died in the line of duty received death benefits for their families, while cops who went to jail for embezzling funds and engaging in criminal activities didn't.

As Shane had said, he was a fuckup, but not a total failure.

Good Shane thought of his three sons. And I could tell when he reached the logical conclusion, because his shoulders came down. His face relaxed.

Shane Lyons looked at me one last time.

"Sorry," he whispered.

"Me, too," I said.

Then, I pulled the trigger.

Afterward, I drove the cruiser out of the driveway and onto the street, eventually pulling in behind a darkened warehouse, the kind of place a cop might go if he spotted suspicious activity. I climbed into the back, ignoring the stench of blood, the way Shane's body still felt warm and pliable.

I dug through his pockets, then his duty belt. I discovered a scrap of paper with digits that resembled GPS coordinates tucked beside his cellphone. I used the computer in the front seat to look up the coordinates, then wrote down the corresponding address and directions.

I returned to the backseat, uncuffing Shane's hands, then placing his duty belt back around him. I'd done him a favor, shooting him with Brian's Glock. I could've used his own Sig Sauer, raising the possibility that his death was suicide. In which case, Tina and the boys would've received nothing.

I'm not that hard yet, I thought. Not that stone cold.

My cheeks felt funny. My face curiously numb.

I kept myself focused on the business at hand. The night was young yet, and I had plenty of work to do.

I moved around the cruiser and popped the trunk. State troopers believed in being prepared and Shane did not disappoint. A case of water, half a dozen protein bars, and even some MREs lined one side. I dumped the food in my duffel bag, half a protein bar already stuffed into my mouth, then used Shane's keys to open the long metal gun locker.

Shane stocked a Remington shotgun, M4 rifle, half a dozen boxes of ammo, and a KA-BAR knife.

I took it all.

37

Bobby and D.D. were halfway to Trooper Lyons's house when they heard the call—*Officer down, officer down, all officers respond...*

Dispatch rattled off an address. D.D. plugged it into her computer. She paled as the local map appeared on the screen in front of her.

"That's right by Tessa's house," she murmured.

"And Trooper Lyons's," Bobby said.

They stared at each other.

"Shit."

Bobby hit the lights, floored the gas.

They sped toward the address in utter silence.

By the time they arrived, ambulances and police cruisers had already bottle-necked the scene. Lots of officers milling about, no one really doing anything. Which meant only one thing.

Bobby and D.D. climbed out of the car. The first officer they came to was a state trooper, so Bobby did the honors.

"Situation?" he asked.

"Trooper Shane Lyons, sir. Single GSW to the head." The young trooper swallowed hard. "Deceased, sir. Declared at the scene. Nothing the EMTs could do."

Bobby nodded, glancing in D.D.'s direction.

"Was he on a call?" she asked.

"Negative. Hadn't reported in yet to the duty desk. Detective Parker"—the kid gestured to a man dressed in a gray heavy wool coat and standing inside the crime-scene tape—"is leading the investigation. Might want to talk to him, sir, ma'am."

They nodded, thanked the kid, and moved forward.

Bobby knew Al Parker. He and D.D. flashed their creds for the uniformed officer handling the murder log, then they ducked under the yellow tape and approached the lead detective.

Parker, a thin, gangly man, straightened at their arrival. He shook Bobby's hands with his leather gloves still on, then Bobby introduced D.D.

The snow was finally slowing down. A couple of inches remained on the pavement, revealing a churn of footprints as officers and EMTs had rushed to assist. Only one set of tire tracks, though. That was D.D.'s first thought. Another vehicle would've left some kind of imprint behind, but she didn't see anything.

She related this to Detective Parker, who nodded.

"Appears Trooper Lyons drove behind the building," he said. "Not officially on duty yet. Nor did he notify dispatch that he was responding to signs of suspicious activity . . ."

Detective Parker let that statement explain itself.

Officers on duty always called in. It was imprinted into their DNA. If you grabbed coffee, peed, or spied a burglary in progress, you called it in. Meaning whatever had brought Trooper Lyons to this remote destination hadn't been professional, but personal.

"Single GSW," Detective Parker continued. "Left temple. Shot fired from the front seat. Trooper Lyons was in the back."

D.D. startled. Bobby, as well.

Seeing their looks, Detective Parker waved them over to the cruiser, which sat with all four doors open. He started with the bloodstain in the backseat, then worked backwards for the trajectory of the shot.

"He was wearing his duty belt?" Bobby asked with a frown.

Parker nodded. "Yes, but there are marks on his wrists consistent with restraints. Bracelets were no longer present when the first officer arrived, but at some point this evening, Trooper Lyons's hands were cuffed."

D.D. didn't like that image—a bound officer, sitting in the back of his cruiser, staring down the barrel of a gun. She hunkered deeper inside her winter coat, feeling cold snowflakes whisper across her eyelashes.

"His weapon?" she asked.

"Sig Sauer is in his holster. But check this out."

Parker led them around to the rear of the cruiser, where he popped the trunk. It was empty. D.D. instantly understood the significance. No cop, uniformed or otherwise, had an empty trunk. There should be some basic supplies, not to mention at least a rifle or shotgun or both.

She glanced at Bobby for confirmation. "Remington shotgun and M4 rifle are standard issue," he muttered, nodding. "Somebody was looking for weapons."

Parker studied both of them, but neither she nor Bobby said another word. It went without saying between them who that somebody was, a person who knew Trooper Lyons, could lure him out to his cruiser, and desperately needed fire power.

"Trooper Lyons's family?" Bobby asked now.

"Colonel went over to notify."

"Shit," Bobby murmured.

"Three boys. Shit," Parker agreed.

D.D.'s cellphone rang. She didn't recognize the number, but it was local, so she excused herself to answer.

A minute later, she returned to Bobby and Parker.

"Gotta go," she said, tapping Bobby lightly on the arm.

He didn't ask, not in front of the other detective. He simply shook Parker's hand, thanked him for his time, then they were off.

"Who?" Bobby asked, once they were out of hearing.

"Believe it or not, Shane's widow. She has something for us."

Bobby arched a brow.

"Envelope," D.D. clarified. "Apparently, Shane handed it to her Sunday evening. Said if anything happened to him, she was to call me, and only me, and hand it over. Colonel has just left. The widow is now complying with her husband's final wishes."

Every light blazed in Shane Lyons's house. Half a dozen cars crowded the street, including two parked illegally on the front yard. Family, D.D. guessed. Wives of other troopers. The support system, kicking into gear.

She wondered if Shane's boys had woken up yet. She wondered if their mother had already broken the news that their father would never again be coming home.

She and Bobby stood shoulder to shoulder at the front door, faces carefully schooled, because that's how these things worked. They mourned the passing of any law enforcement officer, felt the pain of the officer's family, and tended to duty anyway. Trooper Shane Lyons was a victim who was also a suspect. Nothing easy about this kind of case or this kind of investigation.

An older woman came to the door first. Judging by age and facial features, D.D. pegged her to be Tina Lyons's mom. D.D. flashed her credentials; Bobby, too.

The older woman appeared confused. "Surely you don't have questions
for Tina right now," she said softly. "At
least give my daughter a day or two—"

"She called us, ma'am," D.D. said.

"What?"

"We're here because she asked us to
come," D.D. reiterated. "If you could just
let her know Sergeant Detective D. D.
Warren is here, we don't mind waiting
outside."

Actually, she and Bobby preferred
outside. Whatever Tina had for them
was the kind of thing best not shown in
front of witnesses.

Minutes passed. Just when D.D. was
beginning to think that Tina had changed
her mind, the woman appeared. Her
face was haggard, her eyes red-rimmed
from weeping. She wore a fluffy pink
bathrobe, the top clutched closed with
one hand. In the other, she held a plain
white catalog-sized envelope.

"Do you know who killed my husband?" she asked.

"No, ma'am."

Tina Lyons thrust the envelope
toward D.D. "That's all I want to know. I

mean it. That's *all* I want to know. Find that out, and we'll speak again."

She retreated back to the tenuous comfort of her family and friends, leaving D.D. and Bobby on the front stoop.

"She knows something," Bobby said.

"She suspects," D.D. corrected quietly. "She doesn't want to know. I believe that was the whole point of her statement."

D.D. clutched the envelope with gloved hands. She looked around the snowy driveway. After midnight in a quiet residential area, the sidewalk studded with streetlights, and yet pools of darkness loomed everywhere.

She felt suddenly conspicuous and overexposed.

"Let's go," she muttered to Bobby.

They moved carefully down the street toward their parked car. D.D. carried the envelope in her gloved hands. Bobby carried his gun.

Ten minutes later, they'd conducted basic evasive maneuvers around a maze of Allston-Brighton streets. Bobby was content no one had followed them. D.D. was dying to know the contents of the envelope.

They found a convenience store buzzing with college students, not deterred by either the weather or the late hour. The cluster of vehicles made their Crown Vic less conspicuous, while the students provided plenty of eyewitnesses to deter ambush.

Satisfied, D.D. exchanged her winter gloves for a latex pair, then worked the flap of the envelope, easing it carefully open in order to preserve evidence.

Inside, she found a dozen five-by-seven color photos. The first eleven appeared to be of Shane Lyons's family. Here was Tina at the grocery store. There was Tina walking into a building holding a yoga mat. Here was Tina picking up the boys from school. There were the boys, playing on the school playground.

It didn't take a rocket scientist to get the message. Someone had been stalking Shane's family and that person wanted him to know about it.

Then D.D. came to the last photo.

She sucked in her breath, while beside her, Bobby swore.

Sophie Leoni.

They were staring at Sophie Leoni, or rather, she was staring directly at the camera, clutching a doll with one mangled blue button eye. Sophie's lips were pressed together, the way a child might do when trying hard not to cry. But she had her chin up. Her blue gaze seemed to be trying for defiance, though there were streaks of dirt and tears on her cheeks and her pretty brown hair now looked like a rat's nest.

The photo was cropped close, providing only the hint of wood paneling in the background. Maybe a closet or other small room. A windowless dark room, D.D. thought. That's where someone would imprison a child.

Her hand started to tremble.

D.D. flipped over the photo, looking for other clues.

She found a message scrawled in black marker: *Don't Let This Be Your Kid, Too.*

D.D. flipped the photo back over, took one more look at Sophie's heart-shaped face, and her hands now shook so badly she had to set the photo on her lap.

"Someone really did kidnap her. Someone really did . . ." Then her next jumbled thought. "And it's been more than three fucking days! What are our odds of finding her after *three fucking days!*"

She whacked the dash. The blow stung her hand and didn't do a thing to dampen her rage.

She whirled on her partner. "What the fuck is going on here, Bobby? Who the fuck kidnaps one police officer's child, while threatening the family of a second officer? I mean, *who the hell does that?*"

Bobby didn't answer right away. His hands were clutching the steering wheel, and all his knuckles had turned white.

"What did Tina say when she called?" he demanded suddenly. "What were Shane's instructions to her?"

"If something happened to him, she was to give this envelope to me."

"Why you, D.D.? With all due respect, you're a Boston cop. If Shane needed help, wouldn't he turn to his own friends in uniform, his supposed brothers in blue?"

D.D. stared at him. She remembered the first day of the case, the way the state police had closed ranks, even against her, a city cop. Then her eyes widened.

"You don't think . . ." she began.

"Not that many criminals have the cajones to threaten one, let alone two, state troopers. But another cop would."

"Why?"

"How much is missing from the troopers' union?"

"Quarter mil."

Bobby nodded.

"In other words, two hundred and fifty thousand reasons to betray the uniform. Two hundred and fifty thousand reasons to kill Brian Darby, kidnap Sophie Leoni, and threaten Shane Lyons."

D.D. considered it. "Tessa Leoni shot Trooper Lyons. He betrayed the uniform, but even worse he betrayed her family. Now the question is, did she get from Lyons the information she was after?"

"Name and address of the person who has her daughter," Bobby filled in.

"Lyons was a minion. Maybe Brian Darby, too. They pilfered the troopers' union to fund their gambling habit. But somebody else helped them—the person calling the shots."

Bobby glanced at Sophie's photo, seemed to be formulating his thoughts. "If it was Tessa Leoni who shot Trooper Lyons, and she's made it this far, that means she must have a vehicle."

"Not to mention a small arsenal of weapons."

"So maybe she did get a name and address," Bobby added.

"She's going after her daughter."

Bobby finally smiled. "Then for the criminal mastermind's sake, the bastard better hope that we find him first."

38

Some things are best not to think about. So I didn't. I drove. Mass Pike to 128, 128 southbound to Dedham. Eight more miles, half a dozen turns, I was in a heavily wooded residential area. Older homes, larger properties. The kind of place where people had trampolines in the front yard and laundry lines in the back.

Good place to hold a kid, I thought, then stopped thinking again.

I missed the address the first time. Didn't see the numbers in the falling snow. When I realized I'd gone too far, I hit the brakes, and the old truck fishtailed. I turned into the spin, a second-hand reflex that calmed my nerves and returned my composure.

Training. That's what this came down to.

Thugs didn't train.

But I did.

I parked my truck next to the road. In plain sight, but I needed it accessible for a quick getaway. I had Brian's Glock .40 tucked in the back waistband of my pants. The KA-BAR knife came with a lower leg sheath. I strapped it on.

Then I loaded the shotgun. If you're young, female, and not terribly large, shotgun is always the way to go. You could take down a water buffalo without even having to aim.

Checking my black gloves, tugging down my black cap. Feeling the cold, but as something abstract and far away. Mostly, I could hear a rushing sound in my ears, my own blood, I supposed, powered through my veins by a flood of adrenaline.

No flashlight. I let my eyes adjust to

the kind of dark that exists only on rural roads, then I darted through the woods.

Moving felt good. After the first twenty-four hours, confined to a hospital bed, followed by another twenty-four hours stuck in jail, to finally be out, moving, getting the job done, felt right.

Somewhere ahead was my daughter. I was going to save her. I was going to kill the man who had taken her. Then we were both going home.

Unless, of course . . .

I stopped thinking again.

The woods thinned. I burst onto a snowy yard and drew up sharply, eyeing the flat, sprawling ranch that appeared in front of me. All windows were dark, not a single light glowing in welcome. It was well after midnight by now. The kind of hour when honest people were asleep.

Then again, my subject didn't make an honest living, did he?

Motion-activated outdoor lights, I guessed after another second. Floodlights that would most likely flare to life the second I approached. Probably some kind of security system on the doors and windows. At least basic defensive measures.

It's like that old adage—liars expect others to lie. Enforcers who kill expect to be killed and plan appropriately.

Getting inside the house undetected probably was not an option.

Fine, I would draw him out instead.

I started with the vehicle I found parked in the driveway. A black Cadillac Esplanade with all the bells and whistles. But of course. It gave me a great deal of satisfaction to drive the butt of the shotgun through the driver's-side window.

Car alarm whistled shrilly. I darted from the SUV to the side of the house. Floodlights blazed to life, casting the front and side yard into blinding white relief. I tucked my back against the side of the house facing the Cadillac, edging as close as I could toward the rear of the home, where I guessed Purcell would ultimately emerge. I held my breath.

An enforcer such as Purcell would be too smart to dash out into the snow in his underwear. But he would be too arrogant to let someone get away with stealing his wheels. He would come. Armed. And, he probably thought, prepared.

It took a full minute. Then I heard a low creak of a back screen door, easing open.

I held the shotgun loosely, cradled in the crook of my left arm. With my right hand, I slowly withdrew the KA-BAR knife.

Never done wet work. Never been up this close and personal.

I stopped thinking again.

My hearing had already acclimated to the shrill car alarm. That made it easier for me to pick up other noises: the faint crunch of snow as the subject took his first step, then another. I took one second to check behind me, in case there were two of them in the house, one creeping from the front, one stalking from the back, to circle around.

I heard only one set of footsteps, and made them my target.

Forcing myself to inhale through my nose, take the air deep into my lungs. Slowing my own heartbeat. What would happen would happen. Time to let go.

I crouched, knife at the ready.

A leg appeared. I saw black snow boots, thick jeans, the red tail of a flannel shirt.

I saw a gun held low against the man's thigh.

"John Stephen Purcell?" I whispered.

A startled face turning toward me, dark eyes widening, mouth opening.

I stared up at the man who'd killed my husband and kidnapped my child.

I slashed out with the knife.

Just as he opened fire.

Never bring a knife to a gunfight.

Not necessarily. Purcell hit my right shoulder. On the other hand, I severed the hamstring on his left leg. He went down, firing a second time, into the snow. I kicked the gun out of his hand, leveled the shotgun, and except for thrashing wildly in pain, he made no move against me.

Up close and personal, Purcell appeared to be mid-forties to early fifties. An experienced enforcer, then. Kind of guy with some notches on his brass knuckles. He obviously took some pride in his position, because even as his jeans darkened with a river of blood, he set his lips in a hard line and didn't say a word.

"Remember me?" I said.

After a moment, he nodded.

"Spend the money yet?"

He shook his head.

"Shame, because that was the last shopping trip you had left. I want my daughter."

He didn't say a word.

So I placed the end of the shotgun against his right kneecap—the leg I hadn't incapacitated. "Say goodbye to your leg," I told him.

His eyes widened. His nostrils flared. Like a lot of tough guys, Purcell was better at dishing it out than taking it.

"Don't have her," he rasped out suddenly. "Not here."

"Let's see about that."

I ordered him to roll over on his stomach, hands behind his back. I had a pocketful of zip ties from Shane's supplies. I did Purcell's wrists first, then his ankles, though moving his injured left leg made him moan in pain.

I should feel something, I thought idly. Triumph, remorse, something. I felt nothing at all.

Best not to think about it.

Purcell was injured and restrained. Still, never underestimate the enemy. I patted down his pockets, discovering a pocketknife, a pager, and a dozen loose cartridges he'd stuck in his pants for emergency reloading. I removed all items and stuck them in my pockets instead.

Then, ignoring his grimace, I used my left arm to drag him several feet through the snow to the back stoop of his house, where I used a fresh zip tie to bind his arms to an outside faucet. With enough time and effort, he might be able to free himself, even break off the metal faucet, but I wasn't planning on leaving him that long. Besides, with his arms and legs bound and his hamstring severed, he wasn't making it that far, that fast.

My shoulder burned. I could feel blood pouring down my arm, inside my

shirt. It was an uncomfortable sensation, like getting water down your
sleeve. I had a vague impression that I
wasn't giving my injury proper significance. That probably, I hurt a great deal.
That probably, losing this much blood
was worse than a bit of water down a
sleeve.

I felt curiously flat. Beyond emotion
and the inconvenience of physical pain.

Best not to think about it.

I entered the house cautiously, knife
returned to its sheath, leading with the
shotgun. I had to cradle the barrel
against my left forearm. Given my condition, my aim would be questionable.
Then again, it was a shotgun.

Purcell hadn't turned on any lights.
Made sense, actually. When preparing
to dash out into the dark, turning on interior lights would only ruin your night
vision.

I entered a heavily shadowed kitchen
that smelled of garlic, basil, and olive oil.
Apparently, Purcell liked to cook. From
the kitchen, I passed into a family room
bearing two hulking recliners and a giant

TV. From that room, into a smaller den with a desk and lots of shelves. A small bathroom. Then, a long hallway that led to three open doorways.

I forced myself to breathe, walking as stealthily as possible toward the first doorway. I was just easing the door open wider when my pants began to chime. I ducked in immediately, sweeping the room with the shotgun, prepared to open fire on any lunging shapes, then flattening my back against the wall and bracing for the counterattack.

No shadows attacked. I dug my right hand frantically into my pocket and pulled out Purcell's pager, fumbling for the Off button.

At the last second, I glanced at the screen. It read. *Lyons DOA. BOLO Leoni.*

Shane Lyons was dead. Be on the lookout for Tessa Leoni.

"Too little, too late," I murmured. I jammed the pager back in my pocket and finished clearing the house.

Nothing. Nothing, nothing, nothing.

By all appearances, Purcell lived a bachelor life with a big screen TV, an extra bedroom, and a den. Then I saw the door to the basement.

Heart spiking again. Feeling the world tilt dizzily as I took the first step toward the closed door.

Blood loss. Getting weak. Should stop, tend the wound.

My hand on the knob, turning.

Sophie. All these days, all these miles.

I pulled open the door, stared down into the gloom.

39

By the time D.D. and Bobby arrived at Tessa Leoni's father's garage, they found the back door open, and the man in question slumped over a scarred workbench. D.D. and Bobby burst into the space, D.D. making a beeline for Mr. Leoni, while Bobby provided cover.

D.D. raised Leoni's face, inspecting him frantically for signs of injury, then recoiled from the stench of whiskey.

"Holy crap!" She let his head collapse back against his chest. His whole body slid left, off the stool, and would've hit the floor if Bobby hadn't appeared in time to catch him. Bobby eased the big man down, then rolled Leoni onto his side, to reduce the odds of the drunk drowning in his own vomit.

"Take his car keys," D.D. muttered in disgust. "We'll ask a patrol officer to come over and make sure he gets home safely."

Bobby was already going through Leoni's pockets. He found a wallet, but no keys. Then D.D. spied the Peg-Board with its collection of brass.

"Customers' keys?" she mused out loud.

Bobby came over to investigate. "Saw a bunch of old clunkers parked in the back," he murmured. "Bet he restores them for resell."

"Meaning, if Tessa wanted quick access to a vehicle . . ."

"Resourceful," Bobby commented.

D.D. looked down at Tessa's passed-out father, shook her head again. "He could've at least put up a fight, for God's sake."

"Maybe she brought him the Jack," Bobby said with a shrug, pointing to the empty bottle. He was an alcoholic; he knew these things.

"So she definitely has a vehicle. Description would be nice, but somehow I don't think Papa Leoni's talking anytime soon."

"Assuming this isn't a chop shop, Leoni should have papers on everything. Let's check it out."

Bobby gestured to the open door of a small back office. Inside, they found a tiny desk and a battered gray filing cabinet. In the back of the top file was a manila folder marked "Title Work."

D.D. pulled it and together they walked out of the garage, leaving the snoring drunk behind them. They identified three vehicles sequestered behind a chain link fence. The file held titles for four. By process of elimination, they determined that a 1993 dark blue Ford pickup truck was missing. Title listed it as having over two hundred thousand and eight miles.

"An oldie but a goodie," Bobby remarked, as D.D. got on the radio and called it in.

"License plate?" D.D. asked.

Bobby shook his head. "None of them have any."

D.D. looked at him. "Check the front street," she said.

He got what she meant, and jogged a quick tour around the block. Sure enough, half a block down, on the other side of the street, a car was missing both plates. Tessa had obviously pilfered from it to outfit her own ride.

Resourceful, he thought again, but also sloppy. She was racing against the clock, meaning she'd grabbed the nearest plates, instead of burning time with the safer option of snatching plates from a vehicle blocks away.

Meaning she was starting to leave a trail and they could use it to find her.

Bobby should feel good about that, but he felt mostly tired. He couldn't stop thinking what it must've been like, returning home from duty, walking through the front door, to discover a man holding her daughter hostage. *Give us your gun, no one will get hurt.*

Then the same man, shooting Brian Darby three times before disappearing with Tessa's little girl.

If Bobby had ever walked through the door, found someone with a gun at Annabelle's head, threatening his wife and child . . .

Tessa must've felt half-crazed with desperation and fear. She would've agreed to anything they wanted, while maintaining a cop's inherent mistrust. Knowing her cooperation would never be enough, of course they'd betray her first chance they got.

So she desperately needed to get one step ahead. Cover up her own husband's death to buy time. Plant a corpse with baby teeth and homemade explosives as a macabre backup plan.

Shane had originally stated Tessa had called him Sunday morning and requested that he beat her up. Except now they knew Shane had most likely been part of the problem. Made sense—a friend "helping" another friend would just smack her around a little, not deliver a concussion requiring an overnight hospital stay.

Meaning it had been Shane's idea to beat Tessa. How would that play out? *Let's drag your husband's dead body up from the garage to defrost. Then, I'm going to pound the shit out of you for kicks and giggles. Then, you'll call the police and claim you shot your dirtbag husband because he was going to kill you?*

They'd known she'd get arrested. Shane, at the very least, should've figured out how thin her story would sound, especially with Sophie missing and Brian's body having been artificially maintained on ice.

They'd wanted her arrested. They'd needed her behind bars.

It all came down to the money, Bobby thought again. Quarter mil missing from the troopers' union. Who'd stolen it? Shane Lyons? Someone higher in the food chain?

Someone smart enough to realize that sooner or later they'd have to supply a suspect before internal affairs grew too close.

Someone who realized that another discredited officer, a female, as seen on the bank security cameras—say, Tessa Leoni—would make the perfect sacrificial lamb. Plus, her husband had a known gambling problem, making her an even better candidate.

Brian died because his out-of-control habit made him a threat to everyone. And Tessa was packaged up with a bow and handed over to the powers that be as their own get-out-of-jail-free card. We'll say she stole the money, her husband gambled it away, and all will be accounted for. Investigation will be closed and we can ride off into the sunset, two hundred and fifty thousand dollars richer and no one the wiser.

Brian dead, Tessa behind bars, and Sophie . . .

Bobby wasn't ready to think about that. Sophie was a liability. Maybe kept alive in the short term, in case Tessa didn't go along with the plan. But in the long term . . .

Tessa was right to be on the warpath. She'd already lost one day to planning, one day to hospitalization, and one day to incarceration. Meaning this was it. She was running out of time. In the next few hours, she'd find her daughter, or die trying.

A lone trooper, going up against mobsters who thought nothing of breaking into police officers' homes and shooting their spouses.

Who would have the balls to do such a thing? And the access?

Russian mafia had sunk huge tentacles into the Boston area. They were widely acknowledged to be six times more ruthless than their Italian counterparts, and were swiftly becoming the lead players in all things corrupt, drug-fueled, and money-laundered. But a quarter mil defrauded from the state troopers' union sounded too small time in Bobby's mind.

The Russians preferred high risk, high payoff. Quarter mil was a rounding error in most of their undertakings. Plus, to steal from the state police, to actively summon the wrath of a powerful law enforcement agency upon your head . . .

It sounded more personal to Bobby. Mobsters wouldn't seek to embezzle from a troopers' union. They might, however, apply pressure to an insider who then determined that was the best way to produce the necessary funds. An insider with access to the money, but also with the knowledge and foresight to cover his own trail . . .

All of a sudden, Bobby knew. It horrified him. Chilled him to the bone. And made complete sense.

He raised his elbow and drove it through the passenger-side window of the parked car. Window shattered. Car alarm sounded. Bobby ignored both sounds. He reached inside, popped the glove compartment, and helped himself to the vehicle registration info, which included record of the license plate now adorning Tessa Leoni's truck.

Then he trotted back to D.D. and the garage, armed with new information as well as their final target.

40

People were brought down here to die.

I knew that from the smell alone. The deep, rusty scent of blood, so deeply soaked into the concrete floor, no amount of bleach or lime would ever make it go away. Some people had workshops in the basements of their homes. Apparently, John Stephen Purcell had a torture chamber.

I needed overhead light. It would destroy my night vision, but also disorient any gangsters waiting to pounce.

Standing on the top step, my hand on the left-hand wall switch, I hesitated. I didn't know if I wanted light in the basement. I didn't know if I wanted to see.

After hours of blessed numbness, my composure was starting to crack. The smell. My daughter. The smell. Sophie.

They wouldn't torture a little girl. What would they have to gain? What could Sophie possibly tell them?

I closed my eyes. Flipped up the switch. Then, I stood in the deep quiet that falls after midnight, and waited to hear the first whimper of my daughter waiting to be saved, or the rush of an attacker about to ambush.

I heard nothing at all.

I unpeeled my right eye, counted to five, then opened the left. The glare from the bare bulb didn't hurt as much as I'd feared. I kept the shotgun cradled in my arms, and dripping blood from my wounded right shoulder, I started to descend.

Purcell maintained a clutter-free basement. No stored lawn furniture or miscellaneous boxes of junk or bins of Christmas decorations for a man in his line of work.

The open space held a washer, dryer,

utility sink, and massive stainless steel table. The table was rimmed with a trough, just like the ones found in morgues. The trough led to a tray at the bottom of the table, where one could attach a hose to drain the contents into the nearby utility sink.

Apparently, when breaking kneecaps and slicing off fingertips, Purcell liked to be tidy. Judging by the large pink blush staining the floor, however, it was impossible to be totally spill-proof about these things.

Next to the stainless steel table was a battered TV tray bearing various instruments, laid out like a doctor's operating station. Each stainless steel piece was freshly cleaned, with an overhead light winking off the freshly sharpened blades.

I bet Purcell spent a lot of time staging his equipment just so. I bet he enjoyed letting his subjects take in the full array of instruments, their terrified minds already leaping ahead and doing half of his work for him. Then he would strap them to the table.

I imagined most of them started babbling before he picked up the first pair of pliers. And I bet talking didn't save them.

I passed the table, the sink, the washer and dryer. Behind the stairs I found a door leading to the utility room. I stood to one side, reaching around with my hand to pop the door open, with my back still pressed to the wall.

No one burst out. No child cried a greeting.

Still jittery from nerves, fatigue, and a low throbbing sense of dread, I crouched down, bringing up the shotgun to shoulder level, then darting into the gloom.

I encountered an oil tank, a water heater, the utility box, and a couple of plastic shelves weighed down with various cleaning products, zip ties, and coiled rope. And a thick coiled hose, perfect for spraying down the last of the mess.

I rose slowly to my feet, then surprised myself by swaying and nearly passing out.

The floor was wet. I looked down,

vaguely surprised to see a pool of my own blood. Pouring down my arm now.

Needed help. Should go to the ER. Should . . .

What, call the cavalry?

The bitterness of my thoughts pulled me back together. I left the basement, returning to the gloom upstairs, except this time I snapped on every light in the house.

As I suspected, I found a small battery of first-aid supplies in Purcell's bathroom. Guy in his line of work no doubt expected injuries he couldn't report, and had outfitted his medicine cabinet accordingly.

I couldn't pull my black turtleneck over my head. Instead, I used surgical shears to cut it off. Then, leaning over the sink, I poured the hydrogen peroxide straight into the bloody hole.

I gasped in shocked pain, then bit down hard on my lower lip.

If I were a true tough guy—say, Rambo—I would dig out the bullet with chopsticks, then stitch up the hole with dental floss. I didn't know how to do any of those things, so I shoved white gauze into the wound, then taped the bloody bundle with white strips of medical adhesive.

I washed down three ibuprofen with water, then helped myself to a dark blue flannel shirt from Purcell's closet. The shirt was two sizes too big and smelled of fabric softener and male cologne. The hem fell to midthigh and I had to roll up the cuffs awkwardly to free my hands.

I'd never worn the shirt of a man I was going to kill. It struck me as oddly intimate, like sprawling in bed in your lover's button-up Oxford after the first time you'd had sex.

I have gone too far, I thought, *lost some piece of myself.* I was looking for my daughter, but discovering an abyss I'd never known existed inside of me. Would finding Sophie ease the pain? Would the light of her love chase the darkness back again?

Did it even matter? From the moment she was born, I would've given my life for my child. What's a little sanity instead?

I picked up the shotgun, and retreated outside, where Purcell remained slumped against the house, eyes closed. I thought he'd passed out, but when my feet crunched through the snow, his eyes opened.

His face was pale. Sweat dotted his upper lip, despite the freezing temperature. He'd lost a lot of blood. He was probably dying and seemed to know it, though it didn't appear to surprise him.

Purcell was old school. Live by the sword, die by the sword.

That would make my next job tougher.

I squatted down beside him.

"I could take you down to the basement," I said.

He shrugged.

"Let you sample a taste of your own medicine."

He shrugged again.

"You're right: I'll bring the equipment up here. Save me the trouble of lugging your sorry ass around."

Another shrug. I wished suddenly that Purcell had a wife and kid. What would I do if he did? I didn't know, but I wanted to hurt him as much as he'd hurt me.

I placed the shotgun behind me, out

of Purcell's reach. Then I slid out the KA-BAR knife, hefting it lightly in the palm of my left hand.

Purcell's gaze flickered to the blade. Still, he said nothing.

"You're going to die by a woman's hand," I told him, and finally had the satisfaction of seeing his nostrils flare. Ego. Of course. Nothing hurt a man quite as much as being one-upped by a woman.

"Do you remember what you told me that morning in the kitchen?" I whispered. "You told me as long as I cooperated no one would get hurt. You told me as long as I handed over my service weapon, you'd let my family go. Then you turned and murdered my husband."

I ran the knife down the front of his shirt. The blade popped off the first button, the second, the third. Purcell wore a dark T-shirt underneath, topped by the requisite gold chain.

I planted the tip of the knife at the top of the thin cotton fabric and began to tear.

Purcell stared at the blade in rapt fascination. I could see his imagination kicking into gear, starting to realize everything such a large, well-honed blade could do to him. While he sat with his hands tied on his very own property. Helpless. Vulnerable.

"I'm not going to kill you," I said, slicing down the black T-shirt.

Purcell's eyes widened. He stared at me uncertainly.

"That's what you want, isn't it? Dying in the line of duty. A suitable end to an honorable gangster."

Last shirt button. Pop. Last inch of T-shirt. Shred.

I used the blade to peel back his shirts. His stomach was unexpectedly pale, a little thicker around the waist, but defined. He trained. Not a big guy. Maybe a boxer. He understood fitness mattered in his line of work. Got to have some muscle to lug unconscious bodies down to the basement and strap them to the table.

Gotta have some size to snatch a struggling six-year-old girl.

The knife eased back his shirts, exposing his left side. I stared at his bare shoulder in fascination. The goose pimples that rippled across his flesh in the cold. The way his nipple formed a round bud right over his heart.

"You shot my husband here," I murmured, and I used the blade to mark the spot. Blood welled up, forming a perfect red X against Purcell's skin. The razor-sharp blade made for a nice, clean cut. Shane had always taken his equipment seriously.

"Next shot was right here." I moved the blade again. Maybe I cut deeper this time, because Purcell hissed low, quivering beneath me.

"Third shot, right here." This time, I definitely went deep. When I raised the KA-BAR knife, the blood welled at the edge of the blade and dripped down onto Purcell's stomach.

Blood in the clean white snow.

Brian dying in the clean bright kitchen.

The mobster was shaking now. I gazed into his face. I let him see the death in my eyes. I let him see the killer he helped make.

"Here's the deal," I informed him. "Tell me where my daughter is, and in return, I'll remove your restraints. I'm not giving you a knife or anything that crazy, but you can take a shot at me. Maybe you can overpower me, in which case, my bad. Maybe you can't. In which case, at least you go down swinging instead of dying trussed up like a pig in your own front yard. You have until the count of five to decide. *One.*"

"I don't snitch," Purcell snarled.

I shrugged, reached up, and mostly because I felt like it, lopped off a giant piece of his thick brown hair. *"Two."*

He flinched, didn't back down. "Gonna fucking kill me anyway."

Another section of hair, maybe even a bit of ear. *"Three."*

"Fucking cunt."

"Stick and stones may break my bones . . ." I wadded up a big fistful of dark hair at the top of his forehead. Getting into the spirit of things now, I pulled up hard, so I could see his scalp lift. *"Four."*

"I don't have your daughter!" Purcell exploded. "Don't do kids. Told them in the beginning, don't do kids."

"Then where is she?"

"You're the fucking cop. Don't you think you should know?"

I whacked with the blade. I got a lot of hair and definitely some scalp. Blood bubbled up red. Dripped onto the icy ground, turned pink against the snow.

I wondered if I would ever make it through another winter, where fresh snowfall wouldn't make me want to vomit.

Purcell howled, shuddering against his restraints. "You trusted all the wrong people. Now you hurt me? I did you a favor! Your husband was no good. Your police officer friend even worse. How'd I even get into your house, you stupid cunt? Think your old man would just let me in?"

I stopped. I stared at him. And I realized, in that instant, the one piece of the puzzle I'd been missing. I'd been so overwhelmed by the trauma of Saturday morning, I'd never contemplated the logistics. I'd never analyzed the scene as a cop.

For example, Brian already knew he was in trouble. His weight lifting, the recent purchase of the Glock .40. His own jumpy mood and short temper. He knew he'd waded in too deep. And yeah, he'd never open the door to a man like John Stephen Purcell, especially with Sophie in the house.

Except Sophie hadn't been in the house when I'd returned home.

She was already gone. Purcell had been standing in the kitchen alone, holding Brian at gunpoint. Sophie had already been taken, by a second person who must've come with Purcell. Someone Brian would feel safe greeting at the door. Someone who had access to the troopers' pension. Who knew Shane. Who felt powerful enough to control all the parties involved.

My face must have paled, because Purcell started to laugh. The sound rattled in his chest.

"See? I tell the truth," he growled. "I'm not the problem. The men in your life are."

Purcell laughed again, the blood dripping down his face and making him look as crazy as I felt. We were two peas in a pod, I realized abruptly. Soldiers in the war, to be used, abused, and betrayed by the generals involved.

Others made the decisions. We just paid the price.

I set the knife down behind me, beside the shotgun. My right arm throbbed. Using it so much had caused the gunshot wound to bleed again. I could feel fresh moisture trickling down my arm. More pink stains in the snow.

Not much longer now, I knew. And like Purcell, I was not afraid. I was resigned to my fate.

"Trooper Lyons is dead," I said.

Purcell stopped laughing.

"Turns out, you killed him two hours ago."

Purcell thinned his lips. He was no fool.

From the back waistband of my pants, I pulled out a .22 semiauto I'd found taped to the back of the toilet tank in Purcell's bathroom. Strictly a backup weapon for a guy like him, but it would still get the job done.

"I'm guessing this is a black market weapon," I stated. "Serial number filed off. Untraceable."

"You promised a fair fight," Purcell said suddenly.

"And you promised to let my husband go. Guess we're both liars."

I leaned close. "Who do you love?" I whispered in the bloody snow.

"No one," he replied tiredly. "Never did."

I nodded, unsurprised. Then I shot him. Double tap to the left temple, classic gangland hit. Next, I picked up the KA-BAR knife and matter-of-factly carved the word "snitch" into the dead man's skin. Had to obliterate the three Xs I'd formed earlier in his chest, which would've led a savvy detective such as D. D. Warren straight to my doorstep.

My face felt strange. Hard. Grim, even for me. I reminded myself of that tidy basement with its lingering scents of bleach and blood, of the pain Purcell would've happily inflicted upon me, if I'd given him the chance. It didn't help. I was meant to be a cop, not a killer. And each act of violence took something from me that I would not get back again.

But I kept moving, because like any woman, I was good at self-inflicted pain.

Final details: I retrieved Brian's Glock .40 from my duffel bag and wrapped Purcell's right hand around the pistol grip to transfer his prints. Purcell's .22 went into my duffel bag, to be tossed in the first river I passed. The Glock .40 went inside Purcell's house, taped to the back of the toilet as he'd done with the first firearm.

Sometime after the sun rose, the police would find Purcell's body tied to the house, obviously tortured, now deceased. They would search his house, they would discover his basement, and that would answer half their questions— a guy in Purcell's line of work was bound to die badly.

While searching Purcell's house, they would also discover Brian's Glock .40. Ballistics would match the slug that killed police officer Shane Lyons to that firearm, providing a theory that Purcell had once entered my home and stolen my husband's gun, which he later used to kill a highly respected state trooper.

Purcell's murder would go to the back burner—just another thug meeting a violent end. Shane would be buried with full honors and his family would receive benefits.

The police would search for the weapon that shot Purcell, of course. Wonder about his murderer. But not all questions were meant to be answered.

Just like not all people were meant to be trusted.

One-seventeen a.m. I staggered to my feet, made my way back to the truck. I downed two bottles of water and ate two power bars. Right shoulder burned. Tingling in my fingers. A hollow sensation in my gut. A curious numbness to the set of my lips.

Then I was on the road again, shotgun on my lap, bloody hands at the wheel.

Sophie, here I come.

41

"It's Hamilton," Bobby said, pulling D.D. out of Leoni's garage and already jogging back to their car.

"Hamilton?" D.D. narrowed her eyes. "As in State Police Lieutenant Colonel?"

"Yep. Has access, has opportunity, and knows all the players involved. Maybe Brian's gambling problem started the ball rolling, but Hamilton was the brains of the operation—*You guys need money? Hey, I happen to know where there's a huge pot of cash, just sitting there...*"

"Between him and Shane..." D.D.

murmured. She nodded, feeling the first tinge of excitement A name, a suspect, a target. She climbed into the car and Bobby pulled away from the curb, already racing toward the highway.

"Yep," he said now. "Easy enough to work out the logistics of setting up a shell company, with Hamilton pulling strings to cover their tracks from the inside. Except, of course, all good things must come to an end."

"Once the internal investigation kicks into gear . . ."

"Their days are numbered," Bobby filled in for her. "They have state investigators sniffing around, plus, thanks to Shane and Brian continuing to gamble excessively, they also have various mobsters wanting a piece of the pie. Hamilton, of course, grows concerned. And Brian and Shane go from being partners in crime to highly expendable liabilities."

"Hamilton killed Brian, then kidnapped Sophie so Tessa would confess to shooting her own husband and be framed for defrauding the troopers' union?" D.D. frowned, then added, "Or an enforcer did it. The kind of mobster Brian had already pissed off. The kind of guy willing to do one last piece of wet work in order to get his money back."

"The kind of guy who'd mail photos of Shane's family as a warning," Bobby agreed.

"That's the thing about the brass," D.D. said with a shake of her head. "They're big on ideas, but don't like to get their own hands dirty during implementation." She hesitated. "Following that logic, where is Sophie? Would Hamilton risk personally holding a six-year-old girl?"

"Don't know," Bobby said. "But I'm betting if we drop on him like a ton of bricks, we can find that out. He should be downtown, at the scene of Lyons's shooting, hanging out with the colonel and other brass."

D.D. nodded, then suddenly grabbed Bobby's arm. "He's not downtown. Bet you anything."

"Why not?"

"Because Tessa is on the loose. We know it. He knows it. Furthermore, he would've heard by now that Trooper

Lyons's shotgun and M4 rifle are missing. Meaning he knows Tessa is armed, dangerous, and desperate to locate her daughter."

"He's on the run," Bobby filled in, "from his own officer." But then it was his turn to shake his head. "Nah, not a guy as experienced and wily as Hamilton. Best defense is a good offense, right? He's going for Sophie. If she's still alive, he's gonna get his hands on her. She's the only bargaining chip he's got left."

"So where's Sophie?" D.D. asked again. "We've had a statewide Amber Alert for three days. Her picture is plastered all over the TV, her description on the radio. If the girl's around, we should've gotten a lead by now."

"Meaning she's someplace buttoned up tight," Bobby mused. "Rural, no close neighbors. With someone assigned to keep her under lock and key. So a place that is inaccessible, but well supplied. A location Hamilton trusts not to be compromised."

"He'd never stash Sophie in his own house," D.D. said. "Too close to him.

Maybe she's at a friend of a friend? Or a second home? We saw the pictures of him hunting deer. Does he have a hunting lodge, a cabin in the woods?"

Bobby suddenly smiled. "Bingo. Hamilton has a hunting cabin near Mount Greylock in western Mass. Two and half hours away from state headquarters, tucked in the foothills of the Berkshires. Isolated, containable, and distant enough to provide him with plausible deniability—even if he owns it, he can say he hasn't been there in days or weeks, particularly given all the activity that's required his attention in Boston."

"Can you get us there?" D.D. asked immediately.

Bobby hesitated. "I've been there a couple of times, but years ago. Sometimes he invites troopers over for hunting weekends, that kind of thing. I can picture the roads . . ."

"Phil," D.D. stated, pulling out her cellphone. "You get on the Pike. I'll get us the address."

Bobby hit the lights, roaring for the Mass Pike, the quickest route for cutting across the state. D.D. dialed BPD headquarters. It was after midnight, but no-body in the state or Boston force was sleeping tonight; Phil answered on the first ring.

"You heard about Trooper Lyons?" Phil stated in way of greeting.

"Already been there. Got a sensitive request for you. Want full background on Gerard Hamilton. Search under his family members' names, too. I want all known property addresses, and after that, a full financial workup."

There was a pause. "You mean the lieutenant colonel of the state police?" Phil asked carefully.

"Told you it was sensitive."

D.D. heard a tapping sound. Phil's fingers, already flying across the computer keyboard.

"Ummm, if you want some unofficial info, not even water cooler talk, more like urinal gossip . . ." Phil started, as he typed away.

"By all means," D.D. assured him.

"Heard Hamilton's got himself a mistress. A hot Italian spitfire."

"Name?"

"Haven't a clue. Guy only mentioned her . . . derriere."

"Men are pigs."

"Personally, I'm a pig who's in love with his wife and needs her to survive four kids, so don't look at me."

"True," D.D. granted. "Start digging, Phil. Tell me what I need to know, because we think he might have Sophie Leoni."

D.D. hung up. Bobby came to the exit for the Mass Pike. He careened up it at seventy miles per hour and they went squealing around the corner. Roads were finally clear of snow and there wasn't much traffic at this time of night. Bobby hit one hundred on the broad, flat highway as they soared toward western Mass. They had a hundred and thirty miles to cover, give or take, D.D. thought, not all of which could be traveled at top speed. Two hours, she decided. Two hours till finally rescuing Sophie Leoni.

"Do you think she's a good cop?" Bobby asked suddenly.

D.D. didn't have to ask who he was talking about. "I don't know."

Bobby took his gaze off the fast flying darkness just long enough to glance at her. "How far would you go?" he asked softly, his eyes dropped to her belly. "If it were your child, how far would you go?"

"I hope I never have to find out."

"Because I would kill them all," Bobby said flatly, his hands flexing and unflexing on the wheel. "If someone threatened Annabelle, kidnapped Carina. There wouldn't be enough ammo left in this state for what I would do to them."

D.D. didn't doubt him for a minute, but she still shook her head.

"It's not right, Bobby," she said quietly. "Even if you're provoked, even if the other guy started it . . . Criminals resort to violence. We're cops. We're supposed to know better. If we can't live up to that standard . . . Well then, who can?"

They drove in silence after that, listening to the throaty growl of a flat-out engine and watching city lights wink by like bolts of lightning.

Sophie, D.D. thought, *here we come.*

42

Lieutenant Colonel Gerard Hamilton was my commanding officer, but I would never say I knew him well. For one thing, he was several levels above me in the food chain. For another, he was a guy's guy. When he did hang out with the troopers, it was with Shane, and he often included Shane's partner in crime, my husband, Brian.

They'd catch Red Sox games, maybe a hunting weekend, or a field trip to Foxwoods.

In hindsight, it all made perfect sense.

Shane's little excursions. My husband tagging along. Hamilton, too.

Meaning, when Brian started to gamble too much, get in too deep . . . Who would know how badly he needed money? Who would know another option for getting rich quick? Who would be in the perfect position to prey on my husband's weakness?

Shane had never been big in the brains department. Lieutenant Colonel Hamilton, however . . . He'd know how to bring Shane and Brian along. Skim a little here, then a little there. It's amazing how people can rationalize doing bad things when at first you start out small.

For example, I didn't plan on killing Shane when I got out of jail, or murdering a gangster named John Stephen Purcell, or driving through the freezing night to my superior officer's hunting cabin with a shotgun on my lap.

Maybe Brian and Shane told themselves they were merely "borrowing" that money. As union rep, Shane would know all about the pension account and available balance. Hamilton probably knew how to get access, what kind of shell company would be most appropriate for defrauding retired state cops. In the old boys' network, it was probably a matter of a single phone call.

They'd set up a dummy company and they were off and running, billing the pension fund, collecting the funds, and hitting the tables.

How long had they planned on running the racket? A month? Six months? A year? Maybe they didn't think that far ahead. Maybe it hadn't mattered to them at the time. Eventually, of course, internal affairs had figured out the fraud and launched an investigation. Unfortunately for Brian and Shane, once such an investigation started, it didn't end until the taskforce got answers.

Is that when Hamilton had decided to turn me into the sacrificial lamb? Or had that been part of the domino effect? When, even after stealing from the troopers' pension, Brian and Shane had continued to be short on funds, borrowing from the wrong players until they had both internal investigators and mob enforcers breathing down their necks?

At some point, Hamilton had realized

that Shane and Brian might crack under the pressure, might confess their crimes to save their own necks and deliver up Hamilton on a platter.

Of the two, Brian was definitely the bigger liability. Maybe Hamilton had negotiated a final deal for the mob. He'd pay off the last of Brian and Shane's bad debts. In return, they'd eliminate Brian and help frame me for all the crimes.

Shane would remain alive but too terrified to speak, while Hamilton and his cohorts could keep their illicit gains.

Brian would be dead. I would be in prison. Sophie . . . well, once I'd done everything they asked, they wouldn't need her anymore, would they?

So my family would be destroyed, for Shane's survival and Hamilton's greed.

The rage helped keep me awake as I drove three hours west, toward Adams, Mass., where I knew Hamilton kept a second home. I'd been there only once, for a fall barbecue several years ago.

I remembered the log cabin as being small and isolated. Perfect for hiking, hunting, and holding a young child.

The fingers on my right hand wouldn't

work anymore. The bleeding had finally slowed, but I suspected the bullet had damaged tendons, maybe even nerves. Now inflammation had further compromised the injury and I couldn't form a fist. Or pull a trigger.

I would proceed left-handed. With any luck, Hamilton wasn't around. One of his officers had been killed in the line of duty tonight, meaning Hamilton should be in Allston-Brighton, tending to official matters.

I would park at the bottom of the long dirt drive that led to the cabin. I would hike in through the woods, bringing the shotgun, which I could fire left-handed from my hip. Aim would be lousy, but that was the joy of a shotgun—impact area was so large, your aim didn't have to be any good.

I would scope out the cabin, I rehearsed in my mind. Discover it deserted. Use the butt of the shotgun to break out a window. Climb in, then locate my daughter sound asleep in a darkened bedroom.

I would rescue her and we would run away together. Maybe flee to Mexico, though the sensible thing would be to head straight back to BPD headquarters. Sophie could testify that Hamilton had kidnapped her. Further investigation into the lieutenant colonel's affairs would reveal a bank balance far greater than it had any right to be. Hamilton would be arrested. Sophie and I would be safe.

We would move on with our lives and never be frightened again. Someday, she'd stop asking for Brian. And someday I'd stop mourning him.

I needed to believe it would be that easy.

I hurt too badly for it to be otherwise.

Four thirty-two in the morning, I found the dirt road that led to Hamilton's cabin. Four forty-one, I pulled off the road and parked behind a snow-covered bush.

I climbed out of the car.

Thought I smelled smoke.

I hefted up the shotgun.

And heard my daughter scream.

43

Bobby and D.D. had just turned off the Mass Pike for the dark ribbon of rural US 20 when her cellphone rang. The loud chime jerked D.D. out of her groggy state. She hit answer, held the phone to her ear. It was Phil.

"D.D., you still headed west?"

"Already here."

"Okay, Hamilton has two property addresses. First one's in Framingham, Mass., near state HQ. I'm assuming the primary home, as it's listed jointly under Gerard and Judy Hamilton. But there's a second home, in Adams, Mass., solely under his name."

"Address?" D.D. demanded crisply.

Phil rattled it off. "But get this: Police scanner just picked up a report of a residential fire in Adams, near the Mount Greylock State Reservation. Maybe it's a coincidence? Or possibly Hamilton's cabin is the one on fire."

"Shit!" D.D. jerked to attention, fully awake. "Phil, contact local authorities. I want backup. County and town officers, but no state troopers." Bobby shot her a look, but didn't argue. "Now!" she stated urgently, ending the call, then immediately plugging the Hamilton's address into the vehicle's navigation system.

"Phil got us the address, which apparently is near the scene of a fire."

"Dammit!" Bobby pounded the steering wheel with his hand. "Hamilton's already there and covering his tracks!"

"Not if we have anything to say about it."

44

Sophie screamed again, and I jerked into action. I grabbed both the shotgun and the rifle, pouring shotgun shells and rounds of .223 ammo into my pants pockets. The fingers on my right hand moved sluggishly, dumping more ammo onto the snow-covered ground than into my pockets. I didn't have time to pick it up. I moved, relying on adrenaline and desperation to get the job done.

Weighed down with a small arsenal of weapons and ammo, I careened into the snowy woods, heading toward the smell of smoke and the sound of my daughter.

Another scream. An adult cursing. The sizzling sound of wet wood catching flame.

Cabin was straight up. I bounced from tree to tree, struggling for footing in the fresh snow, breathing shallowly. Didn't know how many people might be present. Needed the advantage of surprise if Sophie and I were going to get through this. Don't give away my position, find the higher ground.

My professional training counseled a strategic approach, while my parental instincts screamed for me to charge in and grab my daughter *now, now, now.* The air grew denser with smoke. I coughed, feeling my eyes burn as I finally crested a small knoll on the left side of the property. I discovered Hamilton's cabin on fire and my daughter struggling with a woman in a thick black parka. The woman was trying to drag Sophie into a parked SUV. My daughter, wearing nothing but the thin pink pajamas I'd put her to bed in four nights ago and still clutching her favorite doll, Gertrude, was thrashing wildly.

Sophie bit the woman's exposed

wrist. The woman jerked back her arm and slapped her. My daughter's head rocked sideways. She stumbled, sprawling backward into the snow and coughing raggedly from the smoke.

"No, no, no," my daughter was crying. "Let me go. I want my mommy. *I want my mommy!*"

Shotgun on the ground—couldn't risk it with my child so close to the target. Finding the rifle instead, yanking out the magazine, fumbling in my left pocket. Always load an M4's stack magazine minus two in order to keep it feeding evenly, my police training dictated.

Kill them all, my mother's instinct roared.

I hefted up the rifle, racked the first round.

Fresh blood oozing from my shoulder. Sluggish fingers curling laboriously around the trigger.

The woman towered over Sophie. "Get in the car, you stupid little brat," she screeched.

"Let me go!"

Another scream. Another smack.

Anchoring the butt of the assault rifle

against my bleeding shoulder and sight-ing the dark-haired woman now beating my child.

Sophie crying, arms curled around her head, trying to block the blows.

I stepped clear of the woods. Zeroed in on my target.

"Sophie!" I called out loudly across the crackling, acrid night. "Sophie. *Run!*"

As I'd hoped, the unexpected sound of my voice captured their attention. So-phie turned around. The woman jerked sharply upright, trying to pinpoint the in-truder.

She looked right at me. "Who the—"

I pulled the trigger.

Sophie never glanced behind her. At the body that dropped suddenly, at the head that exploded beneath the on-slaught of a .223 slug and turned into a puddle of crimson snow.

My daughter never turned. She heard my voice and she ran to me.

Just as a gun cocked in my ear, and Gerard Hamilton said, "You fucking bitch."

D.D. and Bobby followed the GPS system through a winding maze of rural roads, until they came to a narrow dirt road lined by fire trucks and grim-faced firefighters. Bobby killed the lights. He and D.D. bolted out of the car, flashing their creds.

News was short and bad.

Firefighters had arrived just in time to hear screams followed by gunshots. Residential home was an eighth of a mile straight up, surrounded by deep woods. Judging by smoke and heat, the building was probably fully engulfed in flames. Firefighters were now waiting for police to secure the scene, so they could get in there and do their thing. Waiting was not something any of them were good at, particularly as one of the guys swore the screaming came from a kid.

Bobby told D.D. to stay in the car.

In response, D.D. stalked to the rear of her vehicle, where she donned her Kevlar vest, then pulled out the shotgun. She handed the rifle to Bobby. After all, he was the former sniper.

He scowled at her. "I go first. Recon," he snapped.

"I'll give you six minutes," she retorted just as sharply.

Bobby donned his vest, loaded the M4, and walked the edge of the steep property. Thirty seconds later, he disappeared into the snowy woods. And three minutes after that, D.D. hit the trail right behind him.

More sirens in the distance.

Local officers finally arriving at the scene.

D.D. focused on following Bobby's footsteps.

Smoke, heat, snow. A winter inferno.

Time to find Sophie. Time to get the job done.

Hamilton yanked the rifle from my injured arm. The M4 fell bonelessly from my grasp and he scooped it up. The shotgun was at my feet. He ordered me to pick it up, hand it over.

From the top of the knoll, I could see Sophie running toward me, sprinting across the property below, framed in white-dusted trees and bright red flames.

While the barrel of Hamilton's gun dug into the sensitive hollow behind my ear.

I started to bend down. Hamilton relented an inch to give me room, and I hurled myself backward into him, yelling wildly, "Sophie, get away! Into the woods. Get away, get away, get away!"

"Mommy!" she screamed, a hundred yards back.

Hamilton pistol-whipped me with his Sig Sauer. I went down hard, my right arm collapsing beneath me. More searing pain. Maybe the sound of something tearing. I had no time to recover. Hamilton hit me again, looming over me, slicing open my cheek, my forehead. Blood pouring down into my face, blinding my eyes as I curled up in the fetal position in the snow.

"You should've done what you were told!" he screamed. He was wearing his dress uniform, topped with a knee-length black wool coat, his wide-brimmed hat pulled low over his eyes. Probably donned the ensemble upon receiving news that an officer had been killed in the line of duty. Then, when he realized it was Shane, and that I'd escaped, was still on the loose . . .

He'd come to get my daughter. Dressed in the official uniform of a Massachusetts State Police lieutenant colonel, he'd come to harm a child.

"You were a trained police officer," he snapped now, looming over me, blocking out the trees, the fire, the night sky. "If you'd just done what you were told, no one would've gotten hurt!"

"Except Brian," I managed to gasp. "You arranged his death."

"His gambling problem was out of control. I did you a favor."

"You kidnapped my daughter. You sent me to prison. Just to make a few extra bucks."

In response, my commanding officer kicked me full-force in the left kidney, the kind of kick that would have me peeing up blood, assuming I lived that long.

"Mommy, Mommy!" Sophie cried again. I realized with horror that her voice was closer. She was still running toward my voice, clambering over the snowbank.

No, I wanted to cry. *Save yourself, get away.*

But my voice wouldn't work anymore. Hamilton had knocked the air from my lungs. My eyes burned with smoke, tears pouring down my face as I gasped and heaved against the snow. Shoulder burned. Stomach cramped.

Black dots dancing before me.

Had to move. Had to get up. Had to fight. For Sophie.

Hamilton reared back with his foot again. He lashed out to hit me square in the chest. This time, I dropped my left arm, caught his foot midkick, and rolled. Caught off guard, Hamilton was jerked forward, falling to one knee in the snow.

So he stopped hitting me with the Sig Sauer and pulled the trigger instead.

The sound deafened me. I felt immediate searing heat, followed by immediate searing pain. My left side. My hand falling down, clutching my waist, as my gaze went up, toward my commanding officer, a man I'd been trained to trust.

Hamilton appeared stunned. Maybe

even a little shaken, but he recovered quickly enough, finger back on the trigger.

Just as Sophie crested the knoll and spotted us.

I had a vision. My daughter's pale, sweet face. Her hair a wild tangle of knots. Her eyes, a bright, brilliant blue as her gaze locked on me. Then she was running, the way only a six-year-old could run, and Hamilton did not exist for her and the woods did not exist for her, nor the scary fire, or the threat of night or the unknown terrors that must have tormented her for days.

She was a little girl who'd finally found her mother and she tore straight toward me, one hand clutching Gertrude, the other arm flung open as she threw herself on top of me and I groaned from both the pain and the joy that burst inside my chest.

"I love you I love you I love you," I exhaled.

"Mommy, Mommy, Mommy, Mommy, Mommy."

"Sophie, Sophie, Sophie . . ."

I could feel her tears hot against my

face. It hurt, but I still brought up my hand, cradling the back of her head. I looked at Hamilton, and then I tucked my daughter's face into the crook of my neck. "Sophie," I whispered, never taking my gaze off him, "close your eyes."

My daughter clung to me, two halves of a whole, finally together again.

She closed her eyes.

And I said, in the clearest voice I could muster, "Do it."

The darkness behind Hamilton materialized into a man. At my command, he raised his rifle. Just as Hamilton placed the barrel of his Sig Sauer against my left temple.

I concentrated on the feel of my daughter, the weight of her body, the purity of her love. Something to carry with me into the abyss.

"You should've done what I said," Hamilton hissed above me.

While in the next heartbeat, Bobby Dodge pulled the trigger.

45

By the time D.D. made it to the top of the property, Hamilton was down and Bobby stood over the lieutenant colonel's body. He looked up at her approach and shook his head once.

Then she heard crying.

Sophie Leoni. It took D.D. a second to spot the child's small, pink-clad form. She was on the ground, covering another dark-clad figure, skinny arms tangled around her mother's neck as the girl sobbed wildly.

Bobby dropped to one knee beside

the pair as D.D. approached. He placed his hand on Sophie's shoulder.

"Sophie," he said quietly. "Sophie, I need you to look at me. I'm a state policeman, like your mother. I'm here to help her. Please look at me."

Sophie finally raised her tearstained face. She spotted D.D. and opened her mouth as if to scream. D.D. shook her head.

"It's okay, it's okay. My name is D.D. I'm a friend of your mom's, too. Your mom led us here, to help you."

"Mommy's boss took me away," Sophie said clearly. "Mommy's boss gave me to the bad woman. I said no. I said I wanted to go home! I said I wanted Mommy!"

Her face dissolved again. She started to cry, soundlessly this time, still pressed against her mother's unmoving body.

"We know," D.D. said, crouching down beside them, placing a tentative hand on the girl's back. "But your mother's boss and the bad woman can't hurt you anymore, okay, Sophie? We're here, and you're safe."

To judge by the look on Sophie's face,

she didn't believe them. D.D. couldn't blame her.

"Are you hurt?" Bobby asked.

The girl shook her head.

"What about your mommy?" D.D. asked. "Can we check her, make sure she is okay?"

Sophie moved slightly to one side, enough so D.D. could see the dark stain on the left side of Tessa's dark flannel shirt, the red blood in the snow. Sophie saw it, too. The girl's lower lip started to tremble. She didn't say another word. She simply lay down in the snow beside her unconscious mother and held her hand.

"Come back, Mommy," the girl said mournfully. "Love you. Come back."

Bobby scrambled down the slope for the EMTs.

While D.D. peeled off her own coat and used it to cover both mother and child.

Tessa regained consciousness as the EMTs went to load her. Her eyes popped open, she gasped sharply, then reached out frantically. The EMTs tried to hold her down. So D.D. did the sensible thing, grabbing Sophie and lifting the child onto the edge of the gurney.

Tessa clutched her daughter's arm, squeezed hard. D.D. thought Tessa might be crying, or maybe it was the tears in her own eyes. She couldn't be sure.

"I love you," Tessa whispered to her daughter.

"Love you more, Mommy. Love you more."

The EMTs wouldn't let Sophie remain on the gurney. Tessa required immediate medical attention and the child would only be in the way. After thirty seconds of negotiation, it was determined that Sophie would ride in the front of the ambulance, while her mother was tended in the back. The EMTs, moving quickly, started to hustle the girl to the front.

She twisted around them long enough to race back to her mother, and tuck something beside her, then ran for the passenger's seat.

When D.D. looked again, Sophie's

one-eyed doll was tucked beside Tessa's unmoving form. The EMTs loaded her up.

The ambulance whisked them away.

D.D. stood in the middle of the snowy dawn, hand on her own stomach. She smelled smoke. She tasted tears.

She looked up to the woods, where a fire was now burning down to ash. Hamilton's last bid attempt to cover his tracks, which had cost both him and his female companion their lives.

D.D. wanted to feel triumphant. They'd saved the girl, they'd vanquished the evil foe. Now, except for a few days of excruciating paperwork, they should be riding off in the sunset.

It wasn't enough.

For the first time in a dozen years, D. D. Warren had reached the successful conclusion of a case, and it wasn't enough. She didn't feel like reporting the good news to her superiors, or supplying self-gratifying answers to the press, or even grabbing a couple of beers to wind down with her taskforce.

She wanted to go home. She wanted to curl up with Alex and inhale the scent of his aftershave, and feel the familiar comfort of his arms around her. And she wanted, heaven help her, to still be at his side the first time the baby moved, and be looking into his eyes when the first contraction hit, and be holding his hand when their baby slid into the world.

She wanted a little girl or a little boy who would love her as much as Sophie Leoni obviously loved her mother. And she wanted to return that love tenfold, to feel it grow bigger and bigger every single year, just as Tessa had said.

D.D. wanted a family.

She had to wait ten hours. Bobby couldn't work—having used deadly force, he was forced to sit on the side-lines and await the arrival of the firearms discharge investigation team, which would formally investigate the incident. Meaning D.D. was on her own as she notified her boss of the latest develop-ments, then secured the scene and be-gan processing the outer fringes, while waiting for the last embers of the fire to cool. More officers and evidence techs arrived. More questions to answer, more bodies to manage.

She worked through breakfast. Bobby brought her yogurt and a peanut butter sandwich for lunch. She worked. She smelled of smoke and sweat, of blood and ash.

Dinner came and went. Sun set again. The life of a homicide detective.

She did what she had to do. She tended what needed tending.

And then, finally, she was done.

Scene was secured, Tessa had been airlifted to a Boston hospital, and Sophie remained safely at her mother's side.

D.D. got in her car and headed back to the Mass Pike.

She phoned Alex just as she reached Springfield. He was cooking chicken parm and delighted to hear she was finally coming home.

She asked if he could change the chicken parm to an eggplant parm.

He wanted to know why.

Which made her laugh, then made her cry, and she couldn't get the words out. So she told him she missed him and he promised her all the eggplant parm in the world, and that, D.D. thought, was love. His love. Her love. Their love.

"Alex," she finally managed to gasp. "Hey, Alex. Forget dinner. I've got something I need to tell you. . . ."

I was in the hospital for nearly two weeks. I got lucky. Hamilton's shot was a through and through that missed most major organs. Hit man Purcell, however, had been a pro to the bitter end. He'd shattered my rotator cuff, resulting in numerous surgeries and endless months of PT. I'm told I'll never regain full range of movement in my right shoulder, but I should get finger function back once the swelling goes down.

I guess we'll find out.

Sophie stayed with me in the hospital. She wasn't supposed to. Hospital policy said children should only be there during visiting hours. Within hours of my arrival, Mrs. Ennis had received word and shown up to assist. But she couldn't peel Sophie off me, and after another ten minutes, the head nurse waved her off.

Sophie needed her mother. I needed Sophie.

So they let us be, two girls in our private room, an unbelievable luxury. We slept together, ate together, and watched SpongeBob Squarepants together. Our own little form of therapy.

Day nine or so, we took a little walk to my former hospital room, where lo and behold, tucked in the back of the bottom drawer, we found Gertrude's missing button eye.

I sewed it on that afternoon with surgical thread, and Sophie made Gertrude her own hospital bed for recovery.

Gertrude would be okay, she informed me solemnly. Gertrude had been a very brave girl.

We watched more SpongeBob after that, and I kept my arm around my little girl and her head upon my shoulder even though it ached.

The hospital arranged for a pediatric psych specialist to visit with Sophie. She wouldn't talk about her captivity and hadn't mentioned Brian's name at all.

The doctor advised me to keep "the channels of communication open" and to let Sophie come to me. When she was ready, the doctor said, she would talk. And when she did, I must keep my face neutral and my comments non-judgmental.

I thought this was funny advice to give a woman who'd committed three murders to save her daughter, but I didn't volunteer that.

I held Sophie. We slept, by mutual consent, with the lights on, and when she drew pictures filled with black night, red flames, and exploding guns, I complimented her level of detail and promised to teach her how to shoot the moment my arm healed.

Sophie liked that idea very much.

Detectives D. D. Warren and Bobby Dodge returned. They brought Mrs. Ennis with them, who took Sophie to the hospital cafeteria so I could answer the last of their questions.

No, Brian had never hit me. My bruised ribs were because I had fallen down icy steps, and, being late for patrol, tended the injury myself. Shane, however, had beat me on Sunday morning, in an attempt to make it look like Brian's death was self-defense.

No, I didn't know Trooper Lyons had been shot. What a terrible tragedy for his family. Did they have any leads at this time?

They showed me photos of a thin-faced man with blazing dark eyes and thick brown hair. Yes, I recognized the man as the one I'd discovered in my kitchen on Saturday morning, holding my husband at gunpoint. He'd told me that if I would cooperate, no one would get hurt. So I had taken off my duty belt; at which time, he'd pulled my Sig Sauer and shot my husband three times in the chest.

Purcell then explained that if I wanted to see my daughter alive again, I had to do exactly what he said.

No, I'd never seen Purcell before that morning, nor did I know of his reputation as a professional hit man, nor did I know why he had my husband at gunpoint or what had happened to Sophie. Yes, I'd known my husband had a gambling problem, but I did not realize it had grown so bad that an enforcer had been hired to deal with the problem.

After Purcell had shot Brian, I'd offered him fifty thousand dollars in return for more time before reporting his death. I'd explained I could freeze Brian's body, then thaw it and call the cops on Sunday morning. I'd still do whatever Purcell wanted, I just needed twenty-four hours to prepare for Sophie's return, as I'd be in jail for shooting my husband.

Purcell had accepted the deal, and I'd spent Saturday afternoon covering Brian's body in snow, then retrieving the dog's body from under the deck, and building a couple of incendiary devices. I tried to rig them to blow back so no one would get hurt.

Yes, I had planned my escape from jail. And no, I hadn't felt it was safe to disclose to anyone, even to the Boston detectives, what was really going on. For one thing, I didn't know who'd taken Sophie and I genuinely feared for her life. For another, I knew at least one fellow officer, Trooper Lyons, was involved. How could I know the taint didn't extend to Boston cops? Or, as the case turned out, to a superior officer?

At the time, I was acting on instinct, carefully trying to do as I'd been instructed, while also realizing that if I didn't escape and find my daughter myself, chances were she was as good as dead.

D.D. wanted to know who had given me a lift from the search and recovery site. I stared her straight in the eye and told her I'd hitchhiked. She wanted a description of the vehicle. Sadly, I didn't remember.

But I'd ended up at my father's garage, where I helped myself to a vehicle. He'd been passed out at the time, in no shape to agree or protest.

Once I had the Ford truck, I'd driven straight to western Mass. to confront Hamilton and rescue Sophie.

No, I didn't know what happened to Shane that night, or how he came to be shot by Brian's Glock .40. Though, if they'd retrieved the Glock .40 from the hit man's house, didn't that imply that Purcell had done the deed? Maybe someone viewed Shane as another *loose end that needed to be wrapped up. Poor Shane. I hoped his wife and kids were doing okay.*

D.D. scowled at me. Bobby said nothing at all. We had something in common, he and I. He knew exactly what I'd done. And I think he accepted that a woman who'd already killed three people probably wasn't going to magically crack and confess, even if his partner used her angry voice.

I did shoot and kill Hamilton's mistress, Bonita Marcoso. The woman had been assaulting my child. I had to use deadly force.

As for the lieutenant colonel . . . In killing him, Bobby Dodge had saved my life, I informed D.D. And I wanted to go on record with that. If not for the actions of state detective Bobby Dodge, Sophie and I both would probably be dead.

"Investigated and cleared," Bobby informed me.

"As it should be. Thank you."

He flushed a little, not liking the attention. Or maybe he simply didn't want to be thanked for taking a life.

I don't think about it much myself. I don't see the point.

So there you have it, I wrapped up for D.D. My husband was not a wife beater or child abuser. Just a gambling addict who'd gotten in way over his head. And maybe I should've done more about that sooner. Cut him off. Kicked him out.

I hadn't known about the credit cards he'd opened in Sophie's name. I hadn't known about his skimming of union funds. There was a lot I hadn't known, but that didn't make me culpable. Just made me a typical wife, wishing fruitlessly that my husband would walk away from the card tables and come home to me and my child instead.

"Sorry," he'd told me, dying in our kitchen. "Tessa . . . love you more."

I dream of him, you know. Not something I can tell Detective Warren. But I dream of my husband, except this time he is Good Brian, and he is holding my hand in his and Sophie is riding ahead of us on her bike. We walk. We talk. We are happy.

I wake up sobbing, which makes it

just as well that I don't sleep much any-more.

Want to know how much the lieuten-ant colonel made in the end? According to D.D., internal affairs recovered one hundred thousand dollars in his ac-count. Ironically, a mere fraction of what he would've received in legitimate retire-ment benefits if he'd just done his job conscientiously, then taken up fishing in Florida.

The lieutenant colonel had ordered my husband's death, and lost money in the process.

They hadn't been able to recover the rest of the funds. No record in Shane's accounts and no record in Brian's. Ac-cording to D.D., internal affairs believed that both men had gambled away their illicit gains at the casino, while Hamilton had saved his share of the scam. Ironi-cally, their bad habit meant Shane and Brian would never be charged in the crime, while Hamilton and his girlfriend Bonita—who'd been positively ID'd as the female who'd closed out the shell company's bank account—would post-humously shoulder the blame.

Good news for Shane's widow, I thought, and good news for me.

I heard later that Shane was buried with full honors. The police determined that he must have agreed to meet with Purcell in the back alley. Purcell had overpowered him, then killed him, maybe to eliminate Shane, just as he'd eliminated Brian.

Purcell's murder remains open, I've been told, the weapon having yet to be recovered.

As I explained to Detective D. D. Warren, I don't know nothing about anything, and don't let anyone tell you otherwise.

Sophie and I live together now in a two-bedroom apartment just down the street from Mrs. Ennis. We've never returned to the old house; I sold it in about three hours, because even if it was once a crime scene, it still has one of the largest yards in Boston.

Sophie does not ask for Brian, nor speak of him. Nor does she talk about the kidnapping. I believe she feels she's

*protecting me. What can I tell you—
she's a chip off the old block. She sees
a specialist once a week. He advises me
to be patient and so I am. I view my job
now as building a safe place to land for
when my daughter inevitably lets go.*

*She will fall, and I will catch her.
Gladly.*

*I made Brian's funeral arrangements
alone. He's buried with a simple granite
marker bearing his name and relevant
dates. And maybe it was weakness on
my part, but given that he died for Sophie, that he knew, standing there in our
kitchen, the decision I would have to
make, I added one last word. The highest praise you can give a man. I had
etched, under his name: Daddy.*

*Maybe someday Sophie will visit him.
And maybe, seeing that word, she can
remember his love and she can forgive
his mistakes. Parents aren't perfect, you
know. We're all just doing the best we
can.*

*I had to resign from the state police.
While D.D. and Bobby have yet to con-
nect me to Shane Lyons's or John
Stephen Purcell's deaths, there's still the*

small matter of me breaking out of jail and assaulting a fellow officer. My lawyer is arguing that I was operating under extreme emotional duress, given my superior officer's kidnapping of my child, and should not be held responsible for my actions. Cargill remains optimistic that the DA, wanting to avoid too much bad publicity for the state police, will agree to a plea where I serve a probationary sentence, or at worse, house arrest.

Either way, I understand my days as a police officer are over. Frankly, a woman who's done the things I've done shouldn't be an armed protector of the public. And I don't know—maybe there is something wrong with me, an essential boundary missing, so that where other mothers would've cried for their child, I armed myself to the teeth and hunted down the people who took her instead.

Sometimes, I'm scared by the image that greets me in the mirror. My face is too hard, and even I realize it's been a long time since I've smiled. Men don't ask me out. Strangers don't strike up conversations with me on the subway.

Bobby Dodge is right—killing someone is not something to be thankful for. It's a necessary evil that costs you a piece of yourself and a connection to humanity you never get back.

But you don't need to feel sorry for me.

I recently started with a global security firm, making more money while working better hours. My boss read my story in the paper and called me with the job offer. He believes I have one of the finest strategic minds he's ever encountered, with an uncanny ability to foresee obstacles and anticipate next steps. There's a demand for those kinds of skills, especially in this day and age; I've already been promoted twice.

Now I drop off Sophie at school each morning. I go to work. Mrs. Ennis picks Sophie up at three. I join them at six. We eat dinner together, then I take Sophie home.

She and I tend the apartment, do homework. Then, at nine, we go to bed. We share a room. Neither of us sleeps much, and even three months later, we're still not ready for the dark.

Mostly, we snuggle together, Gertrude nestled between us.

Sophie likes to rest with her head on my shoulder, her fingers splayed in the palm of my hand.

"Love you, Mommy," she tells me each and every night.

And I say, my cheek pressed against the top of her dark hair: "Love you more, baby. I love you more."

AUTHOR'S NOTE AND ACKNOWLEDGMENTS

With all due respect to Detective D. D. Warren, my favorite part of embarking on a new novel isn't spending time with old characters, but rather, researching new and inventive ways to commit murder and mayhem. Oh, and, um, also spending quality time with law enforcement professionals who remind me why a life of crime really isn't a good idea, and thus I should continue to hope the whole writing gig pans out.

For *Love You More,* I got to fulfill one of my lifelong dreams of conducting research at the University of Tennessee

Anthropology Research Facility, aka the Body Farm. I am deeply indebted to Dr. Lee Jantz, who is one of the smartest people I know, working one of the coolest jobs on the planet. She can look at a pile of cremated bones and tell you within thirty seconds pretty much everything about the person, including gender, age, chronic health issues, and what kind of dental floss he/she used. I had many moments with Dr. Jantz I would've liked to have put in the novel, but I didn't think anyone would believe me.

Readers interested in morbid things like decomp, identifying skeletal remains, and post-mortem insect activity should absolutely check out *Death's Acre,* by Dr. Bill Bass, creator of the Body Farm, and coauthor Jon Jefferson. You can also visit my Facebook page for photos from my very informative research trip.

Oh, this is the part where I add anthropologists are trained professionals, whereas I just type for a living, meaning all mistakes in the novel are mine and mine alone. Plus, just as an FYI, I would never accuse Dr. Jantz, who has a T-shirt reading *Don't piss me off—I'm running out of places to hide the bodies,* of having made a mistake.

I am also deeply indebted to Cassondra Murray, Southern/Western Kentucky Canine Rescue & Recovery Task Force, for her insights into training cadaver dogs and life as a volunteer dog handler. I had no idea that most canine SAR teams are volunteer organizations. These groups and their dogs do amazing work, and we are indebted to them for their hard work, dedication, and sacrifice.

Again, all mistakes are mine, so don't even think about it!

Next up: Officer Penny Frechette, as well as several other female police officers who preferred to remain off the record. I appreciate the time and candor shared by these women, and enjoyed my first ride-along in a police cruiser. I was nervous! She was not. For those of you into police procedure, my character Tessa Leoni's experiences are an amalgamation of different jurisdictions, and not necessarily representative of the life of a Massachusetts State Trooper. The Massachusetts State Police is a fine, upstanding organization and I appreciate their patience with suspense authors who exercise plenty of fictional license.

Under other nerve-wracking and noteworthy experiences, I must thank Superintendent Gerard Horgan, Esquire, and Assistant Deputy Superintendent Brian Dacey, both of the Suffolk County Sheriff's Department for a fun-filled day at the Suffolk County Jail. It's not every day I drive all the way to Boston just to be incarcerated, but boy did I learn a lot (basically, stick to writing fictional crimes, because let me tell you, I wouldn't last a day behind bars). They showed me a first-class operation. I, of course, used the facility for yet more murder and mayhem, because hey, that's what I do best.

Also, my deepest appreciation to Wayne Rock, Esquire, for legal advice and various insights into the BPD. A retired Boston detective, Wayne is always very patient when answering my questions and no longer seems startled when I lead with things like, *So I want to kill a guy but not have it be my fault. What's my best option?* Thank you, Wayne!

I am also indebted to Scott Hale, third generation merchant mariner, for his insights into the life. He agreed to help me out, even after knowing I was going to kill the merchant marine character. Thanks, Scott!

And wrapping things up in the research department, my endless gratitude to gifted doctor and fellow suspense author C. J. Lyons for her medical expertise. Let's face it, not just anyone will respond to e-mails with subject headings such as "Need Advice for Maiming." Thanks, C.J.!

Since writing novels isn't all touring jails and hanging out with cops, I must also thank David J. Hallett and Scott C. Ferrari, who outbid all rivals with a generous donation to our local animal shelter, for the right to include their Soft Coated Wheaten Terriers Skyler and Kelli in the novel. I hope you enjoy Skyler and Kelli's star-making turn, and thanks for supporting our local shelter.

I couldn't let animals have all the fun. Congrats to Heather Blood, winner of the 6th Annual Kill a Friend, Maim a Buddy Sweepstakes, who nominated Erica Reed to die. Also, Canadian Donna Watters for winning the international edition, Kill a Friend, Maim a Mate. She sacrificed her sister, Kim Watters, for a grand end.

I hope you enjoyed your literary immortality. And for those of you hoping to get in on the action, please check out www.LisaGardner.com.

Of course, I couldn't do this without my family. From my own darling child, who quizzed me every day on whether I had saved the little girl yet, to my extremely patient husband, who's gotten so used to having a wife who takes off for prison, he doesn't even ask what time I'll be home anymore. That's love, I tell you.

Finally, for Team Gardner. My supportive agent, Meg Ruley; my brilliant editor, Kate Miciak; and my entire Random House publishing team. You have no idea how many talented and hardworking people it takes to produce a novel. I am indebted to each and every one. Thanks for being on my side, and helping to make the magic happen.

This book is dedicated in loving memory to Uncle Darrell and Aunt Donna Holloway, who taught us laughter, love and, of course, cribbage strategy.

Also, to Richard Myles, aka Uncle Dick, whose love of great books, beautiful gardens, and a good Manhattan will not be forgotten.

We love you, and we remember.

ABOUT THE AUTHOR

LISA GARDNER is the *New York Times* bestselling author of thirteen novels. Her Detective D. D. Warren novels include *Love You More, Live to Tell, The Neighbor, Hide,* and *Alone.* Her FBI Profiler novels include *Say Goodbye, Gone, The Killing Hour, The Next Accident,* and *The Third Victim.* She lives with her family in New England, where she is at work on her next novel.